ESTABLISHING OUR LIFE IN CHRIST

Volume One

By

Rayola Kelley

Hidden Manna Publications

ISBN: 978-09891683-1-1

Establishing Our Life In Christ
Volume 1
By Rayola Kelley

Featuring the following books:
My Words Are Spirit And Life
The Anatomy of Sin
The Principles of the Abundant Life
The Place of Covenant
Unmasking the Cult Mentality

Printed in the USA

Hidden Manna Publications
PO Box 3572
Oldtown, ID 83822

Facebook:
https://www.facebook.com/HiddenMannaPublications/

DEDICATION

I want to dedicate this volume to
a special person who has
been my friend, co-laborer
and sister in the Lord:
Jeannette Haley.
Jeannette, thank you for
sharing my love for both the Living
and written Word
and taking this incredible
journey with me.

ACKNOWLEDGMENT

There was a team effort that went into this volume. Various people help make this book a reality. I want to thank Jo Reaves and Crystal Garvin for editing the different books in this volume. I also want to thank those who helped proofread and check out the references in these presentations.

I want to acknowledge those who have been supportive of the different projects of Gentle Shepherd Ministries such as our team members. Various people have shown their faithfulness, friendship, and support throughout the years. You know who you are. We greatly appreciate you for giving us the opportunity to serve our Lord Jesus Christ in this capacity.

INTRODUCTION

Establishing our Life in Christ is the first volume of seven volumes that are a combination of books related to different themes of the Christian life. These different volumes will complement the Gentle Shepherd Ministries Discipleship course. Five books in this volume present subjects that are vital to establishing a viable life in Christ.

These books deal with the foundation of the Christian life. Understanding how to properly handle the Written Word, recognizing the workings of sin, walking according to godly principles, knowing the place covenant holds in our spiritual status, and being able to start from the premise of truth will establish believers in their life in Christ.

These subjects, which are basic to the Christian life, will establish believers on the right foundation, enabling them to properly assimilate this godly life into their walk. Without the foundation, Christians will not know how to rightly divide the Word.

My Words Are Spirit and Life will help the reader understand the makeup of the Bible in order to properly and skillfully handle it. It will enable the student of the Bible to recognize what he or she is looking at in Scripture so that he or she can get the most out of the Word, and grow in the knowledge of the Lord Jesus Christ.

Another important aspect the Christian must possess is to have a realistic understanding about the ways sin operates in a person's life. Since sin has been, watered down and redefined in various ways, multitudes of Christians lack a correct view and understanding of it. *The Anatomy of Sin* thoroughly exposes and explains every characteristic of this subject. Everything, from the nature of sin, to the forms and types found in this terminal disease of the soul is considered. Although sin is not a popular subject in an age of tolerance and being politically correct, Christians must correctly address it to live a victorious life.

It is important for believers to realize that people walk according to principles that lead to either life or death. *The Principles of the Abundant Life* not only reveals how principles operate according to a law, but this book does so in light of nine principles that constitute the abundant life and encourage growth. These principles are simple, yet profound. They bring a person back to the foundation, and lead him or her to the reality of God through Jesus Christ. It is within the reality of God that a relationship is established. The type of relationship a person has with God will determine the growth and quality of that person's life.

Believers must also come to terms with what it means to be part of a covenant with God if they are going to understand their place and responsibility in His kingdom. *The Place of Covenant* will bring a person into an understanding about the importance that God has put on this binding agreement. It will help the Bible student realize that God has clearly revealed His heart, intention, and desire towards His people.

Since many Christians are not always established in their lives in Christ, they often become prey for cults. As a result, some Christians find themselves battling through the maze created by a cult mentality. *Unmasking the Cult Mentality* represents the various struggles of those who have become victims to a cult. These victims must come back to the center of truth to be set free. Sadly, many Christians do not really understand what they believe in relationship to subjects such as the Godhead. This intense study helps believers to reason out fundamental beliefs according to Scripture. A clear Scriptural foundation is established in this book in order for believers to understand what it means to give a reason for the hope that is in them.

Unmasking the Cult Mentality not only explains how cults indoctrinate people into their heretical beliefs, but how they continue to spoil the authority of God's Word in a cult member's life, even after he or she has left their web of destruction. Betrayed and broken in heart or spirit, these people often try to protect themselves by hiding behind a wall of skepticism. Skepticism causes them to become critical towards all religion regardless of whether it stands on truth or not.

Each book in this volume will clearly bring valuable insights to a believer as to what it means for him or her to properly be established in his or her life in Christ. These books will also complement one another as each subject is considered according to the intent and truth of God's Word.

My prayer is that this volume will bring about the proper understanding of these five areas of the spiritual life. Such understanding is necessary to ensure spiritual maturity.

CONTENTS

Book One:

MY WORDS ARE SPIRIT AND LIFE

INTRODUCTION

As an observer of Christianity in America, I have become increasingly aware that countless Christians are becoming lost in a maze of religious and worldly pursuits, as well as caught up with supernatural counterfeits, while succumbing to spiritual despair and defeat. Upon examination of the possible reasons for this condition, I realize the authority of the Word of God is missing in the lives of these individuals.

Obviously, such people have had no solid foundation upon which to land, stand and test all spiritual matters. They are as Ephesians 4:14 declares, "...tossed to and fro, and carried about with every wind of doctrine." This instability has caused what Amos 8:11 would describe as a famine of the Word of God in the land. How could a nation, such as America, which allows freedom of religion and access to the Word of God, suffer from spiritual malnutrition and biblical illiteracy?

The problem is not that there is a lack of the Word of God, but the fact that there have been various "preservatives" added to it (man's doctrine). In some cases, "poison" (heresy) has been cleverly mixed in with it. In many American homes, the Bible is a sacred ornament that adorns coffee tables, but not people's personal lives. The written Word of God almost serves as some sacred icon that must be observed or honored from a far distance, but never personally applied to our lives. In fact, attitudes towards the Bible vary from its being a religious burden to the response of indifference, flippancy, and skepticism.

The fruits of this state will manifest themselves in a spiritual famine. It can be difficult to find the pure doctrine of the Word being preached and taught with authority and in power. It is difficult at times to find leaders who can impart the words of the Bible as living and powerful *manna* from the throne room of God.

Because there is a growing hunger for spiritual truths, people have opened themselves up to doctrines of demons. The main attraction of these doctrines is that they are marked by the supernatural. If you study the doctrine of demons, you will find contradictions and rhetoric that is neither simple nor practical. It puts much of the responsibility of spiritual success on the shoulders of man, while subtly replacing the redemption of Jesus Christ. Since there is supernatural activity involved, many believe it must be from God. The result is spiritual dullness.

The purpose of this book is to deal with the famine of the Word of God that is taking place in the midst of this "spiritual smorgasbord" that is sweeping the land. Many Christians are spiritually starving to death because they do not know how to partake of the Word of God in a proper way. These victims of spiritual famine are bogged down by facts, knowledge, doctrines, and debates over spiritual matters that neither enlarge nor feed the soul.

My heart's passion is that those who call themselves Christians will stir themselves up to pursue, desire, and fall in love with the Word of God. My hope is that God's Word will become their only source of life as they diligently seek for a deeper relationship with their Creator and Redeemer. My goal is that God's people are established on the immovable Rock, Jesus Christ, so that they will be able to stand, no matter what confronts them.

1

IT IS NOT COMMON

One serious problem that has emerged in our culture is the prevailing attitude that the Bible has been rendered as a common book. Although, in some cases it may be venerated as a special book, it has never been handled or explored as the treasure that it really is. It is treated either as if it is below one's intellect or above the understanding of the common person; yet, its very history refutes both attitudes.

The Bible has survived the intellectual attacks of the most noted scoffers, such as Voltaire. He declared that the Bible would be extinct in 100 years. Fifty years after his death, the Geneva Bible Society used his press and house to produce stacks of Bibles.[1]

A French nurse who tended Voltaire at his deathbed summarized the result of his scoffing, "For all the wealth in Europe I would never see another infidel die." [2] As you study the Bible, you realize Voltaire was a fool, and he died a fool's death.[3]

The Encyclopedia of Sermon Illustrations points out the irony that surrounds such scoffers. For example, the Bible Society of Edinburgh held its first meeting in a room where a man by the name of Hume stated that Christianity would be dead in 20 years. Thomas Paine declared, after landing in New York, that the Bible would be extinct within five years in the United States, but today we know differently.

In spite of being outlawed throughout history because of scoffers and godless societies and nations, the Word of God has survived and outlived blatant attacks. Presently in countries where the Bible continues to be outlawed, it remains prized by those who see it as the source of spirit and life.

Another obstacle that had to be subdued concerning the Bible was religious elitism. Many past religious leaders insisted the common person could not understand the Bible. However, men such as John Wycliffe and John Haus paid a high price for revealing the fallacy of such religious pride. These individuals proved that the Bible's truths were

---

[1] Evidence That Demands A Verdict; Josh McDowell, © 1972, 1979 by Campus Crusade for Christ, Inc., pg. 20

[2] Encyclopedia of Sermon Illustrations; ©1988 Concordia Publishing House; #515

[3] Psalm 14:1; 53:1

simple enough to be grasped by those sincere in heart, simple in mind, and who possessed the curiosity of a child.

Time has confirmed that the Word of God will not go away. History verifies its truth, scientific discoveries confirm its events, and prophecy holds up a mirror that can cause the greatest skeptic to tremble.

Skeptics cannot get around the inevitable fact that there is something about the Bible that is powerful, immovable, and eternal. It covers many different subjects and can attract a wide spectrum of people. It accurately reveals the history of man and the diary of God's heart. It contains prophecies that lead man up to the end of the age as he now knows it. Its oldest book, Job, reveals scientific facts about the beginning of the earth and the makeup of the heavens. The Bible contains some of the most beautiful songs, as well as poetic and philosophical writings. However, what makes the Bible unique from all other historical, scientific, poetic, and philosophic books is its ability to give hope to the hopeless, light to the lost, and comfort to those experiencing sorrow. It is a book, which underneath the surface of facts, debates, and skepticism, serves as a current of unquenchable hope and life.

The reason this book has life is because of its Author. Scripture clearly states that the Holy Spirit, the third Person of the Godhead, is the real source of the 66 books that make up the written Word of God.[4]

The Author of the Bible must be verified and confirmed to determine credibility. Even though historical, scientific, and prophetic proof verifies the consistency and legitimacy of Scripture, its authority rests solely on the One who inspired it. It is on this matter that much rests as to whether there is truly a God with whom man must ultimately reckon with, as well as the reality of an eternal destination. Since the inspiration of the Bible comes from the throne of God, it clearly establishes that it is not a common book. And, to regard the Bible in such a manner, whether through mistranslation, approaching it in a wrong attitude, or by mishandling it, is to profane it.

This debate over the validity of the Bible is made obvious by religious cults who demean the authority of Scripture by accrediting it to men and not God. Man's logic in this debate becomes obvious. If imperfect man is the author of the Bible, then skeptics do not have to regard it as being legitimate. Therefore, people can consider the stories as interesting but mythical, and its instruction as wise but optional.

Once man's logic deems the Bible as another common book, man can define his own god, establish his own moral codes, and create an eternity that is non-existent or that can be adjusted to his self-serving desires. Sadly, this logic cleverly disguises itself even in Christian circles. Most Christians believe the Bible is the infallible Word of God, but at the same time, they reason many of its instructions away. For example, since it was inspired centuries ago, some believe that the principles and

---

[4] 2 Peter 1:20-21

instructions are not applicable for today. This causes many Christians to piece-meal the Bible, disregarding things that do not make sense or seem logical and unrealistic. The problem with piece-mealing the Bible is that its very life and authority are drastically undermined.

If the Holy Spirit is the sole source behind the inspiration of Scripture, then one must decide if He has the ability to maintain the validity of Scripture. In other words, can God maintain the purity of His own book? Most would answer with a resounding yes!

In spite of man's imperfect handling of Scripture, God can maintain the intent of His Word regardless of the seeming discrepancies that are pointed to by the skeptics. The intent of the Bible has to do with its spirit or purpose, not with the technical facts that seem contradictory.

What is the intent of the Word? It is to show man's spiritual plight and God's provision to bring him to salvation. It is in light of salvation that the Creator can unveil His eternal purpose for bringing man forth. However, such salvation cannot occur until man comes back to the one true God and receives His provision of Jesus Christ. This theme of salvation is the fine thread that runs from Genesis through Revelation. It never changes or sways, and it reveals that God is doing everything within His power to draw man back to Himself in order to save him. Through it all, you can see God's mercy and grace being extended in incredible measure. You can see His commitment to and love for man. You can see His patience and faithfulness towards arrogant, rebellious humanity.

The written Word also contains mysteries beyond comprehension that enlarge man's soul and cause greater curiosity. It is like a gold mine that is waiting to be explored with every available means on hand to find treasures that cannot be measured by man's mere standards.

It is a book that is alive! Like its Author, it is eternal and supernatural in nature, making it infallible. Even though it contains what appears to be a veneer of words, it has various layers and depths which are hidden underneath the surface, Each unveiling of its truths can revolutionize the hearts and minds of man, even changing the times and course of history.

There is a story of a man who was raised by his Christian grandmother. She had faithfully prayed for his salvation, but as he got older, he became more self-centered and engrossed with the world. Upon his graduation, she gave him a Bible with his name written in it. Later, when he was a struggling medical student, he sold the Bible, cutting off any real ties to his Christian heritage.

In the eyes of the world, this man was a success as a doctor, but in his personal life, there was emptiness. One day, he was assigned to take care of a destitute man who was dying. As he observed the man, he saw nothing but radiant confidence in God. The man's only request was for a Bible. Eventually, a Bible was located and a week later the ailing man joyously entered into eternal bliss.

The doctor was surprised at the man's attitude about life through his difficult circumstances. As the doctor was going through the man's meager possessions, he came upon the Bible. As he opened the Bible, he suddenly realized the Bible was the one his grandmother had given him years earlier. On that day, at that moment, that man committed his life to the one, true faithful God of his grandmother.

In another incident, a family encountered tremendous loss due to a flood. As they were sorting through the devastation, they discovered a small pocket New Testament, which not only survived the flood, but also was miraculously still brand new in appearance.

The stories surrounding the power of this unique book are many. Each story shows that there is something supernatural behind its existence. This book has survived floods, fires, and persecution. The fact that it can change the heart, attitude, and course of man reveals that it is alive and powerful.

The Word of God may be a common fixture in the homes of America, and in many ways rendered as common by people. However, this book is far from being common in content. By some, it may be considered too sacred to read, but the Word in itself is not sacred. Rather, what is sacred is that the God revealed within its pages must be the One who people possess and venerate in their hearts and minds.

Jesus said this of His words in John 6:63, "It is the spirit that quickeneth; the flesh profiteth nothing: the words that I speak unto you, they are spirit, and they are life."

Sadly, for many who read or study the Bible, the result does not produce life, but pride. It is used to often confirm man's theology, rather than the reality of Jesus, who is the essence of all life. It is debated rather than explored. It is questioned rather than believed. It is used for personal agendas rather than to expose personal failures.

The proofs that the "old man" (the flesh) is involved in the attitudes and handling of the Word of God today are endless. And, whenever the "old man" handles the Word, the person will profit nothing from it because the spirit is wrong. A wrong spirit renders God's words lifeless. Without life, there is no authority and power to change, guide, and encourage. After all, how can something dead give life, guidance, and encouragement? It cannot.

I know from personal experience that the Word of God is alive and well. It is the greatest treasure chest man can possess, and the most profound truth that he can embrace.

What about your attitude toward the Word of God? Is the Word alive to you or is it a burden? Is it simply regarded as a fixture in your home, or is it fixed in your heart? Is it something you look at in regards to others, or does it serve as a personal mirror for you to discern your own heart, attitude, and ways before God? After all, the spirit in which you handle it will determine the type of impact the Word makes on you. Does it bring life or is it just another book? If the Bible does not bring life to your inner man, the problem rests with you, not the Written Word.

2

THE INTENT

Jesus said of His words, "...they are spirit, and they are life" (John 6:63). According to *Strong's Exhaustive Concordance,* the word "spirit" refers to a current of air that cannot be contained. It points to a vital principle, a mental disposition (attitude), or the spirit of man or God.

The fact that Jesus' words are spirit points to the reality that they are meant to touch the spirit and soul of man. His words can change man's perception and attitude towards God by bringing life to his innermost being.

It is important to understand what part attitude plays when it comes to the Bible. Man's attitude towards God's Word will determine how he receives the things of God. This brings us to a very important principle: Everything of God works within two boundaries—spirit and truth.[1] The problem with most people is that they search the Scripture for truth, while ignoring spirit.

The spirit in which we approach something will determine how we handle the truth. The Apostle Paul talked about dividing (or handling) the Word properly in order to prove ourselves as workmen who need not to be ashamed of our lives before God.[2]

In Romans 1:18, Paul spoke about the wrath of God being against those, "...who hold the truth in unrighteousness." It is a serious offense to handle the Word in a wrong spirit or in a deceitful manner.

Spirit points to the motivation and the intent as to why a person is doing something. There are four reasons people read the Bible. They read it to fulfill a religious duty or obligation, to seek spiritual facts, to accumulate biblical knowledge, or to find Jesus.

It appears as if one of the most compelling reasons for people to read the Word comes out of religious duty or obligation. The Word is not meant to be a grave burden. When a person approaches the Word with such an attitude, it will mean that the Word has become dead-letter or lifeless. 2 Corinthians 3:6 explains it in this way, "Who also hath made us able ministers of the new testament; not of the letter, but of the spirit: for the letter killeth, but the spirit giveth life."

---

[1] John 4:24

[2] 2 Timothy 2:15

The right spirit will give life to the Written Word. This is why the writer of Hebrews 4:12 made this statement, "For the Word of God is quick, and powerful, and sharper than any two-edged sword, piercing even to the dividing asunder of soul and spirit, and of the joints and marrow, and is a discerner of the thoughts and intents of the heart."

It is important to acknowledge how Christians can discern if the right spirit is on the scene. If the right spirit is present, Scripture will actually penetrate and dissect their innermost being by establishing proper doctrine for the purpose of reproof, correction, and instruction in righteousness.[3] It will expose personal motives, intents, and agendas as well as separate that which is of self from that which is of God. This separation is necessary so that each person may properly discern that which is good (of God) or evil (of the flesh, the world and Satan).

This discernment does not have to do with outward influences, but with a person's inward spiritual state. Sadly, if people use the Bible, it is usually to judge everything except their own spiritual condition.

In my initial years as a Christian, I approached the Word for the wrong reasons. Any time the motive is wrong, the spirit is wrong. I knew I had to read the Bible, which became my religious duty, but I also wanted to get all the facts in order to impress others with my scriptural understanding. After all, with enough facts and Scriptures, I could intellectually debate any subject or doctrine.

As I studied the Bible, I learned there were more than just facts in God's Word, and I began an intellectual pursuit for myself. In other words, I wanted to impress myself as to how well I knew the Bible. I had a high opinion of my knowledge, but underneath, I knew something was missing. Later, I discovered that a right spirit was missing.

It is important to state that it matters little how much a person can quote Scripture if the spirit is wrong. I have known of people who could deluge others with Scripture. When such a strategy is used, I suspect these individuals are doing one of three things: 1) They are trying to bluff their way to hide their lack of scriptural authority; 2) they have a lot of pride in what they think they know, but no power; and/or 3) they are confusing you in order to promote heresy. Usually these types of handling of the Word lack continuity and the right spirit, producing confusion and weariness.

In my attempts to know more to feed my conceit, I dissected the Word with great fervor. I was probably one of the most dedicated of students, but I was about to discover that I was an unarmed soldier who had fallen prey to the enemies of my soul.

As I grew in the knowledge of the Word, my soul was drying up because there was no life to my religious understanding and activities. I knew much, yet I did not have the authority or power to overcome. My mind was being fed, but my spirit was becoming dry. Eventually, my

---

[3] 2 Timothy 3:16

spiritual state overwhelmed me. There was something drastically wrong with me, but the Word remained silent to my soul. I learned later that the authority of God's Word had been rendered powerless in my life because I had successfully dissected it into pieces in my pursuit of knowledge.

My despairing spiritual state brought me to the foot of the cross, crying out for forgiveness and understanding. God faithfully met me through Jesus. When I encountered Jesus, life came into my being. I suddenly realized that what was missing from my spiritual knowledge was a revelation of the Person of Jesus Christ. Should this have surprised me since Jesus is the Living Word, and Scripture is the Written Word? [4]

As Jesus began to restore me, I watched Him put the sword of the Word back into place. He sharpened the blade and reformed the dull tip. When He was finished, He asked me if I wanted to understand how I could experience the authority and power of His Word in my life. Upon my permission, He pierced my soul and spirit with it.

I will never forget its impact. It forever changed my life. I realized that I could not make any more impact with it in the lives of others than I had allowed it to make in my own life. This is when I recognized that if you only feed your mind, you will only reach the mind of others. If you feed the spirit and soul, you will be able to reach the heart of others.

I made a decision that I wanted to impact souls, so I gave Jesus permission to take the sword through every layer of my soul and expose my heart. I did not realize it then, but He was about to tear up my frame of reference.

The spirit you operate in determines the frame of reference you develop about a spiritual truth. Frame of reference is where you interpret the information you process. This reference determines your focus and inclination.

There are three types of frames of reference in the religious world. The first frame of reference is a *fleshly focus*. It interprets the Word according to how it makes the individual feel about self. People who handle the Word of God in this manner will miss the intent of the Word. As a result, a sturdy spiritual foundation will never be firmly established underneath these individuals. They will be tossed to and fro according to the different waves of religious teachings and movements that catches the attention of their fleshly dictates and preferences.[5]

The second type of reference is made up of *concrete doctrine*. In this case, doctrine, rather than the Spirit of God, determines the interpretation of scriptural truths. Regardless of how right the doctrine may be, a person with this type of reference becomes self-righteous, judgmental, and bigoted because the right spirit is missing. I must state that doctrine without the right spirit becomes a law unto itself or dead-

[4] John 1:1

[5] Ephesians 4:14

letter, but it has no life, authority, or power against Satan. This will leave a person in a vulnerable state, becoming easy prey to enemies.

The third frame of reference is that of the *right spirit* and the *exaltation of truth.* This means that all spiritual conclusions are tested according to the character and Person of Jesus Christ and His work of redemption.

The character of God will not only define how a person perceives spiritual truth, for He will not move outside of who He is, but it will stop the incessant debates that go on about doctrines. In my experience, debates over doctrine exist because there is a great personal arrogance that often hides ignorance about God's character. This is why the command to seek Him is clearly stated throughout Scripture.

I have never found in Scripture where we are to seek doctrine. The reason for this is when doctrine is exalted as a focus, it will determine the character of God, rather than the character of God defining doctrine according to the right spirit. Because man often has his approach backwards, he has a limited perspective of God.

I looked back over my initial pursuits to gain spiritual knowledge and realized how I missed it. I had all my doctrine in place, but it confused the real intent of the Word, which is to know Jesus in all of His glory.

This brings us down to our real teacher. I have had the privilege of having a few great teachers in my life, but there is one teacher who stands out the most. The beauty about this one good teacher is not the information he gave me, but the tools he handed to me which caused an excitement and curiosity in my innermost being to explore God's Word. This is the secret behind all great teachers. Anyone can give information, but few are able to give others the tools that will help them to explore beyond the surface to discover the actual face value of a matter. It is from this premise that one is able to reach beyond nominal, acceptable knowledge.

The next great teacher I was exposed to guided my steps and built up my life in Christ. Jesus talked about this teacher in John 16:13-14,

> Howbeit when he, the Spirit of truth is come, he will guide you into all truth: for he shall not speak of himself; but whatsoever he shall hear, that shall he speak: and he will shew you things to come. He shall glorify me: for he shall receive of mine, and shall shew it unto you.

Romans 11:34 states, "For who hath known the mind of the Lord? or who hath been his counselor?" I already knew God's heart and will for my life: To know Jesus in an intimate way so that He could become my all in all. However, I realized that I needed to know His mind. To know His mind meant that I would be able to walk according to His infinite wisdom or counsel.

Jeremiah 29:11 gives us this promise, "For I know the thoughts that I think toward you, saith the LORD, thoughts of peace, and not of evil, to give you an expected end." It became clear that I must be trustworthy to gain insight into His mind, and only submission to His Spirit would allow me to receive glimpses into it.

There are two ways to discover the mind of God through the leading of the Spirit. The first way can be found in Acts 17:11, "...and searched the scriptures daily, whether those things were so." This Scripture reference in Acts is in regard to the Bereans. These people compared Scripture with Scripture to see if those trying to influence them with spiritual truths upheld the intent or spirit of God's Word. It is important to point out that truth stands alone, but Scriptures do not. They can only stand as a whole in light of the right spirit and in line with the truth of Jesus Christ.

As stated in the first chapter, there is a fine thread that links each book of the Bible, but that same thread also connects Scriptures together. I have watched many people use Scripture after Scripture to prove their point, but there is no life present because the thread is missing. I have also watched heretics use Scriptures to justify blatant heresy, just as Satan did in the temptation of Jesus, but the intent was wicked and evil. This is why Scriptures are unable to stand alone.

You must have the ability to compare Scripture with Scripture, and only the right spirit can bring continuity and understanding to them. This continuity maintains the thread by upholding the truth, Jesus Christ. If you fail to see the thread, Scripture will serve as nothing more than information or doctrine. And, if the right spirit is missing, you will hold the truth in unrighteousness and be subject to God's wrath.

If your motive is to know Jesus, the Holy Spirit will meet you in your search. If your goal is to know doctrine, you will miss that which will personally impact and revolutionize your life.

How do you approach the Word, and what is your frame of reference? Do you compare Scripture with Scripture to ensure the right intent? Or, do you isolate Scripture to fit your own purpose and interpretation?

If you are guilty of mishandling the Word, you will fail to enter into the next stage of discovering the mind of the Lord: that of communion.

3

ACCEPTING THE INVITATION

Jesus made it simple and easy for people to discover God's heart and mind. Matthew 11:28-29 reveals what people's main goal should be, "Come unto me, all ye that labour and are heavy laden, and I will give you rest. Take my yoke upon you and learn of me; for I am meek and lowly in heart: and ye shall find rest unto your souls." (Emphasis added.)

We can also see a similar invitation in John 6:35, "I am the bread of life: he that cometh to me; shall never hunger; and he that believeth on me shall never thirst." (Emphasis added.)

John 7:37 states, "If any man thirst, let him come unto me, and drink." (Emphasis added.)

This brings us to Revelation 3:20, "Behold, I stand at the door, and knock: if any man hear my voice, and open the door, I will come in to him and will sup with him, and he with me." (Emphasis added.)

Jesus' invitation is about communion. Communion entails two types of fellowship. For example, communion is a time of partaking of Him as the living manna or bread from heaven. This communion sustains and strengthens us. It is where we can be refreshed with the rivers of the Living Water of the Holy Spirit. The second type of communion is where we come into agreement. This means we come into a place of communion to know the heart and mind of God in order to carry out His will in a matter.

We often must come by way of the first type of communion, where we learn to partake of the life, teachings, and examples of Jesus, before we can embrace the second point of communion. His clear invitation is to learn of Him, but first we must come to Him and take His yoke upon ourselves. This yoke points to discipline that brings a person into union and servitude to Jesus.

The main motivation of all union and servitude to Jesus is the love of God. God's love produces fellowship and union in the Holy Spirit through Jesus Christ. It is an easy yoke because love causes the commitment and walk to be a matter of privilege. It is selfless and sacrificial in attitude, and points to self-denial and death to the self-life through obedience.

This easy yoke gives believers the liberty to learn of Jesus in an intimate way. As individuals learn of Him, they take on His attitude, bringing glory and honor to God.

Therefore, the purpose of the first type of communion is a time of learning of Jesus. A good example of this form of communion is the dinner table. Communion points to the table, while the Word serves as the food and drink. The chair is symbolic of faith, but a person must sit up at the table by faith to receive what has been prepared. The Holy Spirit is the server as He imparts the food to the individual, but he or she must be prepared to receive and partake of it by faith.

Hebrews 5:12 gives us a description of the Word as being both drink and food. It refers to the drink as milk and the food as meat.[1] Milk represents fundamental truths and pure doctrine. The milk of the Word is designed to establish new Christians upon a proper foundation. 1 Peter 2:2 refers to it as the sincere milk of the Word which enables new believers to graduate to the meat stage.

Meat symbolizes spiritual maturity. The writer of Hebrews reproved the Christians for never getting past the milk stage of fundamental truths and doctrines to the stage of maturity.[2] This stage involves revelation that leads to enlightenment. It is at this level that Christians are equipped to discern between good and evil.

Baby Christians have a hard time discerning between the flesh and the spirit. The Apostle Paul brings this out in 1 Corinthians 3:1-3. He verifies that the fruits of carnality are envy, strife, and division. Carnal Christians are still self-serving in their motives and worldly in their pursuits.

Oswald Chambers said that carnality is produced when the Spirit wars against the flesh. He goes on to stipulate that carnality will disappear when a person begins to walk after the Spirit and not the flesh.[3]

The problem today is that many Christians remain at the milk stage because it is the path of least resistance. These Christians are easily distinguished because they are touchy about their imperfections, and indifferent about their attitudes and actions. They refuse to be properly challenged or corrected because of their pride. They strive to hide their imperfections behind a cloak of self-righteousness as a means to overcompensate for their powerless life. They end up exalting their immature concepts about God into the position of concrete doctrines that stand as their ultimate authority.

Those who get past the carnal stage realize that the Christian walk is not about personal feelings and impulsive conviction, but about a confident, humble, and sober life in Jesus. This life is both satisfying and complete.

---

[1] See 1 Corinthians 3:1-4

[2] Hebrews 6:1

[3] *My Utmost For His Highest*; Oswald Chambers; © 1963 by Oswald Chambers Publications Association, Ltd., March 23rd devotion.

The main pursuit of mature Christians is Jesus. They believe what Scripture states in John 5:39, "Search the scriptures; for in them ye think ye have eternal life: and they are they which testify of me." They have realized that the Christian walk hinges on an intimate relationship with the Son of God. They have also learned that God's words are priceless and add substance to their spiritual life through each new revelation of Jesus. They conclude that their meat is the same as Jesus: Doing the will of the Father.[4]

Each time there is intimate communion with Jesus, a person's perception of God is enlarged, and it brings forth growth and spiritual character. As a result, the individual is able to stand against the onslaught of the enemy, as well as properly discerning good from evil in their own life and in the lives of others.

How does one partake of the Word? The answer is found in 2 Timothy 2:15, "Study to shew thyself approved unto God, a workman that needeth not to be ashamed, rightly dividing the word of truth." It is not enough to read the Word. We must study it to show ourselves approved unto God. In other words, we must study the Word in such a way that it will produce a life that substantiates our claims and will keep us from being ashamed when we face God.

Studying means you must never come to the communion table empty-handed. To ensure you will get a good meal, you should have a good study Bible. My favorite is the KJV Thomson Chain Reference Bible because it has an incredible amount of valuable information. Now that you have the food sitting before you, you should have three items with you, besides pen and paper. They are concordance, dictionary, and curiosity.

A good concordance is the Strong's Exhaustive Concordance of The Bible. This concordance not only allows you to study a topic, but it can give you the Hebrew or Greek meaning of a word. A concordance can also help you to have an overview of the word in Scripture in order to maintain the scriptural integrity of it.

The next item is a dictionary. I have used both a secular and a Bible dictionary. A good Bible dictionary, such as Smith's, gives information from the meaning of a name to historical and archeological information. Secular dictionaries can give you another perspective about the word or topic you are studying.

The final thing is curiosity. The opposite of curiosity is assumption. Assumptions create ignorance when people place their confidence in what they think they know, rather than in Who they need to know.

A child-like faith would include curiosity. Curiosity implies an attitude of awe when it comes to exploring and learning new things. This attitude should be obvious in a Christian because God is infinite, and there is no way one can possess a full comprehension of who He is.

---

[4] Matthew 4:4; John 6:63

Child-like curiosity causes a person to ask questions. These questions can stir up the inclination to probe deeper into a subject. I usually ask three main questions:

1. Do I really understand this subject in the light of God, or am I basing my understanding on assumptions?
2. What is the real intent or meaning of this subject in relationship to the complete Word of God?
3. How must I apply it to myself to make it a living reality in my life?

These questions have opened up the Word to me in wondrous ways. I am shocked at how much my perspective has changed about certain subjects. It has also enabled me to comprehend the depth of other truths that were previously devoid of life in my limited understanding.

Today, healthy curiosity is missing in much of the Church. Many assume, with all of their religious activities, that they know the right truths and doctrines. After all, they have been going to church for many years, have sat under many pastors and teachers, and have it all figured out. As a result, they feel they know enough. Therefore, there is no need to explore further. This conclusion prevents people from exploring the incredible treasures of the Bible. And, if such people do search the Scriptures, it is simply to confirm what they think they already know, not to discover greater truths.

This type of attitude can be seen in Job's companions. They had an understanding about God, but failed to realize that they did not have a clear picture of the situation at hand. They assumed their spiritual understanding would fit into any circumstance. Ultimately, they made foolish conclusions, which brought forth false accusations against Job.

Assumptions are a common occurrence in Christianity. The problem is, when assumptions are reigning there is no amount of reasoning that will change an individual's perspective who is holding tightly to them. In fact, assumptions are reinforced by self-righteous pride that creates a false light. This light often blinds these individuals to their own spiritual condition.

This struggle with truth becomes obvious when you get into a conflict with someone who is clearly standing on this platform of shifting sand.[5] Those who operate from assumptions are often blinded by their pride. As you try to challenge these people's understanding, they become more adamant that they are right, and you are wrong and stupid. These assumptions serve as a judgmental board in these people's eyes.

Through the years, God has dealt with my pride. The conclusions I now have are quite different from the ones I had in my early Christian life. For example, the only assumption I now have is that I do not understand something until I have God's perspective. Even when I gain

---

[5] Matthew 7:24-28

God's perspective, I know the revelation is relevant for that particular time or situation, and may not apply in similar challenges.

Assumptions close down child-like curiosity. This will take the excitement out of exploring God's Word, robbing a person of joy. 1 John 1:4 tells us, "And these things write we unto you, that your joy may be full." The Word of God is designed to bring us joy; rather than burden us down with dutiful obligations or useless pursuits to gain knowledge about the matters of God.[6]

How much of your understanding of the Word is based on assumptions? If your percentage is between 30% and 50%, you probably are devoid of child-like curiosity. Without curiosity, you will not have the inclination to explore the Word or know the joy of discovering its eternal treasures.

Application:

Do a study on forgiveness. Look up the word in your concordance and in a secular dictionary, and then ask the Holy Spirit to reveal its real intent or meaning. I must note that forgiveness, in light of God, does not have to do with the means of dealing with anger, hatred, or bitterness towards an individual. These feelings should not be part of the Christian life, and if they are, the Christian needs to seek forgiveness. There is another meaning attached to forgiveness that will help you gain God's perspective of it, as well as change how you look at it in regards to the forgiveness God has shown every individual who has come to the cross of Christ seeking for it.

Note: Gentle Shepherd Ministries has provided a reference study guide with questions and tests to fine-tune the believer's understanding of the different subjects that are being presented within the different books of the volumes. You can find this reference study guide on our Website where you can download it for your personal edification.

[6] See Ecclesiastes 12:12.

4

THE FOUNDATION

One of the things I have discovered about Christians is that they do not understand how to discern the Word of God correctly. Instead of Christians distinguishing in their mind the different aspects of the Bible, the many facts, concepts, examples, and instructions merge, causing confusion and misappropriation of Scripture.

Four distinct elements make up the Word of God. They are facts, truths, doctrines, and principles. There are also different tools of training that operate in each of these elements that must also be properly considered. They are points of information, examples, instructions, and exhortation. As we are about to see, each element or tool requires a different attitude or approach, to properly receive and assimilate each of them into our lives. For example, information sets up the environment or events that confirm a matter has happened. Such confirmation ensures that we properly discern the correct emphasis in Scripture. Examples reveal personal lessons or consequences that must be considered or instituted for personal edification. Instructions tell us what we need to do, while exhortation warns, admonishes, contends, or encourages us as to how we must walk. If a person does not discern these sources properly, he or she can do a lot of damage to the Word of God, ultimately affecting his or her spiritual life and growth.

The first aspect of Scripture that must be considered is the type of foundation that upholds a person's spiritual life. Foundations determine the level of strength and stability of any structure, kingdom, nation, organization, or religious belief. The designer of a project must determine the type of foundation that needs to be laid according to various factors. For example, the foundations of buildings are laid according to soil, natural elements, and the purpose of the building.

The foundation under religious beliefs is no different. The one who designed it will determine how such religion will be expressed. As a result, the foundations of the many different religious convictions can prove to be distinct from each other. These foundations determine the direction, environment, design, and stability of a person's religious beliefs. If the foundation is wrong, people's ideology will fail them, causing their spiritual life to inwardly collapse. Since religious beliefs can prove to be nothing more than a fragile house of cards that shakes as the different winds blow through the religious worlds, people clearly need to understand the religious foundation on which they stand. Will their spiritual life survive the storms of life, or will it be destroyed because their foundation is weak and defective?

God's Word clearly deals with the subject of foundation. Jesus ended His Sermon on the Mount with the thought-provoking comparison of what it would mean to establish a right foundation that would stand in the storms of life, versus one that would fall. He made it quite clear that the only way a right foundation is firmly established was through obedience to His instructions.[1]

The Apostle Paul identified the true foundation in 1 Corinthians 3:11, "For other foundation can no man lay than that which is laid, which is Jesus Christ." The Person of Jesus serves as the foundation to every believer as well as for the Body or Church. The Christian's foundation is living, and has the ability to determine the quality of life, direction, and purpose of every believer.

This foundation is spiritual in character, and has the capacity to produce a life that finds its purpose in spiritual matters, and not according to worldly influences. It is infinite in nature, which points to eternal stability and endurance. It was designed in the heavenlies; therefore, it naturally leads one upward. It stands distinguished and stable among all other religious beliefs, implying there is no inconsistency in its claims. Because of His foreknowledge, God designed this spiritual foundation before He brought forth His creation. It is the only foundation that will weather every storm, endure all major upheavals and losses, and will stand when all else is shaken.[2]

How did God construct this spiritual foundation? There are a couple of ingredients that make up this unseen, eternal foundation. The first element is facts.

Facts are something that can be proven, thereby give us valuable information. It sets up the environment in which something must be regarded in light of authority and validity. The two greatest biblical facts are the existence of God and the resurrection of Jesus. Romans 1:20 says, "For the invisible things of him from the creation of the world are clearly seen, being understood by the things that are made, even his eternal power and Godhead; so that they are without excuse." This verse states that creation declares that God exists. In fact, science is proving it as it comes into greater understanding about such matters as DNA. These incredible discoveries prove, beyond the shadow of a doubt, that there is a master designer behind creation. Such a declaration makes God's existence a fact that rightfully should be accepted as being trustworthy, rather than foolishly ignored or rejected. Facts will ultimately stand regardless of a person's response, leaving those who reject the evidence that substantiates them without excuse on judgment day.

---

[1] Matthew 7:24-28

[2] Ephesians 1:4; Revelation 13:8; Hebrews 12:26-27

Another fact is the Gospel. The Gospel is that Jesus died for our sins, and was buried, only to be raised up in resurrection power on the third day.[3] It is a historical fact that Jesus died on the cross and was put into a tomb, but the real debate that rages centers around His resurrection.

1 Corinthians 15:14 tells us the significance of Jesus' resurrection, "And if Christ be not risen, then is our preaching vain, and your faith is also vain."

The core of the Gospel and its power rests on the resurrection of Jesus. 1 Corinthians 15:6 states, "After that, he was seen of above five hundred brethren at once; of whom the greater part remain unto this present, but some are fallen asleep." There were various witnesses to Jesus' resurrection. According to the Jewish Law, there needs to be only two witnesses to verify a fact.[4] Through the years, skeptics have tried to prove the fallacy of Christ's resurrection, only to be silenced or to become a believer in it.[5]

The next ingredient that makes up the foundation is found in Isaiah 28:10, "For precept must be upon precept, precept upon precept; line upon line, line upon line; here a little, and there a little." Precept has to do with perception or interpretation of something that will produce godly conduct. It points to the outward structure that was established. Lines imply rulers that will measure or serve as boundaries for that which is being established or constructed. Such lines point to the truths of God. Truths are the second element used to construct the Christian foundation. God is the essence of all truth; therefore, truths consist of His attributes and works. The truths of God's Word are good measuring sticks because they stand on their own merit, but they will present a greater picture when placed alongside other truths. These rulers are basic and immutable. They must be applied to each matter in the same way. These lines serve as a foundation that determines doctrines or precepts.

God's truths are simple, yet profound. A child can understand them, but they also have tremendous depth that reinforces the present foundation as one grows in the knowledge of Jesus Christ. The Holy Spirit is the only One who can reveal the depth of these truths.

People cannot teach truths; rather they are identified and defined according to the nature of God. They bring dimension to facts. For example, God's existence may be a fact, but truths are what identify His character and define His ways. These truths are also upheld by examples that are found in the Word of God. Since truths are unchangeable in nature, there should be no debates, adjustments, or

---

[3] 1 Corinthians 15:1-4

[4] Deuteronomy 17:6; Matthew 18:16

[5] See Josh McDowell's book Evidence That Demands A Verdict, chapter 10, to see the overwhelming evidence of Jesus' resurrection.

intellectual arrogance resonating among believers about these unshakable lines.

This means we must learn to identify the essential qualities and intent of these truths. This is where the Holy Spirit steps on the scene to bring great depth to these lines.

Since these rulers all point to one source: The Person of Jesus Christ, they will remain consistent, regardless of the direction you approach them. Jesus confirmed this by telling His disciples that He is "the truth." Since all truth begins and ends with Jesus, we as believers must conclude that it is only in light of Him that the depth of these truths are revealed by the Spirit, ultimately reinforcing the foundation.

These truths are designed to change or enlarge a person's perception about God. Since these truths are established according to the examples, ways, and workings of God, they must be received by faith. As the individual applies them by faith to his or her life, God's truths will enlarge the person's perception to receive a greater revelation of Jesus.

What are some of the spiritual truths in Scripture? Salvation, mercy, grace, justification, sanctification, forgiveness of sin, and redemption serve as spiritual truths. Keep in mind, these virtues point to the character and work of God. The work of God always brings us back to Jesus Christ who serves as the visible expression of the Godhead.[6] I believe all of these truths have been made visible by the cross of Jesus. And, it is by faith that we receive these truths as our personal reality. This is why Paul declared, "For I determined not to know any thing among you, save Jesus Christ, and him crucified" (1 Corinthians 2:2).

It is the reality of the Person of Jesus that serves as our immovable foundation. Since He is our foundation, everything must be tested and proven according to His character, teachings, and examples. It is within the light of Jesus that something will be established or it will be destroyed.

I have watched many people take biblical truths and try to make them into doctrines that are debatable or controllable. The problem with making a truth into a doctrine is that you take the intent out of it, thus limiting its ability to enlarge you to receive a greater revelation of Jesus.

For example, some have taken grace and made it into a doctrine to confirm some erroneous concepts about salvation. Grace placed into this religious context, had to first be dissected and rendered into a controllable concept. Removing grace from the spiritual foundation closes down a vital avenue in which God's people are able to establish a healthy spiritual life. Ultimately, it weakens people's foundation.

Each time people's foundations are weakened, they will lose their ability to accurately discern the fundamental doctrines that have been

[6] Colossians 2:9

established. As the foundation becomes weaker under these individuals, the structure (or life) becomes vulnerable to collapse.

Today, I am watching different segments of the Church on the verge of collapse. The main reason for this precarious situation is due to Christians taking vital truths from the foundation and making them into doctrines. This procedure has made the church top-heavy as various lines are conspicuously missing from the foundation.

Sadly, as the foundation becomes weaker, it begins to create a crisis as "another Jesus" is erected in the minds of those who are in error or weak in the faith. After all, God's truths not only reveal the Jesus of the Bible, but will also bring all spiritual matters back to His person for the purpose of testing them in light of His character, will, and ways. A weak foundation always implies a weak Jesus to those who are unbelieving, weak, and vulnerable.

A weak foundation produces an identity crisis as people become unstable, which causes them to be tossed to and fro by every wind of doctrine. This instability makes these individuals prey to wolves and heretical teachings.[7] Without an established foundation, there is nothing these people can firmly cling to in times of trouble and challenge. In fact, logical debate or the establishment of another doctrine that will tickle their ears can quickly change the condition of their foundation.

The right spiritual foundation is immovable. This is why truths establish doctrine, instead of doctrine determining truth. Whenever you have people defining truth through doctrine, they will end up with a different Jesus.

Jesus summarized His place and ministry when He stated that He is the way, the truth, and the life. Jesus is the only immovable foundation that will stand the test of time and withstand the onslaught of destruction. He serves as the plumbline to everything man believes. He alone will judge all matters, including the souls of men.[8]

This brings us back to the right foundation. We must know the real Jesus. In Matthew 16:13, Jesus asked His disciples, "Whom do men say that I the Son of man am?"

Peter's reply in Matthew 16:14 was, "Some say that thou art John the Baptist: some, Elias, and others, Jeremias, or one of the prophets."[9] If the understanding you have of Jesus belongs to another person, your foundation will be shaky, regardless of how scriptural the individual may be. You cannot stand, nor can your spiritual life be constructed on another foundation that is already occupied. You must have your own personal, separate foundation.

---

[7] Ephesians 4:14
[8] John 14:6; John 5:22
[9] Matthew 16:14

Jesus then asked the next question, "But whom say ye that I am?"[10] A Christian's spiritual life stands secure because he or she knows the answer to this question. Every Christian is banking his or her eternal destination on Jesus' identity. It is because of who Jesus is that believers are assured of the life God has for them.

What is your answer to the previous question? Could you make the same declaration as Peter because Jesus' identity has been revealed to your spirit by the Father? "Thou art the Christ, the Son of the living God."[11]

This declaration was made at different times throughout Scripture. Instead of walking away from Him in unbelief people declared this reality when they chose to believe Jesus. Interestingly, people like Peter in John 6:69 and Martha in John 11:27 believed Jesus, not because of what they intellectually perceived, but in who they knew Him to be. Because these people chose to believe Jesus' words based on His identity, they could stand in the midst of challenges and crisis.

This is the secret behind every Christian's ability to stand and withstand challenges. Christians cannot stand based on what they know about Jesus, but who they know Him to be. This knowledge can only come through revelation that comes out of obedience and communion.

Is the Person of Jesus your foundation, or is your Christian life top-heavy with intellectual pursuits and doctrine? If your answer is "yes" to intellectual pursuits and doctrine, then your spiritual life will one day collapse around you. It will fail you in a time of spiritual need and crisis. Therefore, repent and ask God to establish you on a right foundation no matter what it may cost you.

Beware! God will tear up and shake everything in your life. Great doubts will raise up to mock your knowledge, and you will feel as if your whole life is out of control. In such times choose to believe Jesus' words because in so doing, you will find yourself clinging to the immovable Rock of Ages. And, through the challenge, you will receive the greatest reward of all: You will learn of Him and begin to possess His glorious life.

Application:

Choose one of the truths and define it according to the character or work of Jesus. Once you understand the intent of it, ask the Holy Spirit to give it life by revealing it in greater ways so that you can learn of Jesus in a greater measure.

---

[10] Matthew 16:15

[11] See Matthew 16:17

5

DOCTRINES

One of the major debates in the Church is what constitutes pure doctrine. Everyone has an opinion, but those with a humble spirit realize that pure doctrine comes down to simplicity more than great explanations. Even though doctrines are debated, exalted, and taught, their main purpose is to prepare the heart to embrace the living reality of the Bible, the Person of Jesus Christ.

I have a tendency to shy away from the word "doctrine" because it has caused a debate in my own soul. Being a member of a former cult has left a very bad taste in my mouth about this word. Yet, the word "doctrine" is a scriptural reality. Like the leaders of my former religion, Christians seem to be quick to create doctrines that abuse the Word and confuse the intent and simplicity behind it. In fact, much of what Christians believe has been improperly lumped into the "concept of doctrine." This practice has prevented people from rightly dividing the Word of truth. It has also robbed the Written Word of its authority to properly instruct according to God's righteous character.[1]

In my attempt to get past my concerns about the word "doctrine," I had to come to terms with what constitutes doctrine. For example, for the Pharisees of Jesus' day, it consisted of a lot of dos and don'ts. Jesus said these doctrines were of men, which translated into traditions of men.[2]

According to *Strong's Exhaustive Concordance*, tradition implies precept, commandment, or ordinance. My dictionary defines it as teaching, instruction, dogma, or a law that has been established through past decisions.[3] Sadly, the many traditions we find in churches have been added on to godly precepts by men, and have become burdens too great to bear for some believers.

Since man's doctrines become traditions that strictly deal with outward performance, rather than inward transformation, they can make the person indifferent to his or her personal condition. Jesus said of these traditions, "This people draweth nigh unto me with their mouth, and honoureth me with their lips; but their heart is far from me" (Matthew 15:8).

---

[1] 2 Timothy 2:15

[2] Matthew 15:8-9

[3] Webster's New Collegiate Dictionary, © 1976 by G. & C. Merriam Co.

This brings us to the concept of precept. Isaiah 28:10 talks about both precepts and lines. As already pointed out in the last chapter, lines point to truths that comprise our foundation, but precepts imply doctrine.

The *New International Version* of the Bible uses the term "do" in the place of precept. This is a good way of confirming that doctrine comes down to doing or man's responsibilities towards God. This is different from the lines or rulers that have to do with establishing a right foundation according to the character and work of God.

The doctrine of the Pharisees created an appearance of righteousness, but the pure doctrine established by Jesus went further than the outward expression of man. It penetrated the mind and reached down to the innermost being of man. Its main goal had to do with confronting and changing the inward man, thereby producing upright conduct. Such conduct would result in the authority to stand before God in confidence, and the power to withstand the enemy. This doctrine also established blessings for those who would accept the challenge of living the righteous life, and consequences and judgment for those who would refuse to respond.

When I studied the concept of doctrine, I discovered there are three elements that ensure pure doctrine: A right spirit, godly philosophy, and upright conduct. The right spirit inspires and enables godly conduct. It is important to point out that no person can live this Christian life in his or her own power. Those who truly decide to follow Jesus need the Holy Spirit's power and leadership in their lives to accomplish such a feat.

It is hard to believe that philosophy is part of doctrine. However, if you look up philosophy, you will find it has to do with the type of attitude or view you have about life. This view will interpret spiritual matters according to what it perceives or understands about God. The Apostle Paul made a distinction about this subject in Colossians 2:8, "Beware lest any man spoil you through philosophy and vain deceit, after the tradition of men, after the rudiments of the world, and <u>not after Christ</u>." (Emphasis added.)

Paul clearly implied that there are philosophies that are of Jesus. In fact, the Sermon on the Mount is a clear example of philosophy. In this sermon, you can actually see Jesus challenging man's attitude or view of life as to what constitutes righteousness to God. He dealt with how people should view their enemies, persecution, self-righteousness, forgiveness, and prayer. He took people beyond outward actions down to inward motives and heart attitudes. For example, adultery entails more than sexual deviation outside the marriage bed. If a married person toys with this sin in his or her mind, he or she has just committed adultery.

A person's motive determines the quality of his or her conduct. Righteous conduct involves godly discipline. It exceeds the traditions of man because it does not settle for an appearance of righteousness.

Rather, it is a visible, living example of it.[4] In fact, we can actually study personal and church disciplines in the epistles, and develop a picture of godly attitudes that ensure upright conduct.

This brings us back to the Sermon on the Mount. The intent of Jesus' doctrine clearly can be observed in this awe-inspiring teaching.

First, let me clarify that the Word clearly identifies Jesus' teachings contained within His sermon in Matthew as doctrine. Matthew 7:28 states, "And it came to pass when Jesus had ended these sayings, the people were astonished at his doctrine." Here, we see that both the people and Matthew recognized His teachings in this discourse as being doctrine. As you study the Sermon on the Mount, you will see where Jesus is dealing with the attitudes, heart, thoughts, and conduct of man. He points out the blessings and consequences. This, once again, confirms the essence of doctrine. It has nothing to do with the character of God, but with the inward condition and outward conduct of man, as well as the reality of reaping what is sown.

This brings us to the purpose of doctrine. It does not define God, rather doctrine gives people a clear understanding of what it means for them to be upright before God and finish the course.

It is also important to point out that truths plus doctrine equal fruits, and the fruits of our lives reveal the spirit or intent of our doctrine. Matthew 7:15-16 tells us we will know people by their fruits. It is easy to discern doctrine inspired by the Holy Spirit because it is living and visible. However, doctrine that lacks the right spirit is arrogant and dead.

It is also significant to point out that precepts involve the senses. This means that doctrine must be personally experienced and walked out before it will have any real impact in the person's life. Therefore, coming to terms with doctrine is more than having a mental assent about Christianity and spiritual beliefs. This is why pure doctrine produces an outward expression of spirit and life. Once again, we must remember the words of Jesus in John 6:63, "The words that I speak unto you, they are spirit, and they are life."

The problem with embracing pure doctrine is that there is much confusion about the concept of doctrine. I have learned that much of what Christians consider doctrine is nothing more than their theological opinions or conclusions to a matter. Even though their beliefs have graduated into a religious theory or system, you can still see the fruits of these beliefs. One of the main fruits of man's theology is arrogance and prejudice.

This is why it is important to understand what constitutes doctrine. It has to do with spirit, attitude, and conduct, not a system of beliefs that govern how a person practices religion. It is not a mental conclusion or evaluation concerning a spiritual matter. Rather, the images or examples that are intertwined into its fiber are understandable, explainable,

---

[4] Matthew 5:20

reasonable, and will produce a righteous response. The power of pure doctrine is that it is supposed to be experienced and walked out; thereby, it has the power to create conviction, passion, change, and even conflict in a person's life.

Conflicts over pure doctrine arise because people have different experiences in their lives when it comes to their spiritual encounters. For example, my understanding or experience of a spiritual matter will be based on what I have encountered in the past or discovered and learned in my Christian walk. Another person will have a different experience in that area and will develop another conclusion. Does one person's experience invalidate another's if the lessons or conclusions are not the same? The answer is no, because people are at different places of maturity. In fact, the different experiences or conclusions can be beneficial if there is agreement in spirit.

This is why doctrines can be greatly debated. Much of our understanding of doctrine is based on the personal experiences and lessons that are attached to them. Ultimately, doctrine determines much of our reality and how we process spiritual information. These doctrines can be alive, enlarging a person's ability to receive, or dead, closing the individual down towards spiritual growth.

The inability to discern pure doctrine results in spiritual dullness. As a result, many Christians cannot properly discern doctrine, which allows for the inundation of the doctrines of demons.[5]

Once a pure doctrine is established, it becomes an avenue for the Holy Spirit to enlarge a person's perception of God, allowing him or her to receive a greater revelation of Jesus Christ.[6] Keep in mind; we each interpret spiritual matters such as experiences and revelation according to the doctrine that is being established. This is why pure doctrine is vital. Nevertheless, the Word of God is clear that our pursuit must never be to acquire doctrine, but to possess the knowledge of Jesus Christ. Since doctrine must be established in light of who Jesus is, it is the presence of His Person in our midst that ensures pure doctrine.

1 Peter 1:13 tells us we must be brought into the revelation of Jesus, and 2 Peter 1:8 warns us that we must not be barren or unfruitful in the knowledge of Jesus. Ephesians 3:3-4 tells us that Jesus is the mystery in the Word. In other words, Jesus Christ is hidden in Scripture, and only the Holy Spirit can unveil Him in greater measure.[7]

As I study Scripture, the Holy Spirit reveals Christ to me in greater ways. Each revelation of Christ must be confirmed by pure doctrine that is being applied and walked out in each of our lives. Notice, truths establish and discern doctrine, while doctrine is meant to confirm truths through practical application. Truths point to the character and work of

---

[5] 1 Timothy 4:1

[6] John 16:13-14

[7] 1 Corinthians 13:9

Jesus Christ, while doctrine can lead to a greater revelation of Him through practical experiences and application. Like the Law, pure doctrine is meant to end with Jesus. Ultimately, the manifestation of His righteous life in us will be a fulfillment of doctrine, revealing that it is alive and it is truth.

If the right spirit is missing in doctrine, it will subdue or stop revelation from taking place. It is also important to point out here that godly doctrine will not capture a complete revelation of the infinite Christ. However, such doctrine constitutes boundaries that He will not step outside of when dealing in our lives, especially when it comes to exposing any moral deviation in our character.

Once Christ is revealed, biblical truths will become a personal reality. They will take on dimension, causing change and growth to take place. This is why the writer of Hebrews made this statement in Hebrews 6:1, "Therefore, leaving the principles of the doctrine of Christ, let us go on unto perfection..."

Doctrine cannot bring perfection or spiritual maturity. Believers who stay at the level of doctrine will not only be stifled in spiritual growth, but there will be no evidence of satisfaction and contentment. When doctrine (even pure doctrine) becomes an end in and of itself, it becomes like the Law, dead letter.

People who insist on staying at the level of doctrine are often self-righteous, opinioned, judgmental, fearful, and unteachable. Sadly, it takes little to offend them concerning their doctrine because they often make it a sacred cow, causing inconsistencies in their lives. This fragile state simply means the person is standing on the shifting sand of their doctrine, rather than on the immovable rock of the Person of Jesus.[8]

The problem with some of the so-called "doctrines" that are being promoted today is that they have nothing to do with a person's spiritual well-being, conduct, or destiny. In other words, believing these concepts one way or the other will not determine the person's eternal destination or present conduct. Instead, what these doctrines often affect are peoples' attitude towards one another.

Upon examining these so-called "doctrines", you realize that they have no point of instruction in righteousness, but are directed at intellectual conclusions. If the instruction in personal conduct is missing, it means that it is nothing more than theological opinions that major in intellectual arrogance.

Although theology is to be the study of God, God is often missing from some of these belief systems, while man's logic often reigns. Any time man's logic plays a prevalent role in establishing spiritual beliefs, such beliefs become nothing more than theories or educated guesses that produce arrogance. Theological arrogance creates a superior air that often results in an elitism that borders on a cult mentality. When I

---

[8] Matthew 7:24-27

encounter this attitude, I become repulsed because it lacks a right spirit, and promotes the intelligence of man over the spirit or intent of God's Word.

As stated in the last chapter, one of the problems is that Christians try to make truths into a doctrine. This is when every angle of a truth is dissected with the goal of putting it into a nice, neat package. This dissection robs the particular truth of its intent and simplicity. Once this happens, there is a breach in the wall of the foundation because there is a vital ruler missing by which to discern doctrine. This creates a weak foundation and an oversized structure.

Today, I watch people make truths into doctrine and doctrine into truths. This makes the Christian life very unstable, as truths become changeable and debatable, and doctrines become the final authority as to what a person believes. This scenario means that Jesus is clearly missing because there is no solid foundation by which to test beliefs.

Another mistake people make is to take a fact and make it into a doctrine. Facts lack dimension. For example, we know there is a God, but who is He? This is where truths come in. As already pointed out, facts establish a reality, but truths define that reality. Facts are tangible; therefore, it is a matter of acceptance or rejection of them. Nevertheless, truths cannot be observed, which means we must receive them by faith.

Doctrine is not for the purpose of acquiring spiritual facts or knowledge, but is meant to establish man in godly conduct. This brings us back to the purpose of doctrine, which is to deal with the inward man to produce upright living.

Doctrine establishes a moral code for man to live by. However, it takes the Spirit of God to transform the inward man to properly live this life within the proper framework. If the right spirit is missing, any code of conduct will become a matter of mere tradition, not spirit and life.

This is brought out as you realize the tradition of man encourages strict conduct, but lacks the spirit and power to live it out. Theology may embrace philosophy, but it can lack the right spirit and righteous conduct to bring it any viable credibility.

With this in mind, check out your doctrine first by testing the fruits of your life. Separate doctrine from facts, truths, and personal theology. Make sure that you are not trying to define God according to your precepts, but that you are allowing the reality of God to establish proper doctrine. Once this separation takes place, begin to examine which of your doctrine promotes upright living, and which doctrine promotes traditions, self-righteousness, and elitism.

Application:

On a piece of paper, make four columns and put the headings of facts, truths, doctrine, and theology. Take the following subjects and put them under the proper heading: Gospel, holiness, consecration, rapture theories, hell, salvation, "once saved—always saved," fornication, and sin. I also encourage you to study the Sermon on the Mount found in *Matthew 5-7*. Observe how Jesus deals with the inward man to create upright living. Note how He outlined the consequences if man fails to earnestly confront wrong attitudes and actions. By properly studying this sermon, you will come out with a better understanding of the purpose and workings of doctrine.

6

THE COMBINATION

As stated, doctrine is a point of interpretation. We actually interpret or consider our Scriptural responsibility in light of what we consider to be doctrine, but it is important to point out that doctrine does not determine our philosophy or view. It is the spirit and attitude towards God that determines how we view and handle doctrine. Therefore, our fruits and conduct will be determined by how we interpret doctrine according to our view of God and life. Without the right view of God, doctrine will lack authority, and without the right view of life, doctrine will prove to be dead-letter or indifferent.

There are four different elements that influence how we interpret or handle doctrine. These elements make up a combination that can be adjusted according to the particular doctrine that is being considered. These elements are: Scripture (S), religion/theology (R), personal preference/experience (P), and culture (C).

Scripture and religion are always opposite of each other in this combination, while personal preference is always facing culture. The particular element that is on the top of the combination will serve as the main emphasis behind our interpretation, while the element on the right points to how something will influence the point of emphasis. The element on the left side serves as a point of consideration or in lieu of, while the bottom requires subjection in some manner.

Consider the following diagram to gain a mental picture:

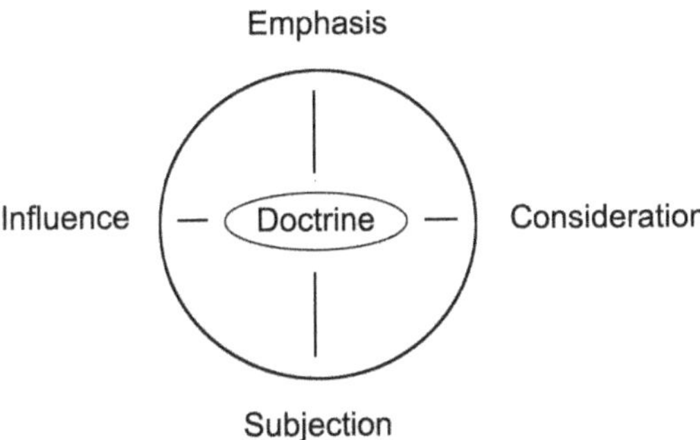

The *emphasis* will determine the spirit in which doctrine will be tested or judged. For example, people are greatly influenced by their particular emphasis as to what they think is important or they want to accomplish.

The power or authority of the point of *influence* in a person's life will determine what will have the greatest impact in interpreting doctrine: emphasis or influence. For example, culture plays a tremendous part in how people view something. If culture is in the place of influence, it will influence the point of emphasis in regards to how a matter must be handled, rather than emphasis overpowering the point of influence. There is only one proper location on the combination where culture will be properly subdued, ultimately serving as a point of contrast, rather than preeminence.

The point of *consideration* on the combination will be either a point of desire, contrast, or instruction, depending on what stands in the position of influence. For example, if Scripture is in this position, it will be considered in light of religion and theology, instead of the other way around. As a result, religion will have the greatest influence.

The final point is that of *subjection*. Depending on what is in this position will determine if the emphasis is coming into subjection to this point, or if the point of emphasis is looking to it for guidance. For instance, if personal preference is in the place of emphasis, it will always look to culture for guidance. However, if Scripture is located in the place of subjection, it will come into subordination to religion or theology.

Now, with this in mind, let us consider how this combination works in light of doctrine. Keep in mind, doctrine also points to attitude and conduct.

Let us consider the combination where religion or theology (R) is the emphasis, and see how it affects how we approach doctrine. Remember, Scripture (S) is always opposite of religion or theology.

Note the following diagram:

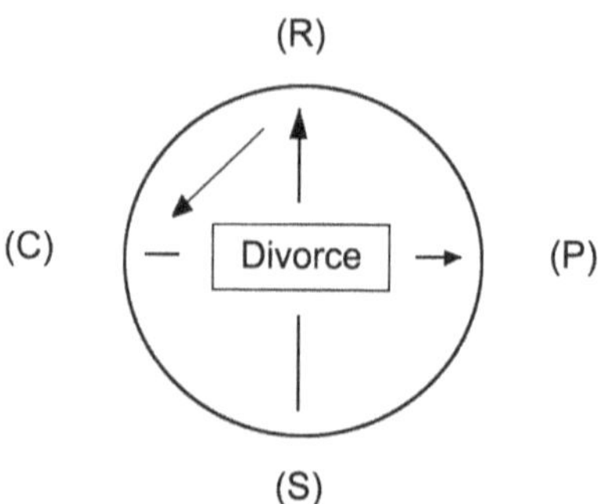

With this diagram in mind, let us consider the controversial doctrine of divorce. Although the teachings of religion may be scriptural concerning this issue, it can lack the right spirit. When the right spirit is missing, the real problem is overlooked. Religion, without the right spirit, calls people to conform instead of facing the root of the problem and properly contending with or confronting it. Religion will sometimes look to the moral practices of the culture to relate to and address personal conduct.

The real problem in divorce is not the action itself. Rather, it is a hard heart. Jesus clearly explained this in Matthew 19:4-9. A hard heart points to a variety of sins such as selfishness, control, anger, and hatred. The fruits of a hard heart are indifference, treachery or unforgiveness. This heart closes down the means in which to properly communicate, resulting in weariness and betrayal.

Jesus also set down the one acceptable ground for divorce: adultery.[1] The problem is there can be many other problems that tear at the fiber of marriage that are beyond a person's control, such as addiction and abuse. Many religions declare that a person, regardless of the circumstances, must not remarry. Sadly, it only takes one self-centered individual to destroy the unity and sanctity of this relationship, leaving many innocent victims paying for other people's actions.

Religion only deals with the outward product of a hard heart in marriage, not the inward condition of it. It only calls people to adhere to rules without addressing the real problem. This results in religion or theology having to swallow a camel while swatting at a gnat.[2]

The problems in marriage are not always obvious, but deeply personal and emotional. I have witnessed this struggle on a personal level. How can a hurting, confused person properly discern in the midst of emotional devastation caused by a breakdown in a relationship? This devastation actually adds to the individual's plight, making him or her feel even more overwhelmed. In such cases, a judgment call needs to be made about the condition of the marriage.

The Apostle Paul talked about making such a judgment call in 1 Corinthians 7. He was not establishing commandments that required obedience. Rather, he was implementing guidelines. For example, he gave another legitimate reason for divorce. That is, if an unbelieving spouse wants to leave the marriage, he or she must be allowed to do so. He stated that God has called us to peace. He also stated that it is better to marry than burn with lust. What is one to do if he or she is divorced because of a bad judgment call that was the result of inexperience? Such a person thought he or she was marrying a believer, only to find a stranger that displayed neither the fruit nor the conduct of a believer. Are such people to burn in their lusts because they dare not remarry? What kind of judgment call should these types of individuals make when their desire is to be right before God in this area, but their heart is to be married? As I studied Paul's instructions, I sensed that he was encouraging both discretion and judgment. In my understanding, remarriage is not prohibited, but it must be done in line with God's will.

---

[1] Matthew 5:31-32

[2] Matthew 23:24

The problem with remarriage is that God is often missing in the equation. It is simply about feeding one's lust.

The one thing that a person caught in this battle does not need is to be judged and lambasted with condemnation and religious platitudes. These responses often raise their head in religious circles. There is nothing gracious about the death of a marriage, but platitudes and criticism will not change the status of such a marriage. The truth of the matter is that the real issues are often ignored as people take sides, and religion hides its inexperience and indifference towards this matter behind a few Scriptures.

As people try to submit to the immovable, harsh demands of religion, the emotional fallout of a broken marriage can cause them to see the religious presentation as unfeeling and unfair. In some cases, the divorce was beyond their control, yet they are left to pay the price of what they perceive to be loneliness because of someone else's actions.

When the condition and reality of the marriage is ignored and people are encouraged to simply conform to some religious masquerade, religion becomes dead-letter and ineffective. This is when those weak in faith will come to the conclusion that religion, with its unfeeling theology, is a farce. If they do not become depressed, they will become a skeptic of religion, thereby, closing themselves off to its influence.

It is at this time that culture will play a big part in such a person's conclusion. Religion, in the position of emphasis, can cause many vulnerable people to become disillusioned, pushing them into the vices of wrong cultural influences. Culture will offer such people a false hope of happiness and a fulfilled life after divorce.

The result of culture stepping into the picture at this point often ends in more wickedness. At the time of this writing, the divorce rate in the Church is as high as in the secular arena. In a way, the Church is part of fulfilling an end-day prophecy, "But as the days of Noe were, so shall also the coming of the Son of man be. For as in the days that were before the flood they were eating and drinking, marrying and giving in marriage, until the day that Noe entered into the ark" (Matthew 24:37-38).

Jesus identified the real problem in the breakdown of marriage, but the Apostle Paul specifically addressed the proper attitude to ensure a godly marriage. In both Ephesians 5 and Colossians 3, he speaks of inward conditions such as a submissive attitude and a loving heart. In 1 Corinthians 7, he talks about benevolence in the marriage. Benevolence is often an expression of good will and kindness. Both Paul and Peter talked about honor in marriage, which is the humble attitude of one preferring another to personal needs and preference.[3]

This brings us to what happens when a person allows religion or theology to be exalted in order to interpret doctrine. Religion or theology

---

[3] 1 Peter 3:5-9

at best makes doctrine a surface, intellectual dogma that has no power to change or give life. It has no vision beyond its own agenda or emphasis. When religion or theology attempts to be the final emphasis or authority in a person's belief system, doctrine becomes a truth that is acknowledged as a fact. The problem with doctrine being made into a truth is that it produces a self-righteous attitude, making the person susceptible to an antichrist or religious spirit.

This brings us to the next combination. There are certain doctrines that are greatly influenced by culture (C). The greatest of these involve sexual conduct. Although Scripture may determine many of our opinions about such matters, the culture is the one which determines many of our attitudes and practices towards personal moral conduct. For example, people look to the culture to determine, logic, or justify practices such as dating, pre-marital sex, and other questionable practices.

Consider the following diagram:

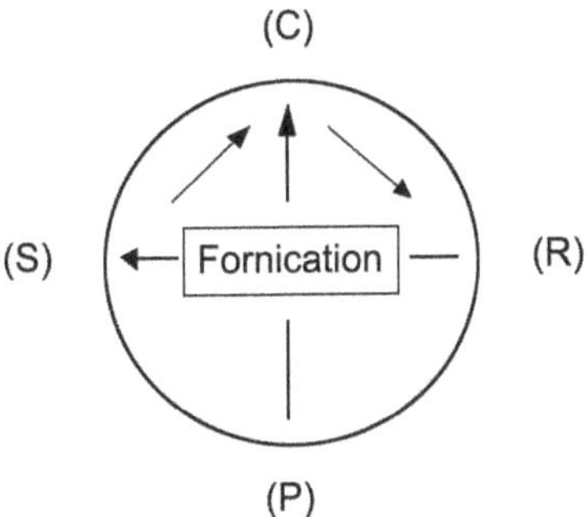

Fornication includes all illicit sex outside of marriage that God clearly instituted between one man and one woman in the Garden of Eden. If you ask most Christians if they believe fornication is a sin, I believe they would say yes. However, the harsh reality is that many Christians are guilty of falling into the subtle traps of this sin, which includes partaking of pornography.

Therefore, Christians who find themselves in the trap of fornication must consider this: Why is much of their personal conduct or practices so far from scriptural beliefs? Simply put, since many have adopted the culture's practices concerning this area, they also unknowingly embraced its attitude about these issues. If these individuals have not allowed the Word of God to transform their minds about moral attitudes and conduct, they will naturally fall into the subtle traps of this sin, especially since it is justified by worldly philosophies. This is why a transformed mind will cause change in a person's conduct.

Our society has effectively indoctrinated us through the different media outlets with both the philosophies, attitudes, and the excuses for improper sexual practices and conduct. This conditioning has erected inclinations and tendencies, whereby, in the right situation, a person will naturally go with the direction he or she is leaning towards. Because of this subtle indoctrination, Christians have no qualms about practices that are nothing more than breeding grounds for fornication.

In our culture, fornication is a justifiable practice in light of desire, love, happiness, personal fulfillment, and expression. In fact, in our society, fornication is no big deal. However, God is clear about how He perceives it. Fornication is a practice of the flesh that will result in eternal damnation.

This brings us down to what happens when culture is the emphasis of a person, causing personal preference to come into subjection to it. Much of religion has established healthy rules in the area of sexual conduct. However, the problem is some people in the religious realm recognize unhealthy practices such as dating as a valid custom. Once again, we see that culture is still setting the trend for conduct. Dating is a cultural practice that has set up many people to fall into the cesspool of fornication. While Christians look to their religion for proper instruction for their conduct, religion considers culture, while trying to work within scriptural instructions to determine practices.

Scripture, on the other hand, is very clear about sexual conduct. It instructs people to flee from youthful lusts. It explains that fornication is a sin against the holy temple of God (man's body) that causes a person to come into agreement with the unholy. It also outlines how a person can defraud a brother or sister by giving them false impressions about feelings or future intentions, which is a frequent happening in the dating game. For example, declarations of love and promises of future bliss have caused many to fall into this devastating trap of emotional and physical fornication. People are often robbed of their innocence, self-respect, and a powerful testimony.[4]

Even though religion may advocate proper sexual conduct, much of it fails to call people to the caliber established by Scripture. In a way, religion unintentionally gives the impression that the instructions in the Bible are antiquated and not realistic for our present challenges.

In this combination, we see that culture overrides Scripture by perverting it. Religion on the other hand, may seek or use Scripture to confirm its stands on such issues, but it often subdues the Scriptures purity and power by adhering to an unholy agreement between cultural practices and moral responsibility.

Culture points to the world and its lusts. Therefore, whenever it stands as a Christian's emphasis, it chokes out the Word of God, and opens a person up to spirits of perversion and lust as he or she gives way to ungodliness through logical excuses and justifications. This produces the fruit of rebellion, which causes a person to become powerless to overcome the spirit of the world and its god, Satan.

Once again, it is time to turn the combination. We need to consider what happens when our emphasis becomes personal preference (P).

[4] 1 Corinthians 6:15-20; 1 Thessalonians 4:3-7; 2 Timothy 2:19-22

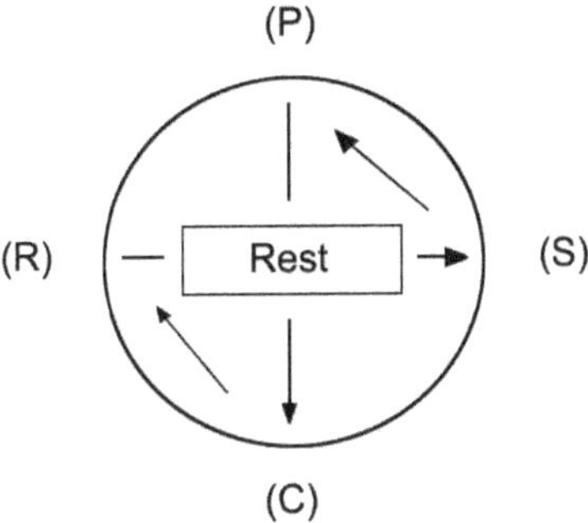

You might be wondering what kind of doctrine would be considered in light of this combination. Let us try the teaching surrounding the subject of rest. The idea of rest has to do with relaxation, enjoyment, entertainment, or pleasure.

The problem with personal preference is that it lacks identity, and will naturally prefer the ways of personal selfishness. Such selfishness becomes subject to what will make it feel good about self. John 3:19-20 tells us that people prefer the darkness of their selfishness because their deeds are evil. However, such personal preference must look somewhere to find out how to act and respond. Therefore, it will usually look to culture for possible options because it serves as its greatest source of identity. If there are religious influences, it will examine the worldly options according to religion. Religion will have some influence on a person's conclusion, but since one presumes that religious positions are always based on Scripture, Scripture is rarely sought out for proper contrast outside of religious influences. Ultimately, God's Word is adjusted or brought into compliance with personal preference.

In America, the idea of rest in many cases has been reduced to the pursuit of what often becomes a useless exercise that we refer to as fun. This exercise often proves to be the very essence of selfishness and vanity, which usually turns into a relentless pursuit of silly fantasies. These fantasies translate into temporary nonsense. It goes without saying that any temporary nonsense leaves a person unfulfilled and disappointed.

Sadly, some of the visible Church has bought into this silly fantasy in the hope of attracting people. In order to do this, it operates from the platform of the world. However, the wrong emphasis on fun brings leanness to the soul, which creates an unexplainable weariness because it leaves a vacuum rather than producing satisfaction. Since the different aspects of the visible Church use worldly means to attract souls, there is no distinction for undiscerning Christians to correctly test their forms of enjoyment.

God encouraged Israel to enjoy life, but it was in a form of celebration, not an exercise in useless activities. This celebration was directed toward man getting in touch with God, which would bring both sobriety and peace to his soul. This sobriety was to help people stop long enough to consider the essence of life, bringing reflection to those things that added substance and virtue to their lives. This reflection would allow them to reevaluate priorities and goals, redefining life and changing their focus from an earthly plane to a heavenly perspective. It is this perspective that brings peace to the soul. Peace produces satisfaction and the much-needed rest and revitalization that man so desperately needs to keep things in a proper, godly perspective.

What brings this type of rest to the soul? It is not useless activities where a person is trying to have fun. A Christian's rest is solely found in the Person of Jesus Christ, but the individual must know what it means to be hid in Christ.

As you consider the average life in America, it is obvious that entertainment has robbed people of their imagination to explore. Pleasure has become a god, enjoyment a facade, while rest to the soul is becoming a foreign concept.

Sadly, this ungodly concept of entertainment and fun has found its way into the Church. The fun concept actually creates an indifferent, unrealistic reality, and is very self-centered and self-serving. Yet, much of religion has bought into this silliness in the name of promoting the kingdom of God. In some cases, religious systems and institutions offer up nothing more than religious entertainment to attract numbers in the name of Christ. However, this attraction is nothing more than a clever means to feed the sensual appetites of people under the guise of promoting salvation.

Culture perverts the things of God, while personal preferences are very fleshly in nature and will defile the things of God. As individuals adjust the things of God to their worldly preferences, they will cloud the issue of uprightness and become lukewarm in their commitment to Jesus. They will lose the ability to discern what is going on in their lives.

This brings us to the spirits that personal preference will give way to: that of the world and rebellion. These influences will cause people to walk in discontentment and condemnation. It will leave them empty or void as each personal preference leads to vanity and compromise. It ultimately robs a person of authority against the enemies of his or her soul.

This brings us to the final combination. The emphasis in the final combination is the right one: that of Scripture. This combination encourages the right spirit and philosophy. If the Holy Spirit is determining a person's interpretation of doctrine, Scripture will influence a person's philosophy and preference. The person will consider culture in light of how it affects his or her relationship with God, while all religious influences will become subject to Scripture.

It is important to note how this correct approach will effectively establish godly doctrine. Consider the following diagram:

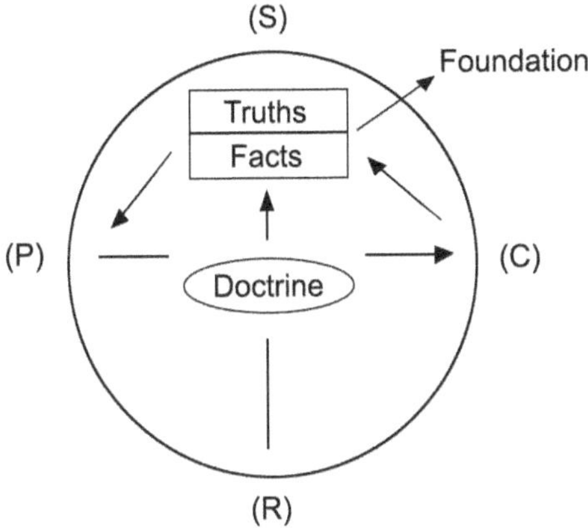

Note how religion or theology is processed through the godly foundation, which we know is the Person of Jesus Christ. This influences personal preference and brings culture into the proper consideration of Scripture. It ultimately instills an upright attitude, resulting in understanding the correct application and life to doctrine. This life and attitude will be in line with the mind and life of Jesus Christ, which will be manifested in and through an individual.

It is the evidence of Jesus in a person that verifies the existence and quality of pure doctrine. Without the evidence of Jesus, doctrine is reduced to nothing more than mental assent or religious tradition, dogma, or theology.

Hebrews 6:1-2 gives us a starting point in establishing pure doctrine. These Scriptures present the principle doctrines of Christ. As you study these doctrines, you will realize that these are the doctrines that have already been established in the Old Testament. The Old Testament cast the shadow of Jesus Christ. When He walked this earth, He became the example, fulfillment, and manifestation of these doctrines to the world. These doctrines are: repentance from dead works, faith towards God, baptisms, the laying on of hands, resurrection of the dead, and eternal judgment.

A person's application of these six doctrines will determine how he or she will view and respond to the Person of Jesus. Each one of these doctrines represents a progression in a person's spiritual walk, beginning with salvation and ending with consecration. The first four are directed at a person's attitude towards God. The last two are reminders that there will be a resurrection where rewards or eternal consequences await believers after their earthly journey. The concept of eternity and rewards, or consequences, is meant to bring sobriety. The attitude of sobriety produces an incentive to conduct our lives in a proper manner.

I will cover these six principles of the doctrine of Christ in the next chapter to observe how doctrine works to deal with the abuses that are taking place in the religious arena. Meanwhile, you need to consider if you are interpreting doctrine according to the proper spirit and combination. It is important to examine this area because if you do not, it will leave you vulnerable, powerless, and prey to the enemies of your soul.

Application:

Consider these following doctrines in light of the emphasis and the combination. Explain how each combination would affect a person's attitude and conduct, and then scripturally examine it and see what the correct view should be.

Faith (Religion/Theology)

Wealth (Culture)

Music (Culture)

Prejudice (Personal Preference)

Happiness (Personal Preference)

Conduct surrounding the gifts of the Spirit. (Religion/theology)

7

THE DOCTRINE OF CHRIST

As Hebrews 6:1-2 states, six principle doctrines of Christ are ranked or placed in order according to the route of salvation. These doctrines were first established in the Old Testament. For example, God has always called His stiff-necked people to repentance. Abraham is the example of faith, the Jewish people practiced baptism, the priests would designate something by laying their hands on it, Job talked about resurrection, and the prophet Daniel made clear statements about eternal judgment. However, each of these doctrines pointed to Jesus Christ. They were fully realized and established as Jesus Christ became the foundation upon which God's people were to establish their spiritual lives.

The idea of six main doctrines should serve as a great relief to Christians, but sadly, it appears as if Christians have no real understanding of these doctrines. In some incidents where there is some knowledge about them, Christians can harbor perverted perceptions about them. It is important that we get these principle doctrines down because they take in various aspects of the Christian life and are capable of developing a proper attitude and response in us.

Repentance from dead works includes acknowledging sin and results in a changed mind, heart, and lifestyle. Repentance was the first message Jesus preached. He declared its significance in Luke 13:3 and 5, "I tell you, Nay: but, except ye repent, ye shall all likewise perish." These verses in Luke show us that spiritual problems that are not dealt with can cause one to perish. The problem that has to be confronted is sin. The dilemma is people can be generic or indifferent about personal sin. They can easily admit to being wrong, but fall short of repenting of, and confessing their personal sins.

People must recognize personal sin in their own lives. Correct recognition of sin will cause a needed radical change in the person's perception in regards to life. This change is necessary if an individual is to overcome this terminal disease of man's soul.[1]

At the heart of all genuine repentance is change. This act has to do with a change in direction from that which is useless and dead to that which is alive. A person turns from a life of slavery to sin, and comes to Jesus seeking mercy, grace, forgiveness, and salvation. Because the

[1] To understand the issue of sin, see the next book in this volume, *The Anatomy of Sin.*

person changes direction and chooses Jesus, he or she will begin to produce another type of work.

This brings us to the concept of repentance from dead works. John the Baptist made this statement about repentance in Matthew 3:8, "Bring forth therefore fruits meet for repentance." Good works cannot save you, but they most definitely are a product of salvation.

Hebrews 6:9-10 make reference to visible fruits or works that must be observed in salvation,But, beloved, we are persuaded better things of you, and things that accompany salvation, though we thus speak. For God is not unrighteous to forget your work and labor of love, which ye have shewed toward his name, in that ye have ministered to the saints, and do minister.

> The Apostle Paul confirmed the need to verify our life in Christ with the physical evidence of good works in Ephesians 2:8-10, For by grace are ye saved through faith; and that not of yourselves: it is the gift of God: Not of works, lest any man should boast. For we are his workmanship, created in Christ Jesus unto good works, which God hath before ordained that we should walk in them.

As you can see, real repentance can only be confirmed by a life of change and good works. This is why Peter made this statement in 2 Peter 3:9, "The Lord is not slack concerning his promise, as some men count slackness: but is longsuffering to us-ward, not willing that any should perish, but that all should come to repentance." Once again, we must remember that without repentance, we face the consequences of eternal judgment.

Faith makes up the second part of the doctrine of Christ but note the wording, "faith towards God" (Hebrews 6:1). Jesus made this statement in Luke 18:8, "I tell you that he will avenge them speedily. Nevertheless, when the Son of Man cometh, shall he find faith on the earth?" It is clear that genuine faith will be an exception, not the rule when Jesus comes back. There are many different types of faiths being promoted, but 99 percent of them must be considered false because according to Scripture there is only one true faith. These false faiths cause people to put their reliance in some aspect of creation rather than the Creator.[2] Today, misguided people are looking to mother earth, man, self, personal words, governments, thoughts, politics, and outward actions to solve problems, but not to the Living God. This erroneous reliance on substitutions that have dethroned God in the hearts and minds of many people has produced the environment of idolatry. [3]

This idolatry invades the souls of men, causing genuine faith to come under attack as more and more inexperienced Christians lose sight of

---

[2] Ephesians 4:5; Romans 1:24-26

[3] If you would like to learn more about unfeigned faith, see the book entitled, *In Search of Real Faith* in the second volume of the foundational series.

the source of it, and give in to popular "faith" movements and formulas. Sadly, this has changed the focus of much of the Church from preaching the Gospel to the unsaved, to contending for the faith that was first delivered to the saints.[4]

There is only one faith and the writer of Hebrews clearly stipulates it must be towards and in the one true God. God establishes a person's faith in His unchanging character. God gives this faith according to the measure one needs to respond to Him in obedience. This is not a mental assent, but an exercise of placing confidence and trust in and towards God. Each step of faith is in light of facts that have been confirmed by truths, but each step of faith will always go beyond knowledge to express itself in the visible conduct of obedience.[5]

The Apostle Paul declared that we walk by faith (in an unseen God) and not by sight. Faith walks hand in hand with the different works of God's salvation such as grace, justification, and sanctification, showing us that it is only by faith that we can grasp and receive the truths of God as a reality.[6]

Hebrews 11:6 states that without faith, it is impossible to please God, and the Apostle Paul stated in Romans 14:23 that what is not of faith is sin. However, the ultimate product of faith is righteousness, as the words echo from the pages of Habakkuk and Romans have declared, "The just shall live by faith." [7]

Righteousness points to right standing before God that will result in upright conduct. In the scheme of things, the walk of faith is about learning to depend on God and discovering His will. It is a life of child-like trust towards a loving Father, and a walk that is in step with the character and will of God. Each step of faith enlarges the person's ability to take larger steps of obedience, refining his or her character, and bringing the individual into a greater relationship with God. At the end of this life-changing and glorious walk is salvation.[8]

Faith that is not established on God's character and fails to respond according to who He is and His will is a counterfeit that will miserably falter in the time of testing. Such pseudo faiths are built on shifting sand rather than on the Rock of Ages.[9]

Do you have genuine faith towards God, or are you standing on shifting sands of judgment?

Baptisms make up the next doctrine of Christ. It is important to note that the word is plural, revealing the fact that there are more than one type of baptism which must be considered. It is also equally important to

---

[4] Jude 3

[5] Ephesians 4:4-6; Romans 12:3; James 2:18

[6] Ephesians 2:8; Romans 3:28; Acts 26:18

[7] Habakkuk 2:4; Romans 1:17

[8] 1 Peter 1:9

[9] Matthew 7:24-28

point out that the word "baptism" implies total immersion by or into something.[10]

The Bible refers to four types of baptism. As you study each baptism, you begin to realize that the combination of these baptisms represents the Christian experience.

The first baptism implemented by John the Baptist, before Jesus' death, burial, and resurrection, can be found in Matthew 3:5, 6 and 11: the baptism of water unto repentance. This baptism was for the purpose of acknowledging sins and turning from them. Such a baptism pointed to conversion or the born-again experience where a person is born of water and of the Spirit, and turns from the hopelessness of an old life to walk out a new birth, and experience a new life in Jesus Christ.[11]

The next baptism is referred to in Matthew 20:22-23 and Luke 22:42. It is known as the baptism of suffering. The purpose of suffering can be found in Hebrews 5:8-9, "Though he were a Son, yet learned he obedience by the things which he suffered; And being made perfect, he became the author of eternal salvation unto all them that obey him."

The experience of suffering produces obedience and maturity, resulting in salvation in a person's life. Acceptable obedience takes place at the point of self-denial. Self-denial points to personal cost that will immerse the person into experiencing the bitterness of loss to the old life in order to obtain something of eternal value.

The Apostle Paul suffered greatly in his life for the sake of Christ. He warned that all who live godly in Christ will suffer persecution, but he also realized the significance of this experience. He knew that through all of his losses, he was gaining Christ and that in the end he would reign with Him.[12]

The baptism of suffering leads us to the third baptism: water baptism. Water baptism represents total immersion in Jesus, resulting in complete identification with Him. This is where the believer decides to make a verbal declaration that Jesus is Lord and Savior through the ceremony of water baptism.

Jesus submitted to this baptism before He went into the wilderness to be tempted. His statement in Matthew 3:15 in regard to His action was that He was fulfilling righteousness. In other words, He was not being baptized because of sin, but to do that which was upright before God. He was preparing the way of righteousness through example for those who followed Him in obedience.

Water baptism points to the death, burial, and resurrection of Jesus. This visible ceremony points to a total identification with Jesus that must be experienced not only physically, but also spiritually in regard to the

[10] Strong's Exhaustive Concordance, #911

[11] John 3:3-7

[12] Philippians 3:7-14; 2 Timothy 2:12; 3:12

new life being brought forth. For example, the water represents the grave, and as the person is submerged into the water, it points to death to the old life. And, when the individual is brought up out of the water, it is signifying his or her resurrection unto the new life. This is not only a powerful picture of identification, but of victory in the believer's life over the grave and death. As 1 Corinthians 15:55 states, "O death, where is thy sting? O grave, where is thy victory?"

It is also during this ceremony that the person is identified with the triune God. During the baptism of Jesus, all three Persons of the Godhead were present. We see the Holy Spirit coming down in the form of a dove, and the voice of the Father was heard as He introduced the Son. According to Jesus' instruction in the Gospel of Matthew at water baptism, these three Persons must be acknowledged as the individual is baptized in the name of the Father, the Son, and the Holy Spirit.[8]

Acknowledging the Godhead at water baptism is a reminder that all three Persons of the Godhead have a significant part in salvation. For example, the Father draws man and reveals the Son; the Son invites and saves or redeems man; and the Holy Spirit convicts man of sin, righteousness, and judgment. Upon salvation, the Spirit seals the believer to a heavenly inheritance and begins the work of sanctification to prepare the Christian for God's work and glory.[9]

The first three baptisms remind us of the two main calls of Jesus. First, He called man to repentance (baptism of water unto repentance). Secondly, He called man to deny self (baptism of suffering), and then pick up his cross in identification (water baptism) in order to follow Him into the abundant life.[10]

The final baptism has to do with the power and authority to fulfill the commission of preaching the Gospel and making disciples of Jesus. John the Baptist first introduced us to this baptism in Matthew 3:11, "I indeed baptize you with water unto repentance: but he that cometh after me is mightier than I, whose shoes I am not worthy to bear: he shall baptize you with the Holy Ghost, and with fire."

Jesus is the one who baptizes the person with the Holy Ghost. This baptism enables a person to become a powerful witness in the dark world, empowering him or her to fulfill the commission to preach the Gospel and make disciples of Jesus.[11]

In the book, *Deeper Experiences of Famous Christians,* James Gilchrist Lawson states that many in the early Church recognized the baptism of the Holy Spirit as a very important doctrine. They referred to it as the Lord's seal. They also distinguished between the spiritual birth

---

[8] Matthew 3:13-17; 28:18-20

[9] Matthew 16:17; Luke 9:56; John 6:44; 7:37; 16:8-11; Romans 15:16; Ephesians 1:13-14; 2 Timothy 2:21

[10] Matthew 4:17; Matthew 16:24-28

[11] Matthew 28:18-20; Mark 16:15

and baptism of the Holy Spirit. It was believed that at the spiritual birth or regeneration, a person became the Lord's, but at the filling of the Spirit, He was setting his seal or brand on them.

Sadly, Christians have many misconceptions about this baptism. They often relate it to the born-again experience, signs and wonders, new revelations, and supernatural intervention. In reality, this baptism is more about being made effective as witnesses of God's salvation and His greatness than it is a show of the supernatural.

Mark 16:17 states that signs will follow those who believe. Miracles were a means to confirm the reality and redemptive work of the Son of God with the intent of bringing glory to God. Therefore, each miracle served as a testimony of the Living God, not as a show of the supernatural.[12]

If a supernatural act does not exalt Jesus Christ, failing to bring glory to God, one must discern that it is a counterfeit of Satan. After all, the whole purpose of this power from above is to carry out the commission.

Have you sought this baptism, and for what purpose? If it is for show or power, your intention is self-centered. But, if it is to live a godly life in order to be an effective living witness, then do as Luke 11:13 says, "If ye then, being evil, know how to give good gifts unto your children: how much more shall your heavenly Father give the Holy Spirit to them that ask him?"

There is much confusion over baptism. Ephesians 4:5 speaks of one baptism. This Scripture verse is in relationship to the Church, or Body of Christ, and not to the believer's conduct. The Holy Spirit must place each believer into the Body. This is a type of baptism or submerging. 1 Corinthians 12:13 confirms this, "For by one Spirit are we all baptized into one body."

The next doctrine is that of the *laying on of hands*. This doctrine points to consecration. Consecration is an act of setting something apart for service. We can study acts of consecration in the Old Testament as sacrifices, priests, prophets, and leaders experienced the laying on of hands, as well as being anointed. These practices designated the calling or purpose of that which was being set apart. The practice of the laying on of hands was also used in the New Testament in regards to those who were being set apart for a specific service and/or as a means to impart gifts.[13]

Consecration points to separation from past activities and total abandonment to the service or commission set before the individual. In the case of Timothy, elders laid hands on him to impart the necessary gift to carry out his calling. Once again, we see the laying on of hands is

---

[12] See John 11:4, 40, 42

[13] Leviticus 1:4; 16:21-22; Numbers 8:10; Deuteronomy 34:9; Acts 6:6; 1 Timothy 4:14

for the sole purpose of consecrating someone or something for a particular calling or duty.

The Apostle Paul gives us this instruction in 1 Timothy 5:22, "Lay hands suddenly on no man, neither be partaker of other men's sins: keep thyself pure." This Scripture verse brings us to another aspect of the laying on of hands, which is agreement. Such agreement is based on spirit or intent. This verse in Timothy shows us that we can expose ourselves to the wrong spirit, which will defile what is pure and make us partakers of another person's sin.

We know that there is power in agreement, especially if the right spirit is present. Matthew 18:19 states, "Again I say unto you, That if two of you shall agree on earth as touching any thing that they shall ask, it shall be done for them of my Father which is in heaven." All laying on of hands must be done in agreement, and it must be for the purpose of advocating a specific aim, whether it be of healing, gifts, calling, or duty.

The next doctrine is resurrection of the dead. St. Chrysostom said that as Christians we are to be taught the mysteries of the resurrection and eternal judgment.[14] Jesus' resurrection was the main miracle that confirmed Him as the Son of God, God Incarnate. It reminds us that this present life is temporary. We see Old Testament writers such as Job referring to it. Jesus said, of this subject, that He was the resurrection and the life, and whosoever believes in Him should live even though he was dead.[15]

The resurrection of Jesus is a fact, but when it comes to the future resurrection of believers, its serves as a doctrine. As a doctrine, it should influence a person's present attitude and conduct. Both concepts of resurrection and judgment should inspire people to be diligent in godly matters, and to live soberly in accordance with these future events.[16]

The reality of these two doctrines should instill a healthy fear of God in people. This attitude not only produces wisdom, but upright conduct, as one lives soberly before God. Sadly, this attitude is lacking in the Church. Too many Christians are flippant or indifferent, about issues concerning godliness as they carelessly continue to live in accordance with fleshly desires and worldly pursuits.

The doctrine of resurrection has been a source of controversy due to the different rapture theories. However, Scripture clearly states that there are two resurrections. The prophet Daniel describes these two resurrections as the resurrection to everlasting life or the resurrection to shame and everlasting contempt.[17]

---

[14] Deeper Experiences of Famous Christians; James Gilchrist Lawson, © 2000 by Barbour Publishing, Inc.

[15] Job 19:25-26; John 8:28; 10:17-18; 11:25; 14:19-20; 1 Corinthians 15:12-17

[16] 1 Peter 5:7-10; 2 Peter 3:10-18

[17] Daniel 12:2; Revelation 20:4-6

Hebrews 9:27 tells us, "And as it is appointed unto men once to die, but after this the judgment." Resurrection will lead to judgment; therefore, these two resurrections also point to two main judgments: the judgment seat of Christ and the great white throne judgment.

Judgment is a form of separation. It is a way of separating the holy from that which is vain and unholy. Separation will always begin in the house of God. This judgment often comes through various trials and testing. However, in the end, all Christians will stand before the judgment seat of Christ where they will receive rewards for the things done in their bodies, whether good or bad. [18]

1 Corinthians 3:12-15 talks about how the Christians' works will be evaluated. Their works will stand as gold, silver, precious stones, wood, hay, or stubble. Obviously, gold, silver, and precious stones will stand the fiery judgment, but wood, hay, and stubble will be consumed in judgment. The individual whose works fall into the last three categories will suffer loss, but will be saved by fire.

What determines the quality of the Christian's work? It comes down to motives, intentions, and focus. For example, if Christians' motives are not the love of God, their intentions not to glorify Him, and their focus not to do God's will, then their work will be nothing more than wood, hay, and stubble before Him. When good deeds lack the reality of Jesus Christ, they will be reduced to fleshly motives, worldly intentions, and religious pursuits, which will be considered humanistic.

The other judgment is the great white throne judgment, which brings us to the final doctrine of Christ: *eternal judgment.* Eternal judgment implies eternal separation. We understand this separation to be in reference to eternal separation from God who is the essence of eternal life.

Revelation 20:11-15 talks about the second resurrection. Those who are part of this resurrection will be judged according to their works, but will be found wanting because Jesus is missing. This sober reality will be brought to the forefront as the books are opened, along with the book of life.

These books will reveal that such works reek with iniquity, and that these people's names are missing from the book of life. The silence of the book of life towards their very existence will identify them as those who will partake of the second death, as they are cast into the lake of fire, along with death and hell, to no longer be remembered.

Sadly, demons capitalize on these six doctrines of Christ. They use them as platforms to promote erroneous doctrines that lead people away from the truths of God into a religious maze of (presumed) self-attained righteousness. These doctrines deify man and humanize God, as they base salvation on man's personal performance. They ride on the

[18] 2 Corinthians 5:10; 1 Peter 4:17

reputation of Jesus, as they demote Him to some religious hero or teacher, but deny that He is the only way to heaven.

Sadly, these doctrines of demons are making great inroads into the Church through humanistic philosophies that make doctrines man-centered rather than Christ-centered. As a result, Christians who have been weakened by such doctrines do not know the right Jesus, and fail to rightly divide the word of truth. These individuals often make Christianity into a fleshly or religious experience, rather than a life established on a right foundation and grounded in righteousness through a relationship with God through Jesus Christ.

Do you properly operate within the principle doctrines of Christ or have you taken a detour away from that which is pure and righteous? Maybe you have bought one of the many doctrines of demons, and now you have lost sight of the real Jesus, the Word has been defiled, and you are now fighting bondage and the invasion of darkness into your soul. If you fit in this last category, know that you can repent, and by faith make your way back to the cross of Jesus. Once there, you can cry out for His mercy and grace, and know that He will reach down and immerse you with His love and forgiveness. You will feel His touch, experience His resurrection power, and be assured that you will be spared His eternal judgment that will come upon all those who walk in the rebellion of unbelief.

Application:

Consider the erroneous doctrines invading the Church today and show how they counterfeit the principle doctrines of Jesus.

8

PRINCIPLES

We have considered facts, truths, and doctrines. This brings us to the next element that must be identified in the Word: that of principles.

Facts serve as evidence, while truths point to the character and work of God. Doctrine comes down to attitude and conduct, while principles have to do with the spirit in which a person applies facts, truths, and doctrine. The spirit will determine the kind of law a person is becoming subject to. Therefore, principles points to the combination of motivation and the boundaries established by the law that is in operation.

Godly principles are powerful and consistent. This brings us to the means by which principles are revealed. Facts are presented, truths are defined, but both doctrine and principles must be properly taught. In fact, I teach more on principles than doctrine. The reason for this is that God works within principles that are subject to an unseen law. Principles actually activate the law that a person is about to come under due to his or her attitude and conduct. For example, if a person is responding in righteousness, he or she will be walking within one of the principles of God, activating the spiritual law that ensures and governs life from above. In some cases, believers who are walking uprightly before God are very unaware that they are operating within the safe boundaries of God's principles or ways. It is only later when they are able to reflect on their walk, and see how God faithfully guided each of their steps within the boundaries established by His righteous ways that they are able to see the beneficial results of His instructions and examples.

As one can conclude, godly principles are higher than doctrine. After all, doctrine is what man operates within. It can prove to be earthly in perspective, whereas godly principles have a heavenly perspective. Doctrine that fails to put a person's feet on the path of God's principles will prove to be powerless and ineffective.

Most Christians never consider that they are living according to principles. As I debated about how important it was for me to explain principles in this book, I asked my co-laborer in the Gospel, Jeannette, what was the significance for people to understand that principles do exist and that they need to recognize them? She kindly reminded me that working within godly principles ensured people that they would come out knowing the real Jesus.

Godly principles are about God. They originate with Him and are maintained by His character and work. The boundaries of God's principles begin with the right Spirit and end with a distinct goal or purpose. A good example of these boundaries can be observed in the first principle of God: That everything must begin with God and end in a revelation of Jesus. This principle is found in Genesis 1:1, John 1:1 and Revelation 1:1. Imagine what a person's life would be like if he or she considered this principle in every decision, as well as walked it out in a practical way?

Let's consider this principle in light of one of the doctrines, that of faith. If you start with God, you will always begin in the right Spirit. This is important because Christians often forget they are part of an eternal plan that often becomes clouded or lost in the midst of earthly, temporal things. Because many become earth-bound, they fail to realize that God is trying to work out His eternal plan in and through their lives. This loss of a heavenly perspective causes them to take detours away from God's main goal, which is to conform them to the image of His Son.[1]

As long as a person's conduct is upright before God, the Holy Spirit will have the liberty to lead him or her down a path that will instill the very mind and character of Christ within his or her life.[2] It is important to point out that this path is anything but a pleasant walk through the park. It is full of obstacles that will test each person's devotion towards God, love for Jesus, and the level of maturity of his or her spiritual character.

This brings us back to one of the principle doctrines of Christ, faith towards God. Every principle of God requires the response of faith because each of us must walk out our Christian life by unseen confidence towards God to discover His heavenly treasures. The problem with the faith walk is that it will immediately cause darkness for us.

Faith begins where personal understanding ceases, causing personal darkness towards a matter. This darkness comes because we will not be able to see, understand, or control the path we are traveling. At times, we will feel as if God is punishing us or toying with our emotions. As a result, we have to put every bit of our energy into clinging to the knowledge of who He is. If we are faithful to take just one-step of faith at a time in what we know about Him in light of the life of Jesus being worked in us, we will come out in the light of truth.

Once in the light, we can reflect on our walk. This is when we are able to see God's ways in a matter as we can clearly see how He faithfully directed us down the path. We will also learn the valuable lessons of life.

There are two main lessons concerning your faith walk. These lessons intertwine and are constantly fine-tuned and reinforced with each

---

[1] Romans 8:28-29

[2] Philippians 2:5

journey of faith. These lessons are: 1) There is no life outside of Jesus and, 2) life does not make sense outside of the reality or truth of Jesus. These vital lessons of life help to redefine what constitutes real life. They change a person's priorities and focus because he or she realizes that there is no life outside of God Incarnate. In fact, most of the principles of God end with these simple lessons of life that often serve as points of exhortation. Exhortation points to being warned, admonished, and contended with, as a means of keeping these lessons in the forefront to remind and encourage ourselves in this challenging walk.[3]

Even though principles automatically determine the boundaries of your path, it is still important to be able to identify them. By understanding the principles of God, a person will be able to discern His ways and discover His will.

Obviously, doctrine determines man's conduct, while principles of God serve as the motivation and boundary to righteous conduct. Doctrines exalted into the place of principles become personal causes or crusades that establish unfair boundaries for others to observe. These causes often serve as the final authority for people in the area of spiritual matters.

Personal causes are self-righteous in attitude, and will use Scripture like impersonal platitudes that can be whipped out and slapped on individuals at any time. These causes become judgmental and harsh as they become burdensome and unrealistic to those who encounter them.

Self-righteous causes hide the fact that those who use platitudes have never actually paid the price to know God. Even though they may have what they perceive as sufficient Scripture to confirm their causes, they lack the heart of Jesus, causing the Scripture to come across as indifferent, dead, and useless.

Any person, who operates within causes, functions in a very small, controlled world where he or she majors in surface, petty issues rather than caring for the souls of others. For example, causes can include such things as strict dress codes or strong but unrealistic opinions about specific doctrines that comply with the religious atmosphere the individual may be promoting or trying to maintain. These codes quickly judge others who fail to live up to them, deeming such culprits as being unacceptable.

These causes hide prejudices and insecurities, and can cause rebellion in those who see them as ridiculous and self-righteous. In fact, victims of such causes can end up rebelling against God because they are unable to discern the difference between these people's causes and God's pure doctrine and principles.

Sadly, immature and inexperienced Christians can fall victim to these causes, making them slaves to the traditions of men, rather than

---

[3] To understand how the principles of God operate, see *The Principles of the Abundant Life* in this volume.

bondservants of Jesus Christ. This bondage will hinder the Holy Spirit from developing them into the servants God intends them to be.

I have also observed how some Christians willingly accept these codes in order to hide inward rebellion by conforming to some outward image. This type of discipline allows them to give a religious appearance without the corresponding inner transformation.

People who operate within personal causes have devised their own personal Christian code by holding on to select Scripture verses that fit their emphasis, while ignoring or missing the intent of the whole counsel of God. This causes them to operate in a wrong spirit.

A good way to test whether something is a personal cause is to ask this question, "Does this conduct determine my eternal destination, or is it an exercise in personal goodness to win the approval of man or God?" If the conduct comes down to exalting your personal goodness, it is a cause, and you will find yourself in unnecessary bondage.

People who operate within religious causes try to serve as the Holy Spirit in people's lives, and as a result, cause a lot of damage. Their style of ministry is cruel because they have never developed the spiritual ears to hear, the eyes to see, and the heart to discern what is going on in a person's life.

Such individuals have no business being in a position where they influence others, but they have such a high opinion of their religious conduct that they believe they can bring proper instruction. The reality of their emphasis makes them nothing more than crusaders on behalf of their own convictions.

Principles will determine how a person applies facts, truths, and doctrines to a situation. Ultimately, principles will produce or determine the result, manifestation, or fruit that others will partake of or witness.

The type of principle a person operates within is based on the spiritual law that he or she has become subject to. According to Romans 8:2, there are only two spiritual laws that are in operation. Every person needs to understand that he or she is subject to one of these two laws.

The first law is that of the Spirit of life in Christ Jesus. The boundaries to this law are the Holy Spirit and life in Christ. The Holy Spirit guides and leads a person to a life in Christ. Jesus' life in us ensures communion with God, produces fruits of righteousness, and will bring glory to God and salvation to man.

The boundaries to the second law are sin and death. This law brings a person under the holy Law of God to be judged, as well as under the influence of the god of the world, Satan. The enemy of men's souls works disobedience in people's hearts, resulting in sin and spiritual death, or separation from God. When people operate according to the ways of the flesh, they will hold the truth in unrighteousness.[4]

---

[4] Ephesians 2:2; Romans 1:18

This once again reinforces an important aspect of principles. The principle you are working within will produce the visible fruit in your life. People may play the religious game and have an appearance of righteousness, but eventually their fruit will tell on them. The reason for this is because the law you are under determines who serves as your head, master, and husband. H. A. Ironside brings this out in his commentary on the book of Romans.

If you are operating under the law of sin and death, you will be working within the framework of iniquity. It is important to explain iniquity before revealing the head, master, and husband of this destructive law.

The Bible talks about sin, transgression, and iniquity. Is there a difference between these three terms? Yes. There are two different meanings behind sin. Sin simply means you have caused some type of offence. However, such offence can occur in two ways. One of the ways points to disobedient actions, while the other way is in reference to unregenerate man. Depending on how it is used, the singular usage of the word "sin" usually has to do with the condition of unregenerate man that is motivated by pride, driven by fleshly lusts, and entanglements with the world. When certain aspects of a Christian's life remain unregenerate, the Christian will prove to be carnal or fleshly in those areas, opening him or her up to spiritual defeat. Here we see this particular idea of sin does not point to what man does, but to his rebellious self-serving disposition. This selfish disposition is the source behind all ungodly actions.

"Transgression" implies one has broken the Law or covenant. This term was used a lot in the Old Testament because of the emphasis on the Law of God. Transgression is a form of trespassing into areas where man has no business treading. At the heart of such acts is treachery against God.[5]

"Iniquity" is the final term that is used in both the Old and New Testaments. Sin is a term used to describe both the unregenerate man and disobedient actions that will offend our holy God. Transgression is the breaking of the Law, which blatantly shows contempt towards our just God. However, iniquity points to immoral actions or conduct that defies and tests our righteous God. Transgression has to do with treachery towards God, while iniquity has to do with treacherous acts against others, including God.

The morality of man not only includes sexual conduct, but his scruples or character. In other words, how he conducts all of his affairs in every area of his life, from his home life to business and religious issues, is a matter of morality. Iniquity is not just a matter of doing something immoral; it also includes the perverted thoughts and attitudes that lead up to morally deviant behavior. If a person is immoral in any of these areas, he or she is committing iniquity in God's sight.

---

[5] Romans 4:15; Hosea 5:7; 6:7

2 Timothy 2:19 states, "Nevertheless the foundation of God standeth sure, having this seal, The Lord knoweth them that are his. And, Let everyone that nameth the name of Christ depart from iniquity." Because iniquity is the outward manifestation of the law of sin and death, an individual who is subject to this law will be operating within the principles of iniquity.

The person who operates within the principles of iniquity comes under the head of Adam, the master of sin, and the Old Testament Law will be serving as the individual's husband. This type of leadership leads to condemnation, slavery, and death.

A person who is under the law of the Spirit of life in Christ has Jesus as his or her head, God as the master, and the risen Christ as the husband. This type of leadership will cause an individual to walk within the principles of godliness.

1 Timothy 4:7 and 9 states, "But refuse profane and old wives' fables, and <u>exercise thyself rather unto godliness</u>. For bodily exercise profiteth little: but godliness is profitable unto all things, having promise of the life that now is, and of that which is to come." (Emphasis added.) Obviously, godliness must be exercised if it is to be evident in a person's life.

Godliness points to piety and holiness. This simply implies that a person's conduct is distinct from that which is considered unholy and defiled, and can be traced back to God's influence and reign. Again, we come down to outward conduct.

Godly conduct points to discipline that will make individuals distinct in their lifestyles.[6] For the Christian, his or her conduct must be beyond the confines of self and the lusts of the world, as well as useless, hypocritical religious exercises that speak of "personal goodness." All holy and acceptable conduct will bring honor to God, not self.

Godly principles fine-tune doctrine. In other words, God's principles set up the boundaries in which doctrine is to operate by determining what constitutes proper attitude and conduct, as well as the final product or fruit of such action.

Doctrine that works within the principles of godliness is practical and realistic. For example, giving a cup of water to someone who is thirsty, helping carry the burdens of your Christian family, and visiting the sick are practical responses when exercising godliness. The problem is that many people spiritualize the practical ways of true ministry, which causes them to become indifferent to the basic needs of others.

Are you operating within godly principles or do causes and lifeless doctrines hinder you? Come higher. Allow the Spirit of God to establish

---

[6] If you would like to understand how to develop godly discipline, see the book, *Godly Discipline* in the third volume of her foundational series.

your character within godly principles, bringing constructive boundaries to doctrine that will make it practical and realistic.

Application:

Take the principle found in Matthew 16:24-26. Identify the boundaries of this principle and explain how it would presently affect or define your Christian walk.

9

POSSESSING THE TREASURE OF HEAVEN

We have considered facts, truths, doctrines, and principles, but now we must understand how each of these working together produces the reality of Jesus in our lives. In order to grasp the workings of these four aspects of the Bible, we must understand the different levels of spiritual comprehension and maturity. There are three such levels of spiritual insight. They are knowledge, revelation and enlightenment.

Each level leads or builds upon the others. Sadly, it appears as if few reach all three levels in their search to know God. As a result, people who fail to reach each level can become limited, self-righteous, opinionated, and in some cases, deluded about what they think they know. This type of individual becomes like the man in James 1:22-24 who is simply a hearer of the word, but not a doer. As a result, this man forgets how the Christian life should be expressed. In fact, individuals who do not operate in all three levels often believe they have arrived in their understanding or perception, when in reality they are far away from the mark.

It is important to understand that these levels comply with the four elements that make up the Word of God. Consider the following table.

Principles	=	Enlightenment
Doctrine	=	Revelation
Truths	=	Knowledge
Facts		

To understand how these three levels work, we must come to terms with the purpose of the Bible. The Word of God is comprised of facts and truths that establish pure doctrine. As a person walks according to pure doctrine, he or she will begin to operate within the principles of godliness. God is able to meet the person at the point of godliness in order to bring a greater reality of Himself to him or her.

In some cases, people have reduced the Bible into one big doctrine in their search for knowledge and spirituality. In other words, they have made it all about man's understanding and religious activities, instead of realizing it is about bringing man to the reality of God. E. Stanley Jones made this comment about the Bible in his devotional, *The Way,* "It is the inspired record of the revelation." "Revelation" in this text points to the unveiling of Jesus Christ. Jesus said of Himself in John 14:9b, "...he that hath seen me hath seen the Father; and how sayest thou then, Shew us the Father?"

Colossians 2:9 states this about Jesus, "For in him dwelleth all the fulness of the Godhead bodily." The Word of God has one major goal, and that is to lead the human race to an intimate knowledge of the One who saves. Such a pursuit will allow every individual to discover the fullness of Jesus in each area of his or her life. Jesus is the visible image of God. If people search the Scriptures to find God and the essence of eternal life, they will find Jesus, God Incarnate, in His glory.

Jesus confirmed this in John 5:39, "Search the scriptures; for in them ye think ye have eternal life: and they are they which testify of me."

When people fail to get beyond self with all of its personal agendas to discover the eternal treasure of heaven, they remain earthly in their perspective and fleshly or carnal in spiritual matters. If a person never gets beyond a carnal view of the Bible, it will be rendered into a book of doctrine that will eventually be categorized into systematic compartments of beliefs. The problem with this scenario is that Christianity will remain a concept rather than becoming a life that is experienced. This condition reveals that it has never been made alive by the reality of the Living Word, Jesus Christ.[1]

Let us now consider the three levels of spiritual development in the area of our understanding.

Knowledge

Knowledge serves as the foundation of our spiritual understanding. This knowledge includes knowing the facts and grasping the truths of God. However, knowledge alone is dangerous because it can turn into an intellectual pride trip.

1 Corinthians 8:1-3 states, "...we know that we all have knowledge. Knowledge puffeth up, but charity edifieth. And if any man think that he knoweth any thing, he knoweth nothing yet as he ought to know. But if any man love God, the same is known of him." Knowledge can operate

[1] 1 Corinthians 2:14-16; John 1:1

without the love of God. This means the person's emphasis is on gaining knowledge about spiritual matters. This type of emphasis can give a person an overrated false sense of his or her spiritual condition.

Scripture is clear. Christians are not identified by what they know, but by whether or not they have love for one another. This love is present because believers have personally encountered the love of God through Jesus, and have embraced it as their compelling motivation behind all they do.[2]

People often think because they know of or about God that they are indeed Christians who are on the right path. However, knowledge alone lacks vital characteristics that clearly mark the person as a blood-bought saint. It can prove to be indifferent and unfeeling because it is not being inspired by God's love, but by intellectual pride. The heart of Christianity is God's love. Such love is ready to show benevolence to others, while knowledge can be aloof from the reality or the struggles of others. Such knowledge will cause a critical spirit that shows condemnation instead of mercy and grace.

Knowledge that is not hedged in by godly discipline and characteristics becomes puffed up because there are no boundaries in which to properly test it. When knowledge lacks godly discipline, it will operate in delusion. People will consider their spirituality in light of what they know instead of by their fruits.[3] This exaltation of the intellect is idolatry in high places, as it brings God down to the level of man in order to understand Him. In fact, if a person walks according to his or her intellect, he or she will fail to walk by faith directed towards God.

2 Peter 1:5-7 gives us the characteristics that must surround knowledge to keep it in the right perspective,

> And beside this, giving all diligence, add to your faith virtue, and to virtue knowledge; And to knowledge temperance; and to temperance patience; and to patience godliness; And to godliness brotherly kindness; and to brotherly kindness charity. (Emphasis added.)

According to Peter in this Scripture, knowledge is in fourth place in the progression that leads to being fruitful in the knowledge of Jesus Christ.[4] It has to be established within characteristics that would keep it in the right perspective. Disciplined knowledge comes out of faith, spiritual strength or character that proves to be excellent, and is tempered by self-control and patience. It loses its importance and glitter in light of benevolence and godly love.

Knowledge may institute the foundation, but the establishment of the structure will determine the value of our lives. For example, when people

---

[2] John 13:34-35; 1 John 4:19

[3] Matthew 7:15-16

[4] 2 Peter 1:8

buy a house, they consider the structure to see if it will fit their needs. It is the fruitful knowledge of Jesus that gives the spiritual structure of our lives the beauty and value that will make them attractive to others. Obviously, the knowledge of Jesus in the text of 2 Peter is not based on knowing a fact, but on knowing the Person of Jesus in an intimate way. It is the fruitful knowledge of Jesus that will inspire the next level of understanding: revelation.

Revelation

"Revelation" means to uncover.[5] God's Word talks about mysteries. Mysteries imply that there are secrets that are hidden in Scripture that can be discovered, but a person must be willing to search the possibilities and depths of the Word to uncover them. One must question what was being veiled from our eyes by these mysteries. Colossians 2:3 gives us an insight into this matter, "In whom are hid all the treasures of wisdom and knowledge."

Revelation 1:1 reveals this treasure and knowledge that needs to be revealed to the minds and hearts of people, "The revelation of Jesus Christ." I must point out that there are no new revelations that need to be uncover as far as truths, doctrines, and principles. Nevertheless, there are greater revelations of Jesus that could be uncovered, and will be revealed throughout eternity.[6]

Today, certain heretics use the idea of "new revelations" to draw people into their deceptive web. Sadly, these heretical so-called "new revelations" tear down the true foundation established by facts and truths, and erect a different Jesus. They subtly develop doctrine that is humanistic, worldly, legalistic, or cultic. They take godly principles and change the course or path, by making the walk so rigid that it excludes Christ, or broad enough to include the latest fads, thereby subtly replacing Christ.

The Word of God is full of the treasure of heaven, but many miss it because they seek to gain knowledge rather than to find and know the true treasure of heaven. They pursue doctrine instead of the Living Word. They get excited about what they know, rather than becoming excited about discovering new aspects about the One who died on the cross for them.

Pure doctrine that works within the principles of godliness will bring a person to new discoveries of Jesus. Greater revelations of Jesus can only occur upon acts of righteousness. Uprightness only occurs when one gets past self, and by faith adheres to what he or she knows is right before God.

---

[5] Strong's Exhaustive Concordance, #601-602

[6] Ephesians 2:7

Sadly, few people deny self to ensure upright conduct. Christians often fail to realize that activities done within personal strength, agendas, and religious piousness will not be regarded as righteousness to God. The reason for this is that whenever self exists, it will pervert or defile the things of God and demand the recognition and glory.

True righteousness involves obedience that will sacrificially cost the right to self. Denying self can prove costly to those who have always given way to its insatiable demands. However, the result of not paying the necessary price is that these individuals never come to terms with real righteousness, which is Jesus Christ.

Once self is out of the way, the Holy Spirit can begin to do the work of sanctification. This work comes down to bringing forth the righteousness of Jesus in a person's life that will be considered acceptable by God.

Once people respond in obedience or uprightness, they are prepared to receive a revelation of Jesus. The preparation involves receiving revelation in the right spirit, without it being defiled by the works of the flesh and perverted by the influence of the world.

Revelation is God's way of enlarging a person's perception about His Son. After all, people are restricted and limited by fleshly, worldly and perverted perceptions. The reason for this perversion is that people continue to run everything through their fleshly minds.[7] Heavenly revelation has the ability to enlarge people's comprehension to understand in greater measure. This enlargement allows a person to embrace greater truths or realities about Jesus.

This enlargement will also change how people perceive or interpret revelations. As their ability to perceive spiritual truths is enlarged, these people's perception will allow the Holy Spirit to bring them to greater depths in their spiritual understanding. These depths will allow these individuals to reach greater heights in God.

Revelations of Jesus not only serve as a means of enlargement for spiritual growth, but they are also great points of testing. Once a person receives a revelation of Jesus, he or she must walk it out in practical experience. For example, I was in a trying situation where God was reaching deep into my character in order to deal with my pride. The impact on my life left me feeling vulnerable and weak. It was at this point that God gave me a choice: Choose the world or choose the narrow path.

I looked at the world and realized it held no significance for me, but as I considered the narrow path, I felt I was too weary to carry on. I even relayed that message to God. Suddenly, I was hit with the reality that both my strength and life are found in Jesus, and all I had to do was grab a hold of Him.

---

[7] Romans 8:5-6

I had always known this truth, but it was a concept and not an inspiration that I personally experienced in the depth of my spirit. Immediately, my perception of Jesus became enlarged and living, causing me to realize that all I had to do was cling to Him.

By faith, I put my confidence in the new revelation that had been entrusted to me. I knew in my heart that God was trustworthy and that He would never leave me nor forsake me.[8] Therefore, I had nothing to worry about because He would get me through my challenging time.

All revelations require the response of faith. By faith we each must walk the revelation out we receive regardless of what we feel, think, or see. Believers try to walk out this Christian life according to what they can see, feel, or logic out. In the end, many of them become disillusioned and depressed. Genuine faith is not based on human senses, but on the unchangeable character of an unseen God.[9]

The walk of faith is both challenging and glorious, but it will also bring saints to a crisis in their spiritual lives. Since faith is based on what people can't see, feel, or comprehend, it causes them to walk in personal darkness. As previously stated, this personal darkness means that a person cannot see where he or she is going, nor can he or she always sense the presence of God or understand what is transpiring. This causes the individuals who are inexperienced to feel vulnerable and out of control. It is this type of darkness that causes many to give up on the deeper walk, and fearfully run back to the artificial light of man-made religion. For this reason, few experience all three levels of spiritual maturity.

Either way, the light of revelation will cause darkness for a person. Nevertheless, that darkness depends on how one responds to the revelation. As stated in the above paragraph, the walk of faith is a walk that is accomplished in darkness because it is beyond man's understanding. After all, God's ways and thoughts are much higher than ours, and few recognize that the gap is great.[10]

Darkness also invades those who fail to respond to a revelation. Faith may cause people to walk in darkness, but this second type of darkness actually invades the souls of man. The first darkness occurs because the light of God's holiness immediately reveals man's depravity and need. However, the second type of darkness is caused by the sin of unbelief.

God does not give revelations to entertain people, but to change and bring them higher in their spiritual life. A person who refuses, or fails, to walk a revelation out will find the darkness of unbelief invading his or her soul. Keep in mind, revelation points to the light of Jesus. Therefore, a person who refuses to respond to this light will come into spiritual

---

[8] Hebrews 13:5

[9] Hebrews 11:1

[10] Isaiah 55:8-9

darkness. Sadly, this darkness can appear as a light. In reality, it is a false light, inspired by Satan, and takes on the form of self-righteousness. This will cause the person to operate within the principles of iniquity. The false light not only deludes it victims, but it also sets them up to fall into the abyss of spiritual ruin.[11]

Obviously, people must be prepared to receive revelation. It will bring judgment upon anyone who becomes rebellious, flippant, or mocking towards it. Therefore, revelation also serves as a point of great testing.

As one considers the pros and cons of revelation, he or she might want to avoid this stage, but there can be no spiritual growth without it. Revelation is not just about gaining a greater understanding of Jesus, but it is also about possessing Him as this valuable treasure of heaven. The more a person possesses Christ, the more He will possess their hearts.

One can gloriously survive this walk, but he or she must learn how to walk by faith. Many Christians have never learned how to walk with child-like confidence in their Father.

To survive this walk, a person must take one-step of faith at a time with the intent to obey. As previously stated, each step of faith that results in obedience will enable the person to take the next step. Psalms 119:105 confirms this concept, "Thy word is a lamp unto my feet, and a light unto my path." This verse shows us that we only have enough light to take the step in front of us, as it guides us along His unknown path.

Christians must not allow the unknown to cause them to give up experiencing the deeper life in Christ. They must not allow the unseen to take them on detours. They also must avoid complacency when the state of despair sets in during challenging times. The unknown, the detours, and despair can cause the wayfarer to sit down in anger or hopelessness, rather than finish the course.

Make the determination that you are going to finish the course by clinging to the Rock of Ages with everything in you. Keep in mind that God is working something out in your character with eternity in view. Therefore, keep taking steps of faith until the veil has lifted.

Once the veil has lifted off from your understanding, you will see clearly and begin to understand why God took you this particular route. The light that will bring this understanding will also lead you to the next level: that of enlightenment.

Enlightenment

The three levels of spiritual understanding can actually be observed in 1 Corinthians 13. The Apostle Paul put knowledge in this perspective, "For we know in part." [12]

---

[11] Matthew 6:22-23

[12] 1 Corinthians 13:9

Revelations of Jesus bring us to this awareness, "For now we see through a glass, darkly."[13]

Enlightenment brings a person to spiritual maturity. Paul made this statement in 1 Corinthians 13:11, "When I was a child, I spake as a child, I understood as a child, I thought as a child: but when I became a man, I put away childish things."

Revelation changes a person's perception by removing the veil, but enlightenment changes the disposition. This change simply means that a person is developing the mind of Jesus.[14]

As the attitude of Jesus is developed, His life becomes apparent in a person's life, thereby reflecting His glory. The Apostle Paul describes the results in 2 Corinthians 3:18, "But we all, with open face beholding as in a glass the glory of the Lord, are changed into the same image from glory to glory, even as by the Spirit of the Lord."

Revelation serves as a means of inspiration to encourage the believer to walk out Jesus' life in child-like confidence. It brings about growth as it enlarges an individual, making Jesus' life a living reality. Once revelation is a reality to a person, it will manifest itself in righteous character. This could be compared to a mountaintop experience for a Christian.

All revelations of Jesus may begin with pinnacles of inspiration. However, these inspirations must be walked out in the valleys of uncertainty and humiliation before these pinnacles become a personal reality. This personal reality is considered enlightenment.

Light points to the concept of enlightenment. "Enlightenment" means that you now understand what God was trying to accomplish in your life. This is what makes revelation a personal reality. Enlightenment involves retrospection or reflection in order for a person to learn the lessons of life, thereby, coming to an understanding concerning the ways of God. It is at this stage that the greatest inward change will take place. Revelation may point to growth, but enlightenment produces spiritual maturity or perfection. This maturity points to the fact that there are certain aspects of the life of Christ that has produced perfection or maturity in a person's life. Maturity fine-tunes the spiritual senses, resulting in the ability to discern both good and evil.[15]

Hebrews 6:4-6 tells us that enlightenment means you have tasted of the heavenly gift. The Apostle Paul reveals this gift in 2 Corinthians 9 as Jesus Christ. He made this declaration in verse 15, "Thanks be unto God for his unspeakable gift."

The verses in Hebrews go on to say that not only have those who have been enlightened have tasted Jesus, but they have also been

---

[13] 1 Corinthians 13:12

[14] Philippians 2:5

[15] Hebrews 5:14

made partakers of the Holy Ghost. This means they have partaken of the Holy Spirit's power and benefitted from His work.

This level of spiritual maturity implies that an individual has tasted the good works of God. This shows that the Word is no longer just a book of platitudes, religious teaching, or doctrine to the person, but that he or she has tasted the Living Word of the Bible, Jesus Christ. As the Living Word, Jesus makes the written Word alive and powerful.

Finally, these verses go on to say that such a person has tasted the powers of the world to come. This means that the person has seen glimpses into the promise of heaven. Such an individual has become receptive to its blessings and touched by its unchanging reality of the Son of God.

Obviously, enlightenment means that you have personally experienced the revelation of heaven, and since it has deeply touched your life, you should never desire to turn back. Your vision is now heavenward; your passion directed towards the throne of God; and your heart belongs to the One who secured your salvation on the cross.

Where are you in these three levels of spiritual progression? Are you at the stage of knowledge, operating on an earthly plane and carnal in your perception? When was the last time you had a revelation of Jesus? Did you walk it out or were you disobedient? How much of the life of Christ has been perfected in you, verifying that the Word is alive, changing your disposition to manifest Jesus Christ? Your level of growth and fruits will tell on you.

Application:

Evaluate what level you are operating in: knowledge, revelation, or enlightenment. If you have not experienced all levels at different times in your spiritual journey, you need to humble yourself before God. Ask Him to go deeper in you to bring you higher in Him.

10

CREEDS

We have been considering the difference between facts, truths, doctrines, and principles. These four elements make up the Word of God.

Man will take these elements and place them into some kind of systematic belief. There are four different belief systems that man works within. We have already touched on two of them, but we now need to understand all four of them, in order to bring a proper comparison. They are traditions, theology, tenets, and creeds.

Traditions are religious rituals that are recognized and practiced. Some of these traditions are Christ-centered, while many others are of men. The traditions of men are legalistic, judgmental, and self-righteous in nature and attitude. They are often man's way of supposedly establishing outward personal righteousness to gain God's approval, but they lack spirit and life.

As previously stated, theology can prove to be man's personal conclusions to spiritual matters. These personal conclusions can become a means to judge all religious activities and teachings. These strict boundaries of understanding can prove to be very indifferent or harsh towards those matters that run contrary to them. They ultimately can serve as the final authority to all religious matters.

When theology serves as the final authority, not only does a person become unteachable, but he or she can begin to harbor a cult mentality. This cult mentality opens the individual up to seducing spirits and doctrines of demons. It is at the point of theology that most arguments occur.

Debates are used as a means of persuasion. It has been my experience, that debates never change the minds of those debating, but only those who are undecided or immature. Therefore, in the spiritual realm, spiritual debates are meant to sway a person to another person's way of thinking, which can be far from God's thoughts and ways.[1]

Some believe such debates are profitable. Debating may stir people up to think about what they believe, but curiosity is much more beneficial. Curiosity also must be stirred up, but it is to encourage people to explore facts, truths, godly doctrines, and principles in order to guide their

[1] Isaiah 55:8-9

thinking towards the reality of Jesus. Debates actually narrow spiritual beliefs down to logical, humanistic conclusions, while curiosity broadens ones understanding to discern the possibilities in light of God.

Debates often start outside of the parameters of spirit and truth, and work towards persuading another person to see the value of a certain belief. This may seem the logical way, but the problem is that wrong beliefs can determine the conclusions to a matter, rather than the Spirit and truth of the Word of God.

After years of debating over spiritual matters, I realize that many people hold to the same opinion. After all, who wants mere man to determine religious beliefs when most people believe they already hold the truth?

The Apostle Paul made this statement in Titus 3:9, "But avoid foolish questions, and genealogies, and contentions, and strivings about the law; for they are unprofitable and vain." Many of our theological stands would not necessarily determine a person's salvation, although these judgments can cause one to become self-righteous and dogmatic.

The Word of God is clear that we need to contend for the pure faith in order to ensure that people walk the narrow path of truth and righteousness. "To contend" means to struggle for a person's soul, by changing his or her direction. This is quite different from trying to persuade another person to believe a certain point of view. Therefore, it is important to recognize matters that will ruin the soul of a person, while avoiding situations that will not change an individual's disposition or eternal destination. [2]

Jesus made this clear to Peter when He got him down to the one predominate issue that would determine a person's eternal destination in Matthew 16:15. "But who say ye that I am?" If a person does not get Jesus right when it comes to his or her perception (understanding), attitude, and approach, it matters little how ironclad or scripturally backed his or her particular belief or theology is. The person is still miserably lost, for only the Person Jesus saves.

Tenets include both doctrine and beliefs. Beliefs can have a profound impact on a person's conduct. In fact, if an individual does not practice what he or she preaches, the person will be a hypocrite. Therefore, when you encounter tenets, you will see beliefs intermingled with doctrine.

In 1991, I wrote a discipleship course that covers what I consider to be the major tenets of faith. I dealt with subjects such as the Godhead, Word of God, faith, sanctification, marriage, divorce, and spiritual warfare. Throughout the course, facts, truths, doctrines, and principles were intermingled to present a complete picture of the Christian faith.

[2] Jude 3; Matthew 10:28

This brings us to creeds. A creed represents a person's fundamental beliefs that they believe to be true. Therefore, such a statement is not subject to change, nor is it debatable. The main purpose of a creed is to establish whether there is agreement. For example, before a person gets involved with a church, ministry, or movement, he or she needs to check out the different creeds of the organizations to see if there is an agreement present. Without agreement, people cannot walk together.[3]

Each aspect of the Word makes a declaration. It is important to compare what each element declares in the following table.

Facts	I know this has been proven; therefore, I accept it
Truths	I know this is a truth; therefore, I receive it by faith.
Knowledge	I know in part.
Doctrine	I know this is an upright response; therefore, I will obey
Revelation	Now I see, but through a glass darkly.
Principle	I know this is the way of God; therefore, I will walk in it.
Enlightenment	Now I understand; therefore, it has become my reality.
Creed	I believe...

The word "believe" is a powerful word in this text. The Apostle Paul expressed the intent of the word "believe" in 2 Timothy 2:12 when he stated he knew in whom he believed. It was this belief that gave him immovable confidence.

This shows us that to "believe" or "believing" is not just a matter of the intellect. Rather, the information has been embraced as an absolute truth in the heart or will area.[4] It is a declaration that will result in action, for it has been verified through personal study, revelation, and experiences.

---

[3] Amos 3:3

[4] Romans 10:9-10. Note, how man believes unto righteousness.

A creed is not like a doctrine that outwardly produces dos and don'ts. Rather, it serves as an immovable anchor in the soul that produces an inward authoritative confidence in what a person perceives to be true. It serves as the foundation and boundary to all a person believes, stands for, and teaches. Everything a person proclaims and abides by will be consistent with his or her creed. If a person sways from his or her creed, it simply means it belongs to another, and serves as a guise for immaturity, false doctrine, or a wrong spirit.

A creed is also known as an article or a statement of faith. I have pondered why the Church has gotten away from the concept of creeds. My conclusion to this matter is that creeds give the impression of beliefs that are forever etched in stone, while the concept of a Statement of Faith would seem more flexible or tolerant.

Personally, I really don't care what term is used, but I believe that a creed or Statement of Faith based on the Word of God will be immovable. This means there will be no room for change or debate. However, this reality does not mean that spiritual growth and experience will not enlarge a person's understanding of his or her creed.

Regardless of what people call their belief system, I believe a person must clearly establish what he or she believes. This is why I encourage people who sit under my teaching to give an account of the hope in them by writing out a Statement of Faith.[5] I want to make sure that their foundation is not based on assumptions, man's traditions, or presumed theology, but on the Person of Jesus Christ and His teachings. After all, He is the foundation upon which each person will eternally stand.

I have known of many Christians who became prey to cults because they were not established in their beliefs. As a result, they had no anchor to hold them fast to the truth of Jesus Christ, causing them to be carried away by other winds of doctrine.

I have also recognized that those who lack proper discipleship also are devoid of such an anchor in their souls. These people have defined Christianity according to their own preferences, insecurities, and prejudices. They have picked and chosen from Scripture verses that support their view on spiritual matters. The results are obvious, as these people often minor in what is important to God, and major in what religiously serves their personal idea of righteousness. They have a form of godliness, but lack inward discipline and the ability to properly discern good from evil.[6]

One of the things I encourage people to do is to check out the Statement of Faith behind any church or religious organization they support. If they find agreement with the Statement of Faith, then the next step is to test the leader's preaching or teachings to see whether he or

---

[5] 1 Peter 3:15

[6] 2 Timothy 3:5

she remains consistent to his or her Statement of Faith. If the leader sways from the foundation, he or she must be considered untrustworthy.

Many heretics hide behind acceptable creeds in order to cover up spiritual discrepancies. Beware of such inconsistencies and flee from any leader who is not up front and living in harmony with his or her Statement of Faith.

A Statement of Faith should include most of the following foundational beliefs, which must be backed up by Scripture:

1. The authority of the Word of God.
2. The identity of God (Godhead).
3. The identity of Jesus including His birth, death, burial, resurrection, ascension, and His return.
4. The provision of salvation through Jesus' shed blood, and what it means for the believers who receive it by faith.
5. The work of the Holy Spirit.

It is important to examine every part of a Statement of Faith to see whether the intent behind it remains the same. I have read articles of faith that appear scriptural, but in the midst of it, subtle errors have been incorporated. I can tell you from experience that the emphasis in the teaching and preaching will be in compliance with the error, not with the Person of Jesus Christ.

All Statements of Faith for Christians must be about who we believe in, more than what we believe. After all, our faith is based on the character of God, not on theological stands. This is why a creed based on the real God serves as an anchor to the soul, immovable and capable of withstanding any attack or storm.

Have you established your own personal anchor? Is it true to Scripture and consistent in intent? If you cannot answer these questions properly, you are probably unable to give an account of the hope in you. This will make you subject to heretical error and to the powerful seductive influences of the doctrines of demons.

Application:

If you do not have a Statement of Faith, you need to take time and write one. You also need to read the Statement of Faith of every church and religious organization you are exposed to or support. Test the leaders to make sure they are consistent with their foundation. Also, check into the Statement of Faith of known heretics and cults. Compare these Statements of Faith with those who are scripturally established, and see if you can discern the error, or whether these erroneous leaders and organizations are hiding behind the veneer of sound creeds.

11

TESTING THE WORD

The next phase of rightly dividing the Word is to be able to test personal biblical conclusions. The difficulty in this area is that we can always scripturally logic out and confirm our conclusions. Therefore, how can we test our understanding of the Word of God to make sure it is correct?

There are four different tests that I have used over the years. These tests have kept me from establishing my own religious system of dead-letter religion. The first test is: You must always test your scriptural conclusions with the whole character of God. Erroneous teachings are not consistent with God's character or His Spirit. They usually present Him in a lopsided or unrealistic light.

For example, people stress either His love or His holiness, but they seem to have a hard time bringing both together to present a proper picture of God. Their idea of love is not based on God, but on the sensual, self-serving, lustful love that is often presented by the world.

When it comes to the subject of holiness, it is often based on man conforming to a strict religious code, instead of the character of Christ being worked into people's lives. Therefore, people often define God according to who they are or striving to become, instead of who God is. In the end, they create their own god who can be understood and controlled by them.

If people would test things in light of the complete character of God, they would see a God who is holy and demands justice, but out of love provided the means for man to escape His wrath.[1] God's character is meant to produce the right attitude in His followers. His holiness is capable of creating a healthy fear, while His love inspires faith and a healthy desire to obey Him.

If God's character is properly maintained, the Word will be kept pure, attitudes will remain teachable, and responses will be upright. Sadly, few know the real character and ways of God. Therefore, they cannot test their beliefs or conclusions in light of Him. As a result, they do not have a heavenly perspective, but an earthly view. This will not only pervert the character of God, but it will develop a frame of reference that will cause the person to be blind towards anything that might challenge his or her perceptions. Ultimately, an earthly view will humanize God, while deifying man in his intelligence, abilities, or strength.

---

[1] 1 Thessalonians 5:9-10

This is why the Word of God instructs us to seek God with all of our hearts, to ensure that our spiritual lives are made alive with His reality.[2] The reality of Jesus implies that the Spirit of God is uncovering bountiful treasures about Him that are being imparted into our spirits as living manna.

It is the impartation of the Word by the Spirit that ensures the intent of God's complete counsel. This means the Word remains consistent to the character, heart, and ways of God at all times.

The second test is: Where is this conclusion spiritually leading me? For example, I had someone tell me that once we are saved, we are no longer sinners. I realize that our new birth positionally makes us saints, but the reality is that we are plagued with the old disposition of sin. Our flesh wars against the Spirit while the entanglements of the world choke out the Word, entice our lust, and give Satan a means to be aggressive.[3]

The reality that Christians must confront is that the old man, or the flesh, must be crucified daily or it will reign with a vengeance.[4] My co-laborer in the Gospel thought at one point in her walk that her flesh was dead, until she met a certain individual who suddenly resurrected it. She learned quickly that if you think the flesh is dead, the Lord will allow it to raise its ugly head to give you a reality check.

Regardless of the position and potential of being saints, we still must deal with the influence of sin in our lives. It will remain a part of our spiritual struggle in this world until our physical death. If we fail to recognize its power and influence, we can become enslaved by it.

Consider what the Apostle John said in 1 John 1:8 and 10, "If we say that we have no sin, we deceive ourselves, and the truth is not in us...If we say that we have not sinned, we make him a liar, and his word is not in us." Clearly, we cannot ignore or deny the sin factor, because if we do, we will deceive ourselves and make God a liar. As Christians our inclination and tendency toward sin should make us poor (humble) in spirit, as well as give us a reality check about our need for God's constant intervention and power to help us overcome. Without such a reality check, our denial of our fallen condition will give us a false security as we hide behind positions, rather than depending on Jesus Christ as our only source, immovable rock, and eternal substance.

This brings each of us to an important point: Where do our conclusions ultimately lead us? If they lead us away from dependency on Jesus, there will be something terribly amiss in our spiritual life. In fact, it often points to idolatry, which means the spirit and emphasis are wrong in our conclusions and heretical in nature.

---

[2] Jeremiah 29:13; 2 Corinthians 3:2-6

[3] Matthew 13:22; Ephesians 2:2-3; 4:27; Galatians 5:9-18; 1 Timothy 2:3; James 1:14-15

[4] Luke 9:23; 1 Corinthians 15:31

We must keep in mind that the thread that binds the Word of God together is Jesus' redemption. If we spiritually get away from this focal point, we can be assured of walking on dangerous ground.

The third test involves maintaining the subject in light of the continuity of the text. It is important to consider the whole of Scripture as well as the theme of each chapter. The problem is that many people read only what they want to read, adjusting Scripture to fit their own beliefs and agendas, thereby, changing the intent of it. This is how cults begin.

Good examples of this are Romans 8:28 and Matthew 19:5-6,

> And we know that all things work together for good to them that love God, to them who are the called according to his purpose... And said, For this cause shall a woman leave father and mother, and shall cleave to her husband and they twain be one flesh? Wherefore they are no more twain, but one flesh. What therefore, God hath joined together, let not man put asunder.

When people quote Romans 8:28, they quote the promise, but leave off the conditions. For example, for all things to work together, believers must love God and adhere to His will for their lives. It is not an unusual practice to partially quote a Scripture verse that will serve personal preferences. People quote what serves their purpose, while ignoring responsibilities that would ensure the fulfillment of the promise. When the promise fails to come to fruition, people often become disillusioned and angry with God.

In Matthew 19:5-6, you will find that I actually misquoted it. It is not the woman who is to leave father or mother, but the man. It is easy to automatically misread or even place words or phrases in a Scripture verse that will comply with cultural or popular religious beliefs. After all, in most cultures, a woman must give up her parents, her identity, and her home, to take on the identity of her husband.

The scriptural concept of a man giving up his identity points to how Christ became of no reputation to identify with His bride, the Church. This sacrifice was an act of love that serves as the motivation for His Church to give up her personal identity, in order to establish a new identity with and in Him.

Because I know I can automatically misread Scripture, I have developed means of forcing myself to acknowledge what I am reading. For example, I color-coded all of my Bibles. Every time I would read a Scripture verse about sacrifice, salvation, or redemption, I underlined it with a red pencil. Each major subject had a different color. This forced me to consider what the Scripture verse was really saying.

I also heard how the late Corrie ten Boom studied her Bible. In each chapter, she would look for the verses that impacted her the most in the areas of inspiration, promises, and warnings. After considering the Scripture passages, she would write a prayer. I found this method thought provoking and rewarding.

My latest method of studying the Word is taking each chapter verse by verse and writing down what stands out the most to me. The result of this practice eventually culminated in my writing a daily devotional, which contains a combination of my thoughts concerning the inspirations, promises, and warnings found in each chapter, along with my prayer. It is vital that we know what we are reading to keep the verses pure and consistent with the text.

The fourth test has to do with historical events and cultural influences. The Word was written to certain people who had different challenges due to the age and cultures in which they lived. This is why the following statement is appropriate to consider when testing scriptural conclusions, "The Bible is not written *to* everyone, but it is written *for* everyone."

For example, the Old Testament was mainly written to the Jews, even though the prophets addressed other nations such as Egypt, Babylon, and Edom. The Jews were chosen to be a holy nation among pagan cultures. They were given strict rules, which if adhered to, would make them very distinct in their beliefs, lifestyles, and practices among these idolatrous cultures.

Much of the New Testament was written to specific local bodies of believers. These churches faced different cultural and political challenges that influence the flavor and instructions found in the epistles addressed to them. In such matters one must seek to understand the environment of the times to properly divide the Word.

A good example of this can be found in the three controversial verses surrounding the subject of women. We find these Scriptures in 1 Corinthians 11:1-16; 14:34-35; and 1 Timothy 2. If you were to consider these verses separately, you would conclude that women must be covered, be only seen and not heard, and they must not teach or instruct men. However, when you compare Scripture with Scripture, it presents a conflicting picture. For example, all Christians, including women, are commissioned to preach the Gospel and disciple people. Discipling involves personal instruction. The New Testament is clear that Priscilla instructed Apollos. The Apostle Paul notified the Roman church to give heed to Phoebe, and Philip's daughters prophesied. The Apostle Paul considered women fellow-workers or co-laborers with him. This means he saw them as equal in importance and work in the kingdom.[5] One must also note that the Apostle Paul stated in Galatians 3:28 that there is no male or female in God, and in 1 Corinthians 14:23-26 he made reference to everyone being able to speak or operate in his or her gift in the Body.[6]

---

[5] Matthew 28:18-19; Mark 16:15-16; Acts 1:14; 2:4-8; 16-18; 18:24-28; 21:9; Romans 16:1-4; 19; 1 Corinthians 9:1-5

[6] If you would like to understand more about this controversial subject, see the book, *Women's Place in the Kingdom of God,* in volume 5.

Comparison of Scripture proves there is more going on than what is obvious to the reader. The problem is that many have made these verses into concrete doctrines that have covered up ignorance and prejudice. It has caused many women to ignore their true calling, and submit to a bitter bondage that can become indescribably abusive.

When you encounter a verse that appears contrary to the intent of the whole counsel of God, do not make it into a truth or doctrine. Rather, put it on the shelf until God brings proper perspective to it. Usually, studying the history, the time, and the culture surrounding the epistles can clear up any confusion.

For example, the Apostle Paul dealt with various issues in the Corinthian body, but one issue had to do with the influence of the Oral Law or traditions of the Jews were having on this local body of believers. Jesus criticized the traditions of the Jews, calling them vain in Matthew 15:1-9. People who promoted this Oral Law were making inroads into the Corinthian church by promoting their customs and practices. The Apostle Paul actually dealt with their customs in 1 Corinthians 11:1-16 (note verse 16), as well as using this Oral Law of the Jews to make a point in 1 Corinthians 14:36-40.

In 1 Corinthians 14, the Apostle Paul is talking about being commanded by the law (not him) concerning women's conduct. Since he made a distinction between the Law of Moses (the Torah) and the traditions of men (the Oral Law of the Jews) in his letter to the Corinthians, one must conclude that he is referring to the Oral Law of the Jews in 14:34, especially since these instructions cannot be located in the Law of Moses.[7] As I studied verse 14:33, I realized that the apostle was talking about order. I believe he simply was using the Oral Law or tradition of the Jews to make a point or bring a contrast about order, and not to establish a doctrine concerning women. This conclusion would maintain the intent of the complete counsel of God, as well as keep the continuity of chapter 14 intact.

According to historical information, the Apostle Paul was dealing with a more serious matter in 1 Timothy 2. We can see that he was addressing the need for a woman's beauty to find its origins from within. The women of Rome were very vain in their physical appearance, while Jewish women were conservative in dress. The liberty of Christ brought the possibilities of greater liberty of dress to the Jewish women, causing the Apostle Paul to call for discretion.

The Apostle Paul also dealt with the issue of women teaching men. It is important to realize that according to their customs, Jewish women were not allowed to learn, let alone teach. Yet, we know Priscilla taught Apollos, which implied that there was an underlying motive for Paul's instruction that we are not aware of.

---

[7] See 1 Corinthians 9:9-11

This brings us back to both historical events and cultural practices. According to Katherine Bushnell in her book, God's Word to Women, the political temperature of that day was causing difficulties for the Church. It was at this time that the persecution of the Church was escalating. Apparently, Roman soldiers looked for any deviant changes in dress and conduct to enable them to locate a local church, bringing possible persecution upon the Christians. The Apostle Paul was simply calling for discretion and restraint, especially on the part of the women.

We do see that the Apostle Paul was clearly stipulating that, in spite of the circumstances that seem to dictate their conduct, women must have the advantage of growing in spiritual knowledge to prevent delusion. He also reminded the church that salvation came by way of woman who experienced childbearing, in order to give birth to Jesus Christ, the Son of God

There are sound explanations for controversial Scripture passages. However, to discover them, one must be willing to break out of acceptable conclusions and beliefs, and search beyond personal understanding, prejudice, and theological boundaries. Such answers are often found in the historical events and cultural practices of the people.

How much of the Bible have you read from a biased perspective? When was the last time you challenged yourself to really consider what the theme of the chapter was and the intent of the Scripture passage? If you approach the Word with an open heart, a child-like curiosity, and the willingness to explore, you will come out with treasures that will enlarge your mind and change your heart.

Application:

Write an epistle to your church about issues that are affecting it. This will help you to see how the flavor and emphasis of your letter will be based on what is happening in your church and community. As a result, your letter might show you how it may not be applicable to other bodies of believers.

12

SPIRITUAL PURSUITS

The Word of God instructs people to seek the Lord and they shall live.[1] This concept is found throughout the Bible, but it is not unusual to discover that people have other religious pursuits that cause spiritual detours and defeat.

These pursuits are not necessarily bad, but given a wrong preference, they can either be abused or become idolatrous in nature. For example, some people are caught up with seeking blessings or claiming promises. This implies that they are caught up with benefits, rather than the real reward or treasure of heaven. In fact, a person's emphasis reveals a lot about his or her spiritual preferences.

Emphasis also determines how people interpret the Word of God. For instance, people will read the Scriptures according to their emphasis. They will only see those things that confirm or compliment their personal emphasis, preventing them from seeing the intent of Scripture.

This chapter will examine what different points of emphasis, or isolated areas of exaggerated importance, reveal about people's motivation, intention, and focus. It will also show how an incorrect emphasis develops a wrong perception of God. Overemphasizing will cause a person to be idolatrous in his or her pursuits.

There are five subjects that can be emphasized in Scripture. They are *covenant*, *blessings*, *promises*, *treasures*, and *gifts*. Two of these clearly emphasize Jesus, while the other three benefit man.

Covenant mainly points to God. Throughout God's dealing with man, He has shown His intentions by making covenants with him. Covenants are agreements or contracts that are binding. These covenants not only express God's commitment towards man, but also expose man's intention towards God. They exhibit whether man is sincere towards God or just playing a religious game.[2]

One of the most well-known covenants God made is found in Genesis 9:11-12. In the presence of Noah, the Lord made a perpetual contract with the earth to never again destroy it with water. He than gave a token to serve as a valuable reminder of this binding covenant, "I do

---

[1] Amos 5:4, 6, 14

[2] To understand the subject of covenant, see the fourth book of this volume, *The Place of Covenant.*

set my bow in the cloud, and it shall be for a token of a covenant between me and the earth."

This brings us to a very important point about covenants. These agreements usually have a visible token that serve as a reminder to all parties concerned. For example, God made a covenant with Abraham concerning his seed in future generations. The token reminder of this agreement on Abraham's part, along with all males that were part of his lineage, was physical circumcision.[3]

Outward tokens of these sacred covenants with God served as a form of consecration or setting apart. It reminded those involved with this agreement that they are part of a covenant with a holy God who requires sobriety and upright responses.

We see these tokens in the covenant of the Law. God instructed the Jewish people to keep the covenant of the Law ever before them, by binding, "...them for a sign upon thine hand, and they shall be as frontlets between thine eyes. And thou shalt write them upon the posts of thy house, and on thy gates" (Deuteronomy 6:8-9). To comply with these instructions, the Jewish people fastened the Scriptures to the doorposts in objects called a mezuzah, and attached phylacteries to their forehead and left arm.

In Numbers 15:38-39 God established another token,

> Speak unto the children of Israel, and bid them that they make them fringes in the borders of their garments throughout their generations, and that they put upon the fringe of the borders a ribband of blue: And it shall be unto you for a fringe, that ye may look upon it, and remember all the commandments of the Lord, and do them.

These verses are in reference to the prayer shawl.

Many of the Jewish practices were to remind the people of the covenant of the Law. They were blessed if they maintained the covenant, but if they failed to adhere to it, they would end up being cursed.[4]

Another important factor in a covenant was sacrifice. We see Abraham offering up five different sacrifices in Genesis 15. God told him to divide these sacrifices. Later, Abraham had to protect them from the fowls, as they sat exposed in the heat of the day. And, when the sun went down, he fell into a deep sleep that ushered him into a great darkness. It was while in this sleep that God revealed that those of Abraham's seed would be afflicted. Then a smoking furnace and a burning lamp passed between the divided pieces of the sacrifice.

This incident pointed to the great sacrifice of Jesus who established the New Testament Covenant. Like the offerings of Abraham, the man's cruel whip would tear His body. His sacrifice would bring great darkness upon the earth as man railed against Him and Satan mocked Him. His

---

[3] Genesis 17:10-13

[4] Leviticus 26

offering would not only bring great affliction upon Him, but it would reveal the captivity that held mankind in unseen chains of rebellion, anger, and hatred. He would be put into the grave to silence the judgment on sin, but would be resurrected to become the light of man's very life and being. Jesus would pass between life and death and judgment and mercy in order to bring grace to every seeking heart.

Jesus' sacrifice would establish a new covenant. Three visible tokens would serve as a reminder of this covenant. The first is *water baptism.*

Water Baptism is a visible sign that a person has entered into the New Testament Covenant by becoming identified with Jesus in His death, burial, and resurrection. This token not only serves as a visual token, but it is a verbal token as well, for it is at water baptism that many make their profession known to others of Jesus being their Savior and Lord.

The second token is *communion*. Communion is a time of remembering what Jesus did on the cross. This token is to be observed until He comes again.[5]

The third token is the *believer*. Ezekiel 36:26-27 gives us insight into this new covenant,

> A new heart also will I give you, and a new spirit will I put within you; and I will take away the stony heart out of your flesh, and I will give you a heart of flesh. And I will put my spirit within you, and cause you to walk in my statues, and ye shall keep my judgments, and do them.

This new covenant points to a new life where there is a circumcision of the heart and the work of regeneration by the Holy Spirit. As a result, Christians serve in newness of spirit and not in oldness of the letter or Law. The Apostle Paul summarized this new life in 2 Corinthians 5:17, "Therefore if any man be in Christ, he is a new creature: old things are passed away; behold, all things are become new". It is not a life of outward conformity as the Law encouraged, but one of inward transformation by the Holy Ghost.[6]

This covenant and token of the new life is established in a relationship with God, "But as many as received him, to them gave he power to become the sons of God, even to them that believe on his name" (John 1:12). Such a relationship points to an eternal inheritance that affords every believer certain rights, especially the right to come boldly to the throne of grace. These rights and benefits are eternal in nature. They give saints authority and power to stand as priests in intercession, and to serve as ambassadors for an unseen kingdom in the midst of great darkness.[7]

---

[5] 1 Corinthians 11:26

[6] Romans 2:29; 7:6; Titus 3:5

[7] Romans 12:2; Ephesians 1:5, 9, 13-14; 2 Corinthians 5:20; Hebrews 4:15-16;

The new life stipulates that the Christian's main intention must be to bring glory to God by being conformed to the image or likeness of Jesus Christ. It will bring character and quality to his or her walk. It must be upright and in line with God's bidding to ensure the integrity of this covenant. In the end, the Christian will actually reflect the very attitude of Jesus.

God's main emphasis is man's salvation. This eternal emphasis will fulfill His plan of making the essence of Jesus and His kingdom a reality in the hearts of His people. He points to His covenant to remind the saints of the binding contract that was made possible by the sacrifice of Jesus. Such an agreement holds responsibilities that must be fulfilled by faith towards Him and obedience to His Word.[8]

The problem is that many people take certain aspects of the New Testament Covenant and claim certain rights, without displaying the outward token of it. This token has to do with identification with Jesus Christ. It is the identification that gives people the necessary authority to claim the benefits of this new covenant.

What is your intention towards God? Are you just claiming the benefits without seeking to know, love, serve, and please Him? Are you lacking the token of identification that must be prevalent in any covenant with God? Or, is your life an outward religious game, rather than an inward transformation based on a living relationship with God?

Blessings

One of the most popular emphasis of many Christians are the blessings of God. In fact, one of the most fashionable religious clubs in America is the "bless me club." This emphasis proves that few understand the purpose of blessings and how they work in God's plan.

In the Old Testament, blessings were associated with land, bountiful harvest, and peace. They pointed to the life that God wanted to give His people. However, these blessings hinged upon obedience, and if it was missing, the blessings were turned into curses that resulted in death.[9]

This brings us to the purpose of blessings. God had two reasons for blessing Israel in an earthly or physical sense. First, the Jewish people were given blessings to fulfill God's promise to Abraham to make them a great nation. Out of this nation would come the Messiah, the Redeemer.

Secondly, Israel was to serve as a holy nation, distinct from the pagan nations. Therefore, blessings were allotted to ensure inheritance and righteous conduct. This righteous conduct included the best of the sacrifices, taking care of the Levites, strangers, widows, fatherless, and

---

1 Peter 2:5, 9

[8] 2 Corinthians 5:7; Hebrews 11:6; John 15:10-14

[9] Leviticus 26

to keep from putting other Israelites under financial burdens and despair. In other words, they were blessed by God so that they could bless others, and freely and liberally display integrity, benevolence, and hospitality. These virtues would stand out as a light in the midst of great darkness.[10]

Biblical history shows us that material prosperity often served as a subtle test to the Israelites' commitment and faithfulness. This test would ultimately expose their priorities. For example, prosperity made Israel slothful and indifferent towards God, forgetting the covenant. During this stage, many of the Jewish people turned from the God of Israel and pursued idols. Because of this disobedience, Israel plummeted down into spiritual poverty, resulting in the blessings of God turning into curses.

Sadly, many Christians think of blessings in terms of worldly possessions. Granted, the purpose for blessings remains the same, but the face of them has changed. The reason for this change is because God is not establishing a physical nation, but a heavenly kingdom. Because of this emphasis, many of the blessings that are available to Christians are spiritual in nature, rather than earthly or worldly. Ephesians 1:3 verifies this fact, "Blessed be the God and Father of our Lord Jesus Christ, who hath blessed us with all spiritual blessings in heavenly places in Christ."

When God blesses the Church with earthly blessings, it becomes a test for faithful and responsible stewardship. He always blesses, so that others will be blessed. It is a way of furthering His plan and purpose on earth. This is why Christians entrusted with such blessings must do the following: 1) Offer them all back to God for His purpose; 2) be faithful, obedient stewards to what He reveals; and 3) avoid heaping them upon self.

The truth is that very few people can be trusted with worldly riches. I cannot tell you how many Christians have told me that if they win the Lotto, they would give ten percent to God. They use this concept as a bargaining chip to gain God's attention or approval, when in reality, such logic is foolishness to Him. Ten percent would be considered crumbs and not a sacrifice. The real crux of the matter is that earthly riches for most Christians have nothing to do with furthering God's kingdom, but heaping the things of the world upon self.

Recently, a friend made a similar statement about winning the Lotto. My co-laborer Jeannette's response not only silenced her, but also put a mirror up in front of her. Jeannette told her if she ever won a large sum of money, she would give ninety percent to God and keep ten percent.

Sadly, giving ten percent in this type of scenario is not a token of commitment, but an immature and selfish way of trying to placate God, so that selfishness is justified. God does not want money from His

---

[10] Exodus 22:21-29; Deuteronomy 15; 18:1-8

people nor does He deserve to receive the leftover of crumbs. He deserves and wants His peoples' hearts and obedience.

Most Christians nobly claim they want money to promote the kingdom of God, but they have their own agendas in mind. In other words, they would not consult God about what He would want them to do with the money. As a result, many Christians foolishly squander money on heretics and charlatans.

This is why New Testament blessings are spiritual in nature, and must become a natural expression of a person's heart and spiritual maturity. These blessings are unseen, but will manifest themselves in attitudes and lifestyles.

We see one of these spiritual blessings in Galatians 3:14. This verse is talking about the blessing that came from Abraham to the Gentiles through Jesus. The blessing points to the promise of the Holy Spirit.

Romans 15:29 states, "And I am sure that, when I come unto you, I shall come in the fulness of the blessing of the gospel of Christ." Here we see blessing is associated with the Gospel. The Gospel is the power of God unto salvation.[11]

Finally, 1 Peter 3:9 tells us that blessings are to be inherited. This relates to a future inheritance, rather than a present reality.

God can prosper His people in various ways, but for the Christian, the real benefits will not be experienced in this present world, but in the next world. This is why Christians are considered sojourners, because their real priority and attraction is not worldly, but heavenly.[12]

Sadly, some Christians are pursuing the things of the world. They are playing spiritual harlotry with the world in the name of Jesus and prosperity. As "kids" of God, they believe their inheritance is worldly and for now. Obviously, these people are not interested in eternity, but are bent on enjoying the present world. In some cases, well-known evangelists and preachers are merchandising men's souls to build extravagant earthly kingdoms. Even though these heretics are facing a greater judgment, people continue to flock into their web of destruction, while blindly filling their coffers in hopes of securing worldly blessings for themselves.

What are you seeking? Are you seeking earthly blessings that will produce spiritual leanness if mishandled, or spiritual blessings that are eternal and satisfying?

---

[11] Romans 1:16

[12] 1 Peter 2:11

The Promises of God

The next popular emphasis of Christians is the promises of God. They love to declare biblical promises to get their way with God. However, promises have a distinct purpose: To work spiritual character or discipline in a person's life.

Promises are always in line with God's character and timing. They are usually conditional and entail a time of waiting or preparation, before they are fulfilled.[13] For example, Abraham waited 25 years before Isaac was born. King David spent years in exile before he became king. And, Jesus, the Son of God, was prepared in obscurity for thirty years before He started His public ministry.

The time spent waiting for the fulfillment of promises serves as a test and a form of discipline that reveals and defines spiritual character or disposition. We see that Abraham passed the test by walking in faith with God, and David overcame by keeping his eyes on God. As for Christians, their test is the same as Abraham's and David's. The test is described by Hebrews 6:11-12, "And we desire that every one of you do show the same diligence to the full assurance of hope unto the end; That ye be not slothful, but followers of them who through faith and patience inherit the promises." In this test, people will find out if they are self-serving or Christ-centered.

Godly promises are unique because they have eternity in mind. We see this for Abraham. God gave him many promises that never came to fruition in his lifetime, but you don't see him losing faith in God nor do you see his commitment waver. Hebrews 11:10 gives insight into his character and his real point of confidence, "For he looked for a city which hath foundations, whose builder and maker is God." Meditate upon Abraham's discipline.

Without proper discipline, people will automatically abuse God's promises, bringing judgment upon themselves, rather than blessings.

What does your attitude towards God's promises say about you?

Treasures

The next area of emphasis is treasures. Treasure reveals motivation of the heart. This brings a person down to what he or she values, the things of the world or the treasure of heaven. Jesus pointed this very fact out in Matthew 6:21, "For where your treasure is, there will your heart be also." A divided heart points to idolatry and spiritual instability.

Sadly, many Christians miss the real treasure of heaven because their hearts are directed in the wrong places. The Apostle Paul reveals

---

[13] Isaiah 40:31

this treasure is the Person of Jesus Christ, "In whom are hid all the treasures of wisdom and knowledge" (Colossians 2:3).

Everything a person needs is found in Jesus. He is the reward to desire and the prize that must be attained. He is the Pearl of Great Price that is so priceless that it is worth selling all to possess Him.[14]

Since the spiritual treasure comes down to the Person of Jesus, many believe they automatically possess this treasure. This belief is based upon salvation. However, salvation is an act of grace and does not constitute possession. Possessing Christ comes out of a growing relationship with God. How much we possess of Him is determined by how much He possesses our heart. Meanwhile, many Christians believe they possess the fullness of the treasure of heaven, even though they are pursuing the world.

The Apostle Paul made this statement in Philippians 3:8, "Yea doubtless, and I count all things but loss for the excellency of the knowledge of Christ Jesus my Lord: for whom I have suffered the loss of all things, and do count them but dung, that I may win Christ."

What does your treasure say about your heart? Do you possess Jesus because He possesses you?

Spiritual Gifts

The final emphasis you can distinguish among Christians is spiritual gifts surrounding the kingdom of heaven. Sadly, often the attraction to these gifts is not for the purpose of glorifying God, but to pursue after and experience the supernatural.

Some Christians are more attracted to the supernatural than to God. The reason for this is that many are seeking power for personal vainglory, rather than seeking to be used by God for His glory. As a result, these people often tap into the power of darkness, opening themselves up to a wrong spirit, a different Jesus, and another gospel.[15]

These gifts have to do with focus and purpose. People's acceptance of counterfeits in the area of gifts has caused them to change their focus from Jesus to the supernatural. This has brought them under the guise of a religious cloak that perverts truth, defiles pure doctrine, and adjusts godly principles.

All godly gifts point to God's supernatural intervention in man's life. In the right perspective, these gifts glorify God and edify the Body of Christ.[16] But, in the wrong perspective, they can cause abuse and spiritualization of the things of God.

---

[14] Genesis 15:1; Philippians 3:8-14;

[15] 2 Corinthians 11:1-3

[16] If you would like to know more about spiritual gifts, see the author's book,

Where is your focus? Is it on Jesus or towards the supernatural? Jesus will lead you in the right direction, while emphasis on gifts will blind you to the destructive path of the supernatural.

Consider the summary of these pursuits in the following table.

Pursuits	Points to Purpose
Covenants	Establish commitment and identification.
Blessings	To fulfill God's plan on earth.
Promises	Work spiritual character or discipline in person.
Treasures	Reveals motivation of the heart.
Spiritual Gifts	Reveals focus.

For the Purpose of Edification, located in Volume 5 in her foundational series.

13

EXAMPLES

The next area that is of utmost importance to understand is the place that the Old and New Testaments should have in rightly dividing the Word of God. Due to misappropriation of the Old Testament, there is much confusion about the New Testament.

Some Christians believe the Old Testament is no longer valid, while others misappropriate certain portions of it to establish a mishmash of beliefs and practices that point to the keeping of the Law, while clinging to some flimsy idea about grace. Such practices show ignorance towards the Law as well as towards God's favor. This hodgepodge of beliefs reveals the establishment of a wrong foundation that will not stand when the real tests come.

The Word of God is clear about the purpose of the Old Testament. In fact, it serves as the foundation, while the New Testament is the visible structure. The Old Testament points to the Law that could only judge, while the New Testament reveals the grace of God that can reach beyond the effects of all sin in order to save.

The Old Testament proves we need a savior, while the New Testament unveils who this Savior is. The Old commences, while the New completes. The Old Testament finds people gathering around Sinai, waiting for the Law, while the New Testament has people bowing before the cross on Calvary to embrace a new way of life.[1] The Old is associated with Moses who gave the Law to Israel, and the New is a revelation of the Lawgiver who serves as the fulfillment of the Law.[2]

The Old Testament is about the Law that revealed the hearts of men, but the New Testament is about how the hearts of men can be changed by the reality of God's intervention. The old exposes the inability of the Law to justify man, while the new shows God's ability to bring forth justification through the death, burial, and resurrection of Jesus Christ.

Without the Old Testament, the New Testament would have no proof of its validity. For example, Jesus and the writers of the New Testament referred to the Old Testament to confirm or verify not only His true identity as the Son of God, but also that He was the prophetic fulfillment

---

[1] Some of the comparisons between the Old and New Testaments were found in, as well as inspired by Henrietta C. Mears book, What the Bible is All About, page 16

[2] Romans 10:4

in regards to being the Promised One or the Messiah. Jesus quoted Deuteronomy when refuting Satan, and Isaiah when He introduced His ministry to those of His hometown. The Apostle Peter quoted the prophets Joel and Isaiah, while the Apostle Paul quoted the prophet Habakkuk and made reference to the Law.

The Old Testament makes up three-fourths of the canon. Its immovable foundation is clearly established both prophetically and historically. It is the history of man's constant failings, and the revelation of God's unchangeable faithfulness. Without its valuable information, man would have no means to understand the present or avenues to test or judge his personal activities or direction in light of eternity.

The Old Testament contains two valuable resources to help people rightly divide the Word. They are examples and shadows. The Apostle Paul made this statement in regards to the events of the Old Testament in 1 Corinthians 10:6, "Now these things were our <u>examples,</u> to the intent we should not lust after evil things, as they also lusted." (Emphasis added.) We have already made reference to how examples bring clarity to doctrines as far as man's responsibility to abide in upright conduct. According to *Strong's Concordance*, example means sampler as in "type" or "model" for the purpose of imitation or in the case of warning.

The Old Testament is full of "samples" that serve as visible examples of what is acceptable to God. These examples are models that leave strong impressions in the spirit. Clearly, the Old Testament is full of instances where one can clearly examine the consequences of wrong actions. In fact, I cannot imagine what it would be like to not have the Old Testament for reference. My understanding of the New Testament would not only be greatly hindered, but there would be no credibility to it.

Jesus and the New Testament writers made reference to Old Testament examples to bring forth comparisons that were vital to the points they were trying to make to their listeners and readers. For example, Jesus made reference to Jonah in regards to His resurrection and to Lot's wife in respect to turning back to the old ways. The Apostle Paul went to great lengths to explain faith in light of Abraham. James mentioned the patience of Job, the faith of Rahab, and the prayers of Elijah. Hebrews referred to the unbelief of Israel, the unheeded tears of Esau, and established a hall of fame for people from the Old Testament who walked by faith. Peter referred to Noah, Lot, and Balaam, while Jude spoke of Balaam and Cain in the same verse, and brought up the prophecy of Enoch.[3]

Can you imagine what a vacuum there would be in our understanding if we could not refer back to the Old Testament to understand these people? We would never discover what made them unique or what caused them to miserably fail before God. At best, we would have a faceless name that had no historical reference or

---

[3] James 2:25; 5:11, 17; Hebrews 3:7-19; 11; 12: 16-17; Jude 11, 14

significance, other than serving as some kind of vague example in the New Testament. Ultimately, the New Testament would lack life, character, and credibility without the examples established in the Old Testament.

As you study the Bible, you will begin to see how the Old and New Testaments work together to bring forth a balanced perspective. The Old Testament lays the groundwork, while the New Testament gives us God's perspective on a matter. For example, the Old Testament tells us how Esau felt about his birthright, but the New Testament tells us what was wrong with Esau. He was a fornicator and a profane person.[4]

Together, these testaments produce a complete picture that can be studied. For example, we would never understand how Abraham became a man of faith who was upheld in the New Testament, unless we follow his steps from Ur of the Chaldeans to the Promised Land in the Old Testament. We would never know the full extent of the test and sacrifice that surrounded Isaac. Nor, could we appreciate Abraham's attitude that made him look beyond earthly blessings to desire, "...a city which hath foundations, whose builder and maker is God" (Hebrews 11:10). We could never understand why he became known as a friend of God, and why Jesus stated that this great patriarch had seen the day that He would walk among man, and was glad for it.[5]

How could we understand the patience of Job, unless we could study his losses and questions in the midst of his great testing? How could we appreciate Rahab's faith, unless we understood her background? How could we know the greatness of Enoch, unless we realized he walked with God? And, what about Esau's tears of self-pity, Balaam's encounter with a talking ass, and Cain's unacceptable actions that were all brought out in the New Testament?

The beauty about the people of the Bible is that they were presented in an honest way. God never blurred the failures of the heroes, and never made the villains appear worse than the righteous. For example, Abraham lied, Noah got drunk, Moses let his anger and pride get the best of him, and King David committed adultery and murder.

When it came to those who were deemed spiritual failures, we see where Cain offered a sacrifice to God. Esau appeared to be a better man than Jacob, and Balaam seemed to be responding in obedience to God.

One of the problems with the Old Testament examples is that people try to fill in the blanks by spiritualizing or transposing their attitudes or conclusions to a matter. For example, Adam and Eve are good examples of transposing personal conclusions. There is a belief that the reason that Adam ate of the tree of the knowledge of good and evil was out of love for Eve because he knew he would be separated from Eve. There is no scriptural basis for this idea. After all, the covenant was made

---

[4] Hebrews 12:16-17

[5] John 8:56; James 2:21-23

between God and Adam. Adam was responsible for keeping the covenant. Eve was deceived, and as a result was in transgression. Instead of giving way to personal rebellion, what if Adam, as the head, had actually interceded for Eve as Jesus did on behalf of Peter when Satan was sifting him? Isn't it possible that God would have restored her back into a right relationship with Him?[6] We can only speculate.

The attempt to make Adam noble in his action is based on personal conclusions and bias. I encountered this biased conclusion when speaking to a group of men wherein reference was made as to how Adam blew it. One man erupted in anger and others became belligerent because it was that terrible woman's fault. The attitudes of these men can be best summarized in this way, "Poor Adam he had no say over his actions, making him a poor, helpless victim, and as a result, all men have apparently been victims of women ever since. After all, it is not their responsibility that they are unhappy, irresponsible, and angry about life."

The Bible is clear that there was deviation in Adam's character. After all, he had dominion over the garden; therefore, why did he let Satan in? He was standing beside Eve when she was being tempted. If he loved her, why didn't he rebuke Satan and lead her away from the tempter? If he was upright, why did he knowingly break the covenant with God? If he was morally responsible, why did he blame both God and Eve for his personal choice and action? After all, he was not deceived; therefore, he understood the implications of his action.[7]

Job and Hosea throw some light on the inward character of Adam. Job 31:33 tells us that Adam had covered his transgression by hiding iniquity in his bosom. Hosea 6:7 tells us that Adam dealt in treachery when he transgressed the covenant.

Another example is that of Rebekah, the wife of Isaac. She has often been presented in a bad light because she helped Jacob secure the blessing in a dishonest way. Esau had already sold his birthright to Jacob and wanted to claim the blessing as elder son. Rightfully, the blessing belonged to Jacob, the one who possessed the birthright. Rebekah had this foreknowledge from God about her two sons when she had Jacob pretend to be Esau in order to receive his rightful blessing from Isaac.[8]

The Bible says nothing more about the incident after Isaac discovered it was Jacob he had blessed and not Esau. Nevertheless, some maintain that Rebekah and Isaac's relationship ceased to be close because of the false pretense, in spite of the fact that nowhere in Scripture is this conclusion maintained. After all, Abraham and Isaac had lied in order to protect themselves, and King David pretended to be

---

[6] Job 31:33; 1 Timothy 2:14

[7] Genesis 1:26; 2:15-17; 3:6; Luke 22:31-34;

[8] Genesis 25:21-34; 27

crazy in order to get himself out of a precarious situation.[9] Interestingly, people point out the incident with Rebekah and Jacob, and try to make something more out of it than it really was in light of the culture of that day.

Some people believe that God punished Rebekah because she never lived to see Jacob and his descendants. Again, there is no scriptural confirmation of this unfounded conclusion. One needs to keep in mind that Isaac never really got to see Jacob and his descendants either, because he was almost blind when he gave the blessing to Jacob. And, like Abraham, Rebekah never got to see the fulfillment of God's promise, but this does not mean that God was punishing her.

A couple of other examples where people transpose their own thoughts or conclusions are concerning Barak and Jonah. Certain people put Barak down because he would not go into battle without Deborah, the judge and prophetess.[10] They accuse him of not having enough faith because he didn't exert his manly leadership and go it alone to face the enemy. To me, Barak recognized that God was with Deborah, and showed both faith and wisdom when he insisted that she be part of the battle. Granted, this could be speculation on my part, except for what Hebrews 11:32-33 states, "And what shall I more say? For the time would fail me to tell of Gideon, and of <u>Barak</u>...Who through faith subdued kingdoms, wrought righteousness, obtained promises, stopped the mouths of lions." (Emphasis added.) According to this verse, Barak was a man of faith who is being accredited with subduing kingdoms in spite of his submission to the leadership of the godly Deborah.

Jonah is another book that is abused by those who transpose their own ideas as to why he did not go to Nineveh. One of the most popular presentations is that Jonah did not want to be considered a false prophet. After all, if he pronounced judgment upon Nineveh and the people repented, God would stay His judgment. This would make it appear that Jonah was a counterfeit.

This may sound reasonable, but it is not scriptural. Jonah clearly states why he did not want to go to Nineveh, and it had nothing to do with his credibility as a prophet. Jonah 4:2 says, "...Therefore I fled before unto Tarshish: for I knew that thou art a gracious God, and merciful, slow to anger, and of greater kindness, and repentest thee of the evil." Nineveh was an enemy of Israel. The people there had a reputation for being cruel and wicked towards the enemies they subdued. The bottom line is that Jonah wanted to see Nineveh destroyed. He knew there was a chance that the people of this wicked city might repent, and he had no intention of giving God the opportunity to warn them and stay any judgment. Clearly, Jonah's concern was not towards maintaining his reputation, but knowing that God would be true

---

[9] Genesis 12:9-12; 26:7-9; 1 Samuel 21:10-15

[10] Judges 4:8

to His character and reputation if the response of the people was that of repentance. It is imperative that we do not read into the lives of people in the Bible, nor take away from their examples.

My understanding of the New Testament has been greatly enriched by the examples of the Old Testament. I truly want to understand the examples that are clearly given to me in this fascinating book. I want to know what makes an Abraham, preserves a Job, causes an Enoch to be great, a mere shepherd to be a chosen leader of God, a prostitute to believe in a God she did not personally know, and people who had much, lose it all for the sake of knowing God. It is my desire to uncover their environment, character, attitudes, and actions. I want to get such a sense of them that they become living companions of righteousness, or distinct examples that keep me from taking destructive detours.

In spite of the growing number of people who think that the Bible is inadequate for today, few realize that neither man nor God has changed. Time and culture have not changed the essence of mankind. People are still confronting the same old problems and issues due to their fallen condition. They still experience the same emotions as King David expressed in Psalms. Their quest to understand life is as real as it was when King Solomon wrote Proverbs and Ecclesiastes. Their desire to experience life is as prevalent as the Israelites in the wilderness. They still must confront giants (obstacles) as David did, conquer the enemies of the mountains (vain imaginations) and of the valleys (the idols of heart) like the Caleb's and the Joshua's. Their questions about suffering are still as intense as Job. Their temptations are as alluring as Delilah was to Samson. Their self-pity is still as inexcusable as it was in Cain, and their failure as great as Adam's in the Garden of Eden.[11]

All of the struggles of man are clearly defined in the black and white pages of the Bible. As Solomon declared, "...there is no new thing under the sun" (Ecclesiastes 1:9*)*. The Bible is a harsh mirror that reveals the very essence of man. It proves that his best is as filthy rags, and that his heart is wicked and deceitful, and only God can know its depths. However, in this mirror is a light of hope that casts a shadow that reaches out of the pages of the Old Testament and becomes a walking, living reality in the New Testament. This incredible reality has a name: Jesus Christ. [12]

As you can see, we can understand man's plight in light of the Old Testament examples. But, we also can actually gain a revelation of Jesus Christ in light of the shadows of the Old Testament. Without the shadows of the Old Testament, Jesus would not have had the verification to prove His identity. Sadly, if we fail to come to terms with the living reality of Jesus in the Old Testament, we will have a limited understanding of Him in the New Testament. The Old Testament is full of

---

[11] The book of Job; Genesis 3:6-24, 4:8-15; Deuteronomy 1:19; Judges 16:1-22

[12] Isaiah 64:6; Jeremiah 17:9-10; James 1:22-25

shadows that point to, reveal, and reflect the Son of God in His humanity, servitude, and glory. The shadows of the Old Testament confirm Jesus as the Messiah, define Him as the Lamb of God, unveil Him as the only begotten Son of God, and reveal His powerful ministry.

In the next chapter, we will consider these shadows of the Old Testament that gave way to the light of the New Testament in order to gain a better understanding on how to properly study the Word of God.

Application:

Take one of the famous people of the Old Testament and do a study on his or her life. Avoid transposing or spiritualizing your thoughts into his or her life. Ask the Lord to reveal this person to you in such a way that he or she becomes a living example and mirror to you on a personal level.

14

SHADOWS

When believers read the Old Testament, many do not realize what they are looking at or looking for in the Scriptures. In most cases, they are looking at an example or shadow that must be rightly discerned in order to receive the proper spiritual nourishment from it.

Some of the examples in the Old Testament cast a shadow that was clearly illuminated in the New Testament. A shadow implies a light that has been obscured in some way. It gives you a sense or a sketchy representation or outline of something, but the form or image is not clear, detailed, or alive.

The Apostle Paul makes reference to this shadow in Colossians 2:16-17, "Let no man therefore judge you in meat, or in drink, or in respect of an holyday, or of the new moon, or of the sabbath days: Which are a shadow of things to come." (Emphasis added.)

Hebrews 8:4-5a says. "For if he were on earth, he should not be a priest, seeing that there are priests that offer gifts according to the law: Who serve unto the example and shadow of heavenly things." (Emphasis added.) Certain lives of people and the things ordained by God cast a powerful shadow that was revealed and explained in the New Testament. The revelation of this shadow can only be embraced by faith, and is made alive through revelation and practical obedience.

This shadow was cast by the very image of the light of the world. However, this image was obscured for years by the veil of flesh, the incredible mysteries of heaven, and God's will and glory. Nevertheless, the shadow was cast. And, when the real image came forth at the appointed time, it ceased to be a representation or outline, but became a living, walking reality. This reality could be heard, seen, touched, and handled in the form of the Son of God, Jesus Christ.[1]

Jesus Christ can be found throughout the Old Testament. His very life cast an indelible shadow upon all that was ordained by God. For example, He is represented by the Tree of Life found in the Garden of Eden, as well as the Passover Lamb whose blood was shed, so death could pass over those who properly applied it. He is the Living Word that was being represented by the fringes (also known as wings) on the borders of the garments of the men of Israel. And, for those who grabbed

---

[1] John 1:4-5; 1 John 1:1-2

a hold of Him, they experienced wholeness as, "...the Sun of righteousness arise with healing in his wings" (Malachi 4:2).[2]

Jesus is an Isaac, the precious son who carried up the mount the very object that would be used to offer Him up as a burnt offering. He is the tabernacle of God, residing in the midst of the barren wilderness of man's soul. He is the sum of the Promised Land to those who possess Him, and an inheritance from heaven that will last forever. He is the Rock that gives living water to refresh the soul, manna that came from heaven to nourish the spirit, and the bronze serpent that was lifted up to save man from the bite of the serpent of sin and death.[3]

Like the Ark of the Covenant that stood in the Most Holy Place, He is the ark that stands at the heart of God's commitment and fellowship with man. He serves as the mercy seat for everyone who comes to God through Him. He is also like the ark that hid Noah and his family during God's judgment on the world. Likewise, every Christian who is hid in Him will be spared from the wrath of God to come.[4]

The life of Jesus can be observed in the lives of men such as Joseph, Moses, and King David. When you study these men's lives, you will find that they have the same type of life as Jesus. For example, each man was a shepherd and rejected by those whom they were to lead. Later, they were recognized as leaders chosen by God. Each of them experienced various hardships. Joseph spent time as a slave and prisoner in Egypt; Moses fled to the wilderness for forty years; David fled Saul; and Jesus was in obscurity for 30 years. After three years of ministry, He then suffered and died on the cross.

After their trying ordeals, God used situations to prepare people to accept them as His chosen leaders. Joseph was exalted as a great leader in Egypt because of pending famine. Moses was sent to Egypt after the Jewish people began to cry about their hard life of oppression. David was made king upon Saul's defeat and death. And, Jesus will come when the world is experiencing great tribulation.

Each of these men were involved in saving God's people. For example, Joseph was used to save his brethren from famine; Moses delivered Israel from slavery; and David led God's people to victory over their enemies. And, when you consider Jesus Christ, you realize He saves His people from inevitable spiritual death, slavery, and unseen enemies.

There are others who point to different aspects of Jesus. Like Joshua, Jesus leads His people into the promises of God. Like Boaz, He

---

[2] John 1:1, 14, 29; 10:10; Matthew 9:18-22. (Notice the woman touched the hem of His garment, the fringes or wings of it and received healing.)

[3] Genesis 22:6 (Refer also to John 19:16-17; John 2:19-21; 3:14-18; 6:32-35; 14:6; 1 Corinthians 10:3-4;

[4] John 14:6; Colossians 3:3; 1 Thessalonians 5:9.

is the dutiful kinsman who redeems back the inheritance of the Church at His own expense.[5]

The shadows are numerous and they bring out powerful examples of Jesus Christ that add dimension to Him in the New Testament. For example, the tabernacle serves as one of the most extensive revelations of Jesus in the Old Testament. This revelation can add depth to His character.

Hebrews 8:5 tells us that the tabernacle was patterned after heavenly things. This implies that it is a pattern after the heavenly tabernacle, but we also know that all aspects of it point to Jesus in some way. Once you understand what each part of the tabernacle typifies, a detailed picture emerges, revealing Jesus' nature, life, and work.[6]

We also know the different Jewish feasts pointed to Jesus Christ. For instance, the feasts of Passover, Unleavened Bread, and First Fruits represent the Gospel as they point to Jesus' death, burial, and resurrection. In the Feast of Pentecost, we see the baptism of the Holy Spirit, while in the Feast of Trumpets, we are reminded of Jesus' advents. For example, the angels proclaim His First Advent, but a trumpet will sound for His Second Advent.[7] The Day of Atonement reminds us of the redemption He secured on the cross and of His future judgment seat, while the Feast of Tabernacles points to His future rule and reign as the King of kings and Lord of lords.

Another example of these powerful shadows is found in the refuge cities. God appointed six cities throughout Israel to serve as refuge cities.[8] These cities were designated to protect strangers and people who accidentally killed someone from being put to death by relatives seeking revenge.

A manslayer who fled to one of these cities for protection had to remain there until the death of the High Priest. Upon the High Priest's death, the individual could return to his or her inheritance without any fear of repercussions.

The refuge city is a type of Jesus, and the manslayer represents the sinner who is under a death sentence, but seeks refuge in Him. The death of the High Priest symbolizes Jesus as our High Priest, dying on the cross as the ultimate sacrifice to set us free from this death sentence.

The shadow cast by the refuge cities is quite clear in light of the New Testament. As a sinner, we must flee to Jesus and hide within His redemption. It was because of His death on the cross that we could embrace an eternal inheritance that can never be taken away from us. What an incredible picture!

---

[5] See Joshua and Ruth

[6] If you want to know more about patterns, see the book, *Follow That Pattern*, located in Volume 2 of the author's foundational series.

[7] Luke 2:8-14; 1 Thessalonians 4:13-18

[8] See Numbers 35

There are other shadows as well. For example, we can see representations of the Church or Body of Christ in Rahab, Ruth, Rebekah, and the young woman in the Song of Solomon. Rahab is symbolic of deliverance from the old life, Ruth, of a new lineage in Christ, Rebekah, of a new life with the bridegroom, and the maiden in the Song of Solomon represents the challenges and maturity surrounding the relationship of the bride with her bridegroom.

We can also see the Godhead in different shadows. For instances, Noah represents the Father; the ark was symbolic of the Son; and the dove Noah sent forth served as the shadow of the Holy Spirit. In the case of Abraham seeking a bride for his son, he was a shadow of the Father; Isaac a shadow of the Son; and Abraham's faithful servant was a shadow of the Holy Spirit, and Rebekah the shadow of the church. [9]

Shadows can also be found in names and in the numbers of God. For example, "Jonah's" name means dove. A dove in Scripture is symbolic of the Holy Ghost. We can see a shadow of His work when Jonah preached against Nineveh's sin, and it resulted in repentance and deliverance from impending judgment.

Other examples of shadows found in names are the names of Jacob's twelve sons. By studying their names and lives in light of the New Testament, some powerful images will emerge. For me, I could see Jesus, the work of the Holy Ghost, and the Christian life being revealed in a powerful way.[10]

Numbers and their multiples also cast an image. The Bible has been mathematically proven.[11] God uses certain numbers to reveal His work, purpose, and mysteries. Consistency can be seen in how these numbers are used. For example, "three" represents completeness; "five" represents grace; "seven" represents perfection; "forty" represents trials and temptation; and "fifty" represents Pentecost.[12] Every time I encounter one of these numbers, I look for its representation to be unveiled in order to bring greater depth to my understanding.

Finally, we have prophecies that have been verified by historical facts and archeological discoveries. The Old Testament is full of prophecies that have been fulfilled concerning people and nations. These prophecies not only prove there is a God, but they identify Jesus as the Promised Messiah.

Jesus fulfilled many prophecies in His lifetime. In the first four chapters of Matthew, the former tax collector pointed out seven prophecies found in Micah, Jeremiah, and Isaiah that were fulfilled by events surrounding Jesus' birth and ministry. When it comes to His

---

[9] Genesis 24

[10] You can find the author's revelation of these names in her second volume of her foundational series in her book, *Revelation of the Cross*.

[11] See the book Theomatics by Jerry Lucas and Del Washburn.

[12] See the book Numbers in Scripture by E.W. Bullinger

death, we see where prophecies found in Psalms and Isaiah have been fulfilled.

This brings me to an important word to remember when studying the Word of God: *connection*. When I am studying the Old Testament, I strive to connect the examples and shadows with the lessons, disposition, revelation, and explanations of the New Testament.

As I study the New Testament, I consider the examples and shadows of the Old Testament to gain a greater insight into my life before God. I have learned that in order to get a complete picture, it is vital to connect the foundation of the Old Testament with the outward structure of the New Testament. The understanding of the Old Testament has brought me to the same conclusion: If I want to gain a greater understanding of God and my relationship and life in Him, I not only look for Jesus in the Old Testament, but I consider my counterparts or examples. For instance, to gain a picture of what it means to be a temple of the Holy Spirit, I study the Old Testament tabernacle and temple, to understand the makeup and purpose of my body as a personal sanctuary. If I want to cleanse my tabernacle, I study the reformation that took place under King Hezekiah. If I want my temple sanctified, I study what the priests did when dedicating it to God. And, if I want to understand what it means to be a New Testament priest of God, I study the instructions, examples of consecration, purpose, and lives of the Old Testament priests.[13]

There are representations in the Bible that serve as both examples and shadows. For example, the tabernacle serves as an example for the Christian, but it also casts a powerful shadow of Jesus. Whenever you have something that serves as both an example and a shadow, you have a picture of a believer displaying the life of Christ in attitude and action. The example will show a Christian what it will take to possess the life of Christ in order to become a reflection of His life or light.

There are various resources that verify the validity, consistency, and fulfillment of Scripture. In fact, there is enough material to reasonably silence the skeptic and unbeliever. However, in spite of the proof, man usually operates in two extremes when it comes to attitudes and the handling of the Word.

The secular world spends much time trying to apply logic by explaining away the validity of Scripture. As you watch their secular presentations, you begin to realize these presentations are nothing more than foolish propaganda. Obviously, those of the world want to do away with God, sin, and its eternal consequences.

The other extreme comes from those who are religious. They use the Word for their own personal agendas, doctrines, and pursuits, while

---

[13] 1 Corinthians 3:16; 2 Kings 18; 2 Chronicles 29; 1 Peter 2:5 & 9; Exodus 28-29

stumbling over the real work of the cross. The Apostle Paul put both extremes in this perspective, "But we preach Christ crucified, unto the Jews a stumblingblock, and unto the Greeks foolishness" (1 Corinthians 1:23).

Today, there is an aggressive move to bring the followers of Christ back under the shadows of the Old Testament. The Apostle Paul put such a move in this perspective,

> But now, after that ye have known God, or rather are known of God, how turn ye again to the weak and beggarly elements, Whereunto into which ye desire again to be in bondage? Ye observe days, and months, and times, and years (Galatians 4:9-10).

The Apostle Paul referred to the Old Testament practices as beggarly elements. These elements simply cast the shadow. Therefore, their purpose was not to keep God's people in the shadow, but bring them to the light to embrace the real image.

This brings us to another shadow, the Law. As in the days of the Apostle Paul, the ignorance and misuse of the Law has caused many to become confused about the grace of God. Before we go on to the New Testament, the gap caused by the Law and grace must be closed, which we will address in the next chapter.

Meanwhile, do you understand the shadow that is being cast in the Old Testament, or is it a book with a lot of facts and foolish people that holds no merit for you? If this is your attitude, you need to repent and ask the Holy Spirit to reveal Jesus to you in the Old Testament. If you embrace the Old Testament in the right spirit, I can guarantee you that both the Old and New Testaments will come alive, as they become pertinent to your spiritual understanding and growth in the knowledge of Jesus Christ.

15

CHRIST, THE END OF THE LAW

One of the greatest points of confusion is what part the Law of the Old Testament plays in the lives of New Testament believers. This confusion has escalated with erroneous theology such as "Replacement Theology" making inroads into the Church. Adding to this problem are the different presentations that make grace appear as if it is cheap, or a free ticket to live irresponsibly without fear of consequences. Both of these extremes are prevalent, and undermine the faith that was first delivered to the saints.[1]

This confusion ought not to be because the Apostle Paul went to great lengths to put both truths into proper perspective. Sadly, people are blinded to these instructions because of indoctrination, as well as defining their Christian lives according to personal, religious, or self-righteous concepts. Because of these extremes, it is important to understand the intent behind both the Law and God's grace.

Psalm 119 gives us insight into the importance and working of the Law. What many of us fail to realize is that whatever God said became Law. Man was to believe it and respond accordingly in light of God's character and ways. On this ground we must conclude that God's Word is law, or the final authority to all matters.

As we will see, the Law of Moses encompasses every aspect of Jewish lifestyle and practices. It was to bring separation, distinction, and life to those who regarded it. There are various terms in Psalm 119 that point to the Law. Such words as testimonies, precepts, statues, commandments, and judgments are used in this descriptive chapter of the Word of God.

To gain a picture of how each of these words point to God's Law, I have studied each of them in the *Strong's Concordance* as well as the secular dictionary.[2] In *Strong's* many of the words intertwine, while in my dictionary they were summarized in such a way that I was able to gain a better picture of how each of them works.

Testimonies point to the fact that the Law is a witness. It is a witness of God's character. It declares that the Judge is holy and that His ways are righteous, and His wisdom trustworthy. However, the Law's witness

---

[1] Jude 3

[2] Webster's New Collegiate Dictionary,© 1976 by G. & C. Merriam Co.

of the character of our just God also makes it a witness against man's disobedience, bringing man under its condemnation. As we will see for the Christian, the Law points to our need for Jesus.

Precepts have already been discussed in a previous chapter. As a reminder, precepts point to the principle of something. Principles include both the spirit and responsibilities of how something must be carried out to ensure the integrity of it. For Christians, this can be related to doctrine. We have a responsibility to maintain the integrity of the Christian life, and to adhere to the pure doctrine of Christ in a spirit that will bring honor to God. How we apply or carry out something will determine what law we come under and the principles we will operate according to.

Statutes refer to the state, condition, or rule in which something is carried out. The Law encourages a state of perpetual obedience before God. To bring about the state, rules were established in which man had to properly comply. These rules involved responsibilities and practices as well as ordinances or rituals that had to be practiced for the purpose of remembrance, distinction, and identification. These statutes included such practices as eating habits and proper dress. Good examples of statutes as far as the Church goes are the ordinances of water baptism and communion. Baptism definitely sets us apart and identifies us to Jesus. Communion, on the other hand, serves as a point of remembrance. It also brings distinction as to our basis for belief, and is a form of identification to Jesus and with each other. The problem with statutes is that man can add his own interpretation, rules, or traditions to a statute of God, and make it ineffective.[3]

Commandments simply mean that such actions or practices are commanded in all situations and at all times. Obedience to such commands are not optional no matter what the circumstances may be. At the heart of the Law are the Ten Commandments. As you study the commandments, they focus in on our attitudes towards God and others. God, in His holiness and goodness, insists on total devotion to Him and moral accountability towards others. It is when we are right before God and doing right by others that we will come to the place of peace or rest (Sabbath) in God.[4] Jesus summarized in two commandments how the whole purpose or intent of the commandments could be properly observed in Mark 12:29-31,

> The first of all the commandments is, Hear, O Israel; The Lord our God is one Lord: And thou shalt love the Lord thy God with all thy heart, and with all thy soul, and with all thy mind, and with all thy strength: this is the first commandment. And the second is like, namely this, Thou shalt love thy neighbour as thyself. There is none other commandment greater than these.

---

[3] Matthew 15:1-9

[4] Matthew 11:28-30

For the Christian, Jesus added one more commandment to clearly bring distinction and define the highest intention of the Law that will bring a point of identification to those who belong to Him, "A new commandment I give unto you, That ye love one another; as I have loved you, that you also love one another. By this shall all men know that ye are my disciples, if ye have love one to another" (John 13:34-35).

Judgments are a formal opinion or decision given by one who is in authority. We see God passing judgments down for the purpose of lining His people up to their moral obligations. True judgment will always lead one to the ability to properly discern in a matter. After all, it is easy for man to compromise in areas that are not obvious to the eye. One interesting judgment that God passed down in order to bring discernment was in regard to a husband's suspicion that his wife had committed adultery. His requirements to determine the innocence or guilt of a woman clearly showed separation between the holy and the profane.[5] It is vital that we understand the intent of the Law, for it will enable us to make sound judgments in areas that have been clouded by other issues.

A good example of a judgment is one that has already been discussed, but let us now consider it in light of the Law. The Apostle Paul made a judgment in regards to divorce in 1 Corinthians 7. Righteous judgments have rules based on both the intent of the Law and the experiences of life. Rules of consideration are put forth in which to make a sound judgment according to one's particular situation. The reason for this is because judgment calls cannot always be fairly applied to every situation; therefore, other instructions or rules must be considered in light of a matter to ensure heavenly wisdom is present to show the proper discretion towards a situation.

Now that we have divided the Law in its purpose, ways, and practices, we can consider how the role of the Law is meant to impact the Christian. The Word is clear that Jesus did not come to do away with the Law, but to fulfill it.[6] There were 613 laws established by Moses in the wilderness. The Jews were reminded of all 613 laws by their prayer shawl. The Hebrew word for the fringes hanging from the shawl is "Tsitizeth." Tsitizeth according to Hebrew numerology equals 600. By adding eight strands and five knots that make up the fringes to the number 600, which is associated to its name, you end up with the number 613.[7]

The Apostle Peter said this of the Law in Acts 15:10 when there was a dispute among the early church leaders about bringing Gentiles under it, "Now therefore why tempt ye God, to put a yoke upon the neck of the disciples, which neither our fathers nor we were able to bear?" Peter admitted that the Law created a yoke that no one could really bear.

---

[5] Numbers 5:11-31

[6] Matthew 5:17-18

[7] Jewish Law and the New Covenant; page 51

However, what aspect of the Law served as such a yoke? As you consider the Law, it was the whole Law that became an unbearable yoke with its many precepts, statutes, and judgments.

Amazingly, Christians are quick to come under this yoke of the Law without fully understanding it. Jesus has already verified the yoke He entrusts believers with as being easy.[8] On the other hand, those who come under the yoke of the Law end up picking and choosing the laws they will adhere to. For example, some hold tightly to the laws concerning food, while others cling to the laws that have to do with dress codes. Although cultural practices and lifestyles governed some of these laws in the Old Testament, these misdirected people simply interpret them according to their modern perspective as to what could constitute personal righteousness. However, as you observe these individuals, they fail to keep the whole Law. According to James 2:10, "For whosoever shall keep the whole law, and yet offend in one point, he is guilty of all." (Emphasis added.)

It is easy for people to adhere to certain aspects of the Law, but no one can maintain the complete integrity of it. After all, the Law dealt with such practices as sacrifices. Therefore, the people who take pride in keeping their own particular code of religious laws are nothing more than lawbreakers. In fact, they bring themselves under a system that can only declare their guilt, not justify them. And, without the right justification, there is no salvation.[9]

The reason for this dilemma is that people are unable to maintain the integrity or intent of the whole Law on a consistent basis. This is why Jesus stated that if a man lusts after a woman, he has just broken the Law by committing adultery in his heart.[10]

The Law was not given as a means by which man could gain God's approval, but as a way to prove that all men are sinners. The Apostle Paul put the Law in this perspective, "Knowing this, that the law is not made for a righteous man, but for the lawless and disobedient..." (1 Timothy 1:9). By coming under the Law, people are not proving their righteousness to God. Rather, they will end up showing their lawlessness and disobedience.

Since the deeds of the Law cannot justify, this righteous code also cannot bring a person to perfection or maturity.[11] Spiritual maturity only comes out of transformation of the inner man. The Law could only demand outward conformity, but could not change or transform the inner man to make an individual acceptable to God. Jesus made this clear when He confronted the Pharisees about their lives, which were all religious show.

---

[8] Matthew 11:28-30

[9] Romans 5:18

[10] Matthew 5:27-32

[11] Hebrews 10:1

The Pharisees were under the Law and thought themselves to be quite righteous. Yet, Jesus called many of them hypocrites and blind fools. They were blinded by their own righteousness that stood as filthy rags before their holy God.[12] Their religion was all an outward show that hid the harsh reality of their spiritual depravity. Jesus described their real condition in Matthew 23:27, "...for ye are like unto whited sepulchers, which indeed appear beautiful outward, but are within full of dead men's bones, and of all uncleanness."

This is why Jesus said in Matthew 5:20, "For I say unto you, That except your righteousness shall exceed the righteousness of the scribes and Pharisees, ye shall in no case enter into the kingdom of heaven." Outward obedience to the Law is often a cover-up of man's real problems. Jesus was advocating righteousness that went beyond outward conformity to the Law.

Hebrews 10:1 states, "For the law having a shadow of good things to come, and not the very image of the things, can never with those sacrifices which they offered year by year continually make the comers thereunto perfect."

Hebrews 7:19 says, "For the law made nothing perfect, but the bringing in of a better hope did; by which we draw nigh unto God." This verse clearly shows the Law is not a person's source of hope, but was a means to bring or usher in a better hope that would allow each of us to draw near to God.

Therefore, the Law was nothing but a shadow that pointed to man's only hope. Colossians 1:27-28 reveals the hope that will bring man to perfection.

> To whom God would make known what is the riches of the glory of this mystery among the Gentiles, which is Christ in you, the hope of glory; Whom we preach, warning every man, and teaching every man in all wisdom; that we may present every man perfect in Christ Jesus.

We know that man's only hope is Jesus, and because of His death on the cross, man can now come near to God.[13]

Galatians 3:24 gives us this valuable insight about the Law, "Wherefore the law was our schoolmaster to bring us unto Christ, that we might be justified by faith." The intention of the Law was to bring people to Jesus Christ for the purpose of salvation.

Romans 10:4 summarized this aspect of Jesus in this way, "For Christ is the end of the law for righteousness to every one that believeth." People who sincerely attempt to be righteous in their own power will be brought to utter vanity and despair because there is no righteousness found or obtained by keeping the Law. The Law reveals that righteousness is outside of man's attempts. In fact, man's righteousness

---

[12] Matthew 23; Isaiah 64:6

[13] Colossians 1:20-22

is not found in the Law, but at the end of it in the Person of the Lord Jesus Christ.

God's terms for acceptable righteousness bring people to the revelation of His grace that was unveiled in Jesus Christ. John 1:14 says this about grace, "And the Word was made flesh, and dwelt among us, (and we beheld his glory, the glory as of the only begotten of the Father), full of grace and truth."

The Apostle Paul summarizes the importance of grace in our salvation, "For by grace are ye saved through faith; and that not of yourselves: it is the gift of God: Not of works, lest any man should boast" (Ephesians 2:8-9). We are saved by grace, not by works or deeds that we do in our own power. This fact takes away the claims that come from the arrogance and self-righteousness of the religious, silencing the vainglory that becomes an expression of the false veneers that hides these people's real wickedness.

Grace is totally contrary to the Law. People cannot be under both grace and the Law at the same time. Galatians 2:21 makes this powerful statement, "I do not frustrate the grace of God: for if righteousness come by the law, then Christ is dead in vain." If people could keep the Law, Jesus would not have had to give up the glories of heaven, take on the form of a servant, be fashioned as a man, and die on the cross.[14]

Religious people who come under the Law make Christ's work on the cross of no affect, bringing them under the unmerciful judgment of the Law. As Galatians 5:4 clearly states, "Christ is become of no effect unto you, whosoever of you are justified by the law; ye are fallen from grace."

If people have fallen from grace and are now under the Law, they stand guilty and condemned. Instead of being under the law of the Spirit of life in Christ Jesus, they are under the law of sin and death, facing a Christless eternity. This is why the Apostle Paul warned in his letter to the Galatians that to emphasize the Law was presenting another gospel. In his letter, Paul was making reference to outward rituals such as circumcision, while advocating that those who give way to the works of the flesh will not inherit the kingdom of God. In other words, our moral obligations (commandments) towards God and others are still in place. He stipulated that the only way people will overcome the flesh is to be led by the Spirit of God. It is not just a matter of outward show, but a change of guard as to who will be reigning in a person.

Regardless of how religious or spiritual the Law may be it does not constitute the Gospel, which is the power of God unto salvation. People who emphasize any other means of justification or righteousness outside of Christ, His cross, and grace are advocating another gospel. Preaching another gospel automatically means the person stands accursed.[15]

---

[14] Philippians 2:4-8

[15] Romans 1:16; 8:2; Galatians 1:6-12; 2:3-4, 11-19; 5:16-21

Why would many Christians choose to come under the yoke of Law when so many New Testament Scriptures oppose such a practice? I believe there are four reasons for this grievous error: 1) Such individuals have never been properly discipled, 2) they have been confused or disillusioned because of how grace has been presented, 3) they do not know the character and ways of God, and/or 4) it serves as a means to discipline or control their spiritual life. Ultimately, these attitudes lead to delusion and produce self-righteousness.

Sadly, much of the presentation of grace has been made into a cheap mockery to those who do not understand their place in Christ. You can tell that those who present this perverted, self-serving picture of grace do not understand how it works because they do not know God or understand salvation.

The way much of grace is presented today is nothing more than a cloak, made up of excuses, to cover up a lack of devotion, the ways of ungodliness, and a lack of love for God and others. It is a way to offer a free ticket to heaven without any responsibility. George Barna, a major Christian pollster, said of the grace and salvation that is being presented that it is a no-brainer. A person can have it all, as far as the world, and still make it to heaven.

Grace is not a free ticket to heaven. It does constitute liberty, but this liberty does not come in the form of living any old way a person may desire. When people understand grace, they begin to realize that it gives them the liberty to live uprightly.

Grace calls for godliness and discipline. As the Apostle Paul stated, God forbid that anyone should continue in sin because of grace, when every believer must consider him or herself to be dead to sin.[16]

Due to the different cheap presentations of grace, many hide behind the presentation of it while ignoring their proper response towards God: that of faith. This perverted teaching about grace establishes unsuspecting people on a faulty foundation that is not based on God's character.

Grace is God's part in salvation, but faith is man's response in this miraculous work. The Apostle Paul pointed out in Galatians 3:24 that man is justified by faith. This means that faith is the proper, healthy, and natural response of any repentant person towards God's work of grace.

Neither grace, nor faith, is inactive. For example, God's grace can be clearly viewed by Jesus' death on the cross. Grace is active as it reigns through righteousness. Faith on the other hand, is evidenced by an obedient life to God's Word.[17] This is brought out in Ephesians 2:8-10,

> For by grace are ye saved through faith; and that not of yourselves: it is the gift of God: Not of works, lest any man should boast. For we are his workmanship, created in Christ

---

[16] Romans 6:1-2

[17] Romans 5:21; James 2:14-26

> Jesus unto good works, which God hath before ordained that we should walk in them. (Emphasis added.)

The logic that a person's salvation hinges simply on a sinner's prayer or declaration is dangerous. Many people are foolishly banking on such concepts, when in reality, their attitudes, fruits, and actions bring their salvation into grave questioning. In my observation, the erroneous presentation of grace not only does away with a walk of faith, but also deludes people regarding their real spiritual condition.

It is important to point out that faith justified people long before the Law. For instance, Abraham lived before the Law, and Romans 4:9 points out that it was Abraham's faith that was reckoned or counted to him for righteousness. Galatians 3:11 reminds us that no man is justified by the Law, and that the just shall live by faith. This declaration about the just living by faith can be found in the book written by the prophet Habakkuk who lived during the time of the Law. Even though the Law was to be upheld in Habakkuk's day, he still recognized that it was faith that justified man.[18]

Galatians 2:16 confirms this point of justification,

> Knowing that a man is not justified by the works of the law, but by the faith of Jesus Christ, even we have believed in Jesus Christ, that we might be justified by the faith of Christ, and not by the works of the law: for by the works of the law shall no flesh be justified.

Before faith was revealed in Christ, man was under the Law.[19] However, the Law was used as a platform by religious leaders, who were blinded to real faith. They used it to encourage their followers to put their reliance in religious practices and activities, rather than believe God. Such belief would express itself in obedience. This is why Galatians 3:12 shows that obeying the Law is not a response of genuine faith, "And the law is not of faith."

Genuine faith is based on God's character and His work on the cross, which are both revealed in Jesus Christ. This is why Hebrews 11:6 tells us that without faith it is impossible to please God. Galatians 2:20 states that the life a Christian lives is by the faith of the Son of God who loved each of us and gave Himself on our behalf.

This brings us down to a person's responsibility to the Law. How can we as Christians properly bring the Law and grace together? Once again, we are reminded that Christ did not do away with the Law.[20] Since He is our example, He has also shown us what we must do in regard to the Law. We must fulfill it.

Obeying and fulfilling the law are clearly different from each other. Obeying something in this fashion is merely adhering outwardly to

---

[18] Habakkuk 2:4

[19] Galatians 3:23

[20] Matthew 5:17-18

something in practice, while fulfilling something actually completes its intent in every way possible.

Jesus, our example, did not simply obey the Law; He fulfilled it.[21] Due to our inability to obey the Law without becoming a lawbreaker, there is no place in the New Testament Scriptures where we are commanded to obey it. However, we are instructed to fulfill or complete it.

How do we fulfill the Law? Jesus gave us insight into the answer to this question in Mark 12:29-31 and John 13:34-35. It comes down to having the love of God operating in us. The Apostle Paul summarized this very thought in Romans 13:10, "Love worketh no ill to his neighbour: therefore love is the fulfilling of the law." (Emphasis added.) As one can see, it is the love of God in operation in believers that fulfills the Law.

People can obey the Law without loving God or their neighbor. In fact, many who adhere to the Law are the most conceited, unloving, critical, and harsh people I have encountered. What is obvious in them is that they take much pride in their outward façade of righteousness, as they lord it over others who does not share their particular view.

Few realize that offences committed against God and people are not a result of not keeping the Law, but of not having the love of God abounding in their hearts.[22] It is easier to keep an outward façade of obedience, than to have the sacrificial love of God reaching out to people in spite of their attitudes and actions. In fact, people who are operating under the Law feel justified in judging and condemning an individual before they ever reach a stage of properly ministering to him or her.

These legalistic people have made the Law a principle unto itself, rather than maintaining it as a truth that brings greater insight into God and establishing their true hope in Him. And, when a truth becomes a principle, it makes it a cause, rather than a point of instruction. Therefore, the main concern of these people is to line others up to their concept about the Law.

As a result, these misguided individuals fail to be effective ministers who will bring healing and restoration. In fact, the best they can offer are religious platitudes and unfeeling Scripture verses that only add burdens, while failing to bring proper instructions or life. To add such burdens in this way is contrary to Galatians 6:2 which states, "Bear ye one another's burdens, and so fulfill the law of Christ." Ultimately, these people not only show their insensitivity, but their spiritual ignorance and foolishness as well.

Such religious people often take pride in keeping the Law based on their perception of it. However, the reality behind keeping the Law is that it is a coward's way out. It is an easy way out because it calls only for outward conformity. This way, individuals can avoid denying self and

---

[21] Ibid

[22] Romans 5:5

picking up their cross. They can outwardly imitate keeping the Law to display personal righteousness without the righteousness of Christ. They can give the impression that they are honorable and good, while covering up the fact that they do not have the goods. In other words, they really do not know and love the real Jesus Christ.

Godly love comes from within the depth of a person's being, and is especially expressed in times of great testing. It does not demand that people line up to a religious code. Rather, it is committed to sacrificially do right by others as a natural outward extension and example of the devotion of God. In a sense, the love of God allows His saints to become an extension of Jesus, as they serve as His mouth, hands, and feet. As Jesus stated, anyone can love someone who treats them kindly. However, the real test of love is the ability to love your enemies in an attitude of meekness and humility, even when you are being persecuted by them.[23]

God's love is going to respond in obedient faith. Since love responds in faith, the Law will automatically be established.[24] This points to the fact that the intent and moral aspect of the Law will be upheld by genuine faith in the attitude of the love of God, thereby, maintaining the intent and character of it.

Once a person is motivated by the love of God, and walking by faith in the Son of God, he or she will be displaying righteousness. As previously stated, the Law is not for the righteous, but the lawless.

Most people obey the Law in order to be considered righteous before God. However, Romans 8:4 makes this statement, "That the righteousness of the law might be fulfilled in us, who walk not after the flesh, but after the Spirit." People, who try to obey the Law in their own power, will do so in their flesh. This will actually kill the things of the Spirit, making people's lives before God merely dead-letter religion.[19]

The flesh is in opposition to God and will result in death. Once again, we must note that the Law must be fulfilled in us by walking after the Spirit. Walking after the Spirit implies that the inward implication of the moral obligation of the Law is being fulfilled in us. This fulfillment points to transformation. Romans 12:2 says, "And be not conformed to this world, but be ye transformed by the renewing of your mind, that ye may prove what is that good, and acceptable, and perfect, will of God."

Ephesians 4:23-24 states, "And be renewed in the spirit of your mind; And that ye put on the new man, which after God is created in righteousness and true holiness."

A transformed mind points to a new disposition. Such a mind means you will look at everything according to the mind of Jesus. Jesus' main goal was not to obey the Law, but to obey the heart, mind, and will of the

---

[23] Matthew 5:38-48

[24] Romans 3:31

[19] Romans 7:6; 2 Corinthians 3:6

Father.[20] It was in His loving obedience to the Father that He fulfilled the Law.

A new mind also indicates that you will be able to receive the things of the Spirit, "But the natural man receiveth not the things of the Spirit of God: for they are foolishness unto him: neither can he know them, because they are spiritually discerned" (1 Corinthians 2:14).

Once your mind has been transformed, you can walk after the Spirit and avoid fulfilling the lust of the flesh. Galatians 5:18 says, "But if ye be led of the Spirit, ye are not under the law." In other words, you have the freedom to walk this life out according to the Spirit of God, rather than operate within the unmerciful boundaries of the Law that will enslave you into a life that will lack the Spirit.[21]

The Christian walk is a walk of faith in the Son of God. It is a walk motivated by the love of God that produces obedience, and is made evident by liberty, godly fruits, and an overcoming life.[22]

Let us now compare grace and Law. Consider the following table (next page) and decide which yoke you are now under.

[20] Philippians 2:5-8

[21] See Galatians 5:1

[22] 2 Corinthians 3:17; Galatians 5:22-23; 1 John 5:4-5

LAW VS. GRACE

Under the Law	Under Godly Grace
Heavy Burdens (Man's attempt to be holy.)	Being led by the Spirit (The Spirit working holiness in us through transformation.)
Desire to impress and please self and others.	Desire to please God.
Bondage (Disillusionment about Christianity.)	Liberty in the Spirit (Freedom to worship and to experience the life He has for us.)
Will walk in the flesh and become cursed.	Will walk in faith by the Son of God and will live.
Will be condemned.	Will be justified.
Will equal dead religion and traditions.	Will equal relationship with the Living God.
Will reap what they sow—pay the consequences.	Will display the Fruit of the Spirit.
Will result in judgment.	Person becomes a new creation.

As Elijah said to the Israelites as they stood between their idols and God, "How long halt ye between two opinions?"[23] Choose now what you will embrace in the name of your Christianity or religion. If you are trying to live under the Law, but claim Christ saves you, you are fooling yourself. You cannot walk the fence between Law and grace without disobeying the intent of the Law and frustrating the grace of God. You cannot continue to delude yourself that you can obey the Law, while clinging to a foreign concept of grace, treating it as if it were some type of option that you can fall back on when all else fails.

[23] 1 Kings 18:21

If you have chosen the Law, Christ will be missing, along with the Spirit and the godly virtues that are much needed to walk out this life. Turn from any self-reliance or personal righteousness, and choose Christ. You will know what it means to respond to His grace by faith, as well as learn how to daily walk this new life out in the power and leading of the Holy Ghost.

In conclusion, each of us must choose whether we will look to the Law to justify us or to genuine faith in the Lord Jesus Christ. The choices are clear. Therefore, let us cease from trying to live under two different covenants or within two different worlds. And, let us accept with our whole heart God's provision of Jesus Christ according to His grace and the measure of faith He entrusted to each of us.[24]

---

[24] Romans 12:3

16

THE FULFILLMENT

Now that we have dealt with the examples and shadows of the Old Testament, we can consider the fulfillment of them in light of the New Testament.

The Old Testament contains the examples, while the New Testament explains the lessons that can be learned by the examples. For instance, you can watch Abraham's faith in action in the Old Testament, but the New Testament explains the disposition behind his faith that made it active and acceptable to God. In the Old Testament, you can study the many shadows, but in the New Testament you can actually see the fulfillment of them in a personal, up-front way. You can study each detail, aspect, or disposition of the shadow, making it alive and real.

This brings us to the beauty and the power of the New Testament. The fulfillment of the Old Testament can be clearly seen in Jesus Christ who was unveiled in the New Testament. Every shadow outlined Him; every sacrifice mirrored Him; and every example pointed to Him. He fulfilled the Law, satisfied the judgment of sin on the cross, and now serves as our High Priest in the courts of heaven.

In the New Testament, we see the words of the Old Testament come alive through Jesus and His teachings. As the Living Word (Jesus) is revealed and applied to the Written Word (Scripture), it causes it to cease from simply being a book. It actually takes on a life of its own that has the power to change a person's disposition. As John 1:1 states, "In the beginning was the Word, and the Word was with God, and the Word was God."

Jesus, as the Living Word, would be the means that communicated God's very heart. He became the visible expression of God's love to man, and became man's living example of what is acceptable to God. He bridged the incredible gap between knowledge and revelation with experience; the Law with mercy and grace; and death and life with salvation.

Like the Old Testament, it is important to know what we are looking at when studying the New Testament, so that we can properly divide the Word of truth. The New Testament is also comprised of teachings, revelations, parables, and idioms.

It is important to understand that there are revelations to be found in the teachings, as well as nuggets of truth in parables. Many of the parables and idioms were greatly influenced by the attitudes and culture of those days.

Although Christians claim they put a lot of stock in the New Testament, few believe its priceless instructions and warnings. For example, it is not unusual to hear Christians declare that warnings of the New Testament do not apply to Christians, but are meant for the non-believer. This concept is absurd because the Word was not written to unbelievers, but to the saints for their instruction in righteousness. All Scripture was given by inspiration for the purpose of righteousness, and is not up for debate according to personal agendas and doctrines. The inspired Word of God has the ability to cleanse a person and bring him or her to perfection, thoroughly prepared unto all good works.[1]

When a person considers the words of correction, reproof, and instruction in 2 Timothy 3:16, he or she will conclude that the warnings are directed at believers. Instruction in righteousness includes correction, which implies the idea of straightening someone up. Reproof points to conviction and admonition, while instruction involves training, chastisement, or discipline.[2]

The Word has no significance or authority to an unbeliever unless the Holy Spirit convicts him or her that it is true. Although I have used the Scriptures in witnessing to those who are not saved, my testimony about Jesus is what usually opens a person's heart up to consider Scripture in the right way.

It greatly amazes me that Christians can claim all of the blessings of the New Testament, while writing off the warnings and admonitions as non-applicable. This type of approach causes people to pick and choose what they will accept or ignore in the New Testament. To me, this is like playing Russian Roulette with one's soul.

Another problem that occurs with the manner in which Christians handle the New Testament is that many take everything literally. There are some Scriptures that can be taken in this manner, while others must be compared with the rest of the Bible in order to ensure a correct perspective. Clearly, it is important to point out that since this book deals with spiritual issues, we must consider it in light of the Holy Spirit who teaches us by comparing spiritual things with the spiritual. To consider spiritual truths from a literal perspective is to only regard it according to limited, personal understanding and indoctrination.[3]

Good examples of taking Scriptures literally instead of comparing them are the few Scriptures concerning women. Many take these Scriptures literally without studying them in light of other Scriptures. The result is that a few misconstrued Scriptures have kept women in bondage and improperly dictate women's place in the kingdom of God.

---

[1] Ephesians 5:26; 2 Timothy 3:16-17; 3:16-17

[2] Strong's Exhaustive Concordance, #1650-1651, 1882, 3809

[3] 1 Corinthians 2:10-14

Therefore, people who take every Scripture literally will end up mishandling the Word, and encouraging erroneous doctrines and practices.

The New Testament is full of teachings and instructions. Jesus taught the most profound philosophy. He wanted people to understand that their lives in God were simple and practical, yet profound and unattainable without the power of the Holy Ghost.

For example, the Beatitudes in Matthew 5 are so simple, yet one cannot possibly walk them out. It takes the power of the Holy Spirit to change the person's disposition. This will enable him or her to walk these teachings out in Spirit and truth.

When you study the teachings of Jesus, they are meant to stir your soul up and inspire your spirit to consider the invisible, omnipotent, omnipresent, and omniscient attributes of God. Every teaching is a door into God's character and ways. Every action of Jesus was a visible expression of the way of righteousness. As the Jews had to acknowledge about Him, "Master, we know that thou art true, and teachest the way of God in truth, neither carest thou for any man: for thou regardest not the person of men" (Matthew 22:16). These men had to admit that Jesus only regarded the ways of God and not man.

Only the Holy Ghost could unveil the depths of heavenly wisdom in Jesus' teachings. The Apostle Paul talked about teaching every man in all wisdom in order to present every person perfect in Christ. His desire was to see the Word of Christ dwell in a person in all wisdom, instruction, and admonition.[4]

We often forget that the Bible is a spiritual book and can only be understood within the boundaries of the right spirit. When the Holy Spirit is not the teacher who is guiding the person into all truth, the individual will be ever learning, but never coming to the knowledge of truth. The truth is Jesus Christ.[5] The final result is that Jesus will simply be a concept or an image, but not a living reality whose very life will change the terrain of the inner person.

The Spirit of God will lead people to a greater revelation of Jesus. John started the book of Revelation with these words, "The Revelation of Jesus Christ..." The Apostle Paul said the Gospel came by revelation of Jesus Christ. He also identified Him as the mystery in the Bible that was kept secret since the world began, but was made manifest just as the writings of the prophets proclaimed.[6] And, Jesus basically said of Himself that He was the revelation of eternal life in John 5:39, "Search the scriptures; for in them ye think ye have eternal life; and they are they which testify of me."

---

[4] Colossians 1:28; 3:16

[5] John 14:26; 2 Timothy 3:7

[6] Romans 16:25-26; Galatians 1:12; Ephesians 3:3-4; Revelation 1:1

Sadly, many people seek the Scriptures for knowledge and not to know the Person of Jesus Christ. The written Word remains lifeless without the revelation of the Living Word. And, without the revelation of Christ, the truth will lack dimension and life. Therefore, the truth will have no power to expose the intents of the heart and bring about inward change.[7]

Another teaching tool Jesus used was parables. Parables are stories that have hidden treasures in them. Jesus confirmed this in Matthew 13:35, "That it might be fulfilled which was spoken by the prophet, saying, I will open my mouth in parables; I will utter things which have been kept secret from the foundation of the world."

In Luke 8:10, Jesus elaborated on parables, "Unto you it is given to know the mysteries of the kingdom of God: but to others in parables; that seeing they might not see, and hearing they might not understand."

The prophet Isaiah explained the significance of people not perceiving, "Make the heart of this people fat, and make their ears heavy, and shut their eyes; lest they see with their eyes, and hear with their ears, and understand with their heart, and convert, and be healed" (Isaiah 6:10).

I once read an explanation about how the parables worked. If a person is pure in heart, he or she would be able to glean the simple gems from them. However, if a person lacks such purity, he or she might sense that the treasures are there, but he or she cannot obtain them. The reason for hiding these truths from people's eyes is an act of mercy on God's part because individuals will be held accountable for everything that they understand but fail to apply.

I have witnessed this myself. The Lord has graciously given me deeper revelations of Himself. Upon sharing these with people, I found that those who were pure in heart embraced the truths, while others who had preconceived notions, struggled to understand, but failed to comprehend the simple truths that were before their eyes.

One of the problems people have with parables is that many fail to recognize that they were based upon the culture of the Jewish people and they were often addressed to them. If you leave this factor out, you may miss the real meanings of many of the parables. As Jesus said to the Syrophoenician woman in Matthew 15:24, "I am not sent but unto the lost sheep of the house of Israel."

A good example of the Jewish influence in Jesus' parables is the parable of the prodigal son in Luke 15. The prodigal son represents Israel, and if you fail to read it in light of these people's beliefs and culture, it will not have the intended impact or meaning. For example, eating with the swine would have caused a Jew to become totally repulsed. Jesus used this example to show how low the young man had

---

[7] Hebrews 4:12

fallen before he became desperate enough to humble himself before his father.

The final element of the New Testament that we must consider are idioms. It is easy to miss the deeper truths of Jesus' teachings. A person may never see the treasures in the parables, or receive a revelation that will change him or her. After all, the whole purpose of God's Word is to prepare believers to live complete, upright, and victorious lives.

Idioms are found in every culture and can cause great confusion and misinterpretation of Scripture. They are also used by every culture to instill a certain impression when communicating a thought or teaching. *Webster's New Collegiate Dictionary* defines idiom as an expression in the usage of a language that is peculiar to itself. Americans use many idioms like, "He lost his head" or "Eat your heart out." These types of statements are in a class of their own in our American language. For example, if you voiced one of these idioms to a person from another culture, it would confuse them. The person would interpret it literally, instead of figuratively. Can you imagine the image that would be incorrectly erected in the individual's mind?

Likewise, there are idioms peculiar to the Jewish culture of that time interspersed throughout Jesus' teaching. All too often, untrained Christians take these idioms and translated them in literal terms, which resulted in the establishment of erroneous doctrines or theology.

One of the idioms that has been misconstrued in a destructive way can be found in Matthew 11:12, "And from the days of John the Baptist until now the kingdom of heaven suffereth violence, and the violent take it by force." There is a certain group in the Christian Church that takes this Scripture out of context and uses it as a mandate to use aggressive force to further the kingdom of God. This interpretation not only goes against the spirit clearly established in New Testament Scripture, but it is contrary to many of Jesus' teachings and examples.

The correct meaning of this Scripture is found in an old rabbinic interpretation of Micah 2:13. It is a picture of a flock of sheep breaking forth after being penned up all night. At night, the shepherd would build a makeshift enclosure for the sheep against a hillside. In order to let the sheep out, the shepherd would make a small breach in the fence, and he himself would lay across this "door". In the morning the sheep would be eager to get out to the pasture. Therefore, they pushed and shoved to get out, which caused a bigger breach in the wall to be made. Jesus was basically saying that the kingdom of heaven was breaking forth as every person who had been restrained by some type of bondage was breaking out in order to follow the Shepherd. Clearly, this is contrary to the literal concept that the violent will take the kingdom by force.[8]

[8] Understanding the Difficult Words of Jesus; By David Bivin & Roy B. Blizzard, ©1983 by Makor Foundation, pgs 123-125

Matthew 16:19 is another idiom that has been badly misrepresented: "...Whatsoever thou shalt bind on earth shall be bound in heaven; and whatsoever thou shalt loose on earth shall be loosed in heaven." This idiom simply points to the practice of Rabbis interpreting scriptural commands by prohibiting (binding) or permitting (loosing) certain activities.[9] In this verse, Peter was given authority to forbid or permit what heaven would forbid or permit.

Another idiom that has been greatly abused by man's interpretation is Luke 18:25, "For it is easier for a camel to go through a needle's eye, than for a rich man to enter into the kingdom of God". I am sure you have heard the popular interpretation of this Scripture that the big gates of Jerusalem had small doors in them. At night, when they were closed, late-night travelers could gain entrance through the door by having their camel kneel and crawl through the smaller opening.

However, according to Dr. Bill Jones, this was definitely an idiomatic expression that referred to an impossible situation from a human standpoint. He goes on to explain that some believe the Jews borrowed it from the Persians who had a similar expression: "It is impossible for an elephant to pass through the eye of a needle."[10]

Today many preachers and teachers are trying to logically explain or spiritualize Jesus' statements. For example, when He made the statement about the impossibility of a camel passing through the eye of the needle, He was presenting a visible contrast to make a point. It is impossible for any person to get into the kingdom of God on his or her own merits. Rather, the entrance into the kingdom of heaven does not hinge on personal merits, but on what God did on the cross through Jesus Christ.

Scriptures surrounding Jesus' teachings that do not fit or make sense are probably idioms. Sadly, many people have interpreted these Scriptures contrary to the spirit of the Word of God, causing confusion and erroneous doctrine.

A few other examples of idioms can be found in Luke 6:22; 9:44; 10:5-6; 12:49-50; and 23:31.

How have you handled the New Testament? Is the New Testament making your Christian life alive or is it dead-letter to you? Has its teachings, revelations and parables made its words a living fulfillment of Jesus in your life or have they become a religion of lifeless facts, rituals, and burdens? How you regard the Bible will determine if you are able to grasp the purpose of its very existence.

---

[9] Ibid, pg. 145-146

[10] Zion's Fire (magazine); January/February 2002, pg. 13

17

REMEMBER

Jesus said of His words that they are spirit and life. His words have the ability to stir up the spirit with spiritual food and renew a parched soul by bringing life to it. They can take the scales off blind eyes and soothe and heal the wounds of those broken in heart and spirit.

As you observe the times in which we live, the Word of God has become a casualty in the midst of man-made religion. This religion is nothing but idolatrous in nature, carnal in practice, and worldly in pursuit. In some cases, the Word is considered obsolete in light of our advanced technology and prudish in light of tolerance. It is often considered insulting as it advocates one God, one way, one truth, and eternal consequences.

You might think that this rebellious attitude towards the Word is only found among unbelievers. Sadly, this attitude is prevalent among those who call themselves Christians.

When you consider the power of the Bible, one would think that the Word of God would be the most priceless physical possession a Christian owns. But, in many cases where the Word is in abundance, it holds no value. As a result, Jesus' words do not become spirit or life to some individuals who consider themselves to be His followers.

It appears that Jesus' words rarely stir up religious people's souls. More often than not, His words become a source of burden, debate, higher criticism, and a matter of opinion where all issues are considered according to man's conclusions instead of the reality of Jesus Christ. The spirit behind the Bible has been replaced with dead-letter religion. This has occurred because His words have been put into the arenas of denominational debate, theological elitism, and personal agendas. Therefore, the power of His words has been buried underneath carnality and idolatry.

In my encounters with Christians, I have discovered that few believe that the complete Word of God is applicable for their lives. This is a tragedy too great to describe. Jesus said in John 5:24-25,

> Verily, verily, I say unto you, He that heareth my word, and believeth on him that sent me, hath everlasting life, and shall not come into condemnation: but is passed from death unto life. Verily, Verily, I say unto you, The hour is coming and now is, when the dead shall hear the voice of the Son of God: and they that hear shall live.

One must ask how many are truly hearing the voice of the Son of God in His Word. In all the years I have ministered to Christians, I would venture to say that only ten percent of them truly believe that the Bible is relevant to every area of their lives. George Barna, a Christian pollster, confirmed a similar figure. For example, his research showed that only 13 percent of adults and seven percent of teenagers base their moral choices on the Bible. According to Barna's findings, the most common basis for moral decision is based on whatever felt right or comfortable in any given situation.

In an interview with Pat Robertson, Josh McDowell found similar figures among teenagers in evangelical churches regarding foundational beliefs. Robertson inquired as to why such a high percentage of our young people do not believe the Word of God. McDowell blamed the epidemic of unbelief on parents.

It is easy to blame the unbelief of our young people on the parents, but I also know the parents have the same struggle. How can parents instill in their children passion and conviction for foundational beliefs when it is clearly missing in their lives?

One has to wonder how the Church could be reduced to such a state. After all, the statistics are consistent. It is clear that Jesus' words carry no credibility with many who claim to be His followers. Why? After extensive study of the Bible, I have discovered four main reasons behind religious people not believing the Word of God.

The first reason is obvious. The world's humanistic and New Age philosophies have made great inroads into the inner sanctuaries of the affections of God's people, their homes, and churches. The world defiles or drowns out the truth, rendering it ineffective.

Secondly, proper instruction is missing. Godly instruction encourages, challenges, and instills obedience in the follower. Without obedience, the Word is unable to become a blessing. Luke 11:28 says, "Yea rather, blessed are they that hear the word of God, and keep it."

Jesus commanded His Church to make people His followers. Today, Christians are made converts to doctrines, denominations, and spiritual leaders. This leaves people without a vision of Jesus, the power of the Holy Spirit, and walking in a state of unbelief towards God and His Word.

The third reason the visible Church is in this state is because of the breakdown of leadership. This breakdown begins at the level of the local church and subsequently leads to the infiltration of the home. The book of Judges is a good example of how the absence of strong, godly leadership leads to idolatry and rebellion. Judges 2:7 and 10 introduced us to this breakdown,

> And the people served the LORD all the days of Joshua and all the days of the elders that outlived Joshua, who had seen all the great works of the LORD, that he did for Israel...And also all that generation were gathered unto their fathers: and there

> arose another generation after them, which knew not the LORD, nor yet the works which he had done for Israel.

This brings us to the final reason why the majority of Christians that were polled do not believe the Word of God: They do not know the God of the Bible. Ignorance of God makes people indifferent towards Him. The stories of His miracles become mythical. We see this in the case of Gideon as he responded to the angel of the LORD, "Oh my Lord, if the LORD be with us, why then is all this befallen us? and where be all his miracles which our fathers told us of, saying, Did not the LORD bring us up from Egypt? but now the LORD hath forsaken us, and delivered us into the hand of the Midianites" (Judges 6:13).

The stories were passed down to Gideon, but Jehovah God seemed deaf, indifferent, or dead. Likewise, the story of Jesus and the cross has been passed down, but to some it seems stupid, unbelievable, romantic, sweet, or heroic, but not real or applicable for today.

The absence of God implies that godly leadership is missing as well. As the leadership breaks down within God's people, each following generation becomes increasingly indifferent to Him and more susceptible to idolatry and the world. As you consider this state, you realize that regardless of all their religious pursuits, some people have eventually forgotten the identity and character of the real God of heaven. They may have various religious encounters and activities, but they do not have a personal reality of God. This is why God said to Israel,

> But thou shalt remember the LORD thy God: for it is he that giveth thee power to get wealth, that he may establish his covenant which he sware unto thy fathers, as it is this day. And it shall be, if thou do at all forget the LORD thy God, and walk after other gods, and serve them, and worship them, I testify against you this day that ye shall surely perish (Deuteronomy 8:18-19).

The reason Jesus' words cease to be spirit and life to a Christian is because he or she has forgotten what the real purpose of the Word is. It is not to establish right theology, but a right disposition. It is not to develop a religion, but a means to experience and be established in a relationship with the Living God. It is not an avenue that enables one to pursue facts about God. Rather, it is the means by which individuals can discover, know, and possess God for themselves.

As the Bible loses credibility, Christians lose sight of the Jesus of the Word of God. This loss of vision has escalated in each succeeding generation as individuals become more indifferent to both God and His Word.

As stated at the beginning of this book, the one thread that runs through the Bible is the redemption of Jesus. We must not forget that this thread holds every Scripture, shadow, and teaching together. 2 Peter 1:8-9 gives us this reality check about this thread,

> For if these things be in you, and abound, they make you that ye shall neither be barren nor unfruitful in the knowledge of our Lord Jesus Christ. But he that lacketh these things is blind, and cannot see afar off, and hath forgotten that he was purged from his old sins.

Believers need to remember their origins: separated from God because of sin, rebellion, and unbelief. As the Apostle Paul stated in Romans 5:8, "But God commendeth his love toward us, in that, while we were yet sinners, Christ died for us." Every time Christians take communion, it is to remember how far away from God they were, and how the cross of Christ brought reconciliation and life.[1]

Christians must not forget that the heart of the Bible is to reveal God to them in a personal way. Colossians 2:9 says, "For in him dwelleth all the fullness of the Godhead bodily." Our understanding of God is found in the revelation of the Son of God. His character and work can be found in every godly example and shadow of the Old Testament. His heart, desire, and mission concerning us can be found in His relationship with the Father along with His teachings and His journey to Calvary.

Even though Jesus can be found in every theme, godly example, shadow, and revelation, He is obscured because of the flesh of man. Even though He is very close, He must be sought out like a priceless treasure that is overshadowed by some object, overlooked because it blends into the landscape, or hidden because it has been buried.

Today, there is a concept that we must chase after God, but this is not scriptural. God is not running from us, He is simply hidden from our physical sight. In fact, He is so near to us that we often trip over His simple clues, overlook the map He has provided, and miss all of the road signs.

This is why the Word commands us to seek after God with all of our heart and He will be found by us.[2] In Amos 5, the prophet's instruction is to seek after God, and you will live. Jesus gave this command in Matthew 6:33, "But seek ye first the kingdom of God, and his righteousness; and all these things shall be added unto you."

What was Jesus telling His listeners to seek after? Was He telling them to seek after a place or a state of mind? If you compare Scripture with Scripture, you will realize that Jesus was instructing people to first seek after Him.

At the core of the kingdom of heaven is Jesus the King of kings. Without a king, there is no kingdom. Therefore, without Jesus, there would be no future hope. When a person embraces the King of kings, he or she becomes part of this unseen kingdom whose authority comes from the throne of God. This kingdom is immovable because it cannot be shaken by events in heaven or on earth.

---

[1] 1 Corinthians 11:23-33

[2] Jeremiah 29:13

The Apostle Paul tells us in 1 Corinthians 1:30 that Jesus is our righteousness. There is no righteousness outside of Jesus. Therefore, when a person seeks righteousness, he or she must seek Jesus Christ in all of His grace, truth, beauty, and glory. When a person fails to seek God, he or she can become lost and will eventually lose sight of his or her need for God. In the midst of confusion and conflict, the person will forget the importance of God in his or her life and fall into idolatry.

Deuteronomy 6:12 and 8:11, 14, and 19 admonished the Israelites to beware lest they forget the Lord. In the Gospels, you see where Peter and the disciples remembered the words of Jesus at different times, which brought conviction, understanding, and comfort to their souls.[3]

In John 15:11, Jesus stated, "These things have I spoken unto you, that my joy might remain in you, and that your joy might be full." Jesus' words brought joy to the hearts of many, set people free, calmed the storms, and raised the dead. His teaching astonished people and revolutionized how many looked at life and the world around them.[4]

Christians, therefore, must not only study the Word, but they must choose to remember what the Word is about. Remembering is a choice of the mind and will. This exercise is a way to discipline one's focus in order to recall something.

People must beware of what they choose to remember. For example, recollection of the past does not constitute reality, but a lopsided presentation of happenings and events. On the other hand, the Word in the right context determines how we view past reality, but how we are going to respond to present reality in order to change the impact of our future reality. It is the connection and summary of this reality that must be sought out in Scripture. We know this reality to be nothing more than truth personified, Jesus Christ.

King David had his way of ensuring that all reality and activities were considered in light of God, "I have set the LORD always before me: because he is at my right hand, I shall not be moved" (Psalm 16:8).

The Apostle Paul had a very disciplined focus that kept his purpose as a man of God ever before him, "For I determined not to know any thing among you, save Jesus Christ, and him crucified" (1 Corinthians 2:2).

In other Scriptures, the Apostle Paul confirmed this focus. For example, Colossians 3:2 instructs believers to set their affections on things above. Throughout Acts and the various epistles, Paul constantly reminded himself of his encounter, calling, and life in Christ. This was made evident in his writings and every time he shared his testimony of what Christ did on his behalf. His conclusion was simple and forthright as seen in the following Scriptures.

---

[3] Matthew 26:75; Luke 24:8; John 2:22; 12:16

[4] Matthew 7:28-29

> This is a faithful saying, and worthy of all acceptation, that Christ Jesus came into the world to save sinners; of whom I am chief. Howbeit, for this cause I obtained mercy, that in me first Jesus Christ might shew forth all longsuffering, for a pattern to them which should hereafter believe on him to life everlasting (1 Timothy 1:15-16).

Acts 5:42 tells us the focus of Peter and the other committed followers of Jesus in the new church, "And daily in the temple, and in every house, they ceased not to teach and preach Jesus Christ."

The reason Jesus must become our reality is because He is the One who will bring us into the desired place: that of communion with the Father. His redemption is about paying a complete price for man who lost his way in the Garden of Eden. His resurrection is about restoring man back into His original place of fellowship with God. His walk on the earth was about bringing the life and glory of God back into the midst of man. [5]

The Christian walk is all about relationship. It is in God's heart that He fellowships, walks, and enjoys man as He did in the Garden of Eden. And, His desire is that man fellowship, walk, and enjoy Him as a means to reflect the beauty, fullness, and power of His life as it is being realized and established in each of His followers. His heart's cry has been the same throughout the centuries, "Adam, where are you." Because of this desire, He sent the Shepherd to find each lost sheep and bring him or her back to the fold.[6]

The Christian life cannot be realized or established outside of this relationship. Everything of value and importance is developed within this fellowship. There are Christians that have failed to realize that this was the whole thrust of Christ's mission, life, death, and resurrection. They have missed the reality that they have the right to be children of God, subject to an eternal inheritance that has been sealed or secured by the Spirit of the Living God.[7]

It is easy to forget that the Christian life is about relationship that allows one to actually put on the very life of Christ. It is not unusual to overlook how spiritual growth depends on sitting at the feet of Jesus as He instructs. It includes sitting up at the table of communion as the Holy Spirit imparts truths, and sitting on the lap of the Father as one learns to enjoy sweet intimacy. This priceless fellowship has a goal: to make every believer one with not only God, but also with each other. This was Jesus' prayer in John 17:21, "That they all may be one; as thou, Father, art in me, and I in thee, that they also may be one in us; that the world may believe that thou hast sent me."

---

[5] John 14:6; Romans 8:14-17

[6] Genesis 3:9; Luke 15:3-7

[7] John 1:12; Ephesians 1:3-14

It is in fellowship that saints are prepared to meet God at every turn in their lives. The one reality Christians must remember is that one day they will meet God, whether it be in death or in the air.[8] The Bible not only reminds us of this fact, but its truths and instructions are meant to prepare us for this meeting.

Jesus said that the Scriptures lead people who were seeking eternal life to Him. In John 17:17, He made this statement, "Sanctify them through thy truth: thy word is truth." His Word is capable of setting a person apart unto good works as it reproves and corrects for instruction in righteousness. [9]

The Word of God is a powerful sword as it cuts away the endless excuses of man and exposes his heart. Hebrews 4:12 confirms this truth, "For the word of God is quick, and powerful, and sharper than any two-edged sword, piercing even to the dividing asunder of soul and spirit, and of the joints and marrow, and is a discerner of the thoughts and intents of the heart."

It is not only a defensive weapon that can be used to protect self from the pitfalls, but it is an offensive weapon that can silence the enemy and cause him to back off. "And take the helmet of salvation, and the sword of the Spirit, which is the word of God" (Ephesians 6:17).

The Word of God is powerful, but that power can be quenched if we do not rightly divide it. Its authority can easily be destroyed in our lives if the Spirit of God is not imparting it into our souls. It can be forgotten when the truth of Jesus is not living in our hearts, active in our lives, evident in our actions, and being exalted in our minds.

Are you remembering what God did for you? Or, have you forgotten because other things have replaced the reality of Christ and His redemption in your life? Maybe your memories reveal that you have never entered into a relationship with God through Jesus Christ. If so, you need to believe in your heart the Gospel of Jesus dying on your behalf because of sins, being buried, but raising three days later to prove Himself victorious over the enemies of your soul. You need to confess He is Lord, implying that you now recognize you have a Lord; therefore, you no longer have the right to call the shots in your life. Submit all to Him and begin to walk in obedience to what you learn about Him in His Word.

If your memories show you that you had a salvation experience, but your life lacks authority, power, and satisfaction, you have left Him behind. As a result, you have forgotten that your Christian life is not about what you do for Jesus, but who you must become in Him. This life is not about some concept or belief about a man named Jesus. Rather, it is the constant reality that He lives to be God, Lord, Savior, and friend in

---

[8] Hebrews 9:27; 2 Corinthians 5:8-10; 1 Thessalonians 4:13-18

[9] John 5:39; 2 Timothy 3:16

your life. It is not about dead religious activities that have no meaning or purpose; rather, it is about a growing relationship with the Living God.

Finally, are you rightly dividing the Word so that you will not be a workman who will be found ashamed? If not, this means your life lacks the disposition and good works that would identify you to Christ and make an eternal difference.

Today, it appears as if some Christians have forgotten their humble beginnings. Let the following Scriptures not only challenge you, but also speak to your spirit as it clearly establishes the validity, work and power of God's Word,

> Glory ye in his holy name: let the heart of them rejoice that seek the LORD. Seek the LORD and his strength, seek his face continually. Remember his marvellous works that he hath done, his wonders, and the judgments of his mouth...Sing unto the LORD, all the earth; shew forth from day to day his salvation (1 Chronicles 16:10-12, 23).

Book Two:

THE ANATOMY OF SIN

INTRODUCTION

A book about sin may seem unnecessary to most believers. However, in my dealings with Christians, I have discovered that many of them do not understand what constitutes sin. This is a frightening prospect because sin lies at the heart of what the Gospel addresses, and the Word of God is clear that believers must overcome sin in their lives.

In examining why people in Christendom do not correctly grasp the concept of sin, I realize that there is a weak presentation of it in light of the Gospel, judgment, and hell. As a result, people fail to identify personal sin. This personal sin not only clings to them, but also stops them from effectively walking out the Christian life.

Hebrews 12:1 gives this description of personal sin, "Wherefore seeing we also are compassed about with so great a cloud of witnesses, let us lay aside every weight, and the sin which doth so easily beset us, and let us run with patience the race that is set before us."

This Scripture verse tells us that there is a visible witness (in the Word) to show that people have the means to put aside any weight and sin to run the race and complete the course.

For example, one of the greatest obstacles in understanding sin is a worldly, warped emphasis of God's love. This ungodly emphasis keeps people from seeing the harsh reality of sin that cost God His best and Jesus His all. Yes, God so loved us that He gave His only Son, but such a concept has been presented as a romantic notion, alleviating any sound understanding of how the holy Law of God demanded such a sacrifice to redeem man from the judgment of death. It is only by understanding personal sin that a person can begin to understand the extent of God's love.

Today, people think of sin in generic terms without coming to a realization of personal sin. This keeps them indifferent about personal sin and how it affects them on a spiritual basis.

This book is meant to deal with generic, unrealistic, and misconceived notions about sin. Its goal is to take you through the many dark corridors of sin to present a clear presentation of it. A clear presentation will enable the reader to not only encounter the depth of God's love, but also experience salvation that is rich and full.

It is vital that Christians make sure that they have a clear understanding of this subject for the sake of others. If a believer has a weak understanding of sin, he or she will be unable to effectively challenge others about it. Sadly, without a proper presentation, it might cost others their very souls.

1

WHAT IS SIN?

What is sin? You would think that most religious people could easily answer this question. The reality is that even in Christendom the answer may prove to vary or be illusive. The answer differs according to how sin has been presented. This subject may have become a point of confusion or lost in a person's philosophies about religion and life. This book is about answering this question.

One might wonder why it would take a whole book to deal with what seems like a simple question. Granted, sin is a fairly black and white subject. It is clear that its effect on man has caused him to be separated from his Creator, as well as bringing him under a death sentence that leaves him hopeless. However, sin proves to be far reaching as it affects every aspect of each of our lives. It actually forms layers that confuse, shroud, and deceive people as to how it has influenced man's inner disposition, how it works through the ways of the flesh, and how it abounds in the activities of the world that surround us.

Although the subject of sin appears to be black and white, it can prove to be very complex. It is not just a matter of what a person does, but also who that person allows him or herself to become. In fact, the greatest manifestation of sin has to do with the lack of character. Those who walk in sin refuse to take accountability for their inner state, attitudes, or actions.

One of the problems with the issue of sin rests with the many misconceptions about it that have been developed through the years. For example, it has been rendered down to an illness, genetics, and mistakes. As a result, some people give the impression that Jesus came to save them *in* their sin, rather than save them *from* their sin. Such misconceptions exist because of the weak presentation of sin that is being advocated in Christendom to avoid insulting people. Such a weak presentation can leave a person indifferent or unclear about this issue.

Properly coming to terms with this issue for many will actually prove to be the difference as to where they will spend eternity. Obviously, the difference between the choices of eternal life and eternal damnation lies at the base of how people perceive salvation. Without having a realistic sense of why each of us actually need to be saved from sin, people will see no need to come to salvation.

Sadly, because of the weak presentation of this subject, many have come to Jesus for other reasons. Some come for worldly benefits, while others come as a means to avoid a place called hell. As a result, many individuals who think themselves to be saved are walking in condemnation because their path or direction has never changed. When judgment day arrives, they will point a finger at those who dared to preach a weak gospel by downplaying the issue of sin.

Salvation is a form of deliverance. This deliverance took place in the past when Jesus paid the price for sin on the cross to provide justification, but it is also present through the work of sanctification, and will be fully realized in the future when God's people are glorified with Him.

As we consider the world around us, it is obvious that people need to be delivered from their personal traps that enslave them into their small worlds of delusion and misery. There are those who are enslaved to their hate. You have seen these individuals; they attack, reject, and mock anyone who dares disagree with them. In essence, they cannot stand their own life; therefore, they transfer their bitterness upon others who might challenge or put a mirror up to reveal their true status. There are those who are trapped by fear, hopelessness, and despair, and cannot see any way out of their situation.

God has offered these people true deliverance, but they prefer the darkness of their own unbelief, rather than the light to expose the source of their real plight. As a result, they reject, shun, or disregard deliverance that is complete and reaches beyond the present to address the past and ensure the future.

To other people salvation appears to be for the future, but it is necessary for the present. Granted, hell is a future place for those who insist on walking in condemnation, but salvation has to do with something that is presently available to those who will embrace it. We need the reality of salvation working within our lives as this moment. This brings us to the harsh reality of sin. The Apostle Paul clearly identified sin as the culprit and influence that each person must be delivered from on a daily basis. It is clearly the enemy of man's soul, opposes God's leadership and demands servitude. Romans 6:12 verifies this, "Let not sin therefore reign in your mortal body, that ye should obey it in the lust thereof."

The real destructive core of sin is not a matter of expressing itself in an outward response, but of an inward disposition. This disposition is influenced by prevailing inclinations and tendencies.[1] Prevailing inclinations and tendencies establish the state of the person. This state, or inward environment that man walks in, came from Adam. Romans 5:12 confirms this, "Wherefore, as by one man sin entered into the world, and death by sin; and so death passed upon all men, for that all have sinned." What is this state? It is death. Man walks in a state of death due to his selfish disposition.

---

[1] Webster's New Collegiate Dictionary © 1976 by G. & C. Merriam Co.

Consider your prevailing inclinations and tendencies. When it comes to doing something that might prove to be inconvenient, what is your natural inclination? Are you inclined towards doing right or will you go with your fleshly, selfish ways? Moreover, if you go along with your natural inclinations, knowing you have failed to do what is decent, is it your natural tendency to somehow justify it?

As you study the inclinations of this fallen state, you will readily see its fruits. The Word clearly defines this fallen condition. Jeremiah 17:9 states, "The heart is deceitful above all things, and desperately wicked: who can know it?" Within man's heart is the tendency to sin. The depth of this tendency is so great that man often walks in denial or delusion about his personal heart condition.

Man's heart defiles him, and causes separation between him and God. Out of the heart come the issues of life; therefore, it either contains the elements of death or life. It is pure or defiled. It determines the quality of life. This quality of life finds its basis in the type of relationship a person has with God.

Jesus confirmed the wickedness of man's heart. "For out of the heart proceed evil thoughts, murders, adulteries, fornications, thefts, false witness, blasphemies: These are the things which defile a man" (Matthew 15:19).

Since people have the tendency to walk in rebellion towards God, they prefer darkness to light, ignorance to spiritual revelation, and delusion to truth. Sadly, this darkness seems reasonable and good to these individuals. Jesus spoke of this darkness as serving as a false light to man.[2] This light is a delusion that blinds one to his or her spiritual condition. Proverbs 14:12 talks about the delusion and destruction of this false light, "There is a way which seemeth right unto a man, but the end thereof are the ways of death."

Even when people have a reality check about their spiritual condition, they still must face the depth of their depravity. For example, many would like to think they have something of worth to offer God. Maybe, they have a winning way about their personality or special abilities that will help God in His endeavors. However, the Word declares differently. The Apostle Paul revealed the depths of this depravity in Romans 3:10-12,

> As it is written, there is none righteous, no not one: There is none that understandeth, there is none that seeketh after God. They are all gone out of the way, they are together become unprofitable; there is none that doeth good, no, not one. (Emphasis added.)

The words "none," "all," "together," and "not one" include you and me. This text reveals seven harsh realities about the fallen condition of man. First, there are none who are righteous. King David brought this

---

[2] Matthew 6:22-23

harsh fact out in Psalm 14. He was talking about those who do not really believe in their heart there is a God. Most people think this statement has to do with people who are Atheists, but in reality, it is also in regard to those who do not believe God. They may claim they believe there is a God, but they do not believe His words.

King David called such people, "fools" because they do not realize that they are corrupt. In Psalm 51:5, King David admitted that he was shaped in iniquity, and that his mother conceived him in sin. He was aware of the inner disposition he had inherited in this fallen world. Clearly, the very origin of each person even from his or her conception proves that there are none who are holy and just before God.[3] Such a state is serious because Hebrews 12:14 states, "Follow peace with all men, and holiness without which no man shall see the Lord."

Holiness is not an option. God is holy; therefore, His followers are commanded to be holy.[4] The problem rests with the fact that there is no base of personal holiness from which man can operate. Every aspect of man has been marred or defiled by sin. Without intervention by God, man stands hopeless and condemned in his unholy state.

Secondly, there is none that understands the real issues surrounding man's depravity and God's holiness. Understanding points to comprehension or wisdom that not only enlightens man in a spiritual way about such matters, but also results in pious or acceptable acts towards God.[5]

Romans 12:3 talks about how people have very high opinions about themselves. These individuals often judge others according to their perception of self. To gain a good example of how such a perception works, all one needs to do is consider Moses' sister, Miriam, in Numbers 12. She considered herself better than Moses. She justified her arrogance at the expense of Moses' wife being from Cush. In her arrogance she presumed God agreed with her. However, God showed her how He perceived her arrogance by causing her to become a leper. She was quickly brought down from her high opinion to face her low, miserable state.

People like Miriam not only walk in great arrogance about their depravity, but they walk in delusion. They see themselves as having something of value to offer God because they have failed to comprehend their real state in light of God's holiness. In reality, they are unable to discern spiritual matters. They simply walk according to their own vanities and conceits.

The Apostle Paul emphasized man's inability to spiritually discern matters if he is walking according to his fallen condition, rather than the Spirit of God. "But the natural man receiveth not the things of the Spirit of

---

[3] Strong's Concordance #1342

[4] 1 Peter 1:15-16

[5] Strong's Concordance #4920

God: for they are foolishness unto him: neither can he know them, because they are spiritually discerned" (1 Corinthians 2:14).

Thirdly, fallen man will not seek after the one true God, because he is in a state of spiritual death. Such a state makes him unable to respond to God; therefore, he is void of such an inclination. A good example of this state can be observed in the three wise men who came to seek Jesus when He was born. Consider the percentage of not only the wise men, but the religious people of Jesus' day. Only three wise men sought out the new King of Israel. People do not naturally seek the true God. Granted, people may turn to some form of known religion, but very few have any inclination to seek out the true God of heaven.

Since man is spiritually incapable of interacting on a spiritual level with the true God, he seeks religion, causing him to erect his own god. Such a god will accept what man perceives is personal worth, while tolerating his inconsistencies, moral irresponsibility, haughty spirit, and insatiable lusts. This substitute god encourages outward compliance, while justifying inward rebellion. We can clearly see this scenario in the case of Israel and the golden calf in Exodus 32. Even though the people of Israel had witnessed God's greatness, they still preferred the lifeless calf to the living God of heaven.

God states that none seek Him. Isaiah 64:7 confirms this, "And there is none that calleth thy name, that stirreth up himself to take hold of thee: for thou hast hid thy face from us, and hast consumed us, because of our iniquities." Once again, the reason man does not seek God is because he is in a state of spiritual death. He may be curious about God, and even have a sense that God could be the missing piece of the puzzle concerning the affairs of life, but he is devoid of the means to seek God in a right way.

Praise God, He has always sought man. He looks for those who will stand in the gap.[6] He even seeks those who never thought about seeking Him. Isaiah 65:1 states, "I am sought of them that asked not for me; I am found of them that sought me not: I said, Behold me, behold me, unto a nation that was not called by my name."

Jesus is the most visible example of God seeking man. We see this in the parable of seeking after the one lost sheep in Luke 15:3-7. He has sought out every believer. It is God's drawing ability that gives people the desire to seek Him out. Jeremiah 29:13 tells us how to seek God, "And ye shall seek me, and find me, when ye shall search for me with all your heart."

Many people search for God out of personal purposes or agendas. However, few seek Him from total deliverance from sin in order to know and serve Him. Those who seek God for personal agendas end up with

---

[6] Ezekiel 22:30

another god or walking in unbelief before the true God of heaven. Those who seek to know God end up possessing the very treasure of heaven.[7]

The fourth harsh reality concerning the fallen inward state of man is that he has gone out of the way. The word "way" points to mode, character, or manner.[8] Man was created to be a reflection of God. Due to sin, he has stepped totally out of this mode or character. Proverbs 21:8 says, "The way of man is froward and strange: but as for the pure, his work is right."

The prophet, Isaiah described this state of enmity with God in relationship to Jesus' crucifixion, "All we like sheep have gone astray; we have turned every one to his own way, and the LORD hath laid on him the iniquity of us all" (Isaiah 53:6). God is the center of life, truth, and purpose. If man does not walk according to the center, he will automatically go astray. Man has become lost in his own ways. Even though he believes that they are leading him in a right direction, he is simply going the natural ways of spiritual death.

The result of man going his own way is that he failing to take on the likeness of Christ, thereby, he is missing the mark of reflecting God's glory. Instead, he is either reflecting the fading glory of the world, the false glory of religion, or the vainglory of man.

To explain the concept of "way" would entail another book. However, there is only one acceptable way to God, and it leads to the true Jesus. All the other ways, regardless of how Christian or religious they may seem, represent the broad path of destruction. Sadly, most people prefer this broad path. They tack enough religion onto their ways to justify and compromise sin. They do just enough good that, in their mind, it changes the balances that weigh their good deeds against their wrong doings. However, like King Belshazzar of Babylon, many will learn too late that they have been weighed in the balances and have been found wanting.[9]

The Apostle Paul confirmed this in Romans 7:18, "For I know that in me (that is, in my flesh,) dwelleth no good thing: for to will is present with me: but how to perform that which is good I find not." "Good" in this text means that there is nothing that is beneficial in the flesh. It cannot add purpose, meaning, or substance to our lives. This shows us that the "way" does not consist of a right or wrong way, but of a disposition that fails to serve its original purpose: To reflect the glory of God, and bring an eternal significance to life.

Since people are failing to fulfill the purpose behind their existence, they have become unprofitable. In short, they have become useless before God. There is no virtue in their flesh that is of value in the scheme of eternity, and no merit in what they do. A good example of this unprofitable state can be found in Matthew 7:21-23. Jesus put forth the

---

[7] Genesis 15:1

[8] Strong's Concordance # 5158

[9] Daniel 5; Matthew 7:13-14; Romans 3:23; John 14:6

warning that many will call Him Lord on the Day of Judgment, but He will not recognize them as His servants. These individuals will attempt to dispute Him by presenting their case based on the good works they did in His name. However, He will consider such works as iniquity because they failed to do the will of God. Isaiah 64:6 summarizes this state, "But we are all as an unclean thing, and all our righteousness are as filthy rags; and we all do fade as a leaf; and our iniquities, like the wind, have taken us away." (Emphasis added.)

The final and seventh pronouncement on man's fallen disposition is that he is unable to do good. This inability to do good points to the cold, harsh reality that there is nothing of use within the fallen man's character or manner in light of that which is holy and eternal. These seven declarations show the hopelessness of man. This is why the Apostle Paul declared this about the state of the unregenerate man that had once been prevalent in his life, "O wretched man that I am! Who shall deliver me from the body of this death" (Romans 7:24)?

The Apostle Paul was not making this statement because he was trying to appear spiritual or humble. He stated it because of the revelation that God gave him concerning his own depraved state before he encountered the Way, Jesus Christ. He had no doubt about this harsh reality. He could honestly face this depravity in light of God's grace and His work of redemption. In 1 Timothy 1:15-16, he made this statement,

> This is a faithful saying, and worthy of all acceptation, that Christ Jesus came into the world to save sinners; of whom I am chief. Howbeit for this cause I obtained mercy, that in me first Jesus Christ might shew forth all longsuffering, for a pattern to them which should hereafter believe on him to life everlasting.

In light of his fallen disposition, the Apostle Paul realized his need for a solution. This solution required God's mercy, grace, and salvation. On the road to Damascus, he met that solution, Jesus Christ.[10]

When Paul met the light of the world, the life of man, and the hope of salvation, the spiritual light came on in his spirit. His encounter with Jesus, the light of the world, resulted in his physical blindness.[11] He had been walking in spiritual darkness until he met God Incarnate. This was not only a turning point in his life, but also a change in his focus, direction, and purpose.

Today, there is an emphasis, by some, on being a saint. When the concept of sin or sinner is present in light of the Christian, it is sometimes shunned or ignored. It is true that Christians are considered saints, but they must be realistic about how sin can operate in their lives.

The idea of being a saint is in relationship to position. Before a position can be a reality, it must be walked out and experienced. For

---

[10] Acts 9

[11] John 1:4-14

example, believers are also positionally dead in Christ, but this does not become a reality until it is walked out in practical ways on a daily basis.

The way a Christian becomes a saint is to walk contrary to the tendencies of the influence, workings, and activities of sin. It is hypocritical to call oneself a saint, while walking as a sinner. This means not hiding behind a title or concept of being a saint, but walking out a righteous life, while neglecting the demands of the tendency to sin and daily mortifying the members of the flesh. Spiritual maturity or growth into sainthood rests on whether sin is properly dealt with. Sin must be recognized, confronted, confessed, and overcome. Ignorance or denial of the workings of sin with its inclinations and tendencies at any level is the fastest way to defeat and destruction.

The question is not whether you think yourself to be a saint or a sinner. Have you properly confronted and dealt with the inward environment that is inclined towards sin? It is easy to tell whether or not this disposition of sin is alive and reigning in your life. Are you self-centered? Are you in destructive cycles that lead to depression and defeat? Do you insist that others honor your way of thinking and doing, causing conflict? Do you insist on becoming a victim in situations, rather than secure victory in Christ? These are a few of the fruits of sin that can be working in our disposition. Such fruit can be easily discerned in the light of integrity and humility, but sin can also quickly deceive those who refuse to take accountability for their own particular disposition. Those who refuse to be accountable for their disposition prefer darkness to loving and choosing the truth.[12] Such a person is already condemned, and walking according to death and destruction in his or her life.

---

[12] 2 Thessalonians 2:10-12

2

THE NATURE OF SIN

What comprises sin? After all, sin expresses itself in opposition to God's rule and reign. Sin is an inherent condition according to Romans 5:12-14. This condition is expressed in the prevailing mood of selfishness that invades, perverts, and motivates man's inner disposition. I am sure you have seen this selfishness in people, and if you are honest with yourself, you have had those selfish moments in your life. Selfishness in any light of truth is hard to face and bear. After all, it is totally focused on self with no real regard or respect for others.

Due to the presence of this selfish mood, foolishness can be found bound in people's hearts. Obviously, it is a condition that each of us born into the human race must properly confront to avoid spiritual death. The fact that sin is a natural tendency gives us insight into the real battle. If sin is a natural response due to our disposition and state of affairs, how can we develop an attitude that will not only recognize it, but also oppose its function in our lives?

Obviously, to confront sin, we must understand how it operates. Romans 3:23 gives us the first indication of what is wrong with humankind. As previously alluded to, man falls short of the glory of God. What does this mean? It means that man falls short of what God intended for him. God formed man in His image in order to manifest His reflection to the world. Sin has marred man's potential to reflect God's glory.[1] In other words, for man to reach his potential, he must overcome sin so he will once again mirror the glory of his Creator.

How does man reflect God's glory? It is a matter of disposition. As pointed out, man's sinful condition points to a wrong or marred disposition. We are once again reminded that disposition is made up of inclination and tendency. Due to our inherent condition, we are inclined to sin, and since it is natural, our tendency is somehow to make it acceptable in our eyes. This state keeps us from properly confronting sin in our lives.

We clearly can see independence working in people lives in the Word of God. Such individuals refuse to come into subjection to God's rule. In Adam's independence, he broke the covenant with God. For Cain, his independence translated into a murderous act. Independence

[1] Genesis 1:27; 2 Corinthians 3:8-18

from God's authority starts from the premise of treachery and ends in rebellious acts.

Independence is at the core of inclination, but pride can be found at the base of our tendency. It is easy to recognize pride in others. In fact, we tend to resist, oppose, and challenge pride in other people, but we have a hard time recognizing it in ourselves. Pride actually blinds us to its presence and activities in our lives.

It has taken me years to recognize my pride. Nevertheless, I have learned how it feels, thinks, looks, and acts. The feeling of pride gave me a sense of incredible confidence that all is well in my world. Such a sense is always based on something making me feel good or happy. However, such feelings are sentimental and temporary.

When pride was operating in my thought process, arrogance reigned in my conclusion. This arrogance stated that there was no way I could be wrong about a particular matter. However, my conclusion was nothing more than an overrated opinion that reeked with the stench of unrealism.

When it came to my look of pride, I would feel disdain as I looked down on those who were not of the same opinion. My arrogant thoughts always made me see such people as inferior or stupid. As a result, I did not feel any real obligation towards these individuals other than to tolerate them at best or placate them when I felt the need to con or use them. My act was all a façade that had no real meaning or honor behind it. It is obvious why God resists pride.

Independence is opposition towards God's rule that expresses itself in rebellion, while pride refuses to submit inwardly to God. Pride will develop an appearance of righteousness and obedience. In a way, pride plays the game of compliance, while protecting rebellion. In the end, rebellion expresses itself in a prideful look, something that God hates. Such expression of pride not only hides selfishness, but self-sufficiency.[2] When self-sufficiency is present, people do not see any need for God. In such a deluded state, these individuals actually feel they are in control and on top of their game in life.

In his first epistle, the Apostle John makes reference to both the inclination and the tendency of sin. As you study the disposition, you realize that the real inclination of man is to be god of his world, and the tendency is to justify himself as god in his own eyes. Justification of this nature gives a person the right to adjust, dictate, or control his or her world regardless of how it affects others.

The inclination to be God of our personal worlds started as a temptation in the Garden of Eden in Genesis 3. Satan tempted Eve to experience evil so that she could possess God's wisdom, thereby, gaining like status. Instead of taking on the status of God, she gave way to the base state of spiritual death.

---

[2] Proverbs 6:16-17; 2 Corinthians 3:5

The pursuit to become God is no longer a simple temptation; rather, it is an inclination that finds its platform in our independency to have life on our terms. The failure to be God in matters is naturally justified by our tendency to avoid the truth that we do not have the means to be God. Such justification excuses us from taking responsibility for the type of person we are becoming in our rebellion.

When people operate within their fallen condition, they often perceive that they are actually determining and controlling reality, thereby, defining what is truth. Such a sinful disposition makes individuals completely wrong in their attitude towards life and their approach towards God. This disposition must be properly recognized and dealt with. Therefore, in his first letter, the Apostle John approaches man's disposition and the delusion he operates within. In order to overcome our deluded, independent state, we, as believers, must understand how sin works in and through our disposition.

At the time that he wrote his first epistle, John was dealing with heretical teachings. Most heretical teachings attack the heart of basic Christianity. The basis of Christianity has to do with who people say Jesus is, (whether they truly know Him), their attitude about sin, and the type of relationship they have with God.

Although most people recognize moral deviation in others, few ever recognize personal moral deviation. The darkness of sin has the capacity to delude each of us about our ways, while our tendency of self-justification allows us to conclude that all of our ways are right. As stated, God has a different way of looking at our ways. They are strange and perverted to Him. The tragedy that befalls man is that his personal way of doing and being may seem right to him, but it leads to death and destruction.[3]

The real test of character comes when a person needs to confront personal sin. Most people live in denial about their own sin, rather than accept God's evaluation. Either they downplay it at the expense of others, or they come across quite noble about it. The deception that plagues their attitude of nobility towards it is that they are trying to change, but are unable to. Often, these individuals flatter themselves about their attempts to make a matter right by convincing themselves that since the problem is now exposed and they actually know about, it has been properly confronted.

People often perceive that they have overcome a prevailing problem after going through a mental evaluation where they call their action wrong and decide never to do it again. Needless to say, in this state the action may be subdued, but the disposition and patterns have not been broken; therefore, these people continue to fall into the same pattern of sin.

---

[3] Proverbs 14:12; 16:2, 25; 21:8; Isaiah 55:8-9

I am sure you have seen this pattern in those you may have been involved with or have contended with, as well as yourself. You may discuss a problem with someone that is destructive, and he or she will agree with you. Perhaps this person's pattern changes for a couple of weeks, but eventually the old ways begin to edge their way to the forefront. To your dismay, you discover nothing has really changed about this person because he or she is back to his or her old patterns.

People who refuse to humble themselves in true repentance concerning the inward working of sin will also take on an attitude of self-pity. After all, they are trying so hard to overcome, but circumstances and people stand in their way of having victory. The fact that they fall in the same pattern is also used to make them victims to something that they have convinced themselves has an unstoppable power over them. In their mind, they make the situation appear unfair. This clearly points a finger at God, and deems Him as being unjust and unfair to make such unreasonable demands on them to give up the deviant ways of such inclinations and tendencies.

Ultimately, in either case of where people either perceive they have intellectually dealt with sin, or that the inclination or tendency is too great for them to confront their inward disposition of sin, such sins are subtly being exalted over God. In the first situation where sin is mentally dealt with, the real affect of sin on the inward disposition is being downplay, causing some type of self-sufficiency. In these people's self-sufficiency to mentally deal with sin without genuine repentance, they are exalting themselves over God's evaluation, rather than becoming subject to it. This means the truth is not in them, causing them to ignore the Word of God concerning their sin.

In the latter state where sin is being deemed to great to overcome, these individuals ultimately exalt themselves over God by appearing noble about His unfair demands for righteousness. In essence, they end up calling Him a liar, verifying that the Word is not in them. Both are the sick, destructive games of sin that put God to a foolish test and result in judgment.[4]

The Apostle John made this statement in 1 John 1:8, "If we say that we have no sin, we deceive ourselves, and the truth is not in us." The natural inclination to sin causes us to deceive ourselves about the spiritual condition of our inward man. We walk in denial about sin's affects on us, giving way to its temptation and coming under the law of sin and death.[5]

In 1 John 3:9, John tells us how to address this inclination, "Whosoever is born of God doth not commit sin; for his seed remaineth in him: and he cannot sin, because he is born of God." "Being born" again means that you now have a new disposition (heart and spirit)

---

[4] Matthew 4:7

[5] Romans 8:2

within you. This disposition has an inclination towards righteousness and not sin, which will change your attitude and approach towards spiritual matters. Therefore, people who continue to walk in sin without conviction of sin and repentance from it must consider whether they have ever been born again of the Spirit and the water of the Word.[6]

If the reality of God is present in a person through the indwelling presence of the Holy Spirit, he or she will not be comfortable in sin. Such individuals will feel the convicting power of God when they fall into the subtle, evil traps of wickedness. They will not be content to remain in any form of wickedness, as it will suck the joy and life out of them. After all, God is holy and He will not tolerate sin in His midst. This is why Jesus came in the form of man to serve as a sacrifice. God could not accept man in his fallen state. In Christ, He provided a means by which man could be born anew with a new spirit and heart.[7] In this new state, sin will repulse the new spirit, and it will break the new heart.

The Apostle John made this statement in 1 John 1:10, "If we say that we have not sinned, we make him a liar, and his word is not in us." This is my simple understanding of this Scripture verse. If we say we have not sinned, when in fact we have, we make God a liar and His Word is not in us. The reason we make God a liar is because we fail to come into agreement with Him about His Scriptural evaluation of a matter. Obviously, if we call God a liar, His Word is not in us.

God's Word has a lot of power to expose and penetrate our lives with its Spirit and truth. It is a revelation of the character and heart of God. It reveals His ways. As a result, application of His Word to our lives keeps us from sinning. It also guides our steps. If it abides in us, we will be able to overcome Satan.[8] It also means that we know what is expected of us. The Apostle John confirmed this in 1 John 3:3-4, "And hereby we do know that we know him, if we keep his commandments. He that saith, I know him, and keepeth not his commandments, is a liar, and the truth is not in him."

The motivating source behind the tendency of the fallen condition is arrogance. Pride at any level sets each of us up to fall into the various traps of sin. It serves as the point of moral deviation as it blinds us to the consequences that will occur due to our actions. Because of it, we are weak and susceptible to the various enticements of the flesh and the temptations of the world. However, pride gives us the feeling of self-sufficiency. It convinces us that we can handle a matter in our own strength. In the end, it serves as the judgmental board in our eye that keeps us from seeing the spirit and fruits of our lives, as well as the traps of destruction that are before us.[9]

---

[6] Ezekiel 36:26-27; John 3:5

[7] Ezekiel 36:26

[8] Psalm 119:11, 15, 105; Hebrews 4:12; 1 John 2:12-14

[9] Matthew 7:1-5; 1 Corinthians 10:12

Since our tendency to sin remains intact even after we are born again, we must recognize our character weaknesses, and humble ourselves under the mighty hand of God. It is at the point of humility that our mind can be transformed.[10] Transformation of the mind is the way to recognize and address the tendency to justify the ways of sin. It actually means that the mind is changed about how we look at a matter or at all sin. Instead of having the tendency to justify sin away, the new mind will recognize it for its destructive ways and reject giving into the foolishness and deception of its pride.

If we do fall into sin, we can be assured that God has provided a way for us to seek out and acquire pardon. In our search, we will find an advocate who can stand in the gap for us, Jesus Christ the Righteous. The only way that He can serve in this capacity is if we confess our sin, acknowledge that we stand guilty and condemned without intervention, and seek Jesus out to stand in the gap for us in the court of heaven. When we do seek Jesus out, He becomes the propitiation or substitute for our sins, thereby, satisfying the judgment or sentence that hangs over us.

This brings us to another point of our tendency to justify sin. Sin hardens us with unbelief towards the reality around us. We see this in the children of Israel. They actually hardened their heart against the conviction and truth of God to possess the Promised Land. The hardening of the heart pointed to unbelief. Every time people refuse to give way to truth, they will become hardened by unbelief in that particular arena. At the core of such unbelief is pride that will put God to a foolish test, rather than simply trust and obey Him.

Pride cleverly tries to orchestrate personal reality to somehow bow down to personal whims and desires. It is arrogant enough to think others must bow down to its way of thinking, and often becomes indifferent to what is really going on around it. When a person is indifferent to reality, he or she will fail to discern or recognize the traps or ways of destruction that are in operation. Such a person will often cause a domino effect in the lives of others, as he or she wreaks destruction along the way.

This brings us to the two sources of sin. Clement of Alexandria identified these two sources, and explained how they work. They are ignorance and inability.[11] The inclination of sin hides behind ignorance towards God, while the tendency of sin claims the inability to do anything about its activities.

Ignorance in the case of people's spiritual plight is opposite of awareness. For people, they need to be aware of their need and responsibility to become cognizant of spiritual matters in order to learn

---

[10] Romans 12:2

[11] The One Who Knows God, Clement of Alexandria, © 1990 by David W. Bercot

the necessary lessons of life and embrace the salvation that has been made available to each of us.

The opposite of inability involves discipline or restraint so as to bring body, thoughts, and actions under proper control. The greatest excuses people have in regards to sin come down to the excuses that they did not know that they were in sin, or that they were unable to control themselves in a matter. However, the Apostle Paul refutes both excuses. He stated in Romans 1:18-23, that we do have an inward knowledge and conscience about God and about sin that will often lead to some type of conviction or guilt. In order to avoid being a castaway, in 1 Corinthians 9:27, Paul told how he brought the members of his body into subjection.

The truth is that people refuse to do away with ignorance about spiritual matters to come to truth, as well as refuse to control their appetites. This is why the Apostle John was adamant in dealing with people's attitude towards personal sin. If they remained ignorant about personal sin, it would be because of preferring such delusion. In their insistence to remain ignorant towards God, these people would also be unable to make sound judgments. In a sense, these individuals will refuse to take accountability for the influence of sin in their lives, as they erect a personal god that will serve their purpose. Such people should heed the Apostle Paul's warning that God will no longer wink at such ignorance in Acts 17:30, but that He is commanding all men to repent.

The claim of inability to overcome sin clearly makes God out to be a liar. Such a person is declaring that God is unfair to declare that man must live righteously before Him since sin can prove to be too great to overcome. Such a claim proves that the Word is not in this person, because the Word declares differently. In Christ we are all able to overcome, but if anyone fails to do so it is because he or she has never repented in the first place. Not only is this person calling God a liar, but he or she also refuses to give way to God's righteous judgments.

As you can see, the way a person deceives him or herself shows his or her real motivation and agendas. The one who insists on ignorance wants to glory in *personal goodness*, and be happy in his or her self-centered reality. Such a premise is humanistic.

The person, who refuses to overcome his or her sin while appearing noble and justified, wants to enjoy his or her personal lusts without facing the consequences. This premise is nothing more than *paganism* hiding behind some kind of veneer or cloak. These points of justification may seem so right to a person, but they are all wrong. Such ways are the ways of darkness, superstition, and death.

In the following chapters, sin will be discussed from every angle. It will be exposed at every level. The inclination and tendency of sin will be identified, along with its claims of ignorance towards God and its so-called "power" that proves greater than God and His truths. Its attitudes, devices, and ways will be unveiled, so that people can see how it works in their lives. It is not a pretty picture. In fact, to the arrogant, it can be an insulting picture. To those in despair, this revelation can be depressing. To those who play at religion, it will cause anger and fear. However, the picture of sin is not meant to bring us to emotionally experience the utter depths of its destruction, but to bring us to realize our desperate need for Jesus because of it.

Jesus is the solution to our sin problem. He is the way to liberty, the truth about deliverance, and the life that brings hope. In order to know Jesus as the solution, we must believe the record that we have about Him. This record is the Word of God, and it shows us who He is, what He did on our behalf, and what He must be in our lives to experience the fullness of His glorious salvation.

Do you possess the real Jesus? Is His life being manifested in and through you, or are you walking according to the inclination and tendency of sin? Are you in ignorance and falsely accusing God in your failures because you have missed the mark as far as coming to the knowledge of the real Jesus?

3

THE DECEITFULNESS OF SIN

Sin is a black or white issue as to what God will accept and honor or reject and judge. People are either operating in sin, or they are recognizing it, repenting of it, confessing it, and walking in the ways of righteousness. Either individuals are walking the broad path that leads to destruction, or they are walking the narrow path that leads to the everlasting glory of God.

In dealing with the issue of sin in people's lives, I have encountered confusion, denial, and arrogance. How can a subject that is so black and white become shrouded in confusion, debate, and denial? Hebrews 3:13 answers this provoking question, "But exhort one another daily, while it is called To day; lest any of you be hardened through the deceitfulness of sin." Sin has a powerful level of deception. People who give into it will walk in this deception.

The deception of sin blinds people to their own spiritual state. You can see this deception in the life of King David when he committed adultery with Bathsheba. We all know the story that can be found in 2 Samuel 11 because it reveals how deep even a righteous person can fall into sin when he or she opens the door to it. For David, the door of temptation he opened was lust. He saw how beautiful Bathsheba was and lusted after her. There is no indication that he tried to reason with himself about it even after hearing that she was a married woman. Obviously, for King David, lust bypassed all common sense and circumvented his heart, while transgressing the righteous Law of God by recklessly pursuing fleshly satisfaction

When King David found that Bathsheba was pregnant, the deceitful web of sin began to take hold in a greater way. Sin can only take hold in darkness. It is one thing to fall into sin's temptation, and another matter in trying to conceal it. To conceal a matter means to hide it. David's goal was to hide the sin, while trying to get Bathsheba's husband to fall into a deceptive trap. When it did not work, David plotted to have the man murdered. During this time, David appeared blinded to the deceptive ways in which he was treading.

David's ways of sin are typical. Sin has the ability to cause a person to walk in indifference to personal rebellion, while judging it or ignoring it in others, as happened in the case of David's older son, Amnon, when he raped David's daughter Tamar. David's sin had robbed him of real authority to address his son's sin.

The delusion of sin can also set a person on a pinnacle of self-righteousness or fake nobility, such as it did in the case of David's son Absalom who tried to take over the kingdom of Israel. It victimizes those who are innocently entangled in its web as it did in the case of Bathsheba's husband. It bruises and wounds the spirits and hearts of people, causing anger, resentment, and unforgiveness, especially when the consequences of it come to fruition as it did for all of Israel when King David almost lost the kingdom to his rebellious, bitter son. Sin claims every aspect of a person's life. Everyone becomes a victim of sin as David's daughter was, as well as a justifier or enforcer of wrong attitudes and ways as we see in his son Absalom. No one will be spared from its far-reaching tentacles, escape its entangling web of hurts and lies, or avoid tasting one of its various forms of destruction.

It is vital that each person recognizes his or her personal sins, and then repents, confesses, and begins to walk contrary to its ways. This is the only way that a person can be set free from its tentacles, loosed from its web of death, and overcome its claims and destruction in his or her life.

To recognize and overcome personal sin, one must understand how it entangles people. Once again, its greatest companion is deception. Deception is a form of darkness that blinds people to the devastation or consequences of their own personal way.[1] Man's heart is the origin of this deception. Jeremiah 17:9 confirms this, "The he is deceitful above all things, and desperately wicked: who can know it?"

Sadly, most people think they know their heart. They believe their heart to be honest and sincere. However, King David had a sense of the real condition of his heart when he asked God to search his heart in Psalm 139:23. In his famous prayer of repentance in Psalm 51:10 after his grave sin with Bathsheba, he asked the Lord to create in him a clean heart.

Unlike David, most people do not realize that their hearts can prove to be very rebellious. Rebellious hearts are treacherous. They are fickle in their commitments, self-serving in their motives, unpredictable in their way of thinking, and untrustworthy in their intentions. Ultimately, such hearts are wicked. This is why God must give people a new heart. There cannot be rehabilitation of the old heart, for genuine life can only come from a new heart or creation.[2]

A deceitful, wicked heart creates a real dilemma. Proverbs 4:23 states, "Keep thy heart with all diligence for out of it are the issues of life." The very essence or quality of a person's life is determined by his or her heart condition. Today, many people claim their lives are lacking or

---

[1] Proverbs 14:12

[2] Ezekiel 36:26-27; 2 Corinthians 5:17

do not make sense. This attitude often reveals that their hearts have remained unchallenged and unchanged. They continue to walk in deceitfulness and wickedness. Such a condition shows that these people have failed to keep their heart with all diligence.

Keeping the heart with all diligence implies guarding, protecting, and obeying.[3] Guarding something implies clinging to that which is righteous. Protecting is overseeing what you have that is acceptable to God. Obedience is in relationship to God's Word and will. Obeying God is the real source of guarding and protecting the things of God. Without obedience and authority, discernment will be missing, while deception will not be far behind.

A good example of a person who failed to guard, protect, and keep what God had entrusted to him was Adam. He was told to dress and keep the garden in Genesis 2:15. It is important to note that the garden was a perfect environment. Therefore, one must wonder in what way he had to guard the garden. The perfection of the garden rested mainly with man maintaining a right environment to ensure his relationship with God. However, Adam let Satan into the garden. When Satan came in so did temptation, deception, and rebellion. Today people are also failing to guard and keep the environments of their inward man, as well as their homes. As a result, there is much temptation to overcome, deception to wade through, and rebellion to confront.

The deception of the heart is clearly manifested in various ways. Hebrews 3:8-15 gives a clear picture of its manifestation. The first manifestation is a hardened heart. "Hard" in this text points to stubborn.[4] Stubborn is more of an obstinate attitude towards authority. It can be unteachable and unreasonable towards spiritual correction. This type of heart has become hardened by temptation that has not been properly subdued through righteousness. Temptation points to a form of discipline.[5] Discipline exposes a person's ways. Therefore, temptation forces an individual to make decisions about his or her perception in regards to a matter, his or her motive towards it, and the handling of it.

The decision will be simple. It comes down to whether the individual is going to insist on his or her way or submit to God. An unwillingness to submit to God is when the clever deception of sin begins to entangle the person into its deadly web. We can observe this in David's sin with Bathsheba. It is easy to follow his digression into total deception to the point that he was even able to justify having an honorable man killed to hide his wretched sin.

An individual can deny, ignore, or justify personal sin. This type of approach to sin does away with the personal reality of sin, making a person indifferent to the extent of his or her deeds. A deceptive approach

---

[3] Strong's Exhaustive Concordance #5341

[4] Ibid # 4645

[5] Ibid #3986

of sin towards any point of accountability, such as God's Law, will make a person an exception to either the rule of honoring the Law, or a victim of unfair circumstances or demands. Ultimately, sin's deception judges God as unfair, inept of possessing true understanding about a situation, or unrealistic.

This brings us to the next manifestation of a hard heart: that of erring in the heart. It is one thing for the heart to be deceptive and wicked, but another matter to err in it. This means that one has wandered from the truth. God said of David in 2 Samuel 12:9 that his sinful actions in regard to Bathsheba showed that he had actually despised the commandment of the Lord.

The Scripture verses in Hebrew 3 were in regard to Israel in the wilderness. The children of Israel experienced God in His power, but because they did not personally know Him, they did not grasp His ways. Such a state revealed their ignorance towards God. Ignorance of this nature is a form of spiritual darkness.

Ignorance leads to disobedience. Disobedience is a product of unbelief. Unbelief will always depart from the living God into the paths of darkness and spiritual ruin. This darkness is a form of personal justification towards sin that causes the heart to become stubborn before God.

A stubborn heart becomes more hardened by the deceitfulness of sin. It becomes dull in hearing, sluggish in response, and unreasonable in correction. Each time it refuses to respond to God and His ways, it becomes more obstinate towards God and that which is right. There is only one way to avoid a stubborn heart and that is to humbly walk before your God and obey Him. By knowing His character, you will know how to obey Him. Godly obedience keeps the heart pliable to God as He changes its focus and desires towards the different issues regarding life.

We know that King David experienced many difficult challenges in his life. He did know the sweetness of victory, but he also knew the bitterness of betrayal, the sorrow of loss, the despair of failure, and the darkness of his own heart. He made this statement about how he actually disciplined the affections and preferences of his own heart, "I have set the LORD always before me; because he is at my right hand, I shall not be moved. Therefore my heart is glad, and my glory rejoiceth; my flesh also shall rest in hope" (Psalm 16:8-9).

Godly obedience is also a daily exercise. It operates in the present, while unbelief operates in the past by clinging to present excuses. Temptation, on the other hand, operates according to the illusive hopes of the future by ignoring or denying the present challenges. Hebrews 3:8 instructs us not to harden our hearts in the day of temptation. Hebrews 3:15 says, "While it is said, Today if ye will hear his voice, harden not your hearts, as in the provocation." This is why exhortation for compliance to God's will, will embrace the present. To fail to obey today means the heart will quickly become stubborn in its temptation as to the various traps of sin, and will ultimately display unbelief in its conduct.

It is vital that people do what is right and acceptable when presented with the choices. An unregenerate heart is primed by deception and bent on wickedness. Discipline that steps on the scene in times of temptation makes the choices black and white. 1 Corinthians 10:13 says, "There hath no temptation taken you but such as is common to man; but God is faithful, who will not suffer you to be tempted above that ye are able, but will, with the temptation also make a way to escape, that ye may be able to bear it."

The way of escape can become shrouded by pride that believes it will successfully stand.[6] Once again, we must realistically consider how personal pride is one of the many idols that blind man to his vulnerable state brought on by sin. In simplicity, 1 Corinthians 13:14 defines the way out of temptation, "Wherefore, my dearly beloved, flee from idolatry."

Idolatry causes spiritual darkness. It is the foundation of all sins. It declares that something is greater or more worthy than God. Reliance on such idols will set people up to believe that the temptation does not exist or it will be easily overcome. Both scenarios are a product of arrogance that will blind the person from seeing his or her need to escape. After all, to escape, you must recognize the necessity for it and begin looking for a way out.

Escape can involve a small window of opportunity. Once the window of opportunity passes, there is no hope of escaping the consequences of disobedience. For King David his small window of opportunity came when the prophet exposed his sins. If David had refused to repent at that moment, his heart would have hardened, and he would have gone into some type of delusion. We see the window of opportunity quickly disappearing in the case of the people who lived during the days of Noah and the flood, Israel in the wilderness, and the five foolish virgins.[7]

Hebrews 3:11 states, "So I sware in my wrath, they shall not enter into my rest." Rest only occurs when one's relationship is right with God. Rest to the children of Israel was the Promised Land, but rest for Christians is the person of Jesus Christ. He said as much in Matthew 11:28-29, "Come unto me, all ye that labour and are heavy laden, and I will give you rest. Take my yoke upon you, and learn of me; for I am meek and lowly in heart: and ye shall find rest unto your souls."

Hebrews 3:14 says, "For ye are made partakers of Christ, if we hold the beginning of our confidence stedfast unto the end." Christ is also our bread. We need to partake of his life constantly.[8]

The Apostle Peter made this statement in 2 Peter 1:4 as to what we will partake of to benefit from the life of Jesus, "By which are given unto

---

[6] 1 Corinthians 10:12

[7] Genesis 7:12-16, Numbers 14; Matthew 25:1-13

[8] John 6:35

us exceedingly great and precious promises, that by these ye might be partakers of the divine nature, having escaped the corruption that is in the world through lust."

Jesus is our immovable Rock who serves as our abiding confidence. We cannot be moved from this Rock if we are established on Him and cling to His promises.[9] This relationship with Him will make us steadfast unto the end. Jesus confirmed this confidence with a promise in Matthew 28:18-20,

> All power is given unto me in heaven and in earth. Go ye therefore, and teach all nations, baptizing them in the name of the Father, and of the Son, and of the Holy Ghost: Teaching them to observe all things whatsoever I have commanded you: and, lo, I am with you always, even unto the end of the world.

Are you walking in the ways of an unregenerate heart or in the ways of God? Is truth guiding you or is sin blinding you? Who are you serving: the ways of the flesh or the Lord Jesus Christ? There are only two masters in this world, and the way you are walking will determine which one you are serving.

---

[9] Matthew 7:24-27; 1 Corinthians 10:4

4

THE CORE OF SIN

Sin has various traits. For example, rebellion, ignorance, and delusion constitute a few of these traits. However, the disposition of sin is inspired or motivated by a sin that gets very little attention. This sin represents the essence of the disposition that is subject to sin's reign, as well as lies at the core of all of its traits.

What is the inspiration behind the fallen condition? It is the sin of unbelief. However, the sin of unbelief expresses itself in idolatry. Sin is not rejection of God, but rebellion against His authority. To rebel against His authority implies that the person has other preferences in regards to leadership and servitude.

The scenario of Adam in the Garden of Eden is a good example of the essence of sin. Adam was not opposed to God's presence. Rather, his action of disobedience was a blatant rejection of God's authority in his life. This rejection was not an impulsive action, but a calculated plan. Job 31:33 confirmed this, "If I covered my transgressions as Adam by hiding mine iniquity in my bosom." There is no doubt that Adam understood the implications of his action. He had been toying with it, as well as debating about this blatant disobedience. The final evidence of his heart attitude towards God was when he ate of the tree of the knowledge of good and evil. His action was considered treacherous for he clearly transgressed the covenant he had with God.[1]

Rebellion dethrones God, while disobedience exalts the desired god on the throne. For Adam, his independence was exalted on the throne, while for others it can be anything from material things, religion, leaders, and entertainment to the worldly environment.

This is why the first commandment sets the one true God apart as deserving worship, while the second commandment forbids exaltation and worship of any other gods.[2] One of God's attributes reinforces this point even more: that of jealousy. Exodus 20:5 says, "Thou shalt not bow down thyself to them, nor serve them; for I the LORD thy God am a jealous God, visiting the iniquity of the fathers upon the children unto the third and fourth generation of them that hate me."

---

[1] Genesis 3:6-7; Hosea 6:7

[2] Exodus 20:1-4

When man dethrones God, who or what does he exalt? This brings us to the foundation of idolatry. Man is what is exalted when God is dethroned. Such dethroning is humanism. This is where man becomes deified and God is humanized. For example, most people consider God's attitude about a matter from the premise of their own attitude about it. Of course, God is far greater and higher in His wisdom and understanding about a subject, but once He has been brought down to our level, He has been humanized in our mind to think as we think.

If people are not looking to God to solve problems, they look to man and his abilities to make their worlds right. For example, people look to education, government, diplomacy, or science to solve the many ailing problems of society and this world. This reliance or dependency on man's means to ensure order in people's world always causes disillusionment and anger. The harsh reality is that man cannot solve problems. His attempts to stop the destruction plaguing homes, societies, nations, and the world are nothing more than futile attempts of putting Band-Aids on bleeding arteries. Lives and relationships continue to become casualties as people continue to look towards men in different positions for a solution.

Jeremiah 17:5-6 talks about the consequences of leaning on the arm of the flesh,

> Thus saith the LORD; cursed be the man that trusteth in man, and maketh flesh his arm, and whose heart departeth from the LORD. For he shall be like the heat in the desert, and shall not see when good cometh; but shall inhabit the parched places in the wilderness, in a salt land and not inhabited.

Dependency on man has terrible consequences. This can be seen in the children of Israel. Moses had gone up to Mount Sinai. God was giving him the Law as well as instructions to the tabernacle. The leader's absence created unrest in the camp of Israel. Without Moses, there was no man who seemed capable of approaching Jehovah God.[3] People needed some type of leader or god to give them hope and confidence.

Since Moses was absent, Jehovah God ceased to be obtainable or real. Therefore, Israel needed another god. Did they look to the heavens to call down another god? No, they looked to Aaron to form a god. This god would not frighten them. They could worship it any old way. In so doing, they could soothe their religious conscience, while feeding fleshly appetites without fear of judgment.

The golden calf came out of the vanity of the children of Israel. After all, they donated the gold. This brings us to the reality of idolatry: It represents the unbelief towards the true God, as well as the vanity and superstition of man in his best religious attempts to reach, understand, and control his idea of God. This is why Isaiah 64:6 declares, "But we are all as an unclean thing, and all our righteousnesses are as filthy rags;

---

[3] Exodus 20:18-21; 24:18; 32

and we all do fade as a leaf, and our iniquities, like the wind, have taken us away."

People are like sheep wanting to be comfortably led to the slaughter.[4] This simply means as long as they are kept content, they will follow whatever or whosoever gives the best appearance of serving their purpose right into the slaughterhouse. Contentment of this nature simply makes a person spiritually dull and unaware of the pitfalls.

Cult leaders understand the idolatrous tendencies of people. They recognize that most people want their flesh or religious pride catered to. They want leadership that will feed their egos. They want religious presentations that bring outward discipline, while inwardly remaining comfortable in their sin. Sadly, many end up selling their souls.

What are people looking for in a god? They are looking for a means to have a religious experience without becoming personally accountable for the moral deviation they are justifying and adopting. These people want a leader who will be responsible for their actions as they blindly hide behind him or her when it comes to personal responsibility and judgment.

Aaron knew what the people wanted. He simply provided it. Today, some churches are geared towards people's preferences. In other words, they provide the convenient "gods" in order to draw people into their buildings. Of course, these religious organizations are doing all of this in the name of Jesus. They are keeping people happily deluded and spiritually inept as they provide a terrible mixture. Like the captives who resettled the land of Samaria, after Assyria brought Israel to her knees, they combined the worship of Jehovah God with the worship of pagan gods.[5]

In this ungodly mixture in Samaria, people failed to bring their gods down in order to worship the one true God of heaven. They simply added the one true God to their entourage of present idols. This always brings a false security to people as they cling to this idolatrous mixture. Meanwhile, the warning that has echoed for centuries is often ignored, "But the fearful, and unbelieving, and the abominable, and murders, and whoremongers, and sorcerers, and <u>idolaters</u>, and all liars shall have their part in the lake which burneth with fire and brimstone: which is the second death" (Revelation 21:8). (Emphasis added.)

God put idolatry in this perspective in Isaiah 2:8, "Their land also is full of idols; they worship the work of their own hands, that which their own fingers have made." Idols are nothing more than products of man's own imagination. For example, Aaron constructed the golden calf with his own hands.

The construction of idols begins within the confines of vain imaginations. They are formed by man's attempts to control that which

---

[4] Isaiah 53:6; Romans 8:36

[5] 2 Kings 17:24-41

he worships. Once formed, they are exalted into a place of importance. Importance implies that the person has now given the idol an identity. Most idols have names, purposes, and responsibilities. Without this identity, they would have no meaning or purpose for their existence. They would simply be an object or a meaningless thing.

It is man that gives his particular idol meaning and purpose. He can give his idol everything but life. There is only one God who is alive. The true God of heaven not only lives, but He is the One who gives life to those who worship Him. What a contrast!

We see Aaron exalting the golden calf and giving it identity. He exalts it by making an altar for it. The altar is a place of worship. Aaron then makes a proclamation in Exodus 32:5 about this idol, giving it identity by associating it with Jehovah God. "And when Aaron saw it, he built an altar before it; and Aaron made a proclamation and said, To morrow is a feast to the LORD." Aaron did not reject Jehovah God, he simply encouraged a spiritual mixture in Israel where God was added on to the religious exercise for credibility.

The children of Israel were quick to accept this silent god in place of the dreadful God of Sinai. They worshipped this false god according to their fleshly terms. There was no sign of holiness coming from this idol that would cause them to fear death and judgment. There was no voice that would make them tremble. There was no eye that would give way to disapproval. This golden idol created a different atmosphere and reality for Israel that was tolerable to their fleshly desires.

Idolatry creates another reality outside of the unchangeable reality of the God of heaven. The fact that idols are a product of imaginations reveals how insignificant they are in light of what is eternal and glorious. This is brought out in the temptations of both Eve and Jesus. These two individuals were tempted in the same way. Eve was being enticed by the fruit, while Jesus was being tempted with bread. Jesus was being tempted to prove Himself as the Son of God, while Eve was being tempted with the possibility of being as God. The tree was pleasant to Eve's eyes, while Satan presented all the beautiful kingdoms of the world to Jesus; that is if He would just bow down and worship him.[6]

Each temptation exalted a different god. The fruit or bread would have made the appetites of the flesh god. Proving or exalting self, exalts pride or the essence of self, while the temptation of the eyes will exalt something as god. These three temptations are tied into the world. When you submit to the temptations of the world, you are submitting to the god of the world, Satan.[7] Keep in mind that the ultimate goal of Satan was to get both Eve and Jesus to worship him by submitting to his temptations. Sadly, Eve did bow down, but Jesus refuted Satan's temptation with the

---

[6] Genesis 3:5-6; Matthew 4:1-11

[7] 2 Corinthians 4:3-4; 1 John 2:15-16

Word. "Get thee hence, Satan: for it is written, Thou shalt worship the Lord thy God, and him only shalt thou serve" (Matthew 4:10).

The author of Hebrews was able to make this powerful declaration because of Jesus' response to each temptation, "For we have not an high priest which cannot be touched with the feeling of our infirmities: but was in all points tempted like as we are, yet without sin" (Hebrews 4:15).

Since the power of an idol has more to do with imagination than with a visible object, the Apostle Paul's words come to life in 2 Corinthians 10:4-5,

> (For the weapons of our warfare are not carnal, but mighty through God to the pulling down of strongholds), Casting down imaginations, and every high thing that exalteth itself against the knowledge of God, and bringing into captivity every thought to the obedience of Christ.

People exalt idols in their minds. This is where the idol's power, deception, and identity lie. These idols serve as a different god by undermining God's true character. God, who represents truth, is exchanged for a figment of a person's imagination. Therefore, idolatry simply rides the high waves of fantasy and delusion. In the end, people exalt another Jesus, as they come under a different spirit, and embrace a different gospel.[8] This type of exaltation serves as an open door to demonic oppression.

The children of Israel could offer sacrifices, dance in a sensual manner, and indulge the flesh before this silent idol. What many of them failed to recognize is that sacrifices had to do with sin. Without proper recognition and accountability, there was no purpose for such sacrifices.

Christians' hearts serve as their altars. To accept the sacrifice of Christ, they must become identified through accountability and confession of personal sin. For, where there is no accountability, there will be no repentance or change. Without identity to a new life, there is no need for the sacrifice of Jesus, making His offering on the cross seem in vain. And, if a religious person remains indifferent about personal sin, his or her heart will become a neglected altar, like the altar of God in Israel in 1 Kings 18.

Because of Solomon idolatrous sins, Israel split into two separate kingdoms. Ten tribes became known as Israel, while the tribe of Judah and Benjamin became known as Judah. The first king of Israel, Jeroboam, feared that he would lose his authority over his particular kingdom of Israel if the children of Israel traveled to Jerusalem to worship God. To prevent this possibility, he erected an idolatrous altar at Bethel.[9] This started Israel into blatant idolatry until its fall as a nation, and the dispersion of its people.

---

[8] 2 Corinthians 11:1-3

[9] 1 Kings 12:26-30

It was in this setting of idolatry that the prophet Elijah stepped onto the scene at Mount Carmel in 1 Kings 18. The broken-down altar of God revealed the spiritual condition of Israel. Jehovah God was still represented in Israel's midst, but the condition of His altar showed the people's preference for their idols. The altar of God will always be neglected when idolatry exists.

Christians must keep this harsh reality before them. Idolatry makes religious exercise an outward show of conformity, while Christianity reveals itself through a transformed life. In idolatry, the heart remains untouched, while in Christianity the heart is replaced with a new heart to become an acceptable altar before God.[10] Elijah illustrated this concept.

Although Elijah repaired the altar of God at Carmel, it was not enough. The old altar represented the tragedy that the real God of heaven was not preferred or considered preeminent in Israel. Idols that had no means to save or change lives were exalted. Therefore, the altar of God was neglected and clearly defiled by idolatry.

After repairing the old, neglected altar of Jehovah God, the prophet constructed a new altar. It was on the new altar that Elijah offered a sacrifice. He was making a point that the reality of God must be clearly reestablished after His altars have been defiled. It is only from a new altar that God can accept sacrifices. Likewise, it is only from the altar of a new heart that Christians are able to present their lives as a living sacrifice.[11] After all, it is the reality of God that gives both the altar and the sacrifice the right identity.

Check out your altar. Can you find evidence of tears of repentance that have washed away the dust from off the altar of your heart? Could you find signs of where you offered your life to God out of devotion and love? Would your altar show sacrifices of praises that have reached the ears of God, and as a result the fragrance of Christ surrounds it?[12]

At the altar of idols, people can also feast on the world and the lust of the flesh in the name of religion without conviction. We see this in the children of Israel's enthusiasm with their new god. They got up early in the morning to pursue this new god. The harsh reality is that you will not find slugs at the altars of idols. Can we say the same about the Christians' altars? Do we rise up early to commune with God, partake of His Word, and enjoy His presence?[13]

It is not unusual for religious people to pursue the things of the world with zealous enthusiasm, but display complacency and apathy towards their lives with God. They can find time to play before or with idols, but they cannot find time to pursue and commune with God on a consistent

---

[10] Ezekiel 36:26-27

[11] Romans 12:1-2

[12] 2 Corinthians 2:15-16

[13] Psalm 63:1-2

basis. In fact, most cult members show more dedication to their idols than Christians do to God.

Idolatry will stop the work of God. Moses had been in the presence of God for forty days and nights receiving instructions. God commanded Moses to return to the camp, because Israel had resorted to idolatry. By the time Moses returned, Israel had been defiled by this sin. It had caused these people to turn aside from the true God, and begin to walk down the broad path of destruction.[14] Sadly, idolatry becomes a contagious disease that engulfs all who have not personally been established on the immovable Rock of God.

As idolatry stirs up the people into a fleshly frenzy, it begins sucking the life of God out of the midst of the people. In other words, it quenches the Spirit of God. This leaves a spiritual vacuum. This empty vacuum is proof that idolatry is of the earth, foolish in nature, and a wide-open pathway to hell.

How could people turn from a Living God to embrace an object that is dead and hides the face of hell? The answer lies in the spiritual condition of being stiff-necked. Those who are stiff-necked refuse to humble self, agree with God's judgment on their sins and idols, repent, and bow before the true God of heaven. Such a response reveals that the essence of man is that he is rebellious in his heart, arrogant in his mind, and deluded about personal goodness and wisdom.

But, praise God! In spite of our rebellion, God desires to reason with each of us about personal sin. This is contrary to idols that have no reasoning power. Isaiah 1:18 brings out the desire of God to reason with us, "Come now, and let us reason together, saith the LORD: though your sins be as scarlet, they shall be as white as snow, though they be red like crimson, they shall be as wool!"

God wants to reason about our sin on the basis of His righteousness. He wants to bring a contrast between vain, useless idols and the reality of His life, power, and majesty. God wants to turn from wrath and show people mercy and grace. The key is to get each of us to completely turn from our idols back to the one true God. Ultimately, people must turn and face Jesus who died on the cross as our substitute.

Jesus Christ gave us the example of turning from that which is the norm, and embrace something greater than self. Jesus left heaven, gave way to the will of the Father, and died on the cross so we could have life. Likewise, we need to turn from our stiff-necked ways to embrace this new life.

If people fail to turn away from their idols to God, they will break the Law and heart of God, resulting in judgment. We have this example when Moses came down from Mount Sinai and encountered the children

---

[14] Proverbs 14:12; Matthew 7:13-14

of Israel's idolatry. He threw down the tablets containing the commandments, breaking them.[15]

Man's sins crushed Jesus, whips broke His skin, beatings bruised His body, and nails fastened Him against the cross. However, what stands out in the end is that Jesus' heart was broken on the cross, just as Moses had broken the tablets. Sadly, man continues to remain blind to his personal preference for and practice of idolatry, breaking his fellowship with God.

When confronted by Moses concerning the idolatry in the camp, Aaron stated that the sin happened because of the mischief of the people.[16] Aaron's flimsy cover-up pointed to treachery and conniving that takes place when idolatry is present. It was true that the golden calf exposed the treachery of the children of Israel. However, conniving occurs when people avoid facing the grave reality and consequences of their idolatry, and end up going with their preferences.

Aaron lied about his part in the idolatry. Idolatry is a lie. The lie goes back to the Garden of Eden that man can be like God and control his life and reality. The reality of idolatry is that it leads to and ends in judgment and consequences. This was brought out in Exodus 32:33, "Whosoever hath sinned against me, him will I blot out of my book." God backed up this judgment by sending a plague among the people of Israel.[17]

Are you in idolatry? Do you have a mixture? If your answer is yes, the true God of heaven desires to reason with you, in order to cleanse and save you from future consequences and judgment.

---

[15] Exodus 32:19

[16] Exodus 32:22-23

[17] Genesis 3:5; Exodus 32:35

5

AVENUES OF SIN

We have been considering the essence of sin. The nature of sin is deceptive, and the base of it is idolatrous. Deception includes such things as lies and ignorance. Ignorance in the religious realm is also known as superstition that operates in unbelief. When you combine ignorance with idolatry, you end up with darkness consuming the soul.

Sin works in every area of people's lives. There is the effect of sin on man, which is death. We see this in the world today. A growing number of young people are fascinated with death as they give way to the workings of death upon their minds and hearts such as witchcraft, gangs, and indifference. These young people seem to be wandering endlessly since they have no initiative to find life, let alone take responsibilities for the type of life they are developing. They walk in the ways of death, and are consumed by its endless darkness of selfishness, hopeless, and despair.

Such workings of death are operating freely through the influence of sin on man through his fleshly appetites. There is no end to how the things of the flesh are enlarged to embrace the complete, utter darkness of ruin and destruction. There is also the ongoing reality that sin abounds in the world in which we live. Therefore, there is no way of avoiding and confronting the issue of sin upon our lives and in our homes and churches. It will break tender hearts, enslave the wills of the innocent, seduce the fickle affections of the ignorant, bruise the thoughts of the pure, and cause such people to walk in the darkness of condemnation,

As you study the makeup of sin, you can begin to see how Satan is able to get a foothold into man's soul. He can only work in darkness. He is called the father of lies.[1] Lies subtly rob a person of faith, kill his or her spiritual discernment, and set him or her up for spiritual destruction. These lies are often half-truths.

Half-truths cause people to look inward at self, rather than upward at Jesus, who is the only source of absolute truth. As they look at self to resolve an issue, they see the possibilities of these half-truths as being true. Keep in mind Satan is always trying to change our reality. He puts pressure on us to change our reality by trying to change, manipulate, or control others or circumstances.

---

[1] John 8:44

These half-truths involve introspection, which often produces condemnation, rather than self-examination that allows for the conviction of the Holy Spirit. The Word clearly instructs people to examine themselves.[2] Such evaluation points to examining the fruits of their lives, not looking inward to gain details as to why a fiasco is occurring. Obviously, such problems will always lead back to the fallen state of man.

Introspection causes depression or delusion or both. In spite of what the Word of God declares about the condition of man, he is, nevertheless, shocked to see the depth of his depravity. Hopelessness begins to invade his soul for he cannot change his condition, no matter how good he tries to be. If he is honest with himself, he will come into a place of agreement with God about his state: that his best is filthy rags before a holy God.[3] There are no redeemable qualities in him.

It is at the point of recognizing the desperation of one's state that introspection can cause such an individual to go into self-delusion, making the work of redemption seem too unobtainable. In such a state God's work on the cross appears that it cannot reach through such darkness; therefore, the person must somehow rise to the occasion by first cleaning up his or her act. At such times, grace becomes a source of mockery, rather than an actual act of God to save man from his hopeless, wretched condition.

Personal examination that takes place in light of the redemption of Christ will also bring a sense of complete depravity; but on the other hand, it will also confidently stand in the glorious hope of Jesus Christ through faith in His redemption. Such a person knows that grace can abound through righteousness, forgiveness is as close as a heart-felt whisper, and deliverance is at hand.

Introspection, no matter how small or great, can become the door through which Satan sends his destructive lies. These lies result in unbelief, struggle, and confusion. This is where idolatry can enter the scene. In the midst of lies, people demote God in their hopelessness, while erecting another god to replace Him. The demotion of God is often done under the guise of fake nobility.

This brings us to the avenues of sin. These openings allow sin to reign with a vengeance. There are three such avenues that allow the work of sin and its consequences to have their way. The first avenue is *temptation*. We have somewhat considered temptation already, but it is vital we have a clear picture of it. Temptation points to the testing of the spirit or the character of a person. Any test can lead to failure and discipline. The one area that temptation exposes in a person's character is his or her level of pride. In the case of King David's adultery, it proved that he was capable of falling into all the traps of sin. His eyes served as

---

[2] Matthew 7:15-16; 1 Corinthians 11:28; 2 Corinthians 13:5

[3] Isaiah 64:6

an avenue of temptation that gave way to lust, his flesh became the avenue in which to experience and partake of sin, and his pride gave him the right to justify his actions.

Pride is an open door to all temptation. It is what often sets a person up to either toy with temptation or fall into it. The Bible makes this clear. 1 Corinthians 10:13 gives us this insight and promise about temptation, "There hath no temptation taken you but such as is common to man: but God is faithful, who will not suffer you to be tempted above that ye are able; but will with the temptation also make a way to escape, that ye may be able to bear it."

Many Christians claim this promise, but fail to understand the source behind such temptation. The clue to the source of temptation is found in the previous scripture verse, "Wherefore let him that thinketh he standeth take heed lest he fall" (1 Corinthians 10:12).

1 Corinthians 10:13 tells us that the temptation that overtakes any person is common. However, pride makes people feel as if they are an exception to the rule when it comes to a enticing situation. This is a lie, but many conveniently buy the lie because they either cannot imagine falling into what they consider a "harmless" trap, or they perceive that their temptation or experience is worse than others, justifying their fall. Both examples are called elitism. Elitism is an attitude of pride that allows a person to become a justified victim in sin, which causes isolation.

Proverbs 16:18 states, "Pride goeth before destruction, and an haughty spirit before a fall." "Haughty" in this verse implies divided.[4] When pride reigns, it brings division, isolates, and then destroys. Whenever there is division, it points to idolatry.

Once again, we must remember that our personal pride is an idol. It exalts the personal strength, abilities, or intelligence of people. This idol sets unsuspecting individuals up to fall into greater idolatry, as it confuses or justifies away moral compromise or deviance. It has the ability to make people feel infallible, while blinding them to the impending destruction. It tempts individuals to either ignore temptation or play with it. For example, a person will perceive him or herself as having the ability to outwit temptation. Ultimately, such a person will put God to a foolish test, as he or she ventures too close to the snares of Satan. Without realizing the danger, he or she will walk right into his trap.

One of Satan's most successful traps is fornication. This trap has ensnared many unmarried couples. I know of couples who did not intend to fall into the trap, but they did not recognize that our culture's practice of dating is a breeding ground in which this trap can easily be set. Couples start out innocently enjoying each other's company. However, if that enjoyment begins to explore greater avenues in a physical and emotional way, it will open the door that allows their affections to turn into

[4] Strong's Exhaustive Concordance of the Bible; #1361 & 1363

passions that are set aflame with overwhelming desire. By this time they are no longer in control of their youthful lusts, they are now riding the incredible wave of desire. Although the wave will crash against the harsh shores of reality of guilt and condemnation, the momentum cannot be stopped. To avoid the momentum created by youthful lusts, the Apostle Paul in 2 Timothy 2:22 instructed people to flee them by changing the direction of their momentum and focus.

James 11:13 states, "Blessed is the man that endureth temptation; for when he is tried he shall receive the crown of life, which the Lord hath promised to them that love him." A person must patiently bear, remain steady, and persevere through temptation, but not toy with it. Ultimately, people's arrogance sets them up to toy with the snares of Satan, only to fall prey to them.

Pride also blinds people to the snares of Satan. This type of pride includes the pride of innocence and that which is clothed in fake nobility. The pride of innocence enjoys its ignorance, as it blindly walks in a type of fantasy towards Satan's snares. It enjoys its naiveté because it never has to take accountability and become mature. Sadly, when this type of pride falls into Satan's trap, it turns into self-pity.

The pride that is clothed in fake nobility walks in deception about its motives. This type of pride operates in a couple of ways. It can become so focused on doing what is right that the person walks around in fear that keeps him or her in a narrow world. This narrow world fears anything that is contrary to its comfort zones. I once ministered to a woman who possessed such fear. She had come out of a cult, and she was afraid of being deceived again. However, she judged everything according to fear, rather than discern according to the Spirit. In trying to help her confront her fear, she just gave way to it. Her fear eventually turned into anger and suspicion towards me.

Sadly, this woman remained enslaved to her fear, rather than experiencing spiritual maturity that comes from walking by faith in the Spirit, and embracing truth that supersedes the enslaving limitations of fear. She could only judge according to personal knowledge, rather than personally discern the spirit, causing her ultimately to reject the very truth that would bring proper authority, love, and clarity to her spiritual life.

The other role in which this type of pride operates is that of the hero. For example, I knew of a woman who went to a religious, New Age meeting to protect a member of her family from deception. She had a high opinion of her ability to discern. She clearly fell into Satan's snare, because she came back with another spirit.

Pride creates blatant weakness in a person's disposition. The key is to recognize our natural tendency to be set up by it. My personal understanding about my pride makes me sober about the weakness it causes in my character. I question my motives and become leery of my intentions. It has been this understanding of the deception and blindness of my pride that has often caused me to fling myself upon the mercy of

God. In other words, I do not con myself about my weak, susceptible character. The Apostle Paul put it this way in Romans 12:3, "For I say, through the grace given unto me, to every man that is among you, not to think of himself more highly than he ought to think; but to think soberly, according as God hath dealt to every man the measure of faith."

To close the door of pride, people must do what 1 Corinthians 10:14 commands, "Wherefore, my dearly beloved, flee from idolatry." A person endures temptation when he or she flees all idols and looks to God. As a person looks to God, He will provide a way out of it.

The Flesh

As already mentioned, the second avenue through which sin operates is the *flesh.* Christians must *endure* temptation, and make sure that Satan is not *enticing* them by way of their flesh. The Bible states that people must flee from the enticements that would be used to ensnare the flesh into Satan's traps. James 1:13-15 gives us insight into this subject,

> Let no man say when he is tempted, I am tempted of God: for God cannot be tempted with evil, neither tempteth he any man: but every man is tempted, when he is drawn away of his own lust, and enticed. Then when lust hath conceived, it bringeth forth sin: and sin, when it is finished, bringeth forth death.

The flesh is the open door to the world. It is driven by carnal appetites, and will only pursue that which brings it pleasure. It wants to be adored, pampered, and fed. It becomes god, as it embraces the different lies and the idols of the world to satisfy its desires. The flesh demands worship, as it feeds its lust, encourages disobedience as it justifies wicked practices, and offers a temporary happiness in place of moral responsibilities for a fleeting moment of satisfaction.

The flesh creates a destructive cycle. It begins at the point where responsibility is shifted from personal conduct to another source. For example, a person will perceive that his or her conduct is God's fault, because He allowed temptation that was too great to overcome him or her. This form of deception rejects the concept of repentance. Yet, Jesus was very clear about the importance of personal repentance in Luke 13:3, "I tell you, Nay: but, except ye repent, ye shall all likewise perish."

Personal justification is a matter of the heart. It is an expression of the desires of the heart. The reality is that man desires to experience the works of the flesh. He simply looks around to find a scapegoat to justify or cover up these personal desires.

In Romans 1:24, the Apostle Paul tells us what happens when man insists on the ways of the flesh, "Wherefore God also gave them up to uncleanness through the lusts of their own hearts, to dishonour their own bodies between themselves." This shows that God simply gives people over to that which entices them. It is a form of judgment.

Once the deception sets in, the means of discipline are no longer in place to bring a reality check. The truths of God become nothing more than unrealistic, indifferent religious burdens of a harsh God, who does not seem to understand or care about the plight of man. This allows the person to give way to fleshly lust without guilt and conviction.

At this point, lust is given rights, conceiving the fruits and consequences of the flesh. The meaning of conception in this text points to capture. The person is literally held captive by the tentacles of their lusts. This is where spirits of perversion and lust enter the scene to enlarge appetites. These appetites end in addictions that will drive and control people.

It is easy to observe the path of sin in the lives of those who struggle from some type of addiction. Sadly, I witnessed many such people when I was involved in jail ministry. One woman, who was just brought in for drunk driving, was suffering from the withdrawal effects of her addiction. As she sat there shaking, I asked her about her life. She admitted she had lost everything including the custody and respect of her two children. She was asked how she got involved in drinking in the first place. Her answer was simple, but it also revealed volumes about how sin entices and enslaves. She had started drinking to receive acceptance from her peers.

Addictive or enlarged appetites cause the natural use or the needs or desires of the flesh to become obsessive. The lust of the flesh begins to operate against the natural order. Such abnormality brings people into a frightening world of slavery and hopelessness. These lusts begin to burn within these individuals, becoming relentless gods. Often the pleasure is not in the satisfying of these lusts, but in the possibilities or imaginations that surround them. However, fulfillment of these lusts ends in emptiness and shame. When you talk to those who are addicted to pornography, they admit that the estimation of the type of expectation and pleasure that such perversion would possibly bring occurs in the imagination. This is why the Bible is clear that as a man thinks, that is who he becomes. However, every fleshly pursuit leads to death.

Death also occurs when people do not develop the ability to relate to their environment realistically. Individuals who function according to this type of fleshly existence are in a survival mode. They have no consensus of anything outside of their self-centered tomb. They cannot properly interact to maintain relationships, and they become deadened to the reality around them. They end up hating their existence, because the god of flesh now owns them. They have given up all of their rights to this tyrant, and the consequence of death is now eating away at them like maggots on a corpse.

Death, for such survivors, begins to change their perception of life. They are not only dead to a healthy existence in which they could enjoy life, but they remain dead to God. They have given in to the lies and snares of Satan. They have justified their conduct, and made their hearts hard towards truth. Delusion has dulled their minds. As a result, they are unable to retain the knowledge of God. This means that God has given them over to a reprobate mind.[5]

A reprobate mind implies that the conscience has been seared towards righteousness. Such people will fill up their minds and lives with wickedness. They will call good evil, and evil good. They might have some recollection that judgment and death await them, but they choose to not care, as they give way to the temporary pleasures of the flesh and the world.[6]

The Bible talks about the works and consequences of the flesh in Romans 1:24-32 and Galatians 5:19-21. Even though I described the extreme manifestations and consequences of the flesh, any subjection to it, even on a minor basis, leaves people desensitized to its destructive tentacles. It serves as an open door to the world, and an invitation for the god of this world to come in and toy with these individuals.

The Word of God clearly gives us two steps to ensure that the flesh remains in the proper perspective. The first way to overcome the flesh has to do with what we pursue or follow. Once again, we need to remember the Apostle Paul's instructions in 2 Timothy 2:22, "Flee also youthful lusts: but follow righteousness, faith, charity, peace, with them that call on the Lord out of a pure heart." People must flee the enticements of the flesh, regardless of how normal they may seem. It is vital that they do not toy with them, but choose to follow that which is godly. This means that they will be walking in the Spirit.

Galatians 5:16 makes this statement, "This I say then, Walk in the Spirit, And ye shall not fulfill the lust of the flesh." Walking in the Spirit means that you are giving way to the Holy Spirit. As individuals give way to the Holy Spirit, He will work the disposition of Christ in them.

Romans 13:14 says, "But put ye on the Lord Jesus Christ, and make not provision for the flesh, to fulfil the lusts thereof." You actually take on the attitude of Jesus towards all matters: that of meekness.[7]

This work of the Spirit also involves self-denial and application of the cross. When self is out of the way, it actually makes a person pliable to the work of the Spirit. However, if self remains intact, there is always a war.[8] If the individual comes under another spirit, he or she will display hardness. At this point, isolation and speculation begin to invade the soul, causing division in the person's relationship with God and other saints.

There was a man that was very fleshly in his pursuits. His real desire was to possess the world. As God's Word began to challenge his fleshly preferences and his worldly attitude, the war between his flesh and the

---

[5] Romans 1:26-28

[6] Romans 1:32; 1 Timothy 4:2

[7] Matthew 11:28-30

[8] Galatians 5:17

Spirit of truth accelerated. He knew in his spirit what the right decision was, but he was not willing to give up the so-called "benefits" that the flesh afforded him and the world offered him. Eventually, he became angry and hardened by the war and the challenge. In the end, he simply gave way to the flesh. No doubt, the war is over for this man, but what is left is nothing but emptiness that surely mocks his foolishness to choose the ways of death to the ways of life found in Christ Jesus.

The life that is established in a person who walks by the Spirit, clearly places him or her under the law of the Spirit of the life of Jesus. However, those who walk according to the flesh are subject to the law of sin and death. They already stand judged and condemned.[9]

Do you walk according to the Spirit or your flesh? Your fruits will tell on you.

The World

The final avenue is the world. The Apostle John said this about the world in 1 John 2:16, "For all that is in the world, the lust of the flesh, and the lust of the eyes, and the pride of life, is not of the Father, but is of the world." This scripture verse shows us that the world is designed to exalt pride, entice the flesh, and stir up fleshly desires. It uses the entrance of the mind, eyes, and ears to honor, entice, and to influence. The world in its philosophies erects various idols that can tempt the pride of man. Due to the various false promises of happiness and success it offers, a variety of appetites can be enticed, leading a person into a world of sensual, but temporary, pleasure.[10] And, last of all, it is clothed in a false standard of beauty that appears glorious to the physical eye.

The world holds much power to entangle its victims. After all, it also possesses what people need to function in each present age. There is a fine line between securing that which is necessary, and pursuing the pleasure of the world that is nothing more than idolatrous. The Word of God reminds us that the cares of the world can choke out the things of God.[11]

Therefore, we must understand the main door of temptation to the world. It lies at the point of a person's affections. The Apostle Paul referred to this in 2 Timothy 2:3-4, "Thou therefore endure hardness, as a good soldier of Jesus Christ. No man that warreth entangleth himself with the affairs of this life; that he may please him who hath chosen him to be a soldier"

Wrong affections can cause a Christian to have divided loyalties. This will make him or her ineffective. This is why the Apostle Paul gave

---

[9] Romans 8:1-2

[10] 1 John 2:17

[11] Matthew 13:22

this instruction in Colossians 3:2, "Set your affection on things above, not on the things on the earth."

Divided loyalties will also cause the war between the flesh and the Spirit to flare out of control. Granted, people may fight the temptation to give in to the world, but if they do not change the direction of their affections, they will eventually return to the world.

Demas is a good example of someone who experienced the reality of Christ through Paul's ministry. He even traveled with Paul on missionary trips, but never changed the direction of his affections. Eventually, he went back to the world. The apostle made mention of this in the last letter he wrote, "For Demas hath forsake me, having loved this present world, and is departed unto Thessalonica..." (2 Timothy 4:10). You can almost hear the sadness and disappointment in Paul. He regarded Demas' action as forsaking him.

How does one deal with the open door of affection towards the world? The Apostle Paul answered that question in Galatians 6:14, "But God forbid that I should glory, save in the cross of our Lord Jesus Christ, by whom the world is crucified unto me, and I unto the world." Paul shows us that a person's affections towards the world must be crucified.

Being crucified to the world is necessary. James 4:4 tells us that if our affections are with the world, we are committing spiritual harlotry that makes us at odds with God. If we have a friendship with the world, it means that we are doomed.

If a person's heart belongs to this world, he or she is subject to the god of this world, Satan. His or her association with it allows Satan to blind him or her to the glorious Gospel.[12] If the Gospel is unable to penetrate a person's spiritual blindness, he or she stands damned for eternity.

What is your relationship with the world? Has it entangled some of your affections?

In Summary

There are various pictures emerging in the first five chapters. For example, we see that the source behind sin is idolatry. Eve was tempted with the concept of being like God, and fell into the trap when she gave way to the appetites of her flesh, the possibilities of her pride, and the attractions of her eyes. Jesus was tempted in the same way by Satan in the wilderness. However, the outcome was different, as He overcame each of Satan's temptations with the Word of God. Consider how the three elements of the world produce idolatry.

---

[12] 2 Corinthians 4:3-6

Flesh:	Something becomes god.
Pride:	Self is exalted as god.
Eyes:	Something is exalted above God.

The avenues of sin have their way of taking something captive. Consider the following:

Temptation/Pride:	Ensnares
Flesh:	Entices
World:	Entangles

As you combine the idolatry with the different forms of entrapment, you will discover the traits and results of sin. They are:

Deception
Division
Destruction
Deadens
Dooms
Damns

Sin covers all the bases of a person's life. It reaches into the far corridors of man's way of thinking, doing, and being. It wreaks havoc at every level of man's life and existence. It is clever, powerful, and effective. Sadly, it claims many victims.

However, there is hope! Sin has one boundary that will stop its destruction. This boundary is found in Romans 5:20, "But where sin abounded, grace did much more abound." We are saved by God's grace through faith that has been clearly put towards God. Therefore, the only limitation to the ongoing consequences of sin is God's grace.

Grace has been cheapened today by presentations that lack the right spirit and perspective. The main point that is missing in cheap grace is repentance that produces a changed life. To experience God's grace, one must stop in his or her sin, turn around and face God in sincere faith, and seek forgiveness of sin and restoration of his or her soul in brokenness. Once a person truly repents, God's grace can reach out and surround him or her. This is how grace abounds in the life of a repentant sinner, regardless of how small or great the sin.

Have you experienced God's grace? If you have, you know the sweetness of victory, as you walk by faith in His authority and power.

6

MENTALITY OF SIN

It is hard to remember that people's ailments and problems can be traced back to sin. Sin is so deceptive and crafty. Its destructive qualities enable people to get cleverly around the guilt and condemnation it causes. They are able to lay personal problems and consequences at the feet of others to avoid accountability. They resort to games to get their godless ways. In their pursuit for personal justification and control outside of Jesus, they perceive themselves as being "okay," regardless of their fruits and the destruction they leave behind.

This brings us to the mentality of sin. People ultimately pay the consequences for their sinful attitudes and deeds.[1] Since most people walk according to the ways of sin, which are darkness and delusion, they automatically give way to the mentality of sin. This mentality insists that the person must come out on top or become a helpless victim in every matter. Either way, these individuals must become the hero because of their godless ways or be considered a victim who stands guiltless in spite of their sinful actions. Therefore, when these individuals reap the true consequences for their wrong actions, they view it as being unfair. This unfairness declares that they are victims, giving them the ammunition to justify ungodly attitudes and actions at the expense of the situation or others. As helpless victims, these individuals are now excused from having to take personal responsibility for their conduct.

There was a woman who had a challenging childhood. She perceived that since no one really cared for her, she would have to watch out for herself. She devised games in which she could play other people in order to survive. Each time she played a person, she viewed it as coming out on top. After all, she had decided that she would never be subject, vulnerable, or emotionally reliant on another person; rather, she would make others need her to the point that they were reliant on her. For some people their relationship with her was parasitic. In her attempt to make others reliant on her, she would almost smother some of them by trying to keep on top of everything.

Her mentality also attracted people who would take advantage of her games by using her. At times she struggled against the bitterness towards the emptiness or betrayals such relationships often left her with.

---

[1] Galatians 6:7-10

Even though she was the one who set up the environment in which people could use and abuse her, she felt like the victim. Tremendous self-pity would rise up in her as she gave way to feeling sorry for herself. Her cycle was destructive, but it clearly showed that her motives were self-serving, while her heart often proved to be hard and indifferent, and her character completely untrustworthy.

The victim mentality is probably one of the most sinister parts of sin's cycle. Obviously, the one characteristic of sin is to keep people from coming to terms with their own fallen, depraved condition. This is why sin takes on the victim mentality. The victim mentality presents itself as a noble, suffering sacrifice, or as being helpless due to unfair circumstances or the unprovoked and unfair actions or attitudes of others. In the first scenario of fake nobility, self is looking for recognition, while in the latter example of the person being the suffering sacrifice, he or she is seeking sympathy and pity in order to be justified, pampered, and exalted.

There is a difference between the victim mentality and being a victim. Every person who has lived will be victimized in his or her journey on earth. After all, this world belongs to Satan. He is a harsh taskmaster. He opposes God's authority and work. His world is made up of various snares that entrap and enslave people into the tentacles of despair and death.

Regardless of the situation, Christians must not give way to this victim mentality. After all, Jesus came to heal every person from the effects of sin, the world, and Satan. Such a healing can only come by way of faith in Jesus. Jesus' healing is complete, which means that Christians are no longer victims, but conquerors or victors. By submitting to Jesus' healing virtue, a person will indeed overcome in every situation in which Christ has His perfect way.

Sadly, we see this victim mentality in those who call themselves Christians. Christians who operate within this mentality subtly insist on being glorified and served. This is contrary to humility and obedience. Such people never get past the influence and reign of the old man who is still subject to his selfish disposition and his fleshly ways. In fact, these people continue to give in to the old man's seduction and enticement. They tack Christ on to their worldly games, they clothe their self-serving ways with a self-righteous cloak, and they cover their treachery with flattery.

Scripture advocates that Christians will have no excuse for failing to overcome. They have been provided the necessary means to ensure victory. Therefore, if a person believes in Jesus, he or she will overcome.[2] The Apostle Peter made this statement, "According as his divine power hath given unto us all things that pertain unto life and

[2] John 16:33; 1 John 5:4-5

godliness, through the knowledge of him that hath called us to glory and virtue" (2 Peter 1:3).

Since Christians have been given the necessary tools that pertain unto life and godliness, they will be without excuse for harboring such an attitude on Judgment Day. Therefore, one must conclude that there are no true victims in the kingdom of God. Individuals, who refuse to overcome in Christ, are those who refuse to be made accountable for their disposition and attitude, thereby, excusing themselves about being losers in their present age

Therefore, Christians need to realize that the notion of being a victim in the Kingdom of God does not represent a state where one is truly being victimized; rather, it is a mentality or mindset that has been developed under the reign of the old man.

It is important to clarify that for a person to be a victim, it must be a present reality, where he or she is helplessly being plagued by overwhelming circumstances. These circumstances involve abuse or disregard of the person's right to common courtesy and decency. Circumstances of this nature do not last forever. Therefore, such things as persecution, irritations, hindrances, or paying consequences for personal actions do not constitute the state of being victimized.

This brings us to another important subject, that of the discomfort and challenges that follow us through life. Suffering for the sake of Christ is a privilege that results in spiritual maturity. It affords each of us, as believers, the opportunity to confirm our words and claims concerning Jesus with godly attitudes and responses. However, worldly irritations and hindrances are a normal reality of life. When these hindrances are turned into a platform where a person becomes a suffering victim due to being uncomfortable, it is nothing more than vain imaginations. When personal consequences are used as a means to present self as a victim, it reveals weak character, irresponsibility, and self-pity. After all, we bring much on ourselves because of vanity, rebellion, and selfishness. Sadly, most people lack the integrity and maturity to take responsibility for their spiritual state; therefore, often giving way to the mentality of sin.

If a Christian gives way to this mentality, he or she is giving way to an evil mindset that is not only unacceptable to God, but is also idolatrous and blasphemous in nature. The reason it is idolatrous is that the mindset will exalt itself over the truth. For example, God's Word proclaims in Romans 8:37, "Nay, in all these things we are more than conquerors through him that loved us." This scripture verse is in relationship to believers being accounted as sheep for the slaughter. It matters little how much God's people are offered up on the altars of the world, they are still more than conquerors because of God's love.

When a Christian possesses the sin mentality, it proves to be blasphemous towards God because it falsely accuses Him of being a liar or a failure. God is true to His nature.[3] If anyone is to be accused of failure, it is man in spiritual matters. He is the one who fails to do that which is right, and, as a result, in his prideful delusion he always ends up blaming God for the consequences that follow.

Since the victim mentality is a mindset of sin, we must understand it. First of all, Jesus serves as our example. He told believers that there would be much tribulation in the world, but not to fear, for He overcame the world.[4] What can Christians learn from Jesus' example? How did He overcome?

The key to overcoming starts with identity. Jesus emptied Himself of His glory as God. He took on the disposition of a servant, and allowed Himself to be fashioned as a man. He actually gave up His rights as God in relationship to His sovereignty, to come into total submission to the Father. Why did He take on a different identity and become lower than the angels in status?[5]

Rights have to do with respect. When rights are disrespected or abused, a person is justified in taking action. Jesus gave up His sovereign rights as God and became a servant. We may not think much about His action. As one of the Persons of the Godhead, Jesus was always in submission to the other members of the Godhead. However, godly submission does not imply obedience, but giving way to that which is worthy or greater in order to come into complete agreement for the benefit of the whole.[6] Likewise, people come into submission to one another because they are working towards a common goal or vision that is worthy of their attention and commitment.

When Jesus took on the disposition of a servant, He came into subjection. Subjection implies coming under authority. When a person comes under authority, it is for the purpose of being lined up to another person's will with the intent to carry it out. In order to come into subjection to the Father, Jesus had to give up His capacity as God, take on the disposition of a servant to come into subjection to the Father's will. He was fashioned as man, so He could obey and carry out the Father's will.[7]

As man, Jesus took on a different identity. His new identity changed the way He functioned. Even though He was divine by nature, He was living and walking in a body. He was now subject to different influences. This new identity put Him in a position of serving, rather than ruling. If He were not in this position, His ordeal on the cross would have required Him to call forth judgment on sin, rather than serve as judgment for sin. Therefore, giving up His rights as God and taking on the body of a man

---

[3] Romans 3:4

[4] John 16:33

[5] Philippians 2:6-8; Hebrews 2:6-8

[6] John 17:18-23

[7] Philippians 2:5-11

ensured that He could become a vessel. As a vessel, He experienced the necessary liberty to carry out His main mission: To die on behalf of man.

At the core of the victim mentality are rights. These rights are based on high opinions of self.[8] They can quickly become offended, angry, resentful, and vengeful, which will translate into treachery. In order to subdue the right to become a victim, a person must give up his or her old identity and take on a new identity.

The purpose of a new identity is to change one's way of thinking. This became a personal reality when I was in boot camp, being prepared to serve in the Navy. My old civilian life was stripped away to make way for a new identity as a sailor. As I consider this time, I realized that they were trying to change my way of thinking from an independent civilian to a soldier who was in subjection to authority. The process was hard because it went against my old way of thinking and doing. Those who fail to make it through boot camp do so because they refuse to allow their mentality to be changed.

New identity means everything. Such a perspective was brought out in a movie called *"Ellen Foster."* It was about an abused girl who had lost her mother, and lived under the abuse and neglect of an alcoholic father. Eventually, she was shoved from one situation to another. Everywhere she turned, she not only remained a victim because of the bitterness, indifference, and selfishness of others, but her challenges escalated. This young girl could have easily given in to the victim mentality, but she desired a new life. At one point, she changed her last name to mark a new identity and held on. At the end of the movie, Ellen finally received her wish of being part of a new (foster) family.

I had a similar situation in my life as a young girl. My parents were divorced. My biological father had some real problems and issues. It was during this vulnerable time that I tasted the prejudice and cruelty of others. I dreamed of a new life and identity. God was gracious to bring me both when my mother remarried. I not only embarked on a new life, but I took my stepfather's name that signified a new identity. The old identity had classified me as a victim, but my new identity gave me hope to acquire a new life.

The victim mentality holds on to the old identity or mentality because it gives it the necessary rights to remain a victim. People can stay in their perverted pigpens, while appearing noble. As victims, they are not responsible for their present spiritual condition, attitudes, and actions. As victims, they perceive themselves as being unable to pay the necessary price to change their pigpens. In other words, they do not have to pay the price and become real, as long as they maintain this façade of being a perpetual victim. They have a right to feel sorry for self and remain a loser who can be admired in their fake suffering. If they ever cease from

---

[8] Romans 12:3

being a victim, they would no longer have any excuses for their present mentality, condition, and lifestyle.

This mentality produces slothfulness and complacency. The presence of slothfulness walks hand in hand with fantasy, while complacency produces indifference to reality. People who operate within the victim syndrome delude themselves into believing that if their situation were different, they would have a different outlook. This is a fallacy, because the problem does not rest with their circumstances, but rather with their outlook. In fact, it is not unusual to see these people waiting for something to drop out of the sky into their lap to make everything right.

Needless to say, these people will be waiting a long time. As long as they insist on being victims, they will continue to be losers. It is up to each person to stir him or herself up from the state of complacency towards the things of God, or awake from spiritual dullness to embrace a new life and a new identity.

The truth is people must overcome before God can meet them. This means that they must overcome the flesh, the world, and Satan to experience all that God has for them. Jesus confirmed this with His own life. He never waited to be delivered from anything. He embraced the challenges of life by facing temptation, betrayal, and the cross. Before Jesus went to the cross, He declared that He had overcome the world. He overcame Satan with the Word; He overcame Judas' betrayal with a kiss, and He overcame the cross with forgiveness and life. As a result, Jesus proved to be the ultimate victor when He was raised up in newness of life and was exalted above all creatures in heaven, on earth, or under the earth.

Regardless of the situation, overcoming a matter is never handed to us. It is always wrought through self-denial and obedience. Jesus lined His will up to the Father and became obedient to the cross. He proved, through His many examples, that His followers have a responsibility to overcome, regardless of the obstacles.

This brings us to the final fruit of the victim mentality: that insidious self-pity. People with this mentality believe that they have a right to feel sorry for self. After all, they are perpetual victims of unrelenting circumstances. Since they are perpetual victims, their plight is worse than others. Such plights make their situation unique, and by suffering silently, they can show how superior they are. This superiority is designed to bring attention to their plight, so others will join them in their pigpens. Since these individuals perceive themselves as helpless victims, they expect you to fight for them and serve them, because it is "the Christian thing to do".

Let us consider the contrast Jesus brings to such a mentality. He did not suffer on the cross to be noticed. Rather, He was lifted up, so that man could be drawn to salvation. He did not go to the cross as a victim, but as a victor, for He had already overcome. He did not go to the cross to show how noble He was. Rather, He went to secure eternal life for each of us. Jesus did not allow Himself the ordeal of Calvary so that He could feel sorry for Himself, and get others to enter into His plight. Instead, He did something utterly foreign to His very person. He became a sin offering, so that those who were enslaved by sin can be made in the righteousness of God.[9]

The cross of Jesus makes one clear declaration to His followers: They have no right to be a victim or feel sorry for themselves. The reason any Christian would hold on to a sinful mentality is because of pride. Underneath their false presentation, they want to be exalted, recognized, or adored. This is idolatrous, but it proves that such people do not love God. Rather, they love themselves. They also love their present wretched life more than they desire the life of God. Through it all, they want to maintain their so-called dignity over the need to possess a new life and identity.

Sadly, these people have a high opinion of themselves. They are impressed with their fake nobility. They delude themselves with the idea that, one day they will overcome, as soon as God delivers them from their unjust circumstances. They claim they want all that God has for them, while maintaining their sick, self-centered identity. Underneath the opinions, delusion, and claims, they cannot afford to pay the price of the old way of life, because as soon as they do, everything will cease to be about them and will become about the reality of God.

To be an overcomer, Christians must deny the old life, and embrace a new identity. This means that they must deny the former self of any rights to rule and reign. They must avoid self-pity by enduring the hardship of self-denial. Such denial will develop inward character. They must face the temptation of their pride, the betrayal of their mentality, and the necessity of the cross, not as a victim or suffering martyr, but as an overcomer. They must give up their right to come out with dignity. Rather, they must be overcome by the shame, despair, and hopelessness of their sin and what it actually cost Jesus. As overcomers, they will be able to embrace a new, powerful life that will reflect the Son of God.

The question is, are you acting as a victim or are you living and walking as an overcomer? I have this to say if you are walking as a victim: Shame on you! How dare you mock what our Lord did on the cross! How dare you compete with His majesty and work! How dare you call Him a liar! How dare you clothe your arrogance with fake humility, while exalting yourself as being special or unique in your suffering! That is exactly what you are doing, and more than that, you expect other people to play your game by getting into your pigpen and becoming defiled with you.

---

[9] 2 Corinthians 5:21; Hebrews 12:2-3

If you are a victim, you need to repent and choose a new life and identity in Jesus Christ. Revelation 21:7 summarizes the victory of overcoming, “He that overcometh shall inherit all things; and I will be his God, and he shall be my son.”

7

THE PRODUCT OF SIN

In the last chapter, we considered the mentality of sin. It must come out on top as being noble, good, and honorable, or it will come out as the helpless, suffering victim. Sadly, what is missing between these two boundaries is reality.

Jesus said in John 8:32 that the truth will make a person free. This statement narrows down what causes the greatest bondage in a person's life: delusion. Man's fallen disposition wallows in and thrives on delusion. Although people may zealously declare that they want truth, most prefer delusion. "Delusion" in this text simply means that most people prefer their own reality.

We see this delusion operating in Judas Iscariot's life. The first thing we must acknowledge about this man is that he had his own personal agendas or ideas as to how Jesus would actually fit into his goals or causes. This type of self-serving agenda produces a false reality in the mind of the person who adheres to such false realities as to the way things should be. In fact, it is man's natural inclination to judge people based on these agendas or ideas.

We know that such agendas existed in Judas' life because he justified personal treachery as a thief, as well as the right to betray the Lord. In the end, he felt bad that an innocent man had been offered up on the cross, but instead of repenting, he went out and hung himself. What amazes me is that some people treat him as a victim. They logic out that someone had to betray Jesus, and Judas was simply in the wrong place at the wrong time. However, if Judas' heart possess integrity and was right before his Teacher and Master, he would have never been tempted to assume such a wicked role. This is why Jesus made this statement about him, "The Son of man goeth as it is written of him; but woe unto that man by whom the Son of man is betrayed! It had been good for that man if he had not been born" (Matthew 26:24).

The reality of sin is that people can never come out on top of life, nor are they continually being victimized. Granted, everyone will become a victim in life, but the reality of most peoples' lives is that they insist on remaining a victim. There is a progression to such a mentality. If these people cannot be exalted for those things that they deem honorable in their lives, they conclude that life is unfair. This is where people begin to con or delude themselves about their real agendas or spiritual condition.

Since life is unfair, these people perceive that they do not have to be fair in their actions. As they give way to this logic, they do things to come out on top, regardless of how it affects others. This selfish pursuit hurts others and compromises personal character. Ultimately, what people sow in the flesh will produce corresponding consequences.[1] Consequences that expose personal corruption make these individuals feel that life is even more unfair, thereby making them greater victims.

Such logic is nothing more than self-delusion. We have talked about the deceitfulness of sin. Sin works in ignorance and darkness. Ignorance is a form of spiritual blindness that prevents a person from seeing the true God of the Bible. The Apostle Paul addressed this blindness in 2 Corinthians 4:3-4, "But if our gospel be hid, it is hid to them that are lost: In whom the god of this world hath blinded the minds of them which believe not, lest the light of the glorious gospel of Christ, who is the image of God, should shine unto them."

Spiritual blindness is a product of unbelief. People choose to give way to this unbelief when they refuse to believe their inward awareness as to the existence and identity of God, as well as the visible witness of God that can clearly be seen in His creation. Both the physical and inward knowledge of God are meant to stir a person up to seek and pursue after the one true God. Instead of seeking God, most people erect a god in their minds. As we know, this god is the product of vain imaginations and speculations.[2]

Much of how people perceive God comes down to their preference of what they want to perceive as reality. These individuals insist that the God of the Bible is not correctly presented, or the presentation is a lie or a myth. Ultimately, these individuals adjust Him to their preferred reality, so they can live happily ever after in their ignorance. This preference is according to the world's philosophies, and we know that the world has been wrapped in Satan's lies.[3]

The lies of Satan have enveloped people's minds with such darkness that any light of truth makes them reel in hatred, false accusations, and mocking. The distinction between light and darkness is becoming more defined even in this present age. The handwriting is on the wall. In the darkness of these people's hatred, they would have no problem justifying any means or method to rid themselves of such light. The Gospel is the only light that can penetrate the darkness of lies and ignorance with the reality of Christ. Jesus is not only the true light that penetrates the darkness of man's soul, but He is also the visible image of the unseen God that has been mirrored in His creation.

Darkness points to delusion. At the heart of the human selfish disposition is pride. Pride is not only idolatrous, but it insists that a

---

[1] Galatians 6:7-8

[2] Jeremiah 29:13; Romans 1:18-28; 2 Corinthians 10:3-5

[3] John 8:44; Colossians 2:8

person must come out on top, or that he or she must become a victim in order to be clear of any personal accountability. Such delusion has to do with the fact that pride refuses to be held accountable for a wrong disposition, or become responsible for wrong actions.

In ministering to people, I have learned that they prefer to believe that their problems are outside of their own way of being. They blame their problems on Satan or circumstances. They seek others out to pray for them, rather than turn and face God about their warped perspective or lack of character. They want the solution handed to them, without confronting their heart condition and spirit. They refuse to consider that their challenges have nothing to do with their circumstances, but with their disposition. They will not make themselves accountable for the way they think, and responsible for the quality of their being.

The idol of pride is always quick to provide the reason and justification for such failures. It removes people from being personally responsible for their attitudes, relationships, and conduct. In fact, pride makes people indifferent to the destruction they leave behind. It makes them insensitive to personal hypocrisy, while, at the same time, extra sensitive towards those things that offend or do not set right in their way of thinking.

Pride simply deludes people into creating their own light. This false light presents itself in the light of honor and glory. The false light of honor is nothing but fake nobility, while the pseudo glory is nothing but useless vainglory. Such glory occurs when people glory in their understanding and abilities, rather than in God. The Apostle Paul clearly stipulated that no flesh will glory in the Lord's presence.[4]

As stated, pride serves as the weak point of character where moral deviation or iniquity can take root in a man. In fact, pride is the reason people do not seek God's forgiveness and salvation. They want to have some hand, or glory, in their spiritual accomplishments. For example, they can consider themselves too rotten to receive forgiveness; therefore, they must make themselves acceptable. On the other hand, they also can see themselves as being too good to be wrong; therefore, they will not humble themselves. This prideful perspective can also cause these people to see themselves as being too smart to be counted as a fool, thereby, remaining unteachable and unreasonable. This proves that the disposition of pride is the biggest hindrance to people receiving salvation. As someone once said, it is not hard to get a man saved, the real challenge is to get him lost in the first place. Pride will not let a person accept such a condition.

The false light of pride blinds people to its existence. Jesus talked about this false light in Matthew 6:23, "But if thine eye be evil, thy whole body shall be full of darkness. If therefore the light that is in thee be darkness, how great is that darkness?" The light of pride is nothing but

[4] 1 Corinthians 1:29-31

darkness. However, those who walk in this darkness believe it to be light. They perceive themselves as being wise.[5] In fact, there is such overwhelming false confidence behind this light that the person cannot perceive him or herself as being wrong in personal conclusions.

I am sure you know what I am describing. If you are married, you know that in a conflict it comes down to either you or your spouse demanding to be right about the matter, while in the mind, the one who is not in agreement is being foolish or unreasonable. As pride takes center stage in both parties, the obstinacy of pride digs in to maintain the right to insist that its particular reality is recognized and properly respected. Even it one person does manage to get his or her way, it leaves behind the fruits of resentment and distrust.

Christians need to realize that personal conclusions inspired by the different false lights of pride are treacherous. They are nothing more than opinions based on personal prejudices. These prejudices are cleverly hidden behind concepts, standards, images, or ideas. The problem is that these conclusions are prejudicial enough to cause a person to believe that he or she possesses the truth about all things. Keep in mind that prejudice is a form of superiority.

People walking in these false lights automatically perceive themselves to be right and superior in their way of thinking. This perception will ultimately make them the final authority in matters. It also makes them unteachable, unreasonable, cruel, and formidable in their judgments against those who will not bow down to such indifferent and wicked demands.

Pride is the self-will that always presumes it is right. People who allow pride to determine their reality will establish a delusion that will ultimately exalt them into the false status that makes them an exception to what is right and proper. Like those who were involved with the building of the Tower of Babel in Genesis 11, these individuals used the different stones of presumptions to build a tower that would supposedly reach the intellectual heights of heaven, thereby, making them divine, only to be brought down into utter confusion by the true God of heaven.

The reality of light is that there are a multitude of counterfeit lights in the world. For example, Satan can come as an angel of light. His false light brings "enlightenment" to people, or gives them "insight" into the supernatural or mysteries. This causes them to either worship him or their own intelligence and knowledge. There are also those who transform themselves into the ministers of righteousness. Righteousness points to a type of light that people are drawn to. It can appear to be morally or religiously upright, but it points people back to the religious leader, rather than to Jesus Christ. The Apostle Paul warned of such

---

[5] James 3:14-15

people as false apostles and deceitful workers, and declared that their end would be according to their works. [6]

There is also the false light of self-righteousness. This is a popular light among religious people. This light points people back to the false idea of personal righteousness, rather than to the righteousness of Christ. It serves as the terrible judgmental board in so many people's eye. This board blinds individuals to their personal condition. It makes them right in their own eyes, while it justifies ungodly actions towards others, and is superior in its wicked disposition. The light of self-righteousness actually blinds people to their personal fruits.[7] They judge themselves according to what they perceive to be moral living. Moral living varies depending on a person's worldview or preferences. Such living may be considered decent, but it does not make a person righteous before God.

Self-righteousness also operates behind the façade of good intentions. Good intentions are simply bones thrown to others, such as flattery. They give an impression of integrity and goodness, but lack substance. Such intentions lack inclination. For example, people may say things out of zeal, but they do not possess the inclination to carry it out. Good intentions are nothing more than hiding the fact that a person is devoid of integrity.

Self-righteous people also test themselves at the expense of those whom they consider inferior. These people have a tendency to exalt leaders whom they perceive as living up to their standards. However, in the next moment, they can bring them down to ridicule and judgment if these leaders fail to uphold these people's ridiculous, hypocritical standards. They also display jealousy and greed towards those whom they perceive as inferior, but who are obviously being bestowed with more blessings than they are by God.[8] Due to their high opinion of self, they perceive such blessings as unfair. After all, they have lived this good life, while the person being blessed has lived a life inferior to them. In the end, these people must be exalted in some way, or they become angry and insulted.

Due to their high opinion of self, these people often try to take the place of the Holy Ghost in others' lives.[9] I cannot tell you how many people have come to me over the years to tell me what is wrong with this ministry, and what I need to do to change it. I listen to their suggestions and pray about them. If the Holy Ghost puts His finger on it, then I submit to His conviction, knowing that He will enable the change. If He does not convict me, then I must consider that the advice does not apply, and let it go to the wayside. Amazingly, many of these people become insulted

---

[6] 2 Corinthians 11:13-15

[7] Matthew 7:15-16; 1 Corinthians 1:30

[8] James 3:11-18

[9] Romans 12:3

because they do not see any change according to their specifications. In their mind, they were speaking on behalf of God and I should immediately bow down to their way of thinking and comply with their suggestions.

Since self-righteous people take pride in being moral in their actions and conclude they are superior in their conduct, they perceive themselves as being okay before God. They do not realize that righteousness is based on a right spirit. Even if the right spirit is missing, a person can still live a moral life, but still fail to be upright before God.[10] A right spirit ensures a right disposition. Nevertheless, because of these people's arrogance, they ignore, avoid, or fail to test their spirit or motivation.

As you examine the spirit behind the disposition of self-righteousness, you will realize that it is nothing more than a disguise for pride. Jesus brought this out in His parable about the self-righteous Pharisee and the publican in Luke 18:9-14.

Jesus Christ is the only true light of the world. His life is actually the light of men. His light has the ability to shine in the midst of man's great darkness, but man is unable to comprehend this light without the intervention of God.[11] People's natural inclination is to chase after false lights, but in their pursuits, they fail to realize that any light outside of Jesus' light is a counterfeit.

Counterfeit lights are treacherous. They actually blind people to the fact that they are walking on the edge of the abyss. These people have no sense as to where they are spiritually. They often flounder in their spiritual lives and pursuits, but they refuse to consider the real light. Their philosophies fail them, but they still prefer their personal reality to the truth. Ultimately, these people's obstinate insistence prevents the liberating truth of heaven from winning out in their lives.

Sometimes people's greatest delusion does not revolve around who God is or the Gospel, but it comes down to them facing their own spiritual condition. This can be true for Christians. I know of Christians who refuse to face their spiritual depravity. It is not that they refuse to admit they have sin, for they do. In fact, they are quite noble about it as they attempt to rectify any deviance in their own power. However, there is nothing noble about sin. Only God can truly resolve the issue of sin. Instead of clinging to the cross and glorying in Jesus' work of redemption, they cling to their dignity as they conform outwardly to some religious code. Ultimately, they put on a different religious cloak.[12] By changing the outward façade or image, they perceive themselves as resolving the sin, and once again, all is well.

---

[10] Proverbs 16:2; 1 John 4:1

[11] John 1:4

[12] John 15:22

Before it can be properly confronted, sin must be unveiled for what it is. Once sin is exposed, there will be no dignity found in its ways. Sin exposed by the light of Jesus Christ will never create pride. Rather, it will break a person, resulting in brokenness, humility, and repentance.

The unwillingness to face one's depravity allows pride to reign with a vengeance. When pride is reigning, it simply means that the old man is alive and well. The old man, who is the manifestation of the fallen, sinful disposition, must survive at any cost.[13] He will confess and process sin on an intellectual basis and call it repentance. He will outwardly comply with religious codes and call it righteousness. He will play dead and call it humility. He will act rehabilitated and call it godliness. Regardless of the religious cloaks he may wear, the unregenerate disposition of the old man will, remain unchanged as long as pride reigns.

This brings us to the reality of pride. It refuses to submit to the sovereign rule of God. It will give the impression of submission, while holding on to its right to determine how, where, and when God will reign. It will declare good intentions, but will fail to carry them out. It will cling to rights, so that it can excuse itself, while appearing noble. It will declare that it is trying to do what is right, while calling God a liar about His power to enable such accomplishments. All of these outward attempts serve as a smoke screen to keep others from seeing the unbelief and rebellion that reigns in the person's soul and heart. Sadly, it deludes the person, keeping him or her from facing the real preference of his or her own heart and soul.

Ultimately, pride will come short of doing the will of God. After all, it has no intention of doing God's will. It will not relinquish its rule to the Lordship of Jesus. It will use God as a way of defusing people from seeing its hypocrisy, but it will always be a matter of show, and not a change of heart and spirit. It will struggle to do right, but it will always fall short of ever accomplishing the task. It will profess its good intentions, but will never pay the price to bring them about. It will run around in religious busyness, but will never enter into the inner chambers of God in humility and obedience. It will verbally give God credit, while inwardly glorying in what is considered personal accomplishments. These are all games of the sin of pride, but they serve as a cloak or smoke screen to cover up the reality that these people have no intention of doing it on God's terms. In fact, they have no intention of doing it at all.

Pride's resistance to God's authority can be clearly seen in Scripture, as well as in the present world. For example, Cain refused to listen to God's warning about sin lying at his door, ready to take him captive. He ultimately insisted on his own way, which ended with him murdering his brother. Instead of humbling himself and taking responsibility for his hateful, murderous action, he left the presence of the Lord and built his own city that he could rule. Man is forever trying to justify his resistance

---

[13] Ephesians 4:22-31; 5:1-13; Colossians 3:5-10

to God's authority in order to embrace the delusion that he truly can be an effective ruler of his own world.

I have heard people confess that they were walking in delusion, but they did not know how to let go of their need to glory in the idea of self. They wanted the glory; therefore, they were not willing to pay the price of regression of self in order to progress in their knowledge of Jesus. They wanted the Christian life handed to them, instead of going through the process of self-denial and applying the cross. They wanted to be a "somebody" in the kingdom of God, subtly laying claim to God's work and glory for their own personal purposes and exaltation.

Are you walking in the light of Christ or in ignorance or delusion? We are prone to walk in the ways of sin and death. In fact, it is natural to want to create our own reality about our spiritual condition, but it is a delusion. Jesus said the truth will make us free, but truth can only be realized when one is honestly and humbly facing reality. It is in reality that God can meet a person and change his or her perspective.

The question each of us must ask ourselves is, "What light am I walking in?" If I am walking in the light of Christ, I have the blessed assurance of possessing His life. However, if I am walking in a counterfeit light, I can be assured of ignorance, delusion, and death.

8

FORMS OF SIN

My co-laborer in the Gospel, Jeannette, stated that until people understand sin in light of God's holiness, they will never come to terms with how devastating and destructive it is. Moreover, sin cannot be fully addressed until individuals come into agreement with God's evaluation about what constitutes sin, and how He looks at it.

The first four chapters of this book dealt with the base, makeup and avenues of sin. The Word of God, which is referred to as both a hammer and a sword, is meant to expose the activities or the influence of sin in a person's life. The Word also reveals how people try to rehabilitate, cover up, or deny this spiritual condition. However, there is nothing that can change the status of the old man, unless sin is forgiven and the old man is crucified. The crucifixion of the old allows the new man or the life of Christ to be resurrected and worked within each area that has been subjected to the bondage of sin. Jesus confirmed this reality in Matthew 9:16-17,

> No man putteth a piece of new cloth upon an old garment, for that which is put in to fill it up taketh from the garment, and the rent is made worse. Neither do men put new wine into old bottles: else the bottle break, and the wine runneth out, and the bottles perish: but they put new wine into new bottles, and both are preserved.

The fallen condition goes back to the Garden of Eden where Adam desired to rule his own life outside of God's sovereignty. The Apostle Paul gives this account of the results in Romans 5:12, "Wherefore as by one man sin entered into the world, and death by sin; and so death passed upon all men, for that all have sinned."

This desire to rule his personal world is encoded into man's rebellious disposition in the form of selfishness and pride. Most people have no problem acknowledging the existence or possibilities of God, but they refuse to face His character, sovereignty, or position in the scheme of life.

It is not our fault that Adam and Eve blew it, but it is our choice to not properly confront this spiritual condition. Man's unwillingness to agree with God's evaluation of this condition is a manifestation of this prideful, unregenerate disposition.

This brings us to what Jesus did at the point of redemption. He came to address sin through example and teaching. He then overcame the consequences of sin by dying on the cross on our behalf. It is at this point of embracing His redemption that each person receives a new disposition by way of a new heart and spirit.[1] Such an individual also stands cleansed and forgiven, opening up a way for him or her to come into fellowship with God.

The problem is, people do not understand the extent of their selfish disposition, nor do they recognize what constitutes personal sin. They want to believe there is some good in them that will outweigh the failures or deviation in their character and thought life. They are often blinded by what is considered to be personal goodness or by comparing themselves with others whose faults are considered greater.[2] Such comparisons create a false light that blinds these individuals to personal sin, and their need for God's constant intervention and deliverance.

Exodus 34:7 makes this statement, "Keeping mercy for thousands; forgiving <u>iniquity</u> and <u>transgression</u> and <u>sin</u>..." (Emphasis added.) Notice how there is a distinction between sin, transgression, and iniquity. It is not unusual to see a separation inserted between these words. Do these three terms represent three forms of sin? If so, it must be important to understand the distinction for personal examination and edification of the Body of Jesus.

Strong's Exhaustive Concordance of the Bible gives a picture of how these terms differ. Let us start with the term *sin.* Sin can refer to the fallen condition of man or the outward manifestation of rebellion. When it refers to the fallen condition, it is referring to something that is missing the mark. As stated previously, we all fall short of God's glory. We were intended to reflect His glory, but because of our fallen disposition, we display the independence of Adam. This shows how we have been sold under sin.[3] We are slaves, not because of our conduct, but due to our spiritual condition. Once again, we are reminded that the origin of sin is an inward problem of the heart, not just a matter of doing something wrong.

Sin is also a generic reference to manifestations of this fallen disposition. In this context, it points to offenses. Offense is an important word to consider. It refers to some type of action that has caused wrongdoing to others.

It is easy for people to become offended. Offense, where some people are concerned, has to do with pride more than what we know to be actual transgression. I am sure you have encountered a few of these prideful people along the way. You feel as if you are walking on eggshells because their pride is so touchy that you never know what will

---

[1] Ezekiel 36:26-27

[2] 2 Corinthians 10:12-14

[3] Romans 7:14

set them off into one of their tyrannical, judgmental, and vindictive moods. Such individuals prove to be unreasonable because they make everything about how they think or feel. And, in the end such individuals prove to be unrealistic because they are unwilling to step outside of their self-absorbed world. Inevitably these people become insulted when they are not being adored or recognized in the way that they perceive is acceptable. Such offense is simply a product of the fallen man, and is idolatrous.

Sin that offends God involves the breaking of fellowship between Him and the person. Breaking fellowship with God is serious. Isaiah 59:2 makes this statement, "But your iniquities have separated between you and your God, and your sins have hid his face from you, that he will not hear."

1 John 1:6-7 makes reference to the breaking of fellowship in this manner, "If we say that we have fellowship with him, and walk in darkness, we lie, and do not the truth: But if we walk in the light, as he is in the light, we have fellowship one with another, and the blood of Jesus Christ his Son cleanseth us from all sin." Sin in this text is not a simple matter of personal offenses, but one of spiritual ruin and devastation. Insulting a person's pride is not a punishable crime. Failing to live up to someone's unrealistic standards will not bring the wrath of God. After all, real love covers such offenses.[4] However, offenses committed against the character, covenant, and Law of God will bring consequences and judgment.

Jesus dealt with how His people were to confront the issue of offences in Matthew 18:15-17. He distinguished the difference between offences that offend the touchy, fickle pride of man, and spiritual offenses that put someone in a position of facing God's judgment. He did this by defining the type of offense that has been committed: that of a trespass. Trespass will be clearly defined later in the chapter, but it has nothing to do with a person's pride being offended.

These guidelines in confronting such offences were set down by Jesus to cause people to first examine personal motives as to why they were offended. If the offense was clearly justifiable, they were to personally go to the person to confront him or her. This was to stop gossip and slander among His people. Sadly, few believers adhere to these disciplines. As a result, gossip is rampant, slander justified, and sin is rarely confronted in order to restore a brother or sister back into a relationship with God.[5]

1 John 5:17 tells us, "All unrighteousness is sin: and there is a sin not unto death." Unrighteousness points to conduct. Obviously, there are some sins that result in death, while others will simply hinder or challenge a person's walk, but not his or her eternal destination.

---

[4] 1 Peter 4:8

[5] James 5:19-20

Faults are also associated with sin. What are faults? Obviously, we all have them. In this text, it is in reference to spots or wrinkles in one's character. Spots and wrinkles point to inconsistencies in a person's character that must be cleansed or ironed out. Consider what the Apostle Paul said about such faults in regard to the Church, "That he might sanctify and cleanse it with the washing of water by the word; That he might present it to himself a glorious church, not having spot, or wrinkle, or any such thing; but that it should be holy and without blemish" (Ephesians 5:26-27). Clearly, the Word of God has the power to work out these faults in the lives of God's people.

Faults often irritate and challenge people's attitudes, often exposing self-righteous, judgmental attitudes. They can serve as personal points of discipline or hindrance. In other words, people find themselves struggling with personal faults that have the potential to work character in them, or these inconsistencies can become a hindrance to their testimony and authority in the kingdom of God. Galatians 6:1 says, "Brethren, if a man be overtaken in a fault, ye which are spiritual restore such an one in the spirit of meekness; considering thyself, lest thou also be tempted."

Every person is subject to like faults. Whenever there is a weakness in character, people are susceptible to fall into the same traps as others. The Apostle Paul warns of this possibility in 1 Corinthians 10:12, "Wherefore let him that thinketh he standeth take heed lest he fall."

There are sins that are not unto death, but there are others that result in death. What are sins that can result in spiritual ruin? There are two categories of sins that fit this criterion. They are known as *transgressions* and *iniquities.*

Transgressions involve the breaking of the Law or covenant. In other words, someone has walked into areas that are off limits or outside of acceptable boundaries, trespassing what is legal. Romans 4:15 confirms this, "Because the law worketh wrath: for where no law is, there is no transgression."[6]

1 John 3:4 says, "Whosoever committeth sin transgresseth also the law: for sin is the transgression of the law." Transgression is a violation against God's Law or covenant. This is a personal offense committed against God in a show of disrespect or rebellion. It actually shows contempt towards His Word. This will break any existing fellowship with Him.

King David actually trespassed into an area that was forbidden by the Law of God when he committed adultery with Bathsheba. He trespassed the second time into an arena in which he had no jurisdiction when he secretly set Bathsheba's husband to be murdered. As a result, he transgressed the Law. In his prayer of repentance in Psalm 51, he acknowledged his transgression, and admitted that his sin was ever

[6] See also Jeremiah 34:18

before him. Since he broke God's Law, he confessed that he had sinned against God.

The prophet Hosea explained the attitude behind transgression. "But they like men have transgressed the covenant: there have they dealt treacherously against me" (Hosea 6:7). Transgression is a treacherous act against God. As a just Judge, He cannot overlook such an act. It calls for both judgment and restitution.

God's Law proves that everyone is a lawbreaker. The Apostle Paul stated in Romans 3:23 that we have all sinned. Scripture also warns of the foolishness, destruction, and hard road for those who insist on walking this route of rebellion.[7] Isaiah 1:28 shows us the consequences for transgressions, "And the destruction of the transgressors and of the sinners shall be together, and they that forsake the LORD shall be consumed."

The Law calls for some type of restitution or judgment when it has been trespassed. In David's case, his acts of adultery and murder required him to pay with his very life, rather than with the sacrifice of an animal. King David understood the judgment that the holy Law of God had pronounced upon him. He even asked God in Psalm 51 to blot out his transgressions and deliver him from his blood guiltiness, the very consequence required by the Law for his godless acts. This is why he made this statement, "The sacrifices of God are a broken spirit; a broken and a contrite heart, O God, thou wilt not despise" (Psalm 51:17). God did not require David's life, but in a way it did cost him the lives of four of his sons, three in a violent way.

Since God is just, there had to be judgment and restitution made for each of us. Praise His Holy Name! He sent Jesus to take on the judgment of our transgressions and pay for restitution for the damage they have caused. The price He paid was His life. Isaiah 53:5 and 8 tell us how He sufficed this judgment and paid restitution, "But he was wounded for our transgressions,...for he was cut off out of the land of the living: for the transgression of my people was he stricken."

The price for our sins was paid at Calvary. The courts of heaven have been satisfied. Does this mean we can continue to trespass against God's Law? NO! Followers of God are told to fulfill the Law. They have been given the very tool by which they can complete the intent or purpose of it: the love of God. Romans 13:10 confirms this, "Love worketh no ill to his neighbour: therefore love is the fulfilling of the law."

Jesus made this statement in John 14:23-24, "If a man love me, he will keep my words: and my Father will love him, and we will come unto him, and make our abode with him. He that loveth me not keepeth not my sayings: and the word which ye hear is not mine, but the Father's which sent me." Obviously, without the love of God compelling a person,

---

[7] Psalm 37:28; Proverbs 13:15; Romans 3:10-31; 8:3-4; Galatians 2:16; 3:11-13, 20-25; James 2:8-11

he or she will commit transgressions against Him. Of course, there will be excuses, justifications, and qualifications as to why such trespasses are taking place, but the real reason will come down to the fact that godly love and devotion are clearly missing.

Iniquity is different from transgression because it involves both perverted and treacherous acts against God and man. This form of sin is often hidden in the heart, and points to moral deviation or perversion. As Proverbs 23:7 declares, "For as he thinketh in his heart, so is he..." This moral deviation begins with toying with some type of sin in the heart. Once the person justifies the sin in his or her mind, it will manifest itself outwardly in transgression of the Law. Therefore, iniquity not only entails conduct, but character or disposition as well.

King David was realistic about the struggles that he encountered with his character throughout the Psalms. He had not let the weak areas of his character give way to iniquity, allowing it to take root and reign. However, iniquity did take root when David fell into sin with Bathsheba. Iniquity came to the center and entrapped him into grave perversion. This is why he asked God to wash him thoroughly from his iniquity in Psalm 51:2.

The first four commandments deal with our attitude towards God and the life He has given us, but the last six have to do with our relationship with others. Sometimes, the moral deviation is obvious with such acts as fornication. However, in some cases, iniquity can prove to be subtle or shrewd, such as is often found in the case of idolatry. It will eventually express itself in ways such as prejudice, playing games with people's emotions, mental or verbal cruelty, or vengeance towards others. Ultimately, it shows disregard towards both God and man.

Interestingly, when the Bible speaks of man's handling of transgression or iniquity, it points out that he tries to cover transgressions and hide any type of iniquity. Job 31:33 brings this out about Adam. "If I covered my transgressions as Adam, by hiding mine iniquity in my bosom." (Emphasis added.) The outward acts of transgressions are a manifestation of the inward presence of iniquity that is beginning to reign.

Since transgression is the breaking of the Law, it cannot be hidden. As a result, the Israelites covered certain transgressions with sacrifices. These sacrifices pointed to surface work that failed to change the inward man if true repentance was missing. If a person did not truly repent, the transgression would remain intact. The prophet Samuel made this statement in 1 Samuel 15:22, "Hath the LORD as great delight in burnt offerings and sacrifices, as in obeying the voice of the LORD? Behold, to obey is better than sacrifice, and to hearken than the fat of rams."

Hosea 6:6 declares, "For I desired mercy, and not sacrifice; and the knowledge of God more than burnt offerings." Obeying God's Word overcomes transgression, while mercy allows this form of sin to be covered. Clearly, it is the knowledge of God's true character that keeps one on the right path.[8]

Iniquity is a different situation. It is part of our very being. It is quietly waiting to be activated by temptation and personal justification. King David understood that moral deviation existed in his character. He recognized that he could not give it audience or toy with it. He stated in 2 Samuel 22:24, "I was also upright before him, and have kept myself from my iniquity."

This form of sin is often hidden behind various religious activities and cloaks without anyone being aware that it exists. It can freely harbor perversion and justify future rebellious actions. Iniquity may be hidden from man, but not from God. Psalm 66:18 confirms this, "If I regard iniquity in my heart, the Lord will not hear me."

Jesus talked about taking away cloaks that cover or hide sin in John 15:22. Luke 12:2-3 gives this warning, "For there is nothing covered, that shall not be revealed; neither hid, that shall not be known. Therefore whatsoever ye have spoken in darkness shall be heard in the light; and that which ye have spoken in the ear in closets shall be proclaimed upon the housetops."

Many transgressions could be covered by sacrifices, but visible acts of iniquity required people to be cut off or put to death. We have considered this in regard to David's sin with Bathsheba, as well as what Adam did in the Garden of Eden when he transgressed the covenant.[9] Once again, we must be reminded of the words of Job 31:33, "If I covered my transgressions as Adam, by hiding mine iniquity in my bosom."

Proverbs 16:6 gives us the solution to the hidden sin of iniquity, "By mercy and truth iniquity is purged: and by the fear of the LORD men depart from evil." King David mentioned in 2 Samuel 22:24 that he was the one who kept himself upright before God, as well as from personal iniquity. As you consider what it takes to keep iniquity at bay, you realize that it is summarized in one word: integrity.

Integrity has qualities that allow the person to not only be convicted and checked towards iniquity, but it also allows him or her to humble his or herself in repentance. We know that David had this characteristic. Once he was made aware of his iniquity and transgression in regards to the incident with Bathsheba, he repented. He clearly acknowledged that there was no sacrifice that could atone for his sins.[10]

These two forms of sin must be properly dealt with. God will judge transgression and reject iniquity. This stern warning about iniquity can be found in Matthew 7:21-23,

---

[8] Proverbs 17:9

[9] Leviticus 18:29-30; 19:8; 20; 2 Samuel 1-12; Psalm 51:2-3; 1 Timothy 2:14;

[10] 1 Kings 9:4: Psalm 51:16

> Not every one that saith unto me, Lord, Lord, shall enter into the kingdom of heaven, but he that doeth the will of my Father which is in heaven. Many will say to me in that day, Lord, Lord, have we not prophesied in thy name? And in thy name have cast out devils? And in thy name done many wonderful works? And then will if profess unto them, I never knew you: depart from me, ye that work iniquity.

The people in these scriptures obviously will think of themselves as righteous. They may have been involved in religious activity, but according to Jesus they were harboring moral deviation. This deviation will put emphasis on works on behalf of God, but will be devoid of any inclination to do His will for His glory. The lack of inclination reveals a wrong motive or spirit behind such people. Since the point of moral deviation is pride, we can assume that these people were doing things in the name of Jesus for self-glorification. Therefore, their works would be considered iniquity before God.

Isaiah 53:10 tells us that Jesus became a substitute for us on the cross. He was made a sin offering.[11] Isaiah 53:5 reveals how Christ dealt with each form of sin, "But he was wounded for our transgressions, he was bruised for our iniquities..."

Through His wounds, He made restitution for our transgressions. His bruises were symbolic of His bearing our iniquities in His body to bring forth justification.[12] As a result, Jesus made forgiveness available to all who will come to Him by faith.

Sadly, people are still refusing to face their sins and accept God's provision. They are covering up transgression by outward conformity. They are hiding their iniquity behind a false light of righteousness, excuses, and justification. As a result, they stand condemned and ready to be rejected and forever cast from His presence.

How can people avoid the type of judgment that stands over those who commit transgressions and maintain iniquity in their hearts? Psalm 32:5 says, "I acknowledge my sin unto thee, and mine iniquity have I not hid. I said, I will confess my transgressions unto the LORD; and thou forgavest the iniquity of my sin."

All sins must be acknowledged, whether they are transgressions or iniquities. This means a person has to comprehend the reality of personal sin. There must be awareness as to what sin does to God and others. Ultimately, a person must take responsibility for the disposition and conduct that caused treacherous attitudes and acts towards God and others.

Iniquity is a matter of the heart, and must be brought to the light.[13] People must confront the deviations in their character, conduct, and

---

[11] 2 Corinthians 5:21

[12] Isaiah 53:11

[13] Psalm 41:6

practices. 2 Timothy 2:19c states, "...Let every one that nameth the name of Christ depart from iniquity."

People must change inclinations that give way to moral deviations. They must do away with any form of personal justification. Forms of sin must be rooted out, and those areas purged. Once again, we are reminded of King David's attitude about his iniquity in Psalm 51:2, "Wash me thoroughly from mine iniquity and cleanse me from my sin."

Titus 2:14 says, "Who gave himself for us, that he might redeem us from all iniquity, and purify unto himself a peculiar people, zealous of good works."

People must confess their transgressions. Confession points to a mournful, repentant attitude. The right attitude ensures a right spirit when it comes to properly confronting personal sins. Transgressions will no longer be acceptable. They must and will cease. Such an attitude points to offering a sacrifice that God can receive.

1 John 1:9 says, "If we confess our sins, he is faithful and just to forgive us our sins, and to cleanse us from all unrighteousness."

If confession is made in the right spirit, a person can make the same declaration as King David, "As far as the east is from the west, so far hath he removed our transgressions from us" (Psalm 103:12).

Take time to examine your disposition and conduct before God. Make sure you are not offending Him because of transgressions or iniquity. If you find either form of sin, cease! Exchange transgression with confession and obedience, and replace iniquity with integrity and mercy. Ask God to root out and cleanse you of all faults, and then, offer the sacrifices that He cannot resist.

9

TYPES OF SIN

There are two types of sin: commission and omission. Most people understand the sin of commission. This is where you commit a transgression against the Law or the covenant. In essence, a person commits an offence against God's rules or agreements or against a person's personal rights as far as showing proper honor and respect for persons and property. The Old Testament Law especially deals with the sins of commission.

Most religious people major in the sins of commission when dealing with the issue of sin. The reason for this is that these sins are visible to the eye. They represent the fruit of blatant rebellion. The problem with only addressing the sins of commission is that it commands that one conform outwardly. In other words, just cease from doing what is wrong, and you will be on the right track.

Such an emphasis can make sin simply a matter of outward action, rather than a matter of the heart. It keeps the disease of man's soul in the physical realm, rather than recognizing that all sin is a spiritual problem. In fact, the outward manifestations of sin reveal the spirit and disposition of a person. This indicates the ways of the old man, and speaks of the law of sin and death, as well as the consequences of hell and eternal damnation.[1]

Jesus brought sin out of just occurring in the physical arena into the unseen realm of spirit and motive. In Matthew 5:27-29, He talked about adultery. The sin of adultery was mentioned in the Ten Commandments as well.[2] Most know that it is morally wrong and a blatant affront against God's original design for marriage. However, Jesus brought the issue of adultery from a physical act to a manifestation of the heart condition. He made this statement in Matthew 5:27, "Ye have heard that it was said by them of old time, Thou shalt not commit adultery: but I say unto you, whosoever looketh on a women to lust after her hath committed adultery with her already in his heart."

It is a grave mistake to solely make sin a matter of what one does, rather than a matter of the intent of the heart and the attitude of the mind.

---

[1] Matthew 15:18-20; Romans 8:2

[2] Exodus 20:14

To keep the issue of sin on the surface ensures self-delusion and separation from God.

Christ came to address the complete issue of sin. When you consider Christianity, it is not a matter of not doing that which is wrong, but a matter of doing what is right. Righteousness is more about being upright before God in attitude and walk, than outward performance.

As you consider the work of the Holy Ghost, you realize that He contends with man by way of outward conduct to reveal inward disposition. For example, the third Person of the Godhead must first convict man of offences that he has committed. Then, He will reprove him of the unrighteousness that is prevalent in his inward disposition. He does this to keep man from facing impending judgment.[3]

Righteousness represents the inward man, while godliness deals with his outward conduct. The Apostle Paul said this about godliness in 1 Timothy 4:8, "For bodily exercise profiteth little: but godliness is profitable unto all things, having promise of the life that now is, and of that which is to come." Godliness is associated with piety and devotion. Devotion always expresses itself in pious living.

This brings us to the sin of omission. The New Testament exposes the face of this common sin. The sin of omission is the failure to do that which is right. James 4:17 confirms this, "Therefore to him that knoweth to do good, and doeth it not, to him it is sin." Sadly, most people do not realize that inaction in the matter of doing right is as much of a sin as wrong action.

A good example of the results of inaction towards sin is King David. He was mad that his oldest son raped his daughter, but he did not confront it. His inaction allowed the seeds of anger, bitterness, and hatred to take hold in his son Absalom. Absalom saw David's inaction as injustice, making David a weak, irresponsible leader in his eyes.

Another example of inaction can be observed in the life of the priest Eli, in 1 Samuel 2:12-36. His sons were wicked in their actions and conduct as priests of Jehovah God. Eli warned them that their actions would bring serious consequences, but he did not take action against their sin by relieving them of all their priestly duties. His complacency towards sin cost the lives of his sons, as well as Israel its precious ark.

Inaction reveals the real heart of the sin of omission. The subject of the heart brings us to another difference between the sins of commission and omission. At the core of the sin of commission is rebellion, but at the heart of the sin of omission is unbelief. Unbelief is the opposite of faith. Romans 14:23c states, "...for whatsoever is not of faith is sin."

People know what is right, but if it is not convenient or if it doesn't serve a purpose, they will figure a way around it. Such an attitude brings us to another difference between sins of commission and omission.

[3] John 16:7-7-11

People justify sins of commission, but they must harden their heart towards the conviction of the Holy Ghost in order to qualify omitting righteousness in a matter.

The story of Pharaoh in the first 12 chapters of Exodus is a good example of a man who was given an opportunity to do right by the children of Israel in light of Jehovah God's request to let them go and worship Him. However, he refused to do the right thing. And, each time he refused the requests of Moses, his heart became harder towards Jehovah God. Eventually, it cost him dearly, including his first-born.

Sadly, the practice of omitting righteousness is not an exception among those who call themselves Christians. I have even heard of Christians using prayer as a means to find a way around doing what is right, even though Scripture is clear about the subject. This type of attitude shows a lack of genuine faith.

Unfeigned faith towards God causes one to have his or her actions accounted to him or her as righteousness. God can only meet a person at the point of righteousness. Acceptable righteousness is not based on the whims of self, but on what is right to God. Righteousness involves the steps of faith. Each step of faith results in walking towards God in obedience. Ultimately, it fulfills the Law. [4]

Righteousness is motivated by love, responds because of faith, and expresses itself in obedience. As you study the ways of righteousness, a picture emerges. It begins with God's grace. His grace produces active faith in those who believe. Faith is the source of right standing before God that produces godly responses. It is only at the point of godly responses that God is able to fulfill His will and promises in a matter.

What one fails to do in regards to righteousness reveals much about his or her spirit and character. A person's heart becomes hardened towards God when he or she fails to simply do what is right.[5] This hardened heart can cause a person to turn away from the reality of God and His work. In such cases, salvation ends up being far away from such an individual.

A good example of the sin of omission can clearly be seen in the rich young ruler in Matthew 19. This young man came to Jesus seeking eternal life. Jesus told him that before He could enter into life, he had to keep the commandments. He declared that he kept the commandments that Jesus quoted. This was his way of saying that he was not guilty of the sins of commission in those areas. Then, Jesus said this to him in Matthew 19:21, "If thou wilt be perfect, go and sell that thou hast, and give to the poor, and thou shalt have treasure in heaven: and come follow me."

In summary, Jesus was saying to this young man that salvation was not just a matter of refraining from doing wrong, but it also included doing

---

[4] Romans 8:4; Galatians 3:6

[5] Hebrews 3:8-19

what is right. The sequence is clearly outlined in this situation. This young man was not instructed to follow Jesus until he did that which was righteous. The reason for this order is because this young man was putting his reliance in personal riches. Before people can truly follow Jesus, they must deal with idolatrous hindrances in their life. Such hindrances prove to be nothing more than worldly dependencies that cause divided loyalties.

When the rich young ruler heard Jesus' statement about giving up his possessions, he sorrowfully went away, for he had many possessions.[6] Jesus had put His finger on what would prevent this young man from going all the way to possess eternal life. The young man proved his dependency and idolatry when he preferred the temporary possessions of the world to eternal life.

Wherever idols reign, there will be weakness in character. Without character, an individual will not be able to stand or withstand the obstacles that confront him or her.[7] Therefore, weakness in character is what hinders many people from finishing the course. Omission means a person will stop in his or her spiritual walk before finishing the course. To stop in this manner implies that a person is giving into unbelief that often expresses itself through fear, compromise, justification, or despair.

Like the rich young ruler, it is easy for people to hide the sins of omission, while advocating personal righteousness. Deviance of character is harder to detect. This is why the sin of omission often proves to be the more dangerous of the two types of sin. People know when they are doing wrong, but they will delude themselves as to why they fail to do what is righteous. They actually trip over what seems to be insignificant, thus plunging headlong into the grasp of hell.

This is what happened to the rich man in Luke 16. The beggar Lazarus seemed insignificant and most likely served as an inconvenient nuisance at the rich man's gate. The rich man probably gave to religious causes, while justifying his indifference to Lazarus' physical condition. Outwardly, this man may have been known as a good citizen, but Lazarus exposed his inward disposition. The rich man may have done right in many ways, but he failed to do right by Lazarus who had become a victim of circumstances. His ungodly attitude and actions towards Lazarus is what ultimately tripped him up. In his pride and delusion, he failed to see Lazarus as the real test to his spiritual condition.

Religious platitudes and activities can cover up ungodly dispositions. However, the problem remains the same: People simply do not believe God. They do not believe what His Word declares. They do not take Him seriously, for they do not fear Him. As a result, they fail to act upon what they know is righteous.

---

[6] Matthew 19:22

[7] Ephesians 6:13-14

The main struggle in the area of disposition rests with man's delusion of self-sufficiency. In its fallen condition, the prideful disposition perceives that it is quite knowledgeable, and deserves to be served rather than to serve. Since it has a high opinion of self, it sees itself as superior, which gives way to complacency, laziness, apathy, and insensitivity to the real needs of others. Such a condition causes spiritual dullness. Therefore, there are always seemingly justifiable reasons for not doing that which is right when it is not convenient, comfortable, and self-serving.

There are three ungodly attitudes towards the Christian life. These attitudes are found among churchgoers who are committing the sin of omission. True righteousness is clearly missing in their lives. Each attitude displays a different heart condition that is revealed by the emphasis of these people's testimony surrounding Christianity. Keep in mind, Christians should have a testimony of Christ, but the people found in these three groups do not possess such a testimony.[8] These three groups can be called associating, assuming, or arrogant Christians.

Associated Christians are those who are associated with Christ through family, friends, and religious affiliations. These people have no personal testimony of Jesus. They talk about their church, testify of their religious leaders, and brag about religious activities and programs, but they appear to have no inclination towards God. In fact, they are ignorant or superstitious when it comes to God.

These Christians maintain Christianity as a religion that has no heart. As a result, they display indifference towards the truths of God. They are often motivated by fear because they do not want to give up their old life or the world that they highly value. Due to their fear, they play on the outskirts of the Christian life, while refusing to become identified with Christ in His death, burial, and resurrection.

Assuming Christians have had some type of religious exposure or experience such as saying the sinner's prayer, or have had some encounter with God. Since they had some type of religious exposure or experience, they assume they are Christians. Yet, their lives have never changed. Self is still reigning, causing them to be inconsistent in their responses. The reason for this inconsistency is due to their Christian life constantly being adjusted to the dictates of self.

When you ask assuming Christians for their testimony, they can only testify of their experience, but not about Jesus. These people walk in denial about their real spiritual condition before God. This denial is the product of these people avoiding truth. Their attitude towards truth causes them to walk in delusion. They display a stony heart that determines when the truth of God will penetrate their lives. This particular group of people insists on holding on to a religious illusion, instead of the Rock of Ages. The main reason for this insistence is because these individuals refuse to pay the price of self to know God.

---

[8] Revelation 12:11

The third group of people is made up of the *arrogant Christians*. The false light of personal self-righteousness deludes these people. This false light has blinded them to truth. Each time truth challenges them concerning righteousness, their heart becomes harder, and their ears grow deafer. These people actually pervert righteousness to confirm or complement their self-righteousness. They may talk the talk, but the power and fruit are missing.[9]

The testimony of arrogant Christians is about their religious discoveries or accomplishments. In other words, their goodness or spirituality is being exalted, instead of Jesus being lifted up in His glory. When you examine these people, you discover that they refuse to submit to the Lordship of Jesus. They want to control their religious worlds.

Each of these groups are guilty of the sin of omission. They may display clean lives outwardly, but inwardly, they are unclean vessels, full of the dead bones of vain, useless religious attempts.[10] Ignorance, fear, self, and erroneous beliefs is what motivates them. These people's attitude towards the Christian life causes them to fail to do that which is right. As they take pride in their religious association, experiences, or personal righteousness, they are failing to do that which is right and acceptable to God. They are committing the sin of omission.

What does your Christian life say about your devotion to God? Are you in rebellion, and are you trespassing against the Law, or is your life revealing character deviance that is being exposed by the sin of omission? Is Christianity a life that you are walking out by faith, or a religion that you are trying to control, in order to hold on to rights, self, and the world?

---

[9] Matthew 7:20; 13:14-15; 2 Timothy 3:5

[10] Matthew 23:26-27

10

PIGPENS

Sin creates pigpens. The most famous pigpen is found in the parable of the "Prodigal Son" in Luke 15. As you study this parable, you can see how people who possess worldly riches can find themselves partaking of a pigpen. It is not a pretty story, but it is a story many people can relate to.

Let us consider the steps of this foolish son. Instead of valuing his true possession, his heritage as a son of a great man, he valued an inheritance that was not yet rightly his. After all, his father was not yet dead, but this son was treating his father as such so he could claim his inheritance. Most pigpens reveal that a person's values are all wrong. Such individuals value temporary things that are only capable of bringing temporary pleasures that end in spiritual poverty.

The second aspect of this foolish son is that he was foolish with the inheritance, rather than a good steward. He used it to partake of the world. No doubt, he accumulated fair-weather friends, but there is nothing lasting in such riotous living. As the Bible tells us, a fool is quickly departed from his money.

Today, many people are foolish with what has been entrusted to them. Either they are using it to heap the world upon themselves, or they are using it to partake of endless worldly appetites. Either way, they are proving to be unfaithful stewards that will lose everything in the end. They will have no treasures waiting for them in the next life.

Since the foolish young man had spent all of his inheritance, he was ill prepared for the famine that came to the land. Sadly, this is true for many people, including some Christians. They are ill prepared for what is about to come upon America. There is already a spiritual famine in the land, and it is just a matter of time before there will be a physical famine. Either way, people who have been foolish with what they have been entrusted with, will find themselves unprepared to face the impending challenge.

The young foolish man became desperate in his plight. He had no means to fall back on. His fair-weather friends had abandoned him when the money ran out. He was now trying to survive in a meager environment. This is when he ended up in the pigpen, scrambling for the same food as the pigs.

This young man was Jewish, and hobnobbing with an unclean animal such as a pig, gave him a wake-up call as to how far he had fallen from his status or heritage as a son. Many people have created pigpens for themselves. They are hobnobbing with that which is unclean, competing for that which is considered garbage, and settling for an environment that reeks with decay and death. However, this is the type of environment that sin creates for everyone who trades their heritage with God for the things of this present age.

These pigpens can be spiritual, mental, emotional, or physical. Good deeds, religious cloaks, and various worldly activities can cover up the stench of these pigpens to those who are living in and partaking of them. Ultimately, these environments will harbor a disposition that demands independence, embraces perversion, and produces rebellion.

These pigpens find their roots in a stony heart. They gain momentum as the Word is either defiled by perversion or drowned out by the attractions or lusts of the world. Those in such pigpens wallow in spiritual slothfulness as they justify their worthless activities or complacent state with excuses.[1]

Pigpens often find their source in the victim mentality. They thrive on the residue of what once was, and operate in fantasies as to what could be. This means those in pigpens never deal in reality. Obviously, they evade reality, so they can avoid facing the stench of their particular pigpen. They insist on walking in delusion about the rotten odor that emits from their lives. They often ignore or cover up the stench of their pigpen, as well as blame others for the condition that surrounds them. Or, they can convince themselves that their particular pen is quite lovely since they are being gracious about living in such mire and filth.

You see this very delusion operating in the prodigal son. He joined himself to a citizen of the country. The citizen sent him out with the pigs. He had to compete with the animals to eat. When the prodigal son came to himself, he began to see his real plight and was able to reason out his options.

There are three main pigpens that people wallow in today. Each of us end up partaking of these pigpens. We ultimately design the pigpen we find ourselves in by determining the type of garbage that we partake of, as well its size, and the depth of depravity we allow ourselves to wallow in.

To say the least, the difference in individual pigpens allows for comparisons. It is not unusual for one whose pigpen may not be as obvious in appearance as the next pigpen to feel superior. Usually, those who gloat over the size of their pigpen are not bothering to examine the depth of it. Those who exalt their pigpen over another pigpen delude themselves about the quality of their garbage. Garbage is garbage. It will eventually rot away in the muck, regardless of its contents.

---

[1] Matthew 13:21-22; Romans 1:18

Let us consider the three main pigpens in existence. The first one is the *religious pigpen*. Jesus referred to this pigpen as being white sepulchers full of dead men's bones.[2] This simply means that the carcass has already rotted away; therefore, the stench is not obvious. However, open this tomb and you will find there is no life or substance. In fact, all you will encounter is darkness of the soul, for there is no real light.

In this sepulcher, you will find dead-letter doctrine. It has an outward appearance of righteousness, but lacks the right spirit. You find a semblance of truth, but it is handled in unrighteousness, defiling the spirit, intent, or power behind it.[3]

In this tomb, you will encounter a false light. Sadly, many are attracted to this false light, but mercy is missing and grace is abused and misused in the name of religion. The false light shows its piousness by swatting at a gnat, while swallowing a camel. In other words, its focus is on religious practices while ignoring the heart that is far from God, and a disposition that expresses the hypocrisy of its practices.[4]

This pigpen is popular among those who think themselves pious. They delude themselves by their own self-righteousness, because they hide their wickedness behind a cloak, while they maintain their religious reputation. They can cling to the world as they claim devotion to God. In fact, they can adjust everything according to their pigpen, while giving the appearance of being godly. Jesus said this, "Ye hypocrites, well did Esaias prophesy of you, saying, This people draweth nigh unto me with their mouth, and honoureth me with their lips, but their heart is far from me" (Matthew 15:7-8).

The next pigpen is *self*. This pigpen can be quite small, but it is filled with the endless waste and residue of the lust of the flesh. This pigpen is marked by disillusionment. It reeks with the stench of rebellion. Even though it is full of things or possessions, it is all a matter of vanity. All such things stand useless for they hold no value. In fact, the things associated with this pigpen are temporary and destined for judgment. The temporary pleasure it brings quickly fades as attractions or lusts are turned toward those things that are newer or out of reach. This brings us to the next harsh reality of this pigpen: the endless pursuit for nothing. As each lust is satisfied, it is enlarged to want more. Lust is like a leech that continues to grow at the expense of others, but can never be satisfied.

In a way, lust becomes an organism in and of itself. It eventually consumes the whole person. Before long, it leaves a carcass that is clearly exposed to the world. In addition, the stench it emits is beyond description. There is no reason or beauty left in the remains, just the

---

[2] Matthew 23:27

[3] Romans 1:18

[4] Matthew 9:13; 15:8-9; 23:24; John 15:22; 2 Timothy 3:5

terrible reality of what the carcass once was, and what it will never become. Obviously, the life of this carcass has not only been offered up on the altars of lust and pleasure, but it has been robbed and wasted away to the point that it has finally destroyed itself. Now it lies in the remaining debris of foolishness and judgment.

It is hard for one to watch as the pigpens consume the life and potential of its occupants. You want to jump in and save these individuals from such a judgment, but such people will turn on you in resentment. Since they do not want to budge from their pigpen, the next tendency is to get in their pigpen with them and try to help clean it up. This is for the purpose of bringing contrast to the bondage such pens will bring to the soul of a person. Instead of serving as a contrast, the people in these pigpens actually believe they are worthy of being made more comfortable in their pens. After all, in their minds, they are victims of these garbage pits, not instigators or inventors of them. These individuals also possess an insatiable lust that only knows how to take, not give. Therefore, no matter how you attempt to change these people's pigpens, they will go back to their original state, and in some cases, become worse. Jesus gives us this insight in Matthew 7:6, "Give not that which is holy unto the dogs, neither cast ye your pearls before swine, least they trample them under their feet, and turn again and rend you."

The Apostle Peter made this statement in 1 Peter 2:22, "But it is happened unto them according to the true proverb, The dog is turned to his own vomit again; and the sow that was washed to her wallowing in the mire."

The third pigpen is the largest of the three pigpens. It is the *world*. It is hard to believe, in all of its glamour and glitter, that the world is nothing but one big, overrated pigpen. Behind the glamour and glitter of the world is an incredible stench of defiance and idolatry. Defiance comes out in self-sufficiency as people bow down to the different idols of the world to find purpose and happiness. Keep in mind that the world offers personal kingdoms where one will supposedly find satisfaction and happiness. Clearly, the world is forever putting forth the proverbial carrot of success that must be obtained in order to receive the benefits of the present age that will bring this desired utopia. However, each kingdom that man obtains in this present world turns out to be nothing more than an overrated pigpen that leaves those wallowing in utter despair.

People who pursue this proverbial carrot of possessing some type of personal kingdom or utopia find there is always another carrot that must be acquired before happiness can be realized. Individuals become so caught up with the chase that they fail to realize that they have become entangled in a web of idolatry and lies. In fact, they lose a sense of what is important. Their perception, priorities, and sense of values are changed.

People in the world's pigpen eventually offer that which possesses a heavenly value upon the altars of selfishness in order to pursue that which is temporary.[5] They not only sacrifice what is valuable for what is useless, but they betray themselves. When they come to the end of this chase, they may have obtained a few "carrots", but they stand in the midst of broken dreams and shattered lives. Sadly, many discover that what is at the end of the world's rainbow is not a pot of gold or success, but failure. Too late, they realize that they are lost and drowning in hopelessness, while the emptiness of the world mocks them.

There are many warnings in Scripture about pursuing or valuing the world. Such preference makes one an enemy of God. If the love of the world is in a person, then the love of God will be missing. Identification with the world reveals that one is committing spiritual harlotry or adultery.[6]

The Apostle Peter referred to God's people as sojourners who will simply pass through the world. They may see the glitter of the world, but they will not partake of it, for they are looking for a city made by God. They may encounter the glamour of the world, but they will remember that it is all temporary vanity in light of the glory awaiting them. They may even experience a few attractions along the way, but realize that they are fleeting or temporary in light of eternity.[7]

Peter said this in 2 Peter 1:3-4,

> According as his divine power hath given unto us all things that pertain unto life and godliness, through the knowledge of him that hath called us to glory and virtue: Whereby are given unto us exceeding great and precious promises: that by these ye might be partakers of the divine nature, having escaped the corruption that is in the world through lust.

Christians have been given the means to live godly in this world." They partake of Jesus' nature because they have escaped the corruption that is in the present age. Escaping the corruption of the world is not a future promise, but must be a present reality.

There are four reactions to the world. We have already dealt with the acceptable response of the sojourner. Like a tourist, they may see the world, but they are simply passing through. They are spiritual pilgrims on their way to discover heavenly territories and treasures that will far outweigh this present world.

The three other attitudes toward the world are destructive. The first attitude is that of the *victim*. This person has become entangled in the web of the world. He or she knows it as the pigpen it really is. After all, this individual has tasted the bitter dregs of it, knowing that it leaves one as helpless prey on an empty street leading to destruction.

The second attitude is that of the *associate*. These people do not want to be directly linked to the world and its destructive entanglements.

---

[5] 2 Timothy 2:3-4; 1 John 2:17

[6] James 4:4; 1 John 2:15

[7] Hebrews 11:8-10; I Peter 2:11

However, they want the benefits of the world without being identified with the perversion of it. Ultimately, they prey on the victims, and spread the filth of the world in various ways for personal gain. They actually cover their self-serving way with foolish glitter, and their false promises and perversion with fading glamour.

The final group is the *pleasure seekers*. They are seeking the god of pleasure. It does not matter what they compromise to partake of the smorgasbord of lust and filth that the world offers. It has little significance to them that such pleasure is temporary, even though residues of it may haunt them the rest of their lives. These people see the seductive, but dangerous fruit of the world as daring and satisfying. They flirt with this fruit, thinking that they are immune or an exception to the poison that lurks with every bite.

It is amazing how Christians flirt with these different pigpens. Jesus talked about how to respond to these filthy environments. For those in the religious pigpen, He clearly rebuked them. He exposed their hypocrisy and condemned them for leading others into this pigpen of religious dry bones. He offered them healing in order to raise them up in newness of the Spirit, but many of them refused and later were involved in demanding His crucifixion.[8]

For the pigpen of self, Jesus left the person in it to suffer its bitter vanity. A good example of this pigpen is the prodigal son. The father never tried to prevent him from going his own way. He never sought after him. When the son realized how far he had fallen in his selfish life, he did come to his senses. When he returned home, broken and repentant, his father embraced him.

Jesus will not seek us out in any of our pigpens. Granted, He looks for the one lost sheep, but you will not find sheep wallowing with the pigs in their pens. His call is simple, "Follow Me to green pastures."[9]

In the final scenario, Jesus exposed the heart that is towards the world in the rich young ruler in Matthew 19:16-23. This young man was seeking a spiritual life he could attach to his worldly lifestyle. However, Jesus put His finger on his real treasures: that of worldly wealth. He exposed the young man's idolatrous heart. When Jesus gave the rich young man a choice between his idol or eternal life, the foolish young man preferred the temporary wealth of the world to the eternal treasure of heaven. He walked away from Jesus in sorrow. Jesus did not chase after him, plead with him to reconsider his choice, or debate with him. He simply let him walk back into the pigpen of the world.

Are you wallowing in one or more of these pigpens, or are you walking the narrow path of eternal life? Jesus may challenge you, leave you behind, or let you walk back to your pigpen after exposing your heart, but He will not wallow in any pigpen with you or try to clean it up

---

[8] Luke 5:17; John 19:6

[9] Luke 15:3-7; John 10:1-11

so you can enjoy it. If you are in a pigpen, it comes down to a matter of personal choice and preference. It is up to you to leave your pigpen behind and choose to follow Jesus into the green pastures of the Christian life.

11

FACING PERVERSION

It is hard for most people to accept that they are surrounded by the perversion of pigpens. Whether it is a pigpen created by the false light of religion, the selfishness of the old man, or the attractions of the world, it is hard to fathom the power and destruction they hold. Pigpens represent one consistent reality, and that is their ability to pervert the character, work, and promises of God. This perversion points to defilement.

"Defilement" means to trample under, contaminate, or to make something unclean or impure.[1] All pigpens find their origin in the way people think. The battle that rages today is for the mind, and in the mind. As in the days of Noah, perversion has found an inroad into the minds of many. The imaginations of many people's thoughts are becoming continually evil. You wonder how long God's Spirit will strive with this present world before He is so quenched and grieved that He withdraws. Once the Holy Ghost withdraws, then judgment clearly awaits to swallow those who insist on being unholy. [2]

Hebrews 12:14 gives us this warning, "Follow peace with all men and holiness, without which no man shall see the Lord." Without holy conduct, one will not see God. This holy conduct involves an upright disposition. Disposition is how one will view, determine, approach, or discern what is holy. It also points to character.

People operate according to three types of what we would consider "respectable" character: 1) There is the character that causes people to take responsibility for ensuring well-being and an honorable or decent lifestyle for themselves as well as others, 2) there is moral character that avoids and flees from sexual deviance, and 3) finally, there is godly character that includes integrity. Character begins with a choice. It is not given, but forged. It is developed as one goes against the grain of what seems natural, pleasant, and satisfying. For the Christian, this means denying self, picking up the cross to ensure discipline and death to the self-life, and following Jesus into a new life.[3]

Christians must have godly character. The reason for this is because God is holy. Godly character entails the other two forms of character of

---

[1] Webster's New Collegiate Dictionary

[2] Genesis 6:5-6; Ephesians 4:30; 1 Thessalonians 5:19; 2 Corinthians 10:4-5

[3] Matthew 16:24

being responsible and moral, but it expresses itself in uprightness before God and honorable conduct towards others. The Apostle Peter made this statement, "But as he which hath called you is holy, so be ye holy in all manner of conversation. Because it is written, Be ye holy; for I am holy" (1 Peter 1:15-16). Since God is holy, all manner of conversation or behavior must be separate from the world and become upright before God. This godly conduct must be apparent in every area of a Christian's life.

Once people give way to unholiness in any form, it invades and permeates their entire being, defiling everything. Titus 1:15-16 confirms this harsh reality,

> Unto the pure all things are pure: but unto them that are defiled and unbelieving is nothing pure; but even their mind and conscience is defiled. They profess that they know God; but in works they deny him, being abominable and disobedient, and unto every good work reprobate.

I have worked with people who have a defiled mind. Everything they see is perverted. For example, perverted minds can consider the kindness of the opposite sex as a come on, rather than the person simply being considerate towards them. Something can be innocently said, but people with dirty minds will pervert it into something that is sick or twisted in meaning. The perception of these people makes them unpredictable and untrustworthy.

If a person has a pure perspective, he or she will only regard things in a sincere way. However, as you can see, people who are defiled will contaminate everything with perversion, treachery, and suspicion. All things become untrustworthy to them, while they become untrustworthy in all of their dealings with others. In fact, those things that are pure or done in purity will be perverted and questioned. Those who are defiled may profess that they know God, but their practices deny Him. The deeds they do on His behalf are considered reprobate.

Reprobate is not mentioned much in the Bible, but it is a hard word that must be reconciled in the hearts of believers. It implies despised, rejected, cast away, and worthless.[4] Romans 1:28 talks about God giving those who are practicing the works of the flesh, over to a reprobate mind. Such a mind will not retain any real knowledge of God. The Apostle Paul also talked about men who were reprobates concerning the faith. Faith of this nature is worthless because the men have resisted the truth, thereby, corrupting their minds.[5] In 2 Corinthians 13:5, Paul identified those who are without Christ as being reprobates.

Unbelief, *disobedience,* and *reprobate* are words that are associated with each other. If a person lacks genuine faith, he or she walks in

---

[4] Strong's Exhaustive Concordance of the Bible; #3988; 96

[5] 2 Timothy 3:8

disobedience before God. Disobedience produces a darkness that will cause one to become a reprobate in mind and deed.

The Apostle Paul made reference to personal concerns about becoming a reprobate in 1 Corinthians 9:26-27, "I therefore so run, not as uncertainly; so fight I, not as one that beateth the air: but I keep under my body, and bring it into subjection lest that by any means, when I have preached to others, I myself should be a castaway."

"Castaway" points to reprobate. The Apostle Paul kept his body or his conduct under subjection to avoid becoming useless to God, and rejected by Him. If Paul was concerned about being a castaway, so should all followers of Jesus.

Defilement is in the same category as unbelief. People who operate in perversion do not fear God; therefore, they do not believe Him. I have even heard some of these people joke about going to hell because they refuse to confront and overcome the perversion in their lives. Obviously, such people do not know God. If they did, they would not joke about the prospect of falling into His hands to taste His wrath upon their disobedience.[6]

There are two popular avenues of defilement: pornography and fantasy. When people think of pornography, they think in terms of hard core pornography, but if you check out the Greek word for fornication, it comes from the word, "ek-porn." Pornography is a form of fornication. In fact, in light of God's holiness He regards all thoughts, acts, and practices of fornication as being pornography. Pornography is any act or practice outside of what is chaste or acceptable conduct. To the Christian, this also includes attitude and practices surrounding the marriage bed.[7]

Fornication not only includes all illicit sex acts, but idolatry. Idolatry is spiritual fornication. It is the one sin that brings people into agreement with the unholy, thus defiling their temple (body), minds, and testimony. The Apostle Paul said this, "Flee fornication. Every sin that a man doeth is without the body: but he that committed fornication sinneth against his own body" (1 Corinthians 6:18).

The Apostle Paul gives this warning in 1 Corinthians 3:16-17, "Know ye not that ye are the temple of God, and that the Spirit of God dwelleth in you? If any man defile the temple of God, him shall God destroy; for the temple is holy, which temple ye are."

Fantasy is the other perversion. Pornography perverts people's perception of sexuality, marriage, and the bed by making everything come into subjection to their sick imagination or reality, but fantasy perverts what constitutes actual reality. Pornography perverts how people look at their sexuality, as well as the opposite sex, while fantasy perverts how people look at life. Pornography demotes the dignity of

---

[6] Romans 1:18; 28-32; Ephesians 2:1-3; Hebrews 10:31; 12:28-29

[7] Hebrews 13:4

humanity, while fantasy exalts a desire or expectation into a place of reality, causing indifference to the actual environment. Pornography causes people to be indifferent to others, while fantasy causes people to be irresponsible toward others. Pornography promises satisfaction of the appetites and desires, while fantasy offers fulfillment in the way of blissful happiness.

These two perverted realities can be clearly observed in people who operate within them. If you have been around people in pornography, you will notice that they are cruel and indifferent as to how their acts are affecting others. I knew of a man whose whole family was devastated by his perversion, but he would not repent and walk away from it.

As for those who operate in fantasy, they become angry because reality will not bow down to their idea of what it means to live out the happiness of their unrealistic fantasies. A good example of this can be seen in the attitude of those who are part of the Hollywood scene. Some of these people think you can direct your life and create a world that will come into compliance with personal ideas of life. When you challenge or dare to intrude into these people's fantasy about life, they will deem you stupid, and will display anger and hatred towards such a challenge or intrusion.

This brings us to how perversion works. It desensitizes a person as to what is holy in order to indoctrinate a person to accept or embrace the unholy. For example, the images erected in the mind begin to determine what will satisfy the appetites. These images have the ability to stir up the imagination to consider the possibilities of how this will create personal satisfaction or pleasure.

Although the image has no substance behind it, evil imaginations give it life and purpose. Now that the imagination is stirred up, the emotions kick in. For pornography, the image has the ability to produce a sensual ecstasy beyond description, while fantasy will stir up the passions in light of the incredible pleasure that will be brought with it. As the emotions ride the high wave of expectancy, a self-centered mentality begins to escalate. This mentality will change any focus, priorities, and inclinations that may have been towards God and what is holy.

In the erection and maintenance of these images, a person's pigpen grows. There are now greater opportunities to taste the forbidden fruit from the tree of knowledge of good and evil. It is surface, self-serving and fleshly, but at this time, it is desired because it is feeding the flesh as to the possible satisfaction that awaits it, while appeasing the pride.

At this point, the person is bowing down to this image, committing idolatry. The person is actually giving this image an identity, purpose, and life. This image becomes more real than the reality that surrounds the individual. In fact, reality becomes unattractive. The individual then makes shrines to this image in his or her mind until the reality around it can be fulfilled. Each time he or she visits the shrine, the desires and possibilities grow until they become driving and tormenting.

As a person toys with the different possibilities, he or she opens him or herself up to spirits of seduction and perversion, as well as a spirit of antichrist. These spirits will produce complacency and laziness. This complacency will be directed towards the things of God, where a person has no desire to respond to God. Laziness on the other hand, will not choose to do what is necessary to overcome. Such lack of initiative is due to the fact that there is also slothfulness.

In dealing with people with grave problems of perversion, you cannot help but notice how steep they are in complacency. You cannot get them to act against their sin. After all, many love the sin of perversion. This love is self-serving, but these deluded individuals can perceive this unholy condition as actually adding to the quality of their life. However, it is a delusion that will create an abyss of depression while sucking them down into the abyss of hell.

There is a tremendous amount of seduction behind perversion. Usually there is a seductive spirit attached to these perverted avenues. This spirit will seduce individuals into a perverted trap, by throwing a covering over their heads, so that they cannot see what it is really doing or where it is taking them. The seductive spirit will ultimately divide people from reality, and isolate them from truth, in order to conquer them.

The Apostle Paul gave this warning, "Now the Spirit speaketh expressly, that in the latter times some shall depart from the faith, giving heed to seductive spirits and doctrines of devils" (1 Timothy 4:2). Seductive spirits will be prevalent in the end days. One can easily see them in operation in movies, music, printed material, the Internet, and heretical teachings.

Perverted spirits are unclean spirits. They will defile the truth, erode away morality, and wear down resolve. They express themselves through lusts, obsession, and unclean acts. They tantalize fleshly appetites. Once a person gives in to these appetites, he or she feels empty and shameful. These feelings wear off as complacency begins to shut down the individual.

Sadly, it does not take much for the imagination to once again be stirred up. It only takes an image, thought, or right situation. The complacency lifts, revealing greater appetites. These appetites become tormenting, wearing down the person's resolve to withstand the temptation. Eventually, he or she gives in. Each time the person gives in, his or her conscience become seared.[8]

An antichrist spirit becomes a substitute for God and His work in many of these people's lives. In fact, everything that belongs to the world is designed to become a substitute for God. Some of the things of the world are necessary for living, such as money, but if exalted, even that which is necessary can become gods that are pursued, while the true

[8] 1 Timothy 4:2

God of heaven is left behind. Other things of the world are meant to pervert reality, such as the philosophy of humanism and the theory of evolution. Such perversion serves as a substitute for truth. There are also the religions of the world that pervert that which is holy and acceptable to God. These religions replace genuine faith in the one true, living God.

Seductive spirits are often behind perversion and the antichrist substitutes. As previously stated, these spirits must first throw an evil covering over people, so that they are unaware of what they are pursuing or being influenced by.[9] This covering allows people to embrace the lie or substitute, as the wicked covering blinds them to destruction.

This brings us to the consequences of sin. People fear and mock these consequences, but they are an impending reality that people must face. These realities are not meant to scare people into the kingdom of God. Such fear tactics are not only counterproductive, but they are unable to change the inward man for salvation to come forth. Rather, these realities are meant to bring sobriety so that people will gravely consider the reality of eternity in light of their present, temporary age of vanity and deception.

[9] Isaiah 25:7; 30:1

12

CONSEQUENCES OF SIN

One cannot talk about sin without talking about its consequences. Oswald Chambers maintains that modern Christianity is leaving out the doctrine of sin. By doing this, Christian leaders end up patronizing Jesus, rather than presenting Him in the light of man's desperate need for redemption.[1]

To downplay sin is a blatant affront against the Gospel. Sin is the reason for Jesus' work of redemption on the cross. He came to buy each of us back from the rights and claims sin has on our souls. Until man's perception and soul are set right by the reality of Christ's redemption, he will patronize, ignore, or reject God's provision.

This brings us to the consequences of sin. Few understand the consequences. Some mock the concept of these consequences or ignore them. Others insist on walking in delusion about the consequences, or they blindly rest in spiritual ignorance that leaves them happy in their unrealistic fantasy. That is until the reality of man's mortality shakes them into a fleeting moment of truth.

Romans 6:23 talks about the initial consequence of sin, "For the wages of sin is death; but the gift of God is eternal life through Jesus Christ our Lord." The first word we must consider is *wages*. "Wages" are what are properly allotted or due to a person because the individual had actually earned it. Remember, wages are not given to freeloaders. The first presentation of sin is that we have earned the wages that come with it, and that the proper allotment it carries with it is that of death.

The wages of sin include such things as darkness, ignorance, rebellion, and delusion. These are the natural preferences of men who walk according to the workings of sin, but each of these works of darkness carry the death penalty. What constitutes death? To many people, death represents finality. There is a distinct finality to death, but it also serves as a beginning. The finality involves life ceasing as one knows it. The reality of physical death is that it serves as a door to eternity where a different existence awaits those who enter in.

Spiritual death points to separation from God. Jesus serves as the only source of eternal life. Without this life, people are spiritually dead.

---

[1] Daily Thoughts for Disciples; Oswald Chambers, © 1990 by Oswald Chambers Publications Association; devotion of June 28

They have no means by which to interact with God. They may believe in God, but they will remain strangers to Him. They may talk about God, but He does not recognize them because they are not sealed with His Holy Ghost.[2]

The Bible is clear that we must be born from above. Eternal life comes from above into a person when he or she believes in his or her heart the Gospel message. At the heart of this Gospel message is the light of the world who exposes sin. As a result, the light walked among darkness to take away the cloak that cleverly hid the depravity of man. Jesus is the light of man. He allowed Himself to be offered up as a sin offering on the cross. Here He bought back men's souls from the domain of sin and death and the harsh taskmaster of Satan, as well as the jaws of hell.[3]

Jesus accomplished this feat with His death, burial, and resurrection. The Gospel message is the power of God unto salvation. It can penetrate the darkest heart and mind with the hope of Christ. The Gospel summarizes what Jesus overcame, so that people can experience spiritual victory. He experienced physical death, so people could experience spiritual birth and life. He was buried, so that each blood-bought saint could be made alive unto God. He was raised from the grave, so that believers could walk in newness of life with resurrected power.[4]

Physical death is the door that leads into immortality. Man was created to live forever. When he enters the door of death, he will put off the corruptible in preparation of putting on the incorruptible.[5] This is why man has a hard time thinking of his physical demise. His spirit and soul have no end to their existence. He is meant to live forever.

What happens to those who refuse to accept God's provision? The prophet Daniel gives us insight into this question in Daniel 12:2, "And many of them that sleep in the dust of the earth shall awake, some to everlasting life, and some to shame and everlasting contempt." The key word is "everlasting."

Jesus confirmed this everlasting punishment in John 5:29, and the Apostle Peter made this statement in 2 Peter 2:9, "The Lord knoweth how to deliver the godly out of temptations, and to reserve the unjust unto the day of judgment to be punished." Everyone will spend eternity in some type of state. Some will experience everlasting life, while others will face everlasting shame and contempt or spiritual death.

---

[2] John 5:39; 14:6: Ephesians 11-14; Colossians 1:20-22

[3] Matthew 10:28; John 1:1-4; 3:3 & 5; 15:22; Romans 8:2; 2 Corinthians 5:21; 2 Timothy 1:10; Hebrews 2:14-17; 9:11-16; 10:10

[4] Romans 1:16; 6:4-5; 10:9-10; 1 Corinthians 15:1-4, 54-57; 2 Corinthians 4:3-6; 2 Timothy 2:11-12

[5] 1 Corinthians 15:49-53

The quality of our eternal existence rests with what we do with Jesus in our present life. We will either be broken by the reality of Who He is and what He did for us on the cross unto repentance, regeneration, and transformation. Or, on Judgment Day, He will crush us. We will embrace His redemption by faith, or it will become a stumbling block to our religious conscience and foolishness to our logic.[6]

The cross of Jesus causes a real division. It looms in the midst of humanity, and there is no way that people can avoid coming face-to-face with it. Either they will bow before it, or they will try to destroy it, only to have it fall upon them in utter judgment.

This brings us to the second part of the consequences. It results in the second death. It has been pointed out that if you are born twice, you will die once, but if you are born once, you will die twice. Revelation 20:6 brings out this second death, "Blessed and holy is he that hath part in the first resurrection: on such the second death hath no power, but they shall be priests of God and of Christ, and shall reign with him a thousand years." The second death points to the judgment of utter separation from God. Separation in this text will be realized at the Great White Throne of Judgment. Those who refuse to accept God's provision by faith will be judged on the basis of their life. Like King Belshazzar in Daniel 5, the Law of God will weigh them in the balance. In the end, each person will be found wanting since God's righteous Law can only condemn, not justify.[7]

To confirm this judgment, the Book of Life will be opened. The Book of Life contains those who have received Jesus Christ as the only means of salvation. Sadly, this book will have many dark blotches or empty spaces. Each mark or empty space represents a name that has been blotted out.[8]

How many assume their names are in this book? How many are simply hoping their names are in this book? Each blot is a sober reminder that we must receive God's provision on His terms. After all, each name blotted out represents a useless life marred by sin, unbelief, and foolishness. Each space will serve as a reminder that the possibilities were great and the hope was bright, but it was sold for temporary pleasures, selfish rights, and worldly pursuits. Who among those that are assuming they are in this book have been forever blotted from the view of God because of their unbelief and rebellion?

Each person will be judged and cast into the lake of fire, but this judgment has not yet happened. Meanwhile, what has happened to those lost souls as they await this fearful judgment? Jesus answered this

---

[6] Matthew 21:44; 1 Corinthians 1:17-23

[7] Galatians 2:16; Revelation 20:11-15

[8] Exodus 32:32: Psalm 69:28; Daniel 12:1; Luke 10:20: Revelations 3:5; 20:15

question in Luke 16:19-31. These lost souls will be sent to a holding place known as hell.[9]

The concept of "hell" embraces eternal separation. It would include the lake of fire, but there is also a place, referred to as Hades or hell that was created as a temporary holding place for fallen angels. These angels are being reserved until judgment day. Sadly, this is where unregenerate man ends up as well. These are the people who choose not to believe God and walk according to their personal preferences. These preferences are the ways of sin and death. The ways of sin and death cause lost individuals to walk in darkness, preventing them from seeing the destruction ahead of them. [10]

Jesus gives us insight into this destruction in Matthew 10:28, "And fear not them which kill the body, but are not able to kill the soul: but rather fear him which is able to destroy both soul and body in hell." The term that Jesus used in regard to hell was "destroy" and not "kill." *Vine's Expository Dictionary of Biblical Words* explains the intent of the word "destroy". It is in relationship to wellbeing. In other words, a soul is not extinguished, but it will be void of satisfaction and peace. Like a broken jaw, the soul will lie in ruin, wretched, and unrecognizable as to its former state.

This type of destruction in hell is described in Scripture. It is primarily a place of punishment. Matthew 5:22 and Luke 9:48 talk about the fire of hell that will never be quenched. Matthew 24:51 speaks of weeping and gnashing of teeth. These scriptures show suffering, torment, and unrest. I once heard that hell is the place where people will forever pursue those things they pursued on earth, but they will never be able to obtain that which is being pursue to know the temporary satisfaction of it. As the Bible says, hell is the place, "Where their worm dieth not, and the fire is not quenched." There is nothing more tormenting than not being able to quench or satisfy a desire. Torment eats at people like worms that work to break down their source of nourishment. I meditated on the idea of this torment, and realized that people suffer in the same way on earth with these desires, but they are temporarily able to satisfy them because they have a body. However, in hell, the corruptible body will be missing.

Jesus clearly dealt with the subject of hell in the story of Lazarus, the beggar and the rich man in Luke 16:19-31. This story not only confirms there is a hell, but reveals the type of person who will end up there, as well as the sin that many will trip over to find themselves flung into this tormenting place. I have already made reference to this story, but we need to consider it in light of torment.

The first person Jesus introduced in the story was the rich man. He was clothed in purple and fine linens. His clothing implied that he was of royalty or affiliated with people of power and prominence. Jesus goes on

---

[9] Revelation 20:14

[10] John 3:19-21; Romans 8:2; 2 Peter 2:4, Jude 6

to say how this man fared sumptuously every day. Obviously, this man lacked nothing. He had the means to help others, and most likely, he gave to people in ways that would be noticed by others, while inwardly holding tightly to his riches. Even though Jesus does not claim that this man is stingy and self-serving with his riches, his attitude would be exposed in a way that he would never have suspected.

The subject of riches can be found throughout the Bible. Jesus said in Matthew 19:23-24, "Verily I say unto you, That a rich man shall hardly enter into the kingdom of heaven. And again I say unto you, it is easier for a camel to go through the eye of a needle, than for a rich man to enter into the kingdom of God." Such a thought inspires a provoking question about what constitutes riches. For the man in the story, it had to be prestige and financial wealth. For other people, it could mean education, homes, respect, and honor. For example, what would make you feel rich, and would others consider you rich?

People value different things. Therefore, people's perception of what is important varies. Jesus tells us how we can determine what we consider to be valuable in Matthew 6:21, "For where your treasure is, there will your heart be also." Our treasure comes down to what possesses our heart. The thing or things that possess our heart will determine our pursuits.

There is only one treasure that deserves to possess our hearts. Such treasure is not a thing, but a person. His name is Jesus Christ.[11] If any other person or possession possesses our heart, it will become a point of idolatrous dependency and self-sufficiency. Self-sufficiency will cause a person to become spiritually indifferent and blind, causing him or her to fail the test in times of temptation.

The Bible is clear, that which constitutes worldly wealth is not good or bad. It is the type of emphasis that we put on it that will determine whether it proves to be a spiritual asset or liability. God gives man everything he possesses. In turn, man must offer it back for God's use to keep it in the right perspective. If it is not properly used for God's purpose, it will be the very thing that will trip us up over that which we will consider to be insignificant.

Jesus then introduced Lazarus. Here he brought a contrast between these two men. The difference was not only on a physical level, but a spiritual one. Lazarus was a beggar. Immediately, we automatically think he was probably some type of loser. He must have been lazy to be in this condition. However, go to the next statement, and you will learn that Lazarus was sick. He was full of sores. In other words, he was not in this state because of slothfulness or irresponsibility. He was in this situation because of circumstances.

Lazarus was at a great disadvantage. He had no money, and he was devoid of good health. This condition put him in the precarious position of

[11] Colossians 2:2-3

having to rely on the mercy of those who were blessed. Jesus tells us that he lay at the gate of this rich man, desirous of the simple crumbs that fell from this man's table. What was this rich man's responsibility?

From the information we have in this story, the rich man was Jewish. After all, he called Abraham, "Father." God established that the reason He blessed the Jewish nation was so they could bless others who were less fortunate. They were to feed the widows, poor, and strangers. As you study the Law of God, you begin to realize that the least fortunate individuals were used to test those who were blessed. The failure to respond properly would bring retribution from God. [12]

The Apostle John equated being sensitive to others' needs with an act of godly love in 1 John 3:16-18,

> Hereby perceive we the love of God, because he laid down his life for us: and we ought to lay down our lives for the brethren. But whoso hath this world's good, and seeth his brother have need, and shutteth up his bowels of compassion from him, how dwelleth the love of God in him? My little children, let us not love in word, neither in tongue; but in deed and in truth.

Lazarus was a test to the rich man. Would the rich man prove to be obedient to what was right or would he deem Lazarus as insignificant? The problem with riches is that they can be greatly abused. The dichotomy is that worldly riches often make people think as paupers. I cannot tell you how many rich people talk about how poor they are, as they lavish the things of the world upon themselves. They moan about limited budgets, as they sit with thousands of dollars stashed in various funds and saving accounts. Indeed, these people are poor, not in worldly goods, but rather in character. The lack of character not only reveals their hypocrisy, but it will trip them up, and cause them to fall into unmerciful judgment since they have conveniently ignored the needs of others around them.

Obviously, the rich man ignored Lazarus. Lazarus died due to the possible neglect or indifference of the rich man. We see this same type of indifference among professing Christians. How many struggling Christians have fallen prey to the same type of neglect from other professing Christians?

In the end, the dogs showed more compassion to Lazarus than the rich man. They at least licked his sores. Jesus tells us that this insignificant man was carried to Abraham's bosom by the angels.

Later, the rich man died. I am sure he was surprised to find himself in hell. He lifted up his eyes to see Abraham and Lazarus. There was a great gulf fixed between the bosom of Abraham and hell. Apparently, those in hell could see those who were experiencing the blessings of

---

[12] Exodus 22:21-24; Leviticus 19:10, 15; Deuteronomy 15:4-11; 1 Samuel 1:7-8; Isaiah 1:17

God. Likewise, those in Abraham's bosom could see hell. The rich man cried out to Abraham to send Lazarus to put cool water on his tongue.

Keep in mind, this rich man never gave a thought to Lazarus when he lay at his gate. He failed to show mercy or compassion to him. Yet, this man asked Abraham to send Lazarus to temporarily relieve him of his great torment. This man was reaping in his after-life what he sowed in his earthly life. His torment was a mirror of his spiritual poverty that was clearly based on his lack of investment in those he considered insignificant.[13] Jesus said it best in Luke 6:38, "Give, and it shall be given unto you; good measure, pressed down, and shaken together, and running over, shall men give into your bosom. For with the same measure that ye mete withal it shall be measured to you again."

Jesus' words should echo in the recesses of everyone's heart. The measure I give here will be given back to me in eternity. Hell was revealing the measure that the rich man had given to Lazarus. The torment of Lazarus' life, which the rich man had conveniently ignored, was now haunting him. Unlike Lazarus, who was now separated by a gulf in the after-life, this rich man had the means to do something about Lazarus' plight during his earthly life. He refused to, and now seeing him from the throes of hell, Lazarus was unable to respond to his plight. Hell had stripped away the man's earthly treasures to reveal their temporary vanity and his foolishness. As the Apostle Paul stated in 1 Timothy 6:7, "For we brought nothing into this world, and it is certain we can carry nothing out."

Hebrews 9:27 states, "And as it is appointed unto men once to die, but after this the judgment." The rich man now had to face the harsh reality of judgment. No one could help him in his plight. He had secured his destination. He had to taste the futility of his life and the emptiness of his ways.

Apparently, the rich man's brothers were at the same spiritual level as he was before his death, hell bound. Suddenly, this man became an evangelist. He asked Abraham to send Lazarus to warn his brothers about the existence of hell. Again, he sees Lazarus as a solution. He never bothered to try to serve as a solution to Lazarus's plight, but he saw Lazarus as a means to warn his brothers about a spiritual fate that was worse than anyone could imagine. All Lazarus needed to do was inform his brothers of this tormenting place, and it would have changed their spiritual direction.

Interestingly, Abraham refuted his conclusion. He told this man that his brothers had Moses and the prophets, and that they needed to hear them. The tormented man was desperate. He reasoned that if Lazarus was raised from the dead that his brothers would repent of their ways. Abraham concluded with this statement, "And he said unto him, If they

---

[13] Matthew 25:31-46; Galatians 6:7-8

hear not Moses and the prophets, neither will they be persuaded, though one rose from the dead."

There are tremendous lessons in this story. In the case of the rich man, he did not find himself in hell because of what he did, but because of what he failed to do. In other words, he was in hell because of the sin of omission. He failed to do right by one man. He had no idea that an insignificant beggar at his gate would be one of the means that would trip him up and cause him to taste the tormenting fires of hell.

This brings us to another important point. According to this story, only one man pretty much tripped up this rich man. This is true for everyone in hell. Those in hell will have tripped over one man, the Man, Christ Jesus. Either they made the fact of Jesus insignificant or they ignored Him altogether. The rich man could not get around noticing or encountering Lazarus at his gate, and likewise, humankind cannot get around Jesus. Jesus is the only door to heaven, and serves as a test for every person. Either each person will be broken and made new in Him, or he or she will trip over Him on his or her way to hell. Regardless of how people want to deny it, Jesus is the pivotal point in every person's spiritual direction, and the only One who closes the gulf between lost man and paradise.

When you realize that hell is about the omission of Jesus in one's life, it can be quite sobering. You can see this omission in three ways. For example, unbelievers will *omit the Son of God altogether.* They will deny His existence as they exalt man's philosophies, the solutions of worldly governments, and the hope of personal intelligence, goodness, and pursuits.

The people in the second group are religious. They tack Jesus on to their various activities, while *omitting faith* in the only begotten Son of God. These people constitute various cults. They proclaim another Jesus, while redefining God and His ways.

The third group professes Christianity, but they are *omitting righteousness* in their conduct. These people fail to obey the Word because they do not love the Son of God. When love for God is lacking, the Christian life becomes a matter of show, rather than one of inward transformation and commitment.

Hell will strip away all the different masks of people's delusions. It will reveal that their treasure is vanity because they do not possess the real treasure of heaven. They will be left spiritually bankrupt, facing the inevitable Great White Throne of Judgment and the lake of fire. These people will taste the bitterness of death, as the essence of real life eludes them. They will be tormented as indifference surrounds them. They will pursue without satisfaction. They will thirst without relief. They will scream without being heard. They will gnash their teeth as they realize there is no end to their torment. In the depth of their tormented spirit, they will know that what they refused to face on earth, they must now face in hell--the loss state of their own spiritual depravity and need.

The final aspect of this story is that unbelief lies at the core of those in hell. These people fail to believe God's Word. Unbelief runs rampant in our cultured, educated society. While the majority of people may own a Bible, few believe it. And, guess what? One of the greatest events that people continue to refute is the resurrection of Jesus.

There are many witnesses to Jesus' resurrection, but people continue to call it a hoax. This brings us to Abraham's comment to the rich man. "If they hear not Moses and the prophets, neither will they be persuaded, though one rose from the dead." The Apostle Paul talked about Jesus' resurrection as being in accordance with the scriptures.[14] Jesus not only was raised from the grave, but He also raised another man by the name of Lazarus from the grave.

In spite of all the evidence, people still refuse to believe the record that has been given about Jesus. And, what is this record? The Apostle John declares this record in 1 John 5:11-12, "And this is the record, that God hath given to us eternal life, and this life is in his Son. He that hath the Son hath life; and he that hath not the Son of God hath not life."

John clearly states that our spiritual well-being hinges on whether we believe the record that God has given concerning His Son. To choose not to believe this record means spending a Christless eternity in torment. This proves that hell is a natural preference for those who refuse to believe this record. They would rather spend eternity in their unbelief and darkness, than humble themselves and pursue the true God to embrace the truth of His salvation.

Is hell your preference or have you chosen to believe the record God has given about His Son? If you have embraced this record as truth, there will be evidence of the reality of Jesus in your life. Is this evidence serving as a living testimony to others?

---

[14] 1 Corinthians 15:1-6

13

REPENTANCE

We have been considering the harsh reality of sin. Now we must consider what needs to be done about this terminal disease of the soul. The first thing we must do is examine our attitude about our spiritual condition. This means determining what our emphasis is. For example, the main issue for people concerning sin is that it is not just to avoid hell, but also to embrace the salvation that has been freely offered to them. Knowing about hell will not keep a person out of hell, but experiencing salvation will not only stop a person from ending up in this tormenting place, but it will result in tasting the reality of eternal life.

Embracing salvation means believing what God has said about sin, and our need for deliverance from its entanglements and influences. Such salvation is an ongoing process where believers have been saved from the claims of sin on their lives, are being saved from the entanglements of sin, and will be saved from the consequences of sin.

I can see the progression of salvation in my own life. When the reality of my sin first penetrated my mind, I realized my need to be saved. This reality brought me to a place of true repentance. When I learned how God loved me enough to send His only begotten Son to address my sins, in desperation I received this message into my heart as truth. At that point, my past sins were taken away by the work of redemption, leaving me justified before God. As I began to walk out the new life, I encountered weaknesses in my character that would give way to sin. It was only when I received the truth of God's words that my present sins were washed away. Such work is also is the work of sanctification. As I began to walk the ways of righteousness by faith, I became aware of the preparation taking place for the time when I would actually realize the fullness of my salvation, at which time I would be glorified with Him.

This is why salvation must be a matter of the heart instead of the mind. Granted, the light of salvation must penetrate the mind. After all, a person must first understand his or her plight and need, but this matter must go from being a fact embraced by the mind to becoming a truth received in the heart.

It is important to point out that a fact has no power behind it. It is something a person simply accepts on an intellectual level. Truth, on the other hand, becomes a point of reality that will not only change how an individual will look at a matter, but his or her emphasis and focus, thereby changing his or her behavior. Therefore, truth is not a matter of the intellect, but of the heart. In other words, it penetrates every fiber of a person's being. In a way, it becomes an absolute, unchanging reality. Upon its immovable foundation, a person not only trusts its contents, but he or she also considers it a guide or determining factor in all that is done.

Jesus summarized truth when He stated that He is the truth.[1] He was not to be considered a mere fact or concept, but He is to become our very reality. As reality, He will penetrate and influence every aspect of our perception, character, and behavior.

The Apostle Paul talked about how we must confess with our mouths the Lord Jesus, and believe in our hearts that God raised Him from the dead.[2] If we do, we will be saved. Notice once again how salvation is a heart reality. Acknowledging who Jesus is comes from the light of His truth penetrating the mind. However, believing is a matter of the heart embracing it as absolute truth.

Paul's reference to Jesus' resurrection stands at the heart of the Gospel. The Apostle Paul summarized the Gospel in 1 Corinthians 15:1-4. Jesus died for our sin, was buried, and three days later rose from the grave. In 2 Corinthians 4:4, he talked about the glorious light of the Gospel. The light he is referring to is Jesus. Jesus is the light in the Gospel. In the Gospel of John, John tells us that His life serves as the light of men.[3] As the light of the world, Jesus brings contrast, hope, and purpose. He reveals man's hopeless plight in light of His redemption.

The Gospel is a fact, but the facts of Jesus death, burial, and resurrection must become truths to a person before it will display the power of God unto salvation.[4] In order for the Gospel to become truth, man must repent to embrace this truth as his reality. Jesus confirmed this in Luke 13:3 and 5, "I tell you, Nay: but, except ye repent, ye shall all likewise perish." Jesus made this statement twice, confirming both its validity and the seriousness of it. A person must repent before he or she can embrace salvation.

What is repentance? I have heard different definitions of repentance, such as an about-face or a change in heart, mind, and direction. In spite of the emphasis some put on repentance, few understand what it really is. They perceive a change must take place, but for many people it appears to be nothing more than outward conformity.

Oswald Chambers addressed the issue of repentance. He talked about how repentance is the bedrock of Christianity, and that an altered life does not signify such repentance. In fact, an altered life may mean a

---

[1] John 14:6

[2] Romans 10:9-10

[3] John 1:4-14

[4] Romans 1:16

person has ceased from ungodly activities because he or she has become exhausted.[5] After all, ungodly conduct leaves people tired of the vanity of it all. Therefore, changed conduct does not imply repentance. Mr. Chambers states that the only truly repentant man is the holy man.[6]

To understand the word "repentance" you must note what word it is associated with, perish. Believing is associated with salvation, while repentance is associated with perishing. The Apostle Peter confirms this association in 2 Peter 3:9, "The Lord is not slack concerning his promise, as some men count slackness; but is long suffering to us-ward, not willing that any shall perish, but that all should come to repentance." Peter reveals that it is God's will that we come to repentance, instead of perishing. The word "come" gives us some insight into repentance. It implies repentance is a place.

Hebrews 12:17 confirms that repentance is a place. It tells us that Esau found, "...no place of repentance though he sought it carefully with tears." Is this place a state or condition, or is it an actual location? Obviously, this means that a person must come to some type of inner state to embrace God's kingdom.

Esau's example also reveals to us that true repentance is more than an outburst of emotional remorse. Remorse in this arena is nothing more than the world's version of getting caught. Such remorse is expressed in self-pity. This is why the Bible talks about two types of repentance in 2 Corinthians 7:10. Godly repentance leads to salvation, while worldly sorrow works death in the individual. In a way, it serves as a sick substitute for repentance, while blinding the person to his or her deluded state. In this state a person is trying to make a wrong right through noble attempts.

John the Baptist's first message was for people to repent, for the kingdom of heaven was near. Repentance in this text points to preparation. In other words, be prepared to encounter and receive the kingdom of God. The reason most people will not truly repent is because they want to glory in their personal attempts to make themselves acceptable, right, or involved in securing their salvation. It is nothing but vainglory, but many prefer this personal glory. That is why cults are attractive. They feed this vainglory with rigid, religious disciplines that change the outward appearance, but never results in inward transformation. As the Apostle Paul clearly stated, "That no flesh should glory in his presence" (1 Corinthians 1:29).

John the Baptist went on to say in Matthew 5:8, "Bring forth therefore fruits meet for repentance." He said this to the Pharisees who were assuming that they were spiritually acceptable because their lineage

---

[5] Daily Thoughts for Disciples; ©1990 by Oswald Chambers Publications Association 1976, devotion of March 21

[6] He Shall Glorify Me; ©1946 by Oswald Chambers Publications Association, this edition 1965, pg. 118

went back to Abraham. John exposed this assumption to be foolish.[7] Acceptability in the kingdom of heaven involves more than association with Abraham. There must be visible fruits that God is truly working life within that individual.

This brings us to the attitude and action of godly repentance. Jesus gives us this first insight into true repentance in Matthew 9:12-13, "They that be whole need not a physician, but they that are sick. But go ye and learn what that meaneth, I will have mercy, and not sacrifice: for I am not come to call the righteous, but sinners to repentance." The first stage of repentance is when a person recognizes his or her spiritual state. Unless this state is recognized, the person sees no need for change to take place in their inward man. Genuine repentance is all about change.

Godly repentance also includes conversion. Conversion is an ongoing process. In my Christian life, I am constantly being converted from an old lifestyle to a new lifestyle. In fact, everything we as believers receive from God as truth must serve as a point of conversion. In conversion, a person is being converted from an old way of thinking, doing, and being to a new way. Conversion will revolutionize attitude, form character, and change function.

Conversion clearly involves a turning. This conversion involves two aspects: that of the intellect and disposition. People must turn from the way they think and respond to something that is totally opposite to their present state. They must regress in the way they perceive themselves. Such change will establish a different attitude. Jesus related this regression to becoming a child.[8]

A child is open to learn and always ready to discover new truths about life. Children begin with a clean slate. They have not developed notions, and are always in the process of growing. This is contrary to those who are not children. They approach God with their personal agendas and expectations. They do not plan to let go of their way of thinking. Rather, they plan to integrate the things of God into what they already know.

Being sincere as a child is the attitude of those coming to repentance. They are not only needy, but they realize they are ignorant about God. This ignorance has caused them to walk in darkness about spiritual matters. In fact, a person must repent of his or her ignorance of God because it often translates into some type of idolatry.[9]

What will people be turning from when it comes to repentance? They will be turning from the path and direction they are walking. The path is the way of sin and death. The final destination of this direction is hell. As a result, it is not enough to cease an action; one must turn to avoid the consequences. As Esau's example showed us, it is not enough to cry

---

[7] Matthew 3:2, 9-10

[8] Matthew 18:2-6; Acts 3:19

[9] Acts 17:29-30

about something. A person must turn from that which simply encourages a visible outburst or mere conformity, to actually change the attitude that resulted in the deed.

People, who say the sinner's prayer, but never change, have not repented. They are still walking down the same old path and doing according to their old ways of sin and death. The only difference now is that they think they possess "fire insurance" that will keep them from burning in the tormenting fires of hell. These individuals do not realize that fire insurance is only good in case of a fire. In other words, it does not prevent it, but it serves as a means to restore what one has lost.

Hebrews 9:27 confirms that there is no policy that will be able to change the eternal state of a person, once he or she departs from this present world. The individual will taste the fires of hell or the glory of heaven. This is why a person must not only cease from walking this path of death, but he or she must turn away from his or her way of thinking, doing, and being in order to embrace life and heaven.

As one can see, godly repentance is not just about turning from the old ways of sin and death, but it is about turning to embrace the new. Acts 26:20c tells us what we must turn to, "...that they should repent and turn to God, and do works meet for repentance." The whole point of repentance is to turn from the old, in order to embrace God Almighty.

It is important to realize that all people initially start out on their way to hell. They may be trying to live a decent life. Some may have ceased from terrible lifestyles, but they are still traveling down the same road of destruction. These people may be deluding themselves as they try to tack on some religion to their life, but nothing has changed as far as their direction because Jesus is clearly missing.

Repentance is all about changing direction in every aspect of our lives, but we first must see the need to do so. This is where delusion and darkness come into play for those who are heading towards destruction. At this point, people can begin to walk in a false confidence. They will take pride in the fact that they have striven hard to change attitudes and actions in order to live decent lives and make themselves acceptable.

The Apostle Paul is a good example of how blinded or deluded people become on their way to spiritual ruin. In the name of God, he was actually persecuting the true Church of Jesus Christ. However, on his way to Damascus in Acts 9, he met the real Jesus. His encounter with the Son of God, not only changed his course and mission, but he ceased to be the Pharisee Saul, who was recognized for his zeal against Christians, and became the Apostle Paul, who understood that he was made small and little in light of Christ. In his spiritual smallness, he became one sent out with a powerful message of salvation and hope.

The harsh reality is, no one can make him or herself acceptable to God. Each person must recognize that he or she cannot change who he or she is. Therefore, the person must turn from such personal attempts and begin to seek the One who addresses his or her hopeless plight.

This is why godly repentance and remission of sins walk hand in hand.[10] People must turn from the hopeless path of sin and death to the one true God who provided the means for their sins to be remitted. "Remitted" means to release someone from the consequences.

Remission cost God a high price. Hebrews 9:22 gives us insight into this price, "And almost all things are by the law purged with blood; and without shedding of blood is no remission." Jesus became the sacrifice. His blood was shed, so that each of us could obtain God's forgiveness. His death on the cross was an act of grace, for out of His death came the promise of eternal life for all those who would repent and believe the Gospel.[11]

Today, many people who think they are on their way to heaven are still on the broad path to hell. This tragedy is due to the easy-believism promoted by some in the Church. The Gospel has been watered down to a "sinner's prayer," rather than a heart revelation that produces change in spirit, mind, and direction.

Due to this cheap presentation of the Gospel, people may happily possess a type of religious policy that may not require changing or turning from doing business as usual, but it holds no protection. Sadly, these people will discover too late that their policy is nothing more than a religious scam or a fraud that gave them a false security and blinded them to the truth.

My co-laborer in the Gospel, Jeannette, addressed the condition that has been created by this erroneous presentation of the Gospel in this statement. "The modern Church has gone to extremes in its effort to overcompensate for decades of hellfire and brimstone, legalistic preaching. What has been lost in the process is the Bible's definition of sin, and what constitutes true repentance, godly living, and salvation. What is left for most people today is a 'Kool Whip' belief system that encourages a lazy type of comfortable religious experience. This sugary diet has left people spiritually emaciated. Even milk is hard for them to swallow. Most preaching that one encounters today is nothing but regurgitated MUSH!"

Even now, the pendulum is swinging back the other way. The "mush" has weakened the Church so much that wolves in sheep's clothing are coming in for the kill. Some of these wolves are actually preaching repentance. Their preaching comes across as refreshing in light of the mush, but the preaching is advocating a false repentance. It does not require people to turn back to God, but to simply cease from old ways and follow the wolf down the road to so-called "holiness." This "holiness" is nothing more than arrogance that operates in delusion, elitism, and self-righteousness.

---

[10] Luke 24:47

[11] Ephesians 2:8-9

The issue remains the same. Have you repented? It does not matter if you said the sinner's prayer, if you have not come to the state where you have embraced the truth about your sin and God's provision. It does not count if you go to church all the time, if you do not have the attitude of Jesus. Perhaps you are living a decent, benevolent life. It does not make any difference if you do moral, kind deeds, if inwardly you are refusing to submit to the work of God in your life. You can only tell that you have repented if you possess fruits of repentance. True repentance will display the attitude and life of Jesus. Therefore, the issue remains the same. Have you truly repented, to ensure salvation that is clearly being reflected in a changed life?

14

RIGHTEOUSNESS

The first step towards God and His salvation is repentance. Repentance speaks of godly wisdom.[1] It requires people to be truthful about their spiritual condition and properly respond to the ways of God. Honesty of this nature leads to the next stage of people recognizing their inability to make it right, and their need to embrace God's provision of Jesus Christ. It actually produces a right attitude in the individual to receive God's provision in sincerity.

This brings us to those who refuse to repent. They are fools. Fools are those who refuse to believe God. They are blinded by their arrogance, and deluded by their spiritual darkness. King David said it best in Psalm 53:1, "The fool hath said in his heart, There is no God. Corrupt are they, and have done abominable iniquity; there is none that doeth good." Many people think David is making reference to only those whom we would consider atheists. This is not a correct evaluation. The people in this Scripture are not verbally saying there is no God; rather they secretly believe in their heart that He does not exist. Keep in mind; it is in the heart where we believe the Gospel.[2] Such fools are the people who choose not to believe God. Ultimately, they will denounce Him by their actions and lifestyles.

Repentance is the first sign of godly wisdom. However, godly wisdom does not stop with an about-face. It puts into practice what it knows to be true. In other words, godly wisdom will walk out the salvation of this newly acquired life. Walking out this new life according to faith towards God, points to righteousness.

Repentance was the place of coming to terms with salvation, but righteousness represents the disposition that will walk it out. Righteousness simply means a person has right standing before God. It implies that he or she is doing right by others and exercising godliness.[3] The contrast of this scenario is wickedness. A person who is considered wicked before God will have no regard for others, and will be evil in his or her conduct.

---

[1] James 3:17

[2] Romans 10:9-10

[3] 1 Timothy 4:7-8

It is important to point out that doing what is right is not noble, as many perceive it. Rather, doing right means people are honorable in their attitudes and conduct. People who do what is necessary often see themselves as doing noble and honorable things that will give them recognition. Those who possess a right disposition realize that the ways of righteousness are not noteworthy; rather it is their reasonable service. Granted, right standing before God will make individuals honorable in the way they think and conduct their lives before God. However, such righteousness is the least we can do in regard to God and His kingdom.

Repentance allows a person to embrace salvation, but righteousness allows God to meet that person in his or her walk. God cannot meet His people at any point, but righteousness. The reason for this is because acceptable righteousness is a matter of both regression and faith. One must regress in their ideas inspired by the self-life in order to progress in their pursuit to know God. Such a pursuit requires unfeigned faith.[4]

We can clearly see this in Abraham's life. Abraham let go of the old life he knew in order to pursue a life that was foreign to him. He regressed, as the Lord became His shield and inheritance. He developed a history with Jehovah God. This process allowed him to respond in faith when God told him to take Isaac, his son, to Mount Moriah and sacrifice him.[5] Abraham obeyed.

The real battle for most people is to hold on to their desired reality. This has been true for my own spiritual life. However, faith allowed me to get past the self-life that forever tries to maintain its desired reality. It was only as the self-life fell to the wayside that I could begin to embrace that which is reality according to God's perspective. Up to this point, I used to lean on my own understanding to come to conclusions. These conclusions kept me from seeking out truth. I could not imagine functioning outside of my reality. Years later, I meditated on how I got past my mind to allow God's truth to penetrate the darkness of my soul. I was aware that it had not been a traumatic experience because it would have made an impact on my life.

When I questioned God, He showed me that I had chosen to believe His Word by faith, and had not tried to fit it into my own understanding.[6] Obviously, it was faith that got me past my perverted reality to embrace God's truth in regard to reality. It was at the point of truth that God met me and set me free from the entanglements of the carnal mind. This freedom was not a result of changing my circumstances, but in changing my perception of Him and the essence of life.

Obedience to God is a righteous act. Such obedience is a product of abiding confidence in God. Abraham knew Jehovah God. He had not only walked in obedience, but He had walked before Him in confidence.

---

[4] 1 Timothy 1:5

[5] Genesis 15:1; 22

[6] Proverbs 3:5-7; John 8:32-36; Romans 10:17; 2 Corinthians 10:5

He chose to believe God. As a result, he witnessed miracles, such as the conception and birth of Isaac, and enjoyed incredible blessings throughout his life.

Faith is not refined unless it is tested.[7] Abraham's faith would not only be refined, but it would allow him to stand and withstand in times of testing. He would not fail the fiery test of his faith. Rather, he would confirm his faith in God. Even though God was asking him to sacrifice the son He had promised him, Abraham obeyed without debate. Hebrews 11:19 states this about Abraham's perception about God's request, "Accounting that God was able to raise him up, even from the dead; from whence also he received him in a figure."

Obedience is nothing more than exercising godliness.[8] In other words, the person is displaying his or her faith in God through godly conduct. The problem with people is that they never exercise what they know is right. Without this exercise, there is no spiritual enlargement or maturity. Without exercising the Christian life, there will be no history with God of knowing His faithfulness and intervention.

Since Abraham had exercised his faith unto godliness, he had encountered God in His faithfulness. He knew God's character and trusted Him in whatever He said. This brings us to the real source of righteousness. Righteousness does not really hinge on us being upright before God, but on the character of God. Man's best is filthy rags. Abraham was simply responding to the character of God. This is why upright acts are not noble, but reasonable. This man's response was not a matter of righteousness, but of faith. As a result, Abraham's faith was accounted unto him as righteousness before God, causing him to be in right standing with God.[9] The Apostle Paul brings this out in Romans 3:22, "Even the righteousness of God which is by faith of Jesus Christ unto all and upon all them that believe."

Acceptable righteousness is of God. This righteousness is imputed to those who believe. The harlot Rahab's example in Scripture confirms this. She had heard how Jehovah God delivered Israel out of Egypt 40 years prior to Israel entering the Promised Land. She must have hid this story in her heart as truth. When the Israelite spies came to her fortified city of Jericho, her faith took on the form of action. She hid the spies and asked them to remember her. They instructed her to hang a red cord out her window to serve as a point of identification. She obeyed. As a result, she and her household were delivered from destruction.[10]

Obviously, Rahab had no claim to personal righteousness. In spite of her moral state she believed in the reality of Jehovah God. Hebrews

---

[7] 1 Peter 1:6-9

[8] 1 Timothy 4:8

[9] Isaiah 64:6; Romans 4:3

[10] Joshua 6; Romans 4:22-23

11:31 says of Rahab, "By faith the harlot Rahab perished not with them that believed not, when she had received the spies with peace."

The reason faith can be counted as righteousness is because it is active. James 2:25 also confirms this about Rahab's faith, "Likewise also was not Rahab the harlot justified by works, when she had received the messengers, and had sent them out another way."

Faith is verified by visible evidence. In fact, it results in a walk or a certain lifestyle.[11] Genuine faith is always walking towards the reality of God. It believes; therefore, it responds. As it responds, it allows God to meet the person. Once God steps on the scene, righteousness is accounted to the individual. God's character is confirmed, while the person's perception is enlarged, adjusting his or her perception of God. This perception changes the person's attitude towards God, thereby, changing the person's disposition.

Once a person's disposition changes due to real repentance, his or her outward life changes before God. Rahab was a harlot, but Scripture tells us that after her deliverance, she lived a different life. She married a Hebrew man, and became part of the lineage of Christ. In a way, Rahab became hidden in the promise of Christ because of her one simple act of faith.

Rahab does not stand alone in Jesus' lineage. She shares this unique position with three other women who had questionable backgrounds as well. As you study these women in the lineage of Jesus found in Matthew 1, you get a complete picture of how righteousness works. For example, Tamara did what was right in spite of her father-in-law Judah. She even faced the possibility of misunderstanding and death. As a result, she not only preserved Judah's lineage, but also ensured the Messiah's lineage.

Rahab, of course, became righteous due to her faith, and is now part of the Son of God's lineage. Ruth, the Moabite, chose the ways of righteousness by choosing her mother-in-law's Jehovah God to her idols. As a result, she was exalted to be part of the lineage of the soon and coming King.

Bathsheba, the wife of Uriah, found herself involved in a scandalous situation, but she stood righteously in the midst of it, as she maintained the integrity of the lineage of the Promised One.

Each of these women revealed a history with Jehovah God that was clearly recorded in Scripture. Each of these women have become identified with God through Jesus Christ. This brings us to what, or who, serves as the Christian's righteousness. We know that God counts His people righteous at the point of active faith. What does this mean for the Christian?

---

[11] 2 Corinthians 5:7

The Apostle Paul identifies the Christian's source of righteousness in 1 Corinthians 1:30, "But of him are ye in Christ Jesus, who of God is made unto us wisdom, and righteousness, and sanctification, and redemption." Jesus serves as the righteousness for believers. This righteousness becomes part of their disposition as His life is worked within the saint by the Holy Spirit. For saints, this actually means that the mind of Christ is being developed in them. It is the transformed mind that changes a person's tendency to justify and give way to the deceit of sin.

The mind of Christ has one focus and that is to do the will of the Father. Once again, we see where godliness is exercised or practiced, due to obedience to what a person knows is right. This righteousness is not based on personal standards, but on God's character. A person, therefore, must personally know God to understand what is His good, acceptable, and perfect will.[12]

Righteousness carries a lot of benefits, but the greatest benefit is knowing God's faithfulness. God's character inspires faith, but faith allows us to witness God in His faithfulness. I have witnessed God's intervention in many ways. I have seen His power, witnessed His greatness, watched His longsuffering, experienced His mercy, and benefited from His grace. However, these incredible attributes are often expressed in His ever-abiding faithfulness.

In each challenging situation as a Christian, I have come to realize that there is something about God's faithfulness that makes Him sweeter. It is because of His faithfulness that I have experienced His miracles, power, greatness, longsuffering, mercy, and grace just at the right time.

God's faithfulness is constantly expressed in His commitment to save and preserve His people. I have noticed through the years that as my history grows with God, no matter what the circumstances, I know that He is faithful to watch over my soul. No matter how overwhelming the demands of life are I know that God is faithful to see me through.

The subject of righteousness would fill volumes. The reason is because God is righteous. There are no means to describe His infinite character. However, I will say this much, salvation is a gift, but righteousness will accompany true salvation. In fact, salvation is worked in us by righteousness that is being established by faith. This righteousness will manifest itself in godliness.

Consider for a moment. Do you display the righteousness of Christ in your disposition, walk, and conduct?

---

[12] Romans 12:1-2

15

HOLINESS

We have been considering how to overcome sin. The Apostle Paul gives us insight into what it will take to overcome the reign of sin in our lives by summarizing the source. It is by finding his or her life in Jesus Christ that a person will overcome sin. "But of him are ye in Christ Jesus who of God is made unto us wisdom, and righteousness, and sanctification, and redemption" (1 Corinthians 1:30).

Jesus Christ is the Christian's source of wisdom, righteousness, sanctification, and redemption. In Him is not only a complete, satisfying life, but also a victorious life. In Him are all the means of overcoming the dictates, influences, and works of sin.

The first three virtues, wisdom, righteousness, and sanctification describe His character, while redemption refers to both His life and work. The first three characteristics are vital for overcoming the entanglements and power of sin, and ensuring the reality of the new life that comes out of His incredible redemption.

As stated, godly repentance is the initial response of godly wisdom for any hell-bound sinner. Righteousness involves establishing a right disposition by doing that which is right, while holiness points to a person's spiritual state in which they are operating.

Holiness involves setting people apart for God's use and purpose. There are two aspects to holiness: the act of consecration and the work of sanctification. Consecration is man's part. It is where he sets himself apart from those things that would defile him with the intent to walk out what is righteous and acceptable to God. Man's initial act of consecration is repentance. This is where he turns from his old way of doing, thinking, and being to embrace a new life. This new life is realized and developed in a person's disposition through righteousness. The right disposition creates the right attitude and approach toward God and will result in godly exercise. This brings us to the work of sanctification.

All three Persons of the Godhead do the work of holiness. For example, the Father positionally places a person in the place of being set apart by setting him or her in Christ, the source of all sanctification. Jesus serves as the actual place of sanctification where the reality of His work and the manifestation of His life are worked into the person. Jesus' life is what actually sets a person apart for God's use. The Holy Spirit does the work of sanctification by working Jesus' life in the saint.[1]

The work of sanctification involves a process. In fact, what God has not sanctified does not belong to Him. Without this claim, God cannot use a person for His purpose and work. The sanctification process starts out with our consecration or repentance. This simply means the turning away from the old way to embrace the new way. Righteousness is the application of God's way to a matter by doing what we know is right. This involves self-denial. Sanctification is actually coming to the state or environment where we express the attitude of holiness or purity. Holiness involves the application of the cross to all that is contrary to God in our lives. It stipulates the state of one walking in the way of humility, forgiveness, reconciliation, and restoration, thereby, always prepared to experience God's work.

This brings us to the process of holiness that must be worked in us. God is holy. This one aspect of His character stipulates our need for repentance, forgiveness, righteousness, and reconciliation. It reveals our spiritual state that can only be changed by God's intervention. In fact, His holiness quickly establishes our need for His forgiveness and reconciliation. It is in this state or condition that we will come to terms with His redemption.

For example, if a person is in a state of opposing something, he or she will not be open to receive or come into agreement concerning a matter. Therefore, this individual will walk in a state of being contrary and unreceptive. In order for a person to truly come to an understanding of redemption, he or she must come to a right spiritual state which begins with true repentance.

Repentance allows one to embrace what is right. Righteousness prepares one to give way to the work of the Holy Ghost. Giving way to the work of the Holy Ghost will allow Him to develop the attitude that will truly sanctify or set a person apart from the unholy. The attitude that will be developed will be the same that was evident in the mind of Christ.[2]

The mind of Christ contains a powerful combination. It will display the fear of God that will walk in humility and meekness before the Lord. We know that the fear of the Lord is the beginning of wisdom. A person's agenda will be to obey God by faith, which is not only righteous, but will please Him. The priority of such an individual will be to glorify God because of who He is. The inclination of such a person will be to worship God for He is worthy, setting God apart in the heart that will be filled with adoration.[3] This holy state will express itself in hatred towards evil. Hatred for evil is what caused God to do something about sin in man's life. He sent His Son to redeem all who will come to Him for redemption.

---

[1] 1 Corinthians 1:2, 30; 1 Peter 1:2; Jude 1

[2] Philippians 2:5-11

[3] Psalm 111:10; Romans 12:2; Revelation 4:8-11

Godly repentance is the opposite of sin and death. Righteousness is contrary to wickedness, while holiness is opposite of evil. By developing the right heart attitude towards evil, individuals will truly be set apart in their way of thinking, being, and doing. Until there is hatred for sin, people toy with it, ignore its existence in their lives, justify it, or deny that it does exist and that it is plaguing them. Moreover, without hatred for sin, people will come into agreement with the unholy, causing them to walk in darkness, delusion, and death.

Holiness is not an option in the Christian life. Peter tells us that since God is holy, we must be holy as well. The writer of Hebrews states that without holiness we will not see God. Holiness lies at the core of coming into agreement with our Holy God without the fear of judgment.[4] Granted, upon our salvation, we are placed in Christ to ensure this state is worked out in our lives. However, we have the responsibility to give way to the vital work of sanctification, in order to possess the mind of Christ, and walk in the ways of godliness. This is necessary if we are to come into this state of being holy before God.

Most people have a vague concept about holiness. They do not understand their part. People cannot sanctify themselves, nor can they make the things in their world holy or acceptable to God. This truth is brought out in Haggai 2. The priests were asked if their holy garment touched an unclean article, would the article become holy. The priests' answer was no. Then the priests were asked if something was unclean, such as a dead body, and it touched a sacred article, would that article become unclean. The answer was yes.

People perceive holiness according to personal standards, rather than the holy character of God. They perceive themselves as being able to walk in the midst of the unholy and still come out with holy lives. This brings us to an important aspect of holiness. It comes down to the type of environment to which people expose themselves. Holiness is not based on what we may intellectually agree with or what we think is right. It is about what we touch or partake of by way of exposure or environment, such as the entertainment we watch.

The issue of holiness comes down to upholding character by guarding our hearts against outside influences that advocate wickedness. For example, the unholy perverts character by distorting our perception as to what is holy and acceptable. Most of us make conclusions about holiness based on whether something embarrasses us or makes us uncomfortable, rather than on the character of God. As we downplay, ignore, fudge, or compromise with the issue of holiness, we become more conditioned to accept the unholy. Our boundaries concerning godliness begin to enlarge. We actually lose our shock value, as we begin to fall into the delusion of the unholy. Eventually, we become more tolerant towards the immoral, defiant, and crass ways of

[4] Hebrews 12:14, 27-29; 1 Peter 1:15-16

the wicked. The more we expose ourselves to what is defiled, the more we become defiled, as our concept of holiness is compromised to embrace those things that are contrary to the holy nature of God. In the end, we are rendered spiritually dull, as the unholy desensitizes and indoctrinates us.

Indoctrination of the unholy invades people's perception of how they consider or perceive the issue of holiness, redefining what constitutes life and morality. If individuals do not recognize the destructive path they are on, they will become reprobates before God. This is where they will call evil, good, and good, evil.[5]

One of the problems is that people perceive themselves as being able to properly handling something that is unholy. This is the sin of pride, but many fail to recognize the danger of any type of arrogance or self-sufficiency. In fact, the sin of pride is what deceives people about the destruction of compromising with the unholy.[6] These individuals cannot imagine that seemingly insignificant things could affect their lives before God. They convince themselves that it is no big deal because underneath they know the difference.

The purpose for knowing the difference between the holy and the unholy in the kingdom of God is not that the individual is able to recognize the state of something in order to beware of it. Rather, the discernment of the unholy should cause one to actually flee from what is perverted, to maintain spiritual discernment and the proper level of hatred towards all avenues of wickedness.[7]

The Apostle Paul tells us what to do when we encounter the unholy, in 2 Corinthians 6:17-18, "Wherefore come out from among them, and be ye separate, saith the Lord, and touch not the unclean thing; and I will receive you, And will be a Father unto you, and ye shall be my sons and daughters, saith the Lord Almighty." We are to come out from that which is unholy if we expect God to receive us unto Himself. It is not a matter of thinking we can recognize or properly handle evil; rather, it is a matter of hating it so much that we will have no part of anything that is contrary to the character of our holy God.

Job was such a man. God pointed him out to Satan as being a perfect and upright man who feared Him and hated evil. Job was pure in his approach and life before God. He stood righteous before God and displayed heavenly wisdom. The result of his upright life is that he was repulsed at evil. He had established a holy environment and developed the same attitude about evil that God clearly displayed towards it. Therefore, Job had nothing to do with that which ran contrary to God. In fact, he stood in the gap for his children, by offering up sacrifices for

---

[5] Isaiah 5:20; Romans 1:28-32

[6] Proverbs 16:18; Jeremiah 49:16

[7] 1 Corinthians 10:12-14; 2 Timothy

them, in the event that they had displeased or offended God in some way.[8]

Job's spiritual state was put to the test. Was he truly a man who maintained holiness in his life or was it all show? Satan set out to prove that even Job would not maintain his spiritual state before God when tested. We all know the story of Job. Even though he struggled before God, he never gave up what he knew to be true about God. In the end, he came out with a greater sense of God's character.[9]

Hebrews 12:10 says, "For they verily for a few days chastened us after their own pleasure; but he for our profit, that we might be partakers of his holiness." We all may have our concept of wisdom, righteousness, and holiness, but we will never know these virtues outside of Jesus. If we are to become holy, we must agree with God's definition of it. Holiness comes from Him. If the Holy Ghost is ever going to develop this state within our being, we must constantly expose ourselves to the ways of God. We must partake of His ways, and walk them out in godliness. We must separate from unholy allegiances, and flee from immoral practices. We must guard against compromise, shun tolerance of any sin or unholy way, and refuse to give evil an audience because of our pride, tendency of self-justification, and rebellion. We must seek God, desire His will, and pursue His ways.

Such responses are acts of consecration on our part. We begin with consecration by separating ourselves from the unholy. Separation allows us to give way to the work of sanctification. As we walk out the work of sanctification, we actively continue to consecrate ourselves for the glory of God.

God will always call us higher, above the filth of this world, the mire of our pigpens, and the smallness of our ways. Every time we accept the challenge to come higher, we will leave more of the tentacles of sin behind. Each new revelation of God will cause us to press towards a higher standard of His holiness. Each encounter with the unholy will cause us to seek God's forgiveness and cleansing, as well as establish the need to become increasingly separated from questionable situations and activities. In the end, the attractions of the world will fade, and the delusion of pride will be exposed as self regresses in importance and sin loses it claims.

What state are you in? Are you being brought higher, or are you in a delusion? Are you soaring above the world, or are you wallowing in your pigpen? Are you discerning towards the things you expose yourself to, or are you more critical of others who hold the line of righteousness? You need to answer these questions, for you will not see the Lord without holiness.

---

[8] Job 1:4-5, 8

[9] Job 42:1-6

16

REDEMPTION

What words could describe or explain Jesus' redemption? Every time I write about Jesus' redemption, I fear I will do it a grave disservice. How can you explain the greatest act to ever occur in history? I have caught glimpses of Jesus' redemption, and it has brought me to my knees in humility. I stand in awe as I realize what this one act means for me: the salvation of my soul. It has produced praise within my soul, as I realize that it is God's visible love and commitment to man. It has brought forth gratitude in my heart as I recognize, in part, the depth Jesus had to reach to make this redemption complete. It has caused me to worship God, as I consider how Christ' redemption closed the gap between lost man and his infinite Creator.

As I consider redemption, I realize that we can only see in part into its incredible depths. Although we have a clearer picture than the angels who desire to look into the spiritual blessings that have been made available to us through Jesus' death on the cross, we are still limited in appreciating it. As long as we are in this earthly tabernacle, we will be limited in embracing its incredible reality. However, in the near future, that will change. One day, we will be in His presence, and we will be able to see His redemption from the heights of eternity. No doubt, it will cause us to cast all of our crowns at His feet, and declare how worthy He is to receive all glory, honor, and power.[1]

We have been considering the attributes of Jesus. He serves as wisdom, righteousness, and sanctification to every born-again saint. Positionally, this is how God must see each of us. He must see Jesus in us, while our lives remain hidden in Christ. However, it is important for each of us to realize that God can only see Christ's wisdom, righteousness, and sanctification in each of us at the point of His redemption. If Jesus had not secured our souls through redemption, there would be no abiding place where His wisdom, righteousness, and sanctification would be realized in our lives.

It is obvious that the complete work of redemption comes out of Jesus' wisdom, righteousness, and sanctification. His wisdom allows us to accept its simplicity. His righteousness allows us to discover its true benefits and His sanctification makes it a living revelation.

[1] 1 Corinthians 13:9-12; 1 Peter 1:12; Revelation 4:10-11

What is redemption? When you examine it in *Strong's Exhaustive Concordance,* such words as ransom, purchase, release, preserve, salvation, and deliverance are associated with this work.[2] When I looked it up in my secular dictionary, it brought even more clarity. Redemption means to buy back or repurchase.[3]

Jesus' death on the cross was a means of buying us back or repurchasing us. It is as if mankind had been kidnapped, and in order to secure our lives and freedom, Jesus had to pay the ransom with His own life. He made mention of this in Mark 10:45, "For even the Son of man came not to be ministered unto, but to minister, and to give his life a ransom for many."

The Apostle Paul referred to the ransom that Jesus paid on the cross. He said this in 1 Timothy 2:6, "Who gave himself a ransom for all, to be testified in due time." The Apostle Paul stated that Jesus provided the ransom for all, but the Lord used the word *many* in Mark 10:45. It is true that Jesus' sacrifice could secure every hell-bound sinner from death, but many fail to allow the ransom to set them free. Sadly, many would prefer to die in their captivity, rather than be set free to discover the eternal and abundant life that comes from God through Jesus Christ.

What must people be bought back from? We must travel back through time to the Garden of Eden to answer this question. God had formed Adam and placed him in the Garden of Eden. Although Adam was given dominion over the garden, he still was subject to God. When Adam rebelled against God, he sold his soul into sin, bringing it under Satan's domain. From that point on, every person was born into the slavery of sin. Sin not only dictates man's walk, disposition, and environment, but it also demands total allegiance and worship.[4]

As you study the characteristics of sin, you will realize that its darkness of sin blinds people to their real master, Satan. It keeps them ignorant about the vanity of their self-serving lives, and it causes them to delude themselves about the destruction and death of the environment in which they reside.

Jesus' redemption was complete. In other words, He had to deliver us from every aspect of sin. This meant He had to change our direction, instill a new disposition, and bring us into a new environment to bring forth the salvation of our soul, reconciliation with God, and restoration of spirit and soul. This complete transformation will be completely manifested in the resurrection of a new body.

From all appearances, this seemed like a tall order, but for Jesus, God Incarnate, it was what He set His course towards. In order to give us a shadow of His complete work, God gave us glimpses of redemption in the Old Testament. These glimpses were to serve as valuable examples

---

[2] OT: #1350, 6299; NT: #629, 3084-3085

[3] Webster's New Collegiate Dictionary

[4] Romans 5:12, 19; 6:12, 18

to us.[5] Few ever take time to see the character, work, and deliverance of God in the many examples we have been given in the Old Testament. However, to understand the purpose of redemption, we must consider these examples.

The first example we have is Israel and Egypt. Israel had become enslaved to the tyrannical arrogance of Egypt. The children of Israel tasted the bitterness of slavery for 400 years. As the slavery intensified, the Hebrews began to cry out to God. God sent a deliverer by the name of Moses.[6]

Before God could deliver the Hebrews from Egypt, they had to begin to hate their slavery. This displeasure caused them to seek God in cries of desperation. God heard their cries and put into motion their deliverance. This is true for those who are in captivity to sin. Sin is very tyrannical, and can cause one to reel under its oppression. When people come to the end of what they consider to be the benefits of sin, and start to taste its incredible slavery, they begin to cry out. For lost humanity, God stepped on the scene 20 centuries ago, and sent a deliverer, Jesus Christ, to rescue people from the unmerciful tentacles of sin.

Egypt, who represented the world, was not willing to let the Hebrews go. God took various measures to break the arrogant, self-serving backs of the Egyptians. There were times when the Pharaoh, who represented the tyrannical, unmerciful, and unpredictable leadership of Satan, considered the idea of letting the Israelites go to serve and worship their God, but at the last minute, he would renege. Before it was over, God would send 10 plagues upon Egypt. Each one proved to be more severe than the last.[7] Each plague exposed the Egyptian gods to be powerless in light of Jehovah God. Each god's identity was exposed to be nothing more than man's vain imagination.

Likewise, sin refuses to let people go. It has such devices as lust that keep people from stepping outside of comfort zones. The vain imagination inspired by sin hides and maintains idols. It has pride that not only exalts a person in his or her mind, but also reinforces rebellion. Sin is also surrounded by lies that either blind people to its true influences in their lives, or it causes them to walk in condemnation. In order for sin to let people go, it must become a stench to them. Its defilement, idolatry, and vanity must be exposed for the destructive environment that it creates.

God's final plague upon the Egyptians broke the back of their stubbornness. This was the death of the first-born male of every Egyptian home, as well as among their flocks. It cost Egypt her sons. What a price to pay to somehow maintain slavery. Yet, their deaths released Israel from Egypt's tyrannical grip. Out of their despair and

---

[5] 1 Corinthians 10:1-10

[6] Exodus 2:23-25; 3:10-17

[7] Exodus 7:17-23; 8; 9; 10; 12

mourning the Egyptians had to let them go because the cost became too high. They had to let go of these people in order to maintain their lives.[8]

Once the heart-felt cry is made to God, sin must let go. Like Pharaoh, sin may hold on in every way, but God knows how to break its back. God's way involved the death of His Son who would become the firstborn among many. Jesus became the Passover Lamb. If His blood is properly applied to the heart and life of every sin-laden soul, slavery and death will lose its power or hold on the person.[9]

There is nothing that points to the cost of redemption like the first Passover. Out of the first Passover, there was the death of a lamb, the burial of the first-born, and the resurrection of a nation. As you observe the present Passover celebration, there is the lamb, the unleavened bread, and the bitter herbs. The bitter herbs pointed to the bitterness of slavery. The bread pointed to Jesus' sinless body that was broken. And, the lamb pointed to His sacrifice.

For the Christian, the Passover began with the broken body of Jesus as He was being offered up as a lamb slain from the foundation of the world. It ended with the Lamb's death and burial, resulting in His resurrection. Out of His side came the beginning of a new and everlasting life. Out of His grave came blessed assurance. And, out of His resurrection came the first-fruits of the kingdom of God.[10]

The success of the sacrifice of the Passover Lamb also hinged on every bit of the lamb being properly utilized. Exodus 12:10, "And ye shall let nothing of it remain until the morning: and that which remaineth of it until the morning ye shall burn with fire." The blood of the lamb was for God. It was a means of atonement. The lamb was for the people. It became the source of nourishment as they prepared to exit from underneath the grips of their unbearable slavery.

For the Christian, the blood of Jesus is the means of cleansing us from all unrighteousness. We must seek His redemption through His blood in humility, as well as in need of forgiveness at the foot of the cross. Partaking of His life daily at the communion table will ensure our strength and endurance as we travel as strangers and pilgrims the challenging path of deliverance that remains before us. Sadly, Christians fail to utilize the Lamb of God. They fail to see that by completely utilizing the lamb was God's way of saving and maintaining His people through the complete work of redemption.

It is important to point out that redemption and salvation are not the same. Salvation means you have been delivered from the restraint of oppression. It is the product of redemption. In other words, there must be a payment before there can be salvation or deliverance. This is why God meets us at the point of redemption, and not salvation.

---

[8] Exodus 12:29-36

[9] Exodus 12: John 1:29; Romans 8:29; Hebrews 9:12-15

[10] 1 Corinthians 15:20, 23; Revelation 5:6; 9; 13:8; 14:4

Salvation or complete deliverance involves a preparation, but it begins at the point of redemption. God buys His people back from slavery. He then begins the process of delivering His people in order to prepare them to properly walk in liberty.

Liberty is frightening to those who have been under such slavery. Such people do not know how to walk. You see this in different situations around the world. Oppressed people are liberated, and they rejoice at their newfound liberty, but they have never been prepared to walk in it. They do not know how to function without tyranny driving them. They must be delivered from their way of thinking and doing in order to change their environment.

God was leading Israel to the Promised Land. But, first He had to take this nation of people through the wilderness. It was in this harsh place that God began the process of delivering them from their mindset of slavery, so they could walk in a new life of freedom. In this freedom, they could choose to love and serve Him. This was the purpose for the wilderness. He wanted the people of Israel to personally know Him as Jehovah God, so that they would allow Him to reign and abide in their midst. While in the wilderness, He gave them the Law, provided them with their needs, showed His miraculous intervention in many ways, and constantly revealed His commitment and intention towards them.

In Numbers 18:15-16, God declared that the first-born was dedicated to Him. This brings us to a very important aspect of redemption. Since redemption involves the purchase of souls, this means that whosoever has been redeemed belongs to the redeemer. The Apostle Paul brings this out in 1 Corinthians 6:20, "For ye are bought with a price: therefore glorify God in your body, and in your spirit, which are God's." Christians do not belong to themselves. They have no say over their lives. In 1 Corinthians 6:18-19, we are told to flee fornication for we are to be the temples of God, holy and set apart for His use.

God also required each person to buy the first-born back from Him. This would cost each person five silver shekels. The number "five" points to grace, while "silver" symbolizes redemption. We are reminded that by grace, Jesus redeemed us on the cross. His redemption was complete. The completion of His redemption is brought out even more so in heaven. As you read about heaven, you cannot help but note the gold and priceless gems that grace this incredible place. However, there is one metal conspicuously missing in heaven: silver. There is no silver in heaven because the redemption of Jesus was completed on the cross. As He said, "It is finished" (John 19:30).

Within the Law, God also set up a time of redemption every seven years. It was referred to as the Sabbatical year.[11] It was not only a time of rest from regular activities, but it was also a time of release. This is

---

[11] Deuteronomy 15

when Hebrew slaves were released by their brethren from all of their debts to go back to their inheritance.

God used this time to test the hearts of people. God had purchased the Israelites. They still belonged to Him, but God is a giving God. He is not only generous, but He ensures the welfare of His people. How will the children of Israel regard the plight of the poor? Will they oppress them more, or will they reach out to them? Would their hearts be closed or open? If their hearts are closed, so will be their hands. If their hands are closed, then they will fail to be an extension of their owner and master, God.

God was also proving another point during this time of release. God brings His people to places of liberty, so they can choose to become His bondservants, knowing that their real inheritance will be realized in the next world. This is brought out in Deuteronomy 15:16-17. If a Hebrew slave wanted to remain as a servant in the household, the master would take an aul and thrust it through his ear to the door. Such an action would signify that from that point on, he would become a loyal bondservant.

Jesus has redeemed us. Through the work of the Holy Ghost, He prepares us through deliverance from the perverted mind, the ungodly walk and the unholy environment, to become a bondservant who is sold out to do His bidding. After deliverance, He sets us free to test our hearts. Sadly, many run back to their former masters of the flesh and sin because they have failed to allow Jesus' wisdom, righteousness, and sanctification to be established in them. They have held on to their old mindset, instead of choosing to pursue God with everything in them. Granted, they may tack on Christ, but they never become bondservants. They simply remain servants who decide when and how they will serve Jesus. This is why the Apostle Paul made this statement in 1 Corinthians 7:22-23, "For he that is called in the Lord, being a servant, is the Lord's freeman: likewise also he that is called, being free, is Christ's servant. Ye are bought with a price; be not ye the servants of men."

There are three necessary qualities needed to become a bondservant or slave. The first one is love. God first loved us. He has shown us commitment, gentleness, and a willingness to share all with us. Such a commitment should result in us loving Him with all of our heart. Christians who fail to become a bondservant have not developed that love for God that is all consuming.[12] A love that, I might add, He is worthy of in every way.

The second quality is total abandonment. Bondservants abandon all life outside of their master's will to serve him with undivided loyalty. In fact, these servants become indebted again, not just for a couple of years, but for a lifetime. Jesus abandoned all, so we could have life. He deserves to have the same response from those who claim that they love

[12] Mark 12:29-30: Romans 5:5; 2 Corinthians 5:14; 1 John 4:19

Him. Anything less than total abandonment will mean divided loyalties and inconsistent service.

Identification is the last quality. For the bondservant of Jesus, it means having His mind, walking as He walked, manifesting His life, and being an extension of Him in this world. It means doing His will and bringing glory to God.[13]

We can declare great things about Jesus and the cross. We can sing about His victory, preach about His sacrifice, and explain what He accomplished for us, but how many people realize that His sacrifice was His way of buying us back from all the dictates of the flesh, the delusion of pride, and unacceptable lifestyles? Due to His redemption, sin is no longer our master. We are free from this tyrannical taskmaster, for now, we belong to Jesus. We have been given the necessary means to experience complete deliverance from all the entanglements of this terminal disease of the soul. We have been given a new heart and spirit. We now have an eternal inheritance.[14]

Redemption is an incredible word, but is it a glorious reality in your life? Have you allowed God to deliver you from all the aspects of sin, as you work your salvation out in fear and trembling?[15] In other words, do you display the wisdom of redemption that reminds you that you do not belong to sin any longer? Do you walk in the righteousness of redemption as an obedient bondservant who has given all to serve your worthy Master? Do you manifest holiness that is found in redemption, by being totally identified to Jesus in attitude and lifestyle? Does redemption lie at the core of everything you are in God, all that you possess in Jesus, and all that you experience in the Spirit, or is it just another word in your Christian vocabulary?

Once again, is redemption a glorious revelation in your life?

---

[13] Matthew 5:16; Romans 8:29; 12:1-2; Philippians 2:5; 1 John 2:6;

[14] Ezekiel 11:19-20 refer Hebrews 8: 10: Romans 6:12, 18; Ephesians 1:11-14

[15] Philippians 2:12

17

MORE THAN CONQUERORS

The tendency for most people is to think that personal problems come from without. In some cases, this could be true, but in many situations, most problems come from within. Some Christians would also like to think that all spiritual challenges come from Satan. They have a hard time facing the fact that Satan must have their permission or some type of agreement to make inroads into their lives.

The Bible describes our greatest enemy. This enemy enslaves us as it works death in us. Its tentacles are far reaching. It reaches into our very being to rob us of life and purpose. The enemy that I am talking about is sin. The truth is that in most cases we do not need to be delivered from Satan, but from the essence of self.

People want to keep everything external and surface. However, sin is from within. As this book has shown, it is not just a matter of doing, but also a matter of being. It is a matter of who we are or allow ourselves to become. Everything in our fallen disposition opposes God's rule and work. Everything about our unregenerate mentality offends God.

The quest for each of us is to come to terms with sin in light of Jesus' redemption. We must honestly confront and contend with this terminal disease of the soul, in light of the power and work of the Holy Ghost. We must overcome its tentacles by coming into an intimate relationship with the Father.

It is in line with the complete work of the Godhead that people can begin to overcome the claims of sin in their lives. The Apostle Paul talked about the condition of his sin and the only solution to it in Romans 7:24-25a, "O wretched man that I am! Who shall deliver me from the body of this death? I thank God through Jesus Christ our Lord."

The Apostle Paul realized that only through Christ could a person overcome the claims, power, and effects of sin. He made this statement about Jesus in Romans 8:37, "Nay, in all these things we are more than conquerors through him that loved us."

Jesus had proved to be victorious over the consequences of sin: that of death and the grave. As a result, Paul could make this powerful declaration in 1 Corinthians 15:55, "O death, where is thy sting? O grave, where is thy victory?" Hebrews 2:14-15 tells us that Jesus actually subdued and destroyed the source of this power of death: Satan.

The realization of Jesus' accomplishments on the cross brought thankfulness and joy to the Apostle Paul. He made this statement, "But thanks be to God which giveth us the victory through our Lord Jesus Christ" (1 Corinthians 15:57).

In 2 Corinthians 9:15, Paul stated, "Thanks be unto God for his unspeakable gift." He appreciated the reality of Jesus. He knew this overcoming power he had over sin was a gift of God. This inspired both awe and thankfulness.

Jesus' work and victory on the cross also brought joy to the Apostle Peter: He stated, "Whom having not seen, ye love, in whom, though now ye see him not, yet believing, ye rejoice with joy unspeakable and full of glory: Receiving the end of your faith, even the salvation of your souls" (1 Peter 1:8-9).

Being a Christian means being victorious over sin. If the victory is missing, a person needs to come to terms with whether he or she has truly embraced Jesus into his or her life as Lord and Savior. Perhaps He has been left behind, allowing the dictates of sin to gain access into the person's life. Maybe the world is crowding out the memories of Jesus' work, as it makes the individual indifferent to his or her spiritual condition.[1] On the other hand, maybe the person is Christian in name only or has a different Jesus, but he or she has never received the Jesus of the Bible as his or her personal Lord and Savior.

The Apostle John is clear. If a person has been born of God, he or she will not be inclined to give way to the devastation and destruction of sin.[2] John confirms this in 1 John 3:6-7, "Whosoever abideth in him sinneth not: whosoever sinneth hath not seen him, neither known him. Little children, let no man deceive you: he that doeth righteousness is righteous, even as he is righteous."

Overcomers in God's kingdom understand what it means to be forgiven because of Jesus' death on the cross.[3] Ultimately, they will overcome the world because the point of attraction towards the world, that of sin, has been taken care of by the blood of Jesus. 1 John 4:4 confirms this, "For whatsoever is born of God overcometh the world: and this is the victory that overcometh the world, even our faith." Overcomers have learned the key of overcoming by faith. They have learned to walk by faith according to the Person of the Son of God.

Studying the Word makes me realize that I am indeed more than a conqueror in Christ Jesus. When all is said and done, there will be no excuse for sin reigning in my life. Now, all I need is the abiding confidence to walk the new life out daily, knowing my victory over sin was truly wrought at the cross by Jesus. Do you possess this incredible confidence?

---

[1] Matthew 13:22; Revelation 3:4

[2] Also see Romans 6:12; 7:5

[3] 1 John 1:7-9; 2:1-2

To have such a confidence means you have truly believed the record that God has given about His Son. The Apostle John reveals this record in 1 John 5:12-13, "And this is the record, that God hath given to us eternal life, and this life is in his Son. He that hath the Son hath life; and he that hath not the Son of God hath nor life." Believing is active. It takes God at His word and acts upon it in confidence and obedience. Ultimately, it will end in righteousness.

Saints are victorious people because they are no longer slaves to sin, but have been made alive unto God by His Spirit.[4] The question is, do you have the testimony of an overcomer? Have you overcome the world, the flesh and the devil because sin no longer reigns in your body? If so, you can joyfully make the claim of Romans 6:22, "But now being made free from sin, and become servants to God, ye have your fruit unto holiness, and the end everlasting life."

---

[4] Romans 6:11-12

Book Three:

THE PRINCIPLES
OF
THE ABUNDANT LIFE

INTRODUCTION

What is a principle? When you understand principles, you realize that everything that properly functions does so because of a principle. Without principles there will be no order or purpose. Without principles there are no sound or safe boundaries. The truth is principles govern our Christian lives at every point. When a person steps outside of constructive principles, his or her life becomes plagued with complications and chaos.

This book is about the principles of God in regards to the abundant life He has prepared for us according to the inward working of the Holy Spirit. These principles constitute our real life in Christ. They are in line with God's character, and can establish believers on the immovable Rock. They are simple, yet profound, as they give each Christian valuable insight into the unchanging character of God.

By understanding these simple principles of God, a person will know how to please Him, for He will not work outside of His godly principles. This actually allows a person to see how He works.

For many years it has been my heart's desire to understand the different principles of God. I was continually aware of them as I studied the New Testament, but I could never summarize them. One morning, the Lord began to show me that some of His basic principles surrounding the abundant life could be found in the first two chapters of Genesis. I was both humbled and excited to see them being illuminated in Scripture.

This book is small, but valuable. Some of the visible fruits of the Church reveal that it has failed in different ways to understand or teach these principles. As a result, it appears as if many Christians are being swallowed up in chaos and despair.

Ask the Lord to open up your heart and mind to embrace these unseen boundaries, in order to grow in the knowledge of Him.

1

MASTER DESIGN

"Therefore leaving the principles
of the doctrine of Christ,
let us go on unto perfection..."
Hebrews 6:1

A principle is a comprehensive and fundamental law. All principles have an origin or source. The purpose or goal of these principles hinges on their creator. For example, principles operate within designs. Therefore, principles constitute a comprehensive design that will not operate outside of its purpose or blueprint.

Principles are made up of laws. These principles are not comprised of just any law. They operate according to natural or basic laws that are subject to a greater order. For example, all natural order goes back to God. Therefore, principles determine the way in which these laws should be applied.

A good example of this is the relationship of the Old Testament to the New Testament. The Old Testament contains the Law, while the New Testament shows how the Law is to be upheld in intent, practice, or application. In the Old Testament, the Law is simply the Law, while in the New Testament, it becomes a living, active revelation of the character of God that must be upheld and fulfilled. Principles actually activate the fruits, or the consequences, based on how the law is being applied.

We know that Jesus Christ is the Lawgiver in the Old Testament. In the New Testament, He teaches man how to properly apply the Law. Much of His teaching includes personal, visible examples of how obedience to the Law will manifest itself in intent and attitude. He, therefore, became an active, living example of the disposition that must be in place to fulfill the Law in spirit and action.

A good example of this can be seen in His Sermon on the Mount. How many laws did Jesus expound on, to only show that outward obedience was not enough in the kingdom of God? He was demonstrating that the Law comprises a bigger picture that embraces the whole of man, from the heart condition to his attitudes.

Laws may govern man's outward actions, but his heart condition and attitudes are influenced by unseen principles that he is actually adhering to. These principles will actually identify or distinguish the law that a person is coming into subjection to.

Principles also find their origins in the spirit that motivates a person. For example, attitude determines the spirit that will motivate a person. Spirit will influence the decisions a person makes. Decisions will set up the environment, or law, that a person will be operating within. This environment will determine the fruits that will manifest themselves. These fruits will reveal the principles a person is walking according to. There are only two types of fruits in the spiritual realm that reveals the principles that are being activated.

The two types of spiritual fruits that are revealed by our lives are godliness and iniquity. Godliness is associated with the character, work, and ways of God. His stamp will clearly distinguish a person in his or her attitudes, conduct, and lifestyle. Iniquity reveals there is some type of flaw within the character of man that will, or is, producing deviant attitudes, conduct, and lifestyles. Such deviance will reveal that man is out of order due to the fact that God is not the center of his life.

As stated, these principles work according to the law that is in operation. One law leads to death, while the other one leads to life.[1] One operates within the confines of truth, while the other one operates under the cloud of darkness and deception. One produces lifeless beliefs and philosophies, while the other one results in life and revelation. The Holy Spirit inspires one, while Satan influences the other one. It is important to realize that you will walk according to the principles of one of these spiritual, unseen laws depending how you walk out your life. These two contrasts show us how important it is to understand how laws and principles operate. This will allow us to properly test the spirit.

Other examples of how laws and principles work are found in nature. Nature's laws actually dictate what is natural in the world in which we live. They are unchanging in how they function and beneficial in practice. A good example of this is gravity.

Gravity is an unseen law that works according to a natural design of the earth. Everything on the planet Earth is subject to this unseen law. Even though everyone is affected by it, it is taken for granted. We never think about how our lives are upheld and maintained by the application of this law, but without it, there would be destruction. The law of gravity is only one example of how an active law operates within a greater master design.

When foundational principles are properly maintained, there is peace and order. However, when these principles are ignored, there is chaos and destruction. For instance, to ignore the law of gravity at great heights means certain death.

---

[1] Romans 8:2

We see this truth in the spiritual realm. There are unseen principles governing every area of our lives. We are given basic principles that uphold godly and moral responsibilities in the Word of God.

The principles in the kingdom of God are made of truths and doctrines that we are to live by. Truths represent the oracles of God, while doctrines point to application of truths in a personal way.

These truths lay a foundation under our spiritual lives. They establish doctrines that manifest themselves in upright conduct. However, Hebrews 6:1 declares doctrine is not enough. Believers must go on to maturity. This maturity means that the principles these individuals are walking according to are adjusting inward disposition as well as outward conduct.

Doctrine is represented by milk. This milk is necessary for the early stage of the Christian's life. In order to encourage proper growth, doctrine must be walked out daily in obedience. Anyone who fails to do this will suffer from spiritual malnutrition. Malnutrition of this nature will cause a person to be unskillful in righteousness and vulnerable to deception. Such a diet will be ineffective to bring a person to full age.[2]

Consider the following example and see how truths, doctrines, laws, and principles lead to each other.

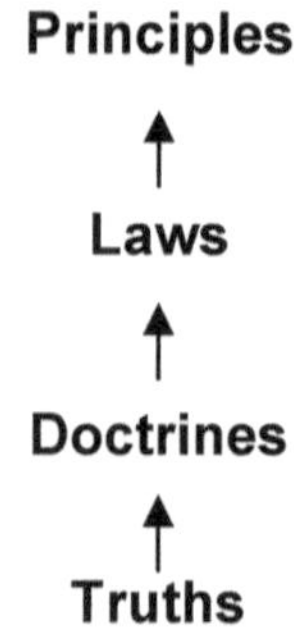

Godly principles actually will activate the spiritual law that will govern us. They will also serve as blueprints for our lives. These blueprints will mean nothing if we do not take the master design and build our lives according to the plan of God. In fact, doctrines that are not properly applied will become dead-letter or great burdens to us. 2 Corinthians 3:6 confirms this, "Who also hath made us able ministers of the new testament; not of the letter, but of the spirit: for the letter killeth, but the spirit giveth life." [3]

Once a doctrine becomes dead-letter, or devoid of the life or revelation of Christ, it will silence the voice of God. This tragedy occurs

[2] See Hebrews 5:11-6:2

[3] See also Romans 7:6

because dead-letter doctrine lacks the right spirit. Without the right spirit, the person will be unable to walk it out in obedience. If this combination is missing, the right principle will be absent in application.

It is only the Holy Spirit who gives life to the things of God and shows individuals how to put the oracles of God into daily practice. He does this by using revelation to reveal the principle.

Revelation in this text means to unveil truths or hidden mysteries about Jesus that become living and life-changing. This type of revelation is only realized through application or obedience to doctrines. However, doctrines ultimately give way to principles. It is the walking out of godly principles that enlightens believers to a particular doctrine's true intentions and purpose for their lives.

Isaiah 28:10 gives us insight into how this design works that is to govern our lives, "For precept must be upon precept, precept upon precept; line upon line, line upon line; here a little, and there a little." The Word is full of good guidelines or truths, but many find themselves in confusion when circumstances create a situation that is beyond their control. This confusion is created because God's Word is not clear on the particular issue. Blurred guidelines are unable to decisively instruct people, which can result in frustration and anger.

A good example of this is the issue of divorce. God's views on divorce do not constitute a truth, but a doctrine. Divorce is an outward symptom of sin reigning in the heart. The outward manifestation of sin reveals that there has been disobedience to godly principles.

The Apostle Paul set down some boundaries to govern marriage, such as submission and love. Application of these godly boundaries maintains the sanctity of marriage. Therefore, proper application of godly principles promotes attitudes that honor and respect God's plan in this area.

Many dedicated Christians have grappled with the subject of divorce. They have unwillingly found themselves part of something that God hates, but they are unable to change the circumstances. They find themselves becoming victims as they struggle with the instructions surrounding divorce in light of unmitigated circumstances that were beyond their control. It all seems so unfair. This is when doctrines in the Bible, such as those concerning subjects like divorce, become shrouded in "gray" or are confusing.

Every Christian must be quick to agree and comply with the Word of God. However, when confusion is on the scene, Christians may find they are now part of a different arena. This arena consists of seeking God's face and coming to terms with the lessons of the past, in order to fulfill the plan of God in the future. In such situations, these individuals must discover the principle that would maintain the correct spirit and intent in their particular situation. It is amazing how understanding the right spirit behind the matter may actually give a person revelation and liberty to step outside of accepted practices to embrace God's personal plan for their lives.

Godly doctrine that produces principles is brought forth as one precept is placed upon another precept. This develops a complete picture. Once a picture takes form, a person will begin to see the principle that must be applied in the "gray" areas.

For example, in light of principles, one can discern that God does not intend all people to remain single once divorced. This implies that there is a greater principle that must be put into practice if a person is to realize God's will for his or her life.

Godly principles work according to one spiritual law. I have already made reference to the two spiritual laws in operation. Romans 8:2 clearly states these two laws, "For the law of the Spirit of life in Christ Jesus hath made me free from the law of sin and death."

People walk according to the laws that govern them. If a person walks according to the law of the flesh (or the law of sin and death), his or her conduct will include such things as compromise, the works of the flesh and the practices of sin. If an individual walks according to the law of the Spirit of life, he or she will display the fruit of the Spirit as he or she follows in the ways of righteousness.[4]

Consider the different foundations, laws, principles, and results in the following diagram.

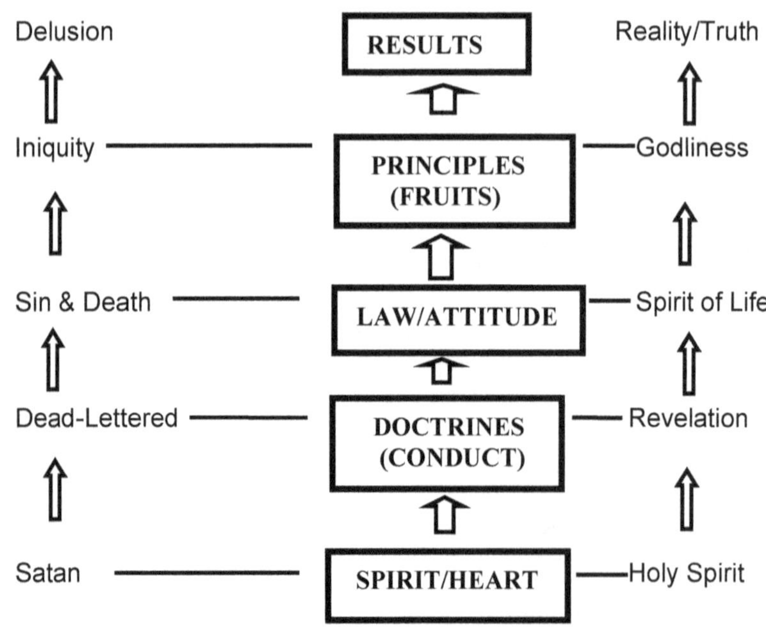

[4] Galatians 5:19-21; 22-23

The Word of God is clear about the conduct of the saint. The Christian life is a choice, not an option or an accident. If believers are to overcome the law of sin and death, they must walk after the Spirit according to godly principles.[5]

The Lord challenged people to follow Him with the word "if." The word "if" is not being used in an optional sense, but rather it states what your natural response would be in those particular areas of your life. For example, if you love Him, you will obey Him. If you truly desire to follow Him, you will deny self and pick up your cross. If you want to gain it all, you must be willing to lose it all. As you can see, "if" stipulates what your natural response will be if you truly belong to Him.

In today's Christendom, it is not unusual to see professing Christians treating the Word of God as optional and insignificant. It is not unusual to see people brush over the word "if" and the truths it promotes when it comes to their personal lives.

There is only one correct path and the word "if" defines that narrow path.[6] It is a word that brings a hard reality check to anyone who will understand the intent behind it. It shows a person if they are really serious about their Christian life or whether they are simply playing the game. It forces a person to choose, exposing not only the spiritual law he or she has become subject to, but also the path that is preferred.

What law have you subjected yourself to? Is it the Spirit of life where you operate within godly boundaries to ensure the life of Christ is being established in you? Or, do you function within the law of sin and death that may guarantee you temporary happiness, but will end in chaos and spiritual death?

Maybe you realize you have never received God's plan of salvation in your heart. God's Word tells us that even though we are doomed because we are subject to the wrong law, God provided Jesus Christ to change our present state and our eternal destination.

Romans 10:9-10 states that if you believe in your heart that Christ was raised from the dead and confess that He is Lord, you shall be saved. Salvation is an act of grace on God's part, but an act of faith when it comes to man.[7] In other words, if a person chooses to believe God about Jesus Christ, he or she will be saved.

Perhaps you know you have been saved, but your life is lacking. You have reserved certain areas of your life for yourself. Turn those areas over to God and let Him have His way. You will find chaos turning into order, confusion into confidence, and turmoil into peace.

---

[5] Romans 8:1-13

[6] Matthew 7:13-14

[7] Ephesians 2:8-10

2

THE ORIGIN

In the beginning God
created the heaven and the earth.
Genesis 1:1

Genesis 1:1 is one of the most powerful verses in the whole Bible. This statement contains volumes. This Scripture could single-handedly bring a person with a searching heart to salvation.

The first three words set a powerful stage for us, "In the beginning." "Beginning" means the principle thing, chief, or first in place, rank, and time.[1] The first statement in this Scripture tells us what must be first in every area of our lives. In fact, it must be chief or become of the greatest importance, significance, or influence to us. These words simply lead us to our only source, God.

Today, there has been a shift in Christendom for there are more and more people within what I considered to be "churchianity" and not "Christianity" adopting the same philosophies and mentality of the world. This mentality makes all matters man-centered, rather than Christ centered. Instead of man pursuing God, he is chasing after the elusive concept of personal happiness. As a result, these people are esteeming self, rather than denying self. They have bought the lie that by exalting the essence of humanity or humanism in different situations, it will help them to understand their place in the scheme of things. The results have proven to be devastating. People end up coming to the end of self, rather than discovering God. This has caused man to be subtly deified and exalted as the solution, while God has been demoted to fit some religious feel-good box or conformed to certain ridiculous concepts. This subtle exaltation of man has been flaunted before God's will and holiness

A. W. Tozer stated that to understand man, people must begin with God. He also said, "Always and always God must be first. The Gospel in its scriptural context puts the glory of God first and the salvation of man second."[2] The order of Genesis 1:1 confirms this order, God first, followed by His creation.

---

[1] Strong Exhaustive Concordance of The Bible; #7225.

[2] Born After Midnight; A. W. Tozer; 1989; pgs. 20 & 23

It is important that we note that there is mention of only one God. This shows a seeking person that there is only one God he or she must make peace with. This God is not just an unseen entity that simply exists. He is Creator of the heavens we see glimpses of, and of the earth that serves as our temporary abode.

This God may appear as a great mystery, but there are three things we can draw from this Scripture. First, He is divine which implies He has incredible attributes. This divine entity is indeed high above finite man and capable of changing circumstances. In fact, His very creation speaks volumes about His perfect order, unlimited capabilities, incredible imagination, and profound artistic abilities.

Secondly, this verse tells us that He is eternal in nature. The mystery of His identity seems as unfathomable as His character. Where does He begin and where can He possibly end? The heavens are said to be ongoing, and this mysterious God created the heavens and formed man to be eternal. The idea of eternity is mind-boggling to finite man. This reality can stir faith in the heart of the most unbelieving soul, and cause some to be willing to lose all to discover his or her Creator.

The third truth about the God of Genesis 1:1 is that He is not a force, but a person. Even though this God is a mystery, He does have a name. God in Genesis 1:1 is translated as "Elohim." According to Ruth Specter Lascelle, a Christian Jewish Bible teacher, "Elohim" is plural, which points to the foundational teaching of the Godhead.[3]

Since God has personality, character, and a name, one must conclude that He can actually be known and understood to some degree. Since one can actually interact with this God, it is up to each of us to personally seek Him. The beauty of the sincere seeker is that such a person will find Him.[4]

John 1:1-5 gives us even more insight into this God. In the first verse of chapter one, we see these words, "In the beginning was the Word." "Word" implies expression. Obviously, this God who existed at the beginning, wants to express Himself or communicate with man. The word, "word" in this Scripture is not pointing to expression that comes in the form of words, thoughts, or statements, but rather in the form of a living person.

We know who this visible expression of God is to humankind. It is His only begotten Son, Jesus Christ. Jesus told Philip in John 14:9, "...he that hath seen me hath seen the Father;..." In the person of Christ, we can see the heart, mind, and will of God. In Him, we can actually see God's love, patience, and commitment to each of us.

---

[3] Jewish Faith and the New Covenant; Ruth Specter Lascelle; 1980; pgs 65-67

[4] Jeremiah 29:13

In John 1:4, we are told that Jesus Christ is the life of men. Life implies the ability to respond to one's environment. In short, Jesus is the essence of real life, and without Him, there is no life.

The life of Jesus can only be realized when an individual is enabled to respond to his or her spiritual environment. A person's spiritual environment is summarized in one word, God. Jesus made it possible for every person to respond to God in spirit and truth. It is the reality of God in an individual that constitutes true life.

The life that Jesus offers is not just any life, it is eternal and complete.[5] First of all, it is a life that foremost seeks and responds to God who becomes the only source of an abundant or whole life. It is a life that is based on the light of Jesus.

Today, there are many people walking in darkness. This darkness causes confusion, chaos, and destruction. Jesus came to bring clarity, order, and hope, but many refuse to accept His life. They prefer their darkness with all of its fleshly deeds, arrogant and self-serving pursuits, and temporary comfort zones.

John 1:14 takes us one step further by telling us this visible expression of God was made flesh and dwelt among man. Twenty centuries ago, Jesus took on the disposition of a servant and was fashioned in the form of a man.[6] He came by way of a manger. He walked among mankind, healing and delivering, in order to change their course. Ultimately, He turned the world upside down in order to turn it right side up.

John 1:14 goes on to tell us that man actually witnessed the glory of the only begotten of the Father. "Glory" means majesty. Christ's majesty was witnessed in His teachings, miracles, and life. Although His flesh veiled His glory as God, He still proved that He was who He said He was, the Son of the Living God, the Messiah, and the Savior of the world.

This Scripture verse goes on to say that Jesus was full of grace and truth. We see Jesus in His humanity showing this grace to the rejected and outcast of society. He showed the same measure of grace towards all on the cross. Sadly, some refuse to see their need for His grace that has been presented to each of us in the form of eternal life.[7]

The Son of God is the essence of truth who will set any captive free. He is the truth about man's spiritual condition. This was made evident when Jesus became sin for each of us on the cross, so that we could be made in the righteousness of God.[8] The cross of Christ exposed how

---

[5] Romans 6:23; John 10:10

[6] Philippians 2:5-11

[7] Ephesians 2:8-10

[8] 2 Corinthians 5:21

man in his sinful condition mocks, despises, rejects, and crucifies the precious things of God, including His precious Son.

Jesus, as the Son of Man, is also the truth about what constitutes true righteousness. Oswald Chambers states that Jesus is what God intended man to be. In other words, Jesus represents the normal man. This is why Christ said He was our example. Therefore, we are not to compare ourselves to anyone but Jesus. He is the only one who can give us a fair contrast in our spiritual life.[9]

Finally, Jesus is the truth about God. He showed man that God could be reached, touched, and identified in practical and personal ways. This brings us to the *first* principle in the kingdom of God: Everything in our life must begin or originate with God. This is constantly made evident through Christ. For example, Christ is the *chief* cornerstone, the *head* of the Church, and the *firstfruits* of the kingdom of God among believers.[10] Colossians 1:18 summarizes this truth in this way, "And he is the head of the body, the church: who is the beginning, the firstborn from the dead; that in <u>all</u> <u>things</u> he might have the <u>preeminence</u>." (Emphasis added.)

Jesus should have preeminence in everything surrounding a person's life. This preeminence means the individual does nothing outside of Jesus' purpose and will. However, it is not enough to simply begin with God, each individual must also end with Him.

The Bible begins with God in *Genesis 1:1*, but the book of Genesis ends in a coffin. The coffin serves as the story of every man, leaving him without hope. Although the first book ends in a coffin, the Bible ends with an incredible revelation. In the first chapter of Revelation, it shows us there is much more to a person's existence. A person must begin with God, but end with the revelation of Jesus Christ.

Genesis starts out establishing a foundation, but Revelation shows us the product of the foundation. Between the knowledge of God and the revelation of Jesus Christ lies the essence of our lives.

Knowledge of something is not enough. In fact, the Apostle Paul tells us that such knowledge puffs up.[11] There are many people with knowledge of God, but few possess a revelation of Him. The people who simply maintain knowledge of Him alone can become quite puffed up about what they think they know. The problem is that knowledge without revelation will be void of life.

Revelation means to unveil something. In the case of God, He wants to unveil His Son to us. The Apostle Paul put it in this manner,

> That the God of our Lord Jesus Christ, the Father of glory, may give unto you the spirit of wisdom and revelation in the

---

[9] 2 Corinthians 12:12-17

[10] Ephesians 2:20; Colossians 1:15-18; 1 Corinthians 15:20 & 23

[11] 1 Corinthians 8:1

> knowledge of him: The eyes of your understanding being enlightened; that ye may know what is the hope of his calling, and what the riches of the glory of his inheritance in the saints (Ephesians 1:17-18).

In Ephesians 1:17-18, we see that Paul desired the combination of wisdom and revelation. The reason for this combination is that without wisdom, there can be no revelation. According to 1 Corinthians 1:30, Christ is the essence of real wisdom. Such wisdom will lead us to greater revelations of Him. Godly wisdom is revealed knowledge being put into daily practice through faith and obedience.

The Christian life is sandwiched in between the knowledge of God and the revelation of Christ. God's part in the establishment of a person's life is to do the vital work through the Holy Spirit. The Spirit will unveil the very life of Christ to, in, and through God's people.[12] It is the manifestation of the life of Christ in and through His people that gives credibility and purpose to their lives and claims.

As you actually study the revelation of Jesus, you will see that He is the Alpha and Omega, the beginning and the end.[13] It may be easy to begin with Jesus, but it is another story to end with Him.

It is not unusual for people to take detours in their spiritual lives and lose sight of their Alpha or Beginning. The reason that many lose sight of the Alpha is they do not keep their eyes on the Omega or the finish line. Christ may start out as a person's Savior, but it is His Lordship that is able to lead individuals to the finish line. His Lordship requires each person to become dedicated servants, humble in attitude, submissive to His voice, and ready to follow, in obedience to His instructions.

As Jesus becomes Lord of a person's life, God will work His likeness into him or her. The life of Jesus is what makes His people greater partakers of His promises.[14]

One must, therefore, realize that a person's life must be prepared between the knowledge of God and the revelation of Jesus. Such a life will be full of communion, worship, and service. It will be a life that is abundant and satisfying to the soul.

Let me ask you: Is your life complete and satisfying? If not, maybe you have not started with God in every area of your life, or ended with the likeness of Jesus coming forth in majesty. After all, it is Jesus' life in you that proves you truly possess His reality, your only hope of obtaining glory.[15] This is the secret of the overcoming, Christian life.

---

[12] Philippians 1:6

[13] Revelation 1:8, 11, 17

[14] 2 Peter 1:3-4

[15] Colossians 1:27

3

BRINGING ORDER

And the earth was without form and
void; and darkness was upon the
face of the deep. And the spirit
of God moved upon the face of the waters.
Genesis 1:2

The first principle of the kingdom of God had to do with the first two manifestations of the Godhead, God the Father and God the Son. It clearly shows how the Father and the Son have manifested themselves in the design and function of creation. The Father has designed creation; therefore, all things consist because of Him. The Son carried out the plans of creation; therefore, all things exist and are maintained by Him.[1] The second principle has to do with the third manifestation of the Godhead in relationship to creation, God the Holy Ghost.

The first part of verse two of chapter one of Genesis tells us the earth was without form, void, and full of darkness. This picture also represents the people who attempt to live without God.

Self-sufficient man deludes himself to believe that his world is fine without God. He conveniently puts God outside of his world in order to be supreme ruler of his own environment. His particular form of godhood remains unchallenged until life shows him how insignificant he is in the scheme of things. This harsh reality sometimes brings the most hardened, self-sufficient individuals to discover that those who live outside of God's rule possess lives that are worthless or without form. All personal actions will take on a useless form that is void of life. In the end, these deluded or misguided souls will find themselves wandering around in desolation, want, and confusion.

A person who does not give way to God will find darkness engulfing his or her life. This darkness has many implications from misery, ignorance, sorrow, destruction, and death. A person who is in such darkness becomes lost in many ways, always groping for the meaning of his or her existence.

---

[1] 1 Corinthians 8:6

This groping leads the individual to various illusive objects or sources. This person will cling to things such as material possessions, earthly relationships, and prestige. However, each object or source lacks substance; therefore, it leads to meaningless dead ends, disillusionment, and despair.

In the last part of Genesis 1:2, we see where the Holy Spirit had to move upon the face of the waters to change the condition of the earth. Here lies the second principle of the kingdom of God. The Spirit of God must move upon the emptiness and darkness of the terrain before the face of something will change. Such work points to *recreation*, and must take place within man.

The word "move" means to brood, to be relaxed, flutter, or shake.[2] The action being described here is consistent with the character of the Holy Spirit. He must move upon the face of something to change it. "Face" in this text means to prepare, land upon, presence, or employ.[3] Obviously, the Holy Ghost must prepare the terrain for the master plan to be carried out. He must move upon the area to allow His presence to be felt. He must employ His power to carry it out.

What is the Holy Spirit preparing? In the case of men, He is preparing their hearts to receive the truth. People are in great darkness, and it is the Holy Ghost's responsibility to try to penetrate their deep darkness with the glorious light of the Gospel. Jesus confirmed this in John 6:44, "No man can come to me, except the Father which hath sent me draw him: And I will raise him up at the last day." The Father draws man with His Spirit.

In Matthew 16:17, Jesus told Peter that flesh and blood had not revealed His true identity to him, but the Father who is in heaven. Once again, we know the Father brings forth revelations of His Son through the Holy Spirit. 2 Corinthians 4:3-6 summarizes this truth. "But if our gospel be hid, it is hid to them that are lost: In whom the god of this world hath blinded the minds of them which believe not, lest the light of the glorious gospel of Christ, who is the image of God, should shine unto them... For God, who commanded the light to shine out of darkness, hath shined in our hearts, to give the light of the knowledge of the glory of God in the face of Jesus Christ."

The Holy Spirit has many symbols in Scripture that associate Him with revealing the glorious Gospel to those in darkness, and once again recreating that which is without form to take on form. He is like the dove that Noah sent from the ark to find dry land. The dove traveled to and fro, looking for a dry place to land. When the dove found none, it came back to Noah. Finally, during one of its excursions, it brought an olive twig

---

[2] Strong Exhaustive Concordance of the Bible; #7363

[3] Ibid #6440

back verifying that the water was receding, and that soon it would find the right place to land.[4]

The Holy Spirit is moving throughout the land, looking for receptive hearts in which to land and make His abode. He will not land on muddy waters for He is holy. Therefore, He will only land where purity is desired and justice will be embraced.

He brings an olive twig representing the peace of God to those who hunger after their Creator and are thirsty for His life. Sadly, many people reject the mild, sweet advances of the Holy Spirit. Such rejection will grieve Him because He knows the heart of the Father, as well as the willingness of the Son to save us.

Like Noah sending forth the dove, our heavenly Father does likewise with the Holy Ghost. After all, it is the Father who draws people to His Son through His Spirit. The Holy Spirit brings the reality of people's sinful condition by convicting them of sin.[5] The knowledge of sin and the hopeless plight it creates for individuals is what brings every heir of salvation to the cross of Christ. Each believer comes to this old rugged instrument on bended knee, broken by the weight of sin, and humbled by the reality of Jesus' substitution. They realize He is the only One who can change their spiritual plight and eternal destination.

Once the Holy Spirit begins to move on the terrain of a person's life, an important order occurs that clearly can be followed in Genesis 1. The first thing He must do is bring forth the light by penetrating the darkness. Once the light is brought to the forefront, the darkness will be revealed and separated from the light.

The Holy Spirit accomplishes this when His light reveals sin, bringing much needed contrast to the person. As the person submits to the Spirit's work, He separates him or her from the darkness of self, the world and Satan.

Once a person receives God's provision of the light of salvation, he or she is translated from the power of darkness into the kingdom of God.[6] "Translated" means to exchange, transfer, remove, put out, or turn away.[7] Obviously, an exchange of some type has to take place in a person's life. Positionally, believers have been removed from under the power of darkness in their lives. But, how is this exchange translated to everyday living?

According to Romans 15:16, the Holy Spirit sanctifies the believer. In fact, He broods over saints like a mother hen. He is gentle towards all of their failures, and flutters over them as they seek God's will. Ultimately,

---

[4] Genesis 8
[5] John 16:8-9
[6] Colossians 1:13
[7] Strong's Exhaustive Concordance of the Bible, #3179

He shakes everything loose that is not established on the right foundation.

Christians must remember that when the Holy Spirit first made His appearance to the believers on the day of Pentecost, He landed on the people in the form of a fire.[8] Fire not only represents holiness, but it is also a form of separation. The separation that took place was evident by the cloven tongues. People's tongues were being separated along with lives to proclaim the glorious Gospel to all of the nations.

This separation is made evident in creation as the Holy Spirit divided waters from the land. He wants to divide that which is of the earth in our lives from that which is designated to be heavenly by our Creator. The Spirit must also sanctify even that which is heavenly.

The truth is that what has not been sanctified by God, does not belong to Him. All things must be translated from the power of darkness in order to be separated for God's use and glory. Problems arise when believers will not allow the Holy Spirit to sanctify the things they possess. Obviously, they are afraid of losing such possessions.

Granted, there will be some things that are burned up in the fire of sanctification, but such things are destructive to God's will and purpose. In my case, hindsight showed me that the Holy Spirit carefully separated me from the dictates of the flesh, the demands of my pride, and the entanglements of the world. This separation has allowed me the luxury of being able to trust God with every area of my life, and to worship Him in spirit and truth.

The Holy Ghost is also beautifully represented by Abraham's servant who sought after a bride for Isaac in Genesis 24. We are not told Abraham's servant's name (in this text) and I believe there are two reasons that God did not make specific mention of his name: 1) His name is never mentioned because he did not exist to promote himself, but Isaac; and 2) God did not want us to know him by his name, but by his character. This servant came on behalf of his master to fulfill an obligation and humbly carry it out.

When you consider the Holy Spirit, you see the same picture. He is unknown to many, even in the Christian realm. He quietly works behind the scenes. His main responsibility is to seek out a bride for the Son of God. He goes far and wide to secure the one who will be betrothed, and once He does, He will present glorious gifts from the storehouse of the Father just as Abraham's servant did to Rebekah.

He is also a committed representative who will not rest until His job is done. In fact, the Holy Ghost woos people to the Son. John 16:8-9 tells us that the Spirit of God reproves the world of righteousness. This means

[8] Acts 2

that He lifts up the real standard of righteousness, which is Jesus Christ.[9] It is this standard of righteousness that admonishes both unbelievers and believers.

Jesus Christ shows man how far away from the mark he is, as well as serving as the believer's example of righteousness. His life shows Christians what is acceptable as far as their heart condition, attitudes, and actions.

Sadly, many ignore, justify away, or reject the advances or convictions of the Holy Spirit. It is during such times that the Holy Spirit is quenched from effectively doing a deeper work in people's lives.

The Holy Spirit also flutters over saints to guide them in their spiritual lives. Romans 8:1 instructs believers to walk after the Spirit. Galatians 5:16 states why followers of Jesus should walk in the Spirit, "This I say then, Walk in the Spirit, and ye shall not fulfil the lust of the flesh."

The Holy Spirit enables believers to become overcomers in God's kingdom. However, His measure of enabling believers is often gentle and sweet. He will not yell at Christians to get their attention, nor will He demand they follow Him.

He lets His presence be known, and then it is up to each person to follow His leading.

John 16:13 tells us where the Holy Spirit leads: He leads into all truth. John 14:6 states that Jesus is the truth. In other words, the Spirit of the Living God will always lead an individual to Jesus, the bridegroom, in order to glorify Him. After all, the Spirit is not here to glorify Himself, nor does He represent any other person or interests on earth.

Today many self-proclaimed apostles, prophets, pastors, and ministers show their true colors because they exalt themselves instead of Jesus. They claim they are anointed of God, but they lead people away from the only standard of truth, the Son of God. They arrogantly try to be the Holy Spirit in people's lives by dictating how their followers must believe, feel, and act.

The Holy Spirit serves as the still, small voice of God in the world. False self-appointed leaders have counterfeited His voice. These heretics realize they must exclusively become the voice of God to their followers in order to negate the sole authority of the Written Word.

As the counterfeits cleverly take the place of the Holy Spirit in a person's life, they know they will drown out any contradictory voice including the Bible. Once they take the place of the Spirit of God, they will have the power to change their followers' belief system or foundations, according to their personal agendas. As these false leaders change the belief system, they can subtly exalt themselves into the place

---

[9] 1 Corinthians 1:30

of the Messiah, or Christ, in their followers' lives. The next step for them is inevitable. They will finally become God to their followers.

The Holy Spirit is not a dictator, but a guide. He is not trying to impress people with His power, but rather woos people to pursue after and fall in love with the Son of God. The purpose for imparting His anointing among Christians is not to exalt them in the kingdom of God, but to give the same power and credibility to all believers to carry out their commission and effectively represent the Lord of lords and King of kings to a dying world.

The Holy Spirit desires that each believer see the bridegroom in His love, beauty, and majesty. His ultimate goal is that Christians fall in love with Jesus and choose to serve Him in total abandonment.

Finally, the Holy Spirit shakes our lives. We see a beautiful example of this in Genesis 26. Isaac set out to once again dig wells that his father, Abraham, had initially prepared. The first two wells caused a battle, while the third well brought him much needed liberty. This liberty allowed him to pursue the fourth well. It was at the fourth well that God introduced Himself to Isaac. Isaac reciprocated by building an altar, calling on the name of the Lord, pitching a tent to establish a dwelling place of communion, and uncovering the fourth well to ensure well-being.

Jesus related the Holy Spirit to Rivers of Living Water.[10] God has provided this water for every believer, but there are conflicts that will always occur when saints seek to uncover these precious rivers. There will be battles with the flesh that will eventually cause waters to become unacceptable. There is the struggle with pride that prevents individuals from partaking of the Holy Spirit's refreshing qualities. The truth is people must cease to strive in the flesh and allow themselves to be brought to a place of liberty. This liberty enables God's people to enjoy the qualities of His endless flow of water.

The Apostle Paul summarized this truth in 2 Corinthians 3:17, "Now the Lord is that Spirit: and where the Spirit of the Lord is, there is liberty." People fail to realize that they cannot worship God if they are in turmoil. Liberty is a necessary ingredient for not only worshipping God, but also enjoying who He is.

Like Isaac, believers go through intense battles before they can come to the place of liberty. The conflicts are intense because they have to do with denying self and applying the cross. But, before this can happen, there has to be a shaking in the areas of the flesh where there is self-sufficiency.

The Holy Spirit actually shakes up our creeds, securities, and perceptions. This shaking is no always like an earthquake, but in most cases, it is like a gentle washing. Titus 3:5-6 tells us this about the type

---

[10] John 7:37-39

of work that takes place, "Not by works of righteousness which we have done, but according to his mercy he saved us, by the washing of regeneration and renewing of the Holy Ghost. Which he shed on us abundantly through Jesus Christ our Saviour."

The Holy Ghost brings forth new life by changing the landscape of our lives. A new life means a recreated or regenerated life. This type of life is fruitful and brings glory to God.

It must be noted that man cannot change the terrain of his heart, mind, and life. It takes the intervention of God through the moving of the Holy Spirit. Without the Holy Spirit moving on the face of our lives, there will be no distinct contrast between the world and the true followers of Jesus.

Today, the Holy Spirit is being accredited with various movements that have rolled through Christendom such as the laughing "revival" and the pursuit of "signs and wonders." These movements are often fleshly, perverted, and mocking towards the real character of God. The contemporary leaders' promotion, acceptance or tolerance towards these movements is backed by their claim that they do not want to quench the Spirit of God. In reality, most of these leaders embrace these strange movements because they serve personal agendas.

Isaac uncovered four wells in his struggle to find a well that served as a source of water. Keep in mind Isaac represented Jesus Christ. Jesus stated in John 7:37 that He is the giver of Living Water. In other words, Jesus is the one who uncovers the fourth well. The fourth well represents the fullness of the Spirit. It is the Living Water springing up and over the face of hearts, minds, and lives that will not only change a person's disposition, but will bring order to his or her shaky, pathetic life.

What about you? Have you allowed the Holy Spirit to move over the face of every area of your life? Maybe you have tried to hold on to wells that are polluted or nearly empty and unacceptable, or are you entangled in situations that prevent you from partaking of the pure rivers of God. If so, you need to relinquish the wells and proceed on until you come to a place of liberty. This liberty will allow you to pursue the reality of Jesus and accept His invitation to come and partake of the fullness of the Rivers of Living Water.

4

A NEW CREATION

...and, behold, it was very good.
Genesis 1:31b

The consistent statement found throughout Genesis Chapter One is, "... and God saw that it was good." According to *Strong's Exhaustive Concordance,* the word "good" has many implications including the word "pleasant." God had created a world that was not only pleasant in every way, but was bountiful, sweet, beautiful, and prosperous.

What was even more amazing is that He created such beauty out of that which had no form. He had taken that which was void or empty and filled it with things that were fruitful. He had overshadowed the darkness with light that encouraged life to grow and reproduce itself.

It was not until after man had been formed on the sixth day that God was able to conclude that His creation was not just good, but it was "very good." It was the presence of man in the midst of God's perfect creation that made all of creation whole, and in a sense, pleasant or beautiful beyond description. This final part of creation allowed God to rest from all of His work. It is true that creation declares God's glory, but it was man who would serve as His crowning glory. Creation's design may give valuable insight to its designer, but it would be man who would be designed to actually reflect the Designer's glory in the world.

Now that God's creation was complete, He could rest and enjoy it. Watchman Nee pointed out that man began life with the Sabbath. This shows the proper order. God works before he rests, while man must rest before he works. This keeps man's life and perspective in the proper working order. He must always begin with his life before God. With this perspective in mind, Nee concluded, "This principle underlies all Christian service."[1]

One would wonder in what way God would enjoy His latest creation of man when He had heaven with all of its beauty, as well as the angels to take pleasure in? It's simple. God would enjoy His handiwork by

---

[1] A Table In The Wilderness (Daily Meditations); July 8th

enjoying man. He would enjoy man as he personally related and responded to his perfect atmosphere. God would rejoice as man communed with Him. He would find the greatest type of pleasure as man served as His unhindered mirror in the midst of His creation.

My co-laborer of the Gospel, Jeannette Haley, confirmed this pleasure created by the existence of man in the Garden of Eden. Jeannette is a professional artist. Her love for the beauty and detail of creation inspired much of her art. One day she was looking at the beauty of a duck on a postage stamp and noticed the Latin name for it. She began to think about the many different species of ducks. This brought her back to the man who named all of the different species of animals in the beginning, Adam. She was thinking how intelligent he had to be to name the array of different types of animal life. As she pondered how God brought each animal to Adam to be named, the Lord sovereignly broke through her thoughts by saying, "And, we had fun."

It is God's heart to watch man enjoy His creation. After all, God created the Garden of Eden for man's good pleasure. He gave man the best so He could enjoy man at his best, without struggles, turmoil or bondage.

The Garden of Eden was a perfect atmosphere with a perfect setup and place for man to experience peace, joy, and communion. It is important to point out how the Word of God puts a shadow over this perfection with the word "was" which is past tense.

It was in the Garden of Eden that man fell into sin. He rebelled against God's authority and disobeyed. This disobedience caused the first man to fall into a lost state of spiritual emptiness and darkness.

Because of sin, man found himself in the same type of condition as the earth was before the Holy Spirit moved upon the face of it. Instead of enjoying a perfect atmosphere, man was ushered into a world of struggle and turmoil. Man found himself only capable of experiencing temporary joy in the midst of great sorrow and suffering. Therefore, is there any real hope for man or is he doomed forever in this state of hopelessness?

The answer is yes; there is hope for man. God provided a way out of this hopeless situation. However, for Him to change man's present lost state, He must now recreate man. This means that the Holy Spirit must move over the face of man's life.

It is as the Holy Spirit moves over the face of a person that he or she will be made into a new creation. As a new creation man will once again be acceptable to God, prepared for His enjoyment, and ready to embrace life in a new way. This is confirmed by what Paul said in 2 Corinthians 5:17, "Therefore if any man be in Christ, he is a new creature: old things are passed away; behold, all things are become new."

This brings us to the *third* principle that real life comes only from God, the Creator. As Creator, God has fashioned all things for the purpose of enjoyment. He created things with a plan in mind. Granted, creation was created for man, but man was formed for God. Today, many people are trying to recreate, to no avail, the perfect atmosphere that was lost by Adam. Obviously, God is the main ingredient to having, experiencing, and enjoying life. Therefore, man must come back into relationship with God in order to line up with His plan for him, before he can discover, know, and enjoy the essence of real life.

It is only as we understand what constitutes real life that we begin to see, that man could not be accepted in his present state of sin, nor could he interact with His Creator. Therefore, a person must be recreated to embrace the life of God. Such a task seems impossible, but creation shows us that it is not impossible to God. How does God recreate man to once again be able to respond to Him as the first man, Adam, did in the Garden of Eden?

Born Again

2 Corinthians 5:17 gives us the first clue of becoming a new creation—that of being in Christ. 1 Corinthians 1:30a states, "But of him are you in Christ." God must place us in Christ. This placement is initially done positionally, giving every believer the right to experience life at greater levels. Such a right gives each saint the ability to grow in a relationship with God through Jesus.

This placement begins with an event that was described by Jesus in John 3:3 and 5, "... Verily, verily, I say unto thee, Except a man be born again, he cannot see the kingdom of God...Except a man be born of water and of the Spirit, he cannot enter into the kingdom of God."

Ruth Specter Lascelle summarizes the necessity of man being born from above: "There are two deaths even as there are two births. If a person is born once, he will die twice, but if he is born twice, he will die only once!"[2]

Since man is spiritually dead because of sin, he must be born from above with the breath of God. The spiritual birth only occurs when the Holy Spirit brings a person to a convicting knowledge of sin. The revelation of sin causes an individual to realize that he or she needs a Savior. As the light of truth begins to penetrate his or her heart, Jesus, the Son of God, is unveiled by the Spirit as God's provision and sacrifice for sins. It is also during this revelation that salvation occurs. Upon believing this as being true, and the person turns in repentance, God gives a new heart and a new spirit to him or her.

---

[2] A Dwelling Place for God; pg. 221

A new heart and spirit points to a new disposition. The heart will be fleshly instead of stony which means it will now be able to respond to God. The Spirit of God will once again become the very breath of life in man, making the person alive unto God, responsive and sensitive to His voice, and desirous to live in communion with Him. Now that the disposition is in place, the Holy Spirit seals him or her, and begins the work of sanctification, as He abides as the Comforter, Guide and Teacher within God's tabernacle or new temple.[3]

Since the Holy Ghost is the breath of the eternal life of God, spiritual life has now been conceived and brought forth in a person's life. This event is known as the "born again" experience. Instead of simply being born of flesh and blood, a person is now born according to the water of the Word and by the indwelling presence of the Spirit of God.[4] The birth not only constitutes a new disposition, but also the beginning of real life. What form will this new creation take on? Our first clue is found in John 3:5, "... man [must] be born of water and of the Spirit."

It is after the Spirit begins to move upon that which must be formed, that the process of recreation begins. There is a separation between light and darkness. This is true for Christians. The Holy Ghost begins to bring a separation between the old life associated with the world, and the new life that is being established in the believer.[5]

Now that there is separation, there will be a division between that which is holy and unholy. In the case of creation, there was a division being made in the waters. For example, there is a distinction made between the firmament and the waters. Obviously, some water would become salt water and other water would become fresh water. For the Christian, this points to discernment. Only the Spirit of God can bring discernment in such matters.[6]

Division brings contrast, which results in identification. It is at this point that God identifies heaven from the earth. We are reminded of how man will reflect the glory of heaven or he will be earthbound and reflect that which is carnal and under judgment. We also know that the Lord will give His saints a new name at the end of their course, written on a white stone that will symbolize their justification in Him.[7]

The work of separation, distinction, and identification points to the work of sanctification. We know that we are positionally sanctified in Christ, but the Spirit of God does the work of sanctification in the inner

---

[3] Ezekiel 36:26-27; John 16:7-14; 1 Corinthians 3:16; Ephesians 1:13-14

[4] John 3:6

[5] Genesis 1:3-5

[6] Genesis 1:6-8; 1 Corinthians 2:13-14

[7] 1 Corinthians 15:40-49; Revelation 2:17

man.[8] The process of sanctification is done in stages as the believer is enlarged to be brought to perfection or maturity in his or her life in Christ.

Cultivating the Seeds of Life

The first man, Adam, was formed from the ground. He was made of the earth, while given heavenly potential when God made him a living soul by giving him the breath of His Spirit. As a living soul, he was designated to not only reflect the glory of his Creator, but to live forever.

When God formed or fashioned Adam, he made him complete or whole. He did not have to go through the stages of conception, birth, growth, and maturity. In his innocent and pure state, Adam stood mature.

Sadly, Adam took the life that he was formed with and used it as an avenue to rebel against God. He, therefore, lost his innocent and pure state as the breath of God lifted from his life. In fact, he fell into another state that resulted in chaos and death.

Therefore, man without the spiritual birth is spiritually dead.[9] In other words, he is the walking dead. He may be able to relate to the earth that he was formed from, but unable to interact with His Creator who is the giver of true and lasting life.

Because man is spiritually dead, he or she must go through the spiritual stages of conception, birth, growth, and maturity. Spiritual conception occurs when the Gospel penetrates the heart. If the seed is conceived by faith in the heart, this conception leads to the next stage--that of spiritual birth.

A newborn baby's only claim to life is that it is alive. A baby has all of the necessary ingredients to grow and mature, but the ingredients are like seeds. These seeds must be nurtured to take on character. This is true for new believers. They have the potential to reach spiritual maturity, but they must be cultivated or nurtured in the right way. The first way new believers must be nurtured is by the Word of God. Ephesians 5:26 says this, "That he might sanctify and cleanse it with the washing of water by the word..."

The Word of God not only cleanses Christians, but it also causes spiritual growth. In fact, the Word has the ability to expose all problem areas that would hinder spiritual maturity.[10] It shows believers what they need to do about those weak areas by revealing how to establish a right foundation (healthy soil), attitudes (healthy plants) and actions (fruits).

---

[8] 1 Corinthians 1:30; 1 Peter 1:3

[9] Romans 6:23

[10] Hebrews 4:12

It is vital at this time to remember one of the important parts of this principle. Every seed planted in the ground can only reproduce itself according to the likeness of its own kind.[11] This truth brings us to another aspect of this third principle--that of the firstfruits.

The Firstfruits

A baby has a genetic code (DNA) that will determine his or her features. As long as this code is not disturbed by destructive factors, the child's makeup will not veer off course. We know that due to sin, the design of man has definitely veered off course, making him unrecognizable, unacceptable, and ineffective to His Creator.

This brings us to a question. Is this scenario true for those who have been born again? Is there some kind of code that should determine their spiritual make-up? The answer is yes.

A seed can only reproduce itself after its own kind. We are given insight into the seed or spiritual code that is to determine every believer's make-up, "For whom he did foreknow, he also did predestinate to be <u>conformed</u> to the image of his Son, that he might be the <u>firstborn</u> among many brethren" (Romans 8:29). (Emphasis added.)

Christians are to be fashioned like the Son of Man, Jesus Christ. With this in mind, we have to consider what factors keep believers from being conformed to Jesus. The main factor to prevent this likeness from coming forth is rebellion.

This was the culprit that caused Adam to fall from his first state. Rebellion finds its origins in a selfish disposition that expresses itself in an independent attitude. This attitude keeps a person from reaching his or her spiritual potential.

Jesus is not only the firstborn of a new creation, but He is the firstfruits as well. The Apostle Paul confirms this, "But now is Christ risen from the dead, and become the <u>firstfruits</u> of them that slept" (1 Corinthians 15:20). (Emphasis added.)

It is easy to get around the idea of being like Jesus Christ, the firstborn. After all, the firstborn only marks an offspring, and most children are different. However, since Jesus is the firstfruits, it sets up the criteria of the fruits that follow. Since every Christian possesses Jesus' life, they should become like Him as they take on His likeness. After all, a seed can only reproduce after its own kind, and the seed is the life of Jesus in a believer.

Jesus in His humanity is the reality of the type of life that will come out of those who truly have been born again of the Spirit. He not only

[11] Genesis 1:11

shows what this life looks like, but the types of fruit that it will produce. In fact, His life must penetrate every aspect of our lives. God's goal is to see every member of Jesus' living Body, the Church, being filled up and overflowing with His Son's life.

If you study both the firstborn and the firstfruits in the Law set up between God and Israel, you will find that both were automatically dedicated to God.[12] Since Jesus is the firstborn and firstfruits of the new creation, He has been totally dedicated or consecrated to God along with every believer.

Each believer is considered the firstborn and firstfruits to God. This means their life does not belong to them, but must be wholly dedicated to God. This is the secret between a nominal Christian life and an effective, powerful life. The latter will make a lasting difference in the kingdom of God.

Next follows the stage of taking on the characteristics of the firstborn or the firstfruits.

Regeneration

A seed goes through a lot of preparation before it can come forth. Every spring seeds and bulbs that have been dormant all winter come forth to display new and exciting life. In the time of dormancy, these plants experience death and the grave in order to reach their potential to shine brightly for a season. This is the miraculous cycle of life. Indeed, there is an incredible process that takes place every year to ensure new life.

You would think this ongoing process would kill the seed or bulb, but each year, it seems to produce more sturdy plants and flowers. Obviously, the life that is being displayed each new season has been enriched by the ongoing challenges of nature that could very well destroy it.

Spiritual birth is just the beginning of a Christian's process. Each new believer must grow and reach his or her potential. Each stage of growth means he or she is taking on the likeness of Jesus.

Like all life, the spiritual life needs nourishment. The Word of God waters these lives with the truths of God. This watering actually allows an individual to take root in the things of God, helping him or her to avoid establishing a wrong heart condition or inward environment.[13]

Once a person takes root in God, he or she can begin to grow in the knowledge of Jesus. This growth implies that the work of ongoing regeneration is taking place. Titus 3:5 gives us this insight, "Not by works

[12] Exodus 22:29-30; Leviticus 2:12

[13] Matthew 13:1-25

of righteousness which we have done, but according to his mercy he saved us, by the washing of regeneration, and renewing of the Holy Ghost." A seed that grows into a beautiful plant is doing what is natural. In other words, it has nothing to do with its own growth. The outside factors such as the ground condition, water, sun, and weather brings forth the final product.

This is true for the Christian. If a person is truly born again, he or she will naturally grow into the likeness of Jesus. A believer cannot bring forth the work of regeneration in his or her own power. The main ingredient for regeneration is the Holy Ghost. He is the one who brings forth the life of Jesus in a believer. It is Jesus' life shining forth in a person that proves regeneration has taken place.

The work of regeneration results in a person being transformed or transfigured. While conformation deals with the outward features, transformation has to do with the inward heart and attitude of man being changed to embrace the characteristics of Christ. Once man takes on the characteristics of the second man, Jesus, both God's plan and His creation once again become complete. As Adam was in the beginning, this new creation in Christ is something to behold. All things have become new in this person's life and all things have become whole.

Man in his lost spiritual state is an empty shell at best. However, in a regenerated state, he becomes the reflection of God's glory in the midst of a dying, lost world.

It is one thing to be a new creation positionally, but another to have the actual evidence of this work of regeneration or new life. The regenerated life is not only an expression of Jesus, but it is a life marked with resurrection power. This resurrection power rises up a new life from that which was absent of form, devoid of substance, and lost in darkness.

Once this new creation is unveiled, it will bring glory to God. God will not only behold this masterpiece, but the world will see glimpses of His reflection and glory.

It is the life of the second man, Jesus, which gives a Christian's testimony credibility or authority. It is the blooming life of the second Man that brings maturity, order, and purpose to a believer's life.

This brings us back to the heart of God. It is His heart for man to enjoy a world of order and purpose as he comes back to center in a relationship with his Creator, and for Him, as Creator, to once again enjoy man. Jesus Christ made this possible. He not only became that ladder that closed the gap between God and man, but He restored man back to his original place with God, as one who would reflect His likeness and bring glory to the Father.[14]

Pleasures and Rest

Psalm 16:11 says, "Thou wilt shew me the path of life: in thy presence is fullness of joy; at thy right hand there are pleasures for evermore." This Scripture shows us there is a path of life. Jesus describes this path as being hard and straight.[15] He also declared that few would find this path. In this verse, in Psalm 16:11, we see that only God can show us this path.

The next part of this verse talks about joy. Real joy can only be found in God's presence. Today many people are looking for excitement. This excitement has become a sick substitute for true joy. Such a substitute is sensual and does not constitute the joy of the Lord. Sadly, few Christians are able to discern the difference.

This misguided search for this so-called "joy" has opened people up to accept counterfeits that are fleshly in nature and inspired by demons. They are unaware that their false joy is leading them into greater spiritual depravity and spiritual ruin.

The final part of the Scripture is where this pleasure can be found—on the right hand of God. According to Hebrews 8:1, Jesus is sitting on the right hand of the throne of the Majesty in the heavens. A Christian's pleasure does not consist of excitement, signs and wonders, church activities, or good works, but of a person named Jesus. Sadly, Christians can miss the real pleasure of being part of the kingdom of God because they have failed to realize it is Jesus becoming all and all to them that gives personal, lasting pleasure. This is the secret to not only embracing God's pleasures, but also coming into a place of great rest. In Matthew 11:28-30, Jesus tells us He is our real place of rest.

At the end of the sixth day of creation, God could look at His work and would know it was complete. In the Jewish Law, He wanted people to recognize the true spirit behind His rest by observing the Sabbath. The rest He was really advocating was not just a day that was absent of work, but also a day that acknowledged all was complete in God's economy. It was a time of celebration and rejoicing, for if God is in His rightful place all will be in order.

It is vital to realize that the first man, Adam, made creation complete. However, due to redemption the second man, Christ, makes man complete. It is this completeness that allows man to enter into rest for he is now at peace with God.

---

[14] Genesis 28:12-13

[15] Matthew 7:13-14

Charles Spurgeon pointed out that Christians need to remember Christ's resurrection.[16] Although many Christians may declare that they have not forgotten the basis of their faith, they still can appear to show a lapse of memory.[17] This lapse is obvious when Christians fail to celebrate Christ's finished work of redemption on their day of rest.

Instead of commemorating a day, Christians are asked to celebrate a person. After all, in Jesus the Law had been fulfilled. In Jesus, all is complete and at rest with God. In Jesus, the work of creation is done, and now it is a time for man to enjoy the blessings of God. It is also a time for God to enjoy His new creation in the beauty and majesty of His Son, Jesus Christ.

Where are you in your spiritual life? Maybe you have not been born again. Or, you might still be a baby who has never grown and matured in your spiritual life. Consider whether Christ has only been ingrained on your lips. Or, is He an ongoing reality in your heart that is being unveiled in your life on a continual basis? Are you still struggling in areas of your old life, or have you come to rest in Jesus Christ, the Son of the Living God in a new transformed life? Examine the fruits of your life, for they will give you a true picture of where you are in your life with God.

---

[16] Jesus Rose for You*;* pg 76

[17] 1 Corinthians 15:14

5

CROSSROADS

And a river went out of Eden
to water the garden; and from
thence it was parted and
became into four heads.
Genesis 2:10

The first three principles involved the work of God on our behalf. The remaining principles encompass the Christian's response towards God's work. People's responses operate according to principles that make them subject to one of the laws: the law of the Spirit of life or the law of sin and death. Therefore, it is only proper for the presentation of the next principle to bring us to the Garden of Eden where man first resided.

Bible scholars and archeologists have been trying to figure out the location of the Garden of Eden for years. Their greatest clue has to do with the four rivers. The two known rivers, the Hiddekel or Tigris and the Euphrates, place the Garden of Eden in locations such as Iraq or Iran.[1]

It is also interesting to note that some of the greatest events took place in the area where man first dwelt. At one of the spots where the Garden of Eden has been traditionally fixed, there is a group of mounds known as Eridu.[2] This place was not only considered the center of the Eastern Hemisphere, but it was the dominating center of the world where the oldest and most valuable inscriptions have been found.

In the Euphrates-Tigris Valley, mounds have been discovered that are 100 feet or higher. They cover the remains of various civilizations and cities. For example, they discovered 20 cities that have been built on top of one another after their demise as a civilization.[3]

These mounds represent the effects of man's fallen state. Destruction and chaos serve as the epitaph of many former civilizations that have been lost in the midst of depravity and debauchery. Today man

---

[1] Halley's Bible Handbook, Henry H. Halley, 24th edition, pg 64

[2] Ibid, pgs 64 & 66

[3] Ibid, pg 42

continues to look for Eden (pleasure), but all he finds is chaos and destruction. This is the sad picture of lost and hopeless man.

Although men may accomplish great feats, they are constantly being reminded that they cannot change the face of their depravity and the failures it produces. Men can strive to build great towers to heaven only to be met with confusion.[4] They can develop advanced cities such as Ur, Abraham's hometown, but eventually they will find it buried in the rubbish of man's perverted lust and failures. They can build great fortresses in the side of cliffs for defense, such as the city of Petra, but in time such sites will silently mock their efforts. They can build great empires such as Rome, but sooner or later they, too, will be reduced to nothing more than ruins, artifacts, and a mere historical description in the pages of history books.

When God formed Adam, He gave him something called free will. God wanted man to have a right to make choices, for good or evil. This brings us to the *fourth* principle: the quality of a person's life is determined by the choices he or she makes along the way.

Although man is quick to blame God for the state of affairs in the world, man, and not God, has always determined the quality of his personal life. God wanted man to have the freedom to choose to love and serve Him. Like the river in Eden that parted into four branches, choices separate those who really want the reality of God from those who simply want to play the game on their own terms.

Each choice reinforces the attitudes and lifestyles of the individual, producing both fruits and consequences. This is why Jesus told people in Matthew 7:16-20 that they would know others by their fruit. The Apostle Paul also reminded people of this basic principle in Galatians 6:7, "Be not deceived; God is not mocked: for whatsoever a man soweth, that shall he also reap."

Today there are those in the Christian realm who would have you believe that Christians have no responsibilities when it comes to their relationship with God. Granted, people cannot earn their salvation, but the Word of God is clear. Believers have a responsibility to choose to embrace the life God is offering them.

God clearly put this choice forth to Israel in Deuteronomy 30:19-20,

> I call heaven and earth to record this day against you, that I have set before you life and death, blessing and cursing: therefore choose life, that both thou and thy seed may live: That thou mayest love the LORD thy God, and that thou mayest obey his voice, and that thou mayest cleave unto him: for he is thy life, and the length of thy days: that thou mayest

[4] Genesis 11:1-9

> dwell in the land which the LORD sware unto thy fathers, to Abraham, to Isaac, and to Jacob to give them.

Obviously, life is a choice of the will, but death is the natural way or preference of sin. If a person chooses life, he or she will experience blessings, but if he or she gives way to death, curses wait to plague such a person.

This choice of life and death was also displayed in the Garden of Eden. There were many trees in the Garden, but there were only two that had the ability to change the quality of Adam's life. These two trees can be found in Genesis 2:9, the tree of life and the tree of knowledge of good and evil.

The tree of life was capable of bringing forth life, but the tree of knowledge of good and evil could only produce death. We know that the first man made the wrong choice, resulting in death.

Jesus used a similar comparison of two distinct gates that lead to different eternal destinations in Matthew 7:13-14. These distinct contrasts reinforced the principle regarding man's choices, "Enter ye in at the strait gate: for wide is the gate, and broad is the way, that leadeth to destruction, and many there be which go in thereat: Because strait is the gate, and narrow is the way, which leadeth unto life, and few there be that find it."

Obviously, Jesus was warning people that their decisions would determine what path they would walk. One path could only be found by entering a narrow gate (through Him), but those who prefer the easy, natural way of self could easily access the other path that was broad, but would lead to utter spiritual ruin.

The great leader, Joshua, brought the concept of choice more into focus in Joshua 24:15. He challenged Israel with these words,

> And if it seems evil unto you to serve the LORD, choose you this day whom ye will serve; whether the gods which your fathers served that were on the other side of the flood, or the gods of the Amorites, in whose land ye dwell: but as for me and my house, we will serve the LORD.

A person who makes choices is not only choosing life or death, but also whom he or she is going to serve. Today we know there are two main authorities in the world. There is the King of kings and Lord of lords, Jesus Christ, or there is the god of this present world or age, Satan.[5] Every man is choosing, directly or indirectly to serve one of these rulers.

The prophet Elijah brought this fact out when he challenged Israel. He said, "How long halt ye between two opinions? If the LORD be God,

---

[5] 2 Corinthians 4:3-4; 1 Timothy 6:14-15

follow him: but if Baal, then follow him. And the people answered him not a word" (1 Kings 18:21).

Choices that one encounters along the way will always force a decision. Indecision is a decision, and inaction is action. This unwilling state produces confusion and usually occurs when people do not what to do what they know is right. For example, indecision is a choice to go the way of least resistance even when the right way is obvious. In my experience, the way of least resistance reveals that a person does not really love God and prefers the broad path of destruction.

Jesus was constantly bringing people to a point of decision. We see this in the case of the rich young ruler in Matthew 19. He told him to choose between his worldly riches or following Him to inherit eternal life. And, with His disciples, He told them the conditions or cost of being His disciples—leaving them to decide what their decision would be.[6]

The river in the Garden of Eden that parted into four branches is symbolic of the choices men make in relationship to God. The number "four" is the number that relates to the function of the earth. For example, there are four seasons, four natural laws, four elements, four points to the compass, four-footed animals, four divisions of mankind, and four types of flesh. It is also a universal number in that it is all encompassing.

As we will see, there are only four distinct responses that affect the terrain of a person's heart and attitude towards God. Like rivers, these responses can change both the course and the terrain of man.

It is important to realize that these four rivers came from one source of water or river. We know that every good and perfect thing comes from God.[7] Therefore, we must consider the history as well as the routes and associations of these rivers to understand the spiritual implications behind them. In fact, the implications of these four rivers represent various aspects of life.

The first two rivers, Pison and Gihon, have not been officially identified, although it has been thought that the Pison is Araxes and the Gihon is the Oxus.[8] A recent, documentary on the Discovery Channel placed the Garden of Eden in modern-day Iran. They showed two rivers with names similar to Pison and Gihon. Obviously, the location of Eden is up for debate. However, since these rivers are not officially identified, we will have to seek understanding based on the information of other scriptural associations for possible spiritual applications.

---

[6] See Luke 9:57-62.

[7] James 1:17

[8] Smith's Bible Dictionary, Sir William Smith, pg. 155

The River That Possesses Riches

According to Genesis 2:11-12, Pison compassed or surrounded the whole land of Havilah or Paradise. This land had great treasures in it such as gold. Although its location is a matter of debate, it is representative of something that must be very much alive in the Christian walk: faith.

The Apostle Peter said this about faith, "That the trial of your faith, being much more precious than of gold that perisheth, though it be tried with fire, might be found unto praise and honour and glory at the appearing of Jesus Christ" (1 Peter 1:7).

Pison surrounded the land that was made valuable by the presence of gold and other gems. Faith in itself is not valuable, but when it ends up possessing the reality of God, it becomes priceless. It is Christ Jesus in us who serves as the priceless treasure that can only be acquired through faith.[9] True faith originates with God, but must embrace His character and ways. Once faith begins to possess God in greater ways, His worth and value will consume the vessel.

Faith comprises an unseen walk that always moves towards one destination—its source, God. Since Pison surrounded the land, it probably found itself coming back to the same source.

Faith is a mystery because it cannot be seen or examined with the naked eye. This is why the Word of God tells us we walk by faith and not by sight.[10] Faith believes the unseen, knows the impossible, experiences the incredible, and walks in expectation in light of a sure hope. It works in obscurity as it stirs the heart to respond, while it is openly expressed in outward obedience.

To walk by faith involves no work or sweat, just submission to the Lord of lords. In fact, faith is the natural response to the grace of God. Grace is an act of God. This glorious act produces the response of faith from those who embrace it. Therefore, initial faith entails believing God about the salvation He freely offers. Once an individual receives the gift of God, faith graduates into an active life of obedience and discovery.[11]

Andrew Murray pointed out that new Christians show zealousness for their salvation, but confusion sets in as they try to bring together the different virtues of the Christian life. Although they have believed that the sinner is justified by faith, they have not yet come to terms with the concept that the just shall live by faith. These new believers know that grace is a life of faith and that all they must do is believe. Believing

[9] 2 Corinthians 4:7

[10] 2 Corinthians 5:7

[11] Ephesians 2:8-9; James 2

serves as the one channel through which grace flows into the heart of man.[12]

Faith must grow to a place where it becomes a natural, daily response of the believer. Growing faith simply means a person is growing in the knowledge of Jesus. This knowledge inspires believers to respond accordingly, causing greater growth. After all, faith is not based on doctrine, but on the person and character of God. This is why it is impossible to please God without faith.[13]

Everything a Christian does must be based on the Person of God. To do anything outside of the character of God is sin. The Apostle Paul made this statement in Romans 14:23, "...for whatsoever is not of faith is sin."

Faith walks hand in hand with other godly virtues and works of God such as love, mercy, truth, hope, justification, sanctification, power, and perfection.[14] As you can see, true faith encompasses a powerful and complete life.

This brings us back to the fact that faith must embrace the character of God to reflect His heart and attitudes. Faith does the impossible because it gives way to the work of our mighty God. It becomes valuable because it ends up possessing the person of Christ.

Faith represents the tree of life, for at the end of it, one can find salvation.[15] This virtue represents the straight path because it will continually bring us back to the same source, thereby, always lining us up to the Person of Jesus Christ.

Are you on the right path or are you taking a detour?

The Lost River

Gihon is the second river that has not been officially identified. Like Pison, there is speculation about it, but nothing that can be confirmed as fact. Genesis 2:13 states that this river compassed the whole land of Ethiopia, also known as Cush. Keep in mind there is speculation about this river's location. However, you cannot help but to think of the inhabitants of the land of Cush. They were the Hamites or the descendants of Ham.[16]

---

[12] Abide in Christ; Andrew Murray, pgs 42-43

[13] Hebrews 11:6

[14] Matthew 23:23; Acts 26:18; Romans 3:28; Galatians 5:6; Ephesians 4:12; I Thessalonians 3:2; Hebrews 11:1; James 2:22

[15] 1 Peter 1:9

[16] Genesis 9:18-25

This bit of information begins to give us an idea where this river will lead in light of spiritual examples. We know the history of Ham. He was one of the sons of Noah with the same inheritance and possibilities as his brothers. But because of his actions, he, along with his descendants became cursed.

Like this river, this is the history of mankind. Every man has potential and possibilities of a great inheritance. Due to a selfish disposition and rebellious actions, humanity has become lost in the mire of sin along with all of its consequences.

We can also find consistent representation of this river in a spring of the same name that is located near Jerusalem. It was at the spring of Gihon that Solomon was anointed and proclaimed king. Here was a man who had great potential, but it all became subdued when pagan foreign wives turned his heart away from God.[17] As a result, King Solomon lost sight of His God; therefore, losing His way. His writings in Ecclesiastes not only referred to how one can lose sight of what is important, but of the vanity of life outside of God.

Gihon, the spring, is still in existence, but because of the debris from Kidron Valley, the spring is not as accessible. It can only be approached by a deep descent of thirty steps down to the water. Apparently, the spring flows strongly, but its potential has been stifled because the flows are intermittent, depending on the season.[18]

As Christians, we have anointing because of the presence of the Holy Spirit.[19] He is the Living Water, which must flow freely through our lives. Sadly, His work is hindered because of the debris of sin filling our lives at different periods of rebellion, worldliness, and complacency. Our potential becomes subdued and the possibilities halted, as we become lost in sin's mire, confusion, and darkness.

Are you hindering the Living Water? If so, you could become lost on your spiritual journey.

The River That Unites

Hiddekel is known as the modern-day Tigris. Unlike the first two rivers, this one does not compass any land. It travels to the east of Assyria and eventually empties into the Persian Gulf.

It is a rapid river and was referred to as the Great River by Daniel in Daniel 10:4. It somewhat runs parallel with the Euphrates River and at different times has become joined with it. According to *Halley's Bible*

[17] 1 Kings 1:33, 38, 45; 11:3-9

[18] The Thompson Chain-Reference Bible; Frank Charles Thompson, Archaeological Supplement, pg 1754

[19] 1 John 2:20

Handbook, the Tigris River now joins the Euphrates River 100 miles above the Persian Gulf.

With this in mind, we might ask ourselves what this river symbolizes in relationship to our spiritual walk. This river represents life. It came from one source just as all life comes from one source, God. Life brings a reality check to each of us because it is comprised of uncontrollable currents or events that can be productive or cause havoc, depending on our response. Most of all, it shows us we are not in control of our lives. God is the one who holds the seasons of our lives.

The places where this river unites with the Euphrates represents the fact that not only do our lives change, but we also can find ourselves being caught up with different currents. For example, there is the current of the Holy Spirit. His leading can be challenging, but He will bring us to calm and peaceful areas of rest. There is also the current of the world. It is fast, exciting, and attractive, but it brings a person to spiritual poverty and ruin.

The fact that this river runs parallel to the greater river shows us that it does not matter how close we come to God, we must come into agreement or union with Him to receive the benefits of His life. How many Christians today run somewhat parallel to God through religious activities, but never touch or encounter Him in order to come into union or agreement?

Jesus talked about how His desire was that we would be one with Him as He is one with the Father.[20] This unity cannot exist unless a person is flowing in the current of the Spirit of God. It is this current that leads a person into the union with God that ends in worship and service.

As we know, rivers change the terrain of the countryside. The current a person flows in will determine the terrain of his or her heart and mind. What does your heart and mind say about the current you are caught in now? Do they display the fruits of godliness or the fruits of the world?

The River of Judgment

The Euphrates River is the largest and longest river of western Asia. It covers a course of 1,780 miles, and its width at the greatest distance is 700 or 800 miles from its mouth. It is considered the most important river in this area.[21]

This river presents a contrast. Some of the greatest civilizations, such as Babylon, presided along its borders. It witnessed great battles on its shores. It not only was a source of life for many, but it also

---

[20] John 17:21-23

[21] Smith's Bible Dictionary, pg 183

humbled and destroyed. For example, two leaders, Cyrus the Younger and Crassus, perished after crossing it.[22]

The Euphrates River also served as one of the boundaries for the Promised Land.[23] This is where the contrast comes to the forefront. On one side of this river stands the Promised Land. On the other side stands the world in all of its false glory. This once again brings us back to the fourth principle: the sum of our lives is comprised of choices, but what will we choose?

Will we choose the narrow path of faith or allow our lives to become lost in sin? Will we choose the current of the Holy Spirit who will bring true, lasting unity in our Christian life, or will we give way to the current of the world that will end in destruction? Will we choose the Promised Land or the false security of the world? Every choice will place us on some type of path. Every decision will put us in a current. Every preference will bring us closer to possessing the Promised Land or closer to tasting the judgment of the world.

The Euphrates River is full of such contrasts. You can travel it and find man's failures. You can stop along the way and witness God's greatness. You can trace the river back to God's perfect creation. You can see how its length represents God's longsuffering and its width, His willingness to reach far and wide to embrace man in love, mercy, grace, and forgiveness. However, this river has limits as well, for it eventually rushes into the Persian Gulf.

It is at this point that the Euphrates River represents judgment. God's Spirit will not always strive with man.[24] His holiness will put an end to rebellion, and His righteousness will demand justice. This is why it is not surprising to see that the last scriptural reference concerning the Euphrates River is that of judgment. This reference is found in Revelation 16:12-14.

The great river that has supplied civilization in abundance will also give way to one of the greatest judgments. The kings of the east will come by way of this river as they converge on Israel for the Battle of Armageddon.

Judgment is a form of separation. Separation forces individuals to decide. The prophet Joel brings this out, "Multitudes, multitudes in the valley of decision; for the day of the LORD is near in the valley of decision" (Joel 3:14). Decisions will reveal people's true heart condition. Therefore, judgment serves as a crossroad that will not allow for complacency or indecision. In the end, it will show a person the strength and source of his or her life. It will all culminate at the point of man's

---

[22] Ibid, pg. 184

[23] Deuteronomy 11:24; Joshua 1:4

[24] Genesis 6:3

relationship with his Creator. The type of relationship he or she has with God will determine the person's quality of life and whether he or she has fulfilled his or her purpose in the scheme of eternity.

Man will always find himself at major crossroads at different times in his life. He will have to decide at these crossroads between right and wrong as he chooses between life and death, Jesus and Satan, faith and sight, the Promised Land and the world. You might be saying, it is not that simple. The truth is, it is that simple. However, because of personal preferences, people confuse the issue by compromising that which is right to justify wrongs.

Are you at a crossroad right now? Often times your present crossroad will give you a good indication as to whether you have made the proper choices in the past. For example, if you have been doing right all along, it will be natural for you to continue on the same path. However, if you have been compromising along the way, the choice to do right will become a great struggle. This struggle will escalate as you fight to resist the tendency to justify away the right choice.

What do the crossroads tell you about your decisions? Where is your walk taking you? Allow the Lord to show you the path you are on. Make sure you are on the right path because each path has a distinct destination that will affect your soul, quality of your spiritual inheritance, and where you will spend eternity.

6

THE PURPOSE

Being confident of this very thing, that he
which hath begun a good work in you
will perform it until the day of Jesus Christ.
Philippians 1:6

Why did God form man? After all, no creator or inventor creates something without a reason. Every invention of man was to fulfill a purpose or need from better communication to transportation. Only when the creation fails to meet that purpose does it become useless in the scheme of things.

This brings us to the *fifth* principle of God: Man must first find his rightful place in God's design before he can reach his potential and be useful in God's plan. It is only when man reaches his potential that he will find peace and purpose.

Today many people are searching for purpose. They have tried to fill their lives with things that have no substance or meaning. They have pursued after various goals only to be disappointed by their futility.

Obviously, people must understand why God formed them. This would be necessary to make sense out of their existence. By coming to terms with the reason for their lives, they will avoid becoming useless in God's design. This truth can be found in the New Testament. Romans 9:20-21 states, "Nay but, O man, who art thou that repliest against God? Shall the thing formed say to him that formed it, Why hast thou made me thus? Hath not the potter power over the clay, of the same lump to make one vessel unto honour, and another unto dishonour?"

Man has not been formed to serve his own purposes, but to fulfill God's plan for his life. The Apostle Paul summarized this thought in 2 Corinthians 4:7 by telling us that we are nothing more than clay jars. Clay jars have no worth outside of the contents they possess. It is the contents that give insignificant vessels value and purpose.

Today many fail to possess the priceless content that brings purpose and value to their lives. This content is not comprised of things, but of a person, Jesus Christ. Therefore, if a person fails to possess Christ, he or she will fail to reach his or her designated potential. I am sure you will agree that there is no greater tragedy than a wasted life.

God gave Adam responsibilities. Obviously, God never intended man to be a sluggard who waited around for the good things to be handed to him. As we will see further in this chapter, man was actually designed to serve, not to be served.

The book of Proverbs has a lot to say about those who are slothful in their ways. Proverbs 21:25 summarizes such an individual in this way, "The desire of the slothful killeth him; for his hands refuse to labour."

2 Thessalonians 3:10 says: "For even when we were with you, this we commanded you, that if any would not work, neither should he eat."

1 Timothy 5:8 states: "But if any provide not for his own, and specially for those of his own house, he hath denied the faith, and is worse than an infidel."

God intended man to work by dressing and keeping what was entrusted to him. Keep in mind that the Garden of Eden was a perfect environment. How much dressing was really required, or was there a greater significance behind God's instruction to Adam?

The word "dress" has to do with working the garden, but according to *Strong's Exhaustive Concordance,* it also has some amazing spiritual implications. It implies work done from the basis of servitude. This term showed that Adam was to serve his Creator.

The fact that man was formed meant that he was to be a servant to the One who designed him. As Creator, God put man in charge of creation. However, man was to understand that his position in the scheme of things was a privilege, not something he deserved. This privilege was to create a proper attitude in Adam in regards to God. In fact, if Adam had truly understood the real implications of the honor he was given, it would have developed into a more intimate relationship with God. Ultimately, he would have become a bondservant.

A bondservant is an individual who willfully, and out of love becomes indebted to his or her master for the rest of his or her life.[1] This bondservant abandons personal rights and identification in order to become solely identified with his or her master's needs, inheritance, and will.

This type of relationship is clearly upheld in the New Testament. God's right to rule over us as master is not strictly based on the fact that He formed us, but because He also has redeemed or bought us back. 1 Corinthians 6:20 says, "For ye are bought with a price: therefore glorify God in your body, and in your spirit, which are God's.

---

[1] See Deuteronomy 15:15-16

1 Corinthians 7:23 states, "Ye are bought with a price; be not ye the servants of men." Every believer has been bought with a high price, the blood of Jesus. Since we have been bought, we do not belong to ourselves, but to God who has the right to use us in the manner He desires.

The beauty about God being our master is that His ways are not only loving, but they are higher and perfect.[2] He will not ask us to do anything that is contrary to our spiritual well-being.

To be a servant of God is a privilege, for we were once far away from Him.[3] This privilege came about because of grace. Grace is God's unmerited favor extended towards people. The favor of God allows individuals to receive unwarranted benefits from HIs throne room. This great privilege has the ability to inspire people to become a bondservant in the kingdom of God. It can produce a heart desirous to become indebted to the One who paid the debt for sins. Such a privilege will redirect people's focus as they give way to total abandonment in regard to the world in order to gain Christ. Out of inspiration and love, they will willingly give up all rights in order to follow Jesus. They will joyfully give up any personal identity, so that they can become identified with the King of kings and Lord of lords.

Identification is everything in the kingdom of God. Jesus became identified with man in order to become sin for each one of us. We must now become identified with Jesus in order to be made in the righteousness of God.[4] Identification of this nature begins with self-denial and taking on the attitude of a servant.

This brings us back to why God formed Adam and put him in the Garden of Eden. Adam was to fulfill two purposes in the garden as well as to obey one commandment. His first responsibility was to dress the Garden, and his second one was to keep it.

To *"dress"* something points to service and execution of duty that will serve as worship. The word *"keep"* means to put a hedge about, protect, guard, attend to, preserve, regard, serve, and watch.[5] Obviously, Adam was to protect the Garden, but from what? It had a perfect atmosphere and did not have the thorns, thistles, and pestilence we have today. Therefore, what could possibly destroy the harmony of this beautiful paradise?

I believe there was only one risk factor that could cause imperfection in the Garden. Such a factor had to do with man's relationship with God. I believe Adam's greatest responsibility in the Garden was to maintain an

---

[2] Isaiah 55:8-9

[3] Colossians1 1:21-22

[4] 2 Corinthians 5:21

[5] Strong's Exhaustive Concordance; #5647 &8104

unhindered relationship with God that would ensure worship and communion with Him. Adam could only rightfully guard the Garden by keeping a right balance in his relationship with his Creator. Therefore, he had to protect the Garden from anything that would disturb this fellowship between God and him.

Obviously, this brings us to the main reason man was formed: to glorify God. Adam, by maintaining an upright relationship with God, would reflect His glory just as Moses did after being in God's presence.[6] To properly understand God's glory, one must also consider another aspect of glorifying God—that of worship. Before a person can glorify God, he or she must learn how to worship God in an intimate relationship. Man was designed to worship his Creator. This is made evident in the Ten Commandments. The first three commandments have to do with worshipping the one true God. The first commandment states that a person shall have no other gods but God. The commandment simply means that a person must not worship any other gods. Jesus confirmed this in the wilderness when Satan was tempting Him to bow down to him. The Lord made this demand, "Get thee hence, Satan: for it is written, Thou shalt worship the Lord thy God, and him only shalt thou serve" (Matthew 4:10).

The second commandment is that man must not make any graven images to bow down to. The reason is because a person must only bow down to God for He is the only One who deserves such adoration.
The third commandment tells us we must not take the name of God in vain. God's name points to His character. Due to His character, His very name must invoke reverence and worship instead of rebellion and disrespect.

Finally, this brings us to the fourth commandment which is to keep the Sabbath. The Sabbath was made for man. The purpose for such rest was to remind man that he must take time to worship and enjoy God. This is what creates true rest in a person's life. Time with God must be a priority regardless of what is going on in a person's life.

When Adam was formed, he was already established in a relationship with God. This relationship was meant to encourage and inspire communion between them and worship on the part of Adam.

True worship will automatically lead into a life of service. For example, when God formed Adam, he clearly established man's purpose in the scheme of things in Genesis 2:15, "And the LORD God took the man and put him into the garden of Eden to dress it and to keep it."

The real test for Adam was not just to serve God, but also to maintain a life of communion and worship before Him. This concept is confirmed by the reality that Adam was to protect the Garden from any

---

[6] Exodus 34:28-30

outside intrusion that would hinder this relationship. Such an intrusion pointed to the enemy of God, Satan.

Satan connives to get man to bow down to him. The day man fell into a lost state, he did so because he submitted and bowed down to the rebellion, temptation, and deception of the enemy of the soul. It was this homage that brought imperfection to the Garden of Eden and spiritual death to man.

By allowing Satan into the Garden, Adam miserably failed his responsibility set forth by God in both areas. As the dresser of the Garden, Adam was to be a nurturer of not only the garden, but of His relationship with God. Instead, he allowed death to enter in. He was to guard the garden and His communion with God, but instead, he allowed entrance to the destroyer.

This is the problem with so many Christian homes. Man has failed as a servant of God to nurture his home and guard it against the wiles of Satan by keeping his life upright. He has allowed the many devices of Satan to flood his home, profane the sanctuary, defile minds, and rob hearts of love and compassion.

Adam had only one known commandment to adhere to. If he had been obedient, not only would he have obeyed the will of God, he would also have overcome temptation. Genesis 2:16-17 gives us this commandment, "And the LORD God commanded the man, saying, Of every tree of the garden thou mayest freely eat: But of the tree of the knowledge of good and evil, thou shalt not eat of it: for in the day that thou eatest thereof thou shalt surely die."

As we know, Adam disobeyed. His disobedience in the garden spoke volumes about what he truly valued. First of all, he did not value his relationship with God. He was willing to sacrifice it for something that had no value or worth. His attitude was not that of a servant, but of someone who wanted to be served. He essentially took the reigns of his life from God to become his own master.

Obviously, Adam did not regard the life that God had given him, for he knew that in the day he took of the tree of knowledge of good and evil, he would die. In essence, he was saying that the life God entrusted to him was useless; therefore, he chose death to any real life with God.

Like those who refuse to receive Christ, I do not believe Adam understood the true consequences of his deed. Sadly, his action showed he lacked fear of the Lord, causing him to blatantly dare and mock God.

Jesus Christ summarized all of the commandments into two commandments in Mark 12:30-31. Followers of God must love Him with everything within them, and love others as themselves. However, He added one more commandment to verify true discipleship, "A new commandment I give unto you, that ye love one another; as I have loved you..." (John 13:34).

Love carries responsibilities. It requires a person to nurture, invest, and do right by the person he or she loves. In reality, true love causes a person to become a bondservant. The first commandment makes believers bondservants to God. And, it is only as bondservants to God, that Christians will reach greatness in the kingdom of God.

As a bondservant, people will love God with all their heart, soul, mind, and strength. In other words, nothing will stand between God and his devoted servant. A servant's priority must be to do the will of God in order to please Him and bring Him glory.

The problem with many believers is that God's will is an option. To treat the will of God as an option will result in disobedience and failure as it did in Adam's case. After all, Adam was treating God's will as an ordinary, common choice clearly profaning it, rather than a priority that needed to hold the utmost importance in his life.

Jesus understood the cost of doing His Father's will. He could have opted not to pay such a great price. To Jesus, His Father's will was not an option, but a priority. It is important to understand that everything in our lives is considered optional until we make it a priority. Therefore, it is vital that we make God's will our priority to ensure a right relationship.

The second commandment requires us to be a bondservant to others. Romans 12:9a, 10 says, "Let love be without dissimulation... Be kindly affectioned one to another with brotherly love; in honour preferring one another." Man cannot love another person correctly until he loves God in the proper fashion. He cannot have a right relationship with others until his relationship with God is right. Man cannot share what he does not possess. Therefore, if there is anything of worth and value in his life, it is because it has come from God. This is why man must get his vertical relationship with God right before he can effectively get his horizontal relationship right with others.

Today many people are caught up with their earthly relationships rather than their heavenly one. The results of this focus are devastating. Yet, many refuse to humble themselves before the cross of Jesus and look upward towards God. Jesus is the only One who can fulfill their real purpose and bring them to their full potential.

Like Adam, believers have two main responsibilities in their life with God. These responsibilities ensure that they will fulfill their purpose on earth and reach their potential. Jesus told His followers, "Ye are the salt of the earth:...Ye are the light of the world" (Matthew 5:13a and 14a).

The salt was to make a difference in the lives of others by nurturing (dressing) them. It was to preserve true Christianity by seasoning the lives of those who are in despair and hopelessness.

Light symbolizes the walk. People who are walking in the light have fellowship with God and others. This light has the capacity to draw people who are lost due to the darkness of their soul and the world.[7] It serves as hope and represents a place of maintenance (keeping), peace, and rest to the weary. As you can see, the salt preserves while the light reveals and upholds the way.

How does a Christian become the salt and serve as the light? Believers are saved from the harsh taskmasters of sin, death, and hell, but these taskmasters must be replaced with the Lordship of Jesus Christ. Salvation is not just a matter of being delivered from something. It also means being saved unto something. For the Christian, it means being saved unto a life of servitude to the real Lord Jesus Christ.

This life of servitude means the Christian is actually being saved unto good works. Ephesians 2:8-10 confirms this, "For by grace are ye saved through faith; and that not of yourselves: it is the gift of God: Not of works, lest any man should boast. For we are his workmanship, created in Christ Jesus unto good works, which God hath ordained that we should walk in them."

Titus 2:13-14 states, "Looking for that blessed hope, and the glorious appearing of the great God and our Savior Jesus Christ; Who gave himself for us, that he might redeem us from all iniquity, and purify unto himself a peculiar people, zealous of good works."

The sole purpose of a servant of God is to do His will. This obedience will always result in good works. Good works verify that a person loves His master. These works serve as visible fruits of a faith that does not disregard or mock God. Ultimately these works will bring honor or glory to God. Jesus confirmed this in Matthew 5:16, "Let your light so shine before men, that they may see your good works, and glorify your Father which is in heaven."

The Christian life that produces works can only come out of a right relationship with God. Nothing of purpose and worth can happen outside of this relationship.

Adam began to hide from God when his fellowship with Him was broken by his rebellion.[8] This is true for man today. He hides behind religion, good acts, and pious causes. Like Adam, his independence has not caused him to find himself, but to lose his way, his purpose, his true identity, and his potential.

God's voice can still be heard as He calls out to the lost. In the cool of the evening, just before the darkness of night falls on the hearts of men, God calls out to them. From the distance He calls, with a voice full

---

[7] 1 John 1:7

[8] Genesis 3:8-11

of longing and expectation. It is close to pleading as He calls out, "Adam, where are you?"

Is He calling out to you because you have failed to fulfill His will and purpose for your life? Are you weary and miserable because you have not realized your potential? The answer is the same. All that you seek and desire can be found in a living, active relationship with God Almighty. He is the only One who can help you find and fulfill the purpose behind your very existence.

7

THE RESPONSE

Behold, to obey is better than sacrifice,
and to hearken than the fat of rams.
1 Samuel 15:22b

The major truth you learn about the principles of God is that they are what constitute and ensure the quality of true life. These principles are about what it takes to possess real life and how to experience it to the fullest. Although this life has been made available to everyone, many refuse it and accept the temporary riches of the world to the eternal, rich life of God.

In the last chapter, we learned that man must understand why he was formed before he is able to grasp the purpose behind his existence. Although his existence intertwines with a physical, temporary world, the essence of his life hinges on a relationship with God.

The definition of life is the ability to respond to one's environment. For example, people who are dead or lack physical life are unable to respond to their physical surroundings. Likewise, people who lack spiritual life are unable to respond to God who is the essence of true life. In fact, they are spiritually dead. They may want to respond to God in a physical arena, but are unable to respond to Him on the spiritual level of Spirit and truth.

This is evident in Adam's life. After his rebellion, he found himself on a different plane than previously. This reality caused him to hide from God, so that he would not have to respond or relate to His Creator in his present state of shame.

You can see this same scenario in many people's lives. They are hiding from God by trying to fill their lives with human relationships, worldly things, and self-centered pursuits. They have a physical life, but they are devoid of a spiritual life. They are empty, condemned, and spiritually dead.

What does it mean to have spiritual life? It means a person will begin to spiritually respond to God on the level of spirit. He or she will realize that God is the summary of the spiritual environment that surrounds a person who is truly born of Spirit and water.

Another interesting evidence of life is movement. People not only show they are alive by interacting with their environment, but by moving forward in some type of physical or emotional growth. This is true for believers. They display spiritual life by moving forward in an active growing relationship with God that brings maturity and discernment. The Apostle Paul made this statement,

> Now we have received, not the spirit of the world, but the spirit which is of God; that we might know the things that are freely given to us of God. Which things also we speak, not in the words which man's wisdom teacheth, but which the Holy Ghost teacheth; comparing spiritual with spiritual. But the natural man receiveth not the things of the Spirit of God: for they are foolishness unto him: neither can he know them, because they are spiritually discerned (1 Corinthians 2:12-14).

Problems occur when man fails to interact with his environment in a proper way. Today much of the world we live in is suffering from diverse consequences because man refuses to recognize that the quality of his life is determined by the respect and consideration he shows the environment around him.

Homes, lives, society, and land are being used, abused, and neglected. Man treats these treasures as if they are here for him, rather than something to be properly regarded. He actually fails to consider that his quality of life depends on having harmony with these different resources. This is true for the spiritual life.

Our spiritual well-being hinges on having harmony with God. This harmony can be easily broken if we use the things of God improperly, abuse the gifts and treasures He has entrusted to us, and neglect the salvation we have been freely given.[1]

How does one maintain harmony with God? The answer is simple, by responding correctly to Him. This brings us to the *sixth* principle: The quality of our life with God can only be maintained with obedience to Him.

The number "six" represents the imperfection of man. Imperfection reminds us that man in his fallen state falls short of perfection. Therefore, the only part man has to overcome is his imperfect state. He does this through obedience to God and His Word.

King Solomon, the wisest man before Jesus, came to this conclusion, "Let us hear the conclusion of the whole matter: Fear God, and keep his commandments: for this is the whole duty of man" (Ecclesiastes 12:13). Solomon understood that everything was vanity outside of fearing and obeying God. He came to this realization after wasting his life on frivolous things.

---

[1] Hebrews 2:3

For the Christian, fearing and obeying God should not be a duty, but a natural response. The Christian life should always be considered a privilege, not a matter of duty. The difference between something that is considered a privilege or duty is attitude. Duty can be a burdensome drudgery, while privilege is an honor. Likewise, serving God should never be considered a duty, but a joyful honor and privilege.

Attitude ultimately determines the type of environment that surrounds a person. Oswald Chambers stated that people should avoid confounding circumstances with environment. He explained that environment is the element in our circumstances that fits our disposition. He concludes that we may not be able to control our circumstances, but we are the deciders of our own environment.[2]

Disposition represents a person's heart attitude, which is of the inner environment of man. God only gave Adam one commandment, and his ultimate action of disobedience showed his heart attitude towards God. The writer Job described Adam's disposition, "If I covered my transgressions as Adam, by hiding mine iniquity in my bosom" (Job 31:33).

Adam's heart disposition showed that he was getting away from God, while his outward action of disobedience simply verified the attitude of his heart. Obviously, there was a separation occurring between God and Adam before he fell into a state of sin and death.

Many people are trying to hide their disposition. Like King Saul, they offer many pious sacrifices, while disobeying God's Word.[3] They exalt their religious activities, while ignoring the simplest responsibilities, such as carrying the burdens of other Christians. They promote love, but show no honor, compassion, or benevolence towards others. They talk about great things of God, while overlooking the basic needs of others. They run from one religious event to another, trying to display their piousness, while they walk around in arrogance and unforgiveness.

Such disobedient actions are exposing the disposition of many. These sick substitutes may be a religious cloak that hides the disobedient attitude from the world, but God clearly sees through such masquerades.[4]

A person must give way to the life of Christ. This giving way to the will of God involves submitting one's will with the intent of changing one's disposition, and coming into obedience. Sadly, many Christians act as if obedience to God and His Word is a duty too great to carry, rather than it being the natural response of someone who truly loves God. This is why the Apostle Paul gave these instructions in Ephesians 6:5-7, "Servants,

---

[2] Still Higher For His Highest, Oswald Chambers, Daily Devotion, April 19.

[3] 1 Samuel 15:22

[4] John 15:22

be obedient to them that are your masters according to the flesh, with fear and trembling, in singleness of your heart, as unto Christ, not with eyeservice, as menpleasers; but as the servants of Christ, doing the will of God from the heart."

Attitude is often revealed by how we respond to God's authority. This attitude, in turn, determines how a person responds to his or her environment. Once again we must remind ourselves that the environment, not circumstances, represents the quality of an individual's life.

The Apostle Paul tells us we must have the mind or attitude of Christ.[5] Jesus' main priority was to do the will of the Father. He obeyed Him at every point and turn in His life. Jesus made this statement in John 5:19, "Verily, verily, I say unto you, The Son can do nothing of himself, but what he seeth the Father do: for what things soever he doeth, these also doeth the Son likewise."

Jesus' life was the will of His Father. He lived and breathed to obey His Father. His disposition would not go along any other line than that of His Father's will. Hebrews 5:8-9 tells us the results of Jesus' obedience, "Though he were a Son, yet learned he obedience by the things which he suffered; and being made perfect, he became the author of eternal salvation unto all them that obey him."

These two Scriptures in Hebrews tell us four things about godly obedience. First, obedience is a learned response. It does not come naturally for those who are new in their Christian faith or still operating in the flesh. It must be a daily determination, discipline, and practice. Each time a person decides to obey and responds in a right attitude, obedience will become easier the next time. As the saying goes, "practice makes perfect." This implies that a person's response has become a natural habit, instead of a struggle.

The second truth about obedience is that it can only be learned through suffering. The suffering Hebrews 5:8 is talking about is the suffering that comes from self-denial. A person cannot obey God until he or she is willing to deny self of what is considered normal or acceptable. Denial of this nature not only causes suffering, but also serves as a form of discipline.

Discipline is an inward strength that allows the person to go beyond comfort zones. People often react according to their comfort zones because they are afraid of the unknown. The unknown implies uncontrollable circumstances and challenges that may lead to personal failure. Even though a person may be willing in their spirit to do the will of God, his or her flesh may override the spirit as he or she resorts to staying in his or her comfort zones.

---

[5] Philippians 2:5

Obedience to God will break the comfort zones, enabling a person to take greater steps of faith in obedience. This happens when a person's focus is directed away from confidence in self to confidence in God. Redirection of focus brings much needed discipline. Discipline that results from change of focus causes a person to first seek out and respond to the Spirit, instead of to the comfortable fleshly impulses that have habitually controlled him or her in the past.

Thirdly, obedience causes a person to come to spiritual maturity. Many Christians remain immature or fleshly because they have never learned obedience. They have failed to come to the point of self-denial, as well as purposed in their heart to do it God's way no matter the cost.

Finally, obedience leads to salvation. Today there are debates among Christians concerning salvation. Some claim that putting any demands on Christians takes away from salvation through grace. Others believe that Christians have godly responsibilities. Godly responsibilities do not earn or ensure salvation, but serve as the outward fruit of this miraculous act.

The idea that real salvation will produce fruits frightens a person who is only clinging to a concept of grace. The reason for this fear is because spiritual immaturity exists in the lives of many Christians. This immaturity lacks the fruits of salvation because it is carnal and not spiritual. The Apostle Paul not only rebuked this condition in the Corinthian church, but also stated that it was an unacceptable condition because the things of God have been made available to every Christian to ensure a quality life.[6]

The problem with carnality is that it is an attitude or a disposition of the heart, and God's grace does not cover up this type of condition. After all, grace does not atone for discrepancies, but it gives a person unmerited favor to do right and to overcome.

Carnality is contrary to God and expresses itself in fleshly acts and abuses. It causes people to major in minors and minor in majors. It makes people spiritually dull, and unable to discern spiritual matters.

The key in salvation comes down to clinging to a person and not to a doctrine or concept. People need to cling to Jesus because in so doing, salvation will be worked out in their lives by the Holy Spirit. Salvation will be made evident in their responses. This evidence will be obedience. Obedience will eventually become a natural response to a person's spiritual environment as he or she falls more in love with God, grows in the knowledge of Jesus, and makes His will a priority.

What about you? Is there evidence that you are spiritually alive, or are you getting further away from God like Adam? Are you trying to hide your true disposition with religious activities, or have you decided to learn

---

[6] 1 Corinthians 2:10-16-3:1-4; 2 Corinthians 2:14

obedience no matter what it costs you? If you are getting away from God, turn around and draw near to Him. If you have a cloak, ask God to remove it, so you can see the real disposition of your inner man. Then, ask Him to give you the mind of Christ, so obedience to God will always be your natural and ultimate response.

8

CONSECRATION

Wherefore come out from among them, and be ye separate, saith the Lord, and touch not the unclean thing; and I will receive you
2 Corinthians 6:17

It is interesting to consider the order of God's principles. The first three start out with the reality of God, the presence of the Holy Spirit, and the Spirit's work in the believer's life. In the first three principles, we talked about the different types of lives that are prevalent in the spiritual realm.

For example, there are those who are devoid of spiritual life because they have not received Jesus Christ. There are the babies who were recently saved, or the carnal Christians who display the fruits of immaturity. Finally, there are those who have apprehended the new or resurrected life.

In the fourth principle, we see how man chooses the type of life he possesses. The fifth deals with the fact that an individual will determine and ensure the quality of life by what he or she does in his or her relationship with God. Then, there is the sixth principle that tells us how this life must be walked out. This brings us to the seventh principle that reveals the actual door that all must enter to apprehend the new, complete life in God.

There is only one door that leads to a different life or existence. We find reference to this door in Genesis 2:21, "And the LORD God caused a deep sleep to fall upon Adam, and he slept: and he took one of his ribs, and closed up the flesh instead thereof:" Katherine C. Bushnell, a learned scholar of Hebrew and Greek, dealt with this Scripture in her book by explaining how Adam and Eve were created at the same time. Eve was in Adam when he was formed and they were physically separated when God put Adam in a "deep sleep".

Bushnell then shows how this relates to Christians. Christ was with us when He walked this earth, but was separated from us by the "deep sleep" of death. It is from Jesus' riven side, by faith in His shed blood that believers came forth. Adam had been separated from Eve so that he might be re-united to her in greater joy. Likewise, one day Christ will come again to be united with His Church. This He promised to the joy of the believer for it was "expedient" for Him to go and return again."[1]

The *seventh* principle is simple: Greater life can only come by way of death. Jesus confirmed this principle in John 12:24, "Verily, verily, I say unto you, Except a corn of wheat fall into the ground and die, it abideth alone: but if it die, it bringeth forth much fruit."

Death, in some cases, represents finality, but for man, it is just a beginning. After all, he was created to live forever. The idea of death, from an eternal perspective, represents a change in man's existence. For example, Adam was put into a "deep sleep" in order for God to bring forth a greater type of life for him. God changed his life by bringing forth woman out of his side in order to serve as a partner in his life.

Physical death has been referred to as a state of sleep in such Scriptures as 1 Thessalonians 4:15 and 5:10. We know that the term "sleep" in these Scriptures does not mean a literal sleep of the spirit and soul, for the Apostle Paul said in 2 Corinthians 5:8, "We are confident, I say, and willing rather to be absent from the body, and to be present with the Lord."

The word "sleep" in 1 Thessalonians means to be deceased, but it is in reference to the body that dies and is buried. According to the Apostle Paul, this part of man, the body, sleeps until it is raised up in immortality.[2] This truth can be seen in the life of Jesus. He gave up His spirit on the cross and His physical body gave way to death, but Jesus was alive. We know that His body waited in the tomb to be raised up in newness of life on the third day, while in His spirit Jesus preached to the prisoners in captivity. Scripture tells us that God would not allow the body of His Holy One to see corruption.[3] Acts 13:37 gives this victorious declaration, "But he, whom God raised again, saw not corruption."

When Jesus identified Himself to Mary, He told her to not touch Him for He had not yet ascended to the Father.[4] Between His resurrection and ascension, Jesus displayed a new glorious body that could be touched and seen.

Since Jesus was the firstfruits, we get a glimpse as to what our new bodies will look like upon resurrection. We can see that we will have a physical appearance that will allow us to interact with the physical environment, while not being subjected to time or space.

It is important to note that we are talking about the seventh principle of God. The number "seven" represents spiritual perfection of the

---

[1] God's Word to Women, Katherine C. Bushnell; Study notes 50 & 51.

[2] 1 Corinthians 15:49-54

[3] Acts 13:35; 1 Peter 3:18-20

[4] John 20:17

Christians. This perfection implies a state of consecration or total separation from the old to embrace the new.

We must recognize that Adam's state of aloneness fell short of perfection as recorded in Genesis 2:18. God noted that it was not good for man to be alone. It was at this time that God began to make man's life full and complete. He put him in a deep sleep and performed "surgery" on him. He took something out of man in order to bring forth a greater life. In a sense, He made man incomplete in order to make his life complete and perfect.

We see this same procedure in Jesus' life. Christ gave up His glory as God and took on a lesser state. In a sense, He became poor in His humanity, so we could be made rich and whole in a new life.[5] He set His face towards the cross in order to give way to its cruelty and suffering, so we could be made whole. He allowed His blood to flow from His sides, and His heart to be broken, so we could be cleansed and made heirs of an eternal inheritance. Why?

Isaiah 53:4-5 tells us why, "Surely he hath borne our griefs, and carried our sorrows: yet we did esteem him stricken, smitten of God, and afflicted. But he was wounded for our transgressions, he was bruised for our iniquities: the chastisement of our peace was upon him; and with his stripes we are healed." Praise God, Jesus gave up His glory, gave way to a cross, and deceased from an earthly life. He did all of this so that you and I could become rich with the reality of God and His heavenly life. We know that before we can experience the fullness of eternal life, most of us will have to enter into it by way of physical death. Like the flesh that veiled Jesus' glory, our flesh veils us from experiencing the fullness of life and God's glory. Physical death is the door that will allow us to step through the limitations of the flesh into His everlasting arms. What a glorious event when flesh no longer limits us, and we are able to experience the majesty of God in its fullness.

What about the life we live on earth? How can we experience the full life that Jesus made reference to in John 10:10? Is there some door of death that we must walk through in order to embrace this life? The answer is yes. The Apostle Paul understood the type of death that gives way to greater life for the Christian. In fact, he stated that he died daily.[6]

The dying process that must take place before one can possess greater life was first described by Jesus in Matthew 16:24-25, "If any man will come after me, let him deny himself and take up his cross and follow me. For whosoever will save his life shall lose it: and whosoever will lose his life for my sake shall find it."

---

[5] 2 Corinthians 8:9

[6] 1 Corinthians 15:31

In order to find this greater life, we must lose the life we presently possess. In short, we must lose the life produced by our fallen or sinful state. The old life is motivated by pride, bent on pleasing the flesh, and is subject to the god of this world, Satan. The Bible calls this the "old life of the flesh" or the "old man."[7]

Jesus was saying we would have to lose the old man if we are going to ensure salvation of our soul. This seems like a drastic measure unless you understand that the old man is the enemy of God. It is rebellious in nature, perverted in its ways, and prefers darkness and delusion to light and truth.

This is why the Apostle Paul was determined to deal with his old man on a daily basis. Paul's goal was to possess the life of Christ, and he knew that in order to obtain this life, he had to die daily to the dictates and reign of this enemy of God.[8]

Jesus actually gave His followers insight into what it takes to die in order to gain life. There are three steps involved in this dying out process which Christians must submit themselves to in order to possess a complete heavenly life in the earthly realm. Believers must first of all deny themselves. Few believers understand what Jesus was referring to as far as self-denial. Sadly, most people, including immature Christians, have an unrealistic or morbid idea of self-denial. Many think of self-denial in terms of disallowing themselves of things or denying themselves of the comforts of life. Both of these ideas are an incorrect interpretation of this Scripture.

When Jesus was telling His disciples to deny themselves, He was telling them that they had to deny the old man of his right to reign and live. This means a person must deny self of its rights to any life or identity outside of Jesus.

The greatest way to deny the old man is to obey the Word of God. We see in Jesus' life that His obedience led Him to the cross and death. We can also see obedience and self-denial in Jesus when Satan was tempting Him in the wilderness.

Once you deny the old man of his rights to reign and live, you must then crucify his ways. The problem is that many want to make friends with the old man by rehabilitating him. They do this by conforming him to act according to some form of religious piousness. However, the Word of God is clear; the old man cannot be rehabilitated. He must be crucified. He must die!

The Apostle Paul made both of these statements in the book of Galatians,

---

[7] Romans 6:6; Ephesians 4:22; Colossians 3:9

[8] Philippians 3:7-14

> I am crucified with Christ: nevertheless I live; yet not I, but Christ liveth in me: and the life which I now live in the flesh I live by the faith of the Son of God, who loved me, and gave himself for me... But God forbid that I should glory, save in the cross of our Lord Jesus Christ, by whom the world is crucified unto me, and I unto the world (2:20; 6:14).

Watchman Nee in his book, *The Normal Christian,* talked about how the cross of Christ was God's instrument to take care of our sins, while our personal cross is the only means of taking care of the old man or the disposition of sin that operates in our inner man. It is true, Christ is the only One who could address sin and its consequences, but we must personally address the old man on a daily basis.

The Apostle Paul knew he had to be emptied of the claims, rights, and dictates of the old man to possess the new man, the life of Christ. He knew that he had to offer up his right to the essence of self through obedience. At this point the old man must give way to his personal cross, and die daily to the influences and ways of the old life. Basically, the Apostle Paul had to cease from interacting with the old man, as well as living according to its whims and dictates. This is what causes the old man to die or cease to play an active part in a person's life.

Death to self is also an act of consecration on man's part, while sanctification is God's act of holiness. To be sanctified means a person actually belongs to God. However, before sanctification can take place, a person must first consecrate him or herself from that which is profane, for the purpose of serving his or her holy God.

This act means a person must set his or her life apart from self that demands the right to rule. A person must turn from the world that entices the flesh to sin, and flee Satan who enslaves man through both of the avenues of self and the world. As Paul said, the world was crucified unto him and he unto the world.[9] Therefore, the world had no influence over him because the old man had ceased to reign.

Once the old man ceases to reign, the believer has the freedom to take the final step towards obtaining the fullness of life, which is to follow Jesus. Following Jesus is also an act of consecration. A consecrated person will be distinct in attitude, conduct, and lifestyle. It is important to note that you cannot follow Jesus until you have denied yourself to live according to the old man, and picked up your cross. The reason is because until the old man is dealt with, a person will be subject to his dictates rather than the Lordship of Jesus.

Many people are double-minded because they desire to follow Jesus, but give way to the reign of the old man who remains alive. As a result, this double-mindedness will cause confusion as to loyalties, goals,

---

[9] Galatians 6:14

and priorities.[10] The biggest sign that the old man still reigns is the defeat that plagues an individual who has never put him in his rightful place.

The life of Christ ensures victory, but the old man leads a person to failure, shame, and defeat. Subsequently, many Christians are frustrated because they have clothed the old man in religious garb, instead of denying him of his rights, and nailing him to the cross. Once the old man rightfully meets his demise, the believer can be clothed in humility as he or she puts on the life of the Lord Jesus Christ.[11]

Like a helpless sheep, a Christian must be led into the abundant life. Only Jesus as loving Shepherd and committed Lord can lead a person up paths of righteousness into the pastures of God's will. This will cause him or her to rest beside the still waters of confidence, peace, and abundance where he or she can experience the complete life of Jesus as He becomes all in all.

What about you? Have you experienced greater life in Christ? Is your life victorious? If the answer is no, examine yourself and see if the old man is still calling the shots. If so, you need to ask the Lord to help you develop a healthy hatred for him so that you can deny him, crucify him, and follow Jesus into His abundant and everlasting life.

---

[10] James 1:8

[11] Matthew 11:28-29; Romans 13:14; 1 Peter 5:5-6

9

A MATTER OF THE HEART

Keep thy heart with all diligence;
for out of it are the issues of life.
Proverbs 4:23

The *eighth* principle in regarding the life God has ordained for His people has to do with the source that motivates an individual in his or her life. It is important that we realize that the source of our motivation serves as the center or mainspring of our lives.

Many people think that the center of our lives is the brain or head. This is why many put much stock in their creeds or beliefs. Yet, in the right circumstances, creeds fail to answer the hard questions of life. They often bring more confusion, throwing people into a spiritual crisis. It is in such crises that people either become hypocrites by pretending their creeds are infallible or avid skeptics who judge all religious matters with a vengeance. They can also realize creeds are as limited as man, and that real understanding lies beyond the world of logic and human reasoning.

If the head does not serve as the center of man's life, what does? Jesus gives us the answer in Matthew 15:18 through 20,

> But those things which proceed out of the mouth come forth from the heart; and they defile the man. For out of the heart proceed evil thoughts, murders, adulteries, fornications, thefts, false witness, blasphemies: These are the things which defile a man: but to eat with unwashen hands defileth not a man.

This truth brings us to the *eighth* principle that simply states that life is a matter of the heart. All issues of life, from our motivations, intentions, and priorities, come from the heart.

Oswald Chambers dealt with the issue of the heart in his book *Biblical Psychology*. He explained how the brain is not spiritual, but a physical thing. This means that thinking actually takes place in the heart. He goes on to explain how Jesus never answered any questions that would originate with the mind because such questions were always borrowed from other sources. Mr. Chambers made this observation, "but the questions that spring from our hearts, the real problems that vex us, Jesus Christ answers those."

It is the heart that is the expression of a man's soul. If the heart is dark, so is the mind. If the heart contains light, then the mind has the capacity to embrace truth and revelation.

How many have you witnessed in the Christian realm whom have made Christianity a matter of the head, instead of the heart? It is nothing more than a mental assent to some facts or religious doctrine. These same people pride themselves in their intellectual conceit, while being devoid of any life. They are immovable about their beliefs, not because they are right, but because they are unteachable.

This type of mind is actually at enmity with God and leads to death. The Apostle Paul called such a mind carnal or fleshly. The problem with this type of mind is that eventually it will exalt its own thoughts or conclusions over the reality of God. In other words, the head or the intellectual conclusions of man often replace the God of the Bible.[1]

The carnal mind does not blatantly debate God's existence. However, it does cleverly redefine God according to its own perverted conclusions, vain philosophies, and deceptive illusions. This type of idolatry deceives a man about his own spiritual condition while it causes the light of life and truth to become hidden underneath a cloak of intellectual foolishness and nonsense. In fact, many people hide behind various cloaks to cover up their real attitude towards God.[2] And, all attitudes about God are inspired by the heart condition.

The battle that rages today is not for the head, but for the heart. It is not the head of man that must be enlightened. It is the heart that must be circumcised by the sword of God's Word before it can rightly perceive and embrace truth, thereby, enlarging man's ability to properly understand and receive spiritual matters.

Many people still believe that if you can change a person's mind, the battle will be won. This is unrealistic because I have changed the minds of people in the past with reasoning, only to watch them fall back into the same traps and patterns because their heart had not been changed. Obviously, as we can see, all issues of life originate with the heart. This is why Jesus' confrontations were not designed to change minds, but to challenge and change hearts.

This eighth principle is also brought out in Genesis 2:22, "And the rib, which the LORD God had taken from man, made he a woman, and brought her unto man." God did not take Eve out of the head of Adam, but out of his side, close to his heart.

---

[1] Romans 1:18-28; 8:5-13; 2 Corinthians 10:3-5

[2] John 15:22

When Jesus came to earth, He did not commit His head to the Father, but His heart. When He was on the cross, it was His heart that was broken. Jesus' example shows us the heart must be broken in relationship to sin. Brokenness must occur before real change can take place. Psalm 34:18 states, "The LORD is nigh unto them that are of a broken heart; and saveth such as be of a contrite spirit."

Psalm 51:17 says, "The sacrifices of God are a broken spirit: a broken and a contrite heart, O God, thou wilt not despise." Brokenness can only happen in the heart, not the head. God accepts a broken heart because it makes a person receptive to receive from Him.

The truth about the heart is also brought out in Jesus' relationship with the Church. Jesus gave His heart to God to be broken on the cross for the benefit of mankind. As a result, He became the head of the Church.[3]

What would happen if a man gave his head and not his heart in the area of commitment and relationship? A good example of the consequences of this scenario can be found in the life of Adam. Adam may have been the head where Eve was concerned, but there is no indication that Adam ever gave his heart to God or Eve. As a result, he rebelled against God and sacrificed Eve when he blamed her for his rebellious actions.[4] This is the same scenario for today. People, who submit their heads to God instead of their hearts, will end up rebelling against Him by sacrificing the truth that cuts against the grain of their hearts.

Do you claim to be a born-again Christian? If so, what have you submitted to God, your head or your heart?

Giving Heart

God's heart can be seen throughout Scripture and was visibly expressed centuries ago. By studying His heart, we can understand what constitutes an acceptable heart.

First of all, God's heart is full of everlasting love. His love expresses itself in mercy, grace, and truth. It covers a multitude of sins. It is sacrificial in nature. The sacrificial nature of His love was made evident when Jesus Christ died on the cross. "For God so loved the world, that he gave his only begotten Son, that whosoever believeth in him should not perish, but have everlasting life."[5]

The cross of Christ is the visible display of God's heart. It was exposed for the whole world to see how far He would go to reach each of

---

[3] Colossians 1:17-22

[4] Genesis 3:9-12

[5] John 3:16; 1 Peter 4:8

us. This is why the writer of Hebrews gave this warning, "How shall we escape, if we neglect so great salvation; which at the first began to be spoken by the Lord, and was confirmed unto us by them that heard him."[6]

The heart of God gives the best. It won't allow any less because of love. For example, He gave Adam the best when He gave Eve to him. He gave humankind the best when Jesus Christ became the sacrificial Lamb on the cross. One day, He will also present a bride to Jesus who will be without spot and wrinkle.

God does not give hand-me-downs or second best. Therefore, as His followers, can we do any less when it comes to our lives? Sadly, many people are like the rich young ruler in Matthew 19.They enthusiastically come up to Jesus seeking eternal life, but when Jesus asks them to give up those things that possess their hearts in order to follow Him, many walk away from Him in great sorrow. Like the rich young man, they may have come to Christ rich in many ways, but they leave spiritual paupers, doomed to face a Christless eternity.

The Apostle Paul knew that a natural response of a heart of love is that of giving. We can see this insight when he gave this instruction in 2 Corinthians 9:7, "Every man according as he purposeth in his heart, so let him give; not grudgingly, or of necessity: for God loveth a cheerful giver."

Paul realized that people could make Christianity a matter of impersonal giving. Giving which simply comes from the pocketbook, guilt, or duty is not of God. Godly giving will be a natural response or expression of a heart that is compelled by the love of God. Giving the best also means it costs you something of value. And, what is the cost of godly giving? It varies with each individual, but you can bank on it costing a person in a beneficial way in order to gain that which is excellent. It is for this reason that whatever the personal cost might be, it will prove worth the price in light of possessing eternal possessions.

King David understood this truth. This was brought out in 2 Samuel 24:24. David had been provoked to number the people, bringing a plague upon them. He was told to offer a sacrifice to stay the plague. He was brought to the threshing floor of Araunah. He asked to buy the property, but Araunah offered to give it to him for free. As king, David had a right to justify accepting the land. He could have even convinced himself that he would be showing good stewardship by allowing Araunah to show his loyalty and citizenship. Instead, King David made this statement, "Nay; but I will surely buy it of thee at a price: neither will I offer burnt offerings unto the LORD my God that which doth cost me nothing."

---

[6] Hebrews 2:3

David knew that life in God was his most valuable asset. He never wanted to cheapen it or take it for granted. King David also knew that the lives of men were precious to God. After all, what is a soul worth? God actually answered that question on an old rugged cross centuries ago.

Jesus made this statement in relationship to paying the price in Luke 14:28, "For which of you, intending to build a tower, sitteth not down first, and counteth the cost, whether he have sufficient to finish it?" Jesus counted the cost of our redemption in the courts of eternity. He knew it would be tremendous, but the rewards would include men and women becoming the children of God, ultimately fulfilling the plan of the Father.[7]

What must each of us offer God to ensure we pay the price? There are four things we must be willing to give to Him. First, we must submit our best to Him. According to Isaiah 64:6, our best is as filthy rags. Presenting our best is necessary if God is going to replace our rags with His robe of righteousness.

Secondly, we must give Him our life. Our life is in bondage to sin, the world, and Satan. It is subject to the flesh and motivated by pride, and it clearly matters to God that the essence of our lives falls short of His holiness. He must have all of our lives if He is going to bring forth new life.

The next object we must present to Him is our hearts. It is wicked and deceitful and only God knows the extent of its great darkness. For this reason, we must offer a heart that is broken by the reality of its own wickedness. God will not be able to resist such a heart. In fact, as the great Physician, He will give us a new heart, capable of containing and expressing His love. It will be a heart where His words are written on it, while His incredible commitment is being reflected through us to others.[8]

Finally, we must offer Him our bodies as a living sacrifice.[9] It must be noted God cannot use our best without making an exchange with that which is excellent. Our lives will remain unacceptable to Him until Jesus becomes a reality in our hearts. Therefore, our hearts must also be broken before He can have His way in our lives.

Interestingly, God can accept our bodies as a living sacrifice. And, what are our bodies? They are nothing more than empty, fragile shells or marred useless vessels that house a soul. God is the great potter who is able to do the impossible with a marred vessel. The blood of Jesus cleanses people from all unrighteousness, and God places a robe of righteousness on them. He will bring forth a new life out of the old life by totally changing the heart or mainspring of man. In short, He will

---

[7] John 1:12

[8] Jeremiah 17: 9-10; Ezekiel 36:26

[9] Romans 12:1-2

resurrect a new life within the empty shell or marred vessels of our bodies. This is why we must present our bodies as a living sacrifice. As we present our bodies as a living sacrifice, God will be able to prove what is His good, acceptable, and perfect will in and through our lives.

As the Apostle Paul stated in 2 Timothy 2:20, there are many vessels in the house of God. However, the quality of those vessels and how God uses them will be determined by whether His Son is the center of all matters in a person's heart.

What does your heart condition say about your relationship with God? After all, the issues of life originate within the heart, and it will always end up telling on you.

10

AGREEMENT

Can two walk together, except they be agreed?
(Amos 3:3)

In the last eight chapters, we have dealt with the principles and characteristics of the Christian life that ensure spiritual well-being. The final principle has to do with the fruits that will be present in the lives of those who are operating within the first eight principles.

We know the number "eight" represents new beginnings, but the number "nine" is symbolic of finality. Once all is said and done, the fruits of a person's life will speak more loudly than any claims or doctrines. Jesus put it this way, "Ye shall know them by their fruits" (Matthew 7:16a).

What do fruits tell about our lives? First of all, they tell us the condition of the soil of our hearts. They also reveal whether our spiritual lives are healthy or are falling short of our potential. Fruits also identify us to our real source of life. Jesus explains this concept in this way in John 15:4-6,

> Abide in me, and I in you. As the branch cannot bear fruit of itself, except it abide in the vine; no more can ye, except ye abide in me. I am the vine, ye are the branches. He that abideth in me, and I in him, the same bringeth forth much fruit: for without me ye can do nothing. If a man abide not in me, he is cast forth as a branch, and is withered; and men gather them and cast them into the fire, and they are burned.

The soil, or our heart must be right before the proper fruit can come forth. Jesus' life must take root in our hearts. As the life of Jesus grows within our hearts, our lives become an extension of the true Vine, our Lord and Savior. Whether the proper fruit comes out of our lives will depend on whether we are totally connected to the Vine.

People who deal with apple orchards admit if the branch is not fully secured to the tree, the flavor of the apples on the branch will be poor. This proves that the fruit is not for the branch; rather it is the product of the branch's relationship to the tree. The fruit has been made available for others to taste and enjoy.

People "taste" our lives on a continual basis. What kind of taste do we leave in their mouths? Is it bitter, sour, sweet, or salty? Is the substance we leave with them comprised of judgmental attitudes, hypocrisy, fluff, or meat? Is it temporary or eternal? Is it the goodness of God or the filthy rags of our religious best?

If you ask me what taste I prefer, I would tell you the salty one. Personally, I have tasted the bitterness of judgmental attitudes, the sourness of hypocrisy, and enough religious fluff to last me a lifetime. However, what I value the most are those who salt my life with the reality of Christ, and challenge my commitment to Him with truth. This type of saltiness will whet my Christian appetite, making me thirsty enough to pursue the Living Waters. This is why Jesus said in Matthew 5:13, "Ye are the salt of the earth: but if the salt have lost his savour, wherewith shall it be salted? It is thenceforth good for nothing, but to be cast out, and to be trodden under foot of men."

Today the spiritual salt is missing in many churches, causing an imbalance. Such an imbalance can be best understood in light of how real salt (not table salt) contains minerals that are needed to balance out some of the body systems. This vital substance not only balances out our body systems, but also gives us a comparison between the things we taste and value. For example, salt shows a person how sweet something really is. If a person's diet consists of nothing but sweets, eventually he or she will develop imbalances that can turn into a form of addiction, not to mention diabetes, obesity, and malnutrition.

Sadly, some church bodies have accepted the fluff over the salt, causing them to become spiritually dull. They swing from one spiritual high to the next, causing "addictive" tendencies and depressing valleys of despair and emptiness. Most of the time, this fluff ends up being nothing more than a temporary, fleshly high.

The fruits from these activities prove to be fruitless or devoid of the life of Christ. They reveal that the Vine is missing, and as a result, the branches are blowing with every wind of doctrine that whet or entice these people's fleshly appetites.

Jesus said we can do nothing outside of Him. But, to benefit from Him, we must be abiding in Him. "Abiding" implies oneness with the Vine. This brings us to the *ninth* principle: *There must be oneness or agreement with God before there can be a fruitful life.*

We see this principle in operation in the lives of Adam and Eve. Genesis 2:23-24 states, "And Adam said, This is now bone of my bones, and flesh of my flesh: she shall be called Woman, because she was taken out of Man. Therefore shall a man leave his father and his mother, and shall cleave unto his wife: and they shall be one flesh." (Emphasis added.)

Eve had been made because there was no other creature that could intimately share in Adam's life. By God taking Eve out of Adam, He could bring them back together in a special relationship, and once again make them one.

It was only after God brought Adam and Eve together as one, that He gave them this commandment: "Be fruitful, and multiply, and replenish the earth, and subdue it: and have dominion over the fish of the sea, and over the fowl of the air, and over every living thing that moveth upon the earth" (Genesis 1:28). God told them to become fruitful in their life together, and to multiply that life.

Fruitfulness in Genesis 1:28 means children. However, we can see where God is telling Adam and Eve to reproduce the life they possess and to multiply it. It is only as Adam and Eve came together as one, could this commandment be fulfilled.

For the Christian, there are two meanings to fruitfulness. The first meaning has to do with the fruit of the Spirit. We read about the characteristics of this fruit in Galatians 5:22-23, "But the fruit of the Spirit is love, joy, peace, longsuffering, gentleness, goodness, faith, meekness, temperance: against such there is no law." These characteristics describe the Person of Christ. The main goal of the Holy Spirit is to reproduce the life of Christ in each of His followers.

The second type of fruit can be found in John 15:8, "Herein is my Father glorified, that ye bear much fruit; so shall ye be my disciples." The fruit mentioned in this Scripture is in reference to the life of Jesus being multiplied in others by those who possess His life. This is the fruit that truly brings glory to the Father.

Every Christian is called to be co-laborers in the harvest field with God.[1] God will bring forth the fruits, but believers must be ready to plant the reality of Christ in the hearts of people. Once the seed of His life has been planted through the preaching of the Gospel, these seeds need to be watered with godly examples and sound teachings. Spiritual investment of this nature establishes a person firmly on the immovable Rock of Ages.

A fruitful life hinges on a person being completely secured in Jesus Christ, the Vine. Such a relationship implies that a person is indeed one in Christ and one with Him.

"Oneness" in the kingdom of God is brought out in Ephesians 4:4-6, "There is one body, and one Spirit, even as ye are called in one hope of your calling; one Lord, one faith, one baptism, one God and Father of all

---

[1] 1 Corinthians 3:6-9

who is above all, and through all, and in you all." There is only one body, not many. There is only one Spirit and one hope. We must only please one Lord, possess one faith, realize that we are baptized into one Body by the Holy Ghost, and know there is only one God who deserves our loyalty and worship. There is only one of each. Whether we embrace the oneness of Christianity or not, comes down to possessing the One who is the head of the body. He is the One whom the Spirit upholds. He is the One who serves as our eternal hope. He is the One who is Lord, God, and the essence of our faith. His name is Jesus Christ.

Watchman Nee shared this perspective concerning this subject. He pointed out that unity solely rests upon a person's union with Christ. This union was wrought by His cross and made real by his indwelling Spirit. Such unity is sound. It is not based on a person's appreciation of the idea of oneness. [2]

This spiritual oneness can only come out of an intimate relationship with God through Jesus Christ. It means there is agreement in spirit and truth. In other words, the people who have oneness, have the same spirit, are walking in the same direction, and have the same focus.

Oneness can clearly be observed in the relationship Jesus had with the Father. In John 10:30, Jesus said, "I and my Father are one."

In John 14:10, Jesus said, "Believest thou not that I am in the Father, and the Father in me? The words that I speak unto you I speak not of myself: but the Father that dwelleth in me, he doeth the works." The oneness between Jesus and the Father was total agreement. Total agreement also points to equality. Without such equality, there is confusion, superiority, and abuse. In His humanity, Jesus possessed the heart of the Father, agreed with His mind, and lined up to His will. As a result, the Father exalted Him and gave Him a name above all names.[3]

This agreement showed that Jesus had the same spirit, focus, and purpose as the Father. In fact, He never acted outside of the Father's plan. Agreement of this nature requires humility and submission. The Son of God visibly showed humility towards the will of the Father when He submitted to the cross as our substitute.[4]

The Church, or Body of Christ is to have the same type of agreement with Jesus as He does with the Father. His Body should possess His heart, take on His mind or disposition, and do His will in the world. However, for the Church to do Jesus' bidding, it must become humble before Him. In humility, it will be able to become His visible extension to this dying world.

---

[2] A Table In the Wilderness, Daily Meditations; March 14

[3] John 5:18; Philippians 2:5-7, 9-11

[4] Philippians 2:6-8

Today there is a move for the Church to embrace another spirit, Lord, God, faith, and hope in the name of peace and unity. Such a move is not only blatant disobedience to God, but it makes a mockery out of His character, Gospel, and will. 2 Corinthians 6:14-17 makes it clear that we must avoid such unholy agreement:

> Be ye not unequally yoked together with unbelievers: for what fellowship hath righteousness with unrighteousness? And what communion hath light with darkness? And what concord hath Christ with Belial? Or what part hath he that believeth with an infidel? And what agreement hath the temple of God with idols? for ye are the temple of the living God; as God hath said, I will dwell in them, and walk in them; and I will be their God, and they shall be my people. Wherefore come out from among them, and be ye separate, saith the Lord, and touch not the unclean thing; and I will receive you.

Agreement does not occur because I agree with someone about different issues, but because we both have the same spirit motivating us. The Apostle Paul brings this important key out in Ephesians 4:3 and 13, "Endeavouring to keep the unity of the Spirit in the bond of peace...Till we all come in the unity of the faith, and of the knowledge of the Son of God, unto a perfect man, unto the measure of the stature of the fulness of Christ."

Watchman Nee spoke about the unity that the Spirit of God brings to the Church. He referred to it as an unbreakable sevenfold cord that binds all believers throughout the world, regardless of their diverse character or circumstances. The one requirement to be part of this incredible union is that they possess the vital oneness conferred by the Spirit's indwelling presence.[5]

The Holy Spirit is the one who leads believers into both the knowledge and fullness of Jesus Christ. He does this by enabling them to securely abide in the Vine. This abiding allows saints to know the abundance of life that comes out of fellowshipping with God through Jesus Christ.

It is important for each of us to understand that a fruitful life with God can only be secured in an intimate relationship with Him. Many Christians believe Jesus came only to save. This is partially true. However, the real reason for Jesus coming was to restore the relationship that had been broken between the first man and his Creator. Jesus made this statement in John 14:6, "I am the way, the truth, and the life: no man cometh to the Father, but by me."

Jesus provided the way for every individual to enter into an intimate relationship with God. It is in an intimate relationship that both the abundant and eternal life is fully realized and secured for the believer for

---

[5] A Table In the Wilderness; March 14

the glory of God. This is the goal of Christianity, where the fullness of Christ's life is truly being unveiled in His people.

As the first principle states, everything must begin and end with God, but the end of all things for man is the restoration of a relationship that was lost in the Garden of Eden. In this restoration the plan of God will be unveiled and brought forth as the very life of Christ is established in His Church. If a Christian fails to realize this, he or she fails to recognize the significance of what Jesus did on the cross. He restored the means for people to reach the ultimate completion or abundance in their Christian life by experiencing an active, unhindered, living relationship with God Almighty.

How about you? Do you have an intimate relationship with God through Jesus Christ? This is the only way that you will be able to fulfill the nine principles in regard to the life God desires to give you. As you embrace and possess this life, you will realize the eternal life He has secured for you, the abundant life He makes available to you on a daily basis, and the satisfying complete life that works in and through you. If this life has eluded you, then like Paul in Philippians 3, may you press forward to apprehend Jesus' very life, so it can seize and consume your heart, mind, and will.

11

SIMPLE IN NATURE

...so your minds should be corrupted
from the simplicity that is in Christ.
2 Corinthians 11:3b

The principles of God are simple in nature. They bring meaning and order to a person's life. They encourage spiritual growth, produce obedience, and inspire godly discipline. In this book, we have been considering the principles that make up a victorious Christian life. However, there are other godly principles that affect a person's life in their relationship and walk with God.

For example, an important principle can be found in Matthew 18:3, "Verily I say unto you, Except ye be converted, and become as little children, ye shall not enter into the kingdom of heaven." Regression is a must to embrace God's kingdom, but the other part of the principle behind this Scripture is simplicity. The things of God are simple in nature, but profound in intent. God's truths are so simple that a child can see them, but so profound that those with great intellect could be confused and stumped by them.

Simplicity is contrary to Satan. He complicates everything. He appeals to the pride of man's intelligence, while God's truth feeds and challenges the spirit of man. Satan confuses the issues and causes people to pursue after greater knowledge, while God's truths help a person to get his or her spiritual bearings, giving him or her a hunger to know more of God.

One of our sayings in Gentle Shepherd Ministries is "keep it simple". In my years, I have found simple truths to be profound as they unveil God's heart and plan. I have also witnessed people taking these simple truths and complicating them, totally losing sight of their meaning and power.

If people are to possess these truths, they must lose their intellectual arrogance. This is hard for many because they pride themselves on what they think they know, rather than putting all their energy to know the true identity of the one true God. Such pride makes them foolish and vain in their understanding, causing them to operate from a carnal perspective, instead of a heavenly one.

Matthew 7:2 gives us insight into another principle, "For with what judgment ye judge, ye shall be judged: and with what measure ye mete, it shall be measured to you again." This shows that the type of judgment a person directs at others will come back to him or her in like manner. It also reveals a person's disposition or inward state. For example, judgment usually comes from the carnal mind of pride, while godly judgment or discernment comes from the spirit and heart.

My encounters with people have confirmed the last part of the principle of judgment many times; and that is ultimately we will end up judging ourselves. The attitude or actions in others that irritate people the most can be found in their own character. This irritation, which is nothing more than a mirror, can cause these individuals to harshly judge the person who is serving as the irritant. As the popular saying goes, "The accuser is the abuser." Therefore, these people's judgment against such offenses or discrepancies is nothing more than a means of judging themselves.

Another popular principle is found in Galatians 6:7-8, "Be not deceived; God is not mocked: for whatsoever a man soweth, that shall he also reap. For he that soweth to his flesh shall of the flesh reap corruption; but he that soweth to the Spirit shall of the Spirit reap life everlasting." Each principle is pretty self-explanatory. This one clearly tells us that whatever we invest in our life with God and others will determine the type of harvest we reap in this life and in the next.

Philippians 4:5 gives us another simple principle to walk in, "Let your moderation be known unto all men. The Lord is at hand." This principle tells believers that they must appropriate what is necessary to keep balance in their life. People have a tendency to operate in extremes. However, moderation in this text points to being mild or gentle.[1] Once again, we are reminded of a state of disposition that is under the influence of the Spirit of God. As the saying goes, too much of a good thing can be destructive.

It is hard to maintain balance, but by keeping Jesus as the focus of our lives, He can maintain this important stability. For example, there must be a balance between work and play, religious activities and quiet times with God, and entertainment and sobriety. There are many fragile lines in our life that can cause one to abuse the life, time, and energy God has given him or her.

One of the keys of maintaining balance is recognizing limitations. This means recognizing strengths and weaknesses. I have found many

[1] Strong's Exhaustive Concordance, #1933

people operating in extremes to compensate for weaknesses or use their strengths to control life and people, or to accomplish unrealistic goals. Sadly, people may put God to a foolish test when they operate in the extremes.

There are other principles in Scripture, but my main purpose for this book is to unveil the principles that will encourage an abundant life in Christ. If a person walks these principles out in the right spirit according to truth, they will automatically put into practice many of the other principles that were not covered. Let us review these principles for the last time. Ask the Lord to make them real to you.

Everything in our life must begin with God and end with a revelation of Jesus Christ. If Christians would daily walk this principle out, they would avoid detours of temptations, pitfalls of the flesh, and the snares of pride and Satan. Life outside of these two boundaries results in delusion, sin, and destruction, and will prevent the saint from being conformed in the likeness of Jesus.

The Holy Ghost must move upon the hopeless terrain of man's heart and mind before he can be changed. The Holy Spirit is the one that changes the personality of something. For man, the Spirit transforms or changes the internal part of man, which will be reflected through his outer countenance.

Real life comes only from God. There are various lifestyles being offered in this world, but there is only one source that can give man true life. This source is God. People constantly seek after a particular lifestyle that they perceive will bring them life and pleasure. Few ever realize that life cannot be found in a lifestyle, but in a relationship with God through Jesus Christ. Eventually, people will realize that the lifestyles they pursue to find some semblance of "life" often leave them empty and disillusioned.

The quality of a person's life is determined by the choices he or she makes along the way. People make choices every day. Some decisions may not be significant in the scheme of things, but other decisions may affect the quality of life and the person's eternal destination. The one choice all people must make to ensure spiritual well-being has to do with Jesus Christ. However, it is not enough to just choose Jesus. A person must choose to follow Him daily. Depending on circumstances, one may make a variety of choices within seconds. Christians must wisely choose to walk in the steps of Jesus regardless of the challenges.

A person first must find his or her rightful place in God's design before he or she can reach his or her potential. Christians have a tendency to go from one impression to another. In other words, they pursue after spiritual things based on feelings, impressions, or fantasies. These pursuits leave them disillusioned with Christianity. After all, they were doing what they thought God wanted them to do. They failed to recognize the real source behind their pursuits. Words such as impressions and feelings often find their origins in the flesh, not in God. Out of mercy, God will close fleshly doors as a means to preserve His people, but in some cases, He allows them to be opened to teach valuable lessons. The latter scenario turns out to be a curse rather than a blessing. Christians must make sure that God is the source behind their direction, instead of discovering that He is the missing link.

The quality of our spiritual life can only be maintained in obedience to God. Christians often substitute religious deeds for obedience. Such deeds are based on personal agendas, while acceptable obedience is based on the will of God. Christians who fail to obey God will never have the authority and power to overcome. Ultimately, they will fail to reach their potential in Christ.

Greater life can only come by way of death. The Christian life can only be reached by death. It is Jesus' death that secured eternal life, and it is our death to the old ways that obtains a greater life in Christ. Death to the self-life is the secret to possessing the life of Jesus. To many people death represents finality, while to the saint it means new beginnings.

Life is a matter of the heart. Christians have a tendency to invest in their minds by seeking spiritual knowledge, but few examine their heart to see what truly possesses it. Christianity is not a matter of logic or the supernatural. Rather, it is a matter of a relationship that should inspire, change, and motivate a person in everything he or she does. This important relationship is with the Living God. He must own our heart. Whether or not God owns our hearts will determine if they will be a stony or a circumcised heart of flesh.

There must be oneness or agreement with God before there can be a fruitful life. There is a real clamor for unity today, but this unity has nothing to do with the quality of life. Its emphasis is for the sole purpose of deceiving the masses by promoting a false environment of love and peace. This unity will quickly collapse when the façade is taken away to reveal the sinister goals of this move. There is no unity for the Christian outside of the Holy Spirit's ability to edify and unite on the foundation of Jesus Christ. The heart of Jesus was to see unity within His Body. This unity would ensure agreement between the Body and the head (Jesus). Once the Body functions properly, then there could be communion within the Body as well as with the Father. Unity of this nature is to exemplify the life, power, and authority of the Body of Christ in the midst of great spiritual darkness.

As you can see, God's principles are simple. They communicate His heart and desire for the Church. They reveal secrets behind the victorious Christian life, and allow believers to see His workings.

How many of these principles do you walk out daily? The fruit of your life will reveal which principles you are abiding within. If you begin with God and end with a revelation of Jesus Christ, you will ultimately reflect the fruit of His life.

Examine your fruit today to see if there is a wrong heart condition due to carnality or disobedience. As Jesus said, "A good tree cannot bring forth evil fruit, neither can a corrupt tree bring forth good fruit" (Matthew 7:18).

Book Four:

THE PLACE OF COVENANT

INTRODUCTION

I have always had a fascination towards the concept of covenant. In most cases, I assumed I understood what I needed to understand about this topic, but I always felt there was more when it came to the role that covenants played in the lives of God's people.

The subject of covenants actually took center stage a few years back in the Christian world. However, like so many Scriptural subjects, some individuals took this topic to the extreme. In fact, the concept of covenants appeared to become another fad that rolled through Christendom. Like all fads, it eventually dissipated. However, it left pockets of confusion behind.

Through the years I would occasionally encounter this subject. Each time, I would get a small glimpse into something that had incredible implications to it, but it continued to remain shrouded in preconceived and half-understood notions. Recently, I was studying a subject that proved to be the key that opened the door to greater insight about this issue.

As I meditated on the insights that I received about covenants, more was unveiled to me. I actually found myself overwhelmed by the simplicity of the purpose and practice of covenant, but also the profound implications behind it. What struck me the most about this subject is that covenant points to a place.

When you study the Christian life, you will realize it is all about coming to a place with God. This place ensures a relationship that allows room for preparation, exploration, and growth into the depths, heights, and incredible attributes and ways of God. Such growth is the means to discover that He is indeed all in all. He is involved with every aspect of the visible and invisible world. He is intimately involved with every detail of our lives. He is working in every arena of the world. Therefore, everywhere a person turns, he or she will encounter the reality, work, and sustaining power of God.

As I studied and meditated on the concept of covenant according to the glimpses I had received, I realized that this practice revealed greater aspects about the character and ways of God. Although, it did not show me anything new about the attributes of God, it did allow me to see deeper into His infinite character. Such revelations always cause me to marvel at the greatness of God, making Him bigger than life as He becomes a greater reality to my spirit.

My goal in writing this book is to remove the confusion and bring balance to this subject. Admittedly, I often feel inept when it comes to doing the matters of God justice, but I also know that I am responsible to share such truths with others. It is up to the Holy Spirit to confirm and bring revelation to individuals as they seek to know our wondrous God.

As you take this spiritual journey into God's Word to discover the place covenants play in the lives of God's people, be prepared to come to a place of awe and worship as you marvel at what this place actually means for us as believers.

1

WHAT IS A COVENANT?

Before we can come to terms with covenants of the Bible, we must understand what constitutes a covenant. According to my *Webster's Dictionary*, covenant is a formal, solemn, and binding agreement or compact. It points to a promise or pledge. It is also sealed by some kind of action.[1]

When you consider the presentation the dictionary presents about covenant, you can see that when actually making one with another individual, it becomes a supremely formal matter. In other words, to enter into a covenant, there must be a right attitude. You will not casually or flippantly enter into such a compact. In fact, it will not only determine what you will do, but it will be a focal point that will stand distinct from all other responsibilities and activities in your life.

For example, the one event that stood out in my mind was my senior prom. I am sure this is true for most people who have graduated from High School. One of the reasons it stood out is because everyone dressed according to the occasion. The occasion marked recognition for an accomplishment in regard to the completion of High School. To commemorate this special time, men wore tuxes and the women formal dresses. The preparations and dress caused this event to stand out. Remember, it took time, energy, and even money to prepare for this auspicious affair.

Since a covenant is formal, a person must solemnly enter into it. The concept of "solemn" points to a ceremony or observance of something that is to stand unique from all other activities that occur in our daily life. In a sense, it is a celebration. However, solemn also points to approach. To come into a covenant requires people to be thoughtful and sober about what they are about to enter into.

One of the most solemn ceremonies in our society is marriage. How many times have you heard the instruction from the officiator of the ceremony that marriage must not be lightly entered into? The couple is clearly admonished to consider what they are doing, and make sure they are ready to come into this binding relationship.

---

[1] Webster's New Collegiate Dictionary; © 1976 by G. & C. Merriam Co.

Initially, the couples that are making a verbal declaration about their intentions towards each other at such a ceremony are often riding on the wave of emotional sentiment. As they ride this wave, they cannot imagine that they will feel any other way about their spouse. However, married couples admit that the wave of emotional sentiment always crashes when the demands and drudgeries of life challenge them. When all such sentiment lies on the shores of vanity and immaturity, the marriage ceremony is to remind them that they solemnly entered into this relationship with the intent of not just experiencing the good fruits from such a bond, but a willingness to also face the challenging times together, and develop maturity as a couple.

Covenant is also a binding agreement. In other words, there is no way out of it short of death. This is why the marriage ceremony declares that these two individuals who are being joined together in this holy bond are obliged to stay in this union until death separates them.

To successfully enter any covenant people must understand the implications involved. They must have a right attitude and approach to ensure that they are solemn and realistic about entering into this place of commitment. This commitment is not temporary, but lasting.

It is important to point out that a covenant is a type of vow, but a vow is not a covenant. In a covenant you are making a vow; however, a vow is something you make in regard to fulfilling a service, act, or condition.[2] For example, devoted Jews would make the vow of a Nazarite.[3] This would bind them to separate unto the Lord for a certain period of time. This vow would be marked by certain outward actions. However, once the vow was fulfilled, the obligation ceased. A covenant differs in that it does not cease because it is not binding oneself to a particular act or service; rather, it has to do with binding oneself in a relationship to ensure that a certain environment will continue to exist between the parties involved. This environment will ensure that the covenant can be carried out in an appropriate way when challenging circumstances arise between the parties that have come into this binding commitment.

A good example of this type of situation can be found in Genesis 21:22-32. Abimelech, the leader of the Philistines, along with the chief captain of the host, Phicol, sought Abraham out to make a covenant with him. These two Philistine leaders recognized that Jehovah God was with this great patriarch, and they wanted to ensure an environment of integrity and peace in their relationship and encounters with Abraham.

Consider the intent of this agreement, "Now therefore swear unto me here by God that thou wilt not deal falsely with me, nor with my son, nor with my son's son: but according to the kindness that I have done unto thee, thou shalt do unto me, and to the land wherein thou hast

---

[2] Webster's New Collegiate Dictionary

[3] Numbers 6:1-8

sojourned." It is important to point out that people made covenants with others as a means to ensure peace. As we will see, the covenants with God are also to ensure a place of peace for man with his Creator. Such peace points to reconciliation and agreement. Notice how this environment established between Abraham and Abimelech was also to be recognized and honored by the generations that followed. In other words, covenants are perpetual or ongoing.

Covenant also points to promises. When you consider covenants in relationship to promises, you realize that you are making a commitment to fulfill your obligation in this agreement by keeping the promises you have made in this pledge. When you consider the covenant of marriage, it contains promises that are being made by the couple to one another. These promises involve regarding one another in honorable and even sacrificial ways.

According to my dictionary, one of the meanings of "pledge" is the state of something being held as security or guaranty. This concept points to the sincerity of one's intention to fulfill an obligation. Commitments are cheap unless they are backed up by a pledge. For example, married couples pledge their hearts and lives to each other, and back it up with a ring that represents their intention to recognize this bond.

Strong's Exhaustive Concordance of the Bible has some of the same meanings as my dictionary, but it also includes that a covenant represents a state or disposition. As we consider the idea of state as far as personal agreement, it brings us to the subjects of inclinations and tendencies. When you combine the inward inclinations of the heart and the outward tendencies towards a matter, you will produce the attitude one must develop about his or her commitments.

Covenants are meant to determine the inclination of a person towards a matter. When a person enters into a covenant, it is with the intention of being constantly bent towards seeing it through. Therefore, the natural tendency of such a person would be to honor the covenant no matter what is challenging his or her personal resolve to break it.

When we consider the determination behind a covenant, we must recognize that to carry out our end of such an agreement will involve the integrity of our will to carry out the responsibilities outlined in the covenant. In other words, we must make a determination that such a contract is of the utmost importance in ensuring the quality of a matter. Without such a determination we will not have the necessary resolve to carry it out.[4]

The concordance also brings out another important word to define covenant, and that is testament. Testament has a couple of meanings.

---

[4] OT, #1285 & 3772; *NT, #1242 & 2476*

One such meaning is that of a witness. A covenant is to serve as a witness of a person's intentions. A credible witness will not be moved from the testimony that he or she has established in such a pact. In fact, the integrity of such covenants not only rests on such witnesses, but these witnesses will not be moved because such agreements have been established on what is real and trustworthy.

This brings us to the foundation of covenants, and that is truth. The Bible tells us truth stands. A covenant cannot be maintained unless it is clearly established on truth. There must be a solid foundation for the agreement to stand in order to have the means to be maintained. Remember, covenants are perpetual or ongoing; therefore, they cannot be fulfilled. They simply bind people in a relationship that will require some type of honor and resolve to maintain such an agreement.

Obviously, we must understand the concept of covenant if we are going to understand the important part it has in our relationship with God. As we will discover, it is a place in which we can truly meet God. If this place were not established, believers would have no real authority in their Christian life.

Since the foundation has been laid in regard to covenant, we can now begin the journey to understand the part and place it must hold in our Christian life. My prayer is that as this aspect of our life in Christ unfolds, it will impact your life as powerfully as it has mine.

2

THE PLACE OF LAW

Understanding covenant is of a great importance to God's people. The concept of covenant has been misunderstood, as well as abused and used in a wrong way. This abuse often comes out of ignorance, but it also is a means to manipulate people into some type of pledge or commitment. It all seems noble, but very few people understand the implications behind such a commitment. In fact, if they did, it is hard to say how many would come into such a pact.

To understand the implications behind covenant, we must consider the very character of God. What most people fail to realize about God making a covenant with man is that He is putting His character, power and reputation on the line. God's covenant with man would have no validity behind it if it was not backed up by the reality of who He is.

This brings us to another important matter. God actually puts His very character and reputation on the line by what He says. God's words are only as valid and good as His character and His ability to back them up. Hebrews 6:17-18 confirms this,

> Wherein God, willing more abundantly to show unto the heirs of promise the immutability of his counsel, confirmed it by an oath, That by two immutable things, in which it was impossible for God to lie, we might have a strong consolation, who have fled for refuge to lay hold upon the hope set before us.

Immutability points to God's unchanging character. He will not move from who He is, and His words serve as an expression of His very character. Unlike man, His words are not based on sentimental hogwash that will ebb away with the tides of emotional fickleness. They are not a means to throw a person a mere bone to keep him or her quiet or content with wishful thinking that has no validity to it. His words are not motivated by so-called "good intentions" that have no integrity or power to adhere to such an agreement. They do not seduce or defraud people into a false reality about their meaning or intention. His words are straight as an arrow. They are truth; therefore, capable of impacting the most indifferent soul by their power.[1] As the psalmist declared, "Forever, O LORD, thy word is settled in heaven (Psalms 119:89).

---

[1] Hebrews 4:12

The prophet Isaiah declared that God's Word would not return void. Jesus stated that the words He spoke contained spirit and life. He also declared that heaven and earth would pass away, but His words would not. The Apostle Peter stated that the Word of the Lord would endure forever. God's words are eternal. Unlike man, there is no deviation in them. As a result, man can bank on them by putting his faith in what God says. After all, faith comes by hearing, and hearing by the Word of God. [2] Such faith allows man to experience consolation as he learns to hide in his real spiritual refuge until matters of life and salvation are fully realized.

This brings us to the revelation of the power of God's words. In Exodus 3:14, God introduced Himself as the "I AM THAT I AM." This term seems impressive up front, but there are greater and more profound implications behind it. This term has to do with present reality. In other words, God always operates in present reality regardless of the past and the future. God is not bound by nor does He deal in terms of time, but in terms of seasons, environment, and circumstances. In God there is no real past or future. In fact, a day to Him is as a thousand years to us.[3] Therefore, His words are forever operating in relationship to the present. Because of His covenant with Abraham concerning His descendants, God was about to make this very agreement a present reality in the life of Moses and the children of Israel. The covenant with Abraham was as real, fresh, and viable at that time in history as it was when it was first made over 400 years before.

Since we are bound by time, this is hard for us to understand how God's reality of the past and the future is always in operation in the present. For this reason, God's words have power. Hebrews 11:3 tells us that the worlds were framed by the Word of God. He will not forget His words because they are as fresh to Him today as when He first spoke them centuries ago. They are going to be as applicable in the future as they are for today in our time. This is the incredible power of God's words. They are always present, and ready to be brought forth according to His plan.

If God could not back up such words, they would have no meaning or purpose to them. They would be much like the words of many men who use them as a means to flatter and con, but there is no substance behind them. In other words, such people have no intention of backing up their words with character and action. Such words are considered idle words.[4]

---

[2] Isaiah 55:11; Matthew 24:35; John 6:63; Romans 10:17; 1 Peter 1:25

[3] 2 Peter 3:8

[4] Matthew 12:36

The Gospel of John tells us that the Word, who was God, became flesh.[5] We know this is in reference to Jesus. He represented the very verbal expression of God in His pre-incarnate state. We know that Jesus was the present reality of God in the wilderness, the great "I AM THAT I AM." It was His train that filled the temple of heaven in Isaiah 6:1. However, twenty centuries ago, He was fashioned as a man and became the visible expression of God in this dark world.

Up until Jesus was manifested in the flesh, God's words were spoken and written, but in Christ they became a living reality, an expression that could be seen, handled, heard, and experienced. This living expression of God challenged hearts, exposed motives, ripped away facades and cloaks, and brought hope to the seeking soul. He was the fulfillment of God's promises and prophecies, as well as the One who would usher in a new covenant.

Jesus in His humanity proved that God's words are true and sure. His words are an expression of His very character. They do not stand idle, empty of substance, and lacking in action or resolve to bring them forth. Obviously, He has the power and means to keep His Word, making it alive and active. The Written Word simply confirms the validity of God's words. If there is any dispute between man and God about a matter, the Apostle Paul declared, "...yea, let God be true, but every man a liar;...(Romans 3:4b).

Obviously, God means what He says, and says what He means. God does not have to really make a covenant with man because He has nothing to prove. However, He chooses to do so. As a result, as His children, we can actually trace His workings in history to the present in regard to His covenants, confirming our certainty about the future.

For example, one of the everlasting covenants He made was with the creatures of the earth. He actually made it before Noah who served as a witness. The covenant is that He would never destroy the entire earth again with water. To confirm His intentions, He set the token of the rainbow in the sky.[6]

To this day God's handiwork and artistry appears in the sky after a rainstorm. It reminds us that all such storms have a stopping point. I remember one time driving down into a beautiful valley after a rainstorm. I counted five different rainbows in this valley. It was as though they were dancing as the rays of the sun broke through the dark storm clouds highlighting each one of them. Their beauty reminded me that these prisms of color give us glimpses into the majesty and heart of God. Even though some people have adopted the rainbow as a New Age symbol, it still remains a visible sign that God is keeping His covenant with every living creature on earth.

---

[5] John 1:1-3, 14; Colossians 2:9

[6] Genesis 9:11-15

God is true to every bit of His word down to the last detail. These confirmations prove that He exists and is active in the affairs of the world to bring forth His agreements. Since God's words are true, it also means they are law.

When we consider the concept of "law," we see, in a way, that a covenant is an unchangeable law that is meant to govern us in how we live and respond. However, covenant is different than actual law. Law tells people how to conduct themselves in society, but covenant outlines one's responsibilities in a personal relationship or matter. Granted, all true covenants stand as truth and law, but they come from the premise of the different parties agreeing to become responsible to abide or conduct themselves according to the agreement that has been made. Law disciplines us in our conduct, but covenant ensures an appropriate environment in which the agreement will be properly honored.

This brings us back to the issue of man. Man often lacks the integrity and power to keep his word. It takes character to learn how to be true to one's words, knowing that it is a visible expression of one's inner resolve to be responsible to the words he or she speaks. The truth is man must become responsible to keep his words, or they will lack power.

Man also lacks the means to bring forth the right environment to ensure such agreements. Jesus brought this out in His sermon on the mount.[7] He knew how cheap words were if not backed up by integrity and action. He instructed that people cease from making oaths before God about issues.

God is not limited in His ability to carry out a matter, but His holy character and His perfect will disciplines His words, commitments, and ways. Man must discipline both his character and his words. His character must be disciplined by godly integrity. Such integrity will ensure that his words will become law to him. In other words, they are binding and cannot be changed; therefore, they must be properly carried out in whatever has been said or agreed upon.

As you consider what Jesus was saying in His sermon on the mount, you discover that man must not swear by those things that he has no power over. Man's simple statement about a matter should be enough. After all, covenants were not made because a man such as Abraham was dishonorable with his words, but because the parties involved were stipulating their responsibilities towards each other to ensure that a peaceful environment co-existed between them.

Jesus instructed people to simply say, "yes" or "no," and to avoid making an oath based on something they have no power to control. For example, man cannot control God, heaven, or earth. The credibility of our words should never be based on something over which we have no

[7] Matthew 5:33-37

power. Such an oath points to actually committing fraud because the real resolve is missing to bring it forth. As a result, man is trying to bind himself to do what is right or honorable by swearing according to something that is real or has power such as heaven. However, the credibility of our words must be based on the fact that we have the means and the resolve to keep them. Therefore, there is no need to take an oath about a situation to prove our intent. In the environment of integrity, it is already done in our minds, and the resolve is present in our hearts to carry it out.

This brings us to the final aspect of God's covenant with us. We will have the means to keep our part of the covenant. God never made a covenant with man that he did not have the means to keep. Man's responsibilities to maintain the right environment were clearly outlined by God in each covenant. However, many failed to see the need to maintain such agreements. As a result, they became covenant breakers, bringing judgment upon themselves.

God's covenant stands as a place of law. It is there to influence, guide, and affect our lives and conduct before Him and with each other. For the Christian, we are not only part of a new and better covenant, but God has also put the means within us to carry out our responsibility in this agreement. We are given insight into what way God has enabled us to keep our part of this pact in Hebrews 10:15-19. Meditate upon these Scriptures, and see what God has provided in order for you and me to experience the fullness of this glorious new covenant.

And the Holy Ghost also is a witness to us: for after that he had said before, This is the covenant that I will make with them after those days, saith the Lord: I will put my laws into their hearts, and in their minds will I write them, And their sins and iniquities will I remember no more. Now where remission of these is, there is no more offering for sin. Having therefore, brethren, boldness to enter into the holiest by the blood of Jesus.

3

THE PLACE OF INTENT

One of the major aspects about covenants is that they truly show the intent of those who make them. Intent represents the purpose of something.[1] Purpose points to the level of determination of a person. We are told that the prophet Daniel purposed in his heart to do right before God, even in the matters of the food he would partake of.[2]

Intent also represents the state of mind in which an act is done. This state points to the will area where a person will carry out a matter under his or her own volition. With such an emphasis there will be great intensity. In other words, the person will have the attention, concentration, or resolve to carry out a matter regardless of the personal cost. After all, he or she has attached significance or importance to the situation.[3]

Another important facet of intent is that it has been clearly formulated or planned.[4] Intention serves as a goal of something that is clearly being aimed at. It has an objective in mind since it has been considered and planned out. As you can see, true intentions will never prove to be idle like false promises that are often handed out by people. Such idle words may be emotional, sentimental, or a means to get people off of a person's back, but they have no real intent behind them to see a matter through to the end.

Sadly, this is the reality of many of the promises people make to one another. They have no real intent behind them. Intent indicates the type of quality of one's character in a matter. This is why broken words or promises end up standing idle, while they clearly expose the absence of the necessary character or resolve to back them up. In other words, the person had no real intention of carrying out such agreement or promises. Without the intention present, a person is basically defrauding someone.

---

[1] Webster's New Collegiate Dictionary

[2] Daniel 1:8

[3] Webster's New Collegiate Dictionary

[4] Ibid

Fraud represents one of the many false ways in which people walk, proving to be unfaithful and treacherous. In fraud, the situation is being perverted by presenting false impressions or intentions. As the saying goes, "The way to hell is paved with good intentions." This is why Jesus stated that every idle word that is spoken will be judged, and that we should keep our commitment towards others to a simple yes or no.[5]

Viable intentions also speak of people's motivation. In Christian terms, motivation points to the type of spirit in which a person will be operating. Without the motivation, there will be no real intent or resolve to carry out a matter. People may have some kind of goal in mind, but they have no real resolve to carry it out because the spirit or motive is missing. The reason for this is because such individuals do not deal in reality. These people deal in grandiose ideas, where in their daydreaming, life is either bowing down to them or falling into their lap. However, there is no connection being made to their present situation. People who operate in such a false way often suffer from anger and depression. As they wait for their fantasy or dream to fall into their lap, life with its lessons and opportunities passes them by, leaving them in depression or despair.

It is okay to have dreams as long as people realize that it will take genuine intent to connect them to such desires. Simply put, they must work towards such dreams by paying the necessary price to secure them. This is how dreams become a reality. People must connect to their present reality, design a plan according to the opportunities that are available, and begin to walk it out in every-day experiences.

This brings us to covenant. God's covenants reveal His intent towards man. Jeremiah 29:11 gives us this insight into God's intention towards us, "For I know the thoughts that I think toward you, saith the LORD, thoughts of peace, and not of evil, to give you an expected end." God clearly knows His intention towards His people. It is for peace, not evil. Therefore, as His children, we can be confident as to the end result of His commitment towards us.

As previously stated, God did not have to make covenants with His people. He is true to His word, and He has nothing to prove. However, He did make covenants with those who are His that would be passed down from generation to generation. In these covenants people learned about His purpose in regard to their very lives. To understand the covenants, we must understand the purpose or the expected end that such covenants intended to bring about in a matter.

We must remember that there is a plan in operation in regard to our lives. Proverbs 20:18 tells us every purpose is established by counsel. We know that our expected end was established in the actual courts of

---

[5] Psalm 119:128; Matthew 5:37; 12:36-37; 1 Thessalonians 4:6-7

heaven. It was a plan that was present before the foundations of the world.

What was the plan? It has to do with peace. When Adam rebelled against God in the garden, man became alienated from God. God's plan was to bring man back into reconciliation with Him. Twenty centuries ago the plan was actually implemented when Jesus came into our midst. He would carry out the very plan of the Father by paying the necessary price for our separation from Him. In so doing, He Himself would become the bridge that would once again bring about peace between God and man by bringing reconciliation into this broken relationship. The Apostle Paul summarized this plan in Ephesians 2:12-16, when he stated that we were far off from God, but were made near to Him by the blood of Jesus. Jesus became our peace by breaking down the middle wall of partition and abolishing the enmity that existed between God and man, as well as the Jews and Gentiles. Then, Paul makes this statement in Ephesians 2:16-17, "And that he might reconcile both unto God in one body by the cross, having slain the enmity thereby, And came and preached peace to you who were afar off, and to them that were nigh."

It is obvious, that God connected His plan of redemption with the reality of our pathetic plight while we were in our doomed state of sin. It was His aim to bring forth the eternal purpose of our salvation. Every work, intervention, and covenant with His people had this one purpose in mind. However, it cost Him dearly, for it cost Him His only begotten Son. It cost Jesus His life, but the connection between lost man and God was brought forth. As a result, it ushered in a new covenant based on redemption. This covenant would allow people to experience this incredible peace by becoming children of God, as well as being placed in one Body that would express the life of Christ.[6]

God's intent allows us to see His determination to do the impossible. In Isaiah 14:27, the question was posed as to who could annul God's purpose or who could turn it back once God puts a matter into motion. We know God will keep His covenant, but it will be based on the environment that is present. The environment is often determined by man's own spiritual condition.

Granted, God has the power to do the impossible, but it would require man's willingness to ensure that it was fulfilled within his particular life or generation. Moses was the great deliverer of the people of Israel out of Egypt, but we must note that they were crying out in desperation for such deliverance. If they were not desperate the environment would have not been conducive for such deliverance to take place.

Obviously, the state of mind must be present in man for God to reveal His state of mind towards His people. The Apostle Paul wrestled

---

[6] John 1:12; Ephesians 3:9-12

over the state of mind in regard to the people of Israel. He made this statement in Romans 9:3-5,

> For I could wish that I myself were accursed from Christ for my brethren, my kinsmen according to the flesh, Who are Israelites; to whom pertaineth the adoption, and the glory, and the covenants, and the giving of the law, and the service of God, and the promises; Whose are the fathers, and of whom, as concerning the flesh, Christ came, who is over all, God blessed forever. Amen.

Paul recognized God's intention towards the people of Israel. After all, the purpose of God was revealed through them. Christ had come forth out of Israel. The people of Israel had all things that pertained to God's glorious promises available to them, yet salvation eluded them. Paul mourned that he could not stand accursed in their place. However, the truth is Jesus already had stood accursed in their place, and many still refused to recognize the gift of salvation.[7]

As we follow God through His covenants with man, we can clearly see the attention to detail He put upon them. We also can note the concentration and resolve that has been clearly put forth through history to bring forth His plan. The fact that He gave His Son to secure and bring about His eternal purpose shows what kind of importance or significance He actually attached to His eternal plan.

For Christians, an inheritance was attached to the new covenant to bring out its significance and magnitude. The reason this significance has been attached to eternal life is because we as believers have been predestinated according to God's purpose to fulfill a high calling that clearly speaks of this incredible life. While we deal in this present world according to the calling upon our lives, we do so in light of an incredible inheritance that is awaiting us. We are also informed that He works all things after the counsel of His own will.[8]

In some cases, His covenants with man revealed the intensity of His intention towards each of us. When you consider that God made covenants that simply bound Him to the work of redemption to confirm the quality behind His devotion and commitment to bring about this plan of redemption, you can see that it was clearly highlighted.

In the covenant with creation, God resolved to never destroy the world again with water. He was making a promise to all creation. In the case of Abraham, He made the covenant without any agreement, sign, or token from Abraham. Granted, by faith Abraham had to leave his former life, but it was for the purpose of witnessing from afar off the covenant that God wanted to bring forth through his seed. The purpose

---

[7] Galatians 3:10

[8] Romans 8:28; Ephesians 1:11

of the agreement was to bring forth the Messiah out of Abraham's loins to secure the plan of redemption.[9]

The reason God could entrust Abraham with this covenant was because he possessed the right inward environment in which faith could be established and brought forth in child-like confidence. Genuine faith will simply respond to God's instruction so He can bring about a matter. In fact, it is genuine faith that allows God the liberty to do the impossible, as well as allow those who possess it to see into the future as far as God fulfilling His end of the agreement. This was true for Abraham. Jesus said of him that he rejoiced to see His visitation, and actually saw it in the representation of the great patriarch presenting his son Isaac as a burnt offering on Mount Moriah.[10]

Genuine faith also recognizes what is important and will cling to it. Acts 11:23 gives us this insight, "Who, when he came, and had seen the grace of God, was glad, and exhorted them all, that with purpose of heart they would cleave unto the Lord." The "he" in this Scripture speaks of Barnabas when he came to Antioch to witness the grace of God in operation. Grace reigns through righteousness, and righteousness is counted or reckoned to those who walk by faith.[11]

Barnabas exhorted those at Antioch to purpose in their hearts to cling to the Lord. The heart reminds us that it is the springboard of our affections. Therefore, our affections must be set upon the Lord in order to possess the sincere confidence of child-like faith towards Him. We are told that faith operates according to love.[12] In fact, without love the trust factor and the faithfulness will be missing in relationships and agreements. Without the character of faithfulness, the intent will not be there to carry out any agreements or promises.

Hence, enters the Apostle Paul's promise concerning God's purpose towards those who are His, "And we know that all things work together for good to them that love God, to them who are the called according to his purpose" (Romans 8:28). As believers we can only be assured that God's purpose will be fulfilled according to His calling upon our lives because we love Him. According to the Romans 8:29 this calling has to do with taking on the life or very likeness of Jesus.

Without genuine love there is no real motivation to carry out a purpose in a matter. Such love reminds us of John 3:16, "For God so loved the world, that he gave his only begotten Son, that whosoever believeth in him should not perish, but have everlasting life." God's intention towards us was carried out by His love.

---

[9] Genesis 12:1-4

[10] Genesis 22; John 8:56

[11] Proverbs 4:23; Romans 4:3, 9; 5:21

[12] Galatians 5:6; Colossians 3:1-2

It is vital to realize that a covenant represents a place of intent. We do not have to guess what God's intentions are towards us. He has clearly outlined them according to His plan of redemption. He has resolved in the past to carry this purpose out by establishing covenants with those who are prepared to walk by faith towards His ultimate goal. He has verified the character of His intentions by an outward display of sacrificial love.

The writer of Hebrews put it best when he stated, "How shall we escape, if we neglect so great salvation, which at the first began to be spoken by the Lord, and was confirmed unto us by them that heard him" (Hebrews 2:3)? Clearly, we will not escape the terrible judgment that will come upon those who refuse to believe and embrace the plan of redemption.

What about you? Have you come to this place of intent as a means to reveal your loving, faithful intentions towards our precious Lord? Even though God has bound Himself to His covenants, we still must come to the place of intent regarding His eternal plan in order to embrace His loving commitment by faith.

4

THE PLACE OF IDENTIFICATION

We have been considering how covenant represents the place of the law as to the authority, wisdom, and righteousness behind those clearly established by God. We also have seen God's intent or purpose regarding mankind in His covenants. God has not hidden His desire, design, or purpose from His people. He has meant what He said, and He has made His purpose behind such agreements known. There is no excuse for people being ignorant about His desire towards them.

This brings us to the next aspect of covenant. It serves as a place of identification. People are lost. They are lost for three reasons. First, they do not know why they are here. Most individuals see themselves as corks floating on the ocean of the world. They are driven by the different winds of influences and decisions that blow upon them from unseen powers. They see themselves consumed by the endless challenges of the different seasons of change that leave them more uncertain about their resolve to survive the extreme conditions that life can send their way.

As people feel themselves being blown around on the ocean of life, it all appears to be useless. All fleshly attempts leave them empty. Worldly accomplishments simply represent a pinnacle that reminds them of how temporary such accomplishments are. After all, life must go on. It cannot remain caught up with one great moment.

Moments always materialize into minutes that will add up to hours. Hours mark one day that eventually will multiply into years. Life goes on, occasionally allowing people a moment to glory in an occasional accomplishment, but after that, it is time to resume in the journey of life in spite of the temporary moments of ecstasy.

Moments of ecstasy will become memories that serve as simple highlights that will mark a particular time in life. Sadly, for some people these moments are not highlights of their life, but the defining moments as to the essence of their present life.

I am sure you have met people who live off of a few highlights of their past, and as a result, they have never matured. They remember that great touchdown they made in high school. Or, perhaps they were a popular cheerleader who was pursued after by the opposite sex. I cannot tell you how many former cheerleaders now blend into the rest of humanity. They no longer stand out, nor are they hotly pursued.

I have also met guys who shined on the basketball court or the football field. Some of these men are now in rescue missions, entangled into the dark world of substance abuse. Angry, disillusioned, and lost, those past moments of glory now mock them.

The second reason people are lost is because they do not know who they are. They are often defined by the influences around them. Their likes and dislikes are based mainly on the culture they grew up in. Their prejudices are aligned to their family's attitudes. The philosophies they maintain are inspired by the type of society, religion, or education that surrounded them. Each influence represented a different avenue in which the matters of life were considered or pursued. However, each of these pursuits usually lead to disappointment, disillusionment, and emptiness.

The final reason people are lost is because they have no real sure purpose in which they can be assured of making a mark on this world. In short, they have not come to terms with their potential. People set goals, but if they do pursue them and manage to reach them, they discover there are other mountains that must be explored and climbed. In other words, goals give a person something to aim at, but each mountain or challenge that is encountered when one is pursuing such goals realistically reveals that there is so much more that can be discovered or accomplished.

In this present world, no one really arrives at their ultimate height of growth or accomplishment. Records can always be broken, and the terrain is constantly changing around us to the point that it always presents new challenges.

Due to these different challenges of life, people find themselves lost in all of it. Who are they; why are they here, and how can they make sense out of this life? Such questions often leave people tormented as they struggle with the meaning and purpose of life.

As you follow God's covenants in the Bible, you realize they are meant to answer these questions concerning life. In fact, they serve as a place of identification. This is quite apparent in the case of the covenant that God made with Abraham.

It has always interested me that God would actually introduce Himself before He reaffirmed His covenant with Abraham, Isaac, and Jacob. In Genesis 17:1, He appeared to Abram (Abraham) and introduced Himself as the Almighty God. God introduced Himself to Isaac as the God of Abraham in Genesis 26:24. When Jacob encountered God at Bethel in Genesis 28:13, the Lord introduced Himself as The LORD God of Abraham, and the God of Isaac.

As we will discuss in a future chapter, the names of God are important when it comes to the place where He must reside in man's life. Notice how with Abraham God reminded him that He is all-powerful. He is able to bring forth His covenant. With Isaac, God reminded him that He was indeed the God, Creator of all he could see. It was He whom his father Abraham worshipped and followed. With Jacob, He emphasized that He was Jehovah, Creator that served as Lord to Abraham, and that was also the God that his father, Isaac worshipped.

It is also important to point out that before God stressed who He was to each of these men, He used the term "I AM." We have already discussed how this term points to the fact that God is ever present in all matters concerning His eternal plan and work. He is not subject to time.

This brings us to Moses. God simply introduced Himself to the people of Israel as the "I AM THAT I AM." No doubt Moses knew of Abraham's relationship with God. The stories of how the Creator of the universe intruded into the life of Abraham were probably widely known by the Hebrew people. After all, their very hope as a people rested on Abraham's encounter with God. Their identity and existence was a matter of God honoring His words to Abraham. As God told Isaac, He was intruding into his life for the sake of Abraham.[1] Clearly, Isaac was experiencing the grace of God because of Abraham's relationship with his Creator.

Now Moses was encountering God in the wilderness. God's very introduction as the "I AM" no doubt became a revelation to Moses' very spirit. This is how God began His introduction to Abraham, Isaac, and Jacob. And, this "I AM' was intruding into Moses' life in the wilderness, to send him forth as His mouthpiece to the children of Israel.

God went on to instruct Moses to explain to the children of Israel that the "I AM" that was sending him forth was the LORD God of their fathers, the God of Abraham, the God of Isaac, and the God of Jacob.[2] The term "fathers" pointed to the great patriarchs of faith in relationship to Jehovah, Lord of all who was their Creator and Maker of all they beheld.

This Lord is the God that sent Abraham forth after making a covenant with him to make his descendants into a great nation. He is the God of Isaac who reaffirmed this covenant. And, He is the God of Jacob, father of the twelve sons from which the nation of Israel was brought forth.

It is important to realize that the covenants that God made always begin with who He is. These covenants represented the impossible.

---

[1] Genesis 26:3-5; Exodus 3:14

[2] Exodus 3:15

However, nothing is too great for Almighty God. Jehovah God is Lord over all. As God, He is in control of the elements, the circumstances, and the matters of life and heaven.

The LORD God alone holds this place. There is no God before Him, beside Him, or after Him. He is Lord over all and God of all. And, He is the one who chose Abraham to do His bidding. He was the One who picked the children of Israel up out of slavery as if they were on the wings of an eagle, and carried them to Himself, eventually guiding them to the land He promised Abraham.[3]

Twenty centuries ago, another voice was heard. This voice introduced Himself as the "I AM." Each introduction as the "I AM" was followed by a simple revelation of Himself to those who would but hear His voice and believe. "I AM" the bread, the good shepherd, the door, the vine, the light, the way, the truth, the life, and the resurrection to name a few of the revelations He voiced in His three-year ministry.[4] At one point He stated: "Verily, verily, I say unto you, Before Abraham was, I am" (John 8:58b).

This man's name was Jesus. The great prophets had introduced Him as the Branch that would make His entrance into the world. Isaiah 9:6 also introduced Him as Wonderful, Counselor, The Mighty God, The everlasting Father, and The Prince of Peace. Many of the Jewish people of Jesus' day understood that He was identifying Himself as the great "I AM" that introduced Himself to Abraham and Moses. They even tried to stone Him for such claims, for they considered them grave blasphemy.[5]

The great "I AM" was establishing not only who He was, but who man needed to be to experience the benefit of His covenant. Abraham had to believe God in order to find his place. At one point, God became Abraham's shield and exceedingly great reward, defining that his real identity and purpose was based on his Creator.[6] As God took His rightful place in Abraham's life, the patriarch's purpose became more defined and his real destination more assured.

King David understood that God was the portion of his real inheritance. He understood that as his portion, real inheritance, or allotment, God maintained the quality of his life.[7] Asaph declared that God was the strength of his heart, and would serve as his portion forever. In the longest psalm in the Bible, it was affirmed that the Lord served as His people's true portion. As their portion, they should be inspired to keep His words.[8]

---

[3] Exodus 19:4; Isaiah 43:10-11; 44:6, 8, 24; 45:5, 18, 21-22

[4] John 6:35; 10:11; 11:25; John 14:6

[5] Isaiah 4:2; 11:1-2; Jeremiah 23:5; 33:15: Zechariah 3:8; 6:12; John 8:58-59

[6] Genesis 15:1

[7] Strong's Concordance, #2506

[8] Psalm 16:5; 73:26; 119:57

As Christians, we are aware that we have a spiritual inheritance that clearly identifies us to our place and purpose in the kingdom of God. Since Jesus needs to be the bread to every believer, we as believers need to become the salt that brings flavor and distinction to the life He is offering others. As our Shepherd, we are His sheep. As the narrow Way, we must become the sojourner and pilgrim in this world. We must seek His truth, discover His life, and possess His resurrection power. Obviously, Jesus is the essence of our spiritual inheritance.[9]

It is not unusual for people to desire a physical inheritance. But those who are of the household of faith realize that their true inheritance is unseen, and will be fully realized in the next world. James put it best when he stated, "Hearken, my beloved brethren, Hath not God chosen the poor of this world to be rich in faith and heirs of the kingdom which he hath promised to them that love him" (James 2:5)? Jesus explained that the poor in His kingdom are those who are truly poor in spirit.[10] These wretched souls recognize their spiritual plight, and are humbled by their need for God's intervention on their behalf. As a result, they are able to discover their place, identity, and purpose in their new, blessed life in Jesus.

Whether we are considering the Old or New Testament, the message remains the same. No one person can find any real semblance, purpose, or meaning to life outside of God. Granted, many are trying to find or acquire some type of life outside of their Creator, but they end up lost and in total despair over the type of existence they experience.

What about you? Where, what, or who are you looking to, to find or acquire life? If you are not seeking out the real God of the Bible, the real essence and purpose of life will elude you.

---

[9] Ephesians 1:11-14

[10] Matthew 5:3

5

THE PLACE OF REMEMBRANCE

One of the reasons I appreciated studying the covenants is because I have discovered greater depths of God's character. So many people affiliated with Christian denominations do not really know God. They know *about* God's capabilities to bring about the impossible. They know *of* His love for the people of the world, but they do not *know* His character. They do not realize that He works according to His character, and that His perfect will testifies about the integrity of who He is.

As a result of people's ignorance towards the God of the Bible, they have failed to develop genuine faith towards Him. How can you trust someone you really do not know? How can you consecrate your total life to someone who you have not developed any real confidence towards? This is why the prophet Daniel, under the inspiration of the Spirit, penned these words in Daniel 11:32c, "...but the people that do know their God shall be strong, and do exploits."

This brings us back to God's covenants. They serve as a place of remembrance. It is important to point out that God does not forget. Granted, He chooses not to remember our sins once they have been addressed by the sacrifice of Jesus.[1] However, choosing not to remember and forgetting are two different states of mind.

Choosing not to remember is a matter of the will. God wills that He will no longer remember those sins that have been removed by Jesus' death on the cross (because His blood cleanses us of sin), in His burial (the sins He took upon Himself remained in the grave of judgment), and because of His resurrection (representing the victory of the new life over the old). He will never allow these sins to become an offence to Him again. As Psalms 103:12 reminds us, "As far as the east is from the west, so far hath he removed our transgressions from us."

Since He is always present and all-knowing, His covenants are always before Him. He is in a state of readiness to bring them forth when the environment is conducive to do so. Once the environment is in place, He chooses to bring the covenant center stage to bring about a matter. If

[1] Hebrews 10:10-18

He recalls something in this manner it is never for His benefit, but for His people's benefit.[2] As a result, His covenants serve as a place of remembrance for His people.

To remember something implies recalling a matter to mind or bringing attention or consideration to it. When God entrusted Moses to bring the children of Israel out of Egypt, He recalled the covenant with Abraham to cause Moses to understand the premise and purpose for Him delivering the people out of such bondage. For the sake of Abraham, God was indeed delivering the people of Israel out of Egypt to take them to the Promised Land. Clearly, God was about to show Himself mighty on behalf of the children of Israel by honoring His covenant with the great patriarch.

Obviously, it is man who so easily forgets a matter. After all, in his limited state, he must contend with the demands of life that often cause him to become consumed with the things of the world. He is bombarded by challenges that cause the real matters of life to become dim or dull to the memory. He is often depressed with the quality of his existence, which causes him to develop select memory. In other words, if a particular memory does not serve his purpose or placates his desired reality, he can easily forget any obligations, agreements, or responsibilities that are attached to it. Such forgetfulness comes down to the type of significance or importance that has been put on an agreement or situation. By deeming a matter as being insignificant or unimportant, one can actually bury, ignore, or delete it from the memory.

The harsh reality we must face is what many of us do with the matters of God. I remember watching two women make an agreement with a church about their responsibilities towards it. This was all in exchange for the church to support them in their overseas missionary endeavors. These women made a verbal agreement, but they put no real significance on it. They were going through the motions so they could go on the missionary trip. No doubt, in light of the trip, the agreement with the pastor of the church seemed silly or insignificant to these women. However, it was serious business to the people of the church, and when these two women showed no regard to their verbal commitment, they lost much credibility. The message they sent is that the only thing this particular church was good for was to use to enable them to go on their missionary trip. Their agreement amounted to nothing more than idle words where these two women were concerned.

The matters of God can become lost in the midst of the demands of the world, personal agendas, and self-serving pursuits. As a result, God must often bring about circumstances that will stir up the memory in regard to Him. This is why man is instructed to remember. The children of Israel were exhorted to remember such things as their humble

---

[2] Leviticus 26:42-45

beginnings as servants in Egypt, the covenants, the commandments, their deliverance, and to remember their God along with His marvelous works and His character.[3]

As Christians, we must also choose to remember. The Apostle Peter talked about those who were barren in the knowledge of Jesus. One of the reasons for such barrenness was because such people became blind and could not see afar off. He goes on to explain that they had forgotten that they were purged from their old sins. He wanted to always bring to remembrance such things to establish the believers in the present truth of Christ. Peter's simple goal was to stir them up by causing them to remember.[4]

God chooses to remember, while men conveniently forget to remember. God is quick to bring the matters of eternity that are before Him to a fruitful place. However, men are quick to let such matters recede into the furthest recesses of their mind. There, they bury them under what they consider to be the more important matters of life. Even though what is taking the back seat in their lives involves eternity, they feel that the present issues take precedence over the eternal, and feel quite excused from keeping them center stage. They console themselves by reminding themselves that they intend to come back to such matters, but eventually they fall out of the habit of even considering them. Such a state represents complacency and indifference towards God.

As a result, man must be stirred up to remember. As you study covenants, you will see how God instituted tokens or practices that would bring His covenants to the forefront of His people's minds. Of course, they would have to be reminded as to the purpose or reasoning for such tokens or practices.

To understand some of the practices that identified people to a covenant, we must go back to the initial concept of covenant. According to Ruth Specter Lascelle, some supposed that the root meaning of the Hebrew word for "covenant" contained the idea of cutting. Cutting of this nature points to some type of division or separation.[5]

We see a certain cutting away from the ties Abraham had to his old life when God called him forth to journey to the land that He promised to his descendants. Clearly, Abraham's seed was being set apart by God to bring forth the blessing of redemption.[6]

In the case of Abraham's sacrifice in Genesis 15, we can witness both the cutting and division or separation. Abraham was struggling with

---

[3] Numbers 15:40-41; Deuteronomy 5:15; 7:18-23; 1 Chronicles 16:11-12; Nehemiah 4:14; Psalm 20:7

[4] 2 Peter 1:8-9, 11-12

[5] Jewish Faith and the New Covenant © 1980 by Ruth Specter Lascelle, pg. 81

[6] Genesis 12:1-3

the covenant God made with him because he had no heirs. God instructed Abraham, who was still called Abram, to look at the stars in the heavens, and know that his seed would be as numerous as the stars. Abraham believed God. Then, Abraham asked for a confirmation or sign that his seed would inherit the land promised to him.

The Lord instructed Abraham to take certain animals for sacrifice. He was required to take the sacrificial animals, except for the birds, and divide them in the middle. Abraham waited before the Lord as he drove away the fowls from partaking of the carcasses. After all, these offerings were consecrated totally to God.

When the sun went down, Abraham fell into a deep sleep. It was in this state that God revealed the future of Abraham's seed. They would not only sojourn in a land that would not be theirs (Egypt), but they would serve as slaves in this land until the fourth generation, or for four hundred years. It would take this many generations for the iniquity of the Amorites to come to maturity. This simply meant that the Amorites, who possessed the Promised Land, would be ripe for judgment at that time.

The other important factor to this prophecy is that Abraham's seed would make up a nation of people that would be able to establish a kingdom within the Promised Land. Keep in mind that when the great patriarch, Israel, came to Egypt with his family, there were only 70 descendants of Abraham. Even in spite of being strangers and slaves in a foreign land, God kept the seed of Abraham separate as his descendants multiplied in an oppressive environment. God clearly allowed Abraham to see that He would keep the covenant He made with him. Generations later God would bring his many descendants into the Promised Land.

This brings us back to the tokens and practices that were used to remind people of God's covenants. We already know about one such token, the rainbow. The rainbow reminds us of the everlasting covenant God made with all of creation. We know that He will never again destroy the earth through the judgment of water. However, it is noteworthy to remember that Noah first built an altar and made a sacrifice to the Lord before God blessed Noah and his sons, and made this covenant with all of creation. Noah's sacrifice represented cutting, and God making a covenant pointed to separation or distinction as to which judgment would be reserved for the future in regards to the world.[7]

Let us now consider Abraham. What token or practice signified the covenant that God made with Him? It was circumcision. God told Abraham that He would establish an everlasting covenant with him and his seed. He instructed Abraham that he and his descendants needed to keep the covenant by circumcising every male among them; hence entered the process of cutting and separation. The foreskin was cut as a

[7] Genesis 8:20-22; 9:12-16; 2 Peter 3:7-11

symbol of God's design to separate His people from those around them, unto Himself.[8]

It is important to understand that by keeping the covenant, one is simply honoring his or her part in it. Therefore, if a Jewish male was not properly circumcised, he would be breaking this covenant with God. This is why Moses almost lost his very life when he failed to do his fatherly duties by circumcising his sons.

God had just reminded Moses that Israel belonged to Him. Circumcision was the mark that visibly set the people of Israel apart as God's special people. Cutting the foreskin not only showed that they were being set apart from the defilement around them and were being consecrated to God, but it also served as His mark of ownership upon them as His people.

In Deuteronomy 10:16-17, God also gives insight that circumcision pointed to another cutting away of the foreskin. In fact, physical circumcision was to point to man's need to be spiritually circumcised to truly belong to God, and to properly be set apart for Him. Consider the area of our inner man that must be circumcised, "Circumcise, therefore, the foreskin of your heart, and be no more stiff-necked. For the LORD your God is God of gods, and Lord of lords, a great God, a mighty, and a terrible, who regardeth not persons, nor taketh reward."

To truly belong to God, He must own our hearts. To insist on separation or consecration to God, He must be our God and Lord. This requires a spiritual circumcision of the heart, where the attachments of the rights of self and the world are cut away from having any inroad into our lives, allowing us to align our affections towards the throne of God. We must be solely committed to Him in every area of our lives.

The Apostle Paul also speaks of this spiritual circumcision. This circumcision is made without hands. It actually puts off the body of the sins of the members of the Church by the circumcision of Christ. Christ's circumcision on our behalf happened on His way to Calvary. It is by becoming identified with Christ in His circumcision that we are made alive unto God. Such circumcision separates us from having any real confidence in the flesh. It allows us to worship God in the Spirit and truth, and to have the liberty to rejoice in our lives in Christ Jesus.[9]

As a Jewish man, Moses' failure to circumcise his sons was breaking the covenant with God. It was a grave dishonor towards God and flippancy on the part of Moses to not recognize the Lord's ownership and mark of distinction. Even Moses' wife seemed to understand the seriousness of circumcising their sons more than Moses did, and

---

[8] Genesis 17:6-14

[9] Philippians 3:3; Colossians 2:11-13

rightfully called him a "bloody" husband.[10] The term "bloody" pointed to the fact that Moses was guilty of something that was worthy of death.[11]

There were also clear tokens, practices or signs to remind the children of Israel about their responsibilities towards the covenant of the Law. When most people think of covenant, they think in terms of the two main covenants: The Old Testament (covenant) of the Law and the New Testament (covenant) of Christ. However, there were other equally important covenants that God made with individuals such as David.

The practices that serve as reminders in the Law are interesting to consider as to what type of distinction they were to bring, not only to the Law, but to the people of Israel. One of the greatest practices of the covenant that was meant to remind Israel of their purpose and identity was the shedding of the blood of innocent animals. There would be no purging or remitting of sins without the shedding of blood. The blood was to remind God's people of the cost of sin, as well as point to the ultimate sacrifice of Jesus Christ.[12]

Another important token of the Old Testament covenant was salt. Salt seasoned the different offerings, especially in the case of the meal offering. The meal offering was considered the most holy of the five offerings presented by the priests. It was to serve as a memorial to God as its sweet fragrance of frankincense reached the throne of heaven.[13]

This meal offering represented the purity and unleavened sacrifice of Christ as the Bread of life on the altar of the cross. This offering was salted, representing cost, value, and purity. Salt was a priceless commodity to these people. It was a valuable antidote to combat the affects of heat upon man and beast, as well as bringing flavor to food.[14]

The New Testament reminds us as believers that we are the salt of the world. Our lives are salted by the very life of Christ that is being established in us. We recognize the cost of Jesus' sacrifice, thereby, striving to bring value to the kingdom of God as we walk in the purity of His wisdom, righteousness, sanctification, and redemption. In His power we will combat the fires of hell with the Gospel, and we will offer necessary healing by standing for His truth.

Another important practice that was to cause the children of Israel to stand distinct was for them to observe the Sabbath. The Sabbath was to remind the children of Israel that they were delivered from the bondage of Egypt. They were to recall their humble beginnings and God's glorious deliverance. In fact, it was to serve as a sign between God and the

---

[10] Exodus 4:22-26

[11] Strong's Concordance, #1818

[12] Exodus 24:8; Hebrews 9:11-22

[13] Leviticus 2

[14] Smith's Bible Dictionary; Thomas Nelson Publishers

people of Israel that they had been set apart or sanctified by Jehovah God. The intent of the Sabbath was to serve as a day of rest from all worldly demands and learn how to enjoy God. For Christians, the Sabbath points to their real place of rest: Jesus Christ.[15]

The other token that reminded the Jewish men of the covenant were the fringes in the borders of their garments.[16] In the days when the Law was established, the men customarily wore a robe called a Tallith, which they wrapped around themselves. Due to the customs, the Jewish men eventually limited the wearing of the Tallith to the synagogue and during prayer. Today, the Jewish men wear what is considered a prayer shawl that is usually made of silk.[17]

The fringes are located on the Tallith or prayer shawl. These fringes remind the Jewish men of the covenant of the Law. There are 613 laws that make up the covenant of the Law. According to the anatomical belief of the Talmudic era, these laws had been broken down to 248 positive commandments, which correspond to 248 parts of the human body, and 365 negative commandments that correspond to the 365 sinews of the human body.[18]

This brings us to the fringes. The word for fringes in Hebrew is "Tzitzith." Tzitzith in numerology equals 600. From this point you would consider how each fringe was comprised of eight strands of string bound together by five knots, which total 613. Therefore, when the Jewish people beheld these fringes, they were reminded of the complete Law, which brought them back to their covenant with God.[19]

The written word of God was to always point to His Living Word. The Living Word of God literally manifested Himself in the flesh two thousand years ago. When the woman with the issue of blood grasped hold of Jesus for healing, many believed she actually grabbed the fringes (also known as wings) that were on His prayer shawl. If so, not only was she identifying herself to the covenant God made with His people, but she was also touching the Living Word of God who fulfilled every aspect of the Law. There she would find healing in His wings or fringes. Is it any wonder that Jesus felt the healing power flow from Him to this woman?[20]

The Jewish men also made phylacteries in order to comply with the instructions found in Exodus 13:9, Deuteronomy 6:8, and 11:18. God commanded His people to bind the words of the Law as a sign upon their hands and frontlets between their eyes. These phylacteries, taken from a

---

[15] Exodus 31:13; Matthew 11:28-30

[16] Numbers 15:38-40; Deuteronomy 22:11-12

[17] Jewish Faith and the New Covenant, pg. 49

[18] Ibid, pg. 50

[19] Ibid, pg. 51

[20] Ibid, pg. 55, along with Malachi 4:2; Matthew 9:20; Mark 5:25-34; John 1:1, 14

Greek word which means "to keep safe" or "to preserve," contained Biblical passages that would remind the Jewish men of such things as the twelve tribes of Israel, the sanctification of the first born, deliverance from Egypt, the unity of God, as well as His sacred name, and rewards and punishments. They were worn on the forehead and on the arm.[21]

The phylacteries between the eyes were to remind the Jews to ever keep God and His Law before them, but the one on the arm reminded them who and where their real strength resided. In Jesus' day He rebuked the religious leaders for their broad phylacteries that served as a means of show, but lacked any real personal meaning.[21]

God's instructions about binding the words between the eyes and on the arm pointed to His desire for His Word to be His people's focus and frame of reference. He wanted them to understand that the source of their strength would be found in His Word. The difference between the Old Testament and the New Testament is that in the new covenant, God promised to put His laws into His people's hearts through the presence of His Spirit, and write them upon their minds.[22]

The old covenant was glorious in its revelation of God's holiness and man's need to find his life, deliverance, and salvation in his Creator. It showed man how he must live *before* God. However, the new covenant is greater because it addresses the inward man and shows him how he must live *in* the glorious reality and work of God through Jesus Christ.

This is why the old covenant of the Law was simply a schoolmaster to believers because it pointed people to Jesus Christ. The symbols of the Law served as shadows that outlined Jesus. For example, the covenant of peace God made with Phinehas, the son of Aaron, pointed to the man Christ Jesus who would stand in the gap to ensure peace between man and His God. Due to Jesus' redemption, He not only stands as the Prince of Peace, but He secured the message that would bring peace to all who would believe the Gospel.[23]

In the covenant of peace, God also mentioned the covenant of an everlasting priesthood. Obviously, this points to the priesthood that would be established by the believer's High Priest, Jesus Christ. Hebrews 7:17 says this of the priesthood of Jesus, "For he testifieth, Thou art a priest forever after the order of Melchizedek." As a priest, Phinehas had been zealous in righteousness for the Lord's sake. In John 2:17 we also see the same type of zeal in the case of Jesus when He went into the house of God, and witnessed that it had been made into a den of thieves. He cleansed the temple, and his disciples remembered that it had been

---

[21] Ibid, pg .45

[21] Matthew 23:5

[22] Ezekiel 36:26-27; 2 Corinthians 3:1-3; Hebrews 10:15-16

[23] Numbers 25:11-13; Psalm 68:11; Isaiah 9:6; 52:7; John 14:27; Galatians 3:24; Ephesians 6:15

written in regard to the Promised Messiah that the zeal for God's house had eaten up His strength.

The question is what token or practice have believers been given in regard to the new covenant established by the blood of Jesus? It is called communion. Every time believers take communion, they are remembering that they are part of an everlasting covenant that has been established by the blood of Jesus. His body was broken open by the hatred of man so that His blood could be poured out as the complete payment for our redemption.[24]

The problem with the tokens and practices that have been put in place to remind us of God's covenant is that people do forget why they are observing them. Such practices often become lifeless ceremonies that have no real meaning. Sadly, this attitude can be passed down to others, proving that we have forgotten.

When was the last time you came to the place of remembrance? The last time you took communion did you truly remember what Jesus did for you? In fact, did you see it as a memorial that must not just be marked as some ceremony that has no real meaning or purpose? Did you take the opportunity to choose to remember, ensuring that the memory of Jesus' redemption was real and fresh to you? In fact, was it so real to you that your heart broke in humility, allowing that moment of worship to inspire an attitude of awe in you? Did the awe you felt actually consume you as you truly remembered the covenant that God established through the precious sacrifice of His only begotten Son? Or, have you forgotten because your Christian life has been reduced to a religious exercise that has no real life, meaning, or purpose?

---

[24] 1 Corinthians 11:23-34

6

THE PLACE OF PROMISE

Covenants are actually comprised of promises. Promises are a popular subject for many Christians. Sadly, some do not understand how the promises of God work. The main reason such understanding eludes them is because they do not understand the real character of God.

God has made promises based on His character and eternal plan. For many people, they simply verbally throw His promises before others to look good or pacify someone. However, God has never thrown His promises out in such a manner. They are not to be treated as if they are candy or manna from heaven that His followers can grab up at any time to partake of the blessings that are attached to them. God's promises have a purpose to them.

The problem is that many people treat God's promises as if they were blessings. As previously stated, there are blessings that are either attached to the promises of God or they are to follow those promises. However, promises are not blessings. It is vital that believers make a distinction between these two subjects to keep them in perspective.

According to my *Webster's Dictionary*, a promise is actually a legal binding declaration. It will stipulate a person's rights in a situation. Therefore, the person can live in expectation that a matter will be brought to fruition as long as the conditions are properly observed.

The *Strong's Concordance* points to promise as something that has been spoken concerning a cause, as well as in regard to a particular affair or business dealing. It is also a platform that serves as a means to bid, command, declare, or to make a pronouncement. Such an announcement declares intent, or serves as a means to make a pledge to bring about a situation. In the case of God, a promise serves as a divine assurance.[1]

Blessings are often associated with divine care, prosperity, or that which benefits our well-being.[2] God blesses people so they can live. A wicked person can experience God's blessings in a worldly way. However, His blessings towards the unsaved allow them to see His

---

[1] OT: #1696 & 1697; NT: #1860

[2] Strong's Exhaustive Concordance of the Bible; OT: 1293; NT: 2129

goodness so that they will recognize their need for Him. If these individuals fail to come to God, these blessings will naturally be heaped upon personal pursuits to feed fleshly lust, causing these blessings to turn into curses, a form of judgment. As we consider these two different avenues of promises and blessings, we must recognize they have different purposes.[3]

God delights in blessing His people with things that will enrich their lives in regard to their spiritual inner well-being. Blessings clearly are to complement our lives. Most people pursue or desire worldly blessings. However, since Christians are called to embrace a spiritual, unseen life that is contrary to the world, they have been allotted spiritual blessings.[4]

Blessings that spiritually benefit God's people will follow His promises. However, promises are conditional. In other words, for a promise to be fulfilled, the conditions of it must be honored. God's covenants are made up of certain promises. However, He cannot honor the promises unless the covenant is being kept.

God will always protect the integrity of His commitment to His people. He will not allow people to improperly use, abuse, neglect, or dishonor His promises. Even though people do not understand why God will not grace their lives with His promises, they can be assured that it is a matter of His mercy.

The more God entrusts to our lives as His people, the greater the level of our accountability to be upright in how we handle such matters. People who misuse, abuse, neglect, or dishonor the matters of God can be assured of judgment, not blessings.

Through the years I have come to understand God's mercy in this very area. I have dealt with people who are quite foolish in their character. Their attitude is that the world owes them certain lifestyles. They often display a slothful disposition and an irresponsible manner. Therefore, if you shower such people with kindness, they will perceive that they actually deserve the blessings that are naturally flowing from benevolence. In their arrogance, they will defile such kindness, robbing the giver of his or her blessing that is attached to such a gesture. These foolish individuals will leave a terrible, bitter taste in your mouth because they remain unclean in their perception, unthankful in their attitude, and wicked in their disposition. In such situations, Jesus' instruction to not cast precious pearls before such individuals (swine) is once again reaffirmed.[5]

These foolish individuals tie your hands because they are untrustworthy when it comes to properly receiving such kindness. This is

---

[3] Psalm 37:16-18; 39:6; Romans 12:14, 20-21

[4] Psalm 109:11-22; Proverbs 10:21-28; Ephesians 1:3

[5] Matthew 7:6

true for God's promises and blessings. Keep in mind that blessings are a matter of God's kindness, while promises are a product of His grace. As His people, we are not worthy to claim either His blessings or promises. However, if we possess a right disposition, attitude, and mind about a matter, God is able to honor His promises in our lives. In fact, in a right state we actually have an assurance and right to benefit from the blessings that His promises will provide for us.

The boundaries that are established within a covenant will ensure the integrity of God's promises within a situation. This brings us to the fact that God's promises are conditional. When God honors His promises, He is showing grace to us. Grace reminds us that God is simply showing us undeserved favor in a situation.

This brings us to the emphasis that is often incorrectly attached to God's promises. The emphasis is on the "idea" of promise and not on the conditions of it. One of my favorite promises that I like to use to drive this point home is found in Romans 8:28, "And we know that all things work together for good to them that love God, to them who are the called according to his purpose."

Most people quote the idea of the promise, "And we know that all things work together for good." However, there are two conditions to this promise. A matter cannot be worked for good unless a person loves God and ensures that the end result lines up to His purpose. If a person lacks love, he or she will not be able to possess the confidence that a situation can prove to be good or beneficial, especially when there is testing, loss, or despair that will unravel and expose weak commitments. James 1:12 confirms this, "Blessed is the man that endureth temptation; for when he is tried, he shall receive the crown of life, which the Lord hath promised to them that love him."

Christians, therefore, must be confident in each situation and circumstance that his or her calling will be established and worked out according to God's purpose. It is when God's purpose is being fulfilled that the blessings attached to the promise will be realized.

As you study each promise, you will begin to see the conditions. In fact, the idea of "if" that preceded Jesus' call to true discipleship can also be seen in line with the concept of promises.[6] *If* we want to see one of God's promises come to fruition, we must meet the requirements that have been clearly set forth in Scripture. And, *if* we care to trace the authority, power, and benefits to the very source of all heavenly promises, we will find a covenant in place.

Hebrews 6:12 summarizes the four main conditions when it comes to possessing God's promises, "That ye be not slothful, but followers of them who through faith and patience inherit the promises." This Scripture

[6] Matthew 16:24

in Hebrews shows us that we must inherit promises. Once again this reminds us that promises are not just for the taking or the claiming. We must come into them by way of possessing the very life of Christ. Inheritance for the Christian points to identification. We must be identified to Jesus. The seal of the Holy Spirit upon our lives spiritually marks and verifies this identification.[7]

The first condition that must be established to inherit our spiritual inheritance is diligence. The Scripture commands believers to not be slothful about the matters of God. We must diligently seek Him if we are going to possess all that He has for us.[8] Sadly, the tendency for most people is to not seek out their Creator to discover their lives. Likewise, Christians can become quite slothful towards the matters of God because they have become half-hearted about spiritual issues.

The second condition is that we must be followers of those who have inherited the promises. We are always taking note of those we expose ourselves to, whether out of friendship, respect, or association. The followers of God exposed themselves to the real matters of heaven. They sought out God in expectation of obtaining His great and precious promises. Although some never witnessed the fruition of such promises, they received the witness of the validity of these promises by faith.[9]

For the Christian, our real example is to follow Jesus. We must follow Him into a new life by way of implementing His example, attitude, and teaching. To do this we must truly become His disciple. After all, a disciple follows the Master into a certain lifestyle. Jesus clearly stipulated that we as His followers must first deny self of its right to reign, pick up our personal cross, and follow Him into this life.

This brings us to the third condition: that of faith. Faith simply believes the promises of God. We see this in the lives of the people of God. Faith in God led Abraham to the Promised Land. Noah's faith caused him to build an ark. Moses' faith caused him to become identified with the suffering of the people of Israel. Rahab's faith resulted in her deliverance from judgment into a new life.[10]

Faith is accounted or reckoned for righteousness. It is in such righteousness that grace will reign in a Christian's life. What does it mean for grace to reign through righteousness? Righteousness points to right standing before God and is expressed in the attitude and conduct of uprightness in which God can show His continual favor to a believer. It allows Him to be God. For this reason, promises are associated with the grace of God that is actually reigning through righteousness. This attitude and standing have been established by unfeigned faith.

---

[7] Ephesians 1:11-14

[8] Hebrews 11:6

[9] Hebrews 11:39; 1 Peter 1:2-9

[10] Hebrews 11:7, 8-10, 24-25, 31

Although, as believers we might be honoring the conditions of God's promises, we still do not deserve His consideration. To honor the matters of God is the least we can do. However, it is God's desire to show such favor or grace to His people. Since faith and its actions are considered righteousness before God, He can honor it with His undeserved favor. We know, according to Peter, that at the end of our faith is salvation.[11] This is why the Apostle Paul made this statement, "For by grace are ye saved through faith; and that not of yourselves, it is the gift of God—Not of works, lest any man should boast" (Ephesians 2:8-9).

The final necessary ingredient to inherit God's promises is patience. Patience is the ability to be long-suffering in a matter. God is long-suffering towards people to give them space to repent.[12] As Christians, patience is the only virtue that will enable us to possess the promises of God. In our instant society, patience is one quality that is often missing.

Patience allows the necessary work to be done in order for a promise to be brought forth. In fact, we know that tribulation is what works the character of patience into us. It enables us to wait in expectation for the promises of God. It allows godly fruit to be developed in us as we are being brought to perfection or maturity. As a result, we as Christians, not only experience in patience the life God has ordained, but it also empowers us to possess our inner man through unfeigned faith.[13]

It is important to note that without diligence, we will fail to follow the examples clearly laid out in Scripture. If we fail to follow, we will never learn what it means to walk by faith in faithful obedience towards the things of God. If we do not walk by faith, we will never develop patience in our character.

This brings us back to promises. God's covenants contain promises that will produce a blessed life of satisfaction. One of the greatest promises given to mankind was that of the Messiah or the Promised One. The promise of the Messiah was attached to a covenant that God made with King David.[14]

In God's covenant with David, He promised him that his seed would sit on the throne of Israel forever. God explained to Solomon the conditions that were attached to the promise of the incredible covenant He had made with his father, David. Solomon would have to walk before God like his father to ensure that the promises of this covenant would be honored through his seed. According to 1 Kings 9:4, we are clearly given insight into David's walk before the Lord. He possessed integrity (godly

[11] Romans 4:3; 5:21; 1 Peter 1:9

[12] 2 Peter 3:9

[13] Luke 8:15; 21:19; Romans 5:3-4; James 1:2-4

[14] 1 Kings 9:4-5; 2 Chronicles 13:5

character) in his heart, was upright in his conduct, and kept God's statutes and judgments.[15]

Sadly, Solomon did not keep the conditions of the promise, thereby, nullifying the covenant. As a result, the throne, along with the kingdom was eventually taken away from Solomon's descendants and given to the descendants of his brother Nathan.[16] We know that Joseph, the stepfather of Jesus, was from the lineage of Solomon. However, if you trace Mary's lineage back in Luke 3:31, you will see that her lineage goes through Nathan, not Solomon. The last true descendants of Solomon, who sat on the throne before Jerusalem fell to Babylon, were taken into captivity where they lived their lives out in foreign lands, far from the throne that had been established in Jerusalem.

We know that the seed of David, who would reign from the throne forever, to be our precious Lord Jesus Christ. Even though Solomon broke the covenant the Lord made with David, God just moved around him, and brought forth His promise of an everlasting king and kingdom through another descendant of David. As a result, we, as believers, greatly benefit from this promise. Our blessing from this covenant is our salvation, which comes through the redemption of our Lord Jesus Christ.

As we study the new covenant established through Jesus' redemption, there are promises that have been outlined in Scripture. These promises are followed by precious blessings that truly benefit the life we have in Christ.

The question is, how do you regard the promises of God? Are you truly possessing them by developing godly character through faith and obedience that will allow the very grace of God to be revealed in His kindness or benevolence? Only you can rightfully answer this question. However, the truth is we are either like King David, who at the end of his life possessed a godly life, or we are like Solomon. He was offered the blessings of the covenant, but because of his idolatrous rebellion, he lost it not only for himself, but also for his descendants!

---

[15] 2 Chronicles 7:17-18

[16] 1 Kings 11:9-13; 1 Chronicles 3:5

7

THE PLACE OF APPROACH

Without a covenant, we cannot rightfully approach God. God approaches man on the basis of His covenant. After all, He wants man to understand His intentions and desires that He possesses towards him. For man, he must approach God on the basis of covenant in order to ensure that he has a right attitude towards God, as well as seek Him in regards to what He desires to accomplish on his behalf, as well as through him.

In order to understand what it means to approach something, we must come to terms with the meaning of "approach." According to my *Webster's Dictionary,* "approach" means to draw close to, and to make advances with the purpose of creating a desired result. Approach points to the preliminary steps toward an accomplishment, or going forward to be located within an approximation of something as a means to gain access or an avenue to a matter.

Obviously, God's preliminary steps toward man are based on covenant. However, the question is will man draw close to God once He makes such advancements towards him? How many times is man instructed to draw near to God in Scripture? When we consider this type of approach, we must recognize that it points to true repentance. One of my favorite Scriptures about drawing near to God is James 4:8, "Draw nigh to God, and he will draw nigh to you. Cleanse your hands, ye sinners; and purify your hearts, ye doubleminded."

The Scripture in James shows us how we are to draw near to God. We are to draw near to Him with clean hands. Hands that touch the unclean things of the world cannot begin to touch the things of God without defiling them. We must purify our hearts. Such purification points to a heart that is singular towards God. Without such a single focus, the heart can become hard as it is blinded by its own obstinacy and unbelief. At this point it becomes a divided heart that proves to be idolatrous.

Hence enters the different types of heart conditions. There is the half-hearted person who lacks vision for God. There is the stony heart that proves to be selfish and self-serving. There is a worldly heart that is hindered by the influences of the world. We could go on and on as to the type of hearts that lack sincere loving devotion towards God, but the reality is that such hearts will always prove to be far away from God. They may claim to love God, but the fruit is missing.

King David talked about how good if was for him to draw near to God. He admitted that he trusted Him, and wanted to declare His wondrous works to others.[1] This shows us David's attitude towards God. He was delighted to encounter his God and rejoice in his works.

God's great desire is to draw near to His people in order to meet with, deliver, and bless them. We know that God actually draws us to Him. Jeremiah 31:3 tells us that God draws His people with loving-kindness. David's request to God was to draw near to his soul and redeem it. Jesus stated that no one could come to Him unless the Father had drawn him or her. In his first epistle, John reminds us that we love Jesus because He first loved us.[2] If God was not drawing us, we would have no real inclination to draw close to Him. Without this drawing God could never meet us at the point of His covenant, ensuring that His purpose would be fulfilled in our lives.

However, the right attitude must be present for people to properly draw near to the Lord. Isaiah brought this out in Isaiah 29:13, when it was revealed that most people draw near to God with lip service, but their hearts remain far away from Him. Jesus also quoted this Scripture in Matthew 15:8. Hebrews 10:22 instructs us to draw near to God with a true heart.

A true heart points to a heart that is established by the full assurance of faith. It has been cleansed by the Word, and walks in complete confidence towards God. Without the heart being true to God, a right attitude will be missing. As a result, God will not be able to draw near to such a person. He or she would not be open enough to properly receive.

Christians must recognize how important their approach is to God. Abraham approached God from the premise of faith. In the case of David, he had a heart that possessed integrity.[3] Not only did he approach God according to his faith, but also like Abraham, he was ready to obey.

Every Christian has one reason to approach God's Word, and that is to believe it. Every saint has one motivation for seeking God's will, and that is to obey it. Every believer has one purpose for serving the Lord, and that is to bring glory to Him.

If the approach is wrong, God will not be able to meet with His people. Consider Moses. God appeared to him in the wilderness. He used a burning bush to get Moses' attention. In other words, Moses had to first turn aside from his normal activities to encounter God. What would God have to do to get us to turn aside from our activities to truly meet with Him?

Once Moses was turned aside to consider the burning bush, God was able to call to him out of the midst of the bush. However, he could

---

[1] Psalm 73:28

[2] Psalm 73:28; John 6:44; 1 John 4:19

[3] 1 Kings 9:4

not draw near until he had removed his shoes. Shoes represent our walk. We are walking through a defiled world that opposes God's reign and rejects His righteous ways. Moses had to first disassociate himself with the world to encounter God.[4]

How did God's encounter with Moses affect his attitude? Moses felt totally undone before the Lord. There was no evidence of self-confidence or self-sufficiency. In fact, he did not feel he had the means to do the job God was entrusting to him. However, God reminded him that He was his total source and strength.[5]

Obviously, we must approach God with a greater sense of who He is. In order to do this we must first be undone so that we can receive the matters of God with a right attitude. For Hannah, she felt undone in her barren state. She approached God as one reproached, only to have God answer the silent cry of her heart about having a child. Her response to her prayer being answered was she promised that she would dedicate the child to Him for His glory. We know that child to be Samuel, the great prophet and last judge of Israel.[6]

As we consider those who effectively approached God, they were often undone by the wildernesses of sin, despair, and hopelessness. Such people would first have to turn aside from the normalcy of life to discover the life God had ordained for them. They often came to God in great need before He could show Himself mighty in desperate times.

God's covenants often reminded His people that it was indeed His work and purpose to deliver them to experience His promises and fulfill His purpose. These agreements also reminded His people that it was all a matter of grace. His grace requires one to respond in faith, humility, and submission in order to properly receive His favor from above.

As you study the Bible, you will realize that God's people did not approach Him from any premise other than that of His covenant. This may see strange because the Bible is not blatant about such an approach. However, it is clearly spelled out if you know what you are looking for.

It was not until recently that I was able to come to terms with the fact that in the Bible the people of God in the Old Testament understood how to approach Him. They not only approached Him from the premise of covenant, but they hid in it, as well as found solace because of it. It is not that God needed to be reminded of His covenants, but His people needed to understand that what was made available to them was not something they deserved. In fact, the reason He honored His covenants

---

[4] Exodus 3:1-6

[5] Exodus 3:10-12

[6] 1 Samuel 1

in the lives of others was for the sake of those He made the covenants with, and not those who often benefited from them.

For example, because of His covenant with Abraham, God honored it in the lives of Isaac and the children of Israel. He made it quite clear to Isaac that the blessings he was experiencing were for the sake of his father, Abraham.[7] This showed Isaac that the blessings were a matter of God's grace due to His covenant with his father.

How did these people approach God on the basis of covenant? To recognize this approach, you would have to consider how they approached God in prayer. Through the years of Bible study, I noticed that God would set a premise by how He introduced Himself, and that people's approaches were also distinguished by how they addressed Him. In other words, the names of God varied in different presentations.

Genesis 1:1 introduces God as *God.* According to E. W. Bullinger's Companion Bible, when *"God"* is used in this text it points to ELOHIM, which identifies God as our Creator and Maker, connecting Him to creation. The "*El*" in the names of God identifies Him as "omni" in His power, knowledge, and presence. He is all in all, and there is no variableness in who He is or what He does.

Whenever God is referred to as *"LORD"* in Scripture, this is pointing to Him as *Yahwe*h (Hebrew) and *Jehovah* (English*). "LORD"* identified God in the context of covenant relationship, to those who have been created. Therefore, when the people of Israel approached God on the premise of Him being *"Yahweh,"* they were appealing to Him according to the basis of covenant.

As we consider how His other names were used, we can also see that God's people were also recognizing Him as their owner, ruler, head, healer, provider, and the One who blesses. However, these positions were often established or confirmed by His covenants. Consider how Bullinger distinguished some of God's names in his companion Bible:
Lord God = Adonai (The Possessor of all who blesses),
GOD = Eloah (connected to His will),
Lord = Adonim (owner),
GOD Almighty = El-Shaddai (All powerful, possessing all strength.)
MOST HIGH = Elyon (possessor of heaven and earth).[8]

The next time you read how God introduces Himself, take note of the position He is placing Himself in, in regard to His covenant. Also consider how Abraham, Moses, Hannah, David, and Daniel approached God. Meditate on how they were addressing Him. It is a fascinating study. Although such a study is only touching the surface of this subject, and

---

[7] Genesis 26:2-5, 24

[8] The Companion Bible, E. W. Bullinger, originally published in 1922; Kregel Publications; Appendix #4

the distinction may not be clearly made by many of the modern translations, the KJ Version of the Bible has made some of these distinctions. These distinctions allow the serious student to meditate upon the different approaches that God's servants have made to Him in their prayers and songs. Such approaches allow His people to see how many of His servants humbly approached Him at the point of covenant, while appealing to Him as their Maker, owner, ruler, and the One who blesses.

This brings us to the covenant of the New Testament. As believers, we are not always taught, or conditioned, to recognize that we, likewise, approach God based on the new covenant that was established on our behalf. We take much for granted because we often start from an immature premise. Therefore, we can find ourselves being ineffective in our approach to God. Granted, we may have some knowledge about the covenant, but there are no dots to connect us to the revelation that all that has been made available to us. These connections have been wrought at the point of Jesus' redemption. His redemption points to the new covenant.

Hebrews 7:19 makes reference to this covenant as representing a better hope, "For the law (old covenant) made nothing perfect, but the bringing in of a better hope did, by which we draw nigh to God." (Parenthesis added.) The new hope or covenant is actually a person. This was clearly brought out by Isaiah 42:6-7. God would actually give Himself as the covenant. We know that this points to Jesus Christ who became the incarnation of this new covenant. God has always been offering Himself as the prized possession, the hope, and the place of identification for His people. However, people are blinded, or refuse to see this place that has been clearly prepared by Jesus.[9]

This new covenant can only be approached and applied at the point of the person and work of Jesus Christ. It was brought forth by His death on the cross. Due to Jesus being lifted up on the cross as God's ultimate sacrifice for our sins, doomed man is now being drawn by the Father through His Spirit to turn aside from his path of utter destruction and consider Jesus. The writer of Hebrews confirms such a consideration when it comes to what the Lamb of God had to endure on His way to the cross.[10]

As Christians, we have drawn near to God by way of this new hope. We each have been drawn to the cross by the promise of Jesus serving as our only real source of Living Water that will spring up into everlasting life in our souls. We surely have been afforded the liberty to boldly approach God because of the covenant secured by Jesus' blood.[11]

[9] John 14:1-3

[10] Hebrews 12:3

[11] Hebrews 4:14-16

Clearly, no man can come to the Father unless it is by Jesus' redemption. Therefore, every man that draws near to God, seeking salvation will do so at the basis of His perpetual covenant. When man approaches God in prayer, he must also come by way of the covenant wrought by Jesus on the cross. Jesus confirmed this fact by stating that all must come by way of Him to ensure reconciliation with the Father and answered prayers. All that is done on our behalf will be for His sake, and not because we are worthy or deserving of any recognition or blessing.[12] Again, it will be a matter of God's incredible favor being shown towards us at the place of covenant.

As we consider what it cost God so that we may boldly approach Him at the place of covenant, it should greatly influence our attitude towards Him. In fact, it should so greatly affect us that we feel undone, totally unworthy to even come to Him in any other state except that of humility. Granted, we may boldly come to the throne of grace, but we must do so from a state of humility that recognizes that such boldness is based on the work of Jesus. We can only approach God because of this incredible covenant that cost Him dearly.

Approach points to our attitude, but attitude will determine the environment that will be established. Keep in mind approach represents our preliminary steps towards God. It is meant to bring us to a certain place that will allow us to go on further in our life in Christ. However, we must get the approach right before we can be assured of entering into the life that has been promised by the blessed covenant wrought by Jesus' redemption.

The question is, are you prepared to go on from the place of approach? Approach is meant to bring us near to God so we can be led to the place of agreement. This agreement has been firmly established by God on our behalf for the sake of His Son.

---

[12] John 14:6; 15:21; 16:23-24

8

THE PLACE OF AGREEMENT

To understand the place covenant should hold in our lives, we as believers must come to terms with where God's covenant will lead us in our relationship with Him. The authority behind God's covenants is based on that which is being established as law. In order to come to the place of covenant, we must agree with the evaluation that has been set forth by the covenant. God's main purpose in His covenants is to deliver His people from the different bondages of this present world to bring them to the place where His purpose will be realized and fulfilled in their lives. Initially, we must all be delivered from sin and death.

By recognizing our need for deliverance, we can come to a place of identification. As law, covenant establishes a place of evaluation in which those involved can come into agreement about what needs to be done. This agreement will highlight the purpose or intent behind the covenant. We already know that the purpose of God was/is to deliver us from the bondage of sin and the consequences of death in order to deliver us to the life He has promised and desires to bring forth. Once the purpose is highlighted and agreed upon, then the parties involved can come to a place of identification.

Jesus Christ represents the place of identification for God with man, and man with God. Jesus became sin so we as believers could be made in the righteousness of God. In identification a person not only establishes identity according to God's plan, but his or her position will also be established in His kingdom. Ultimately, as the life of Christ is established in the believer, he or she will become more like Jesus. As the saint takes on the very likeness of Christ, he or she will begin to reflect Jesus' glory more and more in this dark world.

As we consider Jesus, we realize that Jesus stands as the only place of reconciliation for man and God. God could not identify with man in his sin, and man could not identify with God in His state of holiness. Therefore, a bridge had to be provided that would close the gap between lost man and a holy God. After all, without God, man, who is His creation, has no real identification. Without identification, man has no means in which to discover his position and purpose.

Identification with God in His covenants entails remembering who we are and our place in His kingdom. Within His covenants are tokens or practices that remind us that we must not forget that we have been set apart for a certain purpose. The life of Solomon reminds us that our memory about the matters of God can become quite dim or forgetful in a world that has no real inclination towards the Lord and His ways. We must keep such tokens and practices before us so we do not forget that we must come into a place of agreement with God to experience His promises.

God's covenants are not only about deliverance, but involve the means by which people can truly inherit life. This brings us to the promises of God. They are conditional, but they lead to discovering, inheriting, and embracing the promise of life. We complicate God's promises because we do not understand the main purpose behind them. The main purpose has to do with possessing the quality of life that is not only promised, but will also prove to be abundant and complete, producing true satisfaction and contentment to the soul.

However, the conditions of the promises of God are meant to bring us into a place of agreement with God. The conditions of the promises are designed to prepare God's people to embrace by faith the life that has been made available. It is from the premise of meeting the conditions of the promises of God that we can rightfully approach Him in a right attitude. A right attitude allows us to properly receive from Him.

Most people think that faith is all about doing what is right. However, faith is also about properly receiving matters. This is why Jesus stated that we must take on the disposition of a child in order to receive the things of God in a right state.[1]

As we follow the trail that has been marked by the covenants of God, we can begin to see that they lead us to a place of agreement with God. Jesus summarized the power of agreement among His followers in Matthew 18:20, "For where two or three are gathered together in my name, there am I in the midst of them."

Nothing can be accomplished unless there is agreement. God established covenants as a means to bring people to a place of agreement with Him. They would understand His intention, as well as the conditions that must be adhered to, to see the benefits of such covenants realized in their lives. However, His people would have to agree with His evaluation about their present state in order to be brought to a place of total agreement with Him.

To possess agreement between God and man points to a powerful union. God is the One who has all authority and power to bring something forth. However, man is the one who ensures that the environment is right, which allows God to be God in any circumstance.

---

[1] Mark 9:33-37

This brings us to the reason why such agreement is often missing between God and man. The disposition or state of man is not conducive to God's holy state, ensuring that His character will be honored and His will upheld, ultimately, bringing Him glory. In such cases where real agreement is lacking, the authority of God is undermined, His power is hindered, and His will disregarded. When man's state or disposition is not acceptable to God, then he is unable to properly receive from God.

Through the years, I have been aware that most Christians think that God is concerned about what they are doing. In reality, God is concerned about who they are becoming in their lives before Him. Individuals may appear as if they are doing wonderful or great things for God. However, Jesus exposes the real crux of what is considered in all matters of service in Matthew 7:21-23,

> Not every one that saith unto me, Lord, Lord, shall enter into the kingdom of heaven, but he that doeth the will of my Father, who is in heaven. Many will say to me in that day, Lord, Lord, have we not prophesied in thy name? And in thy name have cast out devils? And in thy name done many wonderful works? And then will I profess unto them, I never knew you; depart from me, ye that work iniquity.

Clearly, the real crux of service is not based on works, but inward character. Iniquity points to inward moral deviation that can express itself in immoral practices such as physical and spiritual fornication. When the inward environment deviates from the holiness of God, outward activities, regardless of how religious and sacrificial they may seem, will be considered iniquity, missing the real mark of righteousness.

This brings us to the inward environment. We know we must approach God by faith. The reason we must approach God by faith is to establish the premise of our inward environment or state: that of holiness that establishes us in an upright life before God.

We already know that the best we have to offer in our humanity is considered filthy rags before the Lord. There is no beneficial quality in our flesh. Our ways may seem right in our own eyes, but they are strange or perverted to God. The light of the unregenerate man is nothing more than the darkness of sin and death upon his soul. There is no agreement between the state of fallen man and the holy state of God.[2] Hence enters the covenant established by Christ. It serves as a place of agreement between man and God. It actually upholds the holy state of God, while providing the solution for man's wretched state of sin and death.

This is why God's covenants are so important. They became places of agreement where the very inward state of man could be properly

---

[2] Proverbs 14:12; 16:2; 21:8; Isaiah 64:6; Matthew 6:22-23; Romans 3:10, 23; 7:18

challenged, channeled, and changed. For man to be properly challenged in his present state, he must change the way he is walking in order to properly channel or discipline the inward man. Consider Abraham. He was living in Ur when God called him to a different land. He was required to separate from the old way of living to embrace a new way. It entailed a path he had never before ventured upon, and a new land that was foreign to his understanding.

Abraham believed that it was God, his Creator who was calling him to this new life. He obeyed. Scripture is clear that it was Abraham's faith that was reckoned as righteousness. In other words, it was Abraham's simple trust in God that caused him to be considered upright before Him. It was for this reason that God could make a covenant with Abraham. He foreknew that Abraham would choose to be a man of faith. Therefore, He could honor the covenant with this great patriarch throughout the generations that followed him.

We know that righteousness must be reckoned or counted to us because, in our humanity, we do not possess any righteousness. This is why, as Christians, our lives must be hid in Christ. It is through the righteousness of Christ that God considers us.[3] Due to our everlasting covenant with God, we believers are now in Christ. In Christ, we positionally stand upright, but because of active faith we are counted as being upright, or as being in right standing before God. It is this right standing that allows God to regard our works or deeds as being acceptable.

As we consider faith and righteousness, we realize that faith properly enables us to walk in that which pertains to God, but righteousness enables us to stand upright before Him. Once again, faith points to our approach, but righteousness has to do with establishing our inward state of holiness before God.

As we consider the holy character of God, we can begin to understand that He can only meet us in a state of righteousness. He reckons our faith as righteousness so that He can meet us in agreement at the place of covenant. Clearly, the state of being upright brings us into agreement with our holy God.

It is vital that we understand how the state of righteousness will operate in our lives. We already know that righteousness points to being upright, or having right standing with God. However, righteousness is a state we must walk in. In other words, our right standing will translate as being righteous in what we do.

The state of righteousness begins with the premise of humility. As believers, we must realize that we do not know how to be righteous in our own power. Faith in God's Word will give us valuable insight into that

---

[3] 1 Corinthians 1:30; Colossians 3:3

which stipulates righteousness in our lives before our Lord. Therefore, in humility we will be ready to do what is right or be obedient when the opportunity is set before us. When righteousness is a natural extension of our inner man, we can do no less than that which is acceptable to God according to His Word.

Once humility is present, then godly submission will be established. Submission in this text proves to be the point of greatest strength. The reason is because godly submission will be quick to give way to that which is worthy. As you consider these two opposing states, you will realize you cannot possess humility and pride at the same time. You cannot have godly submission and selfishness in operation at the same time.

Humility and pride point to what one will immediately regard in a matter. For humility, it will always be the honorable ways of God, but for pride it will be the self-serving ways of the flesh. Submission and selfishness will determine what a person will naturally give way to in relationship to attitudes, alliances, and practices. Humility will never regard the prideful ways of the flesh, and godly submission will refuse to give way to the selfish pursuits of the flesh.

This brings us to the third aspect of righteousness. It has to do with subjection. In the state of pride, man will only come into subjection to his own way of doing, but in the state of humility, man will humble himself before the Lord in order to come into subjection to His perfect will. In pride, man will demand that all bow down to his will, while in humility man will make God's will his will. In such subjection, man will strive to be honorable before God and do that which is honorable in regard to others, while pride will prove to be indifferent, inconsiderate, and cruel where others are concerned.

In His example to man, Jesus was lowly (humble) in disposition and meek in attitude. In this lowly state, His yoke towards others proved to be easy, and His burden light. Such a state is contrary to pride because pride will put a heavy yoke of control on others and load them down with indifferent and unrealistic demands and oppressive burdens.

It is in His lowly state of humanity and servitude that as man Jesus came into agreement with the Father. They became one in spirit (same motivation-love), intent (same purpose-redemption), attitude (ready to give way to that which is greater-doing the work of redemption), and vision (Calvary). There was no deviation in their agreement to establish the new covenant that was founded upon Jesus' redemption.

It is important to recognize how such an agreement came about. Jesus gave up the glories of heaven to be made lower than the angels in order to take on the disposition of a servant. From this premise He came into submission to the Father's plan of redemption, and in subjection to His will as to how it was to be carried out. In His humanity He gave way to that which was far greater.[4] Due to His example, the Apostle Paul instructs us to have the attitude of Christ to ensure our will lines up to God. He also gives this instruction, "Submitting yourselves one to another in the fear of God" (Ephesians 5:21).

Godly submission must be in operation among the people of God to ensure an environment of righteousness. Without such submission, there will be no place of real agreement. Instead of walking in obedience to the ways of God, there will be strife and conflict. Instead of people honoring one another in a godly way, there will be those who will try to control and manipulate those who are weak and vulnerable according to their own self-serving preferences.

Agreement also points to being likeminded. Likeminded implies like attitude about matters, as well as possessing the same vision. As man, Christ possessed the mind of the Father. As Christians, we must have the mind of Christ in order to be likeminded with Him, ensuring that we will walk as He walked.

As Christians, we must clearly be abiding in the state of righteousness. If we are abiding in Christ, we will be abiding in His wisdom, righteousness, sanctification, and redemption. This abiding will express itself in upright conduct towards God and others. This is why righteousness ultimately becomes a state of holiness. We must abide in the attitude and ways of righteousness to ensure a disposition that is upright before God.

In consideration of covenant as a place of agreement, we can begin to see how our approach to God will determine how we will walk out a matter. If we approach God in faith, it will be with the sole purpose of obeying Him. Obedience will bring us to the place of identification where our walk will be disciplined by the attitude and ways of our Lord. In such discipline, we will be reminded of what God has established on our behalf, as we strive to possess His promises. As we walk by faith in God, the Spirit will lead us into the place of agreement. There we will discover the beauty, power, and hope of God's wondrous provision of redemption that has been revealed through His everlasting covenants.

---

[4] Luke 22:42; Philippians 2:5-8; Hebrews 2:7-10

9

THE PLACE OF STATUS

God's covenant points to a place of status. Status has to do with the state in which one is to exist. It can also identify one's position, as well as the state of affairs that will be present in which the promises of God can be brought forth.

It is important to follow the purpose of God's covenants through Scripture. We know that most of them point to redemption. However, they also remind us that a certain environment must be present before God's people can fully embrace their inheritance. Remember, the promise for the children of Israel was the Promised Land, but the inheritance for Christians has to do with eternal life. In each case, God's people had to be redeemed from their former taskmasters (Egypt and sin) in order to be brought to the fullness of God's promise.

As you follow God's covenants, you will realize that they identify His people as possessing a certain status. We speak of status because it points to rights. For example, what rights did the children of Israel possess due to their status? What rights do we, as Christians, have due to our status?

We must also remember that these rights have been allotted to us for the sake of others. In other words, the rights the children of Israel could claim and were to maintain, were due to Abraham. Our rights as Christians are accredited to Jesus' redemption on the cross. But what do these rights entail?

Man often perverts rights. He will use them to get his way with others, which results in him abusing or neglecting the integrity of such rights. Sadly, what most people do not realize about rights is that they find their premise in that which is just, good, or proper. Rights ultimately point to the liberty of doing that which is upright and respectable.

Therefore, the purpose of rights is not to give people a blank check to do as they will, but to give them the freedom to do what is right in a world that often calls good evil, and evil good. Such a wicked attitude inspires the world to oppress and persecute righteousness, while adhering to rebellion. Therefore, to do something outside of the boundaries of that which is just and honorable, is not a matter of rights as the wicked often claim to promote sin, but of rebellion. As the prophet Samuel stated, rebellion is as the sin of witchcraft.[1]

It is often surprising to man to realize that he lives in an environment that is often opposed to righteousness. Isaiah described this environment where people refer to good as being evil, and evil as being good. He goes on to say that in such an environment, the wicked are unduly rewarded, while the integrity of doing right is taken away from the righteous.[2] As a result, honest people find themselves being oppressed in doing what is right. They are encouraged to operate according to the darkness of the world through compromise and indifference. Such an environment takes away the contrast between light and darkness, allowing deluded people to happily remain in their deluded state of sin and death. The tragedy for the righteous is clear. They must sell their souls by shunning integrity, embracing compromise, and practicing shrewdness in order to live peacefully within or beat the wicked system.

God's covenants with His people always established the environment of righteousness. Therefore, His people are guaranteed of experiencing certain rights when righteousness is in place. These rights not only set up the environment, but they will define the status that His people will be operating in.

To understand the place of status in God's covenants, we need to follow the covenant that God established with Abraham. Remember, covenant is a place of identification. There must be identification to be able to claim rights to benefit from the promises of a covenant.

Although the Hebrew people were identified to Israel, their real claim to their rights before God found its source in Abraham. This is clearly brought out in Scripture. In John 8:33 and 39, they were telling Jesus that they were of Abraham's seed; therefore, they claimed him as their father. John the Baptist was also quite aware of their claim to Abraham. John put their claim in this perspective in Matthew 3:9-10,

And think not to say within yourselves, We have Abraham as our father; for I say unto you that God is able of these stones to raise up children unto Abraham. And now also the axe is laid unto the root of the trees; therefore, every tree which bringeth not forth good fruit is hewn down, and cast into the fire.

The children of Israel were claiming their right to their inheritance. Remember, the covenant God made with Abraham was that his seed would inherit the Promised Land. At this point in history, the Jewish people were under the slavery of Roman government in their own land. Since they could prove they were from the seed of Abraham, they were

---

[1] 1 Samuel 15:23
[2] Isaiah 5:20-23

identifying themselves to their right to their inheritance according to the covenant.

Amazingly, the Jewish people have kept their identity distinct from the rest of the world. They are so distinct that they remain a target of the hatred of the world. Regardless of how the world views them, they still have rights according to the covenant God made with Abraham. This association with Abraham identifies them to Jehovah God, the One who not only is their Maker, but He is also the One who keeps His covenants with His people. The people of the world may mock these people's right to exist as a nation within the land of Israel, but God has not forgotten His covenant with Abraham. In due time, He will bring forth the completion of His promises to these people for the sake of Abraham.

As the biological children of Abraham, the Jewish people are peculiar or special. They will never lose their identity. Sadly, much of this distinction has been due to the intense persecution these people have experienced throughout their history and continue to experience today. To this day many continue to wear the tokens, or maintain the practices, that keep them separate. Such separation is not a matter of superiority, but one of rights. They are who they are, and all of the world's attempts to wipe them out will never change their status or identification to Jehovah God and Abraham.

However, the real identifying mark that identifies people to Abraham is not a biological mark. Rather, it is a spiritual mark. This is what John the Baptist was referring to. If God so desired, He could take stones and raise them up as the seed of Abraham. It was not enough to be biologically associated with Abraham; one must become identified with him on a greater plain to truly benefit from the promises of God.

The Apostle Paul gives us the insight into what identifies a person to Abraham, "Even as Abraham believed God, and it was accounted to him for righteousness. Know ye, therefore, that they who are of faith, the same are the children of Abraham" (Galatians 3:6-7). The apostle also pointed out that God would also justify the Gentiles through faith. This would honor the part of the covenant He made with Abraham that in him all nations would be blessed.[3]

The Apostle Paul makes this statement, "That the blessing of Abraham might come on the Gentiles through Jesus Christ, that we might receive the promise of the Spirit through faith" (Galatians 3:14). Obviously, genuine faith is what identifies every true believer of God to Abraham. However, the only avenue in which the blessing of Abraham can flow into the lives of the Gentiles is Jesus Christ. He is the door or way in which the purpose of the covenant made with Abraham connects with the new covenant established in the New Testament. It is through

[3] Galatians 3:8

Jesus, that the promises of heaven are given to those who embrace Him by faith.

Paul goes on to explain how the covenant made with Abraham was four hundred years before the covenant of the Law. The Law could only point to Jesus, but the faith Abraham displayed towards God is what would identify every true follower of God to Jesus Christ. The apostle refers to this point of identification as being a promise of faith that is given to them that believe.[4] Part of this incredible promise also entailed receiving the Spirit through faith.

This brings us to the covenant of the New Testament. The Jewish people claimed their status because of Abraham. They would approach God as Jehovah God or LORD. Such an approach was in relationship to their God establishing a covenant relationship with them through Abraham as their Jehovah or Lord. Sadly, many of them missed the important fact that what made Abraham stand out to God was his faith. His faith was reckoned or counted as righteousness, thereby, establishing a right environment in which rights, promises, and blessings could be allotted to the faithful patriarch, along with those who truly followed his example.

Therefore, the real heavenly blessing did not come through Abraham's actual seed, but through the example of faith that he has clearly left all true believers. Granted, Jesus came through the seed of Abraham, but it is genuine faith that allows believers to benefit from God's promises. Genuine faith is what connects and identifies a true receiver to the promises and blessings of heaven.

In Hebrews 8, we are given a contrast between the covenant of the Law and the new covenant established by the sacrifice of Jesus. We are told that because of the excellent ministry of Jesus, He now serves as the mediator of a better covenant. This improved covenant was established upon better promises—that of an eternal inheritance.[5] The problem with the covenant of the Law is that it was not able to save. It simply pointed out the need for salvation. Therefore, it was not complete, requiring a different and better covenant, which was promised by the Lord.

The writer of Hebrews goes on to explain that instead of the Law being written upon stones, it would now be written upon the minds and hearts of God's people. In other words, it would become not just an intellectual knowledge that disciplined the outer man, but it would become a revelation of the heart that would discipline the inner man in the way he thought and approached the matters of God and life.[6]

---

[4] Galatians 3:17-18, 22-24

[5] See also Hebrews 9:11-15 and 12:24.

[6] Hebrews 8:10

In God's kingdom the old (Law) had to give way to that which was better (Spirit). Although the Law was holy and righteous, it was limited by man's inability to keep it. It could not get man beyond his state of spiritual judgment and ruin. Jesus died on the cross to satisfy the judgment of death declared by the Law upon all men. In Christ, a new, and a more excellent law was established: that of the Spirit of life in Christ Jesus.[7]

In Christ the environment of righteousness was established, clearly paving the way for believers to be recognized in a new status that afforded them rights to discover their true inheritance. The question is what status did this new covenant establish? The Apostle Paul gives us insight into this new status, "For ye are all the children of God by faith in Christ Jesus" (Galatians 3:26).

When you study the status of the Jewish people alongside the status of Christians, there are similarities. Because of God's covenants, the people of Israel and Christians are chosen and considered a holy nation, a special (peculiar) people through which a priesthood would be established.[8] However, for Christians, they have actually been adopted into a heavenly family.

The Jewish people could claim that they were children of Abraham. However, in Christ, each believer can claim that he or she is a child of God. As children of Abraham, the people of Israel approached God from the basis of covenant. Since Christ serves as the believer's place of covenant, he or she approaches God the Father as His son or daughter. This is brought out in Scriptures such as Romans 8:15 and Galatians 4:6-7, as well as in the model prayer found in Matthew 6:9, "After this manner, therefore, pray ye: Our Father, who art in heaven, Hallowed by thy name."

The children of Israel were promised an earthly inheritance: The Promised Land. But, by being adopted into the heavenly family, we, as believers, have the status of children of God, heirs to an eternal inheritance. The people of Israel were delivered from worldly taskmasters, but as children of God, we have been delivered from a spiritual taskmaster: that of sin. In fact, as believers, we have been redeemed from under the Law to receive our status as adopted children of God.[9] The Apostle Paul summarized our position in this way, "And because ye are sons, God hath sent forth the Spirit of his Son into your hearts, crying Abba, Father. Wherefore, thou art no more a servant, but a son; and if a son, then an heir of God through Christ" (Galatians 4:6-7).

In his messages on Galatians, H. A. Ironside pointed out that in the days of the Roman Empire, children held the same status as servants. They had no real rights. The only way the parent could distinguish them

---

[7] Romans 8:2

[8] Exodus 40:15; Deuteronomy 14:2; 1 Peter 2:5, 9

[9] Galatians 4:5

as heirs to an inheritance was that the parent had to take the child when he or she came of age to the forum (courthouse), and officially adopt him or her.[10] It was the legal adoption that actually identified the child as an heir.

We are all born into slavery. We serve the harsh taskmaster of sin. However, we also have the potential to be children of God, but until we are adopted through the born again experience by faith, and legally sealed by the Holy Spirit, we will have no identification or claim to our eternal inheritance.

Let us now consider the two contrasts brought out by the covenant of the Law and the covenant established through Jesus' sacrifice in the following table. Keep in mind, even though the children of Israel would obey the Law, it could not justify them before God. The only way any of us can stand justified before God is through faith.

Covenant	Point of Identification	Promises	Status	Relationship
The Law	**Abraham**	**Promised Land**	**Children of Israel**	**Jehovah God**
Redemption (Grace/ Faith)	**Jesus**	**Everlasting Inheritance**	**Children of God**	**Our Heavenly Father**

For Christians, this is truly a beautiful picture of what it means to be children of God. Clearly it is a better covenant with better promises. Sadly, some Christians are coming back under the old covenant of the Law. The Apostle Paul refers to such an attempt as frustrating the grace of God.[9]

What covenant do you prefer? What covenant are you operating within? If you are operating according to the covenant of the Law, you have brought yourself under the law of sin and death. However, if you are identified to the covenant established through Jesus, you are operating according to the law of the Spirit of life in Christ Jesus.[10] Be of good courage! Your true inheritance will not be fully obtained in this present world, but the fullness of its reality is awaiting you in the next.

---

[10] Expository Messages On the Epistle to the Galatians; H. A. Ironside; Fifteenth printing, September 1978; Loizeaux Brothers, pg. 134

[9] Galatians 2:21

[10] Romans 8:2

10

THE PLACE OF ACCOUNTABILITY

God's covenants also serve as a place of accountability. As you study these agreements, you begin to see that they become a place where God holds Himself accountable to bring about certain matters or events. Consider the first covenant with Noah. God made Himself accountable to never again destroy the earth with water. Clearly, such covenants represent the place where one is required to be honorable in a situation. At such a place, the parties involved will not let each other off the hook, but each party will be called upon to do what is right or responsible according to the agreement.

It is important to point out that without the place of accountability there will be no need to be responsible to do what is just and honorable. As man's character is unveiled more and more, we must realize that the natural preference of the old disposition within each of us is to release ourselves from a place of personal accountability, while calling for everyone around us to be responsible in his or her attitudes and conduct. Needless to say, such attitudes and practices are rightfully referred to as being "hypocritical."

This brings us to the moral deviation of man. It is often referred to as iniquity. Iniquity is deviation from what is ethical and upright. Moral deviation will justify such departure from what is right, making the matter an exception to the rule, rather than the rule. You can clearly see this deviation in matters of the law. Man always finds the excuse as to why he needs not observe certain laws. Immediately, he has made himself an exception to the law, rather than accountable to it. He has reckoned in his mind that he is justified in ignoring the rules.

Each time man justifies himself in such a manner, he gets further away from the center of what is right and true. As he gets further away from the center, he becomes more unbalanced in his perception and conduct. In a way, he becomes indifferent to the reality around him as he insists on a lopsided perspective that will prove him to be foolish and unrealistic.

When man gives way to this moral deviation, he becomes very stiff-necked. He will insist on his way, while purporting that any other way is silly or stupid. As he gives way to the delusion of his deviation, he becomes more certain that he is right in his conclusions. As Proverbs 16:2 tells us, all of man's ways seem clean or right to him, but God is weighing his spirit or motive in a matter. Hence enters the warning of Proverbs 16:25, "There is a way that seemeth right unto a man, but the end thereof are the ways of death."

The harsh reality is man cannot be trusted to be trustworthy in his own accord. There must be a place of accountability in order to make him responsible to his words, for his attitudes, and in regard to his actions. He must be made responsible for who he is and what he is allowing himself to become. Without making man own his attitudes and conduct, he will forever seek ways to skirt around his moral responsibilities. He will put the blame elsewhere, letting himself off the hook from taking accountability for that which ultimately proves to be dishonorable in his character and conduct.

King David understood that he possessed this moral deviation. In 2 Samuel 22:23-25,

> For all his judgments were before me; and as for his statutes, I did not depart from them. I was also upright before him, and have kept myself from mine iniquity. Therefore, the LORD hath recompensed me according to my righteousness; according to my cleanness in his eyesight.

David put his character flaws under control by keeping the ways of God before him. This focus kept him from giving way to personal iniquity. Due to his inward discipline, he created a righteous environment. As a result, God found him trustworthy enough to make a covenant with him. This covenant is referred to as the Davidic covenant. It clearly unveils and promises the eternal reign and kingdom of the Messiah.

Consider Abraham's inward character. We know he was a man of faith. However, his faith translated into obedience. This is important to keep in mind. The Bible is clear that an environment of righteousness must be in place for God to honor His covenants. Nehemiah 9:7-8 tells us that God found Abraham's heart to be faithful or trustworthy; therefore, He made a covenant with him. In 2 Chronicles 16:9a, we are given this insight, "For the eyes of the LORD run to and fro throughout the whole earth, to show himself strong in the behalf of them whose heart is perfect toward him."

King David walked before the Lord according to the integrity or upright character of his heart. The heart of man determines whether he will be trustworthy. God found both the hearts of Abraham and David to be trustworthy. As a result, He made covenants with them that were to be ongoing or perpetual until completed or brought forth.

This brings us to the conditions of God's covenants. God not only used the covenants to show His intentions and character, but He used them as a place of accountability for man. Clearly, there were conditions established in the covenants that man had to keep if he was to be part of the working out of those covenants in his lifetime or generation.

God made a covenant with David, but Solomon had to keep the conditions of the covenant to ensure his seed would remain on the throne. When Solomon failed to keep the conditions of the covenant, the promises of it went to his brother Nathan. It was out of the lineage of Nathan (Mary) that the Messiah was brought forth.[1]

God's covenants can easily pass over the present generation to embrace a person whose heart condition is trustworthy in the next generation. This is why they are considered perpetual, ongoing, or everlasting. God is looking for an upright man to bring forth His promises in each generation. This sad statement was made in Ezekiel 22:30, "And I sought for a man among them, that should make up the hedge, and stand in the gap before me for the land, that I should not destroy it; but I found none." This was in regard to the land of Judah. We know from history that it was destroyed by Babylon.

As you consider God's covenants, you can see that His requirements are clear. By man adhering to them, a right environment is established, allowing God to honor His covenant.

It is interesting to reflect on the different agreements God made with man. Let us consider them. We know about the covenant that God made with the earth about not destroying it with water. We have to admit that God clearly wants to refrain from any judgment. However, judgment comes based on the spiritual environment, and it points to separation, purging, and completeness.

God had an agreement with Adam. The condition of the agreement was that he was to not eat of the tree of the knowledge of good and evil. If Adam obeyed, God's part of the agreement was to maintain a perfect environment, cause fruitfulness and satisfaction, and ensure man's dominion over the earth.[2]

We know that Adam disobeyed. What resulted are the dreadful consequence of sin: that of death was passed down to everyone born in the Adamic race. However, God also promised a redeemer in Genesis 3:15. As Christians, we know who that Redeemer is, and we have entered into an everlasting covenant because of what the Lord Jesus Christ did on the cross.

We know that God made an agreement with Cain after he murdered his brother, that He would not allow anyone to avenge him. However, Cain became a wanderer, a vagabond who never came back to God.[3]

---

[1] 1 Kings 9:4-9; Luke 3:31

[2] Genesis 1:26—31; 2:7-17; 3:14-19, 22-24

[3] Genesis 4:11-15

God even blesses the vagabonds of the world, but many of them never find their way to Him. The darkness upon their souls is great, and they cannot see the light of the Gospel shining through the grave darkness around them.

There was the agreement God made with Hagar concerning her seed, Ishmael.[4] No doubt God made this agreement for the sake of Abraham. Although Ishmael would become a great nation in his own right, he would never inherit the promises made to Abraham. Only Isaac would receive the promises as far as God's covenant with the great patriarch. The Apostle Paul described this distinction between Ishmael and Isaac in this way, "For it is written that Abraham had two sons, the one by a bondmaid (Hagar), the other by a freewoman (Sarah). But he who was of the bondwoman was born after the flesh; but he of the freewoman was by promise" (Galatians 4:22-23)" (Parentheses added.) The contrast between Ishmael and Isaac shows us that the lesser agreement will not outshine the promises obtained through the covenants that have been established according to faith.

We are aware of the covenant God made with Abraham. It contained seven promises: 1) his descendants would be made into a great nation, 2) God would bless him, 3) He would make his name great, 4) Abraham would be a blessing to others, 5) God would bless them that blessed him, 6) He would also curse them that cursed him, and 7) that in Abraham all nations would be blessed.[5] For the male descendants of Abraham, they had to be circumcised in order to be identified to this covenant.

There was the promise of the land to the people of Israel. However, they had to possess the land. Once they possessed the land, they had to obey the Law. As you follow the Lord's instructions and future hope attached to this covenant, you will see that there were seven parts to this agreement that would occur: 1) dispersion for disobedience, 2) repentance in dispersion, 3) the return of the Lord in their midst, 4) restoration in the land, 5) national conversion, 6) judgment upon the enemies of Israel, and 7) national prosperity.[6]

As believers, we must possess our eternal inheritance. The people of Israel had to believe God to enter into the Promised Land, but they also had to obey His instructions to maintain their inheritance. We must possess Jesus to ensure eternal life, and we must walk by faith to maintain our inheritance. Genuine faith always results in obedience to that which is godly and honorable.

---

[4] Genesis 16:7-15

[5] Genesis 12:1-3; 13:16; Exodus 2:23-25; 6:3-8; Deuteronomy 28:8-14; Galatians 3:13-16

[6] Deuteronomy 28:63-68; 30:1-10; Isaiah 11:1-12; Zechariah 12:10-14; 14; Romans 11

This brings us to the covenant made with David. It was contingent on obedience. The covenant with Abraham possessed seven promises. There were seven parts to the covenant concerning the children of Israel inheriting the Promised Land, but there are seven blessings attached to the covenant God made with David. The number "seven" points to something coming to perfection or maturity. The seven blessings in this covenant with David are:

1) David's house (lineage) would last forever.
2) His lineage (Jesus) would sit on the throne forever,
3) There would be an everlasting kingdom.
4) Israel would possess the Promised Land forever.
5) There would be a time that there would be no more affliction allowed against the people of Israel.
6) The people of Israel would be forever assured of the fatherly care of Jehovah God.
7) An eternal covenant would be brought forth.[7]

Finally, we have the New Covenant we enjoy as believers. The conditions have been outlined throughout the New Testament. It truly proves to be a place of accountability. As Christians, this place of the covenant is where our spirit is tested and our character and commitment will be exposed. It is where we will prove to possess the true fragrance of Christ or we will prove to be a stench due to fruits that fall short of our heavenly calling. For example, we are commanded to love, walk by faith, and obey the Word. We must learn to walk after the Spirit, so we can be led into the benefits of possessing eternal life. As we follow the Spirit, we will learn to walk in the Spirit according to the heart and will of God.

As we follow the path of God's covenants, we can see that His great desire was and is to have a relationship with man in order to fulfill His eternal purpose. Adam broke the relationship with God, but Abraham gave us insight into how we could encounter God in a relationship by faith. Moses revealed that we could talk to God face-to-face, and David gave us insight into the type of heart God could honor.

It was Jesus who finally bridged the gap between God and man. He brought much needed forgiveness, reconciliation, and restoration back into the equation so mankind could come boldly to God as His children. But, note that we must come to Him as children, born of the Spirit and the Word, as we ensure that our new disposition is brought to maturity and maintained with a right attitude towards Him, His Word, and others. Are you truly part of the New Covenant, or are you a wanderer like Cain? Perhaps, you have some religion, but you are still wandering in this world. It is time to come home to the Father. The door of Jesus has been provided, but you must accept the invitation to come and partake of the Living Water that will spring up into everlasting life.

---

[7] 2 Samuel 7:10-16; Psalm 89:20-37; Isaiah 9:6-7; Luke 1:32-33

11

THE PLACE OF RELATIONSHIP

As we study the concept of God's covenants, we must recognize God's heart towards His people. He desires a relationship with them. This is what God's covenants are all about. He has put forth these places of agreement for man to come to a place of relationship with Him. In this relationship, man will know the Word of the Lord, along with His intentions towards a matter. He will be able to come to a place of real identification in Christ in order to know the promises of God. Man will be able to approach God in a right way ensuring environment, agreement, and status. He will also know his responsibilities towards God, making him accountable to what is godly and honorable before the Lord, as a means to fulfill His purpose in the kingdom of God.

One of the great revelations I had about God was that the Creator of the universe wanted a relationship with me. Now note, as believers we are encouraged to remember that Christianity is not a religion. It is about having a relationship with God. However, how many have really received a revelation of this incredible privilege?

As believers, we can talk about popular subjects, such as how God loves us, but we often fail to realize that His love or commitment towards us cost Him dearly. We do not recognize how far away from God we are due to the darkness of delusion, sin, and ignorance upon our very souls. Our worldly perception often blinds us to our need for forgiveness, reconciliation, and restoration, and our arrogance deludes us about our status of condemnation and hopelessness, while our self-sufficiency falsely flatters us about our source of dependency: that of the arm of the flesh.

Due to redemption we each can know that Christianity is all about relationship, yet many of us continue to make it a religion. We can know that Jesus provided the way to have a relationship with God, but how many of us have failed to ever enter into a place of true commitment and communion with Him? We can know about glorious truths and promises, but in so many cases there is no life to any of our understanding. There is no life because faith is missing and the Spirit has been hindered by the lack of devotion and the presence of unbelief.

The place of covenant is a place of relationship where one comes into a place of rest. For years I struggled with my flesh warring against the Spirit. I attempted to silence the mocking arrogance that would affront my faith, and the false accusations that the spirit of this present world would often fling against the character and ways of God during times of personal testing and grave doubts. I always knew that there was rest in sweet confidence once it was directed towards the holy character of God and His perfect ways.

Eventually, after years of struggle, I finally came into a place of rest. This is where my confidence came to a place of complete rest in God in spite of the challenges around me. At that time, I discovered that in the place of rest was communion with God. It was a place where I could enjoy the wonders of my Lord, Master, and God. It was a place of relationship. Instead of this relationship just being an incredible experience that occasionally touched my heart, it became a reality to my very being. I knew what it meant to have a relationship with the Creator of the Universe. In such a state I began to explore the possibilities of this relationship.

In order to understand how the place of covenant is about God having a relationship with man, we need to follow His agreement with His people to understand the environment and sincere intention and desire of our God. Let us consider the type of relationship each person had with God.

Adam: The first man gives us a special insight into the type of relationship God desires with us. We know that God made a perfect environment in which man could reside. However, the perfection of this environment was contingent upon Adam walking with his Creator in sweet fellowship. We know that Adam sinned and hid from God in shame. However, God sought out his fellowship in the cool of the day, the time that best represents that which was most pleasant and restful. Adam could hear God's voice as He called out to him to enjoy the garden together. However, Adam could no longer respond because of sin and separation.[1]

It is so easy to miss God. He simply wants to walk with us in sweet fellowship. He wants the fresh wind of His Spirit to blow upon our souls, reviving us to once again walk with Him in the garden of our hearts in sweet communion, while together we enjoy the life He has given us through His work of redemption. Obviously, sin no longer needs to separate us from God. We can come into the perfect environment of rest, and simply learn how to enjoy who He is.

---

[1] Genesis 2:7-8, 15; 3:8-9

Enoch: The next man who gives us insight into having a relationship with God is Enoch. Adam's relationship shows us that God indeed wants to create an environment of fellowship so we can truly walk with Him. However, Enoch shows us where such a walk will lead us. It will lead us to a place where we are no more, for we will have truly been consumed by the very presence of God.[2]

To walk with God as Enoch! We will ultimately know what it means for God to be all in all to us. This should be our desire as saints of the most High God. Jesus clearly instructed each of us as to how we must walk. We must deny ourselves of our right to life on our terms. We must become identified with Him in His death, so that we can become identified in His life. Clearly, we will cease to be as we were, and become what we have been predestinated for: To reflect the life and glory of Jesus. Surely, the life of Jesus must consume us in such a way that we are no more. And, when He comes for us, we will be completely consecrated to Him through identification.

Noah: This man also walked with God. However, the world was facing judgment. Since Noah walked with God, God was able to show him grace or favor. Ultimately, Noah's righteousness would bring judgment upon the world, but God would hide him in His ark. This ark would ride out God's judgment, bringing Noah into a new life and into a new beginning.[3]

Noah's ark reminds us of another ark, the Ark of the Covenant.[4] This was located in the Most Holy Place. It represented the presence of God in the midst of His people. This ark pointed to the fact that God made a covenant to reside in the midst of His people as long as they maintained the ways of His Law. In its inner compartment it contained three articles, the Law, the manna from heaven, and Aaron's rod that budded.

Christ serves as every believer's ark. As His saints, we positionally hide in Him, and He also resides in our midst. As the way, He points to the Law of God that clearly established His righteous, perfect ways. As the truth, He represents the Bread from heaven that serves as the only source that will ensure the satisfaction of our souls. As the life, He points to the budding rod of Aaron. Out of the lifeless grave came eternal life for you and me. [5]

Judgment is upon the face of the earth, but we will be delivered through it, and eventually from it, thanks to our personal Ark. In the end, it will be our faith that will testify of the just ways of God, bringing judgment upon those who also refuse to believe the Gospel. Keep in mind, Noah was one man out of many. Due to his faith, his family also

---

[2] Genesis 5:21-24

[3] Genesis 6:3-9; 2 Peter 2:5, 9

[4] Exodus 37:1-9

[5] John 14:6; Ephesians 2:6; Colossians 3:3

benefited from his walk with God. In the end only the eight souls who made up his family were saved.

Abraham: We have studied the life of Abraham. We think of him as a great man of faith. However, what is most important is how God viewed him. He considered him His friend. We are told that God considered this friendship in light of it lasting forever. After all, Abraham had been chosen due to his faith towards his Maker.[6] His faith in God revealed his faithfulness towards his Creator. Such faithfulness is the virtue that ensures whether one has the ability to prove to be a trustworthy friend. God is not a fair-weather friend who proves to be fickle in His friendships. He is a totally committed friend to those who prove to be His faithful friend.

The salt of the covenant also points to a relationship of friendship. We know that salt was valuable, and used in offering sacrifices, adding flavor and serving as medicine. In fact, without the presence of this valuable substance, sacrifices would not be accepted. However, it was used to make covenants as well. If enemies ate food with salt in it, they became friends. This explains the expression of the Arabs, "There is salt between us."[7] Obviously, when making reference to believers being the salt, it was in relationship with the life of Jesus serving as the real flavor of heaven and the healing virtue of God in each of their lives. The more Jesus' life becomes a precious reality in each of us, the greater affect it will have on others. Therefore, salt also reminds us that this life we have in Jesus allows us to develop a true friendship with Him. Such friendships add personal value to our quality of life.

The Apostle John informs us that, as believers, our Lord has chosen us to bear fruit. His desire is to call us friends. However, this friendship is held together by love and will express itself in like manner to those who belong to the kingdom of God. Clearly, we have been called to an intimate relationship with God. The best type of friendship involves communing together, where two people share their inner desires, struggles, and secrets. Each proves to be trustworthy as they weep and rejoice together. True friendship will also prove to be sacrificial in its commitment.[8] It is God's desire to share this type of intimate friendship with each of us.

Moses: Adam revealed that God desires to walk with us. Enoch showed us that if we do walk with our Lord, we would cease to be as in regard to our former life. Noah confirmed that this type of walk with God creates an environment in which He can show His grace. Abraham revealed that such a walk would end in an everlasting friendship with the

---

[6] 2 Chronicles 20:7; Isaiah 41:8; James 2:23

[7] Dake's Annotated Reference Bible, Finis Jennings Dake, © 1963, pgs. 57-58

[8] John 15:12-14

Lord. However, Moses leads us to the next step in this incredible friendship: talking to God face-to-face as a man speaks to his friend.[9]

God considered Moses a true servant.[10] As believers, we all start out as servants of the Lord Jesus Christ. It is in this status that we learn what it means to be a friend of God. In fact, we should be graduating from the status of servant to one of friendship. Jesus mentioned this in John 15:15, "Henceforth I call you not servants; for the servant knoweth not what his lord doeth: but I have called you friends; for all things that I have heard of my Father I have made known unto you."

A lord will not share intimate matters with his servant, but this is not so for true friends. Our Lord wants to share the matters of the throne with us. But, if we are simply servants, He will not entrust such matters to us. He wants us to not just hear what needs to be done, but He wants us to share His concern, burden, and work. He wants us to come under His yoke out of love and compassion for Him because He is our friend. He wants to not simply call us friend, but He wants us to be friends with Him.

Moses was a servant of God at first, but became a friend. As a friend, he did not want to settle for just experiencing the Lord's presence; he wanted to encounter His glory. He wanted to be exposed to the character or person of God. After all, a true friend will never settle for being left out of an important matter. Friends want to know all they can about their friend so they can compliment, share, and be part of their inner lives.

Moses not only talked to God face-to-face as a friend, but he encountered the glory of God. In his encounter with God, he experienced that blessed Rock of his foundation. While Moses was firmly planted upon the Rock, he was also placed in the cleft of Rock so that he would witness the backside of the unhindered glory of God.[11]

Keep in mind that true friends will greatly influence you. We are told that evil company corrupts good morals.[12] This is why not all friends are "good" friends. Good friends will watch out for our best. They will compliment us in the ways of righteousness, while challenging us in regard to ways that may prove to be destructive. Proverbs 27:6 says it best, "Faithful are the wounds of a friend, but the kisses of an enemy are deceitful."

What an incredible influence Moses' encounter with God had on him. It was God's glory that was reflected from Moses' very countenance

[9] Exodus 33:11

[10] Numbers 12:7-8

[11] Exodus 33:18-23

[12] 1 Corinthians 15:33

when he came down from the mountain. It was so great that no man could come near to him without fear. [13]

This is the type of influence a true friendship with Jesus will have on us. We can speak to Him as a friend. If we prove to be His faithful friend by possessing loving devotion and obedience towards Him, we will be likewise influenced by Him. Such influence will cause us to reflect His glory through our countenance.[14] We will truly represent Him in this dark world as being the One who we know in an intimate way.

Finally, we have the example of King David. He truly knew God. He started out as a humble shepherd who became a servant to King Saul. Out of his humble servitude as a shepherd to sheep and as a servant in the courts of the king, he became a great soldier that continued to be tempered by adversity in the deserts and caves. Out of the adversity came a great king who was trustworthy. As a result, God made a covenant with him that out of his seed the King of Israel would come forth, establishing David's throne forever.

What a glorious picture of Jesus. He started out as a stem that appeared to have no real significance. He became a branch that experienced judgment on our behalf. As a result, He was brought forth as the great Vine who would also come forth as reigning King and righteous Judge. Out of Him would come the realization of an unseen kingdom, as well as an abundant harvest of souls.

As Christians we are part of that harvest. We may be mere branches in the scheme of things, but since we possess the life of the Vine, we have the status of adopted children. Although we were once servants of sin, we are now considered kings and priests in a kingdom that will last forever.[15]

The incredible aspect about our relationship with God is that it was established at the point of covenant. Every great follower of God approached Him at the place of covenant to be established in an intimate relationship with Him. Even in trying times, people like Job had confidence in patience that they could be assured that God would never waver from who He is. The Elijah's of the world knew that in righteousness their prayers would move heaven. The Rahab's were sure about deliverance, and those such as Abraham would always come to rest in their friendship with God, even when they were required to offer up God's very promises to Him as a burnt offering, ready to be consumed in the fires of acceptance.[16]

---

[13] Exodus 34:29-35

[14] 2 Corinthians 3:18

[15] Revelation 1:6

[16] James 2:21-25; 5:11-18

As we come to the end of this journey that we have been taking through the covenants of God, have you come to realize that because of a new, everlasting covenant, we as believers have access as children of God to come boldly to the throne of God? We take so much for granted. The children of Israel understood that their place of reasoning with God was always at the point of His covenant. However, as children of God, we have often failed to recognize that covenant reminds us of the legal procedure that would allow God to consider us as His children, who have been made heirs of an eternal inheritance.

The next time you take communion, remember. Remember that you are recognizing the glorious covenant that was established at the point of Jesus' redemption. As a result, you now can come to God as your Father, ready to commune with Him in Spirit and truth, knowing that you are no longer a servant of sin, but now you are truly a friend of the Lord of lords and the King of kings.

As you take communion, also remember that you are looking forward towards that day when you will stand before God's throne. Like others you will be humbly rejoicing and worshipping Him, knowing that as you peer into His glorious face, you will be assured that the eternal benefits of the new and everlasting covenant that you have benefited from in this present world will be truly unveiled and realized in all of its fullness in the midst of His unhindered majesty.

What a glorious future we have to look forward to. And, imagine—it is all because of God's glorious covenant He made with us through the precious redemption of His Son. The Apostle John said it in a most excellent way as he looked into the future, and stated, "Even so, come Lord Jesus" (Revelation 22:20c). All I can add to such glorious words is, "So be it!"

Book Five:

UNMASKING THE CULT MENTALITY

(An Exposition)

INTRODUCTION

Questions, questions, and more questions continue to flood the minds of those who have tasted the bitterness of a cult. Often bound together by a common religious experience, these individuals find themselves struggling with the same issues. It seems that even after being delivered from their cult's tentacles, they have more doubts than answers. How do they handle a situation where they have been subjected to religious people who have ended up betraying them? In fact, some people would classify their experience as spiritual abuse. Granted, there are hurts and unresolved issues, but what continues to nip at these people's heels comes in the way of suspicions and doubts as to what is true and real.

Religious people had these people's trust, but they used it to promote their own means. These imposters had these individuals loyalty, but they used it to control these innocent receptive souls. They not only have a hold on these people hearts, but they stomped on them through fear and manipulation. They clearly had the attention of their followers' ears, but they had cleverly perverted and poisoned what they told these people, thereby, changing their perspective.

For these poor followers, doubts and questions continue to grow even after time and space has marked their separation from their religious experience. Questions such as how could such leaders be under the right spirit if they were operating according to wickedness (Isaiah 25:7; 30:1; 1 John 4:1)? If they were being influenced by a wrong spirit, how did this spirit affect their understanding of God and what they perceive as Christianity? If the leaders were under a wrong spirit and operating out of a wrong spirit, how much of their teachings were trustworthy?

The one ray of hope out of this is that some of these poor abused souls have concluded that in spite of their religious experience, they still want God. Sadly, there are many people that walk away from God when their religious leaders or experiences fail them. However, God is distinct from man and religion. But, where do such individuals begin in their search for the true God of heaven? How do they discern between the influence of religious leaders and that of truth and righteousness? Who can begin to help these individuals come to terms with the issues that loom before them? After all, they are now suspicious of all religious people. They have seen the insidious control of leaders with personal agendas, riding high on ego trips, but the one question that haunts them is whether there is one person who is willing to step up to the plate to help them wade through the maze of deception without seeking brownie points or personal victories. Is there such a person who will not take advantage of their vulnerability, while being patient with their suspicions? Is there someone who will not be judgmental when it comes to all of their questions?

Clearly these individuals need a revelation of Jesus Christ. But, who can they trust or where can they go to find the space to work through the spiritual and emotional devastation that they must now wade through to come back to the center of truth? They clearly need to be constructively challenged by truth that will set them free.

This book is designed to help Christians understand the debate that rages in the minds of those who have a cult mentality. It is vital that we who claim fundamental ties to the Christian faith have the means to give an account of the hope that is in us. It is this hope that can only be realized in the life and truth of Christ that will wonderfully and gloriously set these people free from their cult mentality.

Section 1

ESTABLISHING A STANDARD OF TRUTH

THE FOUNDATION

As Christians who must contend for the faith that was first delivered to the saints, we need to understand how to help those with a cult mentality. Needless to say, such people must be open to honestly evaluate the shaky foundation and pseudo faith they might still be clinging to due to the influence of their cult. Clearly, these individuals must have a contrast with which to compare, consider, and separate heresy from truth. But, before these individuals can bring a separation through reasoning at the point of Scripture, they must first come to terms with what they believe.

In order to expose their right belief system, the right questions must be asked. But, what are the right questions, especially if you are not sure about what to ask? After all, these individuals may possess some right beliefs that have been cleverly laced with wrong influences and teachings. Or, perhaps they have been exposed to a wrong spirit, while much of their foundation would prove to be stable. On the other hand, maybe their whole foundation is wrong.

The key is foundation. Unsuspecting people test all matters according to the foundation that has been established. If people have a wrong foundation, then nothing will stand under scrutiny or judgment. Therefore, the first challenge to these people's mentality must be taken from *Matthew 7:24-27*. What has their foundation been established upon, the sand of man's ever-changing religion or has it been founded upon the Rock of ages?

Wrong spiritual foundations are often made up of presumptions and assumptions or truths and righteous doctrines. The dictionary states that a presumption is an attitude or belief dictated by probability.[1] In other words, a person presumes that he or she understands a matter based on an assumption. Assumptions or assumed beliefs are comprised of an understanding or belief that the individual assumes is true, but which has never really been personally tested. When an assumed belief is challenged, a person can become confused, angry, and fearful. Peter challenged such assumptions in *1 Peter 3:15* with these exhortations: "But sanctify the Lord God in your hearts, and be <u>ready</u> <u>always</u> <u>to</u> <u>give</u> <u>an</u> <u>answer</u> <u>to</u> <u>every</u> <u>man</u> <u>that</u> <u>asketh</u> <u>you</u> <u>a</u> <u>reason</u> <u>of</u> <u>the</u> <u>hope</u> <u>that</u> <u>is</u> <u>in</u> <u>you</u>, with meekness and fear." (Emphasis added.)

Obviously, if a person quotes what he or she has heard, then it is an assumed belief. If this person is asked why he or she believes a certain way, and responds by referring to a source other than personal conviction established by the Word of God and confirmed by Holy Spirit, then it is obviously presumption on the part of the person. Such a presumption simply reveals that the person who is assuming that a matter is right is operating from the premise of blind hope. In blind hope, this individual will simply hide behind this presumption to relieve self of being responsible for establishing and maintaining a right foundation. However, the Word of God is clear. The truths of God are simple enough for a child to embrace by faith *(Matthew 18:1-4; 2 Corinthians 11:3)*. Therefore, each of us as believers are able and capable of giving an answer for what we see as our hope in regard to all spiritual matters. *Colossians 1:27* clearly reveals what constitutes the hope within each believer.

How can people know how much of their foundation is made up of presumptions and assumptions? By knowing this answer, struggling souls can put their beliefs in the right perspective. In other words, if people's foundation is full of presumptions and assumptions, they must hold lightly to what they believe, and give God permission to shake up their foundation. Shaking foundations will allow individuals to test their personal beliefs with the Word of God to see how well they withstand the shaking. However, such a thought is frightening for most people. After all, what if He shakes everything and nothing is left standing on their foundation? They would have to once again start establishing a new foundation.

It is important to understand what is at risk for these people. They have given their heart, time, resources and energy for what they perceived to be truth. To many of them they have a hard time considering that their religious experiences were a waste of time. They would like to think that there is something that could be salvaged in the devastation of it all. Sadly, what many of these individuals discover is

---

[1] The various meaning of words in this study came from two sources: Strong's Exhaustive Concordance of the Bible and the Webster's New Collegiate Dictionary.

that even those things that have a semblance of truth have been tainted in some way by the poison of heresy.

The battle for these people to simply embrace truth can be intense. It takes everything in them to focus their confusing mind and conflicting heart on one goal and that is to know the truth no matter what. After all, it will be the uncompromised truth that sets them free from the oppression, hurts, and wounds that have been left in their souls by those who have betrayed their trust *(John 8:32)*.

The Bible also brings the contrast as to the urgency for each believer to not just know the truth, but to love it. It warns about the impending destruction to those who do not love the truth. They will be turned over to delusion *(2 Thessalonians 2:10-12)*. In light of this warning, each believer must individually choose the truth in spite of what it might reveal about his or her foundation. Obviously, the only one who can reveal the stability of our foundation is God. It is at this time that we each need to examine our personal foundations. Based on the percentage of 1-100% ask God how much of your foundation is actually made up of presumptions and assumptions.

THE PREMISE OF TRUTH

How concerned should we be if presumptions and assumptions make up over 50% of our foundation? In other words, we cannot give a scriptural answer from the premise of personal conviction and knowledge for 50% or more for what we consider to be our beliefs. Keep in mind, these beliefs may well determine our eternal destination. Therefore, we could be in serious trouble. However, let us say that 20%-40% of our foundation is made up of presumptions and assumptions. In this figure, we are assured of being over 50% right, but is such a percentage good enough when it comes to truth? To understand the seriousness of being even one percent off truth, we first must come to terms with how truth operates in our lives.

It is important at this time to consider that presumptions and assumptions often represent areas of indoctrination. The Bible is clear that we need to be guided into all truth *(John 16:13)*. However, many people associated with religion are not guided; rather, they are indoctrinated by their religious leaders or systems. On a separate sheet of paper for your personal edification, be ready to answer the questions presented in this study. The first question is what is the difference between indoctrination and guidance into the truth?

Here is a statement that we need to get into our spirits. "People are never indoctrinated into truth; rather, they are indoctrinated into man's point of view about a matter." The way people perceive will determine how they will interpret the truth. However, truth does not have to be interpreted; instead, it has to be recognized and believed as being truth.

Therefore, indoctrination involves imbuing a particular opinion, point of view, or principle. In Christianity, such indoctrination often points to an emphasis of certain doctrines or spiritual beliefs as being the truth, rather than the person and life of Jesus. Needless to say, such doctrines can have a personal twist or distortion to them that can oppose truth, rather than adhere to it *(2 Peter 2:1-3; 3:16)*. It is not unusual that doctrine, which finds it origins in indoctrination, to be inundated with Scripture, but when you test the intent or spirit behind it, such doctrine becomes unscriptural. In fact, all one needs to do to change the spirit or intent of God's truth is to change the meaning or emphasis behind a word. For example, take the word meekness. "Meekness" means controlled strength or rage. However, if you take the meaning that is often associated with this word in our culture and apply it to Jesus in His humanity, the definition of Him would be a wimp, rather than one whose very strength and being was under the control of the Spirit.

This brings us to the importance of emphasis. Religious leaders can emphasize good Scriptural points, but still miss the intent of the whole counsel of God's Word. For example, they can emphasize holiness, God's love, grace, works, repentance, sovereignty, etc., but the truth of God's intention and purpose is still absent. These leaders may also have what appears to be the right emphasis, but with the wrong presentation or approach.

The problem with starting from a wrong or biased presentation is that people will end up defining the perspective as to how they look at it according to the spirit that is influencing them. In other words, the particular emphasis will serve as a main theme or point in which all matters will automatically be considered. It is the same concept as looking through rose-colored glasses. Everything will appear rosy, but in reality, it is a false presentation. For cult members to understand how they are defining religious matters, they must consider what their religious leaders emphasized the most in their different religious presentations. Obviously, it would do each of us well to consider the type of emphasis we are exposing ourselves to when it comes to the religious influences in our lives.

How does each of us consider whether the religious theme being purported is correct? Here are some questions to consider. Does it allow God to be God? For example, some themes exalt one aspect of God such as His love, especially in a worldly fashion, while ignoring or downplaying another attribute of God such as holiness. Does it present a balanced picture of God's work and intervention on behalf of man? For instance, an important theme of the Bible is salvation. Clearly, we see where God saves because of His grace, but in some religious circles, it is taught that man's works are a necessary ingredient in order to obtain salvation. In this case, God's grace is being frustrated or made void by the attempts of people who strive to become righteous by their own merits. The fruit of such emphasis are obvious because when challenged, people become vague or confused about God and His salvation *(Galatians 2:21; Ephesians 2:8-10).*

Is there one theme in the Bible that allows for God to be God, presents a balanced picture of His works and ways, and brings the proper contrast as to man's part in salvation, such as faith? The answer is yes. See if you can distinguish this theme by considering the following Scriptures: *Romans 5:10; 2 Corinthians 5:18-19; Ephesians 2:14-18;* and *Colossians 1:20-23.*

God's heart is to establish a relationship with each of us that will promote spiritual growth, joy, peace, and satisfaction. It is a relationship where we will be able to enjoy Him, and He is able to enjoy us. This relationship has many aspects to it, but ultimately it will satisfy all desires of the heart, bring unspeakable joy to the soul, peace to one's being, and produce a hope that will never waver in light of eternity.

By changing the intent of something, you can actually redefine the character and work of God along with His many other truths. Clearly, man is vulnerable to influences and persuasions that could cause him to deviate from the truth, and embrace a lie, even when Scriptures are improperly used as a guise to confirm or verify a matter.

In trying to understand the diligence of the Bereans in *Acts 17:10-12,* it is important to realize that they were comparing scripture with scripture to see if the Apostle Paul's teaching was in line with the intent of the full counsel of God's Word. This comparison was to ensure the integrity of God's Word. However, most indoctrination has to do with how man perceives or interprets the Word. It is important to point out that truth always stands on its own, but Scripture does not. One must always compare Scripture with Scripture to ensure a correct perspective.

Again, it is not unusual for people to use Scriptures to validate their wrong perceptions, but the Scriptures they use are taken out of context to form a biased picture or belief system. In fact, indoctrination of people by using certain phrases or words, along with specific terminology can cause them to close themselves off to any challenge that might set them free to test their foundation and explore God's truth beyond their established comfort zones of indoctrination. Indoctrination of this type is destructive at any level. Undoubtedly, some of the religious leaders of Jesus' day were indoctrinating people by teaching their own traditions. Jesus told them that they made the Word of God ineffective, and their worship a useless exercise *(Matthew 15:3-9).* He also made this statement, "But woe unto you, scribes and Pharisees, hypocrites! For ye shut up the kingdom of heaven against men; for ye neither go in yourselves, neither suffer them that are entering to go in" *(Matthew 23:13).*

Indoctrination closes down a person's ability to discern. It has only one goal and that is to influence and control how a person thinks. On the other hand, God wants to transform our way of thinking. For the sake of avoiding assumptions about this matter, we each need to know the difference between influence and transformation. The answer to this matter can be found in the different meanings of these two words, as well as in *Romans 12:1-2.*

Even if indoctrination has scriptural merit, it still erects a perspective that will only allow people to interpret the Bible according to what they have been systematically taught. It does not encourage the recipients to test such matters, which requires them to think outside of the box.

Thinking outside of their indoctrinated understanding produces confusions and fear. Since indoctrination is influenced by a wrong spirit, those who are held captive by their indoctrination will be prevented from seeing the truth, or when challenged by truth, will quickly become closed to it, rejecting it as a lie.

It is also important to acknowledge two important facts. The first fact is that all of us have been exposed to indoctrination in some way. The second fact we must acknowledge is that we can always find people and teachings to confirm any desired belief, regardless of whether it is truth or not. However, can any of us, as believers, afford to settle for any real interpretation of man in any area of our lives? Indoctrination closes people down to some extent from thinking outside of its presentation. We can clearly see this scenario in much of our public education.

We need to consider how much we have been indoctrinated to believe someone's interpretation of God, the Bible, and life by honestly grading our present belief systems in the following ways: (E) Extremely indoctrinated to the point that terms and words can close me down to any constructive challenge; (C) indoctrinated enough to cause confusion when challenged outside of the box; (M) possess a mixture of indoctrination and truth, but cannot really discern truth from indoctrination; (S) somewhat indoctrinated, causing vagueness in important spiritual foundational beliefs; (O) maintained open mind in spite of any indoctrination, but am struggling with what is true because of the past influence of man or a wrong spirit. (If unsure, ask the Lord to reveal the extent of your indoctrination.)

The question is how can believers know whether something is truth? All lies have a semblance of logic that can be adjusted and presented to appear as if they are truth to man's intellect. The Bible is clear that we can know the truth, but not all are receptive towards it. In some cases, people mishandle the truth, incurring the wrath of God upon themselves. The Bible is clear that we can do nothing against the truth, only for it *(Romans 1:18; 2 Corinthians 13:8)*. *Proverbs 23:23* gives us this vivid instruction, "Buy the truth, and sell it not; also wisdom, and instruction, and understanding."

This brings us down to the premise of truth. Truth is absolute and unchangeable. If people do not start from what is truth, they cannot expect to come out finding or knowing truth. A good example of a premise of truth is creation. The first book of the Bible tells us that God created all that is visible. Therefore, it is from this premise that man must consider all creation. Granted, truth can be confused or discredited by unfounded implications, theories, and lies by those who hate it, but since it is consistent and unable to be refuted, all truths concerning creation fit nicely into the teaching of creationism. However, if you take the humanistic theory of evolution, it can only stand in a class of its own. It sounds logical because it stays away from certain facts and laws. Instead of coming from the center of truth, it has to start on the outside fringes of what is acceptable logic, and work its way towards the center by trying to explain away, ignore, and discredit that which is already established as truth. Evolution can only be upheld in ignorance and maintained within its own perverted arena because it does not fit into the workings of creation. For example, the theory of evolution is not consistent with the Law of Thermodynamics, and discoveries such as DNA. These different laws and discoveries point to Intelligent Design, which clearly refute this humanistic theory.

Therefore, indoctrination unfairly establishes in people the premise in which all things will be judged. This, then, is a perverted view, as opposed to the truth, which serves as the premise by which all things must be considered, weighed, and tested. Indoctrination will cause people to close down to any challenge, while truth will embrace challenge because it will always be confirmed, especially to those who are truly seeking it. Indoctrination insists that the ignorance it is creating is light and not darkness. Truth, on the other hand, serves as the light, and has nothing to fear. Once again, you can do nothing against the truth, only for it. In the end, truth will stand, as all falsehood will crumble under judgment.

The necessary question is, is there one standard of truth that the searching soul can trust? *John 17:17* says, "Sanctify them through thy truth; thy word is truth."

ATTITUDE TOWARDS THE WORD OF GOD

According to the *Gospel of John,* the Word of God serves as the absolute standard in which to test all matters. The most fundamental stand that Christians lay claim to is that the Bible is the only inspired and authoritative written Word of God. But, the question is, how many approach the Bible as if it is the infallible Word of God? *2 Peter 1:19-21* states this case,

> We have also a more sure word of prophecy, unto which ye do well that ye take heed, as unto a light that shineth in a dark place, until the day dawn, and the day star arise in your hearts; Knowing this first, that no prophecy of the scripture is of any private interpretation. For the prophecy came not in old time by the will of man, but holy men of God spake as they were moved by the Holy Ghost.

Do religious people assume, or really believe, that all biblical prophecies are not of any private interpretation? Do they believe it is sure? On the other hand, is it one of those beliefs that they presume is truth, but in reality they are unaware that they are denying it because of a wrong attitude towards the Word? After all, those who interpret the Word for us in preaching and teaching will often become the final authority as to what we believe. Answer the following question. (Yes, I believe it is not of any private interpretation, or no I do not believe it has not been inspired by the Holy Spirit.)

Notice that the word Peter used in his letter was the word "prophecy". The word "prophecy" means prediction. In other words, are the predictions of the Bible sure? This is important because to fulfill prophecy would require powerful intervention. Fulfilled prophecies serve as the means of proving that God is indeed capable of maintaining the integrity of His Word. The integrity of the Word does not address the minor discrepancies that so many skeptics point to as a means to warrant their unbelief; rather, it is a matter of maintaining the intent or spirit of it. If you honestly consider the discrepancies found in the Word, they do not change the main themes of the Bible nor do they alter the character of God, His heart and commitment towards us, His ways concerning truth, and His works on our behalf.

Many prophecies have been fulfilled concerning Tyre, Petra, Nineveh, and Egypt, as well as those surrounding Israel. In fact, one man, when asked how he knew the Bible was true, answered with one word, "Israel." God is not through with Israel, but the fulfilled prophecies concerning this nation are incredible. However, the prophecies that are the most compelling as to the surety of God's Word and power are those that surround Jesus Christ. In his book, *Evidence That Demands A Verdict*, Josh McDowell points out the probabilities of just eight prophecies being fulfilled according to the modern science of probabilities. The probability for eight prophecies to be fulfilled would be 1 in 100,000,000,000,000,000. To comprehend this you would have to take this many silver dollars and spread them throughout the state of Texas. They would actually cover the state two feet deep. You would then mark one of these silver dollars and mix it up in the great mass of coins. Next, you would blindfold a man and ask him to somehow locate and pick up that marked coin. What chance would this man have in locating the marked coin? He would have the same chance that the prophets would have in writing just eight prophecies and having them fulfilled in one man. Yet, according to the book, *All the Messianic Prophecies of the Bible,* by Herbert Lockyer, Jesus fulfilled an estimated 300 prophecies. Each fulfillment of prophecy makes the odds go higher, validating the integrity and validity of the Written Word. Based on prophecy, not the doctrine of man, the Written Word is sure because the author of it is true to His word, and more than able to bring it forth, while maintaining its integrity.

If the attitude of people is wrong about the Bible, they will not believe it to be true. If they do not believe it to be true, then they will strip it of its power to affect their lives properly. Such an attitude will destroy the power the Word must have in their lives to set the record straight as far as personal beliefs. This issue proves to be a real struggle for those who are former cult members because God's Word was not only perverted, it has been stripped of its truth and power by making it subservient to the heretical beliefs that were established as foundational.

It is vital that as Christians we test our real attitude and approach towards the Bible. Former cult members remind me that Christians can take much for granted when it comes to their foundation. We can mentally presume we recognize the authority of the Word, but our attitude or approach towards it could reveal that we really do not regard it as a personal authority in relationship to our lives.

Consider the following Scripture, "All scripture is given by inspiration of God, and is profitable for doctrine, for reproof, for correction, for instruction in righteousness" *(2 Timothy 3:16)*. (Emphasis added.) Does this Scripture say most of the Scriptures are given by inspiration; therefore, we can ignore some? If we can ignore or explain away some, the question remains which Scriptures will we discredit and which ones will we believe? One of the signs of a cult is that it believes the Bible "as far as it is translated" in correlation to the belief system it maintains. If people are indoctrinated, they will automatically discredit those Scriptures that oppose their leader or denomination's point of view. As a result, personal attitudes need to be exposed towards the Word of God in order to see if a person's attitude is correct. In order to properly challenge wrong attitudes, believers need to understand what *2 Timothy 3:16* should mean on a personal basis. At this point, the reader is encouraged to meditate upon and write a summary of what the Scripture in *2 Timothy* means to him or her.

Obviously, the complete Word of God is profitable in establishing right doctrine, to bring proper reproof in the area of error, possesses the authority to bring proper correction in areas of wrong attitudes and practices, and ultimately bring instruction in regard to true righteousness. The issue as to whether the Bible has this type of authority in one's life comes down to how he or she approaches the Bible.

There are different ways in which people approach the Bible. Some approach it from a doctrinal point of view. In the end, such people will adjust the Word according to their doctrine, rather than test and adjust their doctrine to the Word of God. Some approach it from an intellectual level. They want the facts to establish or confirm their present understanding about spiritual matters. As a result, they will only see what they want to see on an intellectual level, while ignoring the other facets of Scripture. In most cases, people approach the Word of God from a self-serving basis to confirm what they consider to be their present truth, but few approach the Bible to find what truth is according to the Word of God.

Romans 10:17 tells us how to approach the Word of God. We are to approach the Word with the intent to receive it as truth by faith. Faith begins where personal understanding ceases. Since personal understanding is not serving as the premise in which a person will view the Word, it will ensure the Word's integrity and powerful impact, while establishing itself as the authority in a person's life. (Also, consider *Romans 14:23; 2 Corinthians 5:7; 13:5; Ephesians 2:8-9;* and *Hebrews 11:6.)*

It is vital we understand what role the Word of God plays in our lives. First, we must consider how it relates to our spiritual growth. *(*See *1 Peter 2:2; Hebrews 5:14.)* Milk points to the pure doctrine of the Word. The Scriptures in *Hebrews 5:13-6:2* bring this out. The writer of *Hebrews* exhorts Christians to graduate from the stage of milk to solid food or meat by leaving the principles of the doctrines of Christ, and going on to perfection or spiritual maturity.

The problem with keeping a person at the level of doctrine is that he or she will remain carnal or fleshly in his or her way of thinking. Since cults establish a false doctrine as a foundation under cult members, these former members cannot even graduate from milk to meat. Instead, they wrestle with the fact that the milk (doctrine) they did partake of was contaminated. In a way, they have to throw out all the milk in order to taste the pure milk of Christ's doctrine. Pure milk is required before a person can graduate from the stage of carnality to a place of being able to walk properly in the ways of righteousness.

The Corinthians were struggling with carnality *(1 Corinthians 3:1-11).* For these Christians, this carnality translated into schisms in the body of believers and cause them to place their value in being associated with men rather than Jesus Christ. Clearly, carnality in the Christian causes inconsistency in his or her walk.

Another problem with keeping people at the milk level where they are dependent on doctrine and man, is that they never learn to discern. *Hebrews 15:12-13* brings this fact out. Discerning is the ability to discern the spirit or intent of a matter to ensure righteousness. Righteousness is not just a matter of doing right, but of being right or having right standing before God. Right standing involves having a right spirit to ensure the integrity of attitudes, approaches, and actions. Such integrity will prevent people from mishandling the truth.

Truth, when it is properly maintained, will have the necessary impact or effect on the way people think and operate. Therefore, discerning is of the utmost importance when it comes to properly identifying the spirit that is operating, not only in others, but also within ourselves. Take a moment to consider *Hebrews 4:12* and *1 John 4:1* in light of discerning the spirit motivating you or that is operating in your present environment.

We do not have to debate as to why some leaders keep people at the milk or diaper stage of Christianity. These people want these poor souls to be ever learning according to their perspective, but never coming to the knowledge of the truth that will enable them to properly discern spirit and take authority over their own spiritual growth *(2 Timothy 3:7).*

Discernment points to the fact that the Word of God is a spiritual book. In other words, the deep truths (meat) of the Bible are only realized in the spiritual realm and not on a natural level. Consider what *1 Corinthians 2:10-14* says about this matter. The Bible is a spiritual book; therefore, only the Holy Spirit can properly discern how its truths must be applied to our lives.

Answer the following question: Why must the Word of God be approached from the perspective of right spirit in order to gain truth? *(See 1 Corinthians 2:5-14; 15:51; Ephesians 1:9; 3:3, 9;* and *Colossians 1:26; 2:3)*

The mysteries contained within the Word of God can be unveiled through revelation, realized in wisdom (that is neither of man nor of this world), and brought forth in knowledge tempered by virtue and self-control *(2 Peter 1:5-7).* In light of this information, do you think that mere man can unveil the depths of these truths to our spirits? *(See John 16:7-13* and *1 John 2:27.)*

The Holy Spirit is the One who leads us into all truth and teaches us the deep things of God. He is the One who inspired the Word and ensured its integrity through the ages. As a result, we as believers have the means to discern between what is good (acceptable) and what is evil (wicked) when it comes to all spiritual matters and practices.

As stated, there are a couple of major themes in the Bible, but one of those themes is that as believers we can, we should, and we must know God. It is from the premise of who God is and His work that all matters must be considered and weighed. The Bible serves as God's diary. We can see into His heart, know His will, hear His cries, and discern His call. The Bible never instructs us to seek doctrine or personal understanding and knowledge, but to seek God, and we will live *(Jeremiah 29:13; Amos 5:4-8).*

The question is, has this study thus far changed your attitude and approach towards the Word of God? If so, in what way?

Section 2

IN SEARCH OF GOD

WHO IS GOD?

Who is God? When you question former members of a cult about how they perceive God, they often present a confusing mixture that may have some truth in it, but it digresses into some abstract or vague notion about God. In most cases, He seems far away from these people's understanding.

As Christians who may encounter former cult members, we need to be able to address this issue clearly. If the Word is dedicated for the purpose of God's saints knowing Him, then as His people, we must make it our priority to seek Him in Scripture and prayer for the purpose of growing in the knowledge of His character and ways. However, how can people know God? If He is whom the Bible says He is, He is beyond mere man's comprehension. Yet, it is clear, we as believers must know Him. The best way is to begin with our personal perception of God. Who is He to me? Who is He to you? Meditate upon this, and then answer the question for yourself.

As believers, can we afford to have a vague idea about God? Can we settle for a concept of God? It is easy to put God into a nice theological box, but in doing so we run the risk of stripping Him of His personality. To keep Him on an intellectual level, as some do, is to demote Him in His majesty. According to *Daniel 11:32b*, "...but the people that do know their God shall be strong, and do exploits." Obviously, any power and authority we possess will hinge on how much we personally know our God. Due to the fact that there are many gods, the real great search for those seeking His truth is to come to terms with who the God of the Bible is. For your personal edification what can you scripturally learn about the different gods? *(Jeremiah 10:6-15; Romans 1:19-28; 1 Corinthians 8:4-5; 2 Corinthians 10:4-5)*

In contrast, what do the following Scriptures say about the God of the Bible? *(Genesis 1:1; Exodus 3:4-6, 14-16; 20:1-5; 34:5-7; Psalm 91:1-9; 92:15; 100:3; Isaiah 43:10-11; 44:6-7; 45:5-9, 14, 18, 21-22; 46:9; 48:12; 49:7; Lamentations 3:22-26; James 2:19)*

When we consider other gods, in most cases, we are talking about idolatry. The big difference between the God of the Bible and other gods is that the God of the Bible created the heavens and the earth, while man creates other gods according to the vain imaginations of his heart and mind. It is man that gives false gods their preeminence in his life by giving them identity, erecting them into a place of importance, and coming under their false authority *(Psalm 115:2-9; Isaiah 2:8; Ezekiel 8:7-12; 14:3-7)*. The problem with idolatry is that it becomes an avenue in which the kingdom of Satan can work in its darkness, play on people's ignorance about God, and replace the true God with the worship of demonic entities. The harsh reality is that demons are behind all idolatry. In *1 Corinthians 8:4-6,* gods also point to magistrates or judges, while lords point to masters.

Scripturally we know there is only one true God who deserves our worship because He is our Creator. In summation, He is the only One who deserves our consideration and service *(Psalms 81:9; Matthew 4:10; Luke 4:8; Colossians 2:18)*. It is important to realize that Satan, the god of this present world, is after our worship, and if he can get us to bow down to any idol, he has succeeded in undermining the authority of God in our lives and directing worship towards himself.

As our Creator, God stands distinct from all other gods. However, He also stands distinct as far as His identity from all other gods. How can we identify God? (See *Galatians 4:8.)* What does the word nature mean? "Nature" means the essence or attributes of something or someone.

There is only one God by nature. He is not God because people refer to Him as God. He is God because of who He is. He is a being, entity, or person. What does it mean for God to be a being, entity or person?

The concept of "being" means that something does exist, while "entity" points to the existence of something as contrasted with its attributes. For example, demons are an entity. Such an entity's attributes identify and distinguish them as wicked. However, the concept of a "person" has to do with personality. Personality serves as the means in which we can interact with another. Scripture stipulates that God is spirit, and in *John 5:37* we are told that no one has seen the shape, or form, of the Father *(John 4:24)*. However, we are also told God has manifested Himself in the man Christ Jesus *(1 Timothy 3:16)*. Even though God is Spirit, He also has a distinct personality that enables others to interact with Him. He communed with Adam, walked with Noah, talked face-to-face with Moses, and met with Joshua. He could not interact with these men if He did not have a personality. We need to consider God according to the context of His person or personality.

In comparison, idols do not exist, except in the imaginations of those who worship them. Those who worship them give them an image, but they have no real personality in which to interact with them. In addition, any relationship with a demon is one sided, ending in grave oppression. Due to the interaction that God desires with us, Christianity is not a religion, but a relationship with the Living God. By understanding God's nature, we will have a sense as to how to properly respond to, as well as interact with Him in a relationship.

The Bible clearly identifies the attributes of God. Again, there is only one true God, and we can personally know Him. Some of His attributes are that He is eternal, holy, faithful, merciful, and full of grace. These are just a few of God's traits. However, the one trait that stands out to me is that He is immutable or unchangeable in His nature, disposition, and ways *(Psalm 102:27; Malachi 3:6)*. When you consider how life is constantly in a state of flux, we can begin to understand how important it is to us, as believers, that God is that immovable Rock. Winds of doctrine may come and go, but God never changes. Religion may change the face of God in the eyes of its followers through its different presentations of Him, but the God of the Bible remains the same. As a result, there should be no confusion about Him and His identity. However, confusion and problems always arise when man defines Him according to theology, doctrine, and personal agendas, instead of by the Spirit and truth of the Word of God.

The great confusion and debates surrounding the identity of the true God is the result of man refusing to simply believe the Bible about Him, and instituting his own understanding and conclusions into some doctrinal or theological presentation. Cults actually redefine God. In the end, the beliefs, practices, or the leader becomes the latest god (idol) in a long line of idols that man exalts in his heart and mind. Eventually these false gods will be defeated and brought down. If they are re-erected, it is because of man's ignorance towards the real God.

Three aspects of God properly identify the one true God. These points of identification begin with the fact that He is our Creator (what He has done), and that He has a distinct nature (Who He is). The final aspect is what He deserves. Because of who He is and what He has done, He alone deserves our worship. It is vital that we keep this presentation about God simple. After all, the Word of God can be overwhelming to those who do not possess a clear understanding about God. People become lost or take detours from the simplicity and truths of God's Word, causing them to lose their ability to properly discern or reason a matter out concerning their Creator. Let us now consider the God of the Bible.

The Father:

The Father is identified as God in *1 Corinthians 8:6*. Clearly, there is one entity known as God, the Father *(Ephesians 4:6)*. As stated, we can know the Person of the Father, due to the fact He has a personality in which we can interact with Him. Nevertheless, what do we need to understand about God being our Heavenly Father? Again, we must somehow bring a contrast as to what we assume we believe about God versus what the Word of God declares.

The first thing that the term "father" brings to mind is the type of relationship He desires with each of us: to be His children. That is simple enough, but who is our Father? What do we need to know and understand about Him to possess a personal sense of who He must be in our lives? What do the following Scriptures show us about God, the Father? *(Matthew 6:1, 4, 8, 14, 26, 32; 7:11; 16:17; Mark 14:36: Luke 6:36: 10:21-22; 12:30; John 5:37; 6:44, 65; Acts 1:4, 7; 2 Corinthians 1:2-3; Galatians 1:1, 3; Ephesians 1:17; Colossians 1:2; 2:2; 1 Thessalonians 1:1; 2 Thessalonians 1:1-2; James 1: 27: 1 John 3:1)*

In these Scriptures, we can learn some interesting facts about the Father. We know He is located in heaven, but how many of us understood until now that no man had really seen His shape, nor had the Jewish people heard His voice. This is interesting to me because people had actual encounters with God in the Old Testament such as Jacob, Moses, Joshua, and Isaiah *(Genesis 28:12-13; Exodus 3:2-6; 24:9-12; 33:9-11; 18-23; Joshua 5:13-15; Isaiah 6)* (Note, Joshua paid homage or worshipped the Captain of the LORD's host). Is there any discrepancy in Scripture concerning the Father? As previously stated, there are mysteries in the Bible. It is up to God to reveal them to us through His Spirit. The challenge is always there. Will each of us allow our logic to dictate to us, or will we choose to believe the Scriptures about the Father as true, and trust that in time the Holy Spirit will make sense out of them?

From these Scriptures, we know that the Father is after what is true and genuine. We also know that Jesus Christ was in total subjection to His will, and that He sent the promise of the Holy Spirit. He is the essence of love, displays mercy, desires to forgive, gives peace, hides spiritual mysteries from those who are prideful, reveals Jesus' identity, draws people to His Son, gives His people the spirit of wisdom and revelation, and He knows what we have need of and provides it. This makes Him Jehovah Jireh, our Provider. He knows the seasons concerning His eternal plan, raised up Jesus on the third day, and that He is part of the mystery concerning Jesus Christ.

1 Corinthians 8:6 calls the Father, God, and states, "of whom are all things." It is because of Him all things exist. This clearly shows us that the Father was involved with creation, which points to Him as the Designer of all things. Without His design, nothing could or would exist. Being the designer of all creation also means that He fits the first criteria of being God in relationship to being our Creator. In *James 1:17*, it tells us that He is immutable or unchanging in His nature and ways, and in *John 4:23-24* we learn that the Father seeks those who will worship Him in spirit and truth. In fact, we are to give Him thanks in the name of Jesus *(Ephesians 5:20)*. *Philippians 4:20* summarizes it best, "Now unto God and our Father be glory forever and ever, Amen." As you can see, the Father fits all three criteria as far as being God.

Has your understanding of the Father changed or become enlarged? Obviously, we are only skimming the surface of who He is, for we know He is eternal. The question is, how do we, as believers, come to a greater understanding of the Father? He actually gives us a valuable key in coming to a greater awareness of who He is in *John 8:19*, "Then said they unto him, Where is thy Father? Jesus answered, Ye neither know me, nor my Father; if ye had known me, ye should have known my Father also."

Jesus stated that He is the way to the Father, the truth about the Father, and the place where life is established in the Father. He told His disciples that because they had known Him, they also knew the Father *(John 14:6-7)*. We see where there was confusion about this issue. We then read these Scriptures in *John 14:8-9*, "Philip saith unto him, Lord show us the Father, and it sufficeth us. Jesus saith unto him, Have I been so long time with you, and yet hast thou not known me, Philip? He that hath seen me hath seen the Father; and how sayest thou then, Show us the Father?"

Obviously, to know the Father, we must come to terms with the Son.

The Son:

Who is Jesus Christ? How important is it for each of us to possess the understanding as to Jesus' real identity? Once again, former cult members will teach you the seriousness of this issue. If you could pinpoint the one Scriptural truth that is under attack when it comes to the majority of the cults, it comes down to Jesus' identity. Most former cult members are people who have greatly struggled with the identity of the Son. Granted, these members may give a basic rundown about how Jesus is the Savior, but, the real difference does not rest in what Jesus did as far as the cross; rather, it comes down to who He is. This conflict has been great among the different theological camps. Is Jesus mere man or is He more? Is He simply a man who serves as a reflection of the Father in godliness and serves as a prophet in word and deed, or does

He possess the very characteristics of the Father? If so, it would also mean that He possesses the very nature of God.

We could easily brush over this issue because we assume that we know what we believe about Jesus and presume that it is a matter that most Christians can agree with; but Jesus clearly warned believers of false Christ's in the end days. He made this statement in *Matthew 24:23-24,* "Then if any man shall say unto you, Lo, here is Christ, or there; believe it not. For there shall arise false Christs, and false prophets, and shall show great signs and wonders, insomuch that, if it were possible, they shall deceive the very elect."

The Apostle Paul made this statement: in *2 Corinthians 11:3-4,*

> For I fear, lest by any means, as the serpent beguiled Eve through his subtilty, so your minds should be corrupted from the simplicity that is in Christ. For if he that cometh preacheth another Jesus, whom we have not preached, or if ye receive another spirit, which ye have not received, or another gospel, which ye have not accepted, ye might well bear with him.

"Bear" in this text means to hold oneself up against. In other words, we need to challenge and bring contrast to one who preaches another Jesus.

The reason for this challenge can be found in *1 John 2:22-23,* "Who is a liar but he that denieth that Jesus is the Christ? He is antichrist, that denieth the Father and the Son. Whosoever denieth the Son, the same hath not the Father; he that acknowledgeth the Son hath the Father also." To believe another Christ implies that a person is under the antichrist spirit, and is rejecting the witness, claims, and reality of the Father. To believe or promote another Christ makes the individual a fraud.

Clearly, we must make sure that our understanding concerning the Son of God is right. The Apostle Paul stipulated that Jesus is the only real foundation upon which people must be established. If we have a wrong Jesus, we also fail to possess the Father. Such a prospect should cause us to tremble at the possibility that we have embraced another Jesus. For if we do not believe and possess the correct Jesus, we will not possess eternal life *(1 Corinthians 3:11; 1 John 5:12).*

At this point, we need to examine honestly the possibility that some, or even much, of our understanding of Jesus may be traced back to man's presentation. We also must discern how much of our understanding is in line with the Word of God. This challenge will bring us to *Matthew 16:13-16.*

Jesus asked his disciples a very simple question in these Scriptures in *Matthew 16*, "But who do men say that I, the Son of man, am?" People's initial understanding of Jesus always comes from another person's presentation. As a result, we need to answer this question for ourselves.

Apparently, the popular belief of Jesus' day was that He was some great prophet like Elijah. Granted, Jesus was a prophet, but He was not Elijah or Jeremiah. Clearly, what the disciples heard from others was incorrect.

Jesus did not stop at the point of other people's personal take on Him. It is common to hear various contradictory witnesses about Jesus from others, making it easy for those who, because of ignorance, assumptions, or presumptions, choose to hide behind these opinions as they presume such presentations to be right. However, inevitably we are going to have to face what we personally believe about Jesus. We are personally responsible to know for ourselves who Jesus is. Jesus made this clear by His second question, "But who say ye that I am?" *(Matthew 16:15).*

If one follows the Scriptures, the answer becomes automatic, "Thou art the Christ, the Son of the living God" *(Matthew 16:16).* What do these two different terms really mean? In many cases, these are well-known terms that are part of the Christian vocabulary, but they hold no real meaning for some in the religious realm. It is generally accepted that Jesus is the Christ, but how many of us are operating from assumptions as to what it means for Jesus to be the Christ? For that matter, what does it mean for Jesus to be the Son of God? For an example as to what I am talking about, let us take the term "Christ".

"Christ" means the Anointed One of God or the Messiah. We know Jesus was anointed to carry out a specific mission *(Luke 4:18-19).* But what significance does the position of Messiah carry? For the Jewish people the term pointed to the Promised One, the Son of David, the Son of man, and their future King who would deliver them. Remember, we need to consider the sure word of prophecy about the Messiah. After all, prophecy was the means used to identify Jesus. He had to fulfill all the prophecies about the Messiah so that He would be recognized as the Promised One.

In *Isaiah's* prophecy about the Messiah, we gain much insight into Him *(Isaiah 9:6-7).* First, He would be born a child and given as a Son. The government shall be upon His shoulders. Clearly, the Messiah would be born of woman, and He would be established as king. It is important to realize that a couple of the Gospels present Jesus from the premise of Him being the Messiah. *Matthew* shows Jesus as the King, while *Luke* shows Him as the Son of man who came to deliver His people. Both of these Gospels clearly trace Jesus back to King David.

From what premise does Matthew present the Messiah? Matthew tells us that the Messiah's earthly name shall be "Jesus" (Jehovah saves) and they shall call His name, "Immanuel," which is interpreted

"God with us" *(Matthew 1:21-23).* The latter is a fulfillment of a prophecy found in *Isaiah 7:14.*

From what premise should we consider Jesus in Luke? Luke is also a fulfillment of *Isaiah 7:14.* Jesus would be born of a virgin. His name was to be "Jesus" and He would save His people. As you study Luke, you will realize this Gospel establishes a testimony as to Jesus' identity. However, Luke also establishes Jesus as the Son of the Highest or the Son of God *(Luke 1:21-32).*

This brings us to the term "Son of God." Those who believe on Jesus are the children of God. Therefore, why is the Son of God unique? He is unique because Jesus was begotten by the Father. Children of God are born into the kingdom of God, but Jesus was not born into the kingdom of heaven, He was begotten by the Father *(John 1:14; 3:3-5, 16).* Since there are cults that see Jesus as simply a "man", as His followers we need to reason out the identity of Jesus by examining whether He was conceived by Mary through some physical encounter with the Father. Keep in mind, no man has seen the Father's shape. Therefore, He does not have a body, and since He is unseen, He must be worshipped in spirit and truth.

It is important we understand Jesus' origins. If He was conceived in a natural way, that would make Him a mere man. According to *Strong's Concordance,* "begotten" implies sole son. Jesus stated that He came from heaven, and that the Father had sent Him *(John 6:33, 38-40, 51, 57-58; 8:23, 29; 12:49; 16:28).* How could Jesus be sent if He did not pre-exist? The main problem that cult members have concerning this matter is that some of them have been indoctrinated by their former cult to believe that Jesus was just a man; therefore, He did not come into existence until He was conceived and born.

As you study the different controversial beliefs claiming to be Christian, you will continually conclude that Jesus' identity is what often separates other beliefs from what is considered mainline Christianity. Almost all unaccepted beliefs rejected by mainline Christianity strip Jesus of His deity, and reduce Him to some type of created being. For example, such beliefs claim that He is a great prophet, an angel, the spiritual brother of Lucifer, a way-shower, a good man, etc.

This brings us to an important aspect that former cult members struggle over concerning this issue. Even though the Word of God can be used to challenge these controversial beliefs, cult members have been indoctrinated to present logical (although twisted) Scriptural arguments to defend their take on Jesus. For this reason, we as believers must be able to reason these matters out, not only for our personal sake, but also for those who are in bondage to heretical indoctrination.

In the past, I have had the opportunity to reason out Scriptural truths with those who have been indoctrinated by cult leaders. It not only allowed the light of Jesus truth to shine through the darkness of confusion and betrayal, but it gave me a greater assurance about the foundation that God established in His Word and in my life.

For example, a former cult member discussed with me the confusion he had concerning Jesus as God Incarnate. To quiet this man's confusion, I scripturally started from the premise of Jesus' pre-existence before He came by way of the manger. When such Scriptures as *John 1:30; 8:58,* and *17:5,* were given to verify Jesus' pre-existence, this man was quick to present the explanation that he had been given by his cult was that the Son was in the bosom of the Father *(John 1:18)*. When I heard this explanation by this former cult member, I asked him how he personally interpreted this Scripture. Did it mean that Jesus was a concept of the Father that He would bring forth in due time, or did it mean He existed, but had not yet been revealed as the Son in human form until God's eternal plan to redeem man was ready to be carried out? Upon his explanation of what it meant for Jesus to be in the bosom of the Father, I then referred him to *Luke 16:23*, pointing out that it was recorded that Lazarus was in the bosom of Abraham. According to this former cult member's vague interpretation of *John 1:18*, Lazarus would have not really existed. He would have simply been a figment of the imagination or concept of the rich man, even though the man in hell could see him, and communicate with Abraham. Just for the record, the word "bosom," implies a bay.

It was also pointed out to this man that Jesus was ascribed as having similar references as God such as those found in *Revelation 1:11:* "I am Alpha and Omega, the first and the last." (Refer to *Isaiah 48:12.)* This man had been indoctrinated well because he had an explanation for that bit of reference. His explanation was that after Jesus ascended to heaven, He was given these titles of being the Alpha and Omega. Upon this explanation, I then challenged him with *Hebrews 13:8:* "Jesus Christ, the same yesterday, and today, and forever." It was pointed out that according to this Scripture Jesus has never changed. Therefore, He always has been the Alpha and Omega. Then, I challenged the former cult member to consider all of *Revelation 1:8*: "I am Alpha and Omega the beginning and the end saith the Lord, <u>who</u> <u>is</u>, and <u>who</u> <u>was</u>, and <u>who</u> <u>is</u> <u>to</u> <u>come</u>, the <u>Almighty</u>." (Emphasis added.) This Scripture is saying the same thing. Jesus has always been the beginning and the end, He will always be the Alpha and Omega, and that He is the Almighty, or all-powerful God. Since Jesus is immutable, He is clearly fitting one of the three criteria that identify Him as God.

As the former cult member was chewing on this information, he was challenged with *John 1:1.* Needless to say, he was not so willing to address this particular Scripture. However, he gave the explanation that he had been given by his former religious teachers. Note, this former cult member's explanation is quite popular among those who denounce Jesus as being both God and man. According to this man's explanation, this particular Scripture had been mistranslated when the Catholics were translating the canon. The former cult member was then asked to explain away *John 1:2-3* while comparing these Scriptures to *1 Corinthians 8:6; Colossians 1:15-17* and *Hebrews 1:2-3*.

These Scriptures reveal Jesus as Creator, meeting the second criterion that clearly identifies Him as being God. Here is the summation of these Scriptures. The Word (Jesus Christ), who was with God from the beginning and who is God, created the world. He also upholds all things by the word of His power. The Apostle Paul tells us that by Jesus all things exist. The Father may have designed all of creation, but Jesus is the One who created everything that we see.

Why is it so important to come to terms with Jesus' origins? As we are about to see in light of the term "Son of God," we will have to conclude that premise is everything if we are going to properly handle the Word of God. For example, if Jesus is simply a man, how can He be the Son of God? If we properly understand the Scriptures, as well as the meaning of nature, Jesus can only be the Son of God if He possesses the nature of God. For example, a child inherits the traits of his or her parents. Being the sole Son of God implies that Jesus possesses the same traits as His Father. He declared that He was in the Father, and the Father was in Him *(John 14:10)*. Remember, it is recorded that the Father sent Jesus, but there are no claims that Jesus is a literal descendant or seed of the Father as He was of the woman, Mary. Clearly, the Father is divine in nature, making that which is of Him, divine in nature as well. The word "of" means origins or derivation. Jesus came from the Father in the position of a Son. As man, Jesus found His source in the Father, but as the Son of God, His deity is clearly established and shows the type of relationship that in His humanity, He had with the Father.

In the beginning, Jesus was not known as the Son, but as the Word, the verbal and visible expression of God in nature and character *(John 1:1)*. According to one article I read, the term "the Word" refers to Yeshua, the One who embodies the Word of God. *John 1:14* tells us the Word became flesh. Jesus actually took on humanity. As we consider this revelation of Jesus, *John 1:1* is the only premise by which we can understand Jesus as the Son of God. If this premise is removed, we are left with terms that have no meaning. Terms without meaning leave us with nothing that is substantial or trustworthy in which to test our beliefs about the Jesus of the Bible.

The key is, the Jewish people understood that the term "Son of God" meant Jesus was God. As you study their reaction toward Jesus being called or considered the Son of God, they thought it to be blasphemy and picked up stones to execute judgment on Him. *John 5:18* gives us this insight, "Therefore, the Jews sought the more to kill him, because he not only had broken the Sabbath, but said also that God was his Father, making himself equal with God."

"Equal" means to be the same as in nature, position, and importance. Does Jesus have the right to make such claims? The Apostle Paul made this statement in *Philippians 2:6*, "Who, being in the form of God, thought it not robbery to be equal with God." According to the "Strong's Concordance", the word "form" in this text means nature. Jesus, who possesses the nature of God, did not think it was robbery when He ceased to be equal with God. What does this mean? When Jesus became man, He emptied Himself (became of no reputation), of His power and authority as God, took on the form of a servant, and was fashioned as a man, thereby, making Him lower than the angels *(Philippians 2:7; Hebrews 2:9-11)*. Jesus never ceased to be God, but His deity was clothed in humanity. The Apostle Paul confirmed this when he stated that in Christ was the fullness of deity in bodily form *(Colossians 2:9)* It was upon the Mount of Transfiguration that His humanity was parted to reveal His true glory as God *(Matthew 17:1-9)*.

Matthew 28:18 tells us that the authority and power He relinquished as God to become man was given back to Him in His humanity. However, this authority would be channeled in a different way, leaving us an important example. Jesus came under the authority of the Father, making His power subject to the Father's will and plan. We get insight into this very fact in *Matthew 26:51-56* and *John 10:18*. Jesus declared that no man could take His life, but He would lay it down as well as raise it again. On the night that He was betrayed He told His disciples He had the authority to request a legion of angels, but He was in subjection to the plan of the Father to fulfill His promise of redemption. In compliance with Jesus' example as man, it is obvious we must receive power from above to carry out our calling as well.

This brings us to the premise in which the Gospel of Mark presented Jesus in *Mark 1:1*, "The beginning of the gospel of Jesus Christ, the Son of God." Mark presents Him as the Son of God. However, there are other entities that recognized Jesus as the Son of God: the demons *(Luke 8:26-29)*.

Consider the actions and words of one of the devils He encountered, "Saying, Let us alone! What have we to do with thee, thou Jesus of Nazareth? Art thou come to destroy us? I know thee, who thou art, the Holy One of God" *(Mark 1:24)*. There are three points that need to be considered in this Scripture. 1) This demon was trembling before Jesus. The Word clearly tells us there is only one being that demons tremble before, "Thou believest that there is one God; thou doest well. The devils also believe, and tremble" *(James 2:19)*. 2) This demon recognized that Jesus had authority over him. It is important to note Jesus did not stand in the authority, name, or power of His Father as we stand in Jesus' authority, name, and power. This brings us to the reason the demon had to give way to Jesus. As Creator, Jesus has pre-eminence over all thrones, dominions, principleities, and powers (Colossians 1:15-18). 3) The final aspect of this Scripture is that the demon referred to Him as the Holy One of God. As you study the concept of holiness, there is only One who is ascribed as being Holy—that is God *(Isaiah 6:3).*

There are also other Scriptures where Jesus is actually referred to as God. In *1 Timothy 1:17* Jesus is called the King eternal and the only wise God. This statement is made about Him in 1 Timothy 3:16, "And without controversy great is the mystery of godliness: God was manifest in the flesh, justified in the Spirit, seen of angels, preached unto the nations, believe on in the world, received up into glory." Paul is pointing out that the mystery that had been hidden is that God would manifest Himself in the flesh. "Manifest" means to make apparent. God had clearly made Himself apparent in human form. We also can read where Thomas called Jesus God in *John 20:28* and the Father even addressed Jesus as God in *Hebrews 1:6-8.*

Ultimately, Jesus was crucified because He was the Son of God. In an indirect way He admitted to the Pharisees that He was the Son of God, sealing His death on the cross *(Matthew 26:63-66).* Yet, all that Jesus experienced was a fulfillment of Scripture to verify His identity and words.

Let me challenge you once again. How important is it to get the Son of God right? The Apostle John put forth this warning,

> By this know ye the Spirit of God: every spirit that confesseth that Jesus Christ is come in the flesh is of God; And every spirit that confesseth not that Jesus Christ is come in the flesh is not of God; and this is that spirit of antichrist, of which ye have heard that it should come, and even now already is in the world *(1 John 4:2-3).* (Emphasis added.)

What is John talking about? We already know that Jesus came into the world as man. There would be no debate about this matter, unless John was presenting this in light of John 1:1. In this case, it would mean that unless a person confesses that Jesus Christ, who is God by nature, actually came in the flesh, he or she is under an antichrist spirit. "Antichrist spirit" points to a spirit who will counterfeit or become a substitute for the real Jesus.

This brings us to another important aspect of Jesus as the Messiah. *Isaiah 9:6* says about the character and work of the Messiah "...and his name shall be called Wonderful, Counselor, The Mighty God, The Everlasting Father, the Prince of Peace." (Emphasis added.) The Messiah is also referred to as The Mighty God and the Everlasting Father. We must not forget the other name that refers to Jesus: "Immanuel," which means God with us *(Isaiah 7:14; Matthew 1:23).* In order to have a proper understanding of the Messiah, we must also consider Jesus Christ, the Anointed One of God in light of His deity.

The prospect of the Messiah being God brings us to a very important aspect of how the Jews handled this concept. They were clearly challenged with it in different ways. We see one of these challenges concerning King David in *Matthew 22:41-46*. Jesus was considered and referred to as the Son of David, a term pointing to the Messiah. Jesus asked the Pharisees, "What think ye of Christ? Whose son is he?" They answered by saying that He would be the son of David. Jesus then asked them how could David in the Spirit call him Lord if the Christ was only his son? This is an important question. Jesus took this reference from *Psalm 110:1.* This *Psalm* has Jehovah (LORD, God) telling David's Lord, (Jesus) to sit on His right hand until His enemies were made His footstool. You have to realize that as a committed Jew, King David would only recognize one to be His Lord—God *(Isaiah 43:11; 45:5, 21).* If you would like to study more about David's Lord, you can refer to *Isaiah 6*, where the prophet encountered Him. Note the spelling of Lord in *Isaiah 6:1-11* as compared to the spelling of it in *Isaiah 6:12.*

Consider both Scriptures in light of *Philippians 2:9-11.* Are you getting the impression that there are great mysteries in the Word of God beyond mere man's comprehension, and because of our finite status as man, we can only know in part? This is why we must approach the Bible to believe it, and not approach it based on personal understanding.

There is also another confrontation in *John 8:48-59* with the Jews. Jesus told them if a person would keep His sayings, he or she should not see death. The Jews took issue with His statement. They declared that He had a demon for those who were righteous such as Abraham and the prophets were dead. These great men could not even give life, nor did they escape death. Then, they asked Jesus if He was greater then Abraham and the prophets. They ended with this challenge "Whom makest thou thyself?"

This important question must be reasoned out. Jesus was claiming to be greater than the great men of faith, and He also claimed that He could give life. This put Him in a different league than what they expected, even from the perspective of Him being the Messiah. Jesus assured them He knew the Father who they claimed they knew. If He acted as if He did not know the Father, He would be a liar. He told them that Abraham rejoiced to see His day, and he saw it and was glad. This was pointing to the incident where Abraham took Isaac to offer him as a burnt offering, giving him a glimpse into God providing His Son as a sacrifice on our behalf. Jesus ended His confrontation with the Jews with these words, "Verily, verily, I say unto you, Before Abraham was, I am."

The Jews' response was to stone Jesus. Their reaction was possibly in relationship to how Moses was instructed to present God to the children of Israel when they asked who sent Him. The Lord told Moses to tell them that *I AM* has sent him unto them *(Exodus 3:14)*. The I AM was the One who gave the children of Israel their Law at Mount Sinai. Jesus was implying that He was the "I AM." This was considered blasphemy by the Jews, for clearly Jesus was claiming to be Jehovah, the great Lawgiver. Did these Jews forget the prophecy about the Messiah in *Genesis 49:10-12?* It said of the Messiah that He would come from Judah. It pointed out that He was the scepter and a lawgiver. (See also *Psalm 60:7.)* Scepter points to a rod that will bring forth correction as well as a ruler. *Isaiah 11:1* tells us that this rod will come out of Jesse (King David's father), and *James 4:12* tells us that there is only one lawgiver. This lawgiver is able to save or destroy us.

Even with all the prophecies about the Promised One, the Jews became confused with Jesus' true identity. It did not make sense to them even though they were given valuable insight into Him. In spite of the miracles they had seen, they refused to believe He was the Christ. Even though He had authority over Satan, they accused Him of being subject to Satan and his kingdom. Sadly, the same arguments have raged over the last 20 centuries about Jesus. Yet, King David believed and acknowledged the reality of the Messiah, and Abraham looked for Him, saw its fulfillment and rejoiced over the day the Messiah would make His entrance into history. And, when you consider that even the angels desire to look into the fulfillment of these promises, you realize that we can only approach and receive these promises by faith *(1 Peter 1:11-12)*.

The next question is why did Jesus have to come in the flesh? He came to be a substitute. There could be no remission (pardon) of sin without the shedding of blood. Calves and goats could not secure such a pardon *(Hebrews 9:11, 22, 10:17)*. No man could offer any sacrifice that would satisfy the Law of God. Therefore, God provided the sacrifice, the Lamb of God. God took on flesh to become that Lamb to secure redemption for our souls, and to serve as the only means of reconciliation back to the Father.

If what we have discovered in Scripture is true, Jesus is fully God and fully man. In *2 Peter 1:4* we are told that we are given great and precious promises that by these we might be partakers of the divine nature. As you consider this Scripture, it is in reference to partaking of Jesus who is divine by nature.

The Word tells us that in His humanity Jesus forgave sin. Forgiveness in this text can only be ascribed to God. As man, He knew the thoughts of men. Once again, only God knows the inner thoughts of man *(1 Chronicles 28:9; Matthew 9:4; Luke 5:20-24; 6:8)*. He commanded the elements of earth such as wind and water *(Luke 8:24-25)*. We know that only the Creator has such power over the elements of this world. As Man in the courts of heaven, He serves as both our mediator and High Priest *(1 Timothy 2:5)*. Jesus also serves as our foundation and the cornerstone. If we fail to come to terms with whom He is to ensure a proper foundation, He will be redefined and replaced as a cornerstone with a different Jesus. He warned that He was the Stone, and that people would fall over Him and be broken, or He would grind them to powder in judgment *(Matthew 21:42-44; 1 Corinthians 3:11; Ephesians 2:19-22 1 Peter 2:6-8).*

It can become quite overwhelming for people to consider these different aspects of Jesus. This presentation merely scratches the surface. If Jesus is eternal, we will only understand in part. If His work is eternal, it will carry a depth too great to comprehend. This study could go on and on in regards to the revelations surrounding the Son of God. *Ephesians 2:7* reminds us, "That in the ages to come he might show the exceeding riches of his grace in his kindness toward us through Christ Jesus."

However, there is one final criterion that Jesus must meet to identify Him as God, and that is worship. Did Jesus receive worship? The answer is yes. The wise men worshipped Him as a baby. Joseph and Mary, who knew the Law, would not tolerate such worship unless they recognized Jesus as their Messiah, the Son of the Highest *(Matthew 2:11)*. The angels worshipped Jesus *(Hebrews 1:5-6)*. As you study the Bible, angels never received worship, but they clearly honor and worship their Creator. Last, but not least, people worshipped Jesus throughout the Gospels. Unlike Peter, Paul, and Barnabas who refused to receive worship in any form because they were mere men, Jesus openly received people's worship *(Matthew 8:2; 9:18; 14:33; 15:25: 18:26; 28:9, 17; Mark 5:6; John 9:38; Acts 9:25-26; 14:12-18)*. We see Him being worshipped around the throne of God as they make this powerful declaration, "Saying with a loud voice, Worthy is the Lamb that was slain to receive power, and riches, and wisdom, and strength, and honor, and glory, and blessing" *(Revelation 5:12 refer to Revelation 4:8; 5:11-14).*

Is Jesus a mere man or is He God incarnate? The issue of Jesus' identity reminds me of the incident that took place in Jesus' hometown, Nazareth *(Luke 4:16-30)*. Jesus had stood up in the synagogue and read the prophecy about the Messiah found in *Isaiah 61:1-2.* He told them that the prophecy was fulfilled that day. These people knew what Jesus was declaring about Himself. Consider what they said, "Is not this Joseph's son?" *(Luke 4:22b).* What were they saying about Jesus? How could He be the Messiah? We know Him as the son of Joseph; therefore, He is of man, and from man, thereby, making Him a mere man. These people reacted in total unbelief towards Jesus. As a result, Jesus declared that the prophecy was fulfilled in their ears, rather than in their lives. Jesus' challenge eventually stirred these people to wrath. They tried to throw Him over a cliff. However, He simply passed through their midst.

We must constantly come back to the correct premise if we are going to properly reason out truths outlined in Scripture. As believers, we have been given sure prophecies in the Old Testament about the Messiah. We have also been given proof of the Son of man's identity through His teachings and miracles. We have been given a record or testimony of the Son of God that is clearly outlined in the New Testament. If we say He is merely a man, how much of the Word of God must we disregard, ignore, or explain away? If He is God Incarnate, can we conclude that all Scriptures concerning Him will fall into line with the full counsel of God's Word? After all, we can do nothing against the truth, only for it.

The Apostle John warns us that if we do not believe the record we have been given concerning Jesus Christ, we will not possess eternal life *(1 John 5:9-13).* If we fail to believe the record that has been given to us concerning the identity of Jesus, we can never be assured of eternal life. If we walk in unbelief towards the Jesus of the Bible, He will pass through our midst, without touching our lives with His salvation or deliverance.

The question remains the same. When you or I stand before Jesus as our Judge, and He asks that question which still rings down through the corridors of time, "Who do you say I am?" What will your answer be? What will my answer be?

The Holy Spirit

Who is the Holy Spirit? Most Christians have some notion, sentiment, or idea about the Spirit of God, but what do each of us really understand about Him? Is He a concept, an ideal, or a point of theology? In some religious arenas He is ignored altogether, while in others He is improperly emphasized and accredited with activity that is void of His fruit,

In the places where the Holy Spirit is improperly sought and overemphasized, it is not unusual to witness manifestations that are accredited to the Holy Spirit, but the fruit of the results leave people in confusion and feeling let down. Therefore, how important is it for believers to know the Holy Spirit? *1 John 4:1* tells us we must test the spirit behind all matters. But, what is spirit? How do the saints test the spirit? Before this question can be answered, people must first come to terms with how they perceive the Holy Spirit.

Spirit comes down to what motivates a person. Motivation will determine the real intentions, causing people to focus on what is intended. The way to know what spirit is in operation is to consider what the real focus or emphasis is of the person.
Christians can know people's spirit or intention by what they emphasize.

Although self-serving intentions may be covered up with religious terms and activities, they will eventually be exposed by what becomes these individuals' focus in a matter. The most popular emphasis for most cults is works. Most of the emphasis on works in these cults are in relationship to the leadership, or in other words, serving the leadership's purpose and goal in building their personal kingdom. Therefore, what does this focus say about the motivation of such leadership? It pretty well says that it is self-serving. It also says something else. It is idolatrous. After all, if something is not about glorifying or honoring the real God (the main purpose for all works), then it must be considered idolatrous. Idolatry is considered one of the works of the flesh, and those who walk in such works will not inherit the kingdom of God *(Matthew 5:16; Galatians 5:16-21)*.

The harsh reality is that the Holy Spirit is merely a vague notion to many Christians. For some believers, they are not sure who the Holy Spirit is. If they do not know who He is, how He works, and the part He plays in their lives, then how can they expect to test or discern what spirit is in operation.

Is the Holy Spirit a force (for He is unseen and works in the spiritual realm), an extension of God (for His origins and source are found in God) or a Person (someone who has a personality that we can interact with). Is the Holy Spirit an extension of the Father and Jesus? (Refer to *Galatians 4:6-; Philippians 1:19; 1 Peter 1:11)*. As you can see, the possibility of confusion can clearly exist about this subject.

Another area that causes confusion is the taboo that can be put on using the term "Holy Ghost. The Bible uses both terms, but there are those who are told not to use the term "Holy Ghost" because there has been some type of superstition attached to it. "Ghost" has the same meaning as "spirit." In fact, in the *Strong's Concordance*, "ghost" and "spirit" have the same reference number in the New Testament (#4151). It also must be noted that spirit points to soul, mind, or mental disposition, which brings us back to motivation, intention, and focus. Emphasizing one term over the other reveals ignorance on people's part, not wisdom. Both terms are Scriptural and both mean the same thing. Granted, different terms may conjure up different images, but people's perception of a subject should not be based on personal images, but on the Word of God.

How does the Word of God present the Holy Spirit? Does it present Him as a force from God that simply moves upon people? "Force" means strength or energy exerted to bring forth a matter. Such energy has the ability to compel, constrain, or force to overcome any type of resistance. In some arenas "force" points to the New Age concept of good overcoming evil or light overcoming darkness. (See *Daniel 11:37-38* for a contrast. Note, our God is not a God of forces, rather He is a God that has power over all of Creation.) Does the concept of force or energy sound like a characteristic of the Holy Spirit? The Holy Spirit is not aggressive; therefore, He can be resisted. In fact, He will not always strive (contend or plea the cause) with man *(Genesis 6:3)*.

Now we come to the second possibility. Is the Spirit an extension of Jesus? There can be a couple of problems with this. First, if Jesus is mere man, how could His Spirit be in operation in the Old Testament without His existence *(Genesis 6:3; 2 Chronicles 15:1-2; 20:14)*? Obviously, for the Spirit to be in existence in the Old Testament, it seems that Jesus would have to be in existence as well.

Another problem is that the Spirit is also associated with God. If God has His own Spirit and Jesus His, this would contradict *Ephesians 4:4* that there is only one Holy Spirit. Of course, this could be possibly explained by the fact that God's Spirit is the same as the Spirit of Christ.

This brings us to the next possibility—that the Holy Spirit is a separate Person who acts distinctively in His duties, but is in submission to the Father's will and in alliance with the Son's mission. Remember personality implies the ability to interact with people. Personality denotes the person of someone. Does the Spirit fit this criterion? Consider the fact that the Holy Spirit is referred to as "he" or "him" in Scripture *(John 14:27; 16:7, 13)*. "He" and "him" are associated to a distinct person, not to a force or extension of something or someone.

It is interesting to note that the Spirit is used in conjunction with Jesus in *1 Corinthians 6:11*. If the Holy Spirit was an extension of Jesus, why did He have to come down and anoint Jesus after His baptism *(Matthew 3:16-17* refer to *Luke 4:18-19)?* If the Holy Spirit was simply an extension of the Father, why did Jesus have to go away before the Spirit could be sent by both Jesus and the Father *(John 14:26; 15:26; 16:7)*? When Jesus was with His disciples, He could simply have extended the Spirit to them if the Spirit was an extension of Him. If the Spirit was an extension of the Father, why is it that He acts as a separate Person in His reactions to a matter? For example, He departed from Saul. *(1 Samuel 16:14). Romans 8:27* also makes reference to the mind of the Spirit, also implying that He is a distinct Person from the Father and the Son.

Does the Holy Spirit have a personality that can be observed in Scripture? We are told that He can be lied to, vexed, tempted, grieved, or quenched *(Isaiah 63:10; Acts 5:3, 9; Ephesians 4:30; 1 Thessalonians 5:19)*. The Word of God tells us He spoke to men in both the Old and New Testaments *(2 Chronicles 20:14-15; Acts 8:29; 10:19). John 16:13* refers to Him as the Spirit of truth. He is the one who leads each of us into all truth about Jesus, and teaches us all things concerning God. He is the Spirit of wisdom, understanding, counsel, might, and knowledge who ultimately reveals mysteries to and through men *(Isaiah 11:2; John 14:26* (refer to *1 John 2:27); 16:13; 1 Corinthians 14:2)*. He is the One who brings to remembrance spiritual truths, and will connect the truths with God's real intent about a matter, bringing forth revelation *(John 14:26; Ephesians 3:3-5)*.

Scripture definitely points to the Holy Spirit being a distinct person from the Father and the Son, but is He simply a spirit or is there more to Him? *John 4:24* tells us God is a Spirit. The Apostle Paul talked about the Lord being that Spirit in *2 Corinthians 3:17*. "Lord" in this text points to supreme in authority as in God, Lord, or master. One of the most interesting Scriptures can be found *in Isaiah 48:16*: "Come near unto me, hear this: I have not spoken in secret from the beginning; from the time that it was, there am I; and now the Lord GOD, and his Spirit, hath sent me." This is in reference to the Messiah. Remember John said that Jesus was the Word in the beginning. In this Scripture in *Isaiah*, the Promised One is declaring that what He spoke from the beginning is not a secret. Clearly, there is a reference to three distinct persons in this Scripture verse. However, note the Lord GOD and his Spirit sent the Messiah. The word "and" points to conjunction with. It implies the equality of both the Lord GOD and the Spirit in sending forth the Messiah. It is also important to note that the Son had to ascend to the Father before the Holy Spirit could be sent.

Do such references point to the Holy Spirit being God? We know that He is of God, but does He fit the criteria of God? How about creation? *Genesis 1:2* tells us: "And the earth was without form, and void; and darkness was upon the face of the deep. And the Spirit of God moved upon the face of the waters." "Form" in this text implies an empty place or waste. "Void" means to be empty or undistinguishable. Jesus may have created everything, but it is the Spirit of God that recreated the face of the world, and garnished the heavens *(Job 26:13; Psalms 104:30)*. He is the One who brought life, order, beauty, and purpose to the world and heavens. *Job 33:4* states that the Spirit of God made man, and that the breath of the Almighty has given life. In summation, the Holy Spirit was the breath of life that was given to Adam in *Genesis 2:7* that distinctively set him apart as a living soul.

The work of recreation and order is consistent with the Spirit's work in the believer and in the Body. For the believer, he or she is born again with the Spirit and with Water (the Word) *(John 3:3, 5,* refer to *Ephesians 5:26* and *1 Peter 1:23* in regards to the Word*; Galatians 4:29)*. The Holy Spirit is the breath of life that comes into a new convert, making the believer a new creation by reviving and renewing the spirit of his or her inner being with new life, as well as transforming his or her mind *(Romans 12:1-2; 2 Corinthians 4:16*; *Ephesians 4:23)*. He is the one who actually establishes the disposition and life of Christ in the believer *(2 Corinthians 3:6, 17-18)*. He is also the One who baptizes and places each believer into the Body of Christ, and gives him or her gifts for the purpose of edification for the whole Body *(1 Corinthians 12:7-13)*. Note, that the Spirit gives these gifts as He wills, pointing to the fact that He is sovereign in His work *(1 Corinthians 12:11)*.

Does the Holy Spirit possess the attributes of God? We know He is completely holy due to His identification as the Holy Spirit, but He is also eternal *(Hebrews 9:14)*. However, can we find in Scripture where He is immutable? Even though He is of God and from God who is unchangeable, it is important to test out this vital characteristic because the Holy Spirit will prove to be consistent in character and manifestation. The Word of God bears out the consistency of the Holy Spirit's character and work. The Spirit of God has always manifested Himself in gifts in both the Old and New Testament. When He came down upon men in the Old Testament, they prophesied, and when He moves among the New Testament Church, gifts such as prophecy are a manifestation *(1 Samuel 10:10-11; 19:20-24; Acts 2:1-17; 1 Corinthians 12:7, 10)*. "Manifestation" in this text means expression or exhibition of the Spirit, which is consistent with Him moving upon men to bring forth the sure prophecy of the Word of God *(2 Peter 1:19-21)*?

The Holy Spirit has never changed as to how He moves and manifests Himself. He has moved in the midst of God's creation. He has always come upon man to bring insight and revelation to God's truths. We see this uniformity in both testaments, but there is one difference. In the Old Testament, the Holy Spirit would only come upon men and move upon them to speak forth the oracles of God, but now He not only comes upon men, but He abides within them through the born-again experience *(John 3:3, 5)*. In fact, believers are known as the temples of the Holy Spirit. The Holy Spirit represents the very presence of God in the midst of His people. He not only moves upon, but He moves in and through man to bring forth the life of Christ in each believer *(1 Corinthians 3:16-17; 6:17-19)*. Since He resides in believers, He has access to move through the Body of believers to bring proper instruction, warning, and encouragement.

It is vital for believers to understand how the Holy Spirit expresses Himself. Remember as believers, we are to test the spirits. The reason we can test the spirits is that their fruits are tangible *(Matthew 7:16-20)*. These fruits can be properly discerned by considering the environment that is being established. The Holy Spirit sets up the environment of righteousness that allows God to have His way. For example, the fruit of the Spirit represents the inward disposition or environment of man *(Galatians 5:22-23)*. Disposition will manifest itself in attitude and approach. If the Holy Spirit is present, a person will be motivated by love, will possess an anchor of abiding confidence due to joy, peace will reign because of a right relationship with God, and the person's attitude will reveal patience, kindness, and moral accountability. Such a person will approach all matters in faith, meekness, and temperance. The result of such an environment is that of order which is made evident by reconciliation with God *(1 Corinthians 14:33)*.

People who operate outside of the Spirit will be plagued by uncertainty, chaos, and confusion. This is brought out in the Old Testament as you consider men such as Saul and David. In the New Testament, you can observe the order wrought by the Spirit of God being upheld in the Body. The Apostle Paul dealt with the attitude as well as the guidelines that the gifts of the Spirit are to operate within *(1 Corinthians 12; 14)*. If the right attitude is missing and the guidelines disregarded, then one can easily conclude that there is a wrong spirit in operation.

This brings us to the subject of order. How does one come into order? The answer is that people must come back to center. The center is God. Therefore, the Holy Spirit will always lead people back to Jesus. When people end with any other sense of someone or something (other than Jesus), such as self (often expressed in emotional hype or impulsiveness), man's-leadership (false security and idolatry), or man-made religion (pious experience), they will quickly find themselves empty, uncertain, and frustrated. Such people give the impression that they have to go back every week to get their regular religious "fix" in order to keep going. The only place where people can find lasting satisfaction is in Christ. Therefore, the Holy Spirit will always lead each of us back to our need, dependency, hope, and life in Jesus *(John 14:6, 26; 16:13-14)*.

As Christians, we must also test the spirit that is not only operating in the Body of believers, but the spirit that is motivating us personally. If our spirit is wrong, we cannot properly receive the things of God. In fact, a wrong spirit always perverts the truths of God, causing confusion. Jesus told James and John that they did not know what spirit they were of when they wanted to call fire down from heaven on the Samaritans *(Luke 9:55)*.

The final criterion that the Holy Spirit must meet is that of worship. There is no place in Scripture where it shows that man worships the Spirit of God. However, if the Spirit is God, then He would receive worship when the Father and Son are being worshipped *(John 4:23-24)*. The other important key to the Spirit besides His character is that He is the one who sets up the proper environment for worship. Only God would know how to worship in a proper way. A study on the Holy Spirit shows us that He is the One who enables us to pray and worship. For example, the disciples asked the Lord to teach them to pray. The woman at the well wanted to know about worship *(Luke 11:1; John 4:19-20)*. We are told to worship God in the right spirit and to pray in the Spirit (*John 4:23-24; 1 Corinthians 14:15; Ephesians 6:18)*. Clearly, the Spirit of God must set up the proper environment to ensure prayers that are effectual and worship that is acceptable.

Another aspect of the Spirit is that communion is associated to Him *(2 Corinthians 13:14)*. In other words, we cannot come into agreement or communion with the Father, except through the Holy Spirit *(Ephesians 2:16-18)*. He is the One that brings unity in the spirit at the point or place of Jesus and His redemption. Unity in the spirit is the environment where communion takes place not only between the Father and believers, but between the church members as well (*Ephesians 4:1-3*).

Regardless of the confusion and debate over the Spirit, we can test a matter to see if He is the breath of inspiration behind it. Clearly, the environment becomes an expression of the spirit in operation. However, one of the greatest joys is that we can personally know the Holy Spirit. We do not have to be vague in our understanding regarding Him. He clearly expresses Himself in a way that He can be properly discerned. He is the One who signifies the new birth (seals us), regenerates (brings forth new life), transforms and renews the inner man (recreates), sanctifies (sets us apart for God's use), anoints (for service), and empowers believers (to be bold witnesses) *(Luke 4:18-19; John 3:3,5; Acts 1:8; Romans 12:1-2; 2 Corinthians 4:16; Ephesians 4:23; Titus 3:5; 1 John 2:27)*. The more Christians learn the character of the Holy Spirit through His work and manifestations, the sharper their discernment will become. As the Apostle Paul explained, the natural man can discern nothing in the spiritual realm. Only the Holy Spirit in each of us as believers is capable of discerning such matters *(1 Corinthians 2:10-14)*.

The Spirit of God is what brings life to the Word of God *(John 6:63)*. If the Holy Spirit is not leading and guiding believers into the truths of God, the Word becomes dead letter *(Romans 7:6; 2 Corinthians 3:6)*. There will be no power for the Word to discern the spirit we are personally operating in, as well as cleanse us, transform, and ensure life. Only the Spirit of God can give each of us greater revelations of Jesus. Consider John in *Revelation*. He was in the Spirit when he received the incredible revelation about Jesus *(Revelation 1:10)*. Clearly, if we are of another spirit, we will never see, know, touch, or realize the Jesus of the Bible. We will end up believing in another Jesus.

Is it important to ensure that as believers we understand, operate within, and possess the correct spirit? It is easy to allow the confusions and abuses that surround the Holy Spirit to steer us away from coming to terms with His Person and work, but the Bible is clear that we must possess the right spirit to ensure the inward witness of our salvation. The Word tells us that the Holy Spirit seals us until we can realize redemption in it fullness. In fact, He serves as the down payment in regards to our spiritual inheritance until redemption is fully realized *(Ephesians 13-14)*. It is the Spirit that bears witness that we are the children of God *(Romans 8:15-16)*. Obviously, as already pointed out it is the Spirit of God that bears record that we are saved *(1 John 3:24; 5:6-12)*. If the Holy Spirit is missing, there is no seal, no witness, and no record to verify our salvation. To believe that we are saved without this heavenly witness is to walk in denial of the truth or in delusion about the real testimony of God in regards to His Son and salvation. Therefore, the challenge is clear, we must know, interact with, and be able to discern the Spirit of God in the midst of the many counterfeits that are present in this world.

The Godhead

As we have studied and reasoned about the concept of the Father, the Son, and the Holy Spirit, there is nothing more we can do but conclude that all three Persons are God. In mathematical terms, this does not make sense. One plus one plus one does not equal one, yet the Word is clear that there is only one God. Now, either the Bible is true or it is the greatest joke in history. After all, many people are betting their eternal destination on this Book.

It has already been pointed out that as believers we must believe the whole Bible or discard all of it. We must consider it as truth in intent and purpose, or we must throw it out as nothing more than fables. Therefore, if we as believers are to believe the Word, there must be an explanation that will maintain the integrity of the complete Word of God without compromising the facts or revelations that are being advocated.

How can three persons equal one God? One of the terms that must be considered is the term "Godhead." The word "God" is clearly a reference to that which is deity, supreme, and mighty, but does the term "Godhead" encompass a greater revelation about the character of God? According to "Strong's Exhaustive Concordance", "Godhead" means divinity. However, Godhead also points to deity or supreme Divinity. It is interesting to note that God has many references in the Old Testament to describe His character, but in the New Testament, the term Godhead is used in three Scriptures.

From the meaning of Godhead can we conclude that the Father, the Son, and the Holy Spirit are deity, but they function within or according to what can be referred to as supreme Divinity? This can all be quite confusing. To Scripturally reason this out, some type of premise or guidelines need to be established in which to regard this subject; The Bible gives us insight as to the premise or guidelines by telling us that God is identified by His nature *(Galatians 4:8)*. "Nature" is the essence of something, or in other words, it identifies who or what something is. Everything in creation has a nature that actually identifies it. The makeup of something can be related to chemistry, rather than mathematics. Divinity points to the fact that God is divine by nature. This means He is supreme in all things. Could we say that within the essence or oneness of the Godhead are three Persons? These three persons are all deity or divine by nature; therefore, they are equal in status, character, power, and position. "Equal" is a mathematical term. It means it is the same as, as far as nature, properties, quantity, and quality; therefore, three will always be equal to that which possesses the same properties, quantity, and quality. Does this equality mean that the one true God manifests (makes apparent) Himself in three different personalities or persons?

For example, in *1 Timothy 3:16* we are told that God manifested Himself in the flesh. Does this mean that the character or nature of God operates in and through three persons or does it mean God simply reveals His person through three distinct personalities that somehow fades into one person or being? There is also the belief of Modalism, which has God manifesting Himself at different times in three distinct modes. However, Scripture refutes the last two concepts of the Godhead. Jesus prayed to the Father. Obviously, He would pray to a distinct person other than Himself. He also would not be seeking the Father's will if there was no distinction or sovereignty between His will and the Father's will. At Jesus' baptism, all three persons of the Godhead were present or made apparent in different ways. Paul also distinguishes the Father and Son as being two distinct persons in *1 Corinthians 8:6.* Based on these examples, it is safe to say that since personality points to the person of someone, that God manifests Himself in and through three persons. Obviously, these three Persons are equal in every way; and since deity or divine attributes are found in all three Persons of the Godhead, can we conclude that one true God is identified and made apparent in three Persons? For example, water always equals water regardless of its location, the size of the lake, ocean, or river, but it can manifest itself in three distinct ways, ice, fog and liquid. Clearly, water will always equal water, for it is what it is and it will never cease to be the complete sum of itself.

Obviously, these three Persons of the Godhead act independently from each other, but always in complete agreement with each other. This agreement would also mean that all three would work in compliance to one goal and purpose. Such agreement would be along the same lines as the concept of married couples becoming one flesh within the institution of marriage *(Matthew 19:5-6; Ephesians 5:28-31).* Although the married husband and wife maintain their separate personalities, they are identified as being one in agreement, purpose, and heart. The fact that the Word of God identifies the Father, the Son, and the Holy Spirit as being divine by nature, and in total agreement in all matters could and would continually equal the sum total of what we refer to as the Godhead.

According to *Romans 1:20,* the concept of the Godhead is seen in creation. As you consider the idea of three in one, a good example is man. Within the human makeup of man are spirit, soul, and body. Each area has its different functions, but they work together as one unit. You have the example of an egg which is made up of the yoke, egg white, and shell. Consider the petals of the Shamrock. These are just a couple of examples of how creation declares this truth, but the reality is that we have examples of this concept all around us.

As a result, we have this warning in *Romans 1:20*, "For the invisible things of him from the creation of the world are clearly seen, being understood by the things that are made, even his eternal power and Godhead, <u>so that they are without excuse</u>." (Emphasis added.) The harsh reality is that there will be no excuse as to why people did not believe and know the true God of heaven.

If there are three Persons that make up the Godhead, then we can understand some of the confusing Scriptures. For example, we have a reference to the plurality of the Godhead in such Scriptures as *Genesis 1:26; 3:22; 11:7;* and *Isaiah 6:8*. In each Scripture God makes reference to Himself with the word "us." We could say He is speaking to angels, but in a couple of these Scriptures it is clear He is speaking to those who are of His likeness or possess the same similitude, not to His created beings such as messengers (angels).

Clearly, we see how the Old and New Testaments approach the character and work of God from different angles, while producing the same picture. For example, the Old Testament shows God in His ways, but the New Testament explains the intent of His ways according to His character. In the Old Testament, we have four Scriptures that clearly refer to the plurality of God, and in the New Testament, we have three Scriptures that reveal the concept of the Godhead to give us insight into this plurality. It is also important to point out that two or three witnesses confirm a matter *(Numbers 35:30; Deuteronomy 17:6; 19:15; Matthew 18:16)*. A good example of this is that at Jesus' baptism John the Baptist, the Holy Spirit, and the Father, confirmed Jesus' identity as the Son of God and the Messiah. Consider *1 John 5:6-9*.

The New Testament also refers to this plurality of the Godhead by using the word "and." This word implies equality with, and is used in conjunction to something for the purpose of connecting the subject, thoughts, or terms. We see this word "and" connect the Father and Jesus together throughout the New Testament in character, purpose, and work. Consider what the Bible tells us about the Godhead in *Acts 17:29-30*, "Forasmuch then, as we are the offspring of God, we ought not to think that the Godhead is like unto gold, or silver, or stone, graven by art and man's device. And the times of this ignorance God winked at; but now commandeth all men everywhere to repent."

What does man need to repent of according to *Acts*? He needs to repent of worshipping false gods. False gods find their idolatrous place in the heart and mind of man because he erects them in a place of importance and worship. The reason for such idolatry is that man is ignorant about the true God of heaven. Ignorance produces superstition about God. How many of our religious practices are nothing more than superstition? Therefore, man often worships God according to the darkness of his ignorance.

The point is, as Christians, we can know God, but we fail to seek Him. The natural response for most people is to look around for some religion or philosophy that feeds their religious pride, soothes their religious conscience, justifies their favorite religious concept, and confirms a certain religious emphasis. Obviously, such a search is not a matter of truth, but a matter of maintaining one's personal ignorance towards God. Because of man's insistence to maintain his own god, he clearly needs to repent about his attitude towards the true God of heaven.

How can we truly know God? *Colossians 2:9* answers this question, "For in him dwelleth all the fullness of the Godhead bodily." This Scripture is in reference to Jesus Christ. In Christ dwells all of the fullness of supreme divinity in bodily form. Was Jesus being a mere reflection of deity or does He possess the full nature and glory of the Godhead? A person cannot consistently reflect an image or thought. Ultimately, he or she will only reflect the inward character of his or her disposition. Therefore, Jesus could not reflect the essence of God unless He possessed God's very character and glory.

One of the confusing Scriptures in the Word of God is the one that says no man has seen God at any time, yet people in the Old Testament had actual encounters with God. For example, who was Abraham communicating with in regard to Sodom in *Genesis 18*? There were three men who came to Abraham, two were identified as angels and the other one he addressed as Lord. Who did Jacob see at the top of the ladder between heaven and earth? He was referred to as LORD *(Genesis 28:12-13).* Who did Moses, Aaron, Nadab, Abihu, and the seventy elders of Israel see in *Exodus 24:9-12?* They declared that they saw the God of Israel. Once again, we are reminded of what Isaiah witnessed in heaven in *Isaiah 6*. He declared that He saw the Lord.

Consider *John 5:37*. Jesus stated that the people of Israel had not heard the voice of the Father nor seen His shape. The only way these incidents in the Old Testament would make sense is that Jesus is God. Since Jesus pre-existed as the Word (visible expression of God), He could have taken on the form of man or spoke to man in the Old Testament. If this is so, then these people of the Old Testament could rightly call Him Lord and declare that they had seen God.

If God is expressed through three persons, then it would mean that man would have to see all three persons of the Godhead to be able to declare that he had seen God. Since Jesus existed as the Word, was ordained to be the Son in the bosom of the Father, and fashioned as man, then we could reason that as Man, He is the only one in His humanity who has seen God in His unhindered glory.

The reason for mentioning the unhindered glory of God is due to Moses' experience in *Exodus 33:18-23*. Moses had communed with God for forty days and nights, but in *Exodus 33:18,* he makes this declaration, "I beseech thee, show me thy glory." The Lord responded by saying that no man could see His face (countenance-character-glory), and live *(Exodus 33:20).* Moses' request was honored, but he had to be put in the cleft of the rock, and then he could only see the back parts of the Lord.

Obviously, God is beyond our comprehension in our present state. Is there any way we can explain the depth of this incredible mystery as to the fact that God did become flesh? Is there any way we will be able to really understand God? The answer is clear, yet we can know this God who is beyond all comprehension by faith. We cannot see Him in the fullness of His glory, but His glory has been revealed in His Son. We cannot see the fullness of His presence, but we can experience His presence in our lives through the Holy Spirit. However, it is up to each of us to seek God with all of our hearts *(Jeremiah 29:13; Amos 5:4-8)*. The reason we must seek Him is that He is obscure. We see through a glass darkly *(1 Corinthians 13:12)*. In other words, we see through our flesh, which hinders our ability to see our great God. It is up to each of us to push through that which hinders us in our flesh, as well as the daunting influences of the world, so we can see the Jesus of the Bible, and know who He is for ourselves. Once we see Jesus for who He is and must be, we will be assured of seeing the fullness of the Godhead in bodily form.

In Conclusion

As you can see, this challenge to discover God can prove to be difficult for those who are limited by their immaturity, but imagine how hard it might be for a former cult member to embrace the true God of heaven. Even in this study, we have waded through much, yet we have only skimmed the surface. There will always be some matters that remain fuzzy. In people's search to know God, they sometimes create more questions, but in the end, as believers we can trust our God that He will answer the questions of our heart in due time; that is, if we desire to know and love the truth.

People who have been members of a cult find it hard to trust God to unveil His truths because the Word was improperly handled and presented to them. Therefore, they have a tendency to reject truth in the areas where it has been abused or wrongly emphasized. It is clear that those who have come out of a cult have been conditioned to rebel or reject any perception outside of what has been established. Since the foundation of what these poor souls believed has been torn up, there is nothing by which they can test a matter. Clearly, the kingdom of God has been closed to these people by heretical teachings and presentations. However, it does not have to remain closed. The truth of God and His Word can make them free—that is if they choose to love the truth and become vulnerable before it.

The question will remain the same for each of us concerning spiritual matters. Do we really want the truth? The truth can prove to be bitter to the stomach when it comes to actually digesting it, salty (burning) to wounds, harsh to our vulnerable spots, and sharp to the weak areas of our theology *(Jeremiah 23:29; Acts 4:10-12; Revelation 10:9-10)*. The problem is that after the improper handling of the Word that has been used to wound people in cults, there are now trigger points that can be activated by different subjects found in the Word of God. These trigger points cause these individuals to shy away, rebel, disregard, or slam the particular truth that is being presented. Needless to say, the Word is stripped of its power to bring proper instruction, healing, and liberty to these wounded people. Such people often become selective about the Word, producing ears that desire to be tickled, rather than challenged *(2 Timothy 4:2-3)*. Ultimately, they will seek counterfeits that will make them feel good about their life, their anger, and their personal justifications for their cynical attitudes towards the matters of God.

The Word of God is clear about all spiritual matters, but we each must approach it to believe it is true, regardless of how unpleasant or challenging it may be. After all, the Word will stand when the fires of judgment consume all else. Therefore, we need to choose to simply believe it is true, and know everything will be properly explained in light of the fullness of Jesus' redemption. Meanwhile as Christians, we have the assurance that in time the true teacher of the Bible will illuminate it to our spirits to bring forth the necessary transformation to our minds.

The problem that remains is unbelief, which can plague each of us at different times. However, it can prove to be even harder for former cult members to trust anything after finding out that people who supposedly were guarding their souls duped them. Such disillusioned individuals have a tendency to give way to feelings about how a matter affects them, personal conclusions when it comes to the Word, and skepticism and scrutiny towards religious matters that do not make sense to them. Rather, than being properly discerned, sound teaching comes under the scrutiny of these people's critical eye, causing its purity to be challenged by suspicion, and its simplicity to be mocked.

As we as believers contend for the true faith in the midst of grave unbelief, we have to come to a conclusion that the conflict does not rest with the Word of God, but with man's presentation. One thing that we humans are good at is putting certain emphasis or terminology on something to explain it. What causes conflict is the wrong emphasis or terminology.

For example, much about God is discredited because of the popular term "doctrine of the Trinity" that is used to explain the concept of the Godhead. There are a couple of reasons for the conflict. The first one is that the concept of the Godhead is not a doctrine, but a truth. Doctrine can be changed, disregarded, or ignored, but a truth is something that we must receive by faith, and apply to the attitude we are developing about God and how we are to approach Him.

The second problem with this term is that it appears to originate within Catholicism. However, it was not the Roman Catholics who coined this term but Tertullian. He was born in 150 A.D. before the conception of the initial (old) Catholic Church under Cyprian in the third century and the establishment of what we now know to be the Roman Catholic Church in the fourth century.[1] Tertullian was fluent in Greek and Latin. He was the first to coin the term "trinity" to explain the concept of the Godhead to the western Christians who only knew Latin.[2] Clearly, the concept of the "trinity" was a belief of the first Christians. The first vicar or pope of the Roman Catholic Church, Constantine, no doubt adopted the concept of the Godhead when he combined Christian beliefs with pagan practices. Moreover, just because the Roman Church has taken an established Christian belief and instituted it into their belief system does not make that belief wrong. In fact, if you study the lives of many of the great reformers, including those who made sure the common people had God's Word made available to them, some were committed believers that recognized the difference between the traditions of the Catholic Church and the truths and teachings of the Word of God. Many of the reformers paid with their very lives for choosing to believe God's Word over a religious system.

As Christians, we do not test something according to how other people have handled a belief or truth, but according to its original source. The concept of the Godhead is found in Scripture. Regardless of how others may have tried to describe or explain it, it does not discredit its validity. It is up to each of us as believers to test out all matters in light of Scripture and to choose to believe it on the basis that it is found in the Word of God.

Obviously, it is easy for people to pick and choose what they will believe. However, as someone once said, if God said it, it is not for us to debate it; rather it is up to each of us to choose to believe it as being true. It is our sole responsibility as Christians to test whether something is of God. Regardless of the instrument used or how it is presented, it is our responsibility to see if a matter is being inspired by the throne of heaven. If it is of God, we must receive it by faith. Active faith will act upon a matter, allowing the Spirit of God to bring confirmation of the truth and revelation of it to our spirit.

As Christians, will we accept the challenge to possess the faith first delivered to the saints, or will we allow Satan to rob us of truth, kill our testimony of the true God, and destroy the faith that ends in salvation? It will be a personal choice on our part as to what master we serve. The master we serve will inspire the type of attitudes we develop towards God's ways, His truth, and the life that He is offering to each of us *(John 14:6)*.

---

[1] The Pilgrim Church; E. H. Broadbend, © 1999; Gospel Folio Press, pgs. 34, 43-47

[2] A Glimpse at Early Christian Church Life; Tertullian, ©1991 by David W. Bercot, pg. 2

After considering this section, has your perception of God changed? If so, explain in what way.

Section 3

THE ISSUE OF SALVATION

WHAT DOES IT MEAN TO BE SAVED?

One cannot help but think that if a person's perception is wrong about God, then he or she must have an incorrect perception about salvation. What does it mean to be saved? Clearly, this matter lies at the heart of fundamental Christianity, and must be properly addressed to counteract the cult mentality. Rather than assume or presume we understand the matter of salvation, we must answer this question, especially since our eternal destination rests on this issue.

To most people the issue of salvation comes down to saying a prayer. This prayer simply invites someone by the name of Jesus to save the individual from condemnation. However, does a prayer save a person, or does the Person of Jesus Christ save the individual? Obviously, we need to clarify what it means to be saved. When you look up salvation or being saved, it means to be delivered from something. Obviously, if people are being delivered from something, one can only reason that we each need to understand what we are being saved or delivered from.

Another important aspect is that the Word of God talks about this deliverance in regards to the past, present, and future. What do we need to be delivered from that affects our past, present, and future? To gain a glimpse into our deliverance, we must consider the Gospel. *Romans 1:16* makes this statement about salvation, "For I am not ashamed of the gospel of Christ; for it is the power of God unto salvation to everyone that believeth; to the Jew first, and also to the Greek." The Gospel, or good news, is the power of God unto salvation.

Therefore, to understand salvation, we must come to terms with the Gospel. When we speak of the Gospel, most people think of *John 3:16*, "For God so loved the world, that he gave his only begotten Son, that whosoever believeth in him should not perish, but have everlasting life."

This Scripture stipulates that man is in trouble and out of benevolence, God gave His only begotten Son to save us from the inevitable. However, what is God saving us from? Clearly, *John 3:16* lays a foundation, or serves as a prelude to the Gospel.

A summary of the Gospel can be found in *1 Corinthians 15:1-4.* The essence of the Gospel is that Jesus died for our sins, He was buried and three days later, He rose from the grave. Why is this message so powerful? There are three major points to the Gospel. 1) It identifies the problem that is plaguing man. 2) This message tells us in what way the problem was dealt with. 3) And, it shows us that Jesus was successful in His mission.

Obviously, we must come to terms with this powerful message that God is using to save the souls of people. But, for the purpose of examining our own understanding about this message, we must consider what the Gospel means to us individually. Write down what this message means to you.

Sin

The problem that plagues man can be identified in the small three-letter word "sin." Before we deal with this subject, it is important for each person to consider how he or she sees sin. In fact, because of sin all men are facing the wrath of God, which will be directed towards all that walk in it *(Matthew 1:21; Romans 1:18; 5:9, 21; 6:20; Ephesians 2:1-3; 1 Thessalonians 1:10)*. What is sin to you?

There are two major affronts against the Gospel. The first affront is against Jesus. Jesus is able to save us to the utmost because of who He is *(Hebrews 7:25).* If a person possesses a different Jesus from what the Word of God advocates, such a Jesus will not be able to save the person.

The second affront against the Gospel is the fact that people have been trying to do away with sin. Sin has been watered down or completely done away with by clothing it in terms that take away its harsh reality. For example, sins are considered mistakes, diseases, and alternative lifestyles that are natural or inherited.

In some ways, these conclusions are right, but they are not being used in the correct perspective. For example, it is a mistake to make light of sin in any way. Sin is not a mistake; rather it is a natural preference of man in his present, fallen state. It is a disease in the sense that it destroys man's relationship with God, thereby, destroying his soul as well. However, man can be healed from its destructive ways. Sin also points to a lifestyle, but it is one of choice or preference. Due to sin, the state of death has been passed down to all men. Death, not life is man's future inheritance in light of eternity, but it is one inheritance that can be changed *(Romans 5:12)*.

How does sin affect us? Sin affects us in three ways: disposition, walk, and works. Sin abounds in its consequences, influences, and activities. Ultimately, sin causes us to reject and rebel against God's authority, walk in delusion about God, and in denial about its effects in our lives. Let us now consider these effects of sin on our lives. This is vital if we are to understand what we are being delivered from.

Disposition

Man is in a fallen condition because of Adam's rebellion against God *(Romans 5:12)*. This fallen condition is not based on who man is, but what he fails to become. In other words, man is human by nature. This will not change, but what man allows himself to become as far as the character or inner state of his being comes down to who or what he allows himself to be influenced by. What is your understanding about the inner state of man?

"Disposition" represents the inner state of man. This inner state is reflected through each of our attitudes towards God and life. Ultimately, it will be manifested in our lives by the type of fruit that is being produced *(Matthew 7:16-20)*. *Romans 3:23* tells us how our disposition was affected by sin, "For all have sinned, and come short glory of God." The first man was created to reflect the glory of God in the midst of creation.

Man's initial disposition or state was that of innocence before God. He had communion with God, thereby, having the ability to reflect the influence of God to the rest of creation. This was brought out in the case of Moses. After being in the presence of God, his countenance shone with the affects of God's presence and glory *(Exodus 34:29-35; 2 Corinthians 3:7)*.

When Adam gave in to rebellion, his inner state became marred. He became soulish or selfish in his disposition. It was no longer about establishing his life in God, but now it was about finding his own life outside of God. His state no longer reflected the influence of God, but now it would reflect the darkness of a soul that was separated from the one who is the essence of light, God. After all, it is the light of God that served as man's life *(John 1:4)*. However, now man was in darkness. He would taste the consequences of his sin: that of death.

Man would experience death in two ways. Spiritually, he became separated from God, who is the essence of all life. Since man was spiritually dead, he no longer was inclined towards God. The Apostle Paul put it best in *Romans 3:11,* "There is none that understandeth, there is none that seeketh after God." Man was now lost in a quagmire of uselessness as he pursued that which was attractive and desirous to his way of thinking and doing. However, such pursuits would prove to be vanity and bitterness to the soul since all such pursuits were all under a curse of death and destruction *(Genesis 3:17-19; Romans 6:23; 8:18-25; Galatians 3:10-13)*. Not only did man taste spiritual death as he walked according to darkness, he would taste physical death as well.

Since man's inner state had changed from experiencing the life of God to walking in the state of death, he was no longer inclined towards the one true God. In fact, he possessed no real desire towards the God of heaven. His desires were directed elsewhere. He now ceased to value the spiritual aspect of a life that found its satisfaction and purpose in communing with God. However, man was created with a need to worship God. Since Adam's defiant act separated all men from their true Creator, their natural tendency would be to erect a god of their own liking that would justify their selfish ambitions and pursuits. The main god that is erected is self—the image, the intellect, the rights, the arrogance, and self-sufficiency of self. In short, man's religion and focus of worship would become man-centered, rather than God-centered. We call the exaltation of man in this way, humanism.

Needless to say, idolatry has caused man to become ignorant towards God. Man has religion, but it often reveals superstition about God and not knowledge of the true God. Man has his theology, but it often lacks life, authority, and power. Man worships, but he does not know whom he is really worshipping. Man has many altars, but few are dedicated to the real God, nor do they show sacrifices that are acceptable and worthy of who He is *(Matthew 15:3-9; John 4:22-24; Acts 17:22-34; Hebrews 13:15-16)*.

The other aspect of sin is its deception *(Hebrews 3:13)*. Since man is often the subject of his own worship, he cannot possibly see the vanity and destruction of his man-centered religion. Since man's search ends with his own conclusions, he cannot see how he can be wrong about present matters. Since man often compares himself with others who are considered more miserable in their plight, he becomes the final authority in all matters. *Proverbs 14:12* and *16:25* states there is a way that seems right to man, but it leads to death and destruction.

It is hard for man, in his state of self-exaltation, to realize that his ways of doing are perverted towards God; his conclusions often come out of vain imaginations that exalt themselves against the real knowledge of God; and his attempts to take care of a matter amount to nothing more than vanity *(Proverbs 21:8; 2 Corinthians 10:4-5; Ecclesiastes 13:8, 13-14)*.

The Word of God commands us to let the mind or attitude of Jesus be in us. Jesus' disposition was that of lowliness. It was expressed in an attitude of meekness *(Matthew 11:28; Philippians 2:5)*. Once again, we are reminded that we must take on a new disposition that will change our attitude and approach towards God. In fact, the first four Scriptures in

Philippians 2 reveals how such a disposition will express itself in our lives, while *Philippians 2:6-8* shows how it expressed itself in Jesus' life.

Our nature as man is who we are, but our disposition will determine who we become. In other words, who or what we will express in our lives daily.

This brings us to how man lives or walks out his life.

The Flesh

The first man was created as a spiritual being with the very breath of God in him *(Genesis 2:7)*. In other words, he was given the breath or Spirit of God to interact with his Creator, who is Spirit and truth *(John 4:23-24)*. When Adam rebelled in the Garden of Eden, the breath of God lifted from him, closing down the spiritual aspect of his life. Instead of being able to operate on a spiritual plane, he became soulish or fleshly in his way of doing, thinking, and being. Instead of the matters of the soul (the will, mind, and emotions) being influenced and directed by the Spirit towards the matters of God, they became subject to the pursuits, desires, and affections of fleshly appetites as he began to interact with the world around him. In man's attempt to get the world around him to feed and satisfy his inner being, he has become enslaved to it (*2 Timothy 2:4; James 4:4; 1 John 2:15-17)*.

Man, in an unregenerate state, walks according to the flesh. According to the Apostle Paul in *Romans 7:18*, there is no good thing in the flesh. To put this into perspective, we must understand what goodness is. Only God is good *(Matthew 19:17)*. This means that all that originates with God is beneficial. It has the ability to bring pleasure, well-being, beauty, and substance to the person's life. In light of this information, the Apostle Paul stated that anything inspired or originating in the flesh cannot be considered good, because it will not benefit or add to the person's well-being. He confirmed this truth in *Romans 3:12*, "They are all gone out of the way, they are together become unprofitable; there is none that doeth good, no, not one." What does it mean for you and me to walk according to the flesh? (Be sure to write your answer or conclusion to a question to see how well you do understand these issues.)

Galatians 5:21 tells us those who walk according to the works of the flesh will not inherit the kingdom of God. The flesh is not spiritual; therefore, it cannot receive the things of God, without perverting or tainting them *(Romans 8:5-8; 1 Corinthians 2:13-14)*. However, the flesh tries to become spiritual on an intellectual (thinking great things) or an emotional level (the wave of emotional sentiment and experience). Such attempts open people up to the realm of Satan, rather than God.

It is not unusual to see people try to rehabilitate the flesh. They try to reform according to standards; they comply to what they perceive is right; they perform according to requirements; and, they adjust to give the appearance that all is well. However, it is all outward attempts. The inward environment remains unchanged.

As you honestly consider the motivation, the influence, and the activities of the flesh, you realize why the Apostle Paul quoted the Old Testament Scripture: "As it is written, There is none righteous, no, not one" *(Romans 3:10).* Righteousness points to that which is holy and just. It implies that a person's character and actions are coming from a point of innocence or purity. Since the flesh is selfish and self-serving, there is no innocence or purity in it. Therefore, it fails to be upright before God in motivation and action. All that comes from the flesh has already been judged, and will stand condemned. This is also in reference to what we consider good works.

Works

We now come to the issue of good works, and the emphasis that can be improperly put on them. As previously stated, almost all cults have one thing in common. They put a tremendous emphasis on good works. What kind of emphasis do you think works play in the Christian walk?

Most people judge themselves by their works. They believe that if they are doing good works, there must be something good in them. This shows their ignorance towards God. He does not consider us according to our works, but according to our inward disposition. If our inward disposition is that of selfishness, then the purpose for personal good works would be self-centered. For instance, people do things because they want to feel good about themselves, do away with guilt, or earn recognition. Clearly, this is man-centered, not God-centered. It will bring glory to man, not God. Since it is not God-centered, it is not eternal, satisfying, or rewarding.

The Word of God clearly outlines this reality. In *Isaiah 64:6,* it tells us our best is as filthy rags. *Titus 1:15-16* tells us how to the pure all things are pure, but to the defiled and unbelieving their mind and conscience are defiled. Even though profane people may profess they know God, their works show their true spiritual condition. It refers to their works as being reprobate or useless.

Matthew 7:21-23 brings this subject closer to home. Apparently, there will be those on judgment day who will bring up their works before the Lord. However, as believers, we are not justified by works, but by faith *(Romans 4:2-3).* In fact, what is not the product of faith is sin *(Romans 14:23b).* It is our faith towards God that is pleasing to Him, not our works *(Hebrews 11:6).* Although these individuals in *Matthew 7:21-23* will make reference to works, Jesus will not recognize them. He commands them to depart from Him because they worked iniquity, rather than doing the will of the Father.

The final reality about works is found in *1 Corinthians 3:12-15*. Paul tells us all works will be tested by fire. This fire will determine the quality of the works. The quality of works brings us back to whether they are ordained, sanctioned, and blessed by God. Some works will come forth as gold (pure), silver (redemptive) or precious stones (costly). While other works will be exposed as wood (self-righteous works), hay (worldly inspired), and stubble (inspired by the flesh). Needless to say, the wood, hay, and stubble will be consumed in the fires of judgment, but the person will be saved by fire.

Ultimately, all acceptable works will be from God, bring glory to Him, and will be offered back to Him on judgment day. If the flesh, world, or man's religion is associated with any work, it will be considered useless and designated for judgment.

As we consider the indictment against the flesh, we realize why Jesus had to die for us. We are most hopeless and miserable in our plight. We can delude ourselves based on fleshly works, we can justify our selfishness because we think that we deserve happiness, and we can convince ourselves we are not so bad because we are religious. However, the truth is we remain miserably lost unless we receive Jesus as our only hope and solution.

Redemption

The next part of the Gospel is that Jesus died for us. Jesus' death on the cross points to redemption. *Psalm 49:8* tells us the redemption of our souls is precious. Redemption is a theme that runs through the Bible. What does redemption mean to you?

As we study the harsh reality of our plight, we realize that without intervention, we are doomed in our sins. Obviously, man cannot deliver himself from his plight. He lives in an environment of death, where sin abounds; therefore, the activities of sin can consume him. He is a slave to the works, consequences, dictates, and appetites of sin, which are constantly taking him captive *(Romans 5:20-21; 6:20-23; James 1:13-15)*.

How can people be delivered from this terrible doom? The only one who could save any of us from our spiritual plight is God. To satisfy the Law of God, the judgment upon sin would have to be carried out. *Hebrews 9:22* tells us there is no remission of sin without the shedding of blood. Remission points to pardon. We must receive a pardon to be released from the consequences of sin.

In the Old Testament animal sacrifices were offered to make atonement for sin. This simply meant that sin was covered by the blood of these sacrifices, but it was never taken away. Therefore, these sacrifices could not satisfy the judgment on sin. *Hebrews 10:4* confirms this, "For it is not possible that the blood of bulls and of goats should take away sins."

It was not enough to cover the sins; they had to be remitted in order to receive a pardon. Therefore, someone had to be willing to take our place as our substitute to satisfy the Law. This means the substitute must satisfy the judgment pronounced by the Law to its fullest degree. In the case of humanity, man stood cursed by the Law, and the sentence over him was that of death *(Romans 6:23; Galatians 3:13)*. In our case the substitute would have to die in our place to ensure our release from the curse and judgment that hung over each of our heads.

God's plan was to provide the one sacrifice that would satisfy judgment and bring reconciliation between Him and man. As He did in Israel, He would use the death of the first born of Egypt to bring about the necessary release from slavery. Only this time, He would offer up His only begotten Son. Ultimately, it would be God's way of redeeming or buying back His people from the taskmasters of the Law, sin, the world, and Satan *(Exodus 12:12-13; John 3:16-18; Galatians 3:13; 1 Corinthians 6:20; 7:23; Ephesians 2:13-17)*.

Hence, enters Jesus Christ on the scene. *1 John 2:1-2* tells us that Jesus is our advocate and the propitiation for our sins. Jesus became our advocate. This does not mean He is simply our defense attorney, but rather He serves as our very defense in the courts of heaven. Because He took our place and paid the complete sentence for our offences committed against God and His Law, He is able to plead our cause.

The fact that we have been bought back points to the fact that God is now our owner. We do not belong to the world, Satan, or ourselves. We are citizens of heaven, and as our owner, Jesus is our Lord *(Philippians 2:9-11; 3:20)*. The real issue here is whom we decide to serve. Jesus may be our Lord, but we must choose to come under His authority and obey Him. This requires complete consecration on our part. However, many of us have divided loyalties, maintain personal rights, and will determine in what way we will serve Jesus.

The reason for such division in our loyalties and servitude is that very few of us truly become identified with Jesus. This brings us to the next part of the Gospel. Jesus died for our sins and was buried.

Identification

Why is identification of the utmost importance concerning our Christian life? We each need to meditate upon this question before we answer it.

You might wonder in what way Jesus' burial is associated with identification. Everything Jesus did was to identify with man. He was tempted in every way as we are, but without sin. He tasted the challenges of the flesh, but remained in submission to the Father. He was weary, yet He became a place of rest as He calmed the seas and the turmoil of man's heart. He experienced death, so man could possess life. Jesus became identified with man in his sinful plight, so man could become identified with God in His righteousness *(Matthew 11:28-30; 26:36-46; 2 Corinthians 5:21; Hebrews 4:16)*.

The Apostle Paul made reference to this identification in *Romans 6:3-14*. Jesus became sin, or the sin offering to take our sins to the grave with Him *(2 Corinthians 5:21)*. There, these sins would lose their power and influence over our lives. However, we must realize that the message of the cross represents the great exchange. It is not enough to take something away; it must be replaced by something else. The power and influence of sin must be exchanged for a new life. This new life will be the life of Christ. However, this exchange must be marked by death.

The grave clothes in Jesus' day marked the end to the previous life. In Lazarus' resurrection in *John 11,* Jesus commanded the people to loose him from the grave clothes, and let him go. The old life marks oppression, hopelessness, and death. Jesus came to release the hold that the old has on each of us, but there must be a death, a burial, and a loosening from the old.

In water baptism we see the symbolism of the grave. We are taken into the water (grave), and are washed clean (of sins). Therefore, the sins are left in the grave, and when we are brought up out of the water, we are being brought forth in a new life. However, the grave clothes of the old way of thinking, doing, and being can still cling to us. We must be loosed from them. The Word of God shows us we have a responsibility to do away with the old. Commands such as mortifying and putting off are associated with the old life *(Ephesians 4:22-24; Colossians 3:5-9)*. *1 Peter 2:1-2* tells us we must lay aside all malice (hatred), guile (deception), hypocrisies (feigning something), envies (jealousies), and evil speaking (gossip, slander, sarcasm, crude comments etc.), and begin to desire the pure milk (doctrine) of the Word. Obviously, if we try to partake of the pure milk of the Word without first getting rid of the old, it will be defiled.

Just as Jesus died to secure our redemption, we must die daily to the power and influence of sin in our lives. This death means that sin no longer can attract or bring us into bondage. Since the new life that is being established in us by faith is the actual life of the Son of God, sin will continue to lose its power, influence, and attraction in our lives. Ultimately, the mind or disposition of Jesus will be established in us. We will walk in meekness and humility before God, ready to come into submission to Him in all matters *(Luke 9:23-24; Galatians 2:20; Philippians 2:5).*

Such a life is also a life of consecration. Consecration means a person is separating him or herself from that which is unholy, so he or she can be separated unto God, and walk in a life that reflects the glory of Christ in disposition, attitude, and conduct.

Obviously, Jesus went to the grave so we could experience freedom from the old way of doing and being. Such freedom allows us to embrace the new and come under the leading, authority, and power of the Holy Spirit in our lives. It is under the leading and power of the Holy Spirit that deeds of the body will be completely mortified, and the inner man will be transformed *(Romans 8:13; 12:1-2).* The result is that we will actually put on the Lord Jesus Christ *(Romans 13:14).*

Identification will allow believers to realize the significance of the last part of the Gospel message—that of resurrection power.

Resurrection

The final part of the Gospel is that three days after being put in the grave, Jesus rose from it. It is important that as Christians we understand why resurrection is important. What do you think the significance of resurrection is in the Christian life?

The Apostle Paul summarized the importance of the resurrection in this way, "And if Christ be not raised, your faith is vain; ye are yet in your sins" *(1 Corinthians 15:17).*

As you study resurrection in Scripture, you will begin to realize how important this issue is. Jesus talked much about resurrection. He told the Sadducees, who did not believe in resurrection, that they erred because they did not know the Scriptures, or the power of God *(Matthew 22:29-30).*

Scripture shows us that every person will be resurrected. However, in *John 5:29*, Jesus speaks of two types of resurrection, "And shall come forth; they that have done good, unto the resurrection of life; and they that have done evil, unto the resurrection of damnation." As you study what is good, you realize it is associated with God, but evil is associated with the works of the flesh, the world, and Satan. Once again, it comes down to who a person is serving.

The prophet Daniel said this about resurrection in *Daniel 12:2*, "And many of those who sleep in the dust of the earth shall awake, some to everlasting life, and some to shame and everlasting contempt."

Man was created to live forever, but as to the state in which he will exist or live comes down to what he does with Jesus Christ. It is not

God's heart to see man live in a state of eternal damnation. It is God's will that all be raised up to eternal life *(John 5:39-40)*. He provided resurrection power that resides within man through His Spirit. This resurrection power (internal power) will respond to the voice of Jesus and raise up those who believe the Gospel unto everlasting life, while those who are devoid of this internal power will be raised up to eternal damnation. Such power will be an external power that comes from above and not from within. Clearly, it is man's choice as to where he will spend his eternal existence.

Jesus identified this resurrection power in *John 11:25-26,* "Jesus said unto her, I am the resurrection, and the life; he that believeth in me, though he were dead, yet shall he live: And whosoever liveth and believeth in me shall never die. Believest thou this?" The Spirit and reality of Jesus' life in us as believers serve as the source and hope of resurrection power that will raise each of us into eternal life.

Jesus' resurrection proved a couple of major points. First, we serve a risen Savior and Lord. No other religious leader has ever been raised from the dust of the earth, except Jesus. He now sits on the right hand of the Father as our High Priest *(Ephesians 1:19-20; Colossians 3:1; Hebrews 7:17; 8:1)*. The Apostle Paul in his summary of Jesus Christ in *1 Timothy 3:16* talks about Him being received up into glory. Of course, we have the promise that He will return in the same way He ascended *(Acts 1:10-11)*. Clearly, His resurrection verifies His identity, works, message, and the blessed hope of Him coming back for His Body, the Church.

Another aspect of Jesus' resurrection is that He proved to be victorious over the works of the enemy. The Apostle Paul made this declaration in *1 Corinthians 15:55*, "O death, where is thy sting? O grave, where is thy victory?"

Since believers have resurrection power, they have the ability to overcome. The Apostle Paul stated that, "For if we have been planted together in the likeness of his death, we shall be also in the likeness of his resurrection" *(Romans 6:5)*. In *1 Corinthians 15:52-53,* the Apostle Paul declared that when we are raised in the newness of the complete life of Jesus, the corruptible (the flesh) will have been put off, and the incorruptible (the fullness of the life of Jesus) put on. Even King David realized that he would eventually be changed into the likeness of his Creator, "As for me, I will behold thy face in righteousness; I shall be satisfied when I awake, with thy likeness" *(Psalm 17:15)*.

The Apostle Paul put resurrection in this light in *Philippians 3:10*, "That I may know him, and the power of his resurrection, and the fellowship of his sufferings, being made conformable unto his death." Paul's heart desire was to know Jesus and to experience the power of His resurrection. However, He was aware this knowledge could not occur unless he was willing to know the fellowship of His sufferings. In the end, he became identified with Jesus in His death.

Revelation 20:6 tells us, "Blessed and holy is he that hath part in the first resurrection; on such the second death hath no power, but they shall be priests of God and of Christ, and shall reign with him a thousand years." As we already know, there are two types of resurrection. The first resurrection will be unto eternal life, the second to eternal damnation. John is clearly distinguishing that we need to be sure to be part of the first resurrection, and not the latter.

The responsibility to examine ourselves in light of resurrection is a necessity. Do we possess the real Jesus? After all, it is only the Jesus of the Bible who possesses both the resurrection power and the life. If Christ is in us, then we can be sure of the promise found in *Ephesians 2:5-6,* "Even when we were dead in sins, hath quickened us together with Christ, (by grace ye are saved;) And hath raised us up together, and made us sit together in heavenly places in Christ Jesus." Believers have already been raised up in position in high places in Jesus. It is a matter of time before they will experience the fullness of His resurrection power and life in them.

WHAT IS SALVATION?

Has your understanding of salvation changed after studying the previous information? If so, explain in what way it has changed.

Once again, we must remind ourselves that salvation to most people is nothing more than a sinner's prayer. Granted, one must ask Jesus to save him or her before He can step on the scene. However, salvation entails more than just a prayer. *Romans 10:9-10* gives us this insight into salvation, "That if thou shalt confess with thy mouth the Lord Jesus, and shalt believe in thine heart that God hath raised him from the dead, thou shalt be saved. For with the heart man believeth unto righteousness; and with the mouth confession is made unto salvation."

Obviously, salvation is more than a sinner's prayer; it is a heart revelation of what Jesus did for us. He took our place on the cross, but the grave could not hold Him. He died so that we could be delivered from that which is oppressive and destructive. He rose from the dead. His complete work of redemption and the reconciliation with God that it leads to, points to the Gospel and its glorious power to deliver us *(Romans 1:16)*.

As we consider the concept of deliverance, we must recognize it is in regards to sin. We have been saved from the consequences of sin, that of death (past), we are being saved from the influence and workings of sin (the flesh) in our present life, and we will be saved from all of the activities and judgment of sin (eternal separation) that abound in this world in the future.

Such a heart revelation will not stop with the realization of what Christ did. It will make an exchange as to who will now be our master. Since sin has been taken away by Jesus' death, it is no longer needs to be a master that brings us into the entanglements of the world and into the unmerciful claws of Satan. In our deliverance we now have the freedom to choose our master. In our new-found freedom, we acknowledged our new Lord by confessing, "The Lord Jesus Christ."

As stated, "Lord" means Jesus is my owner and I am His servant. As I grow in the knowledge of Jesus, I will become a bondservant. A bondservant is one who chooses to become a servant for life out of love for his or her master. You can read about this bondservant in *Deuteronomy 15.* Like the servants in this chapter, believers have been redeemed or set free from being servants of harsh taskmasters. However, since we, as Christians, must serve something, we can see the benefit of serving our Lord Jesus Christ the rest of our lives. Such a consecrated service will be earmarked by the power, presence, anointing, and distinction of the Holy Spirit.

Now that we understand that salvation begins with the Lord Jesus Christ, we must come to terms with what it means to believe in the heart the salvation message.

Faith

Ephesians 2:8 tells us we are saved by grace through faith. What does this mean to you?

Grace is God's part in our salvation. This means He shows us undue favor by freely offering us the gift of life. Faith is our response. Faith is active and simply believes what the Word declares about a matter, and receives it in the heart as truth *(Romans 10:17)*. Clearly, God's grace can only be realized through faith. As we respond to God in sincere faith, we will properly receive His grace. In fact, all that God does for us is a matter of His grace. In addition, it is only as we receive God's favor by faith, that God's grace can flow freely through every area of our spiritual lives *(John 1:16-17; Romans 1:17)*.

Keep in mind the heart represents the understanding, will, and emotions. All three point to our disposition towards God. Receiving the truth of the Gospel does not mean that we will understand the total implications of Jesus' death, burial, and resurrection. However, what it does mean is we will have a sense of our need to receive the truth of the Gospel as our solution to the problem of our spiritual plight. Faith is a choice of the will. Choosing to believe often requires us to bypass personal understanding and redirect our affections and emotions to come into agreement with a matter.

Once we believe the Gospel, faith of this nature is accounted as righteousness on our part, and we are born again from above *(John 3:3, 5; Romans 4:3, 9)*. This means we are given a new heart and a new spirit, pointing to a new disposition, making us into new creations *(Jeremiah 32:39-40; Ezekiel 36:26-27; 2 Corinthians 5:17; Hebrews 10:15-16)*. The new heart is a heart inclined towards God. It is pliable under God; therefore, He is able to influence it by the Holy Spirit writing His laws upon the heart, making them revelation and life. Such revelations will establish in greater measure the life of Christ in the believer.

Active faith must not simply be considered a "work"; rather it is a sincere and natural response to grace. The Apostle Paul is clear that we are saved by grace through faith and not by any personal works. Deliverance is truly an act of grace on God's part. Faith will respond to God's grace through obedience to the truth that is being advocated. Such obedience will result in good works.

Scripture shows us we are not saved by works; rather we are saved unto good works. What constitutes good works? *Ephesians 2:10* gives us this insight, "For we are his workmanship, created in Christ Jesus unto good works, which God hath before ordained that we should walk in them." First, good works have been ordained by God. Therefore, these works are from God, of God, and for God, thereby, making a person perfect, complete, or mature in every good work *(Hebrews 13:21)*.

We are told that God is able to make all grace abound towards us to ensure that we have what is necessary in all things so we can abound in good works *(2 Corinthians 9:8)*. In other words, God blesses and equip us to ensure we flourish in the good works He has ordained. We are also instructed to walk worthy of the Lord, which will not only please Him, but such a walk will prove to be fruitful in every good work. Clearly, not all works are fruitful or pleasing. In fact, doing what is acceptable and pleasing to God is our reasonable service, but there are times that doing good to others actually serves as a sweet sacrifice to our Lord *(Romans 12:1-2; Hebrews 13:15-16)*.

James declared that he would show his faith by his works. In other words, works are a natural response of sincere faith and will accompany salvation *(Hebrews 6:9)*. As Christians we do not do these works to gain merits or recognition; rather we do these works because we believe and love God, and we know they are not only a matter of our reasonable service, but they are the right thing to do.

Self-Denial

Jesus talked about what it would mean to be His disciple. Before He instructed His disciples to follow Him in obedience, He told them they had to deny self. What does this mean to you?

One cannot walk out the Christian life without first denying self. In other words, we must disown the old way of doing and being in order to grab a hold of the new. The problem is we want to bring some aspects of our old life from the past into the present to justify it activities, as well as try to maintain the false dignity of it that will continually prove to be useless and a waste. There is nothing of the old that can benefit our new life in Christ.

Jesus was clear, we must deny the right of self to maintain the old selfish life, and pick up the cross in order to follow Him. The old will defile the new, and prevent the cross from daily putting down the selfish dictates of the self-life. Obviously, the yoke of the cross is necessary if we are going to properly discipline how we are to walk out the new life *(Matthew 9:16-17; 16:24-25)*. It is important to point out that without self-denial the old man will simply become a noble martyr when the person applies the cross. He will appear noble, rehabilitated, and religious, when in fact nothing has changed about the inward disposition.

Jesus' desire is to lead us to a complete life. This life is satisfying and full. Such a life will stipulate us as His true disciple *(John 8:31-36; 10:10; 13:34-35; 15:7-14)*. There are requirements in being a disciple of Jesus. A true follower of Jesus will abide in Him, love others, obey His commands, and will display the fruit of heaven.

Self-denial is also a form of consecration *(Romans 12:1-2)*. "Consecration" means I am setting myself apart from all that is not of God, so that I can be sanctified or set apart unto God for His purpose and glory. Once I begin to consecrate my life in obedience to the Word of God, the Holy Spirit then begins the work of sanctification within *(1 Peter 1:2)*. As I walk in this sanctification, I become more consecrated in my disposition and lifestyle.

The Leading of the Holy Spirit

Romans 8:1 tells us that those who walk after the Holy Spirit will not be condemned. What does it mean to walk after the Spirit and/or to be led by the Spirit? Walking after the Spirit involves faith and obedience. It is at the point of such faith that it is accounted as righteousness to us. Such righteousness will bring us under the leading of the Spirit *(Romans 8:14; Galatians 5:16-18)*. The more we give way to the Spirit in our walk, the more our lives are established in the wisdom, righteousness, sanctification, and redemption of Jesus Christ *(1 Corinthians 1:30)*.

Walking in the Spirit mortifies the works of the flesh. The Spirit also leads us into all truth about Jesus and into an intimate relationship with the Father as children of God. It is in this relationship we experience true communion *(John 16:13-14; Romans 8:13-17; 2 Corinthians 13:14)*. Communion lies at the core of why Jesus came. He came to restore communion between God and man. It is in the Spirit that the fullness of the life of God is realized in us.

The Holy Spirit is both a gift and promise of the Father *(Luke 24:49; Acts 1:4; 2:38)* Jesus made this statement in *Luke 11:13*, "If ye then, being evil, know how to give good gifts unto your children, how much more shall your heavenly Father give the Holy Spirit to them that ask him?" Do we want more of God? We have to ensure our inward environment is upright, and then we need to ask for more of God. He in turn will give us more of His Spirit. However, we must come to Him seeking more of His life.

Jesus confirmed this when this invitation went out to all who would come to receive, "If any man thirst, let him come unto me, and drink. He that believeth on me, as the scripture hath said, out of his belly shall flow rivers of living water. (But this spoke he of the Spirit...") *(John 7:37b-39a*).

As you can see, faith is the means by which God delivers us from the consequences of sin. Denying self and application of the cross is God way of delivering us from the works of the flesh. The leading of the Holy Spirit is the way God delivers us from the condemnation of the world, as the Spirit leads us away from the influence of its far-reaching tentacles. God's salvation is complete, but are we willing to receive it in its fullness or do we pick and choose what we will receive, so that we can hold on to certain aspects of the flesh and the world? The fruits will eventually reveal the choice of our heart. What does your fruit reveal about your life before God?

In Conclusion

We have only briefly touched on the issue of salvation. However, it is clear that we must receive by faith the Gospel as a heart revelation. In the Gospel we discover the light of this world. The light of the world is the life of Christ in the believer *(John 1:4; 2 Corinthians 4:3-6)*. We can initially accept the message intellectually, but if we fail to possess the Jesus of the Bible in our hearts, we will maintain our ignorance about God and ultimately taste His wrath.

Salvation will also be obvious in our lives. Granted, there may be various battles and some defeats, but if we are truly walking in our deliverance in obedience to the Word and according to the leading of the Holy Spirit, the light of the world (Jesus) will be reflected in and through our disposition *(2 Corinthians 3:18)*.

The question is do we have the witness of salvation in our lives? We must not consider this issue in any other light than the Word of God. We must not leave this up to religion, worldly philosophies, or the words of men. Clearly, the Gospel has been replaced with a feel-good religion that is akin to new-age philosophies and the humanistic religion where man's happiness is subtly being exalted in accordance to his feelings, desires, and pursuits *(Colossians 2:8)*. Needless to say, the Gospel and Christianity are being presented as a man-centered religion where man is being esteemed, reducing God to an entity that must come into subjection to man's fleshly whims and beliefs. Sin has been downplayed with acceptable terms so that Christianity does not appear too legalistic and unloving. Moral accountability has been replaced with tolerance in the name of being politically correct, and the love of God has been repackaged to mean a fleshly love that walks in ignorance. Such love is more concerned with popular opinion and fleshly preference than it is to see men saved from their wretched condition.

Our challenge remains the same. We must find Christ in the midst of man's religion, worldly influences, heretical teachings, and demonic seduction and activities. We must seek out the true God for ourselves. We must answer the question concerning salvation for ourselves. As the Word declares, if we are saved, there will be a witness in our spirit that we have been delivered from the kingdom of Satan, and translated into the kingdom of God's dear Son *(Colossians 1:12-14)*.

Have you allowed such deliverance to take place in your life? Are you reflecting the disposition of Jesus or the disposition of the old man? Is there a deep abiding witness that you are indeed saved because Jesus lives in you by faith? Only you can answer these questions as you humbly bow before the Lord of lords and King of kings and seek His face about this most important matter.

Section 4

CHURCH AND LEADERSHIP

THE MAKEUP OF THE TRUE CHURCH

One of the most confusing issues about Christianity is what constitutes the Church of Jesus Christ. This question must be properly answered in order for people to understand what part fellowship, leadership, submission, and obedience play in the workings of the Body of Christ. What constitutes the real Church of Jesus to you?

To put the concept of church into perspective, a very simple question must be considered. Whom did Jesus die for? Did He die for a denomination, a certain group of people, a creed, or rituals? The right answer to this question will reveal the identity of the true Church of Jesus Christ whom He offered up His life on its behalf. The reason for this question is that Jesus loves His Church. However, the Church will be cleansed by the Word, and one day it will be presented to Him in a holy state, without spot, wrinkle, and blemish *(Ephesians 5:25-27).*

Most of us probably know the correct answer to this question, but the word "church" has been used in such a way that there is much confusion about it. Most people relate to it as being a building, religious system, a certain denomination, or group of people. However, the Word of God is quite clear as to what constitutes the real Church that Jesus died for.

Colossians 1:18 tells us that the Church is made up of the Body of believers. In other words, those who have believed the Gospel of Jesus Christ. Such believers include those of the past, present, and future. According to *Hebrews 12:1,* there is a great cloud of witnesses who not only speaks of those of the Old Testament who possessed enduring faith, but confirms the power and expectation of this living, eternal Body to those of this present age. Therefore, religious association, denomination, leadership, and rituals do not constitute the Church. Even though many people may be involved with Christian associations (parents/relatives/leaders or even terms such as Christian), certain Christian denominations, popular Christian leaders, and practicing regimented, religious rituals, do not make such people part of the true Church of Jesus. What has always made a person part of the Church and continues to identify this individual to this glorious Body is faith in the Person and redemptive work of the Lord Jesus Christ.

As you consider the attitudes of religious people, you will realize that many are displaying a cult mentality. We have been dealing with how a cult mentality is established, but now we need to understand what constitutes how this mentality expresses itself. A cult mentality causes people to see their belief system, denomination, leaders, or practices as making them elite or superior to others in the Christian realm. They may tolerate others, but they will be judgmental towards anything that is contrary to their belief system, leader, or practices. This is nothing more than self-righteousness. Such elitism is prideful, and will delude and isolate these individuals from truth, while causing schism among other believers. Even though believers can be divided by certain beliefs, the true Body of Christ cannot be separated into different parts or pieces. It will always remain intact.

Religious foundations that are not founded on the Jesus of the Bible will not withstand the fiery trials of life. However, how many people assume they are saved because of their religious beliefs, affiliations, and practices? It is easy to fall into this category when your perception of spiritual matters is wrong.

There is no elitism in the Body of Christ. In fact, those who are considered of less importance in the function of the Body of believers by the standards of the world, are actually exalted so that all will stand equal before Jesus Christ who is the head of the Body *(1 Corinthians 12:12-27)*. Distribution of gifts among believers is not based on the talents, financial stability, importance, or outward appearances of people, but according to the working of the Holy Ghost for the purpose of the edification (or profit) of the whole Body *(1 Corinthians 12:4-11)*.

This brings us down to what the real Church of Jesus is. It is truly a living organism made up of believers. *1 Corinthians 3:9* tells us it is God's building. In other words, He resides in it. *1 Peter 2:5* calls believers lively stones that make up a spiritual house, a holy priesthood, establishing that the Church is the corporate body of Christ. Within this house, spiritual sacrifices are being offered that are acceptable to God by Jesus Christ. The apostle goes on to state this royal priesthood is a chosen generation, a peculiar (special) people who will show forth the praises for the One who has called them out of darkness into the marvelous light *(1 Peter 2:9)*.

Obviously, the real Church of Jesus walks according to the light or life of Jesus in it, and not according to the world or the flesh. This is why the Church is also considered a cultivated field *(1 Corinthians 3:9)*. Clearly, God does the work within the hearts and lives of people that will bring forth eternal fruits. The people that make up this building and cultivated field of God will stand distinct from the world by their attitude, life, and fruits *(John 15:7-8; Ephesians 5:1-17)*.

How is this building established? The Word of God tells us one stone (believer) at a time. *1 Corinthians 12:13* tells us that each believer is baptized into this Body by the Holy Spirit. Therefore, God places believers in this building according to His eternal purpose for each person's life, but it will always be in line with His plan for the whole Body of Christ.

This Body is to serve as an extension of Jesus in this present world *(1 Corinthians 12:18)*. No believer is an island unto him or herself. God's plan for each believer was ordained before the very foundation of the world. This body is also eternal and encompasses the world. As separate stones within the living, universal Church, we may not see our importance in the function of the whole Body of Christ, but we can know it is vital and significant in light of eternity.

Now that we understand how the Body is comprised, we need to come to terms with the leadership of this Body. The character of the Church will be based greatly on the leadership that is influencing it. Some of the Body of Christ is being rendered ineffective by improper leadership. It is important we gain the mind of Christ about this subject.

True Leadership

Explain how you perceive true leadership in the kingdom of God. *Ephesians 4:11* tells us that He gave some apostles, some prophets, some evangelists, some pastors, and some teachers. Do these people constitute leadership in the Church? To answer that question we must understand the distinct responsibility that they were given. As you will discover, true leaders in God's kingdom are not being called to a place of exaltation, but to a place of subjection and submission to the plan of God in relationship to the Church.

Leadership in the kingdom of heaven is different from the leadership promoted by the world. Jesus clearly brought this up in *Matthew 20:25-27,*

> ...Ye know that the princes of the Gentiles exercise dominion over them, and they that are great exercise authority over them. But it shall not be so among you, but whosoever will be great among you, let him be your minister, and whosoever will be chief among you, let him be your servant.

What can we learn about great leadership in God's kingdom? Simply put, God never calls His people to greater leadership, but to greater servitude.

A great leader in God's kingdom is not marked by titles, degrees, or places of great authority, but by a humble attitude of servitude before God that is clearly displayed towards His sheep. Jesus did not tell Peter, go forth, and my sheep will feed you. He commanded Peter to feed His lambs (new converts), and to feed His sheep (more mature believers), thereby, feeding His whole flock *(John 21:15-17)* Jesus also clearly left us an example of servitude the night He was betrayed *(Matthew 20:28; John 13:13-17)*

As you study these five positions mentioned in Ephesians, you will realize they must come into subjection to the Cornerstone, Jesus Christ, as a means to ensure every believer is firmly planted on the foundation of Jesus. *Ephesians 2:19-22* confirms this,

> Now, therefore, ye are no more strangers and foreigners, but fellow citizens with the saints, and of the household of God: And are built upon the foundation of the apostles and prophets, Jesus Christ himself being the chief corner stone, In whom all the building fitly framed together groweth unto an holy temple in the Lord; In whom ye also are built together for an habitation of God through the Spirit.

We already know the foundation has been clearly established by the apostles and prophets in their writings. There is only one spiritual foundation and that is Jesus Christ *(1 Corinthians 3:11)*. There is nothing more to establish about this foundation. The building or temple (His people) is now being brought forth, but it is in line with the Cornerstone, Jesus.

According to the information I have read on cornerstones, all other stones are lined up to the cornerstone. Therefore, what we need to understand is that the work of the apostles and prophets are to ensure that the Church is lining up to the Person, work, teachings, and examples of Jesus Christ. The problem today is that many of the so-called "leaders" of the Church are redefining the foundation in order to exalt themselves into the place of Jesus Christ as the cornerstone.

Today there is a flood of so-called "apostles" and "prophets" running around. In fact, leaders are flattering and appealing to people's pride as these unsuspecting individuals are given titles of importance in these leaders' "spiritual kingdoms." As a result, many are being seduced by doctrines of demons *(Ephesians 5:6-7; 1 Timothy 4:1-2)*. There are innumerable people running around with new revelations as well as a word here and a word there because they call themselves apostles or prophets. However, if you study about the true apostles and prophets in the Word of God, they were a rare breed. They were not of this world. They stood distinct and they were not looking for followers. Their uncompromising attitudes brought persecution upon them. They spoke the oracles of God, which cut through the religious kingdoms of men. They were not popular or appreciated because they never fit into the popular religious systems or movements of their day. As you can imagine, this study would take many volumes to do it any real justice.

The goal of this exposition is to bring godly leadership in the proper perspective. True leaders in the kingdom of God will establish people firmly on the Jesus of the Bible, and ensure they are lining up to Him as the Cornerstone. As Jesus stated, those who obey and teach men to observe the commandments of God will be great, but those who fail to obey God's commandments, and likewise teach others to disobey will be considered the least in His kingdom *(Matthew 5:19)*.

As you consider apostles, they were sent forth to establish local bodies of believers. In the case of prophets, they were watchmen who were to warn, guard, and exhort God's people in regard to truth. Their goal was to always point people towards the reality of God in their midst. They would warn against anything that would threaten that reality, and they would guard the truth against the invasion of idolatry, heresy, and evil works, knowing that it was the only means to bring proper contrast. They would exhort God's people to believe, obey, and walk according to His righteous ways.

Evangelists are responsible to stir up the vision of God's people. Once God's people lose their vision for the lost, they will lose sight of their calling and responsibility towards God to fulfill His plan to bring forth a complete revelation of the Son. Evangelists have the calling and ability to once again stir up that vision. This means that God's people will be awakened from the sleep of complacency, the dullness of compromise, and to be stirred up by the quickening of the Holy Spirit to consider the holy, and to once again gain the passion of love for God, as well as set flame that which would inspire them to fulfill His will.

Pastors are the shepherds of the flock. Their main goal is to ensure that the sheep are properly following Jesus. These people may be good preachers or teachers or both, but this does not distinguish them as real pastors. Real pastors possess the heart of Jesus towards His flock. They protect the sheep from wolves, they stand against the infiltration of muddy (heretical) waters, and they know how to bind up the wounds of the sheep. They are the truest example of servants to the sheep, and their goal is to see the sheep mature in their relationship with the one true Shepherd who gave His life for them.

Apostles appeal to the spiritual needs of people, while prophets appeal to the spiritual condition of people, evangelists appeal to the vision of people, and shepherds appeal to the heart of people, but teachers appeal to the understanding of people. The greatest teachers do not tell people how to think; rather they give them the tools that will challenge their way of thinking. Great teachers want to enlarge people's ability to consider the possibilities of a matter. It is not just a matter of enlarging their ability to explore outside of the normal, intellectual boxes that many operate within, but it is about enlarging one's world concerning a matter. This is why the Holy Spirit is the real teacher of the saint. He enables, instructs, enlarges, and leads a person to the truth about the impossible, the incredible, and the eternal *(John 16:13; 1 John 2:27).*

The responsibilities of apostles, prophets and evangelists may change according to the needs and growth of the Church. In other words, these positions will not remain constant in the local Body. Apostles and prophets may be sent elsewhere or placed in different types of leadership positions. The evangelist must move to different harvest fields. However, the positions of pastor and teachers remain constant and necessary in local bodies.

This brings us to the real leadership of local bodies. The Word of God clearly stipulates there are two such positions in the local churches. They are elders and deacons. The Apostle Paul clearly establishes the criteria of these two leadership positions.

Elders are overseers. They oversee the well-being and spiritual growth of the Body. Elders are also called bishops and presbyters. Pastors are also considered elders. We get a sense of elders in *Acts 6.* There was a conflict in the new Church. Those who were overseeing (elders) the Church felt they needed to give themselves to prayer and the ministry of the Word of God to avoid being spread out too thin, thereby, neglecting their duties *(Acts 6:4).* In *1 Timothy 3* and *Titus 1*, you can read about the character and duties of an elder. Here are just a few qualifications of an elder. These leaders must be sober-minded, of good behavior, given to hospitality, and apt to teach. They must not display obsessive behavior, and they must know how to properly rule their own house. Such leaders must be able to exhort and convince with sound doctrine those who oppose truth. They must be a steward of God, and not self-willed.

The word "deacon" means minister or servant. These are the people who minister to the practical needs of the local Body. This is also brought out in *Acts 6.* One of the men who stepped into this position as a minister of the Body was the first martyr of the Church, Stephen. It is said of Stephen that he was full of faith and of the Holy Spirit. Although Stephen was ministering to the practical needs of the local body, it was obvious that to be effective in ministering, a deacon must be led by the Spirit and walk by faith. The criteria of deacons reveal character that would maintain the trust of those they minister too. For example, they could not be double-tongued, they had to be true to their word and discreet about what they said or shared about a matter. They had to be sober-minded, faithful in all things, and bold in their faith. Such a person would also have one spouse, and had to properly rule his or her house *(1 Timothy 3:8-13).*

Today there are people who hold the positions of elders and deacons, but how many fit the qualifications? Many of these people hold these positions because of gifts, associations, or financial status, but not because they fit the qualifications. Elders and deacons make up boards that are often subject to a particular hierarchy (such as the pastor) and deal with financial strategies in order to keep the church doors open to do business as usual. However, these people do not really oversee the well-being or practical needs of the sheep.

Since the integrity of the real leadership of the Church has become compromised by wrong attitudes towards what was clearly set forth in the Word of God, the local churches do not have the necessary strength that comes from godly leadership. When you compromise the integrity of any leadership, the authority will be missing. Without the authority, there is no real protection, causing the local body to become prey to wolves and hireling shepherds.

Clearly, the local body needs to come back to center as to the type of leadership that was designated by God. Men and women who fit the criteria must be put in their perspective places to ensure the health and safety of local churches. For such people, it will not be a matter of prestige, money, or means, but of character, calling, heart, and vision. True leaders do not drive, demand, or torment the sheep; rather they lead in humility and serve as an example, while challenging the sheep in meekness, exhorting them in love, and proving to be long-suffering in instruction.

This gives a summary of true leadership in the kingdom of God. We desperately need to establish godly leadership. Local bodies have become weak and are falling prey to heresies, wolves, and hireling shepherds that couldn't care less about the sheep, but see their position as the means to feed themselves and exalt themselves before men. As a result, they scatter the sheep, which will ultimately bring destruction to God's flock *(Isaiah 56:10-12; Jeremiah 23:1-3; 50:6; Ezekiel 34:2-3* refer to *Zechariah 11:17).* However, abuse of the sheep means greater damnation for these false shepherds.

It is the responsibility of the sheep to seek out the true shepherds. After all, the shepherd is only as good as the sheep and the sheep are only as good as the shepherd. Sheep can complain about their shepherd, but many of the sheep are feeding in the pastures that serve their personal preferences. Sheep must take responsibility for their own spiritual welfare, keep their eyes on the true Shepherd, Jesus Christ, and remain sensitive to the leading of His voice.

Ordinances of the Church

The Church has been given ordinances to observe. Without reading any further, test your understanding of this matter. How many ordinances have been given to the Church, what are they, and who gave them to the Body of Believers?

Jesus gave the Church two ordinances to recognize and practice. Sadly, the practices of these two ordinances are controversial even in the Body of Believers. How important is it for believers to have the right perspective about these ordinances?

"Ordinance" means a practice or ceremony that has been ordained. Something that is ordained has an authoritative decree or direction behind it. Jesus not only ordained these two ordinances, He practiced them, leaving us an example for both of them.

The first ordinance was established at the beginning of His ministry. It is that of water baptism. When John the Baptist was reluctant to baptize Jesus, He made this statement in *Matthew 3:15*, "Suffer it to be so now, for thus it becometh us to fulfill all righteousness." The initial purpose for water baptism was for the remission of sins *(Mark 1:4)*. However, Jesus was without sin; therefore, His baptism represented an act of righteousness.

As Christians, how should we look at baptism, and what should the proper procedure be surrounding this ceremony? There are two reasons behind water baptism: identification and righteousness. A person who is baptized does so as a means of becoming identified with Jesus' death, burial, and resurrection. It is a visible witness and sign of the new life. *Romans 6:3-5* tells us as believers that we have been baptized into Jesus, thereby, we were baptized into His death. Such a baptism allows us to be raised up in newness of life. We are also told that believers are baptized into one Body by the Holy Ghost *(1 Corinthians 12:12-13)*.

Water baptism is also an upright act because it was a commandment given by Jesus to His disciples before He ascended to heaven,

> All power is given unto me in heaven and in earth. Go ye, therefore, and teach all nations, baptizing them in the name or the Father, and of the Son, and of the Holy Ghost, teaching them to observe all things whatsoever I have commanded you; and lo, I am with you always, even unto the end of the world *(Matthew 28:18-20)*.

You would think that the issue of water baptism would not be controversial, but it is. You have infant baptism that "supposedly" ensures that the original sin is addressed, as well as baptism for the dead. These acts of baptism would imply that baptism is part of salvation. In fact, there are those who believe it is a requirement for salvation.

As you study Scripture, there is only one mention of baptism for the dead in *1 Corinthians 15:29.* Examination of this Scripture shows it was in relationship to a pagan practice. Paul was using it as an example to show that even certain pagan beliefs recognize that there would be the resurrection of the dead.

There is no Scripture supporting infant baptism. Children were dedicated to the Lord such as the prophet Samuel, but there is no indication that infants were baptized to ensure their spiritual protection or well-being *(1 Samuel 1:11; 2:11).* For example, God stated about the pending death of the infant son of wicked King Jeroboam that He had found some good thing towards him in the child *(1 Kings 14:12-13).* David did not baptize his infant child, knowing that the child would not survive. Yet, he was assured of seeing his child in the next life, even though the child represented an adulterous act between him and Bathsheba *(2 Samuel 12:13-23).*

When it comes to maintaining that a person must be baptized to ensure salvation, *Mark 16:16* does not confirm such a belief. Granted, people are to be baptized out of an act of identification and righteousness, which is a matter of faith or believing something to be true and upright. However, what will solely cause people to perish in their sins is not believing the Gospel message. The thief on the cross brings out such a concept. He could not come down from the cross to be baptized, but he believed and was assured of being with Jesus in Paradise *(Luke 23:39-43).* This brings us to the promotion of another Gospel, meaning Jesus plus some type of work or practice such as water baptism. Jesus alone saves, and the Word of God is clear, we are saved by grace and not by any personal merits or works. Once again, we are reminded that true salvation will be accompanied by works or acts of righteousness *(Ephesians 2:8-10; Hebrews 6:9).*

There are different ways of baptizing. Some sprinkle water, while others submerge the person into water. Is there a right way and a wrong way? For many it is a subject you dare not touch without incurring tremendous debate or passion and wrath. It is vital to consider how God does something. He never does it part way. For example, Jesus, who is God, became total man in every way, except He was without sin. He was completely submerged into the human race. With this in mind, must we accept symbols and practices that are not complete in their identification or representation? Do we dare believe God would support such practices?

When you consider the word "baptism" in the *Strong's Exhaustive Concordance,* it comes from a Greek word, "baptizo" which means to be fully wet or completely submerged *(# 907-911).* Do we ignore the meaning of words to maintain the practices taught to us by family or denominational preference? The issue is the same. It does not matter what man's conclusions may be to an issue. Rather, how does the Word of God address the issue in teaching and example?

There is also the matter of what words are used at the baptism. There are those who baptize in the name of the Father, the Son, and the Holy Ghost. There are also those who baptize in the name of Jesus only. We have both examples in Scripture *(Matthew 28:19; Acts 8:16; 10:48).* Are there inconsistencies between these two instructions? Once again, is there a right way or wrong way? If there is confusion, what is the safest route to take in such matters? In Matthew, Jesus, our Lord, is giving the instruction as to how to baptize. What must come into submission? Should we bring Jesus' words into submission to examples found in Acts, or should we bring all matters into submission to Jesus' words?

People must remember that Jesus represents the fullness of the deity in bodily form *(Colossians 2:9).* God the Father and the Holy Spirit were unveiled in the Old Testament. However, Jesus was a mystery until He was revealed in the New Testament. By instructing Jesus' followers to baptize in His name, was it their way of ensuring that baptism would be a completed ordinance by pointing to the Person of Jesus Christ? After all, in bodily form He represents the fullness of the Godhead, the Father and the Holy Ghost. Did the people realize that the fullness of the Father and the Holy Ghost were being completely represented in the Person of Jesus when they were baptized in His name? In *Acts 10:48*, it used the term "Lord". Lord points to Jehovah. Once again, are all three persons of the Godhead being represented in this term? It is important to consider that when the man Jesus was baptized, the Holy Ghost came down in the form of a dove and the Father made His presence known by introducing His Son. Can we deduct from this example that all three must be recognized as being a vital part of our identification to Jesus and His redemption? In a way Jesus verified this when He commanded His followers to baptize in the name of the Father, the Son, and the Holy Ghost. Keep in mind, Jesus is the one who serves as our example and Master. He did things according to "righteousness."

When it comes to the ordinance of "Communion," there is also disagreement. What is your understanding of this ordinance?

Water baptism signified the beginning of Jesus' ministry. However, "Communion" signals the end of Jesus' mission on earth. Notice the terms used. Jesus' ministry continues in the courts of heaven. He serves as our High Priest, Mediator, and Advocate. However, His earthly mission was to die for us as God's Passover Lamb. On the night He was betrayed He shared "Communion" as His last act with His disciples before He was offered up as the Lamb of God.

The debates over Communion vary from the type of emblems used right down to its meaning. Some people believe that unleavened bread and wine (grape juice) should be used, signifying that Jesus was without sin; therefore, He stood as a sacrifice without blemish (or leaven) *(1*

Corinthians 5:6-8). Some people believe any old bread or drink, such as water, can be used. Some insist on wine and wafers. Who is right? Can any old emblems do, or should we insist on the purity of the emblems that will not only uphold the meaning of what each one represents, while maintaining the spirit or intent of the ordinance?

The meaning behind this ordinance varies as well. For some people, to partake of communion means they are literally partaking of the actual body and blood of Jesus. For others, the bread and wine are nothing more than symbols that remind them of what Jesus accomplished the night He partook of this ceremony with His disciples. Who is right and who is wrong? Is it important we get it right? For some, it is a matter of salvation.

Is it possible to actually eat of the body and drink the blood of Jesus? Jesus made reference to this concept in *John 6:53-58.* He stated that if you did not eat of His body and drink of His blood, you could not possess eternal life. However, does this mean it is something that can be done literally? It is important to realize that this proved to be a hard saying to many of His disciples. They turned away from Him and followed Him no more *(John 6:60-66).* Why were they offended? I believe they were taking it literally as well. However, Jesus clearly explained what He meant.

In *John 6:32-35*, Jesus was speaking of Himself as the Bread of life that came down from heaven. He makes this statement in *John 6:40,* "And this is the will of him that sent me, that everyone who seeth the Son, and believeth on him, may have everlasting life; and I will raise him up at the last day." Believing is brought up at different points in this chapter. Was Jesus simply telling people that if they believe in Him, it would be the same as partaking of His body and drinking of His blood, which points to identification? If this is the correct perspective, it would make more sense than believing that one must literally partake of His body and drink His blood to be saved. If you think about each perspective, both require some type of faith. Obviously, those who believe that they are literally partaking of His body and blood must have the faith to believe that each time they partake of the emblems from the hands of their leaders, these substances are actually turned into the body and blood of Jesus.

Perhaps *John 6:57* will bring more clarity to this matter: "As the living Father hath sent me, and I live by the Father, so he that eateth me, even he shall live by me." When you consider the concept of "live," it also points to walk. We know we do not walk by sight, but by faith *(2 Corinthians 5:7).*

With this in mind, consider *Galatians 2:20*, I am crucified with Christ: nevertheless I live; yet not I but Christ liveth in me; and the <u>life I now live in the flesh I live by the faith of the Son of God</u>, who loved me and gave himself for me." (Emphasis added.) Clearly, we have the life of Christ in us, and we live according to His life by faith *(Hebrews 10:37-39)*. Our life in Christ is clearly established by faith in all we do when it comes to loving Him and obeying His Word.

On this basis what would make more sense? Let us now consider it from another perspective. Faith is practical, and not based on imagination or fanciful notions. When Jesus was conducting "Communion", He raised the bread and instructed His disciples that it was His body. He did the same with the wine. He declared it was His blood *(Luke 22:14-20)*. Was He saying, "Imagine that these two emblems are my body and blood?"

It is important to point out that faith does not work off the basis of imagination, and just because we imagine something, does not make it reality. Would Jesus say that it was His literal body and blood, when it fact it was clear to all present it was not? The key is found in why they would eat of the bread and drink of the wine—it was in remembrance of Him. Remembrance is a memorial as to a person or event. From this example, are we to conclude that these emblems symbolize Jesus' broken body and shed blood in order to remind us of what He accomplished on the cross?

Those who partake of the ritual of Communion according to Paul's instruction consider the present, the past, and future. For example, each person must examine him or herself before taking of the emblems to see if he or she is presently prepared to take of Communion in a worthy manner *(1 Corinthians 11:28)*. From the basis of preparation, people take of the bread reminding them that Jesus' stripes heal them *(1 Peter 2:24)*. They take of the wine, remembering that it is by His blood that their redemption was acquired *(Hebrews 9:15-22)*.

Each time Christians partake of Communion, they are declaring that Jesus is coming again *(1 Corinthians 11:26)* Communion may be a time to consider our present condition, and remember our spiritual heritage, but it also points to a glorious future. Jesus said it best the night He was sharing this time with His disciples.

> And he said unto them, With desire I have desired to eat this Passover with you before I suffer. For I say unto you I will not any more eat of it, until it be fulfilled in the kingdom of God. And he took the cup, and gave thanks and said, Take this and divide it among yourselves; For I say unto you, I will not drink of the fruit of the vine, until the kingdom of God shall come (Luke 22:15-18).

Scripture shows us that the kingdom of God would abide within the heart of man through Jesus Christ, but one day it will be fully realized in heaven at the marriage supper of the Lamb. The Lamb of God will sup with all of those who belong to Him. It will be a glorious celebration *(Revelation 19:7-9)*.

There should not be any debate about these two ordinances, but there is. You must wonder why there is such a debate. It is simple; man's interpretations and traditions have confused the meanings and practices behind these two ordinances. If we would strip away all man's influences and indoctrination that put all the different twists on Scripture, and simply believe what is written, there would be no debate about matters. It would be clear in its simplicity and easy to respond to in spirit and in righteousness.

Do you have inward debates going on in your soul about these two ordinances? Do not let man, religious traditions, or theology settle them for you. Allow the Word to settle it by believing what it says. Do not make more of a matter by spiritualizing it to mean something it does not mean, but do not strip it of its spirit by failing to gain God's perspective. Seek God's perspective about a matter so that the things of God can be fulfilled in your life in the right spirit and in truth. Such completion will result in peace with God, satisfaction of the soul, and rest to the mind.

Benevolence

One of the main goals behind a cult is not only to spread their erroneous message, but also to gain control of the hearts and minds of people so that they can control their finances. The goal of cult leaders is the same; they are after money as a means of supporting and promoting their so-called "self-serving gospels and kingdoms."

What is your understanding concerning the subject of giving in the kingdom of God?

The main concept many shepherds use to shake the money out of their people is that of tithing. However, if you study tithing it was for the Levitical priesthood and for the upkeep of the temple. Since there is no temple in Jerusalem and the Priesthood is not in place, the Jewish people do not pay tithes. After all, tithes had to do with the Law in regards to the increase of land (crops) and animals. These tithes were used for sacrifices and celebrations, as well as set apart as food for the priests *(Leviticus 27:30-32; Numbers 18:21, 31:9, 27-29).*

It is important to point out that I have nothing against people paying 1/10th of their income to those who watch over their souls, but my problem rests with the fact that many religious leaders use the term "tithes" to forced people to give to the kingdom they are promoting. This is not only unscriptural, but it is not a New Testament practice. The New Testament practice is that of being a good steward of what God has entrusted. The Apostle Paul talks about Christian giving in *2 Corinthians 9.*

The first aspect of giving Paul brings up is the principle behind giving, "But this I say, He who soweth sparingly shall reap also sparingly;

and he who soweth bountifully shall reap also bountifully" *(2 Corinthians 9:6)*. People give for different reasons, but few give for the right reason. Everything belongs to God and everything must be offered back to Him for His use to ensure good and faithful stewardship on the part of His servants. It is only as we offer all back as His servants that it will go through the hands of God. Once it goes through His hands He can bless, sanctify, and multiply it for His glory (*Luke 9:13-17; 2 Corinthians 9:10-11)*.

The second part of godly giving is the right attitude. Giving is a form of ministry. God made this statement in *Deuteronomy 28:47-48a,* "Because thou servedst not the LORD thy God with joyfulness, and with gladness of heart, for the abundance of all things; therefore shalt thou serve thine enemies which the LORD shall send against thee." People give out of duty, out of conscience, and out of show. Such people are giving out of religious pressure, guilt, and for self-exaltation. However, godly giving that will bring pleasure and honor to God is giving that comes out of a heart that is upright towards God, and is cheerful in its service before Him *(2 Corinthians 9:7)*.

The third aspect of godly giving is that it serves as a sacrifice. *2 Corinthians 9:8* talks about how godly giving is a type of good work. *Hebrews 13:15-16* talks about how good works are considered a type of sacrifice to God. God desires to abound in His grace towards every good work. Again, God is able to bless, sanctify, and multiply every good work for His use and glory.

Since we are talking about sacrifice, there are three types of sacrifices when it comes to our giving. The first type of sacrifice is the religious sacrifice. We give that which will satisfy our religious conscience. It has nothing to do with stewardship, but with that of duty. Such giving represents the least we can do to keep religion and God off of our backs.

The second sacrifice is our reasonable service *(Romans 12:1)*. In other words, it is a matter of doing what is right before God. Such righteousness is not a matter of sacrifice, but one of reasonable service, but it will fall into the category of good works that God is able to use for His glory.

The final sacrifice is the one that comes out of our need and not out of abundance or what is considered reasonable. Sacrifices that come out of need cannot be confused with that which we do out of impulsiveness. Impulsiveness proves to be the product of our carnal emotions and foolishness. The real issue behind acceptable sacrifice is not the quantity of it; rather, it is the quality. God does not need our sacrifices, but He desires actions that show our good faith towards Him.

A good example of the type of sacrifice that comes out of our need is the widow and her mites in *Mark 12:41-44*. The widow's two mites may have seemed insignificant to the world's way of looking, but God took note of her giving and used it as an example to others. This widow gave out of her lack by faith in God. This is the type of sacrifice that God deserves from each of us, and desires to see. It is a sacrifice of the heart that gives sacrificially in good faith to a God who is trustworthy in every way.

Godly giving will manifest itself in liberal giving *(2 Corinthians 9:13)*. The reason for this is due to benevolence. Our God is a God of benevolence. His desire is to bring good will or kindness. We should manifest this same benevolence due to the fact we actually owe others good will or kindness. Such good will and kindness are because of what Jesus did on the cross. We have been bought with a price and we owe all to our Master, Lord, Savior, and God. Jesus brought this out when He gave His followers a third commandment in *1 John 13:34-35*, "A new commandment I give unto you, that ye love one another; as I have loved you, that ye also love one another. By this shall all men know that ye are my disciples, if ye have love one to another."

Jesus gave His best, He gave His all, and He gave it on our behalf. His sacrifice showed the good will and kindness of God towards humanity. As believers, can we do any less when it comes to those who are part of the Body of Jesus? Paul said it best when he gave this instruction in *Galatians 6:2*, "Bear ye one another's burdens, and so fulfill the law of Christ."

The problem with the subject of giving is that many members of cults gave it all out of religious duty to only be betrayed. As they look back, the idea of the waste of time, energy, and resources can be overwhelming. They can look back and see how they often sacrificed the well-being of their family, as well as themselves. As they look at the emptiness, the lies, and the deception of it all, they must do all they can to fight back the anger and bitterness that can erupt like a volcano, spilling out despair in their souls. They must make sure they do not become a victim a second time to the darkness and false world of Satan and his counterfeits.

Those coming out of cults must seek God to heal them and put all matters in perspective including their giving. In fact, God could have accepted such giving as a sweet sacrifice. After all, the widow put her mites into the coffers of a religious system that stood condemned *(Matthew 3:9-10)*. However, she was not giving it to the religious system, but to God. Once she gave it to God for His glory, it was no longer her concern, but those to whom she entrusted it.

It is vital we do not look back like Lot's wife on that which is already judged. We must go forward in our life with God by learning the lessons of the past to change the terrain of the present. By changing the present terrain of our life according to the Lord's good pleasure, we will be assured of the glorious future with Him.

Regarding my own situation, I have many different markers from the past that represent certain aspects of my life. At one time, those markers represented my terrible failures, but when I realized that they possessed valuable lessons that needed to be learned, they began to mark spiritual growth rather than past failures. In the process of changing my markers, I learned it is how you look at a matter. In God's economy, there are no failures or waste, just markers that mark a passing of an old life and the establishment of a new life.

Let us rejoice over the markers of the old life, knowing we will never have to pass by their way again, recognizing that such markers of the past now represent the maturity of our present character, experience, change, and wisdom *(Romans 5:3-5).*

Section 5

CONFRONTING THE CULT MENTALITY

EXPOSING THE CULT MENTALITY

Most people are interested in what a cult is, but few are interested in how cults affect their victims. Cults establish what I call a cult mentality. When I was first saved, I remember one of the concerns of those who were involved with me was, "She may have come out of the cult, but did the cult come out of her?" The first time I heard this statement, I was confused. What did they mean about the cult being out of me?

It took years before I realized what this statement means. When you consider what a cult is, you realize that it is a belief or teaching that often runs close to and parallel with what is true. In other words, it may sound like truth, it may look like truth, and it may feel like truth, but it is not truth. Obviously, cults can be exposed based on what they promote or present as truth.

However, it is not that easy to confront the affects a cult has on people. You can identify something as being wrong, but the real battle is not at the point of something being wrong, rather the real battle comes down to the extent or level that such wrong has managed to influence the heart and mind of a person. The heart will display loyalty towards the cult or leader regardless of how it may be proven wrong. The mind has usually been influenced in such a way that when the foundation of a cult is proven wrong, such knowledge will be rendered useless because it cannot penetrate through the indoctrination that has been firmly set into place.

The battle for a person's soul does not rest on proving that a cult's belief system is wrong, rather the real battle rages over the blind loyalty and idolatrous affections that have enslaved these individuals into a darkness that will pervert the purity of the light when it is present. When people come out of a cult, the darkness of it will prevent these people from being properly challenged to know, seek out, and find the truth. The deadly seeds of deception and heresy will undermine any good seed. What many people fail to realize is that we learn our behavioral patterns according to our thinking and conduct by that which has influenced our lives *(Deuteronomy 18:9; Psalm 106:33-40; Proverbs 22:24-25)*.

Those who have come under the spirit and indoctrination of a cult have been conditioned to reject truths that do not compliment or reinforce the teachings of the leader or creeds. Truth will seem foreign, offensive, and repulsive to such a person. Therefore, most people coming out from under the influences of a cult are already conditioned to walk in total rejection of any truth that is affiliated with true religion, as well as being susceptible to come under the spirit and influence of another counterfeit. In fact, such people will be naturally attracted to anything that will reject or oppose true religion.

For example, people who have been hurt by a cult already feel betrayed by religion. At this point, they are suspicious of everything. They do not trust the Word of God, because it has been improperly handled. Since they have been indoctrinated to see or interpret the Word from an erroneous point of view, truth will be perverted, preventing it from making the necessary impact. Due to their spiritual captivity, such people do not trust unfeigned leadership or the Word. They have no foundation in which to test anything. This leaves them judgmental, rather than discerning. On this basis, how does one test a matter? Since these people feel so miserable about a matter, the greatest attraction will be to that which makes them feel good about self or life.

In ministering to such people, I have to keep in mind that they are fragile when it comes to religious matters. You never know what point of truth in the Word of God will set them off. They can become immediately insulted over a Scripture or teaching, and put up a wall. Since they feel bad, hurt, or betrayed, they will fight against, argue with, or reject the truth. It is a terrible state indeed. Rejection of the truth reveals that such people are not inclined towards the truth. They prove to be angry and rebellious about all religious matters. As a result, they walk in unbelief towards what is true. They end up rejecting the very thing that could set them free from their plight.

Just because something in the Word has been misused or improperly presented, does not make it any less truth. We are clearly told that we will be judged by every Word of God. The Word of God will stand when all other philosophies, erroneous beliefs, and religious preferences are consumed in the fires of hell. Sadly, many of these people keep exchanging one empty, destructive religious package for another. As Jesus said, those who make converts or disciples out of their particular way of thinking, make such people two-fold the children of hell *(Matthew 23:15)*.

Another aspect about cults is that they use a lot of Christian platitudes and terminology. Sadly, Christianity has been reduced to a subculture within the American culture. We have our own language and way of doing things. However, very few Christians have a grasp on Christian terminology. The reason for this gap is that many Christians assume people understand the meanings behind Christian terms. These assumptions have even caused people in leadership positions to be lax in teaching the correct meaning to ensure integrity and the right spirit behind the words or terms. As a result, people have been left to fill in the blanks. Even though there are fruits that indicate that words or terms hold different meanings for cults, it is not unusual for believers to assume that there is an agreement. However, cult members will associate words or terms to their particular cult's twisted presentation. When the correct presentation challenges these people's foundation it causes them to become closed or skeptical.

The other tactic that is used is platitudes. Platitudes are used when people do not know how to address a real issue or problem. These platitudes can be select Scriptures or what we would consider words of wisdom or popular terms. However, platitudes just reveal our ignorance and not our wisdom. They come across as indifferent, unfeeling, and judgmental. I cannot tell you how many times people have whipped platitudes on me to put me in my place, exalt their so-called "superior wisdom" or to get me off their back. Platitudes are nothing but bones people throw out as a distraction.

One might wonder how people fall into cults. We need to realize that cults are designed to be attractive to our pride, as well as our desire to experience a religious fantasy. These individuals are also religious enough that they appeal to our religious conscience. Let us consider how cults are geared to attract our pride.

One aspect of a cult is that it makes you feel elite. For example, a cult maintains it has a corner on truth and all other beliefs are wrong. This is elitism and it attracts our pride. Being part of the elite causes people to feel superior over those who are part of what is considered mainline Christianity or the so-called "blind stupidity" of the ignorant religious masses. It is important to point out that there are no new truths, just greater revelations of the Jesus of the Bible. God has maintained that His Word is true. If anything proves to be contrary to the intent or teachings of His Word, it must be considered a lie from hell *(Romans 3:3-4)*. I might add that elitism is a tactic that Hitler used on a generation of people, and six million Jews died as a result.

Another area that attracts our pride is how cults use titles, prophecies, gifts, and positions. Cults leaders are notorious for handing out titles and positions to people they want to influence and control. Such people feel that the leader is seeing their worth and potential; therefore, they feel not only special but also obliged to follow that leader into hell itself.

Another area is that of gifts. Gifts are handed out like candy to the people. It goes like this: "You have the gift of healing." "You have a gift of prophecy." "Now that your gift has been identified, you need to operate in this gift among the people." At this point, the individual feels special, and has the promise of serving God. They see this allotment as personal recognition and exaltation as well as the means to influence people. The problem with this presentation is that the Bible tells us the Holy Spirit gives gifts, as He wills, not as man delegates. A person may be used in a certain gift at different times, but he or she does not have a corner on the gift. Gifts are a sovereign manifestation of the Holy Spirit *(1 Corinthians 12:7-11)*. They are for the purpose of edification for the whole Body and not a matter of identification to the importance or personal exaltation of a person. The problem with the misuse of gifts among people who have not been properly instructed in this matter is that religion becomes a matter of experience. This experience supersedes truth and becomes a fleshly, emotional wave that anyone can get caught up in when the flesh, not the Spirit, so moves them in their religious fervor to operate in their so-called "gifts."

The problem is escalated when these people take their positions or gifts seriously. In other words, they pride themselves on their position or gifts, and feel that they are in a leadership position because they are elite or special. When this pride reaches it pinnacle, it becomes superior. Due to the open door of pride, this person is now operating in a religious spirit or under an antichrist spirit.

Such people border on fanaticism about their mission, calling, gifts, or positions. They cannot handle present reality and resent anyone who would dare challenge them about their wrong spirit or belief. They prove to be unteachable; therefore, all they hear will be perverted and quickly rejected unless it feeds their religious fantasy.

The religious spirit demands attention, consideration, and exaltation. When the person who is motivated by such a spirit fails to get the desire recognition, he or she becomes angry and disillusioned with the church. Since this spirit must be recognized, the person will leave the local church in search of a religious platform that will honor him or her. Therefore, the heresy and spirit that is in operation in this individual is spread to the unsuspecting Body of Believers. If the pastor is not strong in faith, Spirit-led and inspired, the leader will not be able to discern the cancer that is confronting the congregation. This cancer will cause a mixture (mixed spirit) or confusion. Ultimately, it can cause division.

Another means that is used involves fear and guilt. Cults know how to manipulate misguided devotion and trust. They cause people to rely on them for their spiritual direction and credibility. Approval from the cult leader and members of the cult becomes a necessary pursuit. Therefore, it is easy for cult leaders to classify questions about their teachings as rebellious. Opinions that differ outside of the cult leader's beliefs are considered independence or pride. To have a life outside of the "elite" group is to undermine the authority of the leader. Fear and guilt not only keeps the person operating in superstition about God, but it also can be effectively used by the cult leader to keep the person under control.

Cults also play with the emotions of their members through the avenues of a merit system. For example, keep the approval of the cult leader or organization at all cost, and all is well. Lose that approval, and fear of rejection or chastisement along with guilt will raise its head. Cult leaders effectively use fear and guilt to gain and maintain control of people.

The greatest obstacle when it comes to the cult mentality is the person's perception of God's Word. All cults present a different God, redefine Jesus, and undermine the authority of the Word of God. Since the cult mentality sets up a perverted perception of God and His Word, there is no standard that can be presented to these people that is able to bring them to a place of discernment and accountability. Without the standard, there is no means by which a person can come to terms about what he or she believes, knows, or understands.

This brings me to my own struggles to ensure the cult mentality was no longer influencing my way of thinking or evaluating a matter. Although the cult I belonged to undermined the Word of God, I realized I had to choose it as a standard by which I would test my beliefs. In order to do this I had to repent in three areas. "Repent" means I had to change my mind, thereby, changing my direction. As I changed my direction, I changed my focus. It was as I changed my focus that my mind began to be transformed, producing godly conduct.

The first area I had to repent in was for my choice as to what I considered my standard of truth. I did not agree totally with the cult to which I had belonged. Therefore, I picked and chose what I would believe to be truth. Although the cult had influenced some of my thinking, it was not the final authority in my thought process. Later, I discovered people, such as my mother, became my final authority in what I considered to be truth or trustworthy. As I evaluated my standard of truth, I realized I went on the basis of what sounded correct to me. Much of my idea of truth was based on how I was conditioned by those who influenced my life the most.

When I started the spiritual journey to discover truth, I had no idea how deep such influences ran in my life. Granted, the cult may have not greatly influenced my way of thinking, but I still possessed a cult mentality because I did not possess truth. I had my own perverted idea of religious truth that made my way of thinking seem wise, elite, and special. This perverted way of thinking served as blinders, which kept me from seeing its hypocrisy. I had to realize that what I understood to be truth was wrong. I even had to stay away from the idea that there were some things that could be salvaged in my belief system. Although, I did not understand it at the time, even the right conclusions had been tainted by a wrong spirit and erroneous indoctrination. Therefore, I had to consider it all as dung and start anew from the right foundation in order to establish a correct belief system. In fact, it was not until 15 years after my conversion that the hidden affects of the cult were completely uprooted out of my life.

The second claim I had to make is that my family was wrong. In our initial innocence, we look to family to establish truth for us. We assume that they know what is true. As they write their form of truth on our clean slates, it takes on an identity of its own. In fact, what we believe becomes a part of our identity. When our beliefs are challenged, it becomes a matter of family pride or honor. If the beliefs are wrong, then my family is wrong. If my family is wrong, where does that leave me? When a person's foundation is being torn up in such a manner, it must be defended or held on to in order to maintain identity, family unity, and a sense of belonging and purpose.

For most people, separation from family based on truth and religion is frightening and overwhelming. However, the Christian life is found outside the camp of family and religion. Sadly, few ever make the separation or cut that allows them to discover their life in God outside the family or religious camps of what has been considered "normalcy" according to their particular influences.

The final claim I had to make is that I was wrong. We each have to take responsibility for what we choose to believe and how we choose to hear such matters *(Luke 8:18)*. I was told that my cult was right, but I discovered it was wrong. I assumed my family knew what was right, but I found out they were wrong. Obviously, I was misinformed and deceived. My foundation was definitely wrong, and I was wrong for not testing it. I was also wrong to assume those around me knew what they were talking about. I was wrong, and to be made right I had to take accountability for what I believed. I not only had a responsibility to know the truth for myself, but I had a responsibility to line up to it in faith and obedience.

In order to ensure I had a right foundation, I chose the Word of God as my authority as to what is true. Although its authority had been undermined by the cult I was involved in, and replaced with man's theology and explanations, I knew that I had to have one standard of truth in which to test all things. Regardless of the attack on the validity of God's Word, I chose by faith to believe it as God's Word, and to believe it as absolute truth in anything concerning God, life, and spiritual matters. Although I did not understand it, I chose to study it to come to an understanding of its truths *(2 Timothy 2:15)*.

When I considered the Word, I did not see how big of a book it was or whether it was boring. I saw it as God's Word that would stand when all else would be considered a lie, a counterfeit, heretical, or worldly. I saw it as a challenge. Its pages contained those things I needed to know to keep me from falling into deception and to live an upright life *(2 Timothy 3:16)*. I did not see reading or studying the Word as a religious duty; rather, I regarded it as the very lifeblood to my well-being. In those initial years of my new life, I readily partook of the Word's pure milk, and in time I developed a hunger for its meat.

At times I would stop and ponder about the possibility that my new life in God was a bad joke. Occasionally, I questioned the logic of putting all of my hope in one book, the Bible. Each time, I was reminded of a very important fact. Since I encountered God as my hope, and His Word as my truth, I had found satisfaction and peace. When I thought about the risk of believing God and His Word, I was reminded of what I told my grandmother the day I debated with her about our differences. The statement I made was, "Grandma, if you are right, I am living a decent life; therefore, I will end up in one of your heavens on the basis of merit. But, Grandma if I am right, you will end up in hell."

As I consider the risk of believing the God of the Bible, and believing His Word as truth, I realize that there was no way I could lose. In fact, to take the other side was to risk everything for something that could not stand, save, or defend a person on judgment day.

Through the different debates over the subject of God, His identity and His Word, I have discovered that faith in the God of the Bible and in His Word is a daily choice. I choose to believe when I do not understand. I choose to believe when logic mocks me for believing God's Word. I choose to believe when circumstances seem more powerful than God. I choose to believe when nothing makes sense to my intellect. I choose to believe because I will not find God in each circumstance without such faith.

Finding God is a daily choice. This means I choose to seek God in each matter and challenge. Through it all, I have found God. In fact, I have found the God described in His Book, the Bible. He has confirmed His identity, authority, and power. He has shown Himself in the small things as well as the big things. In my three decades of being a believer, I have never found God to be a liar, or His Word to be untrue.

Those who come out of a cult with a cult mentality are often like corks bobbing on a sea of confusion, fear, anger, and doubt. The wind of suspicion drives them, the undercurrents of judgmentalism sweep them away from the stability of the Rock, and the waves of uncertainty keep them from ever finding rest, assurance, and healing.

Many cult members struggle with their past, unable to let go of it. Yet, they must let go to seek, discover, and embrace the life God has for them. They keep their past before them to remind them not to trust any religion, rather than learn the lessons of their past so that they can have the liberty to walk in light of the ever abiding present reality of Jesus. They fail to realize the Christian life is never behind us, rather it is discovered on a daily basis in light of a future, eternal hope.

Are you a former member of a cult? Do you have a cult mentality? I have good news for you. You do not have to continue to be a victim of the cult or a false leader. Jesus came to bind up the wounds of the sheep. However, to bind up your wounds, you must come to Him *(John 7:37-38)*. You need to give up your right to be a victim, and recognize the authority and power of the Victor. His truth will set you free, His anointing will heal your heart, His authority will subdue the enemy, and His power will enable you to overcome. However, you must come to Him to be healed. You must come to Him to set the record straight about all that was wrong. You must come to Him to transform your perception about God and life. You must come to Him to exchange your present state of mind with His disposition in order to be reconciled to that which is true and liberating.

As a wounded sheep, a person can claim his or her right to remain skeptical towards all that is associated with God. As an angry sheep, individuals can maintain their right to determine their own standard of truth. As offended sheep, people can bring accusation against all that reminds them of their religious experience, and feel justified in their rebellion towards God and His Word. As sheep in despair, they can rant and rave about all the injustices they have experienced at the hands of these counterfeits, but in the end all such rights and offences will have to stand before the One who bears the scars that were imposed upon Him by the religious counterfeits of His day. No doubt when such sheep come face-to-face with the reality of these scars, all such rights and offenses will fall silent. Each of these individuals will realize that the goal of every counterfeit of God is to produce counterfeits in His kingdom. It will be at that terrible moment that each person will realize he or she has become the counterfeit.

On this grave day of reckoning, the everlasting Word of God will ring through the corridors of time and eternity. What will the Word declare in the courts of heaven? Perhaps it will be *Hebrews 2:3,* "How shall we escape, if we neglect so great salvation?"

Or, maybe the words *of Hebrews 6:5-6*, "And have tasted the good word of God, and the powers of the world to come, If they shall fall away, to renew them again unto repentance seeing they crucify to themselves the Son of God afresh, and put him to an open shame."
Maybe the words of Peter will be heard,

> For if, after they have escaped the pollutions of the world through the knowledge of the Lord and Savior, Jesus Christ, they are again entangled in it, and overcome, the latter end is worse with them than the beginning. For it had been better for them not to have known the way of righteousness than, after

> they have known it, to turn from the holy commandment delivered unto them. (2 Peter 2:20-21)

Finally, we cannot forget the words of Jesus found in *Matthew 7:23*, "And then will I profess unto them, I never knew you; depart from me, ye that work iniquity."

The truth is Satan is using cults to win the battle raging for the souls of men. However, we do not have to accept such a defeat in our lives. We can choose life with its blessings, by choosing the real Shepherd of our souls. We can choose the way of faith, freedom, and healing by believing the Word of God. We do not have to accept Satan's way, we can choose to believe, trust, surrender, and put all of our hope in Jesus, and He will raise us above the snare and destructive paths of the counterfeits. As our place of refuge, He will then set us in a large place, a place of rest, victory, and hope *(Psalm 118:5)*.

Prayer

If you can identify with the text of this study and the above testimony, the question is has the cult come out of you so that you can experience the healing and liberty of Christ Jesus? If not, why not consider the following prayer. Let it be heartfelt as you resolve this issue. Do not remain a victim of a cult, and do not allow it to determine your attitude towards God and the life He offers you. Do not let it undermine the authority of His Word, or strip His truth of its ability to set you free with His eternal perspective. Choose to believe what the Word says, and you will never be ashamed.

Lord,

What can I say? I sincerely searched for You, only to find that which has mocked Your Word, undermined Your authority as God, and made You into a powerless Creator. I am confused. I wanted true religion to only taste of that which was false. I have been wounded, betrayed, and brought to the place of utter despair. I do not know how to believe, and I do not believe I have anything left in me to even reach out to embrace the truth.

However, I have been told that You understand. I have been told that for counterfeits to exist there has to be that which is real. On that basis I choose to believe You are real.

Lord, I have become your lost sheep, but I realize that as a lost sheep, I am unable to find You. However, I am promised according to the parable in Luke 15 that You are the One who will find me.

Lord, hear my cries. I choose to believe You are real, but help me in my unbelief to see You for who You are. I am weary with religion, I am weary with dead-letter doctrine, and I am weary with encountering the same lifeless religious activities. I want what is real, satisfying to the soul, and lasting to the Spirit. I now know I do not want some type of religion; I want You in all of Your glory.

I now come to You in need of mercy, forgive me for settling for the counterfeit. I come to you seeking Your grace, now meet me in your abounding favor to reconcile me back into a living relationship with the one true God. Forgive me for losing sight of Your salvation. Forgive me for neglecting the gift of life, the altar of Your cross, and the benevolence of Your outreached arms.

Forgive me for not loving Your Word, but now I humbly ask that You give me a love for Your truth. Put reins on my walk and bring me under Your liberating yoke. Forgive me for my idolatrous life and ways. I now know Lord, that You are a jealous God and I have exalted idols above You. As a result, I lost sight of You.

Forgive me for the injustices I have shown towards You as God. However, I now know more than ever, I need You. You are the One who will keep my feet on the right path. You are the One who will lead me in the paths of righteousness. You are the One who will heal me in my despair, and lift me out of my hopeless pit. And, it is You alone who deserves my total love and devotion.

As You have promised, give me a new heart that is no longer divided or inclined towards the idolatrous. Give me a new spirit that will be sensitive to Your voice and ways. Cleanse me from all my wicked ways and restore the joy of my salvation.

I choose to believe by faith that you have heard my cries. I have come to You in repentance, in great need of Your grace, desirous of Your salvation, poor in spirit, and broken by the false ways of my life. I not only choose the life You have for me, but I choose to walk in the ways of Your righteousness. Lord, I commit all to You. I offer up my body to You for Your use and glory. I offer up my mind to be transformed by Your Word and Spirit. I offer up my feeble hands to be used for Your work. I offer my ways to You to be lined up to Your will and purpose. Lord, I offer all to You, and ask You to become my all in all. Lord, just have Your perfect way in my life.

Thank you for hearing my cries, meeting me in my need, answering my heart desire to know You, and honoring me with Your mercy, grace, and forgiveness. Thank You for being the one true, unchangeable God of creation. I now bow before You in humility, knowing You will lift me up, enabling me to see You in Your glory.

I say all this in light of Your character, ways, truth, and life. Amen.

Bibliography

Strong's Exhaustive Concordance of the Bible; James Strong; World Bible Publishers

My Utmost For His Highest; Oswald Chambers; © 1963 by Oswald Chambers, Publications Association, Ltd.

Webster's New Collegiate Dictionary; © 1976 by G. & C. Merriam Co.

Encyclopedia of Sermon Illustrations; ©1988 Concordia Publishing House

Evidence That Demands A Verdict; by Josh McDowell ©1972, 1979 by Campus Crusade for Christ

Deeper Experiences of Famous Christians; by James Gilchrist Lawson; © 2000 by Barbour Publishing Inc.

The Way; (Devotional) by Stanley Jones © 1946 by Stone & Pierce

God's Word To Women; by Katharine C. Bushnell; obtained from Ray Munson.

Jewish Faith and the New Covenant; by Ruth Specter Lascelle; © 1980

Zion's Fire; (magazine) January/February © 2002

Understanding The Difficult Words of Jesus; By David Bivin & Roy B. Blizzard , ©1983 by Makor Foundation

Romans, H.A. Ironside. 25th Printing, Published by Loizeaux Brothers, Inc.

What the Bible is All About; Henrietta C. Mears, Second revised edition © 1997 by Regal Books

The One Who Knows God, Clement of Alexandria, © 1990 by David W. Bercot

He Shall Glorify Me; © 1946 by Oswald Chambers Publications Association, this edition 1965

Daily Thoughts for Disciples; Oswald Chambers, © 1990 by Oswald Chambers Publishing Association.

Vine's Expository Dictionary of Biblical Words, ©1985 by Thomas Nelson, Inc., Publishers

Still Higher For His Highest; Oswald Chambers; © D. W. Lambert

Biblical Psychology; Oswald Chambers; © 1995 by Oswald Chambers Publications Association Ltd.

Born After Midnight; A. W. Tozer; © 1989 by Christian Publication

A Table in the Wilderness, (Devotional) by Watchman Nee; © Angus I Kinnear 1978; Tynadale House Publishers

The Normal Christian Life; Watchman Nee; © Angus I Kinnear, reprinted 1972

A Dwelling Place For God; by Ruth Specter Lascelle; ©1973

Halley's Bible Handbook; ©1965 by Halley's Bible Handbook Inc. 24th edition

Jesus Rose For You; Charles Spurgeon; © 1998 by Whitaker House

Smith's Bible Dictionary; William Smith, L.L.D.; Thomas Nelson Publishers

Abide in Christ; Andrew Murray; H.M. Caldwell Co., Publishers

The Thompson Chain-Reference Bible; © 1988 by B. B. Kirkbride Bible Company. Inc.

The Companion Bible, E. W. Bullinger, originally published in 1922; Kregel Publications

Expository Messages on the Epistle to the Galatians; H. A. Ironside; Fifteenth printing, September 1978; Loizeaux Brothers

Dake's Annotated Reference Bible, Finis Jennings Dake, © 1963

A Glimpse At Early Christian Church Life; Tertullian, ©1991 by David W. Bercot

The Pilgrim Church; E. H. Broadbend, © 1999; Gospel Folio Press

Other books by Rayola Kelley:

Hidden Manna
Battle for the Soul
Stories of the Heart
Transforming Love & Beyond
The Great Debate
Post to Post: (1) Establishing the Way
Post to Post: (2) Walking in the Way

Volume Two: Putting on the Life of Christ

He Actually Thought it Not Robbery
Revelation of the Cross
In Search of Real Faith
Think on These Things
Follow the Pattern

Volume Three: Developing a Godly Environment

Godly Discipline
Prayer and Worship
Don't Touch That Dial
Face of Thankfulness
ABC's of Christianity

Volume Four: Issues of the Heart

Hidden Manna (Revised)
Bring Down the Sacred Cows
The Manual for the Single Christian Life
Parents are People Too

Volume Five: Challenging the Christian Life

The Issues of Life
Presentation of the Gospel
For the Purpose of Edification
Whatever Happened to the Church?
Women's Place in the Kingdom of God

Volume Six: Developing Our Christian Life

The Many Faces of Christianity
Possessing Our Souls
Experiencing the Christian Life
The Power of Our Testimonies
The Victorious Journey

Devotions

Devotions of the Heart: Books One and Two
Daily Food for the Soul: Books One and Two

Gentle Shepherd Ministries Devotion Series:
Being a Child of God
Disciplining the Strength of our Youth
Coming to Full Age

Nugget Books:
Nuggets From Heaven
More Nuggets From Heaven
Heavenly Gems
More Heavenly Gems

Gentle Shepherd Ministries Series:
The Christian Life Series:
What Matter Is This?
The Challenge of It
The Reality of It

The Leadership Series:
Overcoming
A Matter of Authority and Power
The Dynamics of True Leadership

www.ingramcontent.com/pod-product-compliance
Lightning Source LLC
Chambersburg PA
CBHW031228090426
42742CB00007B/112

* 9 7 8 0 9 8 9 1 6 8 3 1 1 *